Lecture Notes in Computer Science 4143

Commenced Publication in 1973
Founding and Former Series Editors:
Gerhard Goos, Juris Hartmanis, and Jan van Leeuwen

Ralf Lämmel
João Saraiva
Joost Visser (Eds.)

Generative and Transformational Techniques in Software Engineering

International Summer School, GTTSE 2005
Braga, Portugal, July 4-8, 2005
Revised Papers

 Springer

Volume Editors

Ralf Lämmel
Microsoft Corp.
One Microsoft Way
98052 Redmond, WA, USA
E-mail: Ralf.Lammel@microsoft.com

João Saraiva
Joost Visser
Universidade do Minho
Escola de Engenharia
Departamento de Informática
Campus de Gualtar
4710-057 Braga, Portugal
E-mail: {jas,Joost.Visser}@di.uminho.pt

Library of Congress Control Number: 2006932840

CR Subject Classification (1998): D.2, D.1, D.3, F.3, K.6.3

LNCS Sublibrary: SL 2 – Programming and Software Engineering

ISSN   0302-9743
ISBN-10   3-540-45778-X Springer Berlin Heidelberg New York
ISBN-13   978-3-540-45778-7 Springer Berlin Heidelberg New York

Springer is a part of Springer Science+Business Media

springer.com

© Springer-Verlag Berlin Heidelberg 2006
Printed in Germany

Typesetting: Camera-ready by author, data conversion by Scientific Publishing Services, Chennai, India
Printed on acid-free paper   SPIN: 11877028   06/3142   5 4 3 2 1 0

Preface

The international summer school on Generative and Transformational Techniques in Software Engineering (GTTSE 2005) was held in Braga, Portugal, on July 4–8, 2005. In this volume, you will find an augmented selection of the material presented at the school, including tutorials, technology presentations, and contributions to the participants workshop.

The GTTSE summer school brings together PhD students, lecturers, technology presenters, as well as other researchers and practitioners who are interested in the generation and the transformation of programs, data, models, meta-models, and documentation. This concerns many areas of software engineering: software reverse and re-engineering, model-driven approaches, automated software engineering, and generic language technology, to name a few. These areas differ with regard to the specific sorts of meta-models (or grammars, schemas, formats etc.) that underlie the artifacts involved, and with regard to the specific techniques that are employed for the generation and the transformation of the artifacts.

The 2005 instance of GTTSE offered 8 tutorials, given by renowned representatives of complementary approaches and problem domains. Each tutorial combines foundations, methods, examples, and tool support. The program of the summer school also featured 10 invited technology presentations, which presented concrete support for generative and transformational techniques. These presentations complemented each other in terms of the chosen application domains, case studies, and the underlying concepts. Furthermore, the program of the school included a participants workshop to which all students of the summer school were asked to submit an extended abstract beforehand. The Organization Committee reviewed these extended abstracts and invited 14 students to present their work at the workshop.

This volume contains extended and reviewed versions of the material presented at the summer school. Each of the 7 tutorials included here was reviewed by 2 members of the Scientific Committee of GTTSE 2005. The 8 technology presentations included were reviewed by 3 members each, as were the 6 selected participant contributions. Review was selective and involved multiple rounds of improvements.

We are grateful to all lecturers and participants of the school for their enthusiasm and hard work in preparing excellent material for the school itself and for these proceedings. Due to their efforts the event was a great success, which we trust the reader finds reflected in this volume.

May 2006   Ralf Lämmel, João Saraiva, and Joost Visser

Organization

GTTSE 2005 was hosted by the Departamento de Informática, Universidade do Minho, Braga, Portugal.

Executive Committee

Program Co-chair: Ralf Lämmel (Microsoft, Redmond, USA)
Program Co-chair: João Saraiva (Universidade do Minho, Braga, Portugal)
Organizing Chair: Joost Visser (Universidade do Minho, Braga, Portugal)

Scientific Committee

Paulo Borba, Universidade Federal de Pernambuco, Brazil
Mark van den Brand, Technical University Eindhoven, The Netherlands
Jim Cordy, Queen's University, Canada
Krzysztof Czarnecki, University of Waterloo, Canada
Andrea DeLucia, Università di Salerno, Italy
Jean-Luc Dekeyser, Université des Sciences et Technologies de Lille, France
José Fiadeiro, University of Leicester, UK
Stephen Freund, Williams College, UK
Jeff Gray, University of Alabama at Birmingham, USA
Reiko Heckel, University of Leicester, UK
Görel Hedin, Lund Institute of Technology, Sweden
Pedro Rangel Henriques, Universidade do Minho, Portugal
Y. Annie Liu, State University of New York at Stony Brook, USA
Cristina Lopes, University of California at Irvine, USA
Ralf Lämmel, Microsoft Corporation, USA
Marjan Mernik, University of Maribor, Slovenia
Oege de Moor, Oxford University, UK
Pierre-Etienne Moreau, INRIA Lorraine & LORIA, France
Peter Mosses, University of Wales Swansea, UK
José Nuno Oliveira, Universidade do Minho, Portugal
Jens Palsberg, UCLA, USA
João Saraiva, Universidade do Minho, Portugal
Andy Schürr, Technical University Darmstadt, Germany
Anthony Sloane, Macquarie University, Australia
Peter Thiemann, University of Freiburg, Germany
Simon Thompson, University of Kent, UK
Eelco Visser, Utrecht University, The Netherlands
Joost Visser, Universidade do Minho, Portugal
Eric Van Wyk, University of Minnesota, USA

Organizing Committee

José Bacelar Almeida, Universidade do Minho, Braga, Portugal
Mark van den Brand, Technical University Eindhoven, The Netherlands
Maria João Frade, Universidade do Minho, Braga, Portugal
Pedro Rangel Henriques, Universidade do Minho, Braga, Portugal
Ralf Lämmel, Microsoft Corporation, Redmond, USA
Marjan Mernik, Maribor University, Maribor, Slovenia
João Saraiva, Universidade do Minho, Braga, Portugal
Joost Visser, Universidade do Minho, Braga, Portugal

Sponsoring Institutions

Centro de Ciências e Tecnologias de Computação Enabler
Fundação Oriente
Fundação para a Ciência e a Tecnologia
Luso-American Foundation
Microsoft
Software Improvement Group
Taylor's Port

Table of Contents

III   Participants' Contributions

Part I

Tutorials

A Tutorial on Feature Oriented Programming and the AHEAD Tool Suite

Don Batory

Department of Computer Sciences
University of Texas at Austin
Austin, Texas, 78712 U.S.A.
batory@cs.utexas.edu

Abstract. *Feature oriented programming (FOP)* is the study of feature modularity and its use in program synthesis. AHEAD is a theory of FOP that is based on a fundamental concept of generative programming that functions map programs. This enables the design of programs to be expressed compositionally as algebraic expressions, which are suited for automated analysis, manipulation, and program synthesis. This paper is a tutorial on FOP and AHEAD. We review AHEAD's theory and the tool set that implements it.

1 Introduction

Software engineering (SE) is in a perpetual crisis. Software products are increasing in complexity, the cost to develop and maintain systems is skyrocketing, and our ability to understand systems is decreasing. A basic goal of SE is to successfully manage and control *complexity*; the "crisis" indicates that SE technologies are failing to achieve this goal. There are many culprits. One surely is that today's software design and implementation techniques are simply too low-level, exposing far more detail than is necessary to make a program's design, construction, and ease of modification simple. Future software design technologies will need to do better, and it should not be surprising that they will be different from those of today.

Looking to the future, SE paradigms will likely embrace:

- *generative programming (GP)*
- *domain-specific languages (DSLs)*
- *automatic programming (AP)*

GP is about automating software development. Eliminating the task of writing mundane and rote programs is a motherhood to improved programmer productivity and program quality. Program synthesizers will transform input specifications into target programs. These specifications will not be written in Java or C# — which are too low-level — but rather in high-level notations called DSLs that are specific to a particular domain. DSL programs are known to be both easier to write and maintain than their low-level (e.g., Java) counterparts. Ideally, DSLs are declarative, allowing their users to define *what* is needed and leave it up to the DSL compiler to produce an efficient program automatically that does the *how* part. But placing the burden of program synthesis on a DSL compiler should not be taken lightly. This involves the

R. Lämmel, J. Saraiva, and J. Visser (Eds.): GTTSE 2005, LNCS 4143, pp. 3 – 35, 2006.

problem of AP; it is a technical problem of great difficulty, as little progress has been made in the last 25 years to produce demonstrably efficient programs from declarative specs. Advancement on all three fronts (GP, DSLs, and AP) are needed before the crisis in SE will noticeably diminish.

While it is wishful thinking that simultaneous advances on all three fronts is possible, it is worth noting that a spectacular example of this futuristic SE paradigm was realized over *25 years ago* — ironically around the time when most people were giving up on AP . Furthermore, this work had a fundamental impact on commercial applications. The example is relational query optimization . SQL is a prototypical DSL: it is a *declarative language* for retrieving data from tables. An SQL compiler translates an SQL statement into a relational algebra expression. A query optimizer accomplishes the goal of *automatic programming* by applying algebraic identities to automatically rewrite — and hence optimize — relational algebra expressions. The task of translating an optimized expression into an efficient program is an example of *generative programming.*

Relational optimizers revolutionized databases: data retrieval programs that were hard to write, hard to optimize, and hard to maintain are now produced automatically. There is nothing special about data retrieval programs: all interesting programs are hard to write, optimize, and maintain. Thus if ever there was a "grand challenge" for SE, it would be to replicate the success of relational query optimization in other domains.

AHEAD is a theory of *feature oriented programming (FOP)* that shows how the concepts and framework of relational query optimization generalize to other domains. ATS is a suite of tools that implement the AHEAD theory.

1.1 Background

How do you describe a program that you've written to a prospective customer? You are unlikely to recite what packages you're using — because the customer would unlikely have any interest in such details. Instead, you would take a more promising approach of explaining the *features* — increments in program functionality — that your program offers its clients. This works because clients know their requirements and can see how features satisfy requirements.

Programs come in different flavors, e.g., entry-level through deluxe. The differences between these categories are the presence or absence of features (or more commonly, sets of features). Entry-level versions have a minimal feature set; deluxe advertises the most.

But if we describe programs by features or differentiate programs by features, why can't we build programs (or program families) from feature specifications? In fact, we can. This is the area of research called *product-lines*. The ability to add and remove features suggests that features can be modularized. While it is possible to construct product-lines without modularizing features (e.g., through the extensive use of `#if-`
`#endif` preprocessor declarations), we focus on a particular sub-topic of product-line research that deals with feature modularization. By making features first-class design and implementation entities, it is easier to add and remove features from applications. (In fact, this is a capability that most of us wish we had today — the ability to add and remove features from our programs. We don't have it now; the purpose of this paper is to explain how it can be done in a general way). It happens that feature modularity

goes far beyond conventional notions of code modularity. This, among other things, makes it a very interesting topic.

Feature oriented programming (FOP) is the study of feature modularity and programming models that support feature modularity. A powerful form of FOP is based on a methodology called *step-wise development (SWD)*. SWD is both simple and ancient: it advocates that complex programs can be constructed from simple programs by incrementally adding details. When incremental units of change are features, FOP and SWD converge. This is the starting point of AHEAD and ATS. But what is a feature? How is it represented? And how are features and their compositions modeled?

1.2   A Clue

Consider any Java class c. A class member could be a data field or a method. Class c below has four members m1—m4.

```
class C {
    member m1;
    member m2;
    member m3;
    member m4;
}                                                         (1)
```

Have you ever noticed that there is no unique definition for c? The members of c could be defined in a single class as above, or distributed over an inheritance hierarchy of arbitrary height. One possibility is to have class c1 encapsulate member m1 and c23 encapsulate members m2 and m3:

```
class C1 { member m1; }
class C23 extends C1 {
    member m2;
    member m3;
}
class C4 extends C23 { member m4; }
class C extends C4 {}                                     (2)
```

From a programmatic viewpoint, both definitions of c, namely (1) and (2), are indestinguishable. In fact, we could further decompose c23 to be:

```
class C2 extends C1 { member m2; }
class C3 extends C2 { member m3; }
class C23 extends C3 {}
```

and the definition of c would not change; it would still have members m1—m4. Moreover, there's nothing really special about the placement of member m1 (or m2 ...) in this hierarchy. If method m1 references other members, as long as these members are not defined lower in the inheritance chain than m1, m1 can appear in any class of that chain.

If you recall your high school or college courses on algebra, you may recognize these ideas. Consider sets and the union operation. We can define the sets:

```
C1 = { m1 }
C2 = { m2 }
C3 = { m3 }
C4 = { m4 }

C23 = C2 ∪ C3

C = C1 ∪ C23 ∪ C4 = C1 ∪ C2 ∪ C3 ∪ C4
```

Union is commutative, which means that the order in which the union of sets is taken doesn't matter. This is similar to, but not the same as, inheritance because as we saw, a method can be added only as long as members it references are not defined in subclasses.

Something a bit closer to inheritance are vectors and the vector operations of addition($+$) and movement($\rightarrow$). Suppose we define vectors in 4-space:

```
C1 = (m1,0,0,0)
C2 = (0,m2,0,0)
C3 = (0,0,m3,0)
C4 = (0,0,0,m4)
```

You know about vector addition; vector movement is the path that is followed when laying vectors end-to-end. Vector addition is commutative; vector movement is not:

```
C = (m1,m2,m3,m4) = C1 + C2 + C3 + C4
C1 + C2 + C3 + C4 = C4 + C3 + C2 + C1
C1 → C2 → C3 → C4 ≠ C4 → C3 → C2 → C1
```

Inheritance has the flavor of both vector arithmetic and vector movement.

When you think about an *operation* for inheritance, what you are really defining is an operation for class extension. A *class extension* can add new members and extend existing methods of a class. Here's an example. Suppose a program P has a single class B that initially contains a single data member **x**:

```
class B { int x; }                        // program P
```

Suppose an extension R of program P adds data member **y** and method **z** to class B. Let us write this extension as:

```
refines class B {     // extension R
   int y;
   void z() {...}
}                                                        (3)
```

where "**refines**" is a keyword modifier to mean extension. The composition of R with P defines a new program N with a single class B with three members:

```
class B {                      // program N
   int x;
   int y;
   void z() {...}
}                                                        (4)
```

In effect, this composition is expressed by the following inheritance chain, called an *extension chain*:

```
class B_P { int x; }

class B_R extends B_P {
   int y;
   void z() {...}
}

class B_N extends B_R {}                                 (5)
```

where subscripts indicate the program or extension from which that fragment of B is defined.

We can express these ideas algebraically by "values" and "functions". Program P is a *value* (or constant function) — it defines a base artifact. An extension is a *function* that maps programs, so R is a function. A composition is an expression. We can model (5) as the equation $N = R(P)$ or $N = R \bullet P$, where $\bullet$ denotes function composition.

We can express our previous example about class C in this manner. Here is one way: let C1 be a value and C2, C3, and C4 be the extensions:

```
class C { member m1; }              // value C1
refines class C { member m2; }      // function C2
refines class C { member m3; }      // function C3
refines class C { member m4;   }    // function C4
```

Now, class C of can be synthesized by *evaluating* the expression C4$\bullet$C3$\bullet$C2$\bullet$C1. The expression — C4$\bullet$C3$\bullet$C2$\bullet$C1 — is called the *design* of C. Taking this idea further, we see that C23 has a representation as a composite function or composite extension:

```
C23 = C2•C3
```

which represents the code:

```
refines class C {
    member m2;
    member m3;
}
```

There are loose ends to tie up before a bigger picture emerges. First, there's scalability. The effects of a program extension need not be limited to a single Java class. In fact, it is common for a "large-scale" extension to encapsulate multiple class extensions as well as new classes. That is, such an extension would augment existing classes of a program with new members and extend existing methods, but would also introduce new classes that could be subsequently augmented.

Second, program extensions have meaning when they encapsulate the implementation of a feature. Have you ever added a new feature to an existing program? You discover that you often have to extend a number of classes, as well as add new classes to a program. Well, a feature is a "large scale" program extension.

Third, in product-line design, features are stereo-typical units of application design that can be composed with other features to produce customized programs. A model of a product-line — called a *domain model* — is a set of values and functions each representing a particular feature, that can be composed to synthesize customized programs.

Fourth, recall that a key to the success of relational query optimizers is that they use expressions to represent program designs. That is, a data retrieval program is defined by a composition of relational algebra operations. To see the generalization, a domain model is an *algebra* — a set of operations ("values" and "functions") whose compositions define the space of programs that can be synthesized. Given an algebra, there will always be algebraic identities among operations. These identities can be used to optimize algebraic expression definitions of programs, just like relational algebra expressions can be optimized. (Some domains will have more interesting optimizations than others).

Fifth, what is *design*? If you think about it, this is a *really* hard question to answer, because it is asking for a clear articulation of a deeply intuitive idea. Our discussions offer a simple answer: a program is a value. The design of a program is the expression that produces its value. If multiple expressions produce the same value, then these expressions represent equivalent designs of that program.

Now, let's consider a more precise way to express these ideas.

2 A Model of FOP

Salient ideas of FOP as expressed by two models: GenVoca and its successor AHEAD.

2.1 GenVoca

GenVoca is a design methodology for creating application families and architecturally-extensible software, i.e., software that is customizable via feature addition and removal . It follows traditional step-wise development with one major difference: instead of composing thousands of microscopic program extensions (e.g., $x+1 \Rightarrow inc(x)$) to yield admittedly small programs, GenVoca scales extensions so that each adds a feature to a program, and composing few extensions yields an entire program.

In GenVoca, programs are *values* and program extensions are *functions*. Consider the following values that represent base programs with different features:

```
f                  // program with feature f
g                  // program with feature g
```

A program extension is a function that takes a program as input and produces a feature-augmented program as output:

```
i•x                // adds feature i to program x
j•x                // adds feature j to program x
```

A multi-featured application is an *equation* that is a named expression. Different equations define a family of applications, such as:

```
app1 = i•f         // app1 has features i and f
app2 = j•g         // app2 has features j and g
app3 = i•j•f       // app3 has features i, j, f
```

Thus, the features of an application can be determined by inspecting its equation.

Note that a function represents both a feature *and* its implementation — there can be different functions with different implementations of the *same* feature:

```
k₁•x               // adds k with implementation₁ to x
k₂•x               // adds k with implementation₂ to x
```

When an application requires the use of feature k, it is a problem of *expression optimization* to determine which implementation of k is best (e.g., provides the best performance)[1]. It is possible to automatically design software (i.e., produce an expression that optimizes some criteria) given a set of constraints for a target application . This is automatic programming.

---

[1] Different equations represent different programs and equation optimization is over the space of semantically equivalent programs. This is identical to relational query optimization: a query is represented by a relational algebra expression, and this expression is optimized. Each expression represents a different, but semantically equivalent, query-evaluation program.

Although GenVoca values and functions seem untyped, constraints do exist. *Design rules* are domain-specific constraints that capture syntactic and semantic constraints that govern legal compositions. It is common that the selection of a feature will disable or enable the selection of other features. More on design rules later.

2.2 AHEAD

AHEAD, or *Algebraic Hierarchical Equations for Application Design*, embodies four key generalizations of GenVoca. First, a program has many representations besides source code, including UML documents, makefiles, BNF grammars, documents, performance models, etc. A model of FOP must deal with all these representations.

Second, each representation is written in its own language or DSL. The code representation of a program may be represented in Java, a machine executable representation may be bytecodes, a makefile representation could be an **ant** XML file, a performance model may be a set of Mathematica equations, and so on. An FOP model must support an open-ended spectrum of languages to express arbitrary program representations.

Third, when a feature is added to a program, any or all of the program's representations may be updated. That is, the source code of a program changes (to implement the feature), makefiles change (to build the feature), Mathematica equations change (to profile the feature), etc. Thus, the concept of extension applies not only to source code representations, but other representations as well.

Fourth, FOP models must deal with a general notion of modularity: *a module is a containment hierarchy of related artifacts*. A class is a module (1-level hierarchy) that contains a set of data members and methods. A package or JAR file is a module (2-level hierarchy) that contains a set of classes. A J2EE EAR file is a module (3-level hierarchy) that contains a set of packages, HTML files, and descriptor files. Going further, a client-server program is also a module (a multi-level hierarchy) that contains representations of both client and server programs.

Given the above, a generalization of GenVoca emerges. A "value" is a module that defines a containment hierarchy of related artifacts of different types written in potentially different languages. An "extension" is a function that maps containment hierarchies. Thus, whenever an extension is applied to a program (i.e., an AHEAD value), any or all of the representations in this module (containment hierarchy) will be updated and new artifacts added. Thus, as AHEAD extensions are applied, all of the representations of the resulting program remain consistent. This is exactly what we need.

The notations of AHEAD extend those of GenVoca. A model **M** is a set of features that are "values" or "functions" called *units*:

```
M = { a, b, c, d, ... }
```

Individual units may themselves be sets, recursively:

```
a = { x, y, z }
z = { r, q }
...
```

The nesting of sets models a containment hierarchy or module. The composition of units is defined by the *Law of Composition*. That is, given units **x** and **y**:

```
X = { aₓ,  bₓ,  cₓ        }
Y = { aᵧ,       cᵧ,  dᵧ  }
```

The composition of Y and X, denoted $Y \bullet X$, is formed by "aligning" the units of X and Y that have the same name (ignoring subscripts) and composing:

$$Y \bullet X = \{ a_y \bullet a_x,\ b_x,\ c_y \bullet c_x,\ d_y \} \qquad \qquad // \text{ Law of Composition} \qquad (6)$$

That is, artifact a of $Y \bullet X$ is the original artifact a_x composed with the extension a_y; artifact b of $Y \bullet X$ remains unchanged from its original definition b_x, etc. Composition is recursive: if units represent sets, their compositions are expanded according to (6).

To see the connection with inheritance, consider the following inheritance hierarchy which is a class representation of (6). Assume a and c are methods, where a_y and c_y extend (or override) their super-methods a_x and c_x:

```
class X {
        member aₓ;
        member bₓ;
        member cₓ;
}
class Y extends X {
        member aᵧ;
        member cᵧ;
        member dᵧ;
}

class Y•X extends Y {}
```

How the composition operator • is defined depends on the artifact type. • is polymorphic: it can be applied to all artifacts (i.e., all artifacts can be composed/extended) but what composition/extension means is artifact type dependent (i.e., how makefile artifacts are extended will be analogous to but not the same as how code artifacts are extended). This means that different tools implement • for code and makefiles.

AHEAD representations lead to simple tools and implementations. While there are many ways in which containment hierarchies can be realized, the simplest way is to map containment hierarchies to file system directories. Thus a feature might encapsulate many Java files, class files, HTML files, etc. Feature composition corresponds to directory composition.

Recognize what AHEAD represents: it is a *structural theory of information* — it is not just a theory of code synthesis. Its premise is that if a program can be understood in terms of features, so too can all of its representations — code and otherwise. We can choose to interpret individual terms of AHEAD expressions as code files or code directories, but we are free to consider other representations as well. A familiarity with relational query optimization bares this out: the optimizer reasons about a program in terms of performance representations of relational operations (i.e., cost functions), while the code generator produces a program from code representations of these same operations . Reasoning about programs often relies on different representations of programs. AHEAD provides a mathematical foundation for expressing their inter-relationships.

We'll explore examples of these ideas in the following sections.

3 A Simple Example

Consider a family of elementary post-fix calculators that are modeled after Hewlett-Packard calculators. Calculators in this family are differentiated on (a) the arithmetic values **BigInteger** (an unlimited precision integer) or **BigDecimal** (an unlimited precision, signed decimal number) that can be specified and (b) the set operations that can be performed on them, which includes addition, division, and subtraction.

An AHEAD model that describes this family is **c**:

C = { Base, BigI, BigD, Iadd, Idiv, Isub, Dadd, Ddivd, Ddivu, Dsub }

The lone value in this model is **Base**, which defines an empty **calc** (short for "calculator") class (Figure 1a). The extensions **BigI** and **BigD** introduce a 3-level stack of **BigInteger** or **BigDecimal** objects, respectively (Figure 1b-c). **BigI** and **BigD** are mutually exclusive as the stack variables introduced by both have the same name, but are of different types. Thus, calculators either work on **BigInteger** or **BigDecimal** numbers, but not both.

```
class calc { }
```
(a) Base/calc.jak

```
refines class calc {
   void divide() {
      e0 = e0.divide( e1 );
      e1 = e2;
   }
}
```
(d) Idiv/calc.jak

```
refines class calc {
   void add() {
      e0 = e0.add(e1);
      e1 = e2;
   }
}
```
(e) Iadd/calc.jak
and Dadd/calc.jak

```
import java.math.BigDecimal;

refines class calc {
   void divide() {
      e0 = e0.divide( e1,
         BigDecimal.ROUND_DOWN );
      e1 = e2;
   }
}
```
(f) Ddivd/calc.jak

```
import java.math.BigInteger;

refines class calc {
   static BigInteger zero = BigInteger.ZERO;
   BigInteger e0 = zero, e1 = zero, e2 = zero;

   void enter( String val ) {
      e2 = e1;
      e1 = e0;
      e0 = new BigInteger(val);
   }

   void clear() {
      e0 = e1 = e2 = zero;
   }

   String top() { return e0.toString(); }
}
```
(b) BigI/calc.jak

```
import java.math.BigDecimal;

refines class calc {
   static BigDecimal
      zero = new BigDecimal("0");
   BigDecimal e0 = zero, e1 = zero,
      e2 = zero;

   void enter( String val ) {
      e2 = e1;
      e1 = e0;
      e0 = new BigDecimal(val);
   }

   void clear() {
      e0 = e1 = e2 = zero;
   }

   String top() { return e0.toString(); }
}
```
(c) BigD/calc.jak

Fig. 1. Files from the **C** model

The extensions **Iadd**, **Idiv**, and **Isub** respectively introduce the **BigInteger** addition, division, and subtraction methods to the **calc** class (Figure 1d-e). The extensions **Dadd**, **Ddivd**, **Ddivu**, and **Dsub** do the same for **BigDecimal** methods (Figure 1f-g). Note that there are two mutually exclusive **BigDecimal** division extensions: **Ddivd** and **Ddivu**. **Ddivd** rounds answers down, **Ddivu** rounds up.

As you may have already noticed, these files look like Java programs, but the language that we are using is not Java but an extended Java language called *Jak* (short for "Jakarta"). Jak files have .jak extensions, like Java files have .java extensions.

A calculator is defined by an equation. Here are a few calculator definitions:

```
i1 = Iadd•BigI•Base

i2 = Isub•Iadd•BigI•Base

i3 = Idiv•Iadd•BigI•Base


d1 = Dadd•BigD•Base

d2 = Dsub•Dadd•BigD•Base

d3 = Ddivd•Dadd•BigD•Base
```

Calculator **i1** offers **BigInteger** addition. **i2** also supports subtraction. **i3** has **BigInteger** addition and division. **d1**—**d3** are the corresponding calculators for **BigDecimal** numbers using rounded-down division. The code generated for the **i3** **calc** class is shown in Note the term "**layer**" in Figure 2 is used interchangeably with "**feature**" in AHEAD.

```
layer i3;

import java.math.BigInteger;

class calc {
    static BigInteger zero = BigInteger.ZERO;
    BigInteger e0 = zero, e1 = zero, e2 = zero;

    void add() {
        e0 = e0.add(e1);
        e1 = e2;
    }

    void clear() {
        e0 = e1 = e2 = zero;
    }

    void divide() {
        e0 = e0.divide( e1 );
        e1 = e2;
    }

    void enter( String val ) {
        e2 = e1;
        e1 = e0;
        e0 = new BigInteger(val);
    }

    String top() { return e0.toString(); }
}
```

Fig. 2. i3/calc.jak

Model Exercises

[1] What other calculator features could be added to **c**? What would be their Jak definitions? Look at the **BigInteger** and **BigDecimal** pages in the J2SDK
documentation for possibilities.

[2] Suppose the size of the stack was variable. How would this be expressed as an
extension? What modifications of existing extensions would be needed?

[3] Modify model **c** so that **BigDecimal** round-up and round-down are features,
which could parameterize operations like division.

[4] How would **c** be modified to permit the synthesis of a program that would invoke
the calculator from the command-line? From a GUI?

Tool Exercises

An AHEAD model **c** corresponds to a directory **c**, and each unit **u** in **c** corresponds to
a subdirectory of **c**, namely **c/u**. The contents of a unit in our example is merely a
calc.jak file. The AHEAD directory structure of **c** is:

```
C/Base/calc.jak              // see Figure 1a
C/BigI/calc.jak              // see Figure 1b
C/BigD/calc.jak              // see Figure 1c
C/Iadd/calc.jak              // see Figure 1d
C/Idiv/calc.jak              // see Figure 1e
C/Isub/calc.jak
C/Dadd/calc.jak              // see Figure 1d
C/Ddivd/calc.jak             // see Figure 1f
C/Ddivu/calc.jak
C/Dsub/calc.jak
```

Although we provide no **calc.jak** files for **Isub** and **Dsub**, they are easy to write. In
fact, they are almost identical to the **calc.jak** files for **Iadd** and **Dadd**.[2]

The **composer** tool is used to evaluate equations and has many optional parameters.
For our tutorial, we need to reset one of these parameters. Create in the model directory a file called **composer.properties**. Its contents is a single line (which says when
composing Jak files, use the **jampack** tool):

```
unit.file.jak : JamPackFileUnit
```

To evaluate an equation, run **composer** in the model directory. The order in which
model units are listed on the **composer** command line are inside-to-outside order, and
the name of the composition is given by the **target** option. Thus, to evaluate **i3** use:

```
> cd C
> composer --target=i3 Base BigI Idiv Iadd
```

The result of the composition is the directory **c/i3**, which contains a single file,
calc.jak, shown in Figure 2. Note that the order in which units are listed on the **composer** command line is in *reverse* order in which they are listed in an equation —
base first, outermost extension last. (This is a legacy oddity of AHEAD tools that has
never been changed. Sigh.)

[5] Validate your Model Exercise solutions by implementing them using AHEAD
tools.

---

[2] So why not just define one layer to represent both? This could be done with our current tools,
as they are preprocessors. In future tools, these files will be different, because the types of
variables for **e1**—**e3** will need to be explicitly declared. When this occurs, the corresponding files will indeed be different.

3.1 Translating to Java

The `jak2java` tool converts Jak files to their Java counterparts:

```
> cd i3
> jak2java *.jak
```

The above command-line translates all Jak files (in our case, there is only one file — `calc.jak`) to their Java equivalents. Of course, these generated files can be compiled in the usual way:

```
> javac *.java
```

Note there are Jak files (i.e., those that refine classes and interfaces) that cannot be translated to Java, as they have no Java counterpart. `jak2java` translates only Jak classes and interfaces.

3.2 Design Rules

New arithmetic operations could be added to `c` to enlarge the family of calculators. At the same time, it becomes increasingly clear that not all compositions are meaningful. In fact, it is quite easy to deliberately or unintentionally specify meaningless compositions, but `composer` is usually quite happy to produce code for them. We need automated help to detect illegal compositions.

This is not a problem specific to calculators, but rather a fundamental problem in FOP. The use of a feature in a program can enable or disable other features. *Design rules* are domain-specific constraints that define composition correctness predicates for features. *Design rule checking (DRC)* is the process by which design rules are composed and their predicates validated. AHEAD offers two different tools for defining and evaluating design rules: `drc` and `guidsl`. `drc` is a first-generation tool ; `guidsl` is a next-generation tool that we will highlight here.

The theory behind both tools is the use of grammars to define legal sequences (i.e., compositions) of features. A grammar for model `c` is:

```
C     : Type Base ;
Type  : BigInt+ BigI
      | BigDec+ BigD ;
BigInt  : Iadd | Idiv | Isub ;
BigDec  : Dadd | Ddivu | Ddivd | Dsub ;          (7)
```

where tokens are units of `c`. A sentence of this grammar specifies a particular sequence or composition of features. The set of all sentences defines the model's *product-line*, i.e., the set of all possible expressions or compositions of features.

Like any grammar, some sentences are semantically invalid. To weed out incorrect sentences, a grammar is augmented with *attributes*. Conditions for correct sentences (or correct compositions) are predicates defined over these attributes. That is, these predicates filter out syntactically incorrect sentences. The core theory behind both tools are *attribute grammars*, a well-understood technology.

In the case of our `c` model, syntactic correctness is almost all that is needed. The only additional constraint — which is simple enough to have been expressed by an additional grammar rule — is the mutually exclusive nature of `Ddivu` and `Ddivd`; at most one of these features can appear in a decimal calculator.

As an aside, product-line researchers are familiar with feature diagrams, i.e., trees whose terminal nodes are primitive features and non-terminal nodes are compound features. So what is the connection between grammars and feature diagrams? Although feature diagrams were introduced by Kang, et al in the early 1990s and "GenVoca" grammars, like (7), were introduced in 1992 , it was not until 2002 that de Jonge and Visser noticed that feature diagrams are graphical representations of grammars . In fact, grammars provide an added benefit beyond feature diagrams in that they tell us the *order* in which features are composed, which is important to AHEAD and step-wise development. So if you're a fan of feature diagrams, you will see that the tools and ideas we present here are directly applicable to your interests.

3.2.1 The guidsl Tool

guidsl is a next generation tool for design rule checking . The key idea is that a tree grammar (i.e., a grammar where each token appears at most once in a sentence and which itself can be depicted as a tree) can be represented as a propositional formula. Moreover, *any* propositional constraints on the use of features can be added to this formula. Amazingly, an FOP domain model reduces to a single propositional formula, whose variables correspond to primitive and compound features!

Here's why this is important. First, we have a compact representation of an FOP domain model: it is a grammar (which encodes syntactic/ordering constraints) plus a set of propositional formulas that constrains sentences to legal compositions. The entire guidsl specification for the c model is shown in Figure 3. The :: Name phrase in a guidsl specifica-tion is a way to assign a name to a pattern.

```
C     : Type Base :: Main ;

Type : BigInt+ BigI :: BigInteger
     | BigDec+ BigD :: BigDecimal ;

BigInt : Iadd | Idiv | Isub ;

BigDec : Dadd | Ddivu | Ddivd | Dsub ;

%% // arbitrary propositional formulas below

Ddivu or Ddivd implies not (Ddivu and Ddivd);
```

Fig. 3. C.m -- the guidsl Model of C

Second, one of the hallmarks of feature oriented designs is the ability to declaratively specify programs in terms of the features that it offers. guidsl takes a model specification (a .m file) and synthesizes a Java GUI. As a user selects features in the GUI, guidsl uses a logic truth maintenance system to propagate constraints so that users cannot specify incorrect programs. (guidsl is, in effect, a syntax-directed editor that guarantees compilable programs). Further, because a domain model is a propositional formula, satisfiability solvers (or SAT solvers) can be used to help debug models. (A *SAT solver* is a tool that determines if there is a truth assignment to boolean variables that will satisfy a propositional formula). We believe that SAT solvers will be invaluable assets in future FOP tools.

To generate a declarative language for our calculator, run guidsl on the c model file:

```
> guidsl c.m
```

The GUI that is synthesized is shown in Figure 4.

Model Exercises

[6] How would you change the `guidsl` file if both Add and Subtract operations were always included if either is selected? Similarly for Divide and Multiply?

Tool Exercises

[7] Implement your solution to [6].

[8] To see an explanation (in the form of a proof) why certain features have been automatically selected or deselected, run `guidsl`, go to **Help**, and select "**Display reason for variable selection**". Now drag your cursor over a variable that has been greyed out (i.e., whose value was automatically selected). In the text area at the bottom of the selection panel, you'll see the explanation/proof for that variable's value.

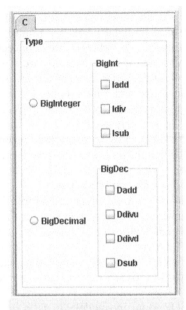

Fig. 4. Declarative GUI for Model C

[9] Alter the `c.m` file of Figure 3 by eliminating the propositional constraint and modifying the grammar specification to account for the mutual exclusion of `Ddivd` and `Ddivu`. Test your solution to see the impact of this change. (Hint: your GUI front-end will change).

4   Other ATS Tools and Program Representations

So far, you have seen the `composer`, `jampack` (which is called by `composer`), `jak2java`, and `guidsl` tools. Now let's look at the `mixin`, `unmixin`, and `reform` tools.

4.1 `mixin`

`mixin` is another tool, besides `jampack`, that can compose Jak files. Edit the `unit.file.jak` line in the `composer.properties` file to be:

```
unit.file.jak : MixinFileUnit
```

This is the default setting for `unit.file.jak`. If `composer` doesn't see a `composer.properties` file, it uses `mixin` to compose Jak files.

Let's re-evaluate the `i3` equation to see how `mixin` works:

```
> cd C
> composer --target=i3 Base BigI Idiv Iadd
```

This is the same command as before. However, the `calc.jak` file that is produced is quite different and is shown in Figure 5.

```
layer i3;

import java.math.BigInteger;

SoUrCe RooT base "../base/calc.jak";
abstract class calc$$base {}

SoUrCe BigI "../BigI/calc.jak";
abstract class calc$$BigI extends  calc$$base {
    static BigInteger zero = BigInteger.ZERO;
    BigInteger e0 = zero, e1 = zero, e2 = zero;

    void add() {
        e0 = e0.add( e1 );
        e1 = e2;
    }

    void clear() {
        e0 = e1 = e2 = zero;
    }
    void divide() {
        e0 = e0.divide( e1 );
        e1 = e2;
    }

    void enter( String val ) {
        e2 = e1;
        e1 = e0;
        e0 = new BigInteger( val );
    }

    String top() {
        return e0.toString();
    }
}

SoUrCe Iadd "../Iadd/calc.jak";
abstract class calc$$Iadd extends  calc$$BigI {
    // adds BigIntegers
    void add() {
        // adds BigIntegers
        e0 = e0.add( e1 );
        e1 = e2;
    }
}

SoUrCe Idiv "../Idiv/calc.jak";
class calc extends  calc$$Iadd {
    void divide() {
        e0 = e0.divide( e1 );
        e1 = e2;
    }
}
```

Fig. 5. mixin-produced.jak file

The idea behind **mixin** is simple: each extension is mapped to a class in an extension (inheritance) chain. Each class is prefaced by a **soUrce** statement which indicates the name of the feature and the actual file from which the class was derived. Thus, in Figure 5 four Jak files were composed to yield the **calc** class; this class is the terminal class of a four-class extension chain. All other classes are abstract — meaning that they can't be instantiated and whose purpose is only to contribute members to the final class in the chain. Note that class names are *mangled* (i.e., by appending $$<featureName>) to make them unique.

The intent of `mixin` and `jampack` is that you can use either tool to compose Jak files. As you'd expect, the programs of Figure 2 and Figure 5 are functionally equivalent.

Both `mixin` and `jampack` can compose files that they themselves have produced. That is, a `jampack`-produced Jak file can be composed with another `jampack`-produced Jak file. The same holds for `mixin`. Because `jampack`-produced Jak files have the same format as uncomposed Jak files, `mixin` can compose files produced by `jampack`. However, the reverse is not true: `jampack` cannot compose `mixin`-produced files.

4.2 `unmixin`

So why use `mixin`? Why not always use `jampack`? Consider a typical debugging cycle: you compose files, use `jak2java` to translate Jak files to Java files, compile and run the Java files to discover bugs. The *composed* Jak files are patched and the cycle continues. Eventually, you'll want to back-propagate the changes you made to the composed files to their original feature definitions. Knowing what feature files to update won't always be easy — and the problem becomes worse as the number and size of the Jak files increases. Back-propagation is a tedious and error-prone process.

Because `mixin` preserves feature boundaries, it is easy to know what features to update. In fact, with `SoUrCe` statements, the propagation of changes can be done automatically. That's the purpose of `unmixin`. The idea is that you compose a bunch of Jak files, edit the *composed* files, and run `unmixin` on the edited files to back-propagate the changes to the original feature files. For example, suppose we add a comment to the bottom-most class in the extension chain of Figure 5:

```
SoUrCe  Idiv "../Idiv/calc.jak";
class calc extends  calc$$Iadd {
   void divide() {
      // *new* divide and pop stack
      e0 = e0.divide( e1 );
      e1 = e2;
   }
}
```

By running `unmixin`, this change is propagated back to the `Idiv/calc.jak` file:

```
> cd C
> unmixin calc.jak
```

See for yourself that the change was made. Here are things to remember about `unmixin`:

- *it can take any number of Jak files on its command line,*
- *the body of the class or interface in the command-line file will replace the body of the class or interface in the original file,*
- `implements` *declarations are also propagated, and*
- *don't change the contents of the* `SoUrCe` *statements!*

`unmixin` updates the original uncomposed files only if changes to its composed counterpart have been updated.

4.3 `reform`

`reform` is a pretty-printing tool that formats unruly Jak files (and Java files!) and makes them unbelievably beautiful. Consider the 1-line `calc.jak` file:

```
refines class calc { void divide() { e0 = e0.divide( e1 ); e1 = e2; } }
```

By running:

```
> reform calc.jak
```

`reform` copies the original file into `calc.jak~` and updates `calc.jak` to be:

```
refines class calc {
    void divide() {
        e0 = e0.divide( e1 );
        e1 = e2;
    }
}
```

4.4 Equation Files

As we said earlier, AHEAD is a theory for structuring and synthesizing documents of all kinds by composing features. We introduced Jak file (i.e., code) representations earlier, and now we introduce a second.

Typing in equations on the command line to `composer` can be tedious, particularly if equations involve more than a few terms. `composer` takes an alternative specification, called an *equation file*, which is a list of units. The order in which the units are listed is from inside-out, and the name of the equation is the name of the equation file.

For example, the equation $A = B \bullet C$ would be represented by the equation file `A.equation` whose contents is:

```
# base feature listed first!
C
B
```

Where any line beginning with `#` is a comment. Like other AHEAD artifacts, equation files can be composed. File `A.equation` above is a "value". An equation file that is an extension has the special term `super` as one of its units. An extension of `A.equation` that puts `E` before `C` and `F` after `B` is `R.equation`:

```
E
super
F
```

A composition of the above files is:

```
> composer --target=c.equation A.equation R.equation
```

and yields file `c.equation` with contents:

```
E
C
B
F
```

Intuitively, an equation file defines an *architectural representation* of a program as an expression. As all program representations are extendable, we now have a means by which to specify and manipulate program architectures. We will see how such representations are useful later.

5 More Features of Jak Files

There are three additional features of the Jak language that you should know: `Super()` references, extension of constructors, and local identifiers.

5.1 The Super Construct

To invoke a method `m(int x, float y)` of a superclass in Java, you write:

```
super.m(x,y);
```

In Jak files, use the `Super` construct instead:

```
Super(int,float).m(x,y);
```

`Super(<argument types>)` prefaces a `Super` call and lists the argument types of the method to be called. Consider the class `foo` and an extension:

```
class foo {
    void dosomething() { /*code*/ }
}

refines class foo {
    void dosomething() {
        /* more before */
        Super().dosomething();
        /* more later */
    }
}
```

In this example, the `Super` references the `dosomething()` method prior to its extension. A `jampack` composition of these definitions is shown in Figure 6a. Observe that the original `dosomething()` method is present in `foo`, except that it has been renamed, along with its references. The corresponding `mixin` composition is shown in Figure 6b. When `jak2java` translates Figure 6b, `Super(...)` references are replaced by "`super`". In general, always use the `Super(...)` construct to reference superclass members; ATS tools do not recognize "`super`".

```
class foo {
    final void dosomething$$one()
    { /*code*/ }

    void dosomething()
    { /* more before */
        dosomething$$one();
        /* more later */
    }
}                                    (a)
```

```
SoUrCe ...;
abstract class foo$$one {
    void dosomething()
    { /*code*/ }
}

SoUrCe ...;
class foo extends  foo$$one {
    void dosomething() {
        /* more before */
        Super().dosomething();
        /* more later */
    }
}                                    (b)
```

Fig. 6. jampack and Mixin compositions

5.2 Extending Constructors

A constructor is a special method and to extend it requires a special declaration in Jak files. Consider the following file that declares a constructor:

```
class test {
    int y;
    test() { y = -1; }
}
```

An extension of **test** and its constructor is:

```
refines class test {
    int x;
    refines test() { x = 2; }
}
```

where "**refines <constructor>**" is the Jak statement that extends a particular constructor. The **jampack** composition of these files is shown in Figure 7a. That is, the actions of the original constructor are grouped into a block and are performed first, then the actions of the constructor extension are grouped into a block and performed next. The semantically equivalent **mixin** composition is shown in Figure 7b.

```
class test {
    int y;
    int x;
    test() { { y = -1; } { x = 2; } }
}
                                    (a)
```

```
SoUrCe ...;
abstract class test$$t1 {
    int y;
    test$$t1() { y = -1; }
}
SoUrCe ...;
class test extends  test$$t1  {
    int x;
    refines test() { x = 2; }
}
                                    (b)
```

Fig. 7. Another jampack and Mixin composition

5.3 Local Identifiers

Variables that are local to a feature are common. Such variables are used only by the feature itself, and are not to be exported or referenced by other features.

Suppose a class **bar** declares a local variable **x**, and an extension of **bar** declares a local variable, also named **x**:

```
class bar {
    int x;
}
```

```
refines class bar {
    float x;
}
```

jampack is smart enough to alert you that multiple definitions of **x** are present; **mixin** isn't that smart — and you will discover the error when you compile the translated Java files and see there are multiple definitions of **x**.

The problem we just outlined isn't specific to AHEAD. In fact, it is an example of a classic problem in metaprogramming, and in particular, macro expansion. The problem is called *inadvertent capture* — i.e., multiple distinct variables are given the same names as identifiers. A general solution is to make sure that distinct variables are given unique names[16].

The way this is done in AHEAD is by using a `Local_Id` declaration. This declaration lists the set of identifiers (i.e., variable names and method names) that are *local* to a feature; ATS tools will mangle their names so that they will always be unique. So a better way to define the above is:

```
Local_Id x;

class bar {
    int x;
}
```

```
Local_Id x;

refines class bar {
    float x;
}
```

The `jampack` and `mixin` composition of the above two files are:

```
class bar {
    int x$$one;
    float x$$two;
}
```

```
SoUrCe ...;
abstract class bar$$one {
    int x$$one;
}

SoUrCe   ...;
class bar extends  bar$$one  {
    float x$$two;
}
```

where local names are replaced with their mangled counterparts so that their names no longer conflict.

6 A More Complex Example

Consider model `L`, which defines a set of programs that implement linked lists:

L = { sgl, dbl, sgldel, dbldel }

The lone value is `sgl` which contains a pair of classes, `list` and `node`, that implement a bare-bones singly-linked list (Figure 8a-b).

An extension of `sgl` is `dbl`, which converts the program of `sgl` into a doubly-linked list. `dbl` is a crosscut that augments the `node` class with a `prior` pointer, adds a

```
class list {
    node first = null;

    void insert( node n ) {
        n.next = first;
        first = n;
    }
}
```
(a) L/sgl/list.jak

```
refines class list {
    node last = null;

    void insert( node n ) {
        if (last == null)
            last = n;
        if (first != null)
            first.prior = n;
        Super(node).insert(n);
        n.prior = null;
    }
}
```
(c) L/dbl/list.jak

```
class node {
    node   next = null;
}
```
(b) L/sgl/node.jak

```
refines class node {
    node prior = null;
}
```
(d) L/dbl/node.jak

Fig. 8. The **sgl** and **dbl** Layers

last pointer to the **list** class, and extends the **insert** method so that the values assigned to the **last** and **prior** pointers are consistent (Figure 8c-d).

The composition **both = dbl•sgl** yields the doubly-linked list program of Figure 9. The code underlined originates from the **dbl** extension.

```
class list {
    node first = null;
    node last = null;

    final void insert$$sgl( node n ) {
        n.next = first;
        first = n;
    }

    void insert( node n ) {
        if (last == null)
            last = n;
        insert$$sgl(n);
        x.prior = null;
    }
}
```

(a) L/both/list.jak

```
class node {
    String constant;
    node    next = null;
    node prior = null;
}
```

(b) L/both/node.jak

Fig. 9. Composition dbl•sgl

Now suppose we want to enhance the design of our list programs by adding a **delete** method. **sgldel** does exactly this for singly-linked lists: it adds a **delete** method to the **list** class (Figure 10a). We can use **sgldel** in a composition **slist** that defines a singly-linked list with both **insert** and **delete** methods:

> **slist = sgldel • sgl**

To create a doubly-linked list that has both **insert** and **delete** methods requires an extension **dbldel** (Figure 10b). **dbldel** converts the singly-linked list deletion algorithm of **sgldel** to a doubly-linked list deletion algorithm by replacing (or overriding) the **findAndDelete** method.

The following equations yield identical programs for inserting and deleting elements from a doubly-linked list. The reason why they are equivalent is that the extensions **dbl** and **sgldel** are independent of each other, and thus can be composed in any order.

$$\text{dlist} = \text{dbldel•dbl•sgldel•sgl} \tag{8}$$

$$= \text{dbldel•sgldel•dbl•sgl} \tag{9}$$

Model Exercises

[10] Suppose other operations for traversing the list are added. How would this impact model **L**? What about the operation **reverse()**, which reverses the order in which nodes are listed?

[11] Suppose an "ordering" feature is added to a list, meaning that nodes have keys and are maintained in ascending key order. How would this feature impact **L**?

[12] Consider a "monitor" feature, which precludes more than one thread to access a list at a time. How would this feature impact **L**? How would it be defined?

```
refines class list {

   void delete( node n ) {
      if (n == first) {
         first = first.next;
      }
      else
         findAndDelete(n);
   }

   void findAndDelete(node n) {
      node prev = first;
      while (prev != n)
         prev = prev.next;
      prev.next = n.next;
   }
}
```

(a) L/sgldel/list.jak

```
refines class list {

   void findAndDelete(node n) {
      if( n== last)
         last = last.prior;
      if (n.prior != null)
         n.prior.next = n.next;
      if (n.next != null)
         n.next.prior = n.prior;
   }
}
```

(b) L/dbldel/list.jak

Fig. 10. The `sgldel` and `dbldel` Layers

Tool Exercises

The directory structure for L is:

```
L/sgl/list.jak          // see Figure 8a
L/sgl/node.jak          // see Figure 8b
L/dbl/list.jak          // see Figure 8c
L/dbl/node.jak          // see Figure 8d
L/sgldel/list.jak       // see Figure 8a
L/dbldel/list.jak       // see Figure 8b
```

The files of Figure 9 are the result of evaluating the equation `both = dlb•sgl` using the `composer` tool:

```
> cd L
> composer --target=both sgl dbl
```

The generated directory structure is:

```
L/both/list.jak         // see Figure 9a
L/both/node.jak         // see Figure 9b
```

[13] What is a `guidsl` model of L?

6.1 Multi-dimensional Models and Origami

There remains a fundamental relationship among the features of L that we have not yet captured. Consider the following incorrect compositions:

```
error1 = dbl•sgldel•sgl
error2 = dbldel•sgldel•sgl
```

Both define programs that are partially and thus incorrectly implemented. `error1` is a program whose `insert` method works on a doubly-linked list, but whose `delete` method works only on a singly-linked list. `error2` is a program whose `insert` method works on a singly-linked list, but whose `delete` method works for a doubly-linked list.

The problem is that if a data structure is extended (i.e., a singly-linked list becomes doubly-linked), then *all* of its operations should be updated to maintain the consistency of this extension, and not just some. That is, if a singly-linked list has both `insert` and `delete` operations, when the structure becomes doubly-linked, both operations must be updated to work on doubly-linked lists. Equivalently, if a feature adds a new method to a data structure, then that method must work for that data structure and not some other structure.

Although this is an elementary example, it is representative of a large class of problems in FOP, namely that a model defines a group of features that are not truly independent and this group must be applied in lock-step — all or nothing — manner. Whenever you notice this phenomena, realize that these groups represent features of multidimensional models, which we explain further and illustrate in the following paragraphs.

Create a matrix, called an *Origami matrix* (which is a 2-dimensional model), where rows represent operations (`insert`, `delete`), and columns represent structure variants (`singleLink`, `doubleLink`). Entries of this matrix are the features of L (see Table 1). This matrix can be extended to handle other operations (sort, find) and other structure variants (ordered-lists, monitors, etc.).

Note: what we have done is to identify orthogonal feature sets as 'data structure operations' and 'data structure variants'; these feature sets define the units of different dimensions of a 2-dimensional model or matrix.

Table 1. Origami Matrix for L

	doubleLink	singleLink
insert	dbl	sgl
delete	dbldel	sgldel

Suppose the rows of this matrix are composed (or *folded* — hence the name "Origami"), where the corresponding entries in each column are composed (Table 2):

Table 2. Row-Composed Origami Matrix

	doubleLink	singleLink
delete•insert	dbldel•dbl	sgldel•sgl

Study the entries of Table 2. Consider the entry in the `singleLink` column: `sgldel•sgl` defines a singly-linked program `s` that has both an `insert` and `delete` method. The entry in the `doubleLink` column, `dbldel•dbl`, defines an extension of `s` that converts its `insert` and `delete` methods to work on a doubly-linked list. Thus by composing the `delete` row with the `insert` row of Table 1, we synthesize a data structure that has multiple methods, and an extension of that data structure that consistently updates these methods. This interpretation holds if more rows (operations) or more list features (columns) are added.

The columns of Table 2 can be composed to yield a 1×1 matrix whose entry is an expression that defines a doubly-linked list with insert and delete methods (Table 3). This expression is identical to equation (8).

Table 3. A Completely Folded Matrix

	doubleLink•singleLink
delete•insert	dbldel•dbl•sgldel•sgl

Now instead of composing rows of Table 1, let's compose the columns, where corresponding entries in each row are composed (Table 4):

Table 4. Column Composed Origami Matrix

	doubleLink•singleLink
insert	dbl•sgl
delete	dbldel•sgldel

The entry in the insert row, dbl•sgl, defines program D that implements a doubly-linked list with an insert method. The entry in the delete row, dbldel•sgldel, defines an extension of D that adds a delete method. By composing the columns of Table 1, we have synthesized a data structure with a single (insert) method, and an extension that adds a delete method to this structure. Again, this interpretation holds if we add more rows (methods) or more columns (features) to Table 1. By folding the rows of Table 4, a 1×1 matrix is produced whose lone entry is equation (9). As a general rule, as long as the order in which rows and columns (that is, 'data structure operation' features or 'data structure variant' features) are composed is legal, the resulting equations in a fully-folded matrix should be equivalent. (If they are not, then a dimension is missing in the design).

Origami matrices capture fundamental relationships among groups of features: to build consistent and correct programs, it is often necessary to apply an entire group of features at once [6]. A matrix representation of these relationships works because the set of features along one dimension are *orthogonal* to those of another. In our example, the set of methods that can be used with a data structure is orthogonal to the set of data structure variants.

Although this is a simple example, Origami applies at much greater levels of granularity. For example, ATS has five tools — including jampack, mixin, and unmixin — each having over 30K LOC, and totalling over 150K LOC. These tools are synthesized by folding a 3-dimensional (8×6×8) Origami matrix, where the dimensions are: language features × tool features × language feature interactions [6].

6.2 The Meaning of Origami

Why is Origami significant? There are several reasons, all of which capture important generalizations of equational program specifications.

In earlier sections, we defined a program by a single equation. Origami generalizes this idea, so that a program is defined by a set of k equations, one per dimension. This has a significant impact on reducing the complexity of a program specification. Suppose each of the k equations has n terms. Thus, a program specification in Origami is of length $O(nk)$. Yet, the matrix that is folded into a single expression would have $O(n^k)$ terms! That is, *Origami exponentially shortens specifications of product-line programs* [6]. Or stated another way, Origami enables very simple specifications for very complex programs.

Here's another interesting question: what is the algebraic meaning of matrix folding? The answer is evident when we interpret the composition operator (•) as addition [12].

Composition in AHEAD is similar to summation. Suppose to build program P, we start with a base feature F_0 and progressively add on features F_1, F_3, and F_7. Instead of using •, we use + to denote composition:

$$P = F_7 + F_3 + F_1 + F_0 \tag{10}$$

Here's another way to represent P. Suppose F is the model that contains features F_0, F_1, F_3, and F_7. In general F_i is the ith feature of model F. Let E be the sequence of subscripts whose features we are to sum. For equation (10), $E = (0,1,3,7)$. We could equivalently write (10) as a summation:

$$P = \sum_{i \in E} F_i$$

Now suppose our model is two dimensional. Let M denote a two-dimensional Origami matrix, where M_{ij} is the element in the ith row and jth column. When the matrix is folded first by rows then by columns, this corresponds to summing the matrix by columns then by rows. When the matrix is folded by columns and then by rows, this corresponds to summing by rows and then columns. Let R be the sequence of subscripts in which rows are folded; let C be the sequence of subscripts in which columns are folded. Origami expresses the equivalence of the summation of elements of a matrix in different orders:

$$P = \sum_{i \in R} \sum_{j \in C} M_{i,j} = \sum_{j \in C} \sum_{i \in R} M_{i,j}$$

That is, an Origami matrix is a k-dimensional "cube", which when summed across different dimensions yields a program in a product-line. Summation of matrix entries and permuting the order in which entities are added, are familiar ideas in mathematics. The name "Origami" is really a visual interpretation of matrix summation.

Finally, it is worth noting that Origami and multi-dimensional models are historically related to a fundamental problem in program design called the "expression problem", which has been widely studied within the context of programming language design where the focus is achieving data type and operation extensibility in a type-safe manner [22][18]. The FOP contribution to this is to show how the idea scales to the synthesis of large programs [6].

6.3 Metamodels and Model Synthesis

How are Origami matrices represented in AHEAD? Before we can answer this question, we need to introduce an important concept in modeling called metamodels. A *metamodel* is a model whose instances are themselves models. Consider model M, which has units a, b, and c:

```
M = { a, b, c }
```

Consider metamodel MM, which also has three units, each being a set with a single unit:

```
MM = { AAA, BBB, CCC }
   = { {a}, {b}, {c} }
```

A model can be synthesized by composing metamodel units. The MM equation for model M is:

```
M = AAA•BBB•CCC
```

In this particular case, because there are no units in common with AAA—CCC, composition reduces to set-union. The interesting thing about metamodels is that they are identical to models. That is, a model or metamodel is a set of units, where each unit may be a set. Further, the composition operator for units of metamodels (•) is the same operator for units of models (•).

An Origami matrix is a metamodel. Consider the example of an $n{\times}m$ matrix o where o_{ij} denotes the row i column j element of o. There are two ways to represent this matrix as a tree, i.e., as a model of models. One way is to decompose the matrix first into rows, and then each row into columns (Figure 11a). Another way is to organize by columns first, and then rows (Figure 11b). This idea scales to arbitrary dimensional matrices.

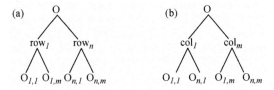

Fig. 11. Matrix Embeddings in Trees

6.4 Representing Origami Matrices

Now lets consider how to represent Origami matrices. Consider a row-dominant decomposition. Figure 12a shows our example matrix, where entries are equation files that have the same name (eqn.equation). Entry subscripts denote (to us) their true identity. Figure 12b is the corresponding row-oriented metamodel; Figure 12c is its AHEAD directory structure. Figure 12d-g are the contents of the equation files.

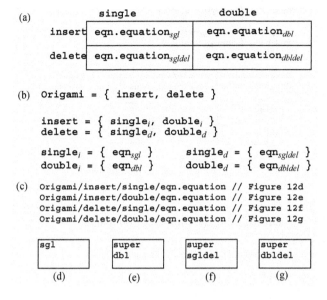

Fig. 12. Row-Dominant Embedding of a Matrix

Why do we use this particular representation of a matrix? Why use equation files, rather than embedding the actual feature directories themselves? The answer: convenience. Try to create such a hierarchical directory yourself, where instead of equation files, you have feature directories. It's hard to navigate such a directory structure, let alone maintain it. The simpler the representation the better. So it is common that we have a flat model directory (where features are immediate subdirectories), and a separate Origami directory which defines the multi-dimensional relationship among features using equation files.

Model Exercises

[14] Expand the Origami matrix to handle more data structure operations and variants, such as list element updates and key ordered lists.

Tool Exercises

To fold a 2-dimensional matrix, you need to invoke **composer** twice: once to compose rows and a second time for columns. (For a k-dimensional matrix, we would invoke **composer** k times). So to produce the AHEAD equivalent of Table 2, we compose the rows of the **Origami** model to produce model **Table2** = **delete•insert**:

```
> cd Origami
> composer --target=Table2 insert delete
```

The resulting model **Table2** is depicted in Figure 13a, and its synthesized AHEAD directory structure in Figure 13b, and the contents of the equation files in Figure 13c-d.

(a) `Table2 = { single, double }`

$single = \{\ eqn_{sgldel}\bullet eqn_{sgl}\ \}$
$double = \{\ eqn_{dbldel}\bullet eqn_{dbl}\ \}$

(b) `Origami/Table2/single/eqn.equation // Figure 13c`
`Origami/Table2/double/eqn.equation // Figure 13d`

(c)
```
sgl
sgldel
```

(d)
```
super
dbl
dbldel
```

Fig. 13. AHEAD Origami Metamodel

To produce the 1×1 matrix of Table 3 or equation **(8)**, we compose the columns (named **single** and **double**) using the following command:

```
> cd Table2
> composer --target=both single double
> cd both
> jak2java *.jak
```

[15] Represent the matrix of Figure 12a by columns, and repeat the above folding.

Model Exercises

[16] Create two different GUIs for a calculator: one uses the standard 2D keypad, a second uses text fields to enter values and operations. A calculator will use one (but not both) of these GUIs. Operations on both GUIs are buttons. So when a calculator is extended by a new operation, its GUI will be extended also. Express this relationship between operations and GUIs as an Origami matrix.

[17] Generalize the model in [16] that permits multiple GUIs per calculator. One idea would use tabs, one tab per different GUI. Implement your model.

7 What's Next?

There are many interesting topics and capabilities that we have yet to explore (or develop) for AHEAD. Here are just a few. If you are interested in learning more about these topics, see [1][5].

7.1 Extensible Languages

There are all sorts of non-Java extensions to the Jak language that we haven't talked about, including:

- *metaprogramming — the ability to assign code fragments to variables, the ability to compose code fragments via escape substitutions, hygienic macros.*
- *state machines — an embedded DSL for supporting the definition and extension of state machines* [7].

7.2 Compiler-Compiler Tools

ATS has a sophisticated set of compiler-compiler tools that are used to (a) define base grammars, (b) define grammar extensions, and (c) to synthesize grammars by composing base grammars with extensions. Grammars are yet another representation of a program, in this case, a compiler, and ATS has tools for defining and composing grammars and generating Java files from them [1].

7.3 Generating and Optimizing MakeFiles

The idea of modules as hierarchical collections of related artifacts is powerful. A paradigm of AHEAD that we have explored so far is that of *composition*: that artifacts of a program can be composed from previously defined artifacts. But there is another way in which program artifacts can be produced: by *derivation*. For example, Java files can be produced from Jak files by the **jak2java** tool; class files can be produced from Java files by the **javac** compiler, and so on. A general paradigm is depicted in Figure 14: an artifact can be produced by first composing it from more elementary artifacts, followed by a derivation. Or equivalently, it can be produced by deriving a set of artifacts from more elementary artifacts, and then composing the derived representations[3]. This leads to the following fundamental distributive algebraic relationship (11).

```
derive( artifact_i • artifact_j ) =
derive( artifact_i ) • derive( artifact_j )                    (11)
```

Ultimately, we want to specify an entire program — all of its composed and derived representations — as a set of equations. Although ATS does not yet have such a tool, one can imagine a specification like:

```
Using L;
i3 = javadoc( javac( jak2java( sgldel( sgl ) ) ) );           (12)
```

where the **Using** clause tells this tool that **sgldel** and **sgl** are units in model **L**, and by inference, **composer** should be used to compose them. The resulting module will have **.jak**, **.java**, **.class** and **.html** files. The **jak2java** tool, when applied to the module of **sgldel(sgl)**, translates all Jak files to Java files and adds them to the module. Similarly, the **javac** operation compiles all Java files and adds their **.class** files to the module. The **javadoc** operation will generate JavaDoc **.html** files from the generated Java files, and so on, progressively enlarging the contents of that module/directory. In effect, (12) is really an equational representation of a makefile! More on this shortly.

The lesson that we learned from relational query optimizers is that an expression represents a program design and expressions (and hence designs) can be optimized. In this particular example, there really isn't anything to optimize. There is, though, a particular sequencing of the application of the **javadoc, javac,** and **jak2java**

---

[3] Figure 14 can be generalized further, so that multiple output artifacts can be derived from a single input artifact, and vice versa.

operations that must be imposed. (In fact, this really is the only legal ordering of these operations for this equation). So notions of design rules also apply to tool operations. But as equations become more complicated, there is the possibility of optimization. In some of our larger examples using Origami, generating common subexpressions among different sets of tools arises. Evaluating common subexpressions once, and not many times, is an important optimization that a tool should be able achieve automatically [14].

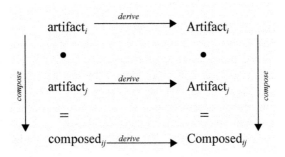

Fig. 14. Compose vs. Derive

The big picture is depicted below. Given an equational representation of a program that specifies both the artifacts that are to be composed and those that are to be derived, a tool will expand the equations and perform optimizations to synthesize the resulting program in an efficient manner. The tool will then produce an optimized set of equations, and a generator will translate these equations into a *makefile* — a functional-like language that efficiently executes equational specifications [14].

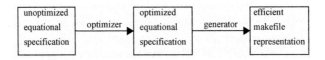

Fig. 15. Generation and Optimization of MakeFiles

7.4 Type Systems

As mentioned earlier, extensions are functions that appear untyped. In fact, function inputs and outputs have definite constraints. Our tools assume that the correct types are both being input and output. In general, this is bad assumption.

Question: how does one type a program? Should Java interfaces be used? How does typing generalize to, say, grammar files or equation files? What is a general mechanism for typing arbitrary artifacts and their extensions? At the present time, there are no solutions to these problems.

7.5 Aspect-Oriented Programming

Aspect-Oriented Programming (AOP) is closely related to FOP. Both deal with modules that encapsulate crosscuts of classes, and both express program extensions. FOP uses a subset of the "advising" capabilities of AOP, namely those that use execution pointcuts. However, the primary difference between AOP and FOP is their composition models. FOP treats aspects as functions that map programs, and uses function composition as the means to compose aspects. This leads to algebraic representations of programs and a simple means to perform program reasoning with aspects.

In contrast, AOP uses a complex model of aspect composition (e.g., precedence rules) that complicates program reasoning using aspects and makes step-wise development difficult [19]. AOP and FOP are thus not directly comparable, but are instances of a more general paradigm of automated software development — one that composes aspects by FOP function composition and uses the full power of AOP pointcuts.

8 Conclusions

Just as the structure of matter is fundamental to chemistry and physics, so too must the structure of software be fundamental to computer science. Unfortunately, our understanding of software structure is in its infancy. Today, software design is an art. As long as it remains so, our ability to automate rote tasks of program design and synthesis will be limited. And software engineering will be more of a craft than a discipline.

Software designs can be given mathematical precision when expressed as a composition of features. We have presented a simple and elegant theory of program design, backed by years of implementation and experimentation, that brings together key elements in the future of software development: generative programming, domain-specific languages, automatic programming, and step-wise development. Generative programming gives our theory its mathematical backbone: functions can map programs. Domain-specific languages give programming artifacts their form: these are the artifacts that functions transform. Automatic programming underscores AHEAD as a simple model that relates automated reasoning, compositional programming, and design optimization by algebraic reasoning. And step-wise development is a practical way of controlling complexity. AHEAD provides an algebraic foundation for understanding program development on a larger scale.

This paper has explored basic concepts of FOP and a (small) subset of the tools of the AHEAD tool suite. For the most recent results, see our web site [17] and consult the AHEAD documentation [1].

Acknowledgements. This work is sponsored by NSF's Science of Design Project #CCF-0438786. I thank the referees, Ralf Lämmel, João Saraiva, and Joost Visser for their helpful comments.

Suggested Reading

[1] AHEAD Tool Suite, `http://www.cs.utexas.edu/users/schwartz/ATS.html` `ATS documentation`.

[2] R. Balzer, "A Fifteen-Year Perspective on Automatic Programming", *IEEE Trans. Software Engineering*, November 1985, pp. 1257-1267. `Mid-80's state-of-art-report on automatic programming`.

[3] D. Batory and S. O'Malley. "The Design and Implementation of Hierarchical Software Systems with Reusable Components". *ACM Trans. Software Engineering and Methodology*, October 1992, pp. 355-398. `The GenVoca Model`.

[4] D. Batory: "The Road to Utopia: A Future for Generative Programming". *Domain-Specific Program Generation 2003*, Lecture Notes in Computer Science #3016, pp. 1-18. `Relationship of query optimization to AHEAD`.

[5] D. Batory, J.N. Sarvela, A. Rauschmayer, "Scaling Stepwise Refinement", *IEEE Trans. Software Engineering*, June 2004, 355-371. `The AHEAD model`.

[6] D. Batory, J. Liu, J.N. Sarvela, "Refinements and Multi-Dimensional Separation of Concerns", *ACM SIGSOFT 2003*, pp. 48 - 57. `A sophisticated example of Origami`.

[7] D. Batory, C. Johnson, R. MacDonald, and D. von Heeder, "Achieving Extensibility Through Product-Lines and Domain-Specific Languages: A Case Study", *ACM Transactions on Software Engineering and Methodology*, April 2002, 191-214. `A product-line that needs both extensions and embedded DSLs`.

[8] D. Batory, G. Chen, E. Robertson, and T. Wang, Design Wizards and Visual Programming Environments for GenVoca Generators, *IEEE Transactions on Software Engineering*, May 2000, 441-452. `Explains relationship between automatic programming and GenVoca equation optimization`.

[9] D. Batory and B.J. Geraci. Composition Validation and Subjectivity in GenVoca Generators, *IEEE Transactions on Software Engineering*, February 1997, pp. 67-82. `Early form of design rule checking`.

[10] D. Batory, "Feature Models, Grammars, and Propositional Formulas", *Software Product-Line Conference (SPLC) 2005*, pp. 7-20. `Generalizes results in` .

[11] M. de Jong and J. Visser, "Grammars as Feature Diagrams", 2002. *Workshop on Generative Programming (GP2002)*, Austin Texas, USA. April 15, 2002. `Relates feature diagrams to grammars`.

[12] E.J. Jung, "Feature Oriented Programming and Product Line Architectures for Open Architecture Robot Software", M.Sc. Thesis, Dept. Mechanical Engineering, University of Texas at Austin, 2004. `Application of FOP ideas to robotics, Origami`.

[13] K. Kang, S. Cohen, J. Hess, W. Nowak, and S. Peterson. "Feature-Oriented Domain Analysis (FODA) Feasibility Study". Technical Report, CMU/SEI-90TR-21, Software Engineering Institute, Carnegie Mellon University, Pittsburgh, PA, November 1990. `First significant paper on features and product-lines.`

[14] J. Liu and D. Batory, "Automatic Remodularization and Optimized Synthesis of Product-Families", *Generative Programming and Component Engineering (GPCE)*, October 2004, pp. 379-395. `Shows how sets of equations can be optimized`.

[15] R. E. Lopez-Herrejon and D. Batory, "A Standard Problem for Evaluating Product-Line Methodologies", *Generative and Component-Based Software Engineering* (GCSE 2001), Erfurt, Germany. pp. 10-24. `A simple product-line defined using the GenVoca model`.

[16] E. Kohlbecker, D.P. Friedman, M. Felleisen, and B. Duba, "Hygienic Macro Expansion", SIGPLAN '86 *ACM Conference on Lisp and Functional Programming*, pp. 151-161. **Classic paper on the inadvertent capture problem.**

[17] Product-Line Architecture Research Group. **http://www.cs.utexas.edu/ users/schwartz/**

[18] R. Lopez-Herrejon, D. Batory, and W. Cook, "Evaluating Support for Features in Advanced Modularization Technologies", *European Conference on Object-Oriented Programming (ECOOP)*, July 2005, pp. 169-194. **Using the expression problem to evaluate different modularization technologies.**

[19] R. Lopez-Herrejon, D. Batory, and C. Lengauer, "A Disciplined Approach to Aspect Composition", *Program Evaluation and Program Manipulation (PEPM)* 2005, pp. 68-77. **Formalizes the AspectJ composition model.**

[20] P. Selinger.P, M.M. Astrahan, D.D. Chamberlin, R.A. Lorie, and T.G. Price, "Access Path Selection in a Relational Database System", *ACM SIGMOD 1979*, pp. 23-34. **Classic paper on relational query optimizers.**

[21] T. Teitelbaum and T. Reps, "The Cornell Program Synthesizer: a Syntax-Directed Programming Environment", *CACM*, v.24 n.9, pp. 563-573, Sept. 1981. **Classic paper on syntax-directed editors.**

[22] M. Torgersen, "The Expression Problem Revisited. Four New Solutions Using Generics", *ECOOP 2004*, pp. 123-146. **A recent paper on the Expression problem.**

Model Driven Engineering: An Emerging Technical Space

Jean Bézivin

Atlas Group: INRIA, and LINA
University of Nantes
2, rue de la Houssinière - BP92208
44322 Nantes Cedex 3, France
Jean.Bezivin@univ-nantes.fr

Abstract. As an emerging solution to the handling of complex and evolving software systems, Model Driven Engineering (MDE) is still very much in evolution. The industrial demand is quite high while the research answer for a sound set of foundation principles is still far from being stabilized. Therefore it is important to provide a current state of the art in MDE, describing what its origins are, what its present state is, and where it seems to be presently leading. One important question is how MDE relates to other contemporary technologies. This tutorial proposes the "technical space" concept to this purpose. The two main objectives are to present first the basic MDE principles and second how these principles may be mapped onto modern platform support. Other issues that will be discussed are the applicability of these ideas, concepts, and tools to solve current practical problems. Various organizations and companies (OMG, IBM, Microsoft, etc.) are currently proposing several environments claiming to support MDE. Among these, the OMG MDA™ (Model Driven Architecture) has a special place since it was historically one of the original proposals in this area. This work focuses on the identification of basic MDE principles, practical characteristics of MDE (direct representation, automation, and open standards), original MDE scenarios, and discussions of suitable tools and methods.

Keywords: Model Driven Engineering; MDE; MDA; Metamodeling; Technical Spaces;

1 Introduction

In November 2000 [32] the OMG proposed a new approach to interoperability named MDA™ (Model-Driven Architecture). MDA is one example of the broader Model Driven Engineering (MDE) vision, encompassing many popular current research trends related to generative and transformational techniques in software engineering, system engineering, or data engineering [6], [11]. Considering models as first class entities and any software artifact as a model or as a model element is one of the basic principles of MDE. The key ideas of MDE are germane to many other approaches

R. Lämmel, J. Saraiva, and J. Visser (Eds.): GTTSE 2005, LNCS 4143, pp. 36–64, 2006.

such as domain specific languages (DSLs), software factories, model-integrated computing (MIC), model-driven software development (MDSD), model management, language-oriented programming and much more. The OMG MDA initial proposal may be defined as the realization of MDE principles around a set of OMG standards like MOF, XMI, OCL, UML, CWM, and SPEM. Most of these acronyms will be referenced later in the document. Their important number is due to the initial normative aspect of the field. A list of some common ones is provided in an appendix.

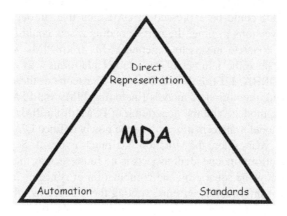

Fig. 1. The three IBM manifesto tenets

The IBM manifesto [15] makes the claim that MDA-based approaches are founded on three ideas: Direct representation, Automation and Standards. Direct representation allows a more direct coupling of problems to solutions with the help of Domains Specific Languages (DSLs). Automations means that the facets represented in these DSLs are intended to be processed by computer-based tools to bridge the semantic gap between domain concepts and implementation technologies and not only for mere documentation. This should be complemented by the use of open standards that will allow technical solutions to interoperate. These three complementary ideas are central to the development of MDE approaches. Models should be exchangeable and for this we need to agree on consensual standards. Many models would however need to be written by human agents, very often non computer scientist agents. In this case, these models (or programs) will be written in domain specific languages, restricted in size and precisely defined. The mapping of these models written in precise DSLs onto operational technology by using generative and transformational techniques is one important aspect of MDE. Another major issue is to solve the fragmentation problem resulting from the coexistence of a high number of small DSLs. The answer to this problem is the existence of a global representation system (for example the MOF OMG M3 level), and the support of libraries of various correspondences between models (e.g. transformation or weavings). However this is not sufficient and we need also to invent registries and global links between entities like models and metamodels to escape fragmentation problems.

Historically in year 2000, the MDA had a specific goal: preserving the IT investments of companies through the constant and rapid evolution of platforms. At that time the middleware and the component solutions alone were no more in a position to achieve this goal. The proposal was thus to capture in PIMs (Platform Independent Models) the part of the investment that should not be affected by major or minor changes in platforms. The idea was then that it should be possible, by some means, to generate PSMs (Platform Specific Models) from these PIMs. How this problem could be concretely solved was not completely clear at the time. The main idea was that a PIM could be expressed in UML and that, through the supposedly stability of UML versions in time, the corresponding assets could be preserved over long periods. The concrete means to generate PSMs from PIMs were not precisely stated at the time since the number of such target platforms was rather limited and similar (mainly CORBA, J2EE/EJB and DotNet). The scope of these target platforms was then broadened, the notion of models (including PIMs and PSMs) was extended beyond mere UML models, and the generation of PSMs from PIMs was suggested to be automated by model transformations using the newly defined QVT standard [29].

More than five years after, the situation has much evolved. Separating platform dependent from platform independent aspects is no more seen as the unique goal. The major problem is now the separation and combination of concerns in the construction and maintenance of information systems. Among these concerns, platform dependent and independent aspects remains important in the agenda, but these are more and more considered as a special case of a general problem including for example separation of functional and non-functional requirements. MDA and DSL solutions are now more and more closely related. What MDA is bringing to DSLs is this idea of using a collection of metamodels to capture the various facets of a system under construction or under maintenance. What DSLs is bringing to MDA is that a unique general purpose language, even a very large one like UML 2.0, is not able and will never be able to capture all the needs of the designers, administrators, and users of a given system.

The notion of direct representation [15] is very important. This means that instead of performing themselves directly certain tasks in general purpose languages like Java, computer scientists may instead concentrate on defining specialized languages and handling these to final users that will be able to express precisely their contributions in these languages in a non-ambiguous manner. The computer scientists will be in charge of mapping these contributed expressions (often of a declarative nature) into executable structures i.e. target platforms. We recognize here the common objective of MDA and DSLs. But a DSL may address a lot of needs, corporate or organizational for example. A typical DSL, that has been very successful for a long time, is Excel that addressed in early stages, with products like VisiCalc, the domain needs of basic accounting. Excel is now an example of a language defined by computer specialists to solve the problems of non specialists. Using such tools, many tasks may be solved now by non-specialists, without the help of specialists that are becoming more and more language engineers. The form of these languages may vary in their concrete appearance and they could be defined by conventional grammars, by DTDs or XML schemas, by ontologies, by graphical representation or by metamodels. One central contribution of MDE is about the possible expression of DSLs by metamodels.

The three tenets mentioned in the IBM manifesto are essential to MDE. However, to make it practical we need to extend this definition in two directions First we need to build MDE on a sound set of principles. Next we need to implement MDE on practical platforms of wide usage. We propose an initial set of kernel principles that could serve as a proposal for a foundational set of principles. We also suggest an architectural style that could be used as a guide to implement these principles on current industrial platforms.

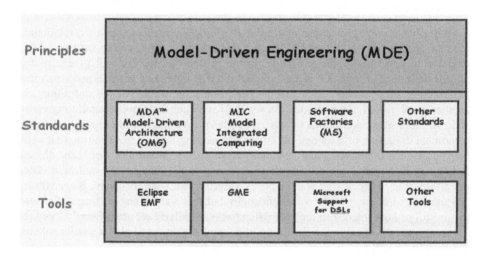

Fig. 2. Principles, Standards, and Tools

This text proposes some ideas on the present rapid evolution of the MDE scene. The basic set of MDE principles is based on two concepts (system and model) and two basic relations (conformance and representation). This allows giving a first definition of what is a model in the MDE context. In another section we propose to situate MDE with respect to other possible solutions. Our organization of the solution space is based on the notion of "technical space". This will help us to give an extended definition, more general and precise, of what is a model. In the rest of the document we come back to the strict MDE technical space. We also propose an initial inventory of possible operations on models. Model transformation will obviously be one important example of an operation on models. The consequences of a transformation being itself considered as a model will be much emphasized. We also propose an architectural style for implementing an MDE platform respecting the basic principles. This will be given in the form of an abstract architecture composed of four complementary functional blocks addressing the issues of model transformation, model weaving, global model management, and model projection onto other spaces. As an illustration of this architectural style, we will present the AMMA prototype [1] available in the Eclipse GMT project [19].

2 Basic MDE Principles

2.1 Prerequisites

In order to discuss the broad view of MDE, we need a suitable common notation. Among many possibilities, we use the now conventional UML class diagrams and the Object Constraint Language. UML and OCL do not bring new expressive power to MDE, but they are standards (OMG standards) that may facilitate interoperability of solutions and common understanding.

2.2 Introduction

A model is a complex structure that represents a design artifact such as a relational schema, an interface definition (API), an XML schema, a semantic network, a UML model or a hypermedia document [4]. In the present section we will give a more limited definition of a model, in the context of MDE only, as a graph-based structure representing some aspects of a given system and conforming to the definition of another graph called a metamodel. As we shall see later there are several contextual and complementary definitions of what a model is. We are not interested here by a theoretical definition of a model, but by an engineering one, i.e. a definition that will help users to implement and maintain systems. The parallel between object technology and model engineering that was made in [7] may be relevant here. The definition of an "object" that was given by pioneers like Dahl, Nygaard, Kay, Meyer and others had nothing to do with philosophy but this was an engineering definition that is still of high interest to the profession today. Similarly we are presently looking for an operational engineering definition of a "model" that could play a similar role in the coming period.

2.3 Basic Entities

The present trend in model engineering [7] is to consider that models are first class citizens. This approach seems to be the only possibility to deal with ever-increasing complexity in information and software systems. It will hopefully allow to separate and to combine different aspects in a more regular way. Among these aspects we may mention platform dependent and independent features. As a corollary of this principle stating "that everything is a model", we may infer for example that "a model transformation should also be considered as a model". The basic principle and its corollaries build the foundation of third generation model transformation frameworks. However there is still an important amount of work to be done before fully understanding MDE environments and putting them to work.

In [31], Ed Seidewitz writes: "…In any case, without this well-grounded foundation, our models are, in the end, just pictures that don't really mean anything at all…"

Models are now commonly used to provide representation of real-world situations. A model is said to *represent* a system. Fig. 3 provides an example of a relational model that defines a possible representation for a set of books in a library. On the right side of Fig. 3, we have a relational representation of part of the world (a library). Other different representations of this same library are possible, e.g. an event-based representation capturing book creation, lending, returning, destruction, etc.

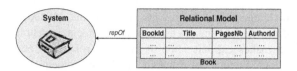

Fig. 3. The "representation" relation between a system and a model

Each model is defined in conformance to a metamodel. Metamodels define languages enabling to express models. A metamodel describes the various kinds of contained model elements, and the way they are arranged, related, and constrained. A model is said to *conform to* its metamodel. Thus, our Book relational model conforms to the relational metamodel (Fig. 4). Representation and conformance relations are central to model engineering [7].

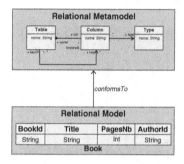

Fig. 4. The "conformance" relation between a model and its metamodel

As models, metamodels are also composed of elements. Metamodel elements provide a typing scheme for models elements. This typing is expressed by the *meta* relation between a model element and its *metaelement* (from the metamodel). We also

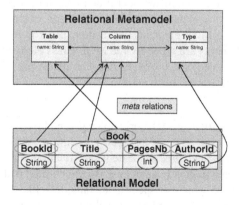

Fig. 5. The "meta" relation between model and metamodel elements

say that a model element is *typed* by its metaelement. A model conforms to a metamodel if and only if each model element has its metaelement defined within the metamodel. Fig. 5 makes explicit some of the *meta* relations between Book model elements and relational metamodel elements: the Book element is typed by the Table metaelement, BookId and Title are typed by the Column metaelement, and String is typed by the Type metaelement.

The growing number of metamodels has emphasized the need for an integration framework for all available metamodels by providing a new item, the metametamodel, dedicated to the definition of metamodels. In the same way models are defined in conformance with their metamodel, metamodels are defined by means of the metametamodel language. A metamodel is said to conform to the metametamodel. As an example, we can consider the MOF (Meta-Object Facility), which is the OMG proposal for metamodels definition [28]. The relational metamodel may conform to the MOF metametamodel.

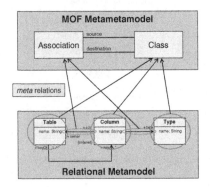

Fig. 6. The "meta" relation between M2 and M3

As models and metamodels, the metametamodel is also composed of elements. A metamodel conforms to the metametamodel if and only if each of its elements has its metaelement defined in the metametamodel. Some *meta* relations between relational metamodel elements and MOF elements are made explicit in Fig. 6. Thus, the Table, Column, and Type elements are typed by the MOF Class element, whereas relational links elements are associated with the MOF Association element.

2.4 Extensions

The previous characterization of MDE principles given above is minimal. It does not cover all aspects necessary for a workable definition. Other relations between metamodels like a clean and precise "extension" relation may be necessary. One reason this has not been completely and consensually defined is that there are ways to solve this problem when you use specific metamodels like UML. The notion of profile for example allows some kind of extensibility in this context.

2.5 Structuring Metamodels

Before engaging in the following section about comparing technologies, we see here that the strong concept in model engineering is the concept of a metamodel. As a consequence a metamodel brings engineering facilities different from grammars, XML schemas, ontologies, etc. Even if the notion of metamodel is still evolving in structure and application, we can say that a metamodel helps defining a language (DSL). This covers however a lot of different facets, some of them being described below.

Basically, as we have seen, a metamodel is a graph composed of concepts and relationships between these concepts. From a usage perspective, a metamodel is a concrete representation of a shared conceptualization. Some of these conceptualizations may be normative (e.g. OMG) and some are not. A metamodel acts as a filter to extract pertinent elements from a system in order to build a corresponding model. Any feature (concept or relationship) not present in the metamodel will be ignored when building the model representing the system.

Metamodels are used to define formalisms or languages (DSLs). To define a formalism, we may need to provide different kind of information for example structure knowledge, assertion knowledge, execution knowledge, display knowledge, etc. The fact that these information are provided by separate parts of a metamodel contribute to a clear separation of concerns. The fact that they are provided by separate metamodel parts combined together goes one step beyond in the direction of modularity and reusability.

Let us consider for example a classical PetriNet formalism. A Petri net is a bipartite directed graph with two kinds of nodes: Places and Transitions. It is an edge-labeled and node-labeled graph. A number of Tokens may be associated to each Place. We may define a Petri Net in four steps:

- The structural knowledge may be captured by a class diagram with concepts of *Pnet* (the global graph), *Place*, *Transition*, *Token* and relations *basicRelation* and *numberOfToken*.

- The assertional knowledge may be captured by OCL descriptions stating that the value attribute of *Token* may never be negative and that a *basicRelation* may link a *Place* to a *Transition* or a *Transition* to a *Place* but never a *Place* to a *Place* or a *Transition* to a *Transition*.

- The execution knowledge may be captured by the following description:
<u>function</u> fireable (t:Transition)
    {return true if every directly incoming Place has at least one Token else false}
<u>context</u> Pnet <u>action</u>;
    <u>repeat</u>
        select from pNet one arbitrary Transition t such that fireable(t);
        decrement the number of tokens for every incoming Place of t;
        increment the number of tokens for every outcoming Place of t;
    <u>until</u> no Transition t in pNet verifies fireable(t);

- The display knowledge may be captured by the following description:
- represent a *Transition* by a *Rectangle*
- represent a *Place* by a *Circle*
- represent an *Edge* by an *Arrow*

Now we may see in this description that any part is based on a separate metamodel for example the OCL metamodel or the AS (Action Semantics) metamodel or a drawing metamodel composed of concepts *Arrow*, *Circle* or a *Rectangle*. So the formalism of Petri Nets is defined not by a single but by an aggregation of metamodels. This way of "decorating" a model with another one based on a different metamodel is quite powerful and goes beyond the classical distinction between abstract and concrete syntaxes. It allows achieving separation of contents from presentation. If we wish to define an extension to Petri nets, for example colored Petri nets, then reusability may be achieved thanks to this clean separation.

We just mentioned in this example that a model may be decorated with assertions to make it more precise, but that it may also be decorated with execution annotations to provide it with some animation capabilities (e.g. simulation but not only). Models are not naturally executable, but by using some available language with precisely defined execution semantics, it is possible to animate them. In [5] the language to write execution annotations was Smalltalk but variants of Java have also been used. The OMG invest efforts in trying to standardize action semantics for UML or even for MOF.

A more regular definition of a DSL may be given as a coordinated set of models. Among these, a central domain metamodel would define the central concepts like *Place*, *Transition* or *Token* in the example above. Most of the other models will be correspondence or transformation models mapping the domain metamodel onto other DSLs, in order to provide various concrete syntaxes, to define executability or other properties. This external way to define executability by a mapping to another executable language (like Java for example) is very general.

2.6 Summary

The basic assumption in MDE is the consideration of models as first class entities. A model is an artifact that conforms to a metamodel and that represents a given aspect of a system. These relations of conformance and representation are central to model engineering [7]. A model is composed of model elements and conforms to a unique metamodel. This metamodel describes the various kinds of contained model elements and the way they are arranged, related, and constrained. A language intended to define metamodels and models is called a metametamodel. Models may be decorated in various ways in order to associate additional properties. The declaration itself is a model, i.e. conforms to a metamodel. The precise mechanisms for composing the various models are not yet completely understood.

3 Engineering: Structuring the Solution Space

Technical spaces were introduced in [24], in the discussion on problems of bridging different technologies. A technical space is a working context with a set of associated concepts, body of knowledge, tools, required skills, and possibilities. It is also a model management framework usually based on some algebraic structures like trees, graphs, hypergraphs, categories, etc. Although technical spaces may be difficult to define formally, they can be easily recognized (e.g. XML, MDA). In the three-level conjecture, each technical space can be seen as based on a metametamodel (explicit or implicit) and a collection of metamodels. For the OMG/MDA the MOF and the collection of standard metamodels and UML profiles play this role.

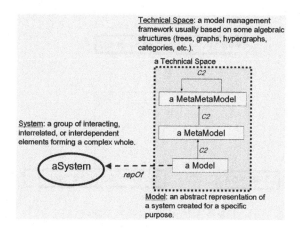

Fig. 7. Systems, models and technical spaces

As illustrated in Fig. 7, the basic notions that we consider are now Systems, Models and Technical Spaces (abbreviated TSs). When we talk about a model, we should say which kind of model we are referring to. For example we could say that an XML-document is an XML-model or that a Java program is a Java-model. Proceeding in that way saves a lot of time by solving a lot of endless discussions about a Java program being or not being a model. The notion of model is a contextual one and to be non-ambiguous we need to prefix the model by its context. A TS denotes such a notion of a context. To take once again the object analogy, Smalltalk objects, Eiffel objects and C++ objects were different kinds of objects, not even able to communicate directly in the absence of some kind of Middleware support like CORBA. However Smalltalk programmers were used to talk about objects in their particular context. Similarly a MDA-model is a model that conforms to a metamodel that conforms to the MOF. When the context is clear, we may talk about a model, often meaning here MDA-model. Such a model will have specific properties, i.e. being able to be serialized in the XMI 2.1 format. When we talk about a Microsoft/DSL-model like in Fig. 8, this will be a different kind of model, not based on the MOF or directly serializable in XMI [30]. We may generalize this prefixing convention when we have to talk about models pertaining to different TSs. If we consider TSs that are organized according to the three level conjecture, we may even talk about a Java program as EBNF/Java/myProg or about an XML document as XML/MusicML/myMusic as naturally as we could talk above ECORE/UML2.0/ myModel or about MOF2.0/CWM/MyData.

Several TSs may thus be considered as based on a three level organization like the metametamodel, metamodel and model of the MDA. One example is grammarware [23] with EBNF, grammars and programs but we could also consider XML documents, RDF documents, Semantic Web, DBMS, ontology engineering, natural

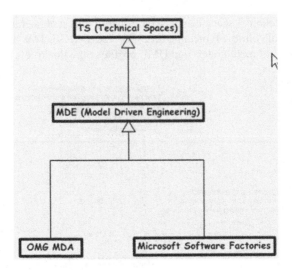

Fig. 8. Two MDE Technical Spaces

language processing systems, etc. In order to get a synergy of different technical spaces we should create conceptual and operational bridges between them, and some of these bridges are bi-directional.

The main role of the M3-level in a TS is to define the representation structure and a global typing system for underlying levels. The MOF for example is based on some kind of non-directed graphs where nodes are classes and links are associations. The notion of "association end" plays an important role in this representation system. Within the grammarware space we have the specific representation of abstract syntax trees while within the XML document space we also have trees, but with very different set of constraints, for example with possibilities to have direct references from one node to another node (REFs and IDREFs). In Fig. 9 we see how a simple system may be represented as an XML document corresponding to a Petri Net XML schema. We represent in this figure the *conformsTo* relation between the document, the schema, and the schema definition. We also represent the fine grained *meta* relations presented earlier (section 2) between elements and metaelements.

As we can see, there are a lot of similarities between the XML TS and the MDA TS. To get even more convinced, we may compare this situation with a similar one expressed in the MDE TS. Here, in Fig. 10, we have chosen another specific variant of MDE called sNets based on typed, reflective, and partitioned semantic networks [8], [9].

Associated to the basic representation system, there is a need to offer a navigation language. For MDA the language that plays this role is OCL, based on the specific nature of MDA models and metamodels. OCL for example know how to handle association ends. For the XML document space, the corresponding navigation notation is XPath that takes into account the specific nature of XML trees. As a matter of fact OCL is more than a navigation language and also serves as an assertion language as we have seen earlier and may be even used as a side-effect free

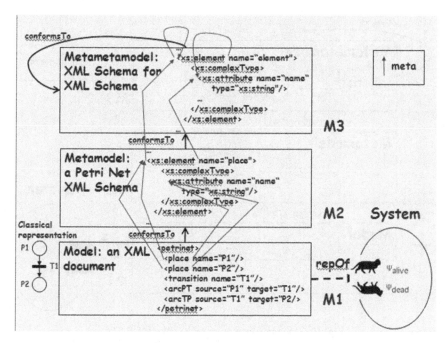

Fig. 9. Three level structure in an XML TS

programming language for making requests on models and metamodels. At the M3-level when the representation system and corresponding navigation and assertion notations are defined, there are also several other domain-independent facilities that need to be provided. In MDA for example generic conversion bridges and protocols are defined for communication with other technical spaces:

- XMI (XML Model Interchange) for bridging with the XML space
- JMI (Java Model Interchange) for bridging with the Java space
- CMI (CORBA Model Interchange) for bridging with the CORBA space

Obviously these facilities may evolve and provide more capabilities to the MDA TS. We may even see many other domain-independent possibilities being available at the M3-level like general repositories for storing and retrieving any kind of model or metamodel, with different access modes and protocol (streamed, by element navigation, event-based, transaction based, with versioning, etc.).

We see here the high potential impact of considering these technical spaces as explicit and semi-formal entities. In most of these spaces we have internal transformation tools (e.g. XSLT and XQuery for XML, QVT for MDA, etc.). Some of these internal transformation tools are general and other are specialized (a compiler can be seen as a specialized transformation tool of the EBNF/Grammarware space). These transformation tools have evolved in their own context to fit with specific objectives and main representation system of the corresponding space. There is no reason to change that. Now we have to consider another kind of transformation: across technical space boundaries. We call these transformations "projectors" in order to distinguish them from other transformations internal to one technical space.

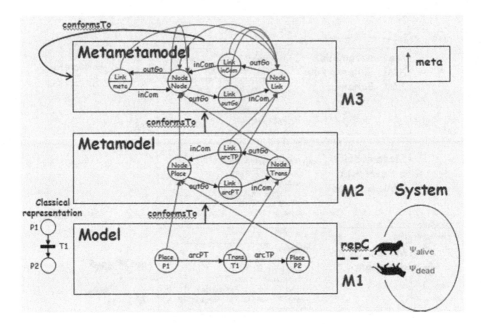

Fig. 10. Three level structure in the sNet MDE TS

The responsibility to build projectors lies in one space. The rationale to define them is quite simple: when one facility is available in another space and that building it in a given space is economically too costly, then the decision may be taken to build a projector in that given space. There are two kinds of projectors according to the direction: injectors and extractors. Very often we need a couple of injector/extractor to solve a given problem.

In order to illustrate this situation, let us look at the MDA technical space. The main entity there is a model (a metamodel may be considered as a kind of model). A model contains very useful and focused information, but by itself it is very dull and has no much capability. If we want MDA models to be really useful we have to give them these capabilities. There are two ways to do this: either to build them in the MDA space or to find them in another space. In the latter case what we will have to provide is some set of projectors.

An MDA model is a graph (non directed graph with labeled edge ends). Since there was no possibility to exchange MDA models, the OMG initiated a RFP called SMIF (Stream-based Model Interchange Format). The objective of SMIF was to find a serialization scheme so that any kind of MOF model could be exchanged by simple means (by mail, or a USB key, etc.). After some months of study, the group leading this initiative identified several solutions based on well known graph serialization algorithms. The solution was then to select and standardize some of these algorithms and to suggest building software extensions to handle these standards as part of the major CASE tools. This was the time when some people realized the importance that the XML TS was taking and the growing availability of XML tools in various industrial environments. Many people then realized that it would be economically much more interesting to define standard serialization in XML, i.e. that instead of directly serializing graphs on text flow or binary streams, it was more interesting to serialize graphs as trees and the let the remainder of the work being handled in the XML TS. As a consequence a bidirectional projector was defined by the XMI convention.

Each MDA projector has a specific goal, i.e. it consists in providing new facilities to models that are available in other TSs. XMI brings the capability of global model exchange to the MDA space and this capability is found in the XML space. Global model exchange means only the possibility to have batch-style of communication between tools. This is an interesting facility, but in many occasions it is not sufficient because we have to provide a fine grain access to model elements. XMI is of no use to do this. Here again the problem of adding new capabilities to models arose. Building intra-MDA tools for doing this was considered very costly. So, as part of the Java community process program, a standard projector with the Java technical space was defined under the name JSR #40. The capability to access models elements in MDA was given with the help of the Java TS. This projector is known today under the name JMI (Java Metadata Interface Specification [33]).

As we may see, each projector has a specific purpose. In the UML standard, the diagram interchange part deals partially with the separation of content and presentation for MDA models. In order to help model presentation, specific tools could have been added to the MDA space, but with a high implementation cost. Here again a solution was found in the XML space, by using the SVG standard for scalable vector graphics. Although the solution is limited to only certain kind of models, here again we see the interest of using important investments of other TSs to bring economically and rapidly functionalities to a given space (here the MDA) with the help of projectors.

Many other examples could be found showing the need for a very precise definition of the goal of any projector. For example, after the introduction of XMI, it was rapidly found that this projector was not bringing the facility of easy textual reading to the MDA space. Many solutions were possible, including applying XSLT transformation to XMI-serialized models to make them more usable for human operator (considering that XMI is sufficient for computer operators). Then the OMG decided to address this problem separately and a solution involving the EBNF space was defined under the name HUTN (Human Usable Textual Notation). HUTN offers three main benefits: (1) It is a generic specification that can provide a concrete language for any MOF model; (2) the HUTN languages can be fully automated for both production and parsing; (3) the HUTN languages are designed to conform to human-usability criteria. In the same spirit, OMG is today studying more general kinds of projectors between the MDA and the textual technical space (Model to Text RFP).

So we can see all the gain that could be reaped from the homogeneous consideration of bridges between TSs with the help of generic projectors. There are many activities presently going on in this area with TSs like data base (SQL projectors, E/R diagram projectors), in the OS TS (Unix projectors), in the legacy technical spaces (Cobol, ADA, PL/1 projectors to name only a few of them), in the ontology TS, for example with Protégé, in the natural language processing TS for requirement engineering applications, in the semantic Web TS, etc.

4 Some Examples of Technical Spaces

In this part, we give some rapid examples of TSs related to model engineering.

4.1 The OMG MDA Technical Space

We have already mentioned many of the characteristics of this MDA TS which was one of the first to explicitly state its clear foundation on some notion of concrete model. It should be noted that this TS borrowed much inspiration from the CDIF achievements as well as from the Microsoft OIM framework. CDIF and OIM are two examples of previous TSs, now extinct.

A typical presentation of the OMG/MDA organization is shown in Fig. 11. This may be used to illustrate the various roles that UML is playing in the global picture.

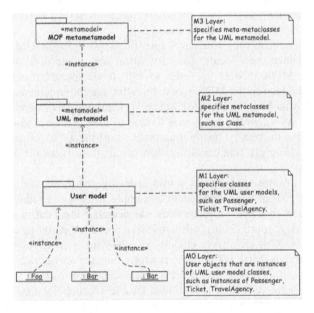

Fig. 11. Typical illustration of OMG MDA Organization

There has been a lot of reorganization at OMG on the occasion of the move to UML 2.0. The idea was to achieve some simplification by taking this opportunity to align other standards as well (OCL 2.0, MOF. 2.0, XMI 2.0, etc.). The result may be considered as mitigated. For various reasons there have always been two camps at OMG, according to the role devoted to UML. For the MOF camp, UML is only one ordinary metamodel among many (CWM, SPEM, etc.) while for others UML has a special and central role in MDA; the latter view UML as a rather universal language covering most of the software engineering needs, either directly or through its profile extension mechanism. The two camps have made a working compromise stating that 1) the UML conforms to MOF but also that 2) MOF is aligned on UML. Keeping the balance between these two political views has always been a complex exercise. The fact that UML is separated in infrastructure and superstructure was a help in defining the alignment, but is not sufficient. MOF itself is now composed of two parts, EMOF (for essential MOF) and CMOF (for complete MOF).

One sub-area of the MDA work at OMG is called ADM (Architecture-Driven Modernization) and deals with model-based reverse engineering and software modernization. In this very active area, the notion of TS projector between legacy spaces and the MDA space are of paramount importance. ADM mainly deals with the utilization of metamodeling techniques for recovery PIMs from PSMs corresponding to platform of the past.

4.2 The EMF Technical Space

In theory EMF (Eclipse Modeling Framework [17]) and OMG/MDA are aligned and should be considered as only one TS. As suggested in Fig. 2, MDA may be viewed as a set of standards while EMF should be an implementation based on these same standards. In practice this is not completely true and the two may be somewhat evolving independently. The M3 level in EMF is called ECORE (see Fig. 12), and corresponds approximately to EMOF mentioned above. Another view is to consider EMF as a sophisticated projection of MDA onto the Java TS, and to a lesser extent onto the XML TS.

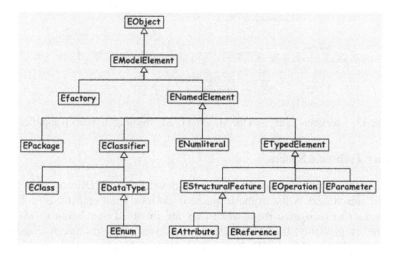

Fig. 12. The EMF ECore metametamodel

4.3 The Microsoft DSL Tools Technical Space

A general description of the concept of software factories has been presented in [20]. Starting from there, several sets of tools are being regularly released as beta-versions since December 2004. This allows us to understand in which direction the modeling activities are leading at Microsoft.

In order to define a DSL toolkit for a specific purpose (e.g. for a business of deigning airports), one will proceed as follows:

- Define the 'object model' (abstract syntax or metamodel) of the language -- that is, the concepts and relationships you want to handle in it.
- Define a graphical concrete syntax for the language -- the boxes, lines, etc that represent the concepts on-screen.
- Create a graphical editor for the language that you will use to design a specific airport.
- Develop code generators that will create software, configuration files, reports and other artifacts from the graphical model.

The choice of Microsoft DSL Tools has been to map mainly to the XML technical Space for handling models and metamodels. Executability is provided by mapping to the Dot Net TS. The M3 level at Microsoft is left implicit, but could be reified somewhat as illustrated in Fig. 13. An operational bridge between EMF and Microsoft Software factories may be found in [12].

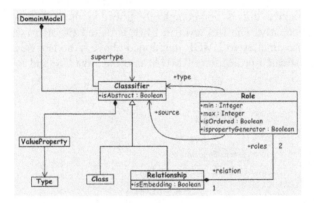

Fig. 13. A tentative to explicit the M3 level of Microsoft DSL Tools (simplified)

4.4 Other Technical Spaces

There are plenty of other technical spaces besides the three MDE ones that we have just briefly introduced. A list of these spaces is obviously not realistic here. However it is important to recognize them when they are involved in relation to MDE. The major one is probably the XML Document space that has taken considerable importance in the last decade. We have seen how the OMG has established links with this space through standards like XMI. This is even more important in Microsoft DSL Tools that are making more usage of XML mappings.

Another very important technical space is programming languages, e.g. Java. We can even say that EMF is mainly concerned with the bridging of MDA and Java. This had previously been achieved with JMI in other environments like MDR/NetBeans, but to a much less ambitious scale.

An interesting reading about technical spaces in the domain of web services is [21]. Although not naming explicitly the concept of technical space, this paper considers three complementary ones, namely objects, SQL and XML. The author notices that each of these solutions has strengths and weaknesses when applied to the inside and outside of web service boundary. He then concludes that the strength of each of these solutions in one area is derived from essential characteristics underlying its weakness in the other area. In other words, the multiplicity of technical space is not only a fact of life but it has also many positive effects.

Bridging to another technical space is interesting if it has something interesting to bring. We have already seen the advantage of using XML or Java instead of reinventing the wheel.

Interesting bridges could also be built with ontology engineering and web semantic. Some functionalities may be easier to provide in a TS with a M3 based on OWL than on the MOF. For example name management seems superior in OWL where a given object may be referred by several different names. Also in OWL the possibility to infer from the properties of an individual that it is a member of a class may be of interest. Through this example we understand more clearly the fundamental relations between representation and reasoning. Reasoning on a model is usually considered a more complex operation than just querying this model. It would be unwise to try implementing in the MDA TS all the reasoning facilities available in the ontology engineering or description logic TS for example. It seems much more valuable to build specific projectors when needed.

Having surveyed the basic MDE principles and having placed them in the context of multiple TSs, it remains now to prove that this approach may lead to real and usable implementations. We will use the example of AMMA (ATLAS Model Management Architecture), a platform built in our team to demonstrate the feasibility of these model-centric approaches to software engineering, system engineering, and data engineering.

5   Architectural Style for an MDE Platform

This section will describe an architectural style for MDE composed of four functional blocks illustrated with prototypes running in the AMMA platform:

- Model transformation (ATL)
- Model weaving (AMW)
- General model management (AM3)
- Model projection to/from other technical spaces (ATP)

This architectural style and the feasibility of its implementation will be illustrated by the description of the AMMA platform. The architecture of the current EMF-based AMMA implementation is described in Fig. 14. The transformation tool of AMMA, ATL, uses the basic features of EMF to handle both source and target models and metamodels, as well as the transformation model and metamodel. An Integrated Development Environment (IDE) has been developed for ATL on top of Eclipse. Based on EMF, it makes use of many other features, such as the code editor and the code debugging frameworks. AMW, the AMMA model weaving tool, uses more advanced EMF features. Since it is built as a model editor, AMW can benefit from editing domains facilities for complex model handlings (including undo-redo). It also reuses some components of the Eclipse default views to display models.

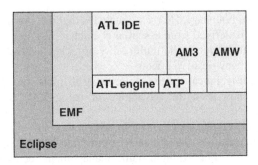

Fig. 14. Architecture of the AMMA platform

Eclipse is mostly used as an IDE for software development. As such, it includes facilities enabling to navigate the code, to keep track of the files that need rebuilding, etc. The megamodel tool (AM3) is used as a model-oriented extension of these abilities. As a matter of fact, using the relations between models (such as the source and target relations between a transformation model and its source and target metamodels), and between models and tools (such as those provided by ATP), AM3 makes it possible to easily carry on complex weaving, transformation and projection tasks.

5.1 MMA: A Model Engineering Platform

AMMA has both local and distributed implementations and is based on four blocks (Fig. 15) providing a large set of model processing facilities:

- the Atlas Transformation Language (ATL) defines model transformation facilities;
- the Atlas ModelWeaver (AMW) makes it possible to establish links between the elements of two (or more) different models;
- the Atlas MegaModel Management (AM3) defines the way the metadata is managed in AMMA (registry on the models, metamodels, tools, etc.);
- the Atlas Technical Projectors (ATP) defines a set of injectors/extractors enabling to import/export models from/to foreign technical spaces (Java classes, relational models, etc.).

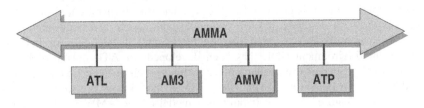

Fig. 15. The AMMA platform

5.2 ATL: Transforming Models

5.2.1 ATL Presentation

ATL is a model transformation language, having its abstract syntax defined using a metamodel. This means that every ATL transformation is in fact a model, with all the properties that are implied by this. Fig. 16 provides the scheme of the transformation of a model M_a (conforming to MM_a) into a model M_b (conforming to MM_b) based on the M_t transformation (which itself conforms to ATL transformation language).

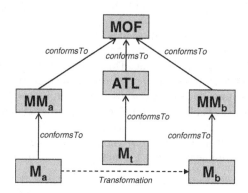

Fig. 16. An ATL transformation

What appears on Fig. 16 is the postulate of the existence of this common family of model transformation languages. This is exactly what OMG is presently trying to define through MOF/QVT. A given transformation operation is thus represented as follows:

$$Mb \leftarrow f\,(MMa, MMb, Mt, Ma)$$

This means that a new target model Mb based on metamodel MMb is obtained from the source model Ma based on metamodel MMa, by applying a transformation Mt based on the standard transformation language.

5.2.2 The ATL Metamodel

The ATLAS transformation language is defined by the way of a metamodel (Fig. 16) taking inspiration from the OCL 2.0, which may be considered here as an assertion and as a navigation language at the same time.

ATL transformations are stored in QVTUnits. QVTUnits are composed of QVTOperators, which are composed of TransformationDescription. A TransformationDescription is an abstract class, which has two sub classes: Action and Context.

Context: The context is used to store the variables and models manipulated by the transformation.

Action: The Action class is the element of the language that will describe the action needed to perform a transformation. The actions have to be executed in specific order, which is defined in the position attribute. This notion of order is necessary. We cannot for example set an attribute to a class if the class has not been created.

There are three types of Actions: CreateInstance, PropertyOperation, AddTransientLink.

The rest of ATL metamodel is the description of Expression sub-classes. ATL expression classes are a copy of a part of OCL Expression sub classes. An important extension has been made: the QueryTransientLinkExp that is a sub-class of CallExp. It is used to navigate through the transient links.

5.2.3 An Example of a Transformation in ATL

Several examples of model transformation in ATL are provided as an open source contribution on the Eclipse/GMT Website. This is a tentative to build a first library of reusable model transformations. Among the fifty examples currently available, we chose one particular for illustrative purpose here: http://www.eclipse.org/gmt/atl/ atlTransformations/#Java2Table. The complete code and documentation is available from the Web site. This example aims to compute a static call graph from a Java program and to present it in a tabular way (in an Excel spreadsheet or in an HTML Table). The following comments on this example are typical of ATL transformations.

a) Although a conventional transformation from UML 2.1 to UML 2.1 (e.g. refactoring) with source models and metamodels in XMI, target models and metamodels in XMI may be written in ATL without much difficulties, many examples are usually more diverse and more specific.

b) Here we describe in the source metamodel only a small subset of Java programs. More precisely we consider that a Java program is composed of class definitions, each one being composed of methods definitions and each method definition in turn being composed of a number of method calls. The other characteristics of a Java program are not captured by this metamodel.

c) The process of practically getting this Java metamodel expressed in XMI is rather complex, besides the fact that XMI exists in many non compatible versions. As a standard procedure we should define a specific UML class diagram with a standard tool like Poseidon, then get the corresponding XMI output file and input it to a "model promotion" tool like UML2MOF available in the MD/NetBeans tool suite. The resulting XMI output file could serve in the transformation as the definition of the java metamodel. As we can see this procedure is rather cumbersome. As an alternative we have defined a DSL for specifying metamodels called KM3 (Kernel MetaMetaModel [2]). This is a textual language with a Java-like syntax and basic support available in the Eclipse/GMT project, for example XMI conversion tools. ATL accepts the source and target metamodels in KM3.

d) As already noticed, the source metamodel does not cover much details of the Java syntax and this is an advantage on using a Java metamodel corresponding for example to the full Java grammar. We see here one additional characteristics of model transformation: the metamodels should be tailored to the transformation task at hand. Using an over-dimensioned source Java metamodel would have made the transformation more complex and less secure. The metamodels play the role of type and the models of variables. It is of high importance to use the most accurate metamodel for reasons of clarity and reliability of the transformation. A theoretical scheme would allow building a transformation μ taking as input a metamodel Ms and a transformation α and producing as output a new metamodel Mt, reduction of Ms to the only exact needs of transformation α.

e) Now that we have discussed the source metamodel characteristics, we have to face the real situation that Java programs are naturally and usually expressed as plain source text programs and not as XMI representations. As a matter of fact, there is a very restricted number of information naturally expressed in standard XMI in the real world. So what we have to consider here is a bridge between the Java and the MDA TS, i.e. a projection. We suppose that such a projection exists in the ATL projection library (see ATP below). However if we look at the actual Java2Table example, we realize that such projections have not been realized directly but instead that the author found more convenient to cross another TS (XML) to achieve the transformation. Among various reasons for this decision, the existence of the JavaML DTD that allowed to consider all the class definitions in one single file. This is an example of a possible implementation choice.

f) Now that we have discussed the source model, metamodel and projector we may turn our attention to the corresponding target items. The first work is to define a metamodel for Excel, obviously not provided with the tool. Here again we notice that we don't need a full metamodel but a very simplified one, tailored to our transformation needs. Formulas are not needed but a *Spreadsheet* could be considered as composed of *Rows*, each being composed of a *Cell* with a contained value.

g) Once we have defined the target metamodel, we need to build the corresponding projectors. This could be implemented with specific MS tools like Visual Basic or more likely again through the XML import/export facilities available in the MS Office suite. In the process of doing this we realize that the target metamodel could as well correspond to HTML or XHTML tables. As a consequence this is the final implementation choice in the provided example. More precisely the target metamodel is an abstract definition of tabular presentation. The result of this transformation could then be chained to another transformation generating specific XHTML or Excel tables, with the metamodels specific to these tools. Of course chains of transformations are important in many practical situations.

5.3 AMW: Weaving Models

Model weaving operations are performed between either metamodels (two or more), or models. They aim to specify the links, and their associated semantics, between elements of source and target models. Concerning the set of links to be generated, the following issues may be considered:

- this set of links cannot be automatically generated because it is often based on human decisions. The generation can however be partially automated by means of heuristics;
- it should be possible to record this set of links as a whole, in order to use it later in various contexts;
- it should be possible to use this set of links as an input to automatic or semi-automatic tools.

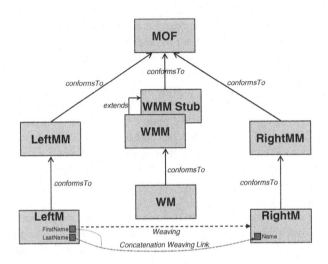

Fig. 17. The model weaving scheme

As a consequence, we come to the conclusion that a model weaving operation produces a precise model *WM*. Like other models, this should conform to a specific metamodel *WMM*. The produced weaving model relates to the source and target models *LeftM* and *RightM*, and thus remains linked to these models in a megamodel registry.

Each link element of the produced weaving model *WM* has to be typed by an element of a given *WMM* metamodel. There is no unique type of link. Link types should provide weaving tools with useful information. Even if some links contain textual descriptions, these are valuable for tools supporting documentation, manual refinements or applying heuristics.

One may assume that there is no standard metamodel for weaving operations since most developers define their own. However, we suppose there is a stub weaving metamodel, and that this stub is extended by specific metamodel extensions. Thus, a given weaving metamodel may be expressed as an extension of another weaving metamodel. This allows building a general weaving tool able to generically deal with weaving tasks. Fig. 17 describes a simple model weaving scheme in which an explicit weaving link (of type *Concatenation*) associates two source elements (*FirstName* and *LastName*) with an only target element (*Name*).

Mapping heterogeneous data from one representation to another is a central problem in many data-intensive applications. Examples can be found in different contexts such as schema integration in distributed databases, data transformation for data warehousing, data integration in mediator systems [25], data migration from legacy systems [14], ontology merging [18], schema mapping in P2P systems [22], workflow integration [27], mapping between context and ontologies [16].

A typical data mapping specifies how data from one source representation (e.g. a relational schema) can be translated to a target representation (e.g. a XML schema). Although data mappings have been studied independently in different contexts, there are two main issues involved. The first one is to discover the correspondences between data elements that are semantically related in the source and target representations. This is called schema matching in schema integration [3] and many techniques have been proposed to (partially) automate this task, e.g. using neural networks. After the correspondences have been established, the second issue is to produce operational mappings that can be executed to perform the translation. Operational mappings are typically declarative, e.g. view definitions or SQL-like queries. Creating and managing data mappings can be very complex and time-consuming if done manually. Recent work in schema integration has concentrated on the efficient management of data mappings. For instance, Clio [26] provides techniques for the automatic generation of operational mappings from correspondences obtained from the user or a machine learning technique. ToMAS [34] also provides techniques for the automatic generation of operational mappings as well as their consistency management while schemas evolve. This work is significant as it can be the basis to general purpose data integration tools.

5.4 AM3: Global Model Management

The Atlas MegaModel Management tool, AM3, is an environment for dealing with models or metamodels, together with tools, services and other global entities, when considered as a whole. For each platform, we suppose that there is an associated megamodel defining the metadata associated to this platform. Within the content of a given platform (local or global), the megamodel records all available resources. One may also refer to these resources as "model components" [10]. The megamodel can be viewed as a model which elements represent and refer to models and metamodels [13]. Represented as models, available tools, services, and services parameters are also managed by the megamodel. There are plenty of events that may change the megamodel, like the creation or suppression of a model, or a metamodel, etc. A megamodel is associated with a specific "scope" and conforms to a specific metamodel.

5.5 ATP: Projection Between Technical Spaces

The Atlas Technical Projectors, ATP, define a set of injectors and extractors, which can be seen as import and export facilities between the model engineering Technical Space and other TSs (databases, flat files, XML, etc). Indeed, a very large amount of pre-existing data that is not XMI compliant would greatly benefit from model transformation. In order to be processed by a model engineering platform, this data needs injection from its TS to the model engineering TS. The need for extraction is also quite important: many existing tools do not read XMI. A simple example is the Java compiler. What we need here is code generation, which may be seen as a specific case of model extraction. Many other TSs require both injectors and extractors: database systems provide another example in which database schemes have to be generated from model definitions.

5.6 Conclusions

What appear in this presentation are the high complementarities between all four presented functional blocks (ATL, AMW, AM3, and ATP). There are plenty of applications that make use of these four kinds of functionalities at the same time.

6 Conclusions

We have presented in this paper our definition of MDE basic principles and our view of an MDE implementation architectural style. The basic principle on which this work is based (Models as first class entities) is common to many current research communities (Model Management, Model Integrated Computing, etc.) and similar goals and means may be found in other TSs. This is summarized in Fig. 18.

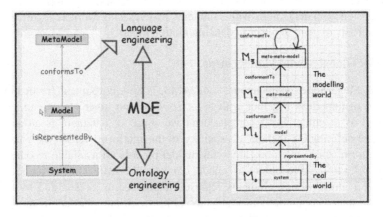

Fig. 18. Summarizing the Basic Principles

We have taken here a broad view of model engineering as encompassing not only the MDA™ OMG proposal or the Microsoft SoftwareFactories/DSL view, but also other approaches like Model Integrated Computing, Generative Programming, Model Management and many more. We distinguished the three levels of principles, standards, and tools to facilitate the discussion. We suggested the idea that there may exist a common set of principles that could be mapped to different implementation contexts through the help of common standards. We have illustrated our claim with AMMA, an architectural organization that is currently mapped onto the EMF extension of the Eclipse platform.

One contribution of this work has been to propose a precise and minimal definition of a conceptual MDE technical space. This space may be considered as a general graph where partitions are composed of model, metamodel and metametamodel entities. We have not committed here to a particular kind of graphs. The OMG/MOF graphs, the EMF/Ecore graphs or the Microsoft/SoftwareFactories/DSL graphs are not completely identical but we believe these systems share one common set of principles and definitions corresponding to the MDE abstract global typing system presented here. As a consequence this work should be useful not only to relate different technical spaces like XML, Grammarware, etc., but also to compare variants of the MDE space.

One contribution of this work is the AMMA conceptual architecture, seen as an intermediary level between model engineering basic principles and executable systems running on operational platforms like EMF/Eclipse. The main advantage of proceeding in this way is that we may more clearly evaluate the gap between principles and implementation. From our initial experimentations, we came to the conclusion that building a model engineering platform is much more demanding than simply providing a RPC-like mechanism for allowing tools to exchange models in serialized format (e.g. XMI-based), with the corresponding services and protocols (e.g. Web Service-based). The present state of AMMA with the four functional blocks is only one step in this direction and still needs many extensions.

There are many variants of model engineering. Our attitude has been to find the set of basic principles common to all the dominant model engineering approaches and to make them explicit. We are then in a position to clearly separate the principles, the standards, and the tools levels.

One of the contributions of our approach is also to take explicitly into account the notion of technical space. Instead of building a lot of different ad-hoc conversions tools (modelToText, textToModel, ontologyToModel, modelToOntology, XMLToText, textToXML, modelToSQL, SQLToModel, etc.), we have proposed, with the notion of projectors (injectors or extractors), a general concept that may be used in various situations. These projectors can be selected as either front-ends or back-ends for classical transformations.

Acknowledgements

I would like to thank Freddy Allilaire, Marcos Didonet del Fabro, Frédéric Jouault, Ivan Kurtev, David Touzet, Patrick Valduriez and all the members of the AMMA group for their numerous contributions to this document. This work has been supported in part by the IST European project "ModelWare" (contract 511731).

References

1. ATL, ATLAS Transformation Language Reference site http://www.sciences.univ-nantes.fr/lina/atl/
2. ATLAS Group KM3: Kernel MetaMetaModel. Available at http://dev.eclipse.org/viewcvs/indextech.cgi/~checkout~/gmt-home/doc/atl/index.html

3. Batini, C., Lenzerini, M., and Navathe, S. B. 1986. A Comparative Analysis of Methodologies for Database Schema Integration. ACM Computing Surveys 18, 4, 323–364.
4. Bernstein, P.A., Levy, A.Y., Pottinger, R.A., A Vision for Management of Complex Systems, MSR-TR-2000-53, Microsoft Research, Redmond, USA, ftp://ftp.research.microsoft.com/pub/tr/tr-2000-53.pdf.
5. Bézivin J., Lemesle R. The sBrowser: a Prototype Meta-Browser for Model Engineering. Proceedings of OOPSLA'98, Vancouver, Canada, 18-22 October 1998. (http://www.metamodel.com/oopsla98-cdif-workshop/bezivin2/)
6. Bézivin, J. From Object Composition to Model Transformation with the MDA TOOLS'USA 2001, Santa Barbara, August 2001, Volume IEEE publications TOOLS'39. http://www.sciences.univ-nantes.fr/info/lrsg/Recherche/mda/TOOLS.USA.pdf
7. Bézivin, J. In search of a Basic Principle for Model Driven Engineering, Novatica/Upgrade, Vol. V, N°2, (April 2004), pp. 21-24, http://www.upgrade-cepis.org/issues/2004/2/up5-2Presentation.pdf
8. Bézivin, J. Lemesle, R. Towards a true reflective modeling scheme LNCS, ISSN: 0302-9743, Vol. 1826/2000, http://www.springerlink.com/media/3G267U4QVH5RRJ47VBFT/Contributions/2/8/4/W/284W7VGQC302VR5W.pdf
9. Bézivin, J. sNets: A First Generation Model Engineering Platform. In: Springer-Verlag, Lecture Notes in Computer Science, Volume 3844, Satellite Events at the MoDELS 2005 Conference, edited by Jean-Michel Bruel. Montego Bay, Jamaica, pages 169-181.
10. Bézivin, J., Gérard, S. Muller, P.A., Rioux, L. MDA Components: Challenges and Opportunities, Metamodelling for MDA, First International Workshop, York, UK, (November 2003), http://www.cs.york.ac.uk/metamodel4mda/onlineProceedingsFinal.pdf
11. Bézivin, J., Gerbé, O. Towards a Precise Definition of the OMG/MDA Framework ASE'01, San Diego, USA, November 26-29, 2001 http://www.sciences.univnantes.fr/lina/atl/publications/ASE01.OG.JB.pdf
12. Bézivin, J., Hillairet, G., Jouault, F., Kurtev, I., Piers, W. bridging the MS/DSL Tools and the eclipse EMF Framework. OOPSLA Workshop on Software Factories, http://softwarefactories.com/workshops/OOPSLA-2005/Papers/Bezivin.pdf
13. Bézivin, J., Jouault, F., Valduriez, P., On the Need for Megamodels, OOPSLA & GPCE, Workshop on best MDSD practices, Vancouver, Canada, 2004.
14. Bisbal J., Lawless D., Wu B., Grimson, J. Legacy Information Systems: Issues and Directions. IEEE Software, September/October 1999, pp. 103-111, Vol. 16, Issue 5. 1999.
15. Booch G., Brown A., Iyengar S., Rumbaugh J., Selic B. The IBM MDA Manifesto The MDA Journal, May 2004, http://www.bptrends.com/publicationfiles/05-04%20COL%20IBM%20Manifesto%20-%20Frankel%20-3.pdf
16. Bouquet P., Giunchiglia F., Van Harmelen F., Serafini L., Stuckenschmidt H.: Contextualizing Ontologies. Journal of Web Semantics, 1(4):1-19, 2004
17. Eclipse Modeling Framework (http://www.eclipse.org/emf/)
18. Ehrig M., York Sure: Ontology Mapping - An Integrated Approach. ESWS 2004: 76-91
19. GMT, General Model Transformer Eclipse Project, http://www.eclipse.org/gmt/
20. Greenfield, J., Short, K., Cook, S., Kent, S., Software Factories, Wiley, ISBN 0-471-20284-3, 2004.
21. Helland, P. Data on the outside versus data on the inside.2005 CIDR Conference.
22. Kementsietsidis A., Arenas M., Miller, R. J. Mapping Data in Peer-to-Peer Systems: Semantics and Algorithmic Issues. In Proceedings of the SIGMOD International Conference on Management of Data (SIGMOD'03), San Diego, USA, pages 325-336. 2003.

23. Klint, P., Lämmel, R. Kort, J., Klusener, S., Verhoef, C., Verhoeven, E.J. Engineering of Grammarware. http://www.cs.vu.nl/grammarware/

24. Kurtev, I., Bézivin, J., Aksit, M. Technical Spaces: An Initial Appraisal. CoopIS, DOA'2002   Federated   Conferences,   Industrial   track,   Irvine,   2002 http://www.sciences.univ-nantes.fr/lina/atl/publications/

25. Lenzerini M., Data integration: a theoretical perspective, Proceedings of the twenty-first ACM SIGMOD-SIGACT-SIGART symposium on Principles of database systems, June 03-05, 2002, Madison, Wisconsin

26. Miller, R. J., Hernandez, M. A., Haas, L. M., Yan, L.-L., Ho, C. T. H., Fagin, R., and Popa, L. 2001. The Clio Project: Managing Heterogeneity. SIGMOD Record 30, 1, 78–83.

27. Omelayenko B. RDFT: A Mapping Meta-Ontology for Business Integration, In: Proceedings of the Workshop on Knowledge Transformation for the Semantic Web (KTSW 2002) at the 15-th European Conference on Artificial Intelligence, 23 July, Lyon, France, 2002, p. 76-83

28. OMG/MOF Meta Object Facility (MOF) Specification. OMG Document AD/97-08-14, September 1997. Available from www.omg.org

29. OMG/RFP/QVT MOF 2.0 Query/Views/Transformations RFP, OMG document ad/2002-04-10. Available from www.omg.org

30. OMG/XMI XML Model Interchange (XMI) OMG Document AD/98-10-05, October 1998. Available from www.omg.org

31. Seidewitz, E. What do models mean? IEEE Software, IEEE Software,September/October 2003 (Vol. 20, No. 5)

32. Soley, R., and the OMG staff, Model-Driven Architecture, OMG Document, November 2000, http://www.omg.org/mda

33. Sun Java Community Process JMI Java MetaData Interface Specification Available from ftp://ftp.java.sun.com/pub/spec/jmi/asdjhfjghhg44/jmi-1_0-fr-spec.pdf

34. Velegrakis Y., Miller R. J., Popa L., Adapting Mappings in Frequently Changing Environments, Int. Conf of Very Large Databases (VLDB), Sep 2003.

Appendix: Acronyms

Due to the initial normative aspect of the field, we have used an important number of acronyms in this document. We provide below a list of more common ones with their definitions.

ADM	Architecture-Driven Modernization
AS	Action Semantics
CDIF	CASE Data Interchange format
CORBA	Common Object Request Broker Architecture
CIM	Computation Independent Model
CWM	Common Warehouse Metadata
DTD	Document Type Definition
EAI	Enterprise Application Integration
EBNF	Extended Backus-Naur Form

EDOC	Enterprise Distributed Object Computing
EJB	Enterprise Java Beans
HUTN	Human Usable Textual Notation
IDL	Interface Definition Language
JSR	Java Specification Request
JMI	Java MetaData Interface Specification
MDA	Model Driven Architecture (OMG™)
MDE	Model Driven Engineering
MDD	Model Driven Development (OMG™)
MDSD	Model Driven Software Development
MDSE	Model Driven Software Engineering
MIC	Model Integrated computing
MOF	Meta-Object Facility
OCL	Object Constraint Language
OIM	Open Information Model
OMA	Object Management Architecture
OMG	Object Management Group
PIM	Platform Independent Model
PSM	Platform specific Model
RFP	Request for Proposal
RAS	Reusable Asset Specification
RUP	Rational Unified Process
SMIF	Stream-based Model Interchange Format
SPEM	Software Process Engineering Metamodel
TS	Technical Space
UML	Unified Modeling Language (OMG™)
XMI	XML Model Interchange
XML	eXtensible Markup Language

Program Transformation with Reflection and Aspect-Oriented Programming

Shigeru Chiba

Dept. of Mathematical and Computing Sciences
Tokyo Institute of Technology, Japan

Abstract. A meta-programming technique known as reflection can be regarded as a sophisticated programming interface for program transformation. It allows software developers to implement various useful program transformation without serious efforts. Although the range of program transformation enabled by reflection is quite restricted, it covers a large number of interesting applications. In particular, several non-functional concerns found in web-application software, such as distribution and persistence, can be implemented with program transformation by reflection. Furthermore, a recently emerging technology known as aspect-oriented programming (AOP) provides better and easier programming interface than program transformation does. One of the roots of AOP is reflection and thus this technology can be regarded as an advanced version of reflection. In this tutorial, we will discuss basic concepts of reflection, such as compile-time reflection and runtime reflection, and its implementation techniques. The tutorial will also cover connection between reflection and aspect-oriented programming.

1   Introduction

One of significant techniques of modern software development is to use an application framework, which is a component library that provides basic functionality for some particular application domain. If software developers use such an application framework, they can build their applications by implementing only the components intrinsic to the applications. However, this approach brings hidden costs; the developers must follow the protocol of the application framework when they implement the components intrinsic to their applications. Learning this framework protocol is often a serious burden of software developers. A richer application framework provides a more complicated protocol. Learning the protocol is like learning a new domain-specific language since software developers must understand the programming model or the underlying architecture.

A program translator has a potential ability to simplify such a framework protocol. If framework developers use a program translator, they can provide a simpler but not-real framework protocol for the users. The users can implement their application-specific components with that simple protocol. Then they can translate their components by the program translator into ones following a complex but real protocol of the application framework. Their translated components

R. Lämmel, J. Saraiva, and J. Visser (Eds.): GTTSE 2005, LNCS 4143, pp. 65–94, 2006.

can actually run with the application framework. A challenge of this idea is to make it easy for framework developers to implement a program translator for their framework. Since framework developers are normally experts of not compiler technology but the application domain of the framework, the easiness of developing a program translator is a crucial issue in this scenario. Furthermore, if the development cost of a program translator is extremely high, it would not be paid off by the benefits of the simple protocol.

Reflection [35, 34, 24] can be regarded as one of the technology for making it easy to implement such a program translator for simplifying a framework protocol. The power of meta programming by this technology allows framework developers to implement a simple protocol without directly developing a program translator for their framework. The framework developers can describe the algorithm of program transformation with high-level abstraction and the actual program transformation is implicitly executed by the underlying mechanism for reflective computing. They do not have to consider source-code parsing, semantic analysis, or other messy details of implementation of a program translator. Although reflection used to be known as the mechanism involving serious performance overheads, today there are several implementation techniques for efficient reflective computing. Carefully designed reflective computing does imply zero or only a small amount of overhead.

Aspect-oriented programming (AOP) [21] is relatively new technology; as well as reflection, it is useful for simplifying a framework protocol. One of the roots of AOP is the study of reflection and thus AOP is often regarded as a descendant of the reflection technology. AOP is not another new name of reflective computing or technology hype. AOP is new technology for reducing dependency among software components. If components have strong dependency on each other, the protocol of interaction among the components will be complicated and difficult to learn. AOP reduces the dependency among components, in particular, between components implemented by application developers and components provided by an application framework. Reducing the dependency makes the framework protocol simpler and easier to use. AOP does not directly help implementing a program translator but it is a programming paradigm that provides language constructs for simplifying a framework protocol. The ability of those constructs are quite equivalent to what we want to achieve by using a program translator.

In the rest of this paper, we first discuss how program translators can simplify the protocols of application frameworks. Then this paper presents overviews of the reflection technology. It also describes AOP. We discuss what are benefits of AOP and the unique functionality of AOP, which is not provided by the reflection technology.

2   Program Translator

To illustrate our motivation, this section first presents the complexity of the protocols of application frameworks. Then it mentions how a program translator can simplify the protocols.

2.1 Simple Example: Graphical User Interface Library

Application frameworks are class libraries that can be a platform for building application software in a particular application domain. Since they provide basic building blocks in that domain, they significantly improve efficiency of software development. However, to exploit the power of application frameworks, application developers must learn the protocols of the frameworks. Unfortunately, those protocols are often complicated and thus learning the protocols is often a time consuming job. It is hidden cost of software development with application frameworks.

The complications of a framework protocol mainly come from the limited ability of programming languages to modularize software. For example, we below show a (pseudo) Java program written with the standard GUI framework. It is a program for showing a clock. If this program does not have GUI, then it would be something like the following simple and straightforward one (for clarifying the argument, the programs shown below are pseudo code):

```
class Clock {
  static void main(String[] args) {
    while (true) {
      System.out.println(currentTime());
      sleep(ONE_MINUTE);
    }
  }
}
```

This program only prints the current time on the console every one minute.

Now we use the standard GUI library as an application framework to extend this program to have better look. To do that, however, we must read some tutorial books of the GUI library and edit the program above to fit the protocol that the books tell us. First, we would find that the Clock class must extend Panel. Also, the Clock class must prepare a paint method for drawing a picture of clock on the screen. Thus you would define the paint method and modify the main method. The main method must call not the paint method but the repaint method, which the tutorial book tells us to call when the picture is updated. The following is the resulting program (again, it is pseudo code):

```
class Clock extends Panel {
  void paint(Graphics g) {
    // draw a clock on the screen.
  }
  static void main(String[] args) {
    Clock c = new Clock();
    while (true) {
      c.repaint();
      sleep(ONE_MINUTE);
    }
  }
}
```

Note that the structure of the program is far different from that of the original program. It is never simple or straightforward. For example, why do we have to define the paint method, which dedicates only to drawing a picture? Why does the main method have to call not the paint method but the repaint method, which will indirectly call the paint method? To answer these questions, we have to understand the programming model or the underlying architecture of the framework provided by the GUI library. This is hidden cost that application developers have to pay for exploiting the power of application frameworks.

2.2   Enterprise Java Beans

Enterprise Java Beans (EJB) [36] is a popular application framework for building a web application in Java. This framework provides basic functionality such as transaction, distribution, and security, for software components developed by the users. Since the cost of implementing such functionality for each component is never negligible, the use of EJB significantly reduces the development cost of application software.

However, the benefits of EJB are not free. The developers must follow the protocol of EJB when they develop their software components. This protocol (at least, before EJB 3.0) is fairly complicated whereas the power of the EJB framework is strong. Only the developers who spend their time on mastering the framework protocol of EJB can enjoy the power of EJB. For example, to implement a single EJB component, the developer must define three classes and interfaces in Java. Suppose that we want to implement a component for dealing with registration of summer school. Ideally, the definition of this component would be something like this:

```
class Registration {
  void register(String who) { ... }
  void cancel(String who) { ... }
}
```

However, to make this component be EJB-compliant, we must define the following class and interfaces (again, these are pseudo-code):

```
class RegistrationBean implements SessionBean {
  void register(String who) { ... }
  void cancel(String who) { ... }
}

interface RegistrationHome {
  Registration create() throws .. ;
}

interface Registration extends EJBObject {
  void register(String who) throws .. ;
  void cancel(String who) throws .. ;
}
```

Note that Registration is now the name of the interface extending EJBObject although it was the class name in the ideal version. The name of the class implementing the component functionality is now RegistrationBean. The protocol is not only the names; the reason why we must define extra interfaces is not clear unless we know the underlying architecture of EJB.

2.3   Use of Program Translators

The complications of framework protocols we showed above can be simplified if the application frameworks are distributed with custom program translators. The framework designers can define a simple but not-real protocol, with which the framework users implement their components. These components *as is* cannot work with the application frameworks but they can be translated into the components that follow the real protocols of the application frameworks. In fact, this idea has been adopted by upcoming EJB 3.0. EJB 3.0 provides an extremely simple protocol; it allows developers to implement EJB components as regular Java objects. The developers do not have to follow any protocol when they implement EJB components. So the developers can write the ideal code we have seen above:

```
@Session class Registration {
  void register(String who) { ... }
  void cancel(String who) { ... }
}
```

The components described as above are translated by a sort of program translator into the components that follows the real but hidden protocol of the framework so that they can work with the framework.

However, this approach using a program translator has not been widely used yet. A main reason would be that implementing a program translator is not easy. Only application frameworks that have a large user base can adopt this approach since the cost of implementing a program translator is paid off by the benefits that the users can receive. EJB is a typical example. To make this approach widely used for simplifying a framework protocol, we have to study technologies for easily implementing a program translator customized for each application framework. One of such technologies is reflection and another is aspect-oriented programming (AOP). In the following sections, we discuss these two technologies.

3   Reflection

Reflection, or reflective computing, is one of meta-programming technologies originally proposed by Brian C. Smith in the early 1980's [35, 34]. He presented this idea by showing his Lisp language called *3-Lisp*. This idea was extended and applied to object-oriented languages by Pattie Maes, who proposed the *3-KRS* language [24], and others during the 1980's. Smalltalk-80 [17] is also recognized today as one of the early reflective languages [14] although it was not intended to enable reflective computing when it was designed.

3.1   Reify and Reflect

Reflection allows a program to access the *meta-level view* of that program itself. If an entity in that meta-level view is changed, the corresponding entity in the original program is really changed. Therefore, reflection enables a program to transform (parts of) that program itself within the confines of the language. Self-reflective languages, that is, programming languages that enable reflective computing are like surgeons who can perform an operation on themselves for cancer.

The primitive operations of reflective computing are *reify* and *reflect*. Reifying is to construct a data structure representing some non-first-class entity in a program. It is also called *introspection*. That data structure can be queried for the structure of the represented entity. For example, the standard reflection API of Java provides a Class object representing a class. Such an object as the Class object is often called a *metaobject* since it is part of the meta-level view of a program. The Class object can be queried for its super class, methods, and so on. Constructing the Class object is a typical reifying operation since a class is a non-first-class entity in Java. That is, the forName method in Class is the reifying operation provided by the reflection API of Java. Here, the first-class entity means a data value that a program can deal with. The non-first-class entities are the rest of the entities included in a program. For example, an integer and a String object are first-class entities. On the other hand, a class and a method are non-first-class entities since variables cannot hold them or refer to them.

Reflecting is to alter the structure or the behavior of a program according to the changes applied to the metaobjects (or some data structure representing the meta-level view if the language is not object-oriented) obtained by the reifying operation. Note that a metaobject is a regular object although it represents part of the meta-level view of a program. It does not have to be identical to a meta-level entity of the program; it can be a mirror image [3]. Therefore, it is not obvious that changes in a metaobject are reflected on the structure or the behavior of the program. To emphasize that the changes are reflected on the program, a reflective language has *causal connection* between a program and metaobjects (or data structures representing the meta-level view). The reflection API of Java does not provide this type of reflecting operation. The metaobjects such as Class, Method, and Field objects provide only getter methods but not setter methods. Thus, any changes cannot be applied to the metaobjects.

Another type of reflecting is to execute base-level operations, such as object creation and method invocation, through a metaobject. The reflection API of Java provides this type of reflecting operation. The Class class includes the newInstance method, which makes an instance of the class represented by the Class object. The Method class includes the invoke method, which invokes the method. The computation by these methods is also the reflecting operation since it is reflected on the real program execution.

3.2 Metaobject Protocol

CLOS [1] is known as an object-oriented language that has strong ability with respect to both reifying and reflecting operations. The reflection API of CLOS is called the CLOS *Metaobject Protocol* (MOP) [20]. CLOS is an object system built on top of Common Lisp and thus an object in CLOS is implemented by using a data structure of Common Lisp, for example, an array. If a class is defined in CLOS, an object representing a class is created at runtime. This object contains the information of the class definition. Note that this fact does not cause infinite regression. From the implementation viewpoint, this fact just means that the runtime data structure representing a class is the same data structure of Common Lisp that is used for representing an object. However, we interpret this fact as that a class is an object in CLOS as we say that a class is an object in Smalltalk-80.

The class definition in CLOS is expanded by a macro into an expression that makes an object. Recall that Lisp macros are powerful programmable macros. This architecture of CLOS is illustrated by the following pseudo Java code:[1]

```
public class Point {
  int x, y;
  void move(int newX, int newY) { ... }
}
```

This class definition is expanded by a macro into the following expression:

```
Class pointClass
  = new Class("Point",
              new Field[] { new Field("int", "x"),
                            new Field("int", "x") },
              new Method[] { new Method("void", "move", ... ) });
```

Here, pointClass is sort of a global variable. For each class definition, a Class object is created at runtime and it contains the information about the class definition. Note that there is no syntactical distinction among expressions, statements, and declarations in Lisp. Thus transforming a class declaration into an expression as shown above is valid macro expansion in Lisp.

An expression for making an instance of Point is also expanded by a macro. For example, this expression:

```
Point p = new Point();
```

is transformed into this:

```
Point p = (Point)pointClass.newInstance();
```

newInstance declared in the Class class is a method for making an instance. Furthermore, the following expression for calling a method in Point:

```
p.move(3, 4)
```

is transformed into something like this:

```
pointClass.getMethod("move").invoke(p, new Object[] { 3, 4 });
```

---

[1] The object model of CLOS is quite different from that of Java. So the following explanation is not exactly about the CLOS MOP. We try to show the basic idea of the CLOS MOP with the context of Java since most of the readers would be familiar to Java.

The resulting expression first obtains a Method object representing move and then invokes the method with arguments 3 and 4. In principle, since the resulting expression consists of two method calls (getMethod and invoke), it would be also expanded by the same macro. However, this macro expansion performs different transformation; the expression is transformed into a Lisp expression implementing the normal behavior of method call. It does not include a method call or any other object-oriented operators. If the macro expansion were naively applied, it would cause infinite regression.

As we showed above, all the operations related to objects in CLOS are always transformed into method calls to Class objects, at least, in the programming model of CLOS. Therefore, if we call a method on the Class objects and change the states of those objects, the changes are immediately *reflected* on the behavior of the operations related to objects.

For example, we can dynamically add a new method to the Point class by explicitly calling a method on the Class object representing the Point class:

```
pointClass.addMethod(new Method("String", "toString", ...));
```

This expression first makes an instance of Method that represents a toString method. Then it adds the method to the Point class by calling the addMethod method.

If a subclass of Class is defined and some methods in Class is overridden, the behavior of the operations such as object creation and method calls can be altered. This alteration is called *intercession*. For example, let us define the following subclass:

```
public class TracedClass extends Class {
  public Object newInstance() {
    System.out.println("instantiate " + getName());
    return super.newInstance();
  }
}
```

Then define a Point class as following:

```
public class Point is_instance_of TracedClass {
  int x, y;
  void move(int newX, int newY) { ... }
}
```

Here is_instance_of is a keyword for specifying the class of the class metaobject. This class definition is expanded by the macro into the following statement:

```
Class pointClass = new TracedClass("Point", ... );
```

Now the class metaobject that pointClass refers to is an instance of TracedClass. Hence, if an instance of Point is made, a trace message is printed out.

3.3   Operator Interception

Reflection enables developers to define a method that is executed when an operator such as method call and field access is executed. If the thread of control reaches such an operator, the program execution is intercepted and then that defined method is invoked instead of the operator. The TracedClass example shown above is an example of such an intercepting method. We defined a method intercepting a new operator in the TracedClass class.

Although such an intercepting method has a large number of practical applications and it is provided by most of reflective languages, an intercepting method is not a unique mechanism of the reflection technology. It is also provided by other technologies such as aspect-oriented programming. A unique feature of the reflection technology is that it enables an intercepting method to access the contexts of the intercepted operator through a meta-level view so that the intercepting method could be *generic*.[2]

For example, the newInstance method in the TracedClass example can intercept the new expressions (object-creation expressions) of making an instance of any class type. It can intercept a new expression for either Point or Rectangle. This is because the newInstance method is at the meta level and hence the class type of the created object is *coerced* to the Object type. Another example is the invoke method in Method. This method receives arguments in the form of array of Object independently of the types and the number of the arguments. This enables a generic intercepting method, which can intercept different kinds of method calls. The following example illustrates the invoke method overridden in a subclass so that it will print a trace method:

```
public class TracedMethod extends Method {
  public Object invoke(Object target, Object[] args) {
    System.out.println("method call " + getName());
    return super.invoke(target, args);
  }
}
```

The invoke method is an intercepting method, which is executed when a method represented by a TracedMethod metaobject is called. This invoke method can intercept any method calls, no matter how many parameters or what type of parameters the method receives. This is because the list of arguments is *reified* by using an array of Object.

How the base-level entities such as the number and types of method arguments are reified depends on the reflective language. For example, OpenC++ (version 1) [9] uses an instance of the ArgPac class for representing the method arguments at the meta level since there is no root type of all the class types in C++.

---

[2] This feature is also provided by an aspect-oriented programming language AspectJ. However, it is a reflection mechanism of AspectJ according to the documents of AspectJ.

3.4   Structural Reflection vs. Behavioral Reflection

Reflective programming is classified into two categories: structural reflection and behavioral reflection. Structural reflection is to alter a program structure, that is, a class definition in Java, through a metaobject, for example, defining a new class, adding a new method to an existing class, removing an existing field, and changing a super class. Structural reflection enables straightforward implementation of program transformation while keeping simple abstraction for describing the transformation.

Behavioral reflection is to alter the behavior of operations in a program. Typical behavioral reflection is to define a subclass of Class or Method and override methods for executing operations such as object creation, method calls, and field accesses. For example, in Section 3.3, we defined a subclass of Method for altering the behavior of method invocation to print a trace message:

```
public class TracedMethod extends Method {
  public Object invoke(Object target, Object[] args) {
    System.out.println("method call " + getName());
    return super.invoke(target, args);
  }
}
```

This is typical behavioral reflection since it alters the semantics of method invocation through a metaobject instead of transforming a program to print a trace message.

The main difference between structural reflection and behavioral reflection is a programming model. The expressive power of the two kinds of reflection is, in principle, equivalent to each other. For example, a program can be evolved to print a trace message by either structural reflection or behavioral reflection. If behavioral reflection is available, the tracing mechanism can be implemented as we have already showed above. On the other hand, if structural reflection is available, statements for printing a trace message can be embedded at appropriate places in the method bodies included in the program. A method metaobject would allow substituting the body of the method or instrumenting statements included in that body. Suppose that a Method object provides an insertBefore method, which inserts a given statement at the beginning of the method body. Then the following statement transforms the move method in the Point class so that it will print a trace message when it is called:

```
pointClass.getMethod("move")
         .insertBefore("System.out.Println(\"method call\");");
```

Note that the variable pointClass refers to the Class object representing the Point class.

This discussion is analogous to how to implement language extensions. If we want to extend a programming language, we have two approaches for the implementation. The first one is to implement a source-to-source program translator from the extended language to the original language. The other one is to extend a compiler or interpreter of the original language so that it can deal with the new features of the extended language. The structural reflection corresponds to the former approach while the behavioral reflection corresponds to the latter approach.

The programming model of structural reflection is easily derived from the program structure of the target language. If the target language is Java, the metaobjects are classes, methods, constructors, and fields. On the other hand, the behavioral reflection has a variety of programming models. In one programming model, the metaobjects are classes, methods, and so on. In another model, each object is associated with a metaobject representing a virtual interpreter that is responsible to the execution of the operations, such as method calls, on that object. Developers can customize that metaobject to alter the behavior of only the particular object instead of all the instances of a particular class. There is also a programming model in which a garbage collector and a thread scheduler are metaobjects. Developers can customize their behavior through the metaobjects [39, 28]. Another model uses a metaobject representing a message exchanged among objects [13] or communication channels [4].

3.5 Typical Applications

A typical application of reflective computing is to implementing a program translator. Structural reflection is obviously useful for that purpose. It allows developers to concentrate the procedure of program transformation at the source-code level. They do not have to implement a program parser or to transform an abstract syntax tree.

For example, structural reflection can be used to implement a program translator that automatically transforms a program written as a non-distributed program so that it can run on multiple hosts as a distributed program. The essence of such program transformation is to produce the class definitions for proxy objects and modify the program to substitute a reference to a proxy object for a reference to a local object when the local reference is passed to a remote host. To produce the class definitions for proxy objects, the class definitions for the original objects that the proxy objects refer to must be investigated; the names and the signatures of the methods declared in the class must be obtained. The reifying capability of metaobjects helps this investigation. Structural reflection allows developers to easily produce the class definitions for proxy objects by constructing new class metaobjects. Substituting object references can be implemented by modifying method bodies through method metaobjects.

Behavioral reflection provides a direct solution for program translators that implement some language extensions such as distribution, persistence, and transaction. It is useful to transform a program so that those non-functional concerns will be appended to classes in the program. For example, it can be used to implement the synchronized method of Java. Some languages like C++ do not provide the language mechanism of the synchronized method but it can be implemented by a customized method metaobject. If Java did not provide synchronized methods but supported behavioral reflection, the class for the customized method metaobject would be as following:

```
public class SynchronizedMethod extends Method {
  public Object invoke(Object target, Object[] args) {
    synchronized (target) {
      return super.invoke(target, args);
    }
  }
}
```

The synchronized statement locks the target while the following block statement is being executed.

If a language supporting behavioral reflection provides a metaobject representing a thread scheduler, the metaobject can be used to implement an application-specific scheduler. In the area of scientific computing with parallel processing, thread scheduling optimized for particular application software can often significantly improve the execution performance of that software [26]. Suppose that a tree data structure must be recursively searched in parallel. For some applications, the depth-first search approach should be used while for other applications the breadth-first search approach should be used. If the thread scheduler can be customized through a metaobject, the application software can adopt the most appropriate scheduling policy. In general, the maximum number of concurrent threads should be decreased for the depth-first search whereas it should be increased for the breadth-first search.

3.6   Implementation Techniques

Reflection was regarded as a mechanism that was useful but too inefficient to use for practical purposes. The most significant problem was that a language supporting reflection tended to imply a serious performance penalty even when the reflection mechanism was not used at all. If a language fully provides the reflection capability, any parts of the program structure and the behavior of any operations must be changeable through metaobjects. A naive implementation of the language processor for such a language is an interpreter and thus it cannot run the program efficiently.

To avoid this performance problem, several implementation techniques have been proposed so far. A simple technique is to restrict a kind of metaobjects available. For example, if we know in advance that only a limited number of classes are reified, the other classes that are not reified can be normally compiled into efficient binary code. Otherwise, the language processor can first run a program with the compiled binary code and then, when classes are reified, it can stop using the compiled binary code and start executing those classes with an interpreter [26].

If the reflection capability allows only intercession, efficient implementation is relatively easy. The whole program can be normally compiled into efficient binary except that *hook code* is inserted around the operators customized by metaobjects [9, 40, 18]. When the thread of control reaches one of those operators, the hook code intercepts the execution and switches the control to the metaobject, which executes extended behavior of the intercepted operator. Although the execution of the operators customized through metaobjects imply performance penalties, the execution of the rest of the operators does not involve an overhead due to intercession.

Another technique is to partly recompile a program whenever the structure or the behavior of the program is altered through a metaobject. For example, if a class definition is changed, the runtime system of the language can recompile that class definition on the fly so that the changes of the class will be reflected. Note that this technique makes it difficult to perform global optimization. Suppose that a method is inlined in other methods at compilation time. If the body of that inlined method is changed through a metaobject at runtime, all the methods where that method is being inlined must be also recompiled during runtime.

Curring and Memoizing. The CLOS MOP adopts the *curring and memoizing* technique [20] for efficient implementation. This technique is similar to the dynamic recompilation technique above. To illustrate the idea of the curring and memoizing technique, first let us consider the following naive implementation of the newInstance method (written in Java for readability). Assume that we implement an object as an array of Object:

```
public class Class {
  public Object newInstance() {
    int size = getSuperclass().computeFieldSize();
    size += computeFieldSize();
    return new Object[size];
  }
    :
}
```

Although newInstance in Java is a native method, that method is a regular method in the CLOS MOP so that it can be customized by subclassing the Class class.

Unfortunately, this implementation is too slow since it repeatedly computes the object size whenever a new instance is created. To avoid this inefficiency, the curring and memoizing technique uses a function closure. See the improved version of newInstance below:

```
public class Class {
  private Closure factory;
  public Object newInstance() {
    if (factory == null)
      factory = getFactory();
    return factory.newInstance();
  }
  public Closure getFactory() {
    int s = getSuperclass().computeFieldSize();
    final int size = s + computeFieldSize();
    return new Closure() {
      public Object newInstance() {
        return new Object[size];  // size is constant
```

```
      }
    };
  }
      :
}
```

The getFactory method is a sort of compiler since compilation is a process of transforming a program to an efficient form by using statically available information. Indeed, that method transfomrs a new expression and returns a function closure[3] that efficiently makes an instance. Notc that the computeFieldSize method is called only once when the closure is created. The returned closure is memoized in the factory field to avoid redundantly calling getFactory. From the next time, the newInstance method creates an instance by calling this function closure.

Now let us define a subclass of Class so that a trace message is always printed out when a new object is created. We override the getFactory method:

```
public class TracedClass extends Class {
  public Closure getFactory() {
    final Closure c = super.getFactory();
    final String name = getName();
    return new Closure() {
      public Object newInstance() {
        System.out.println("instantiate " + name);
        return c.newInstance();
      }
    };
  }
}
```

Note that super.getFactory() and getName() are called only once when the closure is created.

In the CLOS MOP, a subclass of Class does not directly specify how to create an instance. Rather, it specifies how to construct an efficient function for creating an instance. Hence the class metaobject of that subclass can be regarded as a compiler. The runtime system of the CLOS MOP calls that metaobject to obtain the "compiled code" and then continues to use it until another reflecting operation is performed.

The CLOS MOP requires metaobject developers to describe how to construct an efficient function for doing basic operations such as object creation. Hence the programming style is not simple or straightforward although the runtime overhead is low.

Partial Evaluation. A number of applications do not need full reflection capability. They need the reflecting operation only at the beginning of the program execution. Once the reflecting operation is performed, they do not need to alter program structure or behavior again during runtime. In fact, altering program structure during runtime is not a simple job. For example, if a new field is added

---

[3] In the CLOS MOP, getFactory really returns a closure.

to an existing class, we must also specify how the existing instances of that class are dealt with. Is the new field also added to those existing instances? If so, what is the initial value of that added field?

If a program does not need the full reflection capability and some reflecting operations are statically determined, we can compile the program into efficient code. A few researchers [25, 27] have proposed using the technique called *partial evaluation* for compiling away metaobjects. Their idea is to apply partial evaluation [12, 16] to the class definitions for metaobjects. The static input for the partial evaluation is the program running with the metaobjects.

From a pragmatic viewpoint, partial evaluation is a theoretical framework for agressively performing constant propagation and code inlining. We below illustrate the basic idea of partial evaluation from the pragmatic viewpoint. For example, suppose we have the following simple class definition for metaobjects:

```
public class TracedClass extends Class {
  public Object newInstance() {
    System.out.println("instantiate " + getName());
    return super.newInstance();
  }
}
```

Then suppose that a program includes the following statement:

```
Point p = new Point();
```

This statement is first translated into the following statement calling a metaobject as in the CLOS MOP:

```
Point p = (Point)pointClass.newInstance();
```

pointClass refers to the class metaobject representing the Point class. Then the partial evaluator inlines the newInstance method in TracedClass:

```
System.out.println("instantiate " + pointClass.getName());
Point p = (Point)pointClass.super.newInstance();
```

Next, let us inline getName() and newInstance():

```
System.out.println("instantiate Point");
int size = pointClass.getSuperclass().computeFieldSize();
size += pointClass.computeFieldSize();
Point p = (Point)new Object[size];
```

Since the resulting values of getSuperclass() and computeFieldSize() are constant, those method calls turn into constants. Let the value of size be 5. Thus the resulting statement is as following:

```
System.out.println("instantiate Point");
Point p = (Point)new Object[5];
```

This statement is the result of partial evaluation but it does not include any calls to the metaobject.

Although partial evaluation is a powerful technique for efficiently implementing the reflection mechanism, developing a partial evaluator is extremely difficult. The articles [25, 27] reported that the authors succeeded in developing a partial evaluator for their Lisp-based ABCL/R3 reflective language. Unfortunately, no article has yet reported that a partial evaluator can be used to efficiently compile reflective computing in C++ or Java as far as the author knows.

Compile-Time Reflection. If the reflection capability is necessary only at the beginning of program execution and not necessary during runtime, we can use another compilation approach, which is called *compile-time reflection*. It was developed by the author's group for reflective languages OpenC++ [5, 6] and OpenJava [38]. The compile-time reflection allows reflective computing only at compile time — therefore, a code block performing reflective computing must be separated from the rest of the program, which performs normal base-level computing. The *meta* program performing reflective computing is executed by a compiler at an early stage of the compilation process as macro expansion is.

The meta program can directly describe program transformation. Suppose that pointClass refers to the metaobject representing the Point class. If the meta program includes the following statement:

```
pointClass.addField(new Field(intType, "z"));
```

this meta program is separately compiled in advance and then executed at the compile time of the target (base-level) program. If executed, the meta program appends a new int field named z to the Point class. After that, the resulting target program is normally compiled into binary code.

An advantage of the compile-time reflection is that the overhead due to reflective computing is negligible or zero. To implement a program translator, the compile-time reflection is an appropriate tool since it provides high-level abstraction, such as class metaobjects and method metaobjects, with negligible overheads. The developers do not have to directly manipulate an abstract syntax tree for program transformation.

The meta program for the compile-time reflection can also include user-defined classes for metaobjects. However, as the metaobject of the CLOS MOP returns a function closure, the metaobject of the compile-time reflection returns transformed source code. For example, see the following class:

```
public class TracedClass extends Class {
  public String newInstance() {
    return "(System.out.println(\"instantiate " + getName() + "\"),"
         + super.newInstance() + ")";
  }
}
```

The compiler for the compile-time reflection first reads a target program and, when it finds an expression for object creation, method call, or field access, it queries the corresponding metaobject about how the expression should be transformed. The compiler uses the static type of the expression for selecting the metaobject. Then the compiler replaces the original code with the source code returned from the metaobject. After finishing the replacement of all the expressions, the compiler compiles the program into binary code.

For example, suppose that a target program includes the following statement:

```
Point p = new Point();
```

and the class metaobject for Point is an instance of TracedClass. When the compiler finds this object creation, it calls the newInstance method in TracedClass and requests it to transform "new Point()". Since the newInstance method in Class returns "new Point()" (*i.e.* no transformation), the newInstance method in TracedClass returns the following code:

```
(System.out.println("instantiate Point"), new Point())
```

Note that we use for readability the comma (,) operator of C++. If an expression "(*expr1, expr2*)" is evaluated, *expr1* and *expr2* are evaluated in this order and the resulting value of *exp2* becomes the resulting value of the whole expression. The returned code above is substituted for the original expression "new Point()". After this substitution, the target program becomes:

```
Point p
  = (System.out.println("instantiate Point"), new Point());
```

Finally, this program is normally compiled. The resulting binary code will not include any metaobjects.

Load-Time Reflection. We have also developed a variant of the compile-time reflection. It is *load-time reflection* and it was adopted for designing our Java bytecode engineering toolkit named *Javassist* [7, 10].

The load-time reflection allows reflective computing only at load time whereas the compile-time reflection allows at compile time. Both types of reflection do not allow reflective computing during runtime. From the programming viewpoint, there is no differences between the two types of reflection. However, from the implementation viewpoint, there is a significant difference between them: the target program of the compile-time reflection is source code but that of the load-time reflection is compiled binary.

OpenC++, which is based on the compile-time reflection, reads source code and constructs metaobjects. Changes to the metaobjects are reflected back to the source code before compilation. On the other hand, Javassist reads a Java class file (*i.e.* Java bytecode obtained after source code is compiled) and constructs metaobjects. Changes to the metaobjects are reflected on the class files before the JVM (Java Virtual Machine) loads them. This architecture is possible at least in Java since Java class files contain rich symbol information.

Note that the users of Javassist does not have to learn the internal structure of Java class files or the instructions of Java bytecode. They can enjoy the source-level abstraction provided by metaobjects as they can in OpenC++. The changes to the metaobjects are described with Java source code and, when they are reflected on the class files, Javassist automatically translates them into the changes described at bytecode level. For example, the following meta program appends a new method toString to the Point class:[4]

```
Method m = new Method(
  "public String toString() { return this.x + \",\" + this.y; }");
pointClass.addMethod(m);
```

pointClass refers to the class metaobject representing the Point class. Note that the method body is given in the form of Java source code. This source code is compiled by the internal compiler of Javassist and then embedded in a class file. The users do not have to construct a sequence of Java bytecode for specifying a method body. Providing source-level abstraction is an advantage of Javassist against other naive bytecode engineering toolkits such as BCEL [11].

4 Aspect-Oriented Programming

Aspect-oriented programming (AOP) [21] is an emerging paradigm for modularizing a *crosscutting concern*, which is strongly relevant to other concerns and thus cannot be implemented as an independent component or module in a traditional language. The implementation of a crosscutting concern in a traditional language, for example, an object-oriented language like Java, often consists of not only a normal independent component but also code snippets spread over the components implementing other concerns. Therefore, such an implementation of a crosscutting concern is difficult to append and remove to/from software without editing the implementations of other concerns when the requirements of the software are changed. The goal of aspect-oriented programming is to provide language mechanisms to solve this problem.

From the viewpoint of program transformation, AOP languages such as AspectJ [22] provide several useful mechanisms for more simply achieving the goals that we have been doing with typical program transformation tools or reflection mechanisms. In fact, one of the roots of AOP is the reflection technology. Describing rules or algorithms for program transformation is never easy but it is often error-prone. For example, one algorithm for program transformation might be not general enough to cover all possible programs and thus it might not work if a particular program is given as the input. AOP languages like AspectJ provides mechanisms integrated into the language semantics and thereby they let us avoid directly describing error-prone rules for program transformation.

4.1 AspectJ

To illustrate the overview of AOP, we show a simple program written in AspectJ. A famous example of AOP is logging, which is a typical crosscutting concern.

---

[4] This is not a real program for Javassist.

Suppose that we want to print a logging message when the paint method is called.

Example. The main body of the implementation of the logging concern can be modularized into a single class, for example, in Java:

```
public class Logging {
  private PrintStream output = System.out;
  public static void setStream(PrintStream out) {
    output = out;
  }
  public static void print(String m) {
    output.println(m);
  }
}
```

This component encapsulates which output device is used for printing a logging message.

The rest of the work is to edit the paint method so that the print method in Logging will be called:

```
public class Clock extends Panel {
  public void paint(Graphics g) {
    Logging.print("** call paint method");    // edit!
    // draw a clock on the screen.
  }
  public static void main(String[] args) { .. }
}
```

Although this is a very typical Java program, the implementation of the logging concern cuts across other components such as Clock. It is not an independent component separated from other components. Some of the readers might think that the implementation of the logging concern is separated into the Logging class. However, that thought is wrong since the implementation of the logging concern also include the expression for calling the print method. This caller-side expression specifies when a logging message is printed out. The argument of the call specifies the contents of the printed message. Although these issues are part of the logging concern, that expression is not encapsulated in Logging but embedded in the paint method in Clock.

Using an Aspect. An AspectJ, the logging concern can be implemented as a single independent module called an *aspect*. See the following program:

```
aspect Logging {
  private PrintStream output = System.out;
  public void setStream(PrintStream out) {
    output = out;
  }
  public void print(String m) {
    output.println(m);
  }
```

```
// before advice
before(): call(void Clock.paint(Graphics)) {
  print("** call paint method");
}
}
```

Note that Logging is now not a class but an aspect and it includes before advice:

```
before(): call(void Clock.paint(Graphics)) {
  print("** call paint method");
}
```

This specifies that the print method is called just before the paint method in Clock is called. An instance of the Logging aspect is a singleton and automatically created. The AspectJ compiler automatically modifies the definition of the Clock class to implement this behavior. Thus the developer can write the Clock class without considering the logging concern:

```
public class Clock extends Panel {
  public void paint(Graphics g) {
    // draw a clock on the screen.
  }
  public static void main(String[] args) { .. }
}
```

The paint method does not include an expression for calling the print method in Logging. Hence Logging and Clock are completely separated from each other. They can be combined and disconnected on demand without editing the source code of those components.

Joinpoints. The key concepts of AOP is joinpoints, pointcuts, and advice. In this programming paradigm, program execution is modeled as a sequence of fine-grained events, such as method calls, field accesses, object creation, and so on. These events are called *joinpoints*. *pointcuts* are filters of joinpoints. They select interesting joinpoints during program execution. Then, if a joinpoint selected by some pointcut occurs, the *advice* associated to that pointcut is executed. In the case of the example above,

```
call(void Clock.paint(Graphics))
```

is a pointcut. It specifies method calls to the paint method in Clock. call is one of the primitive pointcut designators provided by AspectJ. There are various pointcut designators for selecting different kinds of joinpoints. Pointcut designators can select joinpoints that match a given pattern. The advice is the declaration beginning with before and ending with a block {..}.

A crosscutting concern is implemented as a set of advice in an aspect. The connection between the aspect and other classes is described by pointcuts. Joinpoints can be regarded as execution points at which an aspect and a class are connected to each other.

Intertype Declaration. An aspect of AspectJ may contain an intertype declaration as well as regular methods and fields, pointcuts, and advice. The intertype declaration declares a method or a field in another class. Developers can use intertype declarations for appending methods and fields to existing classes. For example, the following aspect appends the paintCount field to the Clock class:

```
aspect Counter {
  int Clock.paintCount = 0;
}
```

An intertype declaration can be also used to modify inheritance hierarchy. It can change the super class of an existing class and add an interface to an existing class. For example, the following aspect adds SessionBean interface to Registration class (remember the example in Section 2.2):

```
aspect EJBCompliant {
  declare parents: Registration implements SessionBean;
}
```

The modification by declare parents is highly restricted. If a super class is changed, the new super class must be a subclass of the old super class. Although a new interface can be added to an existing class, removing an interface from an existing class is not allowed.

4.2   Dependency Reduction

AOP is a technology for implementing a crosscutting concern as a separate component. A component implementing such a concern in a traditional language is tightly coupled with other components so that it cannot be treated as an independent component. It cannot be disconnected from the other components when it is not necessary any more during software life cycle, or it cannot be connected to the existing software on demand. In other words, AOP languages provides language mechanisms for loosing this dependency among components so that the components can be treated as an independent one. Those components independently described are connected to each other at compile time or runtime to constitute complete software. This connecting process is called *weaving*.

Reducing inter-component dependency simplifies a framework protocol. Developers can describe their components without considering that the components are connected to other components provided by a framework. The connections among components are separately described. This reduces the amount of protocol that developers have to consider when they implement a component since the protocol is a rule for connecting components.

Dependency Injection. AOP is one of the latest approaches for loosing dependency among components. It provides more powerful mechanisms than other existing approaches such as dependency injection [15].

The dependency injection is a popular mechanism of recent component frameworks for web applications. It is a simple helper mechanism for intensively using so-called *factory method pattern* to create a component. The use of dependency injection improves the reusability of the components built on top of other lower-level sub-components. Suppose that an component contains other components. The idea of the dependency injection is that, when a factory object creates a component, it also creates the sub components contained in that component and automatically sets the fields of that component to those sub components. This makes the source code of the component independent of the code for creating the sub components. For example, a component implementing business logic may contain a sub component for accessing a database:

```
class Registration {
  DbAccessor da;
    :
  void setDbAccessor(DbAccessor obj) { da = obj; }
  void register(String who) { ... da.commit(who); ... }
  void cancel(String who) { ... da.commit(who); ... }
}
```

When the factory object creates an instance of Registration, it also creates an appropriate sub component for that instance. Then it calls the setDbAccessor method to set the da field to that sub component. Note that the definition of Registration does not include the code for creating the sub component. The type of the sub component is specified in a separate file, normally written in XML.

The dependency injection enables switching the sub component without editing the source code of the component for business logic. Sub components can be switched by editing only a separate specification file in XML. This feature allows the reuse of the components without the sub component. If the dependency injection is not used, the source code of the component would include the initialization code for creating the sub component for accessing a particular type of database. It would heavily depend on that particular type of database and thus the source code of the component must be edited to be reused with another type of database. Otherwise, the component must be always reused with the original sub component together. For example, the definition of Registration would be changed into the following if the dependency injection is not used:

```
class Registration {
  DbAccessor da;
    :
  Registration() { da = new MySQLAccessor(); }
  void register(String who) { ... da.commit(who); ... }
  void cancel(String who) { ... da.commit(who); ... }
}
```

The constructor must explicitly create a sub component. MySQLAccessor is a class type implementing the DbAccessor interface. To change the type of the sub component, the definition of Registration must be edited.

Sources of Dependency. Although the dependency injection addresses code dependency with respect to the initialization of the links between a component and its sub components, the code dependency is not limited to that. According to our observation, the sources of the inter-component dependency are the following three:

- Declaration of fields referring to sub-components,
- Creation of sub-components, and
- Method calls to sub-components.

The dependency injection addresses only the creation of sub-components. It does not address the dependency due to a field declaration. For example, the Registration class shown above includes a filed da of type DbAccessor. This field declaration must be explicitly included even though the field will be unnecessary if the Registration is reused without a DbAccess sub-component. Registration may be always reused with a DbAccess sub-component but, if Registration contains a Logger sub-component as well, then Registration will be sometime reused without the Logger component.

Another source of the dependency is a method call. If a Registration components calls a method on a DbAccess sub-component, the source code of Registration depends on the DbAccess. It must include an expression for the method call. If a sub-component is modified and a new parameter is appended to the called method, for example, for passing a hint on performance tuning, then the method-call expression in Registration must be also modified. If Registration also contains a Logger sub-component, developers might want to reuse it later without Logger sub-component. In this case, the source code of Registration must be modified; all occurrences of the method calls to Logger must be removed from the source code so that Registration can be solely reused.

Aspect-Oriented Programming. Unlike the dependency injection and other existing techniques, AOP addresses the three sources shown above. If we regard an aspect as a sub component above, the dependency due to method calls can be clearly separated from the source code of the component by the pointcut-advice mechanism of AOP. Developers do not have to include a method-call expression in the source code of the caller-side component. Moreover, developers do not have to explicitly declare a field referring to a sub component or create the sub component. Note that here a sub component is an aspect. AOP languages such as AspectJ automatically deal with such declaration and creation. In AspectJ, the field referring to an aspect instance is not visible but the value of that field can be obtained by the aspectOf() operator.

However, the dependency reduction by AspectJ is limited since an aspect in AspectJ is not equivalent to a regular class. An aspect instance cannot be treated in the same way as a component constructed as an object. For example, developers do not have full control of the creation of aspect instances. They must choose one of the pre-defined options to specify how an aspect instance is created. AspectJ provides issingleton (an aspect instance is a singleton), perthis (an aspect instance is created per this object), pertarget (created per target object), and so on. It does not enable some (but not all) components to share the same aspect instance. Furthermore, AspectJ does not provide a direct mechanism for initializing the value of an existing field. Although an inter-type declaration of AspectJ can declare a new field and define its initial value, it cannot define the initial value of an existing field.

To overcome this limitation of AspectJ, several AOP systems such as Caesar [29], JAsCo [37], The Aspect Markup Language [23], JBoss AOP [19], and Classpects [31], have been developed. They divide the description of an aspect into two parts: aspect implementation and aspect binding. This separation improves the reusability of aspects. An aspect implementation defines a sub component, which is connected by AOP to a target component, and an aspect binding defines at which joinpoints the sub component is connected to the target components. Roughly to say, the aspect implementation corresponds to advice of AspectJ and the aspect binding corresponds to pointcuts of AspectJ. Their description of aspect implementations are quite indistinguishable from that of regular components. For example, JBoss AOP lets developers use plain Java for describing an aspect implementation while an aspect binding is in XML. Classpects also let them use a regular class for describing an aspect implementation although an aspect binding is also defined in a class by extended syntax. However, in these AOP systems, the creation of an aspect implementation, that is, a sub component is implicitly executed by a runtime system. Developers do not have full control of it.

Association aspects [32] gives developers better control of creation of an aspect instance. Developers can use the new operator to explicitly create an aspect instance and connects it to a set of components, that is, objects. However, an association aspect must be connected to a fixed number of components, normally two or three, since it was designed to model a relationship among components.

Caesar [29] is a dynamic AOP system and hence it allows developers to explicitly create an aspect instance and connect it to a target component. Developers can activate an aspect binding only during a specified period and thereby an aspect implementation explicitly created is connected to a target component only during that period. However, the aspect implementation may be connected to multiple target components that the aspect binding selects; the developers cannot fully control those connections. Furthermore, the runtime systems of dynamic AOP imply not negligible performance overheads [30, 33] unless a custom JVM is used[2].

GluonJ. GluonJ [8] is our prototype AOP system designed for separating the three sources of inter-component dependency from the implementation of components. The design goal of GluonJ is to develop an AOP system that provides a flexible way to describe connections among components written in plain Java. Unlike typical architecture description languages, GluonJ allows creation of new components during runtime.

In GluonJ, an aspect is divided into an aspect binding and an aspect implementation. An aspect implementation, that is, a component is described in plain Java while an aspect binding is described in XML. GluonJ gives developers full control of creation of an aspect instance. Another unique feature is that GluonJ enables an aspect binding to directly define how to initialize an existing field. Therefore, it can be used as a substitute for the mechanism of dependency injection. GluonJ is categorized into static AOP systems; it does not need a runtime weaver.

A basic idea of GluonJ is to open up how an aspect implementation is created and connected to a target component. Although other AOP systems encapsulate it in the implementation of the system, GluonJ lets developers directly describe it in plain Java. Thereby, GluonJ gives greater flexibility to the developers. How an aspect implementation is created and connected is described in an aspect binding, which we also call *glue code*.

The Logging **Concern in GluonJ.** The aspect binding of GluonJ includes glue code written in Java. It connects an instance of an aspect implementation to a target component. The following XML code is an aspect binding of GluonJ for Logging:

```
<glue>
  <injection>
    Logging Clock.aspect = new Logging();
  </injection>
  <advice>
    <pointcut>
      execution(void Clock.paint(Graphics))
    </pointcut>
    <before>
      Logging.aspectOf(this).print();
    </before>
  </advice>
</glue>
```

The block surrounded by the injection tag specifies how an Logging object is connected to a Clock object. It represents that a new instance of Logging is created for each Clock object and it is assigned to an aspect field of Clock. The aspect field is a special field, which is available without declaration. The value of the aspect field can be obtained by aspectOf().

The pointcut block above selects as joinpoints method calls to the paint method in Clock. When the thread of control reaches these joinpoints, the code surrounded by the before is executed. Although this code block seems similar to AspectJ's before advice, it is not executed on an instance of Logging since it is glue code. Rather, it is executed on an instance of Clock as part of the paint method. Thus this represents the Clock object. The code block obtains a Logging object connected to the Clock object and then calls the print method on the Logging object. Logging.aspectOf(this) represents an Logging object assigned to the aspect field of this object. The definition of the Logging is a regular class definition as following:

```
public class Logging {
  private PrintStream output = System.out;
  public void setStream(PrintStream out) {
    output = out;
  }
```

```
  public void print(String m) {
    output.println(m);
  }
}
```

Note that the code blocks surrounded by injection and before are written in plain Java. This fact provides the full control of creation of aspect implementations. The injection block may connects any instance of Logging to a Clock object; it does not have to create a new instance of Logging for each Clock object. It can connect an existing Logging object to a Clock object.

The injection block can assign a Logging object to an existing field of a Clock object. For example,

```
<injection>
  Logging Clock.logger = new Logging();
</injection>
```

A Logging object is assigned to a logger field of Clock. If there is no such a field declared in Clock, the logger field is automatically declared as an intertype declaration of AspectJ declares it.

The before block does not have to call a method on the object returned by aspectOf(). It may call a method on the object pointed to by another field of Clock.

GluonJ vs. AspectJ. Some readers might think that an aspect binding in GluonJ could be easily translated into an equivalent aspect described in AspectJ. For example, the aspect binding for the Logging concern could be translated into the following aspect in AspectJ:

```
aspect LoggingGlue {
  private Logging Clock.aspect = new Logging();
  before(Clock c): execution(void Clock.paint(Graphics)) && this(c) {
    c.aspect.print();
  }
}
```

The second line is an intertype declaration, which declares an aspect field in the Clock class. The initial value of the aspect field is a newly created instance of Logging. We do not have to change the source code of the Logging class. The third line is a before advice, which is executed before a call to paint in Clock. It calls the print method on the Logging object that the aspect field of c refers to. The variable c is bound to the Clock object that is going to execute the paint method.

This AspectJ program also implements how an Logging object is created and connected to a Clock object. Although the two programs are similar among GluonJ and AspectJ, there are a few differences. First, in AspectJ, an instance of the LoggingGlue aspect is created at runtime and it is placed between a Logging object and a Clock object. This aspect is being used as an entity implementing not a logging concern but a forwarder of method calls to a Logging object. On the other hand, in GluonJ, any intermediate object for method forwarding does not exist. The Java code surrounded by before is executed by a Clock object and it directly calls the print method on a Logging object. Obviously, the semantics of the AspectJ program is more complex since an aspect is used for implementing an implementation-level *meta* concern — a method-call forwarder — and a logging crosscutting concern is implemented by another class. This does not fit the programming model of AspectJ, in which an aspect should be used for implementing a crosscutting concern. Furthermore, from a performance viewpoint, method forwarding by the LoggingGlue aspect will imply a performance penalty.

Another difference is between an injection block of GluonJ and an intertype declaration of AspectJ. Both can declare a new field in an existing class but only an injection block can assign a value to an existing field. Suppose that the Clock class already includes a logger field and thus we want to use it for storing a reference to a Logging object. In GluonJ, the injection tag will be changed into the following:

```
<injection>
  Logging Clock.logger = new Logging();
</injection>
```

No big change is required. On the other hand, the intertype declaration of the AspectJ program will be replaced with the following advice:

```
before(Clock c): execution(Clock.new(..)) & this(c) {
  c.logger = new Logging();
}
```

This advice is executed when a constructor of Clock is executed. A variable c is bound to the Clock object being created. Thus, a newly created Logging object is assigned to the logger field of c. Again, this advice represents an implementation-level *meta* concern. It never directly represents what we want to do, which is that a Logging object is connected to a Clock object through a logger field.

Module Mechanism or Binding Mechanism? Although AOP is known as a new modularization mechanism, it is rather regarded as a new mechanism for connecting components, modules, or objects. We have designed GluonJ so that it will provide essential operators for representing connections among components.

Providing a right set of language mechanisms is important. An advantage of AOP against reflective computing is that AOP provides mechanisms that are less powerful but relatively safe and easy to use. A disadvantage of reflective computing is that a program for reflective computing is often complicated and difficult to maintain. The reflective computing is powerful enough to write a program that lets you *really* shoot yourself in the foot, that is, break the program itself. For example, it allows developers to wrongly remove a method that is called by other methods. It allows them to change the super class of a class to an irrelevant class.

If readers consider that an aspect of AspectJ corresponds to an aspect binding (*i.e.* glue code) of GluonJ, GluonJ can be regarded as a restricted version of AspectJ. They can consider that GluonJ is a language that enforces AspectJ developers to follow a particular type of programming style, in which an aspect is used only for gluing objects. It is not used for implementing a crosscutting concern; a plain Java class must be used for that. For example, the Logging aspect shown in 4.1 directly implements a logging crosscutting concern. It cannot be translated into a corresponding aspect binding in GluonJ. It must be translated into a set of aspect binding written in XML and aspect implementation in plain Java since an aspect binding does not define an entity that can be instantiated.

5   Summary

This tutorial first discussed that program translators will be able to simplify a framework protocol, which is often complicated in compensation for its func- tionality and reusability. Developing a program translator only for a particular framework is too expensive, but the reflection technology provides a power- ful platform for such a program translator. If an appropriate implementation technique is used, the inefficiency of reflective computing can be reduced. This tutorial also mentions aspect-oriented programming (AOP). It can be also used for implementing a program translator and it provides a simpler programming model than the reflection technology. Although the reflection and AOP tech- nologies significantly improved our ability for simplifying a framework protocol, the current states of those technologies are never perfect. For example, we need further study for dealing with the example in Section 2.1.

References

1. Bobrow, D.G., DeMichiel, L.G., Gabriel, R.P., Keene, S.E., Kiczales, G., Moon, D.A.: Common lisp object system specification. Sigplan Notices (1988) (X3J13 Document 88-002R).
2. Bockisch, C., Haupt, M., Mezini, M., Ostermann, K.: Virtual machine support for dynamic join points. In: Proc. of Int'l Conf. on Aspect-Oriented Software Development (AOSD 2004). (2004) 83–92
3. Bracha, G., Ungar, D.: Mirrors: design principles for meta-level facilities of object-oriented programming languages. In: Proc. of ACM Conf. on Object-Oriented Programming Systems, Languages, and Applications, ACM (2004) 331–334
4. Cazzola, W.: mcharm: Reflective middleware with a global view of communications. IEEE Distributed System On-Line **3** (2002)
5. Chiba, S.: A metaobject protocol for C++. In: Proc. of ACM Conf. on Object-Oriented Programming Systems, Languages, and Applications. Number 10 in SIG-PLAN Notices vol. 30, ACM (1995) 285–299
6. Chiba, S.: Macro processing in object-oriented languages. In: Proc. of Technology of Object-Oriented Languages and Systems (TOOLS Pacific '98), IEEE Press (1998) 113–126
7. Chiba, S.: Load-time structural reflection in Java. In: ECOOP 2000. LNCS 1850, Springer-Verlag (2000) 313–336
8. Chiba, S., Ishikawa, R.: Aspect-oriented programming beyond dependency injec- tion. In: ECOOP 2005. LNCS 3586, Springer-Verlag (2005) pp.121–143

9. Chiba, S., Masuda, T.: Designing an extensible distributed language with a meta-level architecture. In: Proc. of the 7th European Conference on Object-Oriented Programming. LNCS 707, Springer-Verlag (1993) 482–501

10. Chiba, S., Nishizawa, M.: An easy-to-use toolkit for efficient Java bytecode translators. In: Proc. of Generative Programming and Component Engineering (GPCE '03). LNCS 2830, Springer-Verlag (2003) 364–376

11. Dahm, M.: Byte code engineering with the javaclass api. Techincal Report B-17-98, Institut für Informatik, Freie Universität Berlin (1999)

12. Ershov, A.: On the essence of compilation. In Neuhold, E., ed.: Formal Description of Programming Concepts, North-Holland (1978) 391–420

13. Ferber, J.: Computational reflection in class based object oriented languages. In: Proc. of ACM Conf. on Object-Oriented Programming Systems, Languages, and Applications. (1989) 317–326

14. Foote, B., Johnson, R.E.: Reflective facilities in Smalltalk-80. In: Proc. of ACM Conf. on Object-Oriented Programming Systems, Languages, and Applications. (1989) 327–335

15. Fowler, M.: Inversion of control containers and the dependency injection pattern. http://www.martinfowler.com/articles/injection.html (2004)

16. Futamura, Y.: Partial computation of programs. In: Proc. of RIMS Symposia on Software Science and Engineering. Number 147 in LNCS (1982) 1–35

17. Goldberg, A., Robson, D.: Smalltalk-80: The Language and Its Implementation. Addison-Wesley (1983)

18. Golm, M., Kleinöder, J.: Jumping to the meta level, behavioral reflection can be fast and flexible. In: Proc. of Reflection '99. LNCS 1616, Springer (1999) 22–39

19. JBoss Inc.: JBoss AOP 1.0.0 final. http://www.jboss.org/ (2004)

20. Kiczales, G., des Rivières, J., Bobrow, D.G.: The Art of the Metaobject Protocol. The MIT Press (1991)

21. Kiczales, G., Lamping, J., Mendhekar, A., Maeda, C., Lopes, C., Loingtier, J., Irwin, J.: Aspect-oriented programming. In: ECOOP'97 – Object-Oriented Programming. LNCS 1241, Springer (1997) 220–242

22. Kiczales, G., Hilsdale, E., Hugunin, J., Kersten, M., Palm, J., Griswold, W.G.: An overview of AspectJ. In: ECOOP 2001 – Object-Oriented Programming. LNCS 2072, Springer (2001) 327–353

23. Lopes, C.V., Ngo, T.C.: The aspect markup language and its support of aspect plugins. Isr technical report # uci-isr-04-8, University of California, Irvine (2004)

24. Maes, P.: Concepts and experiments in computational reflection. In: Proc. of ACM Conf. on Object-Oriented Programming Systems, Languages, and Applications. (1987) 147–155

25. Masuhara, H., Matsuoka, S., Asai, K., Yonezawa, A.: Compiling away the meta-level in object-oriented concurrent reflective languages using partial evaluation. In: Proc. of ACM Conf. on Object-Oriented Programming Systems, Languages, and Applications. (1995) 300–315

26. Masuhara, H., Matsuoka, S., Watanabe, T., Yonezawa, A.: Object-oriented concurrent reflective languages can be implemented efficiently. In: Proc. of ACM Conf. on Object-Oriented Programming Systems, Languages, and Applications. (1992) 127–144

27. Masuhara, H., Yonezawa, A.: Design and partial evaluation of meta-objects for a concurrent reflective languages. In: ECOOP'98 - Object Oriented Programming. LNCS 1445, Springer (1998) 418–439

28. McAffer, J.: Meta-level programming with coda. In: Proc. of the 9th European Conference on Object-Oriented Programming. LNCS 952, Springer-Verlag (1995) 190–214
29. Mezini, M., Ostermann, K.: Conquering aspects with caesar. In: Proc. of Int'l Conf. on Aspect-Oriented Software Development (AOSD'03), ACM Press (2003) 90–99
30. Popovici, A., Gross, T., Alonso, G.: Dynamic weaving for aspect-oriented programming. In: Proc. of Int'l Conf. on Aspect-Oriented Software Development (AOSD'02), ACM Press (2002) 141–147
31. Rajan, H., Sullivan, K.J.: Classpects: Unifying aspect- and object-oriented language design. In: Proc. of the 27th International Conference on Software Engineering (ICSE'05), ACM Press (2005) 59–68
32. Sakurai, K., Masuhara, H., Ubayashi, N., Matsuura, S., Kimoya, S.: Association aspects. In: Aspect-Oriented Software Development. (2004) 16–25
33. Sato, Y., Chiba, S., Tatsubori, M.: A selective, just-in-time aspect weaver. In: Proc. of Generative Programming and Component Engineering (GPCE '03). LNCS 2830, Springer-Verlag (2003) 189–208
34. Smith, B.C.: Reflection and semantics in Lisp. In: Proc. of ACM Symp. on Principles of Programming Languages. (1984) 23–35
35. Smith, B.: Reflection and semantics in a procedural languages. Technical Report MIT-TR-272, M.I.T. Laboratory for Computer Science (1982)
36. Sun Microsystems: Java 2 Platform, Enterprise Edition (J2EE). (http://java.sun.com/j2ee/)
37. Suvée, D., Vanderperren, W., Jonckers, V.: Jasco: An aspect-oriented approach tailored for component based software development. In: Proc. of Int'l Conf. on Aspect-Oriented Software Development (AOSD'03), ACM Press (2003) 21–29
38. Tatsubori, M., Chiba, S., Killijian, M.O., Itano, K.: Openjava: A class-based macro system for java. In Cazzola, W., Stroud, R.J., Tisato, F., eds.: Reflection and Software Engineering. LNCS 1826, Springer Verlag (2000) 119–135
39. Watanabe, T., Yonezawa, A.: Reflection in an object-oriented concurrent language. In: Proc. of ACM Conf. on Object-Oriented Programming Systems, Languages, and Applications. (1988) 306–315
40. Welch, I., Stroud, R.: From dalang to kava — the evolution of a reflective java extension. In: Proc. of Reflection '99. LNCS 1616, Springer (1999) 2–21

The Transformational Approach
to Database Engineering

Jean-Luc Hainaut

University of Namur, Institut d'Informatique Rue Grandgagnage,
21 B-5000 Namur, Belgium
jlh@info.fundp.ac.be
http://www.info.fundp.ac.be/libd

Abstract. In the database engineering realm, the merits of transformational approaches, that can produce in a systematic way correct, compilable and efficient
database structures from abstract models, has long be recognized. Transformations that are proved to preserve the correctness of the source specifications have
been proposed in virtually all the activities related to data structure engineering:
schema normalization, logical design, schema integration, view derivation,
schema equivalence, data conversion, reverse engineering, schema optimization,
wrapper generation and others. This paper addresses both fundamental and practical aspects of database transformation techniques. The concept of transformation
is developed, together with its properties of semantics-preservation (or reversibility). Major database engineering activities are redefined in terms of transformation
techniques, and the impact on CASE technology is discussed. These principles are
applied to database logical design and database reverse engineering. They are
illustrated by the use of DB-MAIN, a programmable CASE environment that
provides a large transformational toolkit.

1 Introduction

Data structure manipulation has long proved to be a fertile domain for transformational engineering process modelling. Several contributions have made this approach
a fruitful baseline to solve the complex mapping problems that are at the core of many
database engineering processes.

We can mention the normalization theory, which laid the basis for data- and con-
straint-preserving schema transformations [13], but also the now standard 3-schema
data modeling architecture [48] which clearly complied, more than 25 years ago, to
what the SE comzmunity currently calls *Model-Driven Engineering* (MDE). Generally built on these principles, most database design methodologies rely on four expressions of the database structure, namely the conceptual schema, the logical
schema, the physical schema and the DDL[1] code (Fig. 17). According to these approaches, a schema at one level derives from a more abstract schema at the upper

---

[1] Data Description Language. That part of the DBMS language dedicated to the creation of data
structures.

R. Lämmel, J. Saraiva, and J. Visser (Eds.): GTTSE 2005, LNCS 4143, pp. 95–143, 2006.
© Springer-Verlag Berlin Heidelberg 2006

level through some kind of translation rules that preserve its information contents, which clearly are schema transformations. For instance, a logical relational schema can be produced from the conceptual schema by applying to non SQL-compliant conceptual structures rewriting rules that produce relational constructs such as tables, columns and keys. If the rules are carefully selected, the relational schema has the same information contents as its conceptual origin.

An increasing number of bodies (e.g., the OMG) and of authors recognize the merits of transformational approaches, that can produce in a systematic way correct, compilable and efficient database structures from abstract models.

Transformations that are proved to preserve the correctness of the source specifications have been proposed in virtually all the activities related to schema engineering: schema normalization [39], logical design [4, 19, 41], schema integration [4, 34], view derivation [35, 33], schema equivalence [11, 28, 29, 32], data conversion [36, 12, 46], reverse engineering [6, 8, 18, 19], database interoperability [34, 45], schema optimization [19, 25], wrapper generation [45] and others.

Warning

In the database community, a general formalism in which database specifications can be built is called a *model*. The specification of a definite database structure expressed in such a model is called a *schema*. Example: the *conceptuel schema* of the Customer database is expressed in the *Entity-relationship model*, while its *logical schema*, that is made up of table, column and key definitions, complies with the *relational model*.

A First Illustration

Before discussing in deeper detail the concept of transformation and its properties, let us have a look at a first practical application of the concept. The schemas of Fig. 1 show a popular example, namely the production of a relational schema (top right), from a small conceptual schema (top left) that describes a set of books for which a collection of copies are available. The graphical conventions will be described later, but the essence of the schemas can be grasped without further explanation.

The main stream of the process is covered by the two top schemas. The translation rules that have been applied can be identified easily:

1. each entity type is represented by a table,

2. each single-valued attribute is represented by a column,

3. each *all-attribute* identifier is represented by a primary or alternate key,

4. each one-to-many relationship type is represented by a foreign key,

5. each multivalued attribute is represented by a table, comprising the source attribute that is declared a primary key, and by an additional table made up of a foreign key to the table that represents the entity type of the attribute and another foreign key to the new attribute table; both foreign keys form the primary key of their table.

Of course, other, more or less sophisticated, sets of rules exist, but this one is adequate for demonstration purpose.

We can read this derivation process from another, *transformational*, point of view. We do not produce another schema, but we *progressively modify* the source conceptual schema, until it complies with the structural patterns allowed by the relational model.

This interpretation, which will prove much more powerful and flexible than the translation rules approach, is illustrated in the alternate circuit (top → down → right → up) of Fig. 1.

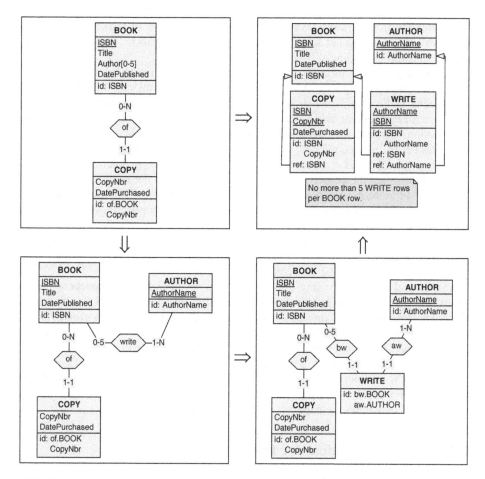

Fig. 1. Two ways to describe the derivation of a relational schema from a conceptual schema

The first modified schema (bottom left) derives from the source conceptual schema (top left) as follows: the multivalued attribute Author has been **replaced** with the entity type AUTHOR comprising the identifying attribute AuthorName, and the many-to-many relationship type write.

Then (bottom right), the new many-to-many relationship type write is **replaced** with entity type WRITE together with two one-to-many relationship types bw and aw. The schema does not include multivalued attributes or complex relationship types anymore.

Finally, each one-to-many relationship type is **replaced** with a foreign key. Hence the final version, at the top right side.

The Structure of This Paper

This short illustration raises several questions and problems, to some of which this paper will try to answer, at least partially. The paper is organized in two parts, that allow two levels of reading.

The **first part**, that includes Sections 2 to 8, develops **practical aspects** of the transformational paradigm. Section 2 positions the role of transformation in the database realm. In Section 3, we show that dealing with multiple databases leads us to introduce a generic pivot model, the GER, that is intended to represent a large variety of operational models. Its graphical representation is sketched and a formal semantics is suggested. In this section, we also show how specific operational models can be defined in the GER. The concept of schema transformation is precisely defined in Section 4, in which the property of semantics-preservation is defined and analyzed. In Section 5, we describe some useful elementary and complex GER transformations, that are then used in Section 6 to revisit the Database Design process, showing that it is intrinsically a (complex) schema transformation. Similarly, Section 7 studies the Reverse Engineering process as an application of the transformational paradigm. Section 8 discusses the role of transformations in CASE tools, and illustrates this point with the toolkit and the assistants of DB-MAIN.

The **second part**, comprising Sections 9 to 12, develops **formal aspects** of transformations that were only sketched and suggested in Part 1. Section 9 describes the ERM, an extended N1NF[2] relational model the semantics of which is borrowed from the relational theory. Section 10 maps the GER onto the ERM so that the former can be given a precise formal semantics. Section 11 described a small set of ERM transformations that can be proved to be semantics-preserving. Finally, Section 12 exploits the GER-ERM mapping to prove the semantics-preservation property of selected practical GER transformations.

Section 13 concludes the paper.

Part 1   Transformations for Database Engineering

2   Transformational Engineering

Producing efficient software by applying systematic transformations to abstract specifications has been one of the most mythical goals of software engineering since the

---

[2] *Non 1st Normal Form.* Qualifies a relational structure that uses non simple domains. Elements of a non simple domain can be tuples and/or sets. In particular, a relation or the powerset of a relation can be a valid domain. A N1NF relational model is a relational model in which non simple domains are allowed.

late seventies. For instance, [3] and [14] consider that *the process of developing a program [can be] formalized as a set of correctness-preserving transformations [...] aimed to compilable and efficient program production.* In this context, according to [37], *a transformation is a relation between two program schemes P and P' (a program scheme is the [parameterized] representation of a class of related programs; a program of this class is obtained by instantiating the scheme parameters). It is said to be correct if a certain semantic relation holds between P and P'.* The revival of this dream has now got the name of Model-Driven Architecture [38], or, more generally, Model-Driven Engineering (MDA/MDE).

It is not surprising that this view has been adopted and developed by the database community since the seventies. Indeed, the data domain has relied on strong theories that can cope with most of the essential aspects of database engineering, from clean data structuring (including normalization) to operational data structures generation.

In particular, producing a target schema from a source schema can be modeled either by a set of translation rules, or by a chain of restructuring operators or transformations. The latter has proved particularly attractive, notably in complex, incremental, processes.

The question of how many operators are needed to cover the current needs in database engineering is still open, though it has been posed for long: in the 80's, authors suggested that four [15] [29] to six [11] were enough, but experience has shown that there is no clear answer, except that surely more transformations are needed, as we will show in the following.

One of the peculiarities of transformational approaches in the database realm is that they must, in all generality, cope with three aspects of the application system, namely the *data structures*, the *data*, and the *programs*. Let us consider a scenario in which a database must be migrated from a technology to another one. Clearly, this database must be *transformed*, whatever the meaning of this term, into another database. This means that three components of the application must be modified.

1. The database schema, that must comply with the data model of the target technology, and, possibly, include additional requirements that have emerged since the last schema modification.
2. The data themselves, that must be restructured according to the new schema, possibly through some kind of ETL process.
3. The application programs, that must interface with the new schema and comply with the new API. This generally involves rewriting some sections of the source code.

Each of these modifications follows its own rules, but we should not be surprised by the idea that the first one should strongly influence the others. This view currently is emerging under the name *co-transformation* [30]. Indeed, it has been proved that it is possible to automatically derive data transformations (ETL) directives, as a SQL script for instance, from schema transformations [27]. Program transformation is much more complex. Automating this conversion has been studied in [26] and [9], and has been proved to be feasible.

One of the arguments of this paper is that one can study all transformations, including inter-model transformations, in the framework of a single model[3]. This raises the question of the nature of this generic model. Two approaches have been proposed, that distinguish themselves by the granularity of the model [24].

One approach, that can be called *minimalistic*, or *bottom-up*, relies on a very simple and abstract formalism, from which one can define more elaborated and richer models. Such a model generally represents the schema constructs specific to a definite model by abstract nodes and edges, together with assembly constraints. AutoMED [7] is a typical representative of this approach.

Another approach, symmetrically called *maximalistic* or *top-down*, is based on a large spectrum model, that includes, though in an abstract form, the main constructs of the set of operational models that are used in the engineering processes. The GER model follows this principle. It has been described in [21] and [24], and will be the basis of this paper.

3   Modeling Data Structures

3.1   Dealing with Multiple Models

Some database engineering processes transform schemas from one model to itself, involvin one model only. Such is the case of relational normalisation, and of XML manipulation. These processes make use of *intra-model* transformations. Being dedicated to this model, their form generally is quite specific (e.g., respectively relational algebra and XSLT) and cannot be reused for other models.

Other processes, on the contrary, produce a result that is expressed into a model that is different from that the source schema. The most obvious example is the so-called *database logical design*, the goal of which is to transform an abstract conceptual schema into an operational (say, relational) logical schema as will be discussed in Section 6.2. In such cases one makes use of *inter-model* transformations. Many comprehensive processes, such as database design, reverse engineering and integration involve several abstraction levels and several technologies (and therefore models).

To master this complexity, several approaches rely on some kind of **pivot** model. The idea is quite simple, and has been adopted as an elegant way to solve the combinatorial explosion in situations in which mappings must be developed from any of M formalisms to any of N formalisms. Theoretically, one would need N x M distinct mappings. Thanks to the introduction of a *intermediate* or *pivot* formalism P, one needs to define M + N formalisms only. Language translation and plateform-independent components are two of the most common examples.

In the database engineering realm, dealing with a dozen models is not uncommon in large organizations. Developing, migrating, integrating, reverse engineering databases or publishing corporate data on the web all are processes that require inter-model schema transformation and, accordingly, data conversion. Considering N operational models, and admitting that the mappings among any pair of models are potentially useful in some processes, we need to define N^2 mappings, while

---

[3] As illustrated in Fig. 1.

the introduction of a pivot model allows us to reduce the number of mappings to $2 \times N + 1$. Fig. 2 identifies the mappings that will, sooner or later, be useful in an organization in which the data are stored in CODASYL and relational databases, that describes its information needs through Entity-relationship schemas, and that produces XML documents. Sixteen inter-model mappings are necessary, while the pivot model reduces the number of mapping to nine only. Moreover, all the mappings but one serve the mere function of formalism conversion ($\Sigma m > m'$, with $m \neq m'$), and therefore are fairly simple, while the power needed to express complex data structure transformation is the responsibility of one mapping only, namely $\Sigma p > p$. Introducing any new operational model M implies the development of two additional mappings $\Sigma m > p$ and $\Sigma p > m$.

An interesting consequence of approaches based on a pivot model is that inter-model transformations reduce to intra-model ones.

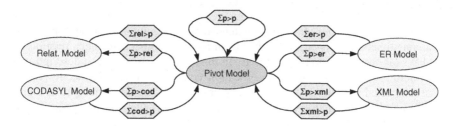

Fig. 2. Introducing a pivot model among N models reduces the number of inter/intra-model mappings

The example of *relational logical design*, that is, producing a relational schema from a conceptual schema, is illustrated in Fig. 3, which is just a subset of Fig. 2. It reads as follows:

1. the source conceptual schema is transformed into the pivot model ($\Sigma er > p$),

2. the resulting schema is transformed through a set of rules ($\Sigma p > p$) such as those that are largely described in the literature (see [4] for example[4]);

3. finally, the transformed schema obtained is expressed into the target relational model ($\Sigma p > rel$).

The next section describes in an informal way the main constructs of a pivot model on which we will base our discussion, namely the GER model.

Remark. The interpretation of Fig. 2, 3 and some of those that follow, needs to be precised a bit further. All schemas that can be expressed in model M are represented by the M-labelled ellipse. The mapping $\Sigma m > m'$ states that any schema expressed in the source model M is transformed through $\Sigma m > m'$ into a schema that complies with the target model M'.

---

[4] Not the most recent reference actually, but still one of the best.

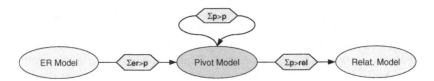

Fig. 3. Modeling *relational logical design* with a pivot model

Remark. The interpretation of Fig. 2, 3 and some of those that follow, needs to be precised a bit further. All schemas that can be expressed in model M are represented by the M-labelled ellipse. The mapping $\Sigma m{>}m'$ states that any schema expressed in the source model M is transformed through $\Sigma m{>}m'$ into a schema that complies with the target model M'.

3.2 The Generic Entity-Relationship Model (GER)

The GER model, GER for short, is an extended Entity-relationship model that includes, among others, the concepts of schema, entity type, domain, attribute, relationship type, keys, as well as various constraints. In this model, a schema is a description of data structures. It is made up of specification constructs which can be, for convenience, classified into the usual three abstraction levels, namely conceptual, logical and physical. We will enumerate some of the main constructs that can appear at each level (Fig. 4).

- A *conceptual schema comprises* entity types (with/without attributes; with/without identifiers), super/subtype hierarchies (single/multiple; total and disjoint properties), relationship types (binary/N-ary; cyclic/acyclic; with/without attributes; with/without identifiers), roles of relationship type (with min-max cardinalities[5]; with/without explicit name; single/multi-entity-type), attributes (of entity or relationship types; multi/single-valued; atomic/compound; with cardinality[6]), identifiers (of entity type, relationship type, multivalued attribute; comprising attributes and/or roles), constraints (inclusion, exclusion, coexistence, at-least-one, etc.)
- A *logical schema comprises* record types, fields, arrays, single-/multi-valued foreign keys, redundant constructs, etc.
- A *physical schema comprises* files, record types, fields, access keys (a generic term for index, calc key, etc), physical data types, bag/list/array multivalued attributes, and other implementation details.

3.3 Formal Semantics of the GER

In this paper, we develop transformational operators and discuss their properties. Many approaches rely on some intuitive rewriting rules expressed graphically. Though this is quite appropriate to allow readers to grasp the idea of the operators, a

---

[5] The role cardinality constraint, denoted by i-j, specifies the range of the number of relationships in which an entity can appear in a definite role. Value N of j denotes infinity.

[6] Same as *role cardinality* applied to the number of attribute values *per* parent instance.

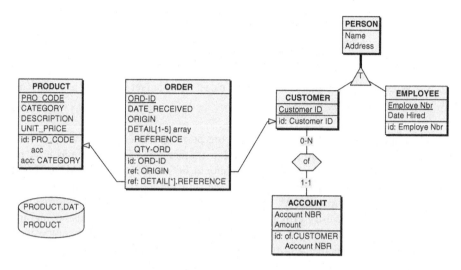

Fig. 4. A typical hybrid schema made up of conceptual constructs (e.g., entity types *PERSON*, *CUSTOMER*, *EMPLOYEE* and *ACCOUNT*, relationship type *of*, identifiers *Customer ID* of *CUSTOMER*), logical constructs (e.g., record type *ORDER*, with various kinds of fields including an array, foreign keys *ORIGIN* and *DETAIL.REFERENCE*) and physical objects (e.g., table *PRODUCT* with primary key *PRO_CODE* and indexes *PRO_CODE* and *CATEGORY*, table space *PRODUCT.DAT*). Note that the identifier of *ACCOUNT*, stating that the accounts of a customer have distinct account numbers (*Account NBR*), makes it a *dependent* or *weak entity type*.

more formal treatment is necessary. In particular, we must base the definition and the evaluation of the properties of each operator on a rigorous basis, that is, a formal semantics of the GER. This is important for at least two reasons. First, formal semantics allows us to reason about transformations, and in particular to state its main properties such as the preservation of the information capacity of the source schemas. Secondly, implementing a set of transformations, for instance in a CASE tool, must rely on a completely defined semantics of both the model and the operators.

In Part 2, Sections 9 and 10, we will give the GER a precise semantics by stating mapping rules between the constructs of the GER and constructs of a variant of the N1NF relational formalism, called Extended Relational Model (ERM). Each GER construct will be given an ERM interpretation, and, conversely, each construct of the ERM will be given a GER interpretation. Basically, these mappings are the inter-model transformations Σger>erm and Σerm>ger depicted in Fig. 5. The ERM is described in Section 9 while mapping Σger>erm and its inverse are presented in Section 10. The reader will find a complete formalization of the GER in [16].

[44] follows another approach. The author associates with HERM, a variant of the ER model, a specific notation with a precise ad hoc semantics, that includes an algebra and a calculus.

Fig. 5. Expressing the semantics of the GER model by a bidirectional mapping with the Extended Relational Model (ERM)

Note. The interpretation of the inverse mapping Σerm>ger is a bit more complex than suggested. Indeed, Σger>erm is **not surjective**, so that some ERM schemas have no GER counterpart. To be quite precise, we should define the subset ERM* of ERM that makes Σger>erm surjective. However, we will ignore this for simplicity sake. This is no problem since ERM* is closed under the set of ERM transformations Σerm>erm that we will use[7]. Proving this is fairly easy but would lead us beyond the scope of this paper. In the rest of this paper, we will admit that the composition Σerm>ger ∘ Σger>erm is the identity mapping without loss of generality.

3.4 Specifying Operational Models in the GER

Popular operational formalisms, that is, those which are in practical use among developers, can be expressed as *specializations* of the GER. In general, deriving model M from model M0 (here the GER) consists in,

1. selecting the constructs of M0 that are pertinent in M;
2. specifying the structural constraints on this subset so that only schemas valid in M can be built;
3. renaming these constructs in order to make them compliant with the taxonomy of M; this step will be ignored in this paper.

This process materializes the mapping ΣM>M0. We will briefly discuss this mapping for two models, namely Entity-relationship model and the SQL2 relational model (Fig. 6). Similar mapping can be (and have been) developed for CODASYL and IMS models, for standard files structures, and for XML DTDs and Schemas.

Fig. 6. Two mappings described in Sections 3.5 and 3.6

3.5 GER Expression of the Entity-Relationship Model

Let us first observe that there is no such thing as a *standard ER model*. At least a dozen formalisms have been proposed, some of them being widely used in popular

---

[7] Σerm>erm is the set of ERM-to-ERM transformations. Applying operators from the subset of Σerm>erm that underlies Σger>ger (as discussed in Section 12) to any ERM* schema produces an ERM* schema.

text books and in CASE tools. However, despite divergent details, they all share essential constructs such as entity type, relationship types with roles, some kind of role cardinality/multiplicity, attributes and unique keys. Due to the nature of the GER, restricting it to a definite Entity-relationship model is fairly straighforward, so that we do not propose to develop the Σer>ger mapping.

The increasing popularity of the UML class model[8] (*aka* class diagrams) incites some authors and practitioners to use them to specify database conceptual and logical schemas. This was not the primary objective of the UML formalism, so that it exhibits severe flaws and weaknesses in database modelling. However, mapping Σuml>ger can be developed in the same way as for other models.

3.6 GER Expression of the Standard Relational Model (SQL2)

A relational schema mainly includes tables, domains, columns, primary keys, unique constraints, not null constraints and foreign keys. The relational model can therefore be defined as in Fig. 7.

relational constructs	GER constructs	assembly rules
database schema	schema	
table	entity type	an entity type includes at least one attribute
domain	simple domain	
nullable column	single-valued and atomic attribute with cardinality [0-1]	
not null column	single-valued and atomic attribute with cardinality [1-1]	
primary key	primary identifier	a primary identifier comprises attributes with cardinality [1-1]
unique constraint	secondary identifier	
foreign key	reference group	the composition of the reference group must be the same as that of the target identifier
SQL names	GER names	the GER names must follow the SQL syntax

Fig. 7. Defining the standard relational (SQL2) model as a subset of the GER model (mapping Σrel>ger)

A GER schema made up of constructs from the second column only, and that satisfies the assembly rules stated in the third column, can be called a *relational GER schema*. As a consequence, a relational schema cannot comprise *is-a* relations, relationship types, multivalued attributes nor compound attributes.

---

[8] The term UML model has a specific interpretation in UML, where it denotes what we call a schema in this paper.

4 Schema Transformation

Let us denote by M the unique model in which the source and target schemas are expressed, by S the schema on which the transformation is to be applied and by S' the schema resulting from this application. Let us also consider sch(M), a function that returns the set of all the valid schemas that can be expressed in model M, and inst(S), a function that returns the set of all the instances that comply with schema S.

4.1 Specification of a Transformation

A **transformation** Σ consists of two mappings **T** and **t** (Fig. 8):

1. **T** is the *structural mapping* from sch(M) onto itself, that replaces source construct C in schema S with construct C'. C' is the target of C through T, and is noted **C'** = T(C). In fact, C and C' are classes of constructs that can be defined by structural predicates. T is therefore defined by the *weakest precondition* **P** that any construct C must satisfy in order to be transformed by T, and the *strongest postcondition* **Q** that T(C) satisfies. **T** specifies the rewriting rule of Σ.
2. **t** is the *instance mapping* from inst(S) onto inst(S'), that states how to produce the T(C) instance that corresponds to any instance of C. If c is an instance of C, then c' = t(c) is the corresponding instance of T(C). **t** can be specified through any algebraic, logical or procedural expression.

According to the context, Σ will be noted either <T,t> or <P,Q,t>.

The nature of the most suited formalism in which P, Q and t could be expressed[9] will not be discussed here. In the following, we will use abstract schema fragments following the graphical convention of the underlying model.

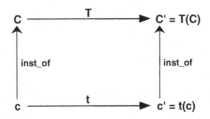

Fig. 8. The two mappings of schema transformation S ≡ <T,t>. The inst_of arrow from x to X indicates that x is an instance of X.

4.2 Generic, Parametric and Instantiated Transformations

Let us consider relation R, the attributes of which are partitioned into non empty subsets I, J and K. Considering Σ, a (lossy) variant of relational decomposition transformation, predicates P and Q as well as instance transformation t can be written as follows:

---

[9] Description logic [2] could be a good candidate for P and Q.

T	P	R(U); {I,J,K} partition of U;
	Q	R1(IJ); R2(IK);
	t	*let r be the current instance of R; let r1, r2 be instances of R1, R2;* *r1 = r[IJ]; r2 = r[IK];*

Σ is *generic*, since it gives an abstract pattern that must be applied to an actual relation before being carried out. Let us apply Σ to relation CUST(C#, CNAME, CADD, CACC) of a supposedly current schema. We observe that there are several ways to instantiate Σ according to the values we assign to variables I, J and K, leading to as many *instantiated* transformations. For this reason, we call Σ a *parametric* transformation. For instance, with assignments I := {CNAME} and J := {C#, CADD}, we get the following fully *instantiated* transformation.

T	P	CUST(C#, CNAME, CADD, CACC); I = {CNAME}; J = {C#, CADD} ;
	Q	C1(CNAME, C#, CADD); C2(CNAME, CACC);
	t	*let c be the current instance of CUST; let c1, c2 be instances of C1, C2;* *c1 = c[CNAME, C#, CADD]; c2 = c[CNAME, CACC];*

A generic transformation can be partially instantiated if some, but not all, variables of P have been instantiated.

Each transformation Σ is associated with an *inverse transformation* Σ' which can undo the result of the former under certain conditions that will be detailed in the next section.

4.3 Semantics Preservation Properties of Transformations

One of the most important properties of a transformation is the extent to which the target schema can replace the source schema without loosing information. This property is called *semantics preservation* or *reversibility*.

Some transformations appear to augment the semantics of the source schema (e.g., adding an attribute), some remove semantics (e.g., removing an entity type), while others leave the semantics unchanged (e.g., replacing a relationship type with an equivalent entity type). The latter are called *reversible* or *semantics-preserving*. If a transformation is reversible, then the source and the target schemas have the same descriptive power, and describe the same universe of discourse, although with a different presentation.

Similarly, in the pure software engineering domain, [3] introduces the concept of *correctness-preserving* transformation aimed at compilable and efficient program production.

We must consider two different classes of transformations, namely reversible and symmetrically reversible.

1. A transformation $\Sigma1 = <T1,t1> = <P1,Q1,t1>$ is *reversible, iff* there exists a transformation $\Sigma2 = <T2,t2> = <P2,Q2,t2>$ such that, for any construct C, and any instance c of C: $P1(C) \Rightarrow ([T2(T1(C))=C]$ and $[t2(t1(c))=c])$. $\Sigma2$ is the inverse of $\Sigma1$, but the converse is not true. For instance, an arbitrary instance c' of T(C) may not satisfy the property c'=t1(t2(c')).

2. If $\Sigma2$ is reversible as well, then $\Sigma1$ and $\Sigma2$ are called *symmetrically reversible.* In this case, $\Sigma2 = <Q1,P1,t2>$. $\Sigma1$ and $\Sigma2$ are called *SR-transformations* for short.

Example

The so-called *decomposition theorem* of the 1NF relational theory [13] is an example of reversible transformation that can be described as follows[10].

T1	P1	R(U); {I,J,K} partition of U; I →→ J|K;
	Q1	R1(IJ); R2(IK);
	t1	*let r be the current instance of R; let r1, r2 be instances of R1, R2;* *r1 = r[IJ]; r2 = r[IK];*

However, there is no reason for any arbitrary couple of instances r1 of R1 and r2 of R2 to enjoy the inverse property r = (r1*r2)[IJ]. We must refine this transformation in order to make it symmetrically reversible. This transformation and its inverse are summarized here below.

T1	P1	R(U); {I,J,K} partition of U; I →→ J|K;
	Q1	R1(IJ); R2(IK); R1[I] = R2[I];
	t1	*let r be the current instance of R; let r1, r2 be instances of R1, R2;* *r1 = r[IJ]; r2 = r[IK];*
	t2	*let r1, r2 be current instances of R1, R2; let r be an instance of R;* *r = r1*r2[IJK];*

4.4 Generating and Studying GER Transformations

The complexity of high-level models, and that of the GER in particular, makes the study of their transformations particularly complex. To begin with, experience shows that several dozens of operators can be useful, if not necessary, to describe the most important engineering processes. Then, identifying and proving the reversibility degree of each of them can be a huge and complex task, notably since there is no agreed upon algebra or calculus to express Entity-relationship queries.

---

[10] Denotes a multivalued dependency, [ ] the projection operator and * the join operator.

The key lies in the ERM formalism that expresses the semantics of the GER. Indeed, the relational model, of which the ERM inherits, includes a strong and simple body of properties and inference rules that can be used to built a relational transformational theory. We can reasonably expect the set of transformations defined for the ERM to be far smaller and simpler than that of the GER.

If this idea proves to be correct, then we will be provided with a nice way to generate, explain, and reason on, GER transformations. Fig. 9 illustrates this approach.

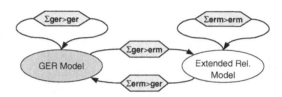

Fig. 9. Generating and specifying GER transformations through their expression in the Extended Relational Model

According to this view, each GER transformation can be modelled as the compound mapping:

$$\Sigma ger{>}ger = \Sigma erm{>}ger \circ \Sigma erm{>}erm \circ \Sigma ger{>}erm$$

Since $\Sigma erm{>}ger$ and $\Sigma ger{>}erm$ are symmetrically reversible, a transformation in $\Sigma ger{>}ger$ is semantics-preserving *iff* there exists a (possibly compound) transformation in $\Sigma erm{>}erm$ that is symmetrically reversible. Section 11 describes the main transformations of $\Sigma erm{>}erm$. Then, Section 12 interprets three popular GER transformations as compound ERM transformations.

5 Typology of Practical Transformations

This section describes several families of GER transformations with which complex engineering processes will be built.

5.1 Mutation Transformations

A mutation is an SR-transformation that changes the nature of an object. Considering the three main natures of object, namely *entity type*, *relationship type* and *attribute*, six families of mutation transformations can be defined. Fig. 10 shows the structural mapping (T) of some representative operators (couples of operators $\Sigma 1$ to $\Sigma 3$) applied to typical schema fragments. The transformations $\Sigma 4$ are not primitive since they can be defined by combining other mutations. However, they have been added due to their usefulness.

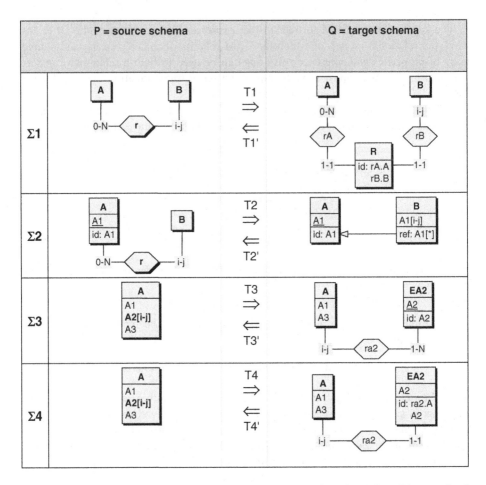

Fig. 10. Six representative mutation transformations $\Sigma 1$ to $\Sigma 3$. Transformations $\Sigma 1$ generalized to N-ary rel-types as will be shown in Fig. 26. Though not primitive, compound transformations $\Sigma 4$ are shown as well. Cardinality constraints [i-j] are arbitrary values.

5.2 Other Elementary Transformations

The mutation transformations can solve many database engineering problems, but other operators are needed to model special situations.

Expressing supertype/subtype hierarchies in DMS that do not support them explicitly is a recurrent problem. The technique of Fig. 11 is one of the most commonly used [4] [23]. It consists in representing each source entity type by an independent entity type, then to link each subtype to its supertype through a one-to-one relationship type. The latter can, if needed, be further transformed into foreign keys by application of $\Sigma 2$-direct.

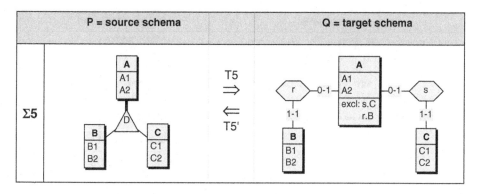

Fig. 11. Transforming an is-a hierarchy into one-to-one relationship types and conversely. The exclusion constraint (excl:s.C,r.B) states that an A entity cannot be simultaneously linked to a B entity and a C entity. It derives from the disjoint property (D) of the subtypes.

Transformations Σ3 and Σ4 showed how to process standard multivalued attributes. When the collection of values is no longer a set but a *bag*, a *list* or an *array*, operators to transform them into standard multi-valued attributes are most useful. Transformations Σ6 in Fig. 12 are dedicated to arrays. Similar operators have been defined for the other types of containers.

P = source schema	Q = target schema
Σ6	

Fig. 12. Converting an array A2 into a set-multivalued attribute and conversely. The values are distinct wrt component Index (id(A2):Index). The latter indicates the position of the cell that contains the value (Value). The domain of Index is the range [1..5].

Attributes defined on the same domain and the name of which suggests a spatial or temporal dimension (e.g., departments, countries, years or pure numbers) are called *homogeneous serial attributes*. In many situations, they can be interpreted as the representation of an indexed multivalued attributes (Fig. 13). The identification of these attributes must be confirmed by the analyst.

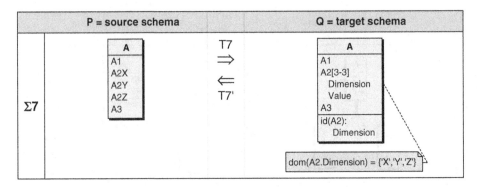

Fig. 13. Transforming homogeneous serial attributes {A2X, A2Y, A2Z} into a multivalued compound attribute A2 and conversely. The values (Value) are indexed with the distinctive suffix of the source attribute names, interpreted as a dimension (sub-attribute Dimension).

5.3 Compound Transformations

A compound transformation is made up of a chain of more elementary operators in which each transformation applies on the result of the previous one. The transformation Σ8 in Fig. 14, illustrated by a concrete example, transforms a complex relationship type R into a sort of *bridge* entity type comprising as many foreign keys as there are roles in R. It is defined by the composition of Σ1-direct (generalized to N-ary rel-types) and Σ2-direct. This operator is of frequent use in relational database design.

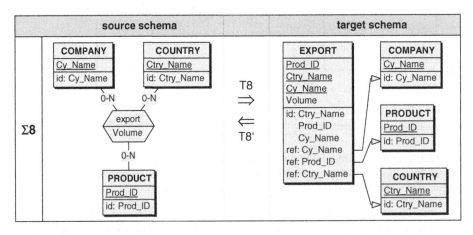

Fig. 14. Transformation of a complex relationship type into relational structures

The transformation Σ9 is more complex (Fig. 15). It is composed of a chain of four elementary operators. The first one transforms the serial attributes Expense-2000, ..., Expense-2004 into multivalued attribute Expense comprising subattributes Year (the dimension) and Amount (transformation Σ7-direct). The second one extracts this attribute into entity type EXPENSE, with attributes Year and Amount (transformation Σ4-direct). Then, the same operator is applied to attribute Year, yielding entity type YEAR, with attribute Year. Finally, entity type EXPENSE is transformed into relationship type expense (Σ1-inverse).

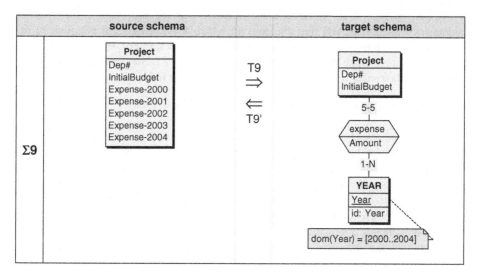

Fig. 15. Extracting a temporal dimension from homogeneous serial attributes

5.4 Predicate-Driven Transformations

A predicate-driven transformation Σp applies an operator Σ to all the schema objects that meet a definite predicate p.

predicate-driven transformation	interpretation
RT_into_ET(ROLE_per_RT(3 N))	transform each rel-type R into an entity type (RT_into_ET), if the number of roles of R (ROLE_per_RT) is in the range [3 N]; in short, *convert all N-ary rel-types into entity types.*
RT_into_REF(ROLE_per_RT(2 2) and ONE_ROLE_per_RT(1 2))	transform each rel-type R into reference attributes (RT_into_REF), if the number of roles of R is 2 and if R has from 1 to 2 "one" role(s), i.e., R has at least one role with max cardinality 1; in short, *convert all one-to-many rel- types into foreign keys.*
INSTANTIATE(MAX_CARD_of_ATT(2 4))	transform each attribute A into a sequence of single-value instances, if the max cardinality of A is between 2 and 4; in short, *convert multivalued attributes with no more than 4 values into serial attributes.*

Fig. 16. Three examples of predicate-driven transformations. *Rel-type* is a short-hand for *Relationship type*.

It will be specified by $\Sigma(p)$. p is a *structural* predicate that states the properties through which a class of patterns can be identified. In general, the inverse of Σp cannot be derived from the expression of Σ and p. Indeed, there is no means to derive the predicate p' that identifies the constructs resulting from the application of Σp, and only them.

We give in Fig. 16 some useful transformations that are expressed in the specific language of the DB-MAIN tool (Section 8), which follows the $\Sigma(p)$ notation. Most predicates are parametric. For instance, the predicate ROLE_per_RT(n m), where n and m are integers such that $n \leq m$, states that the number of roles of the relationship type falls in the range [n..m]. The symbol "N" stands for infinity.

5.5 Model-Driven Transformations

A model-driven transformation is a goal-oriented compound transformation made up of predicate-driven operators. It is designed to transform any schema expressed in model M into an equivalent schema in model M'.

As illustrated in the discussion of the relational model expressed as a specialization of the GER (Fig. 7), identifying the components of a model also leads to identifying the constructs of the GER that do not belong to it. Except when M is a subset of M', an arbitrary schema $S \in sch(M)$ may include constructs that violate M'. Each class of constructs that can appear in a schema can be specified by a structural predicate. Let P_M denote the set of predicates that defines model M and $P_{M'}$ that of model M'. In the same way, each potentially invalid construct can also be specified by a structural predicate. Let $P_{M/M'}$ denote the set of predicates that identify the constructs of M that are not valid in M'. In the DB-MAIN language used in Fig. 16, ROLE_per_RT(3 N) is a predicate that identifies N-ary relationship types that are known to be invalid in DBTG CODASYL schemas, while MAX_CARD_of_ATT(2 N) defines the family of multivalued attributes, that is invalid in the SQL2 database model. Finally, we observe that a set such as P_M can be rewritten as a single predicate formed by *anding* its components.

Let us now consider predicate $p \in P_{M/M'}$, and let us choose a transformation $\Sigma = \langle P,Q,t \rangle$ such that,

$$(p \Rightarrow P) \wedge (P_{M'} \Rightarrow Q)$$

Clearly, the predicate-driven transformation $\Sigma(p)$ solves the problem of the invalid constructs defined by p. Proceeding in the same way for each component of $P_{M/M'}$ provides us with a series of operators that can transform any schema in model M into schemas in model M'. We call such a series a *transformation plan*, which is the practical form of any model-driven transformation. In real situations, a plan can be more complex than a mere sequence of operations, and may comprise loops to process recursive constructs for instance. Transformation plans implement what some authors call *strategies*, that is, deterministic or heuristic reasoning on how to apply transformations to reach a definite goal. [1] propose strategies to convert VDM data types in relational structures while [40] applies semi-procedural strategies to high-level engineering processes.

In addition, transformations such as those specified above may themselves be compound, so that the set of required transformations can be quite large. In such cases, it can be better to choose a transformation that produces constructs that are not fully compliant with M', but that can be followed by other operators which complete the job. For instance, transforming a multivalued attribute into relational structures can be obtained by an ad hoc elementary transformation. However, it can be thought more convenient to first transform the attribute into an entity type + a one-to-many relationship type (Σ4-direct), which can then be transformed into a foreign key (Σ2-direct). This approach produces transformation plans which are more detailed and therefore less readable, but that rely on a smaller and more stable set of elementary operators.

The transformation toolset of DB-MAIN includes about thirty operators that have proved sufficient to process schemas in a dozen operational models. If the transformations used to build the plan have the SR-property, then the model-driven transformation that the plan implements is symmetrically reversible. When applied to any source schema, it produces a target schema semantically equivalent to the former.

6   Modeling Standard Database Engineering Processes as Transformations

Complete database engineering processes, such as database development, database reverse engineering, data warehouse design or database migration comprise several steps, most of which can be viewed as chains of transformations, or, more specifically, transformation plans. This section illustrates the issue by modeling one of the major processes, namely *database logical design*, through the transformational paradigm.

6.1 Database Design

The process of designing and implementing a database that is to meet definite users requirements has been described extensively in the literature [4] and has been available for several decades in CASE tools. It comprises four main sub-processes, namely (Fig. 17):

1. *Conceptual design*, the goal of which is to translate users requirements into a conceptual schema, which is a technology-independent abstract specification[11].
2. *Logical design*, which produces a logical schema that losslessly translates the constructs of the conceptual schema according to a specific technology family[12].
3. *Physical design*, which augments the logical schema with performance-oriented constructs and parameters, such as indexes, buffer management policies or lock management parameters.

---

[11] Or *Platform-Independent Model* (PIM according to the MDA/MDE vocabulary.
[12] The logical and physical schemas can be called *Platform-Specific Model* (PSM in the MDA/MDE vocabulary).

4. *Coding*, that translates the physical schema (and some other artefacts) into the DDL code of the DBMS.

Calling the whole process DB-Design, and the four sub-processes respectively ConcD, LogD, PhysD and Coding, we can describe them with the transformational notation:

DDL code = DB-design(Users requirements)

DB-design = Coding ∘ PhysD ∘ LogD ∘ ConcD

These processes are model-driven transformations that can be described by transformation plans. The level of formality of these processes depends on the methodology, on the existence of CASE support and of non functional requirements such as performance and robustness, that generally require human expertise. For instance, conceptual design is a highly informal process based on human interpretation of complex information sources, while logical design can be an automated process completely described by a transformation plan. Anyway, these processes can be decomposed into sub-processes that, in turn, can be modelled by transformations and described by transformation plans, and so forth, until the latter reduce to elementary operators such as those described in Sections 5.1 and 5.2. Below, we examine the Logical design process in further detail.

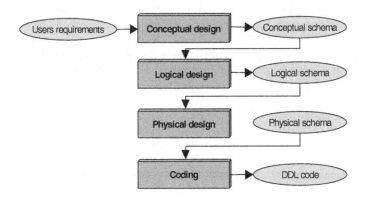

Fig. 17. The main processes of database design

6.2 Database Logical Design

We consider the most popular conceptual source model, namely the Entity-relationship model, and the most popular logical target model, the SQL2 relational model, to which Oracle, SQL Server, DB2, PostgreSQL, Firebird and many others are compliant. The GER expression of the SQL2 model has been developed in Fig. 7. By complementing this table, we identify the Entity-relationship constructs that **do not belong** to the SQL2 model, the four most important of which being transformed as follows.

Transforming *is-a* relations
Transformation Σ5-direct eliminates this structure without semantics loss by introducing one-to-one (functional) rel-types. The latter can then be processed by the mutation transformation Σ2-direct that generates foreign keys.

Transforming relationship types
Two cases must be considered. The easy case is that of *functional rel-types*, that can be replaced by foreign keys through transformation Σ2-direct.

The complex patterns comprise *non-functional rel-types*, that is, those which are *many-to-many*, or *N-ary*, or which *have attributes*. They are first transformed into entity types with operator Σ1-direct. Then, the resulting functional rel-types are transformed into foreign keys (Σ2-direct). Note that the whole process is a compound transformation that has been described as Σ8-direct.

Transforming multivalued attributes
A multivalued attribute that directly depends on its parent entity type (level 1) is transformed into an entity type, through the compound mutation operator Σ4-direct. If

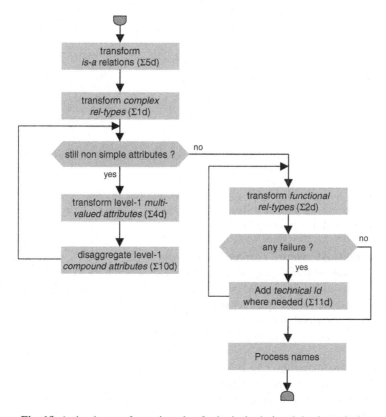

Fig. 18. A simple transformation plan for logical relational database design

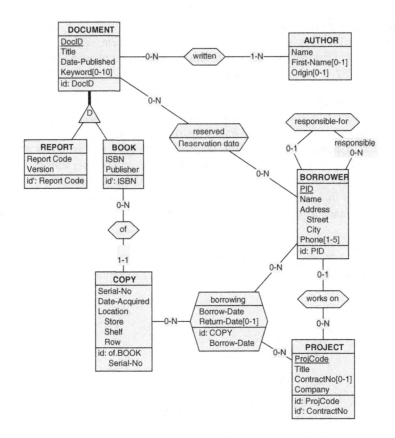

Fig. 19. A representative conceptual schema

the attribute is compound, it is suggested to incorporate its components in the new entity type, and not the attribute itself. This generates a one-to-many rel-type, that is further transformed into a foreign key.

Transforming single-valued *compound attributes*
The simplest way to transform a level 1 compound attribute is to replace it with its components, a technique called *disaggregation* (transformation Σ10-direct, not illustrated). Another technique consists in processing the attribute as if it was multivalued as described here above (Σ4-direct). In this case, it is transformed into an entity type and a functional rel-type, itself transformed into a foreign key.

Note on the transformation of a rel-type into a foreign key
This transformation requires the other entity type to have an identifier made up of attributes. Otherwise, we have to give it a *technical identifier* (transformation Σ11-direct, not illustrated).

Grouping similar transformations and reorganizing the operations logically provides us with a simple but fairly powerful transformation plan that transforms most conceptual Entity-relationship schemas into pure relational schemas (Fig. 18). Since we have used SR-transformations only, the whole process is semantics-preserving[13]. Actual plans are more complex, but follow the same approach. Let us mention some extensions: eliminating optional identifiers, other techniques to implement is-a relations (e.g., by descending or ascending inheritance), instantiating multivalued attributes, concatenating multivalued attributes, concatenating compound attributes, etc.

6.3 Case Study

The conceptual schema of Fig. 19 includes, in a small footprint, several interesting constructs, such as complex rel-types, a cyclic rel-type, is-a relations, multivalued attributes, compound attributes, an entity type without identifier, an optional identifier, a mandatory *many* role (written.AUTHOR [1-N]) and a hybrid identifier.

The application of the transformation plan of Fig. 18, extended to the elimination of optional identifiers[14], produces the relational schema of Fig. 20.

7 Modeling Database Reverse Engineering Process as Transformations

Many database engineering processes, such as maintenance, evolution, migration, integration or federation require the availability of a complete and up to date documentation, that is, for a database, its logical and conceptual schemas. Needless to say that these essential documents most often are missing, specially for legacy databases that can be more than 20 years old.

Database reverse engineering is the process through which one attempts to recover or to rebuild these schemas when they are missing, obsolete or incomplete. We will show that several important aspects of this process can be modelled by transformtions. Intensive research in the last decade have shown that reverse engineering generally is much more complex than initially thought.

We can put forward three major sources of difficulties, namely (1) the absence of systematic design (empirical coding still is the most popular way to design a database), (2) the weaknesses of the legacy (and, paradoxically modern as well) DBMS, that force the developer to resort to various tricks to code the data structures and the integrity constraints and (3) only the DDL code provides a reliable description of the database physical constructs.

---

[13] This assertion is not quite correct if we only use the transformations presented in this paper. In particular, some constraints can be lost, or incompletely translated. Such is the case for cardinality constraints [i-j] where $1 < j < N$. A more comprehensive plan, making use of more precise transformations, can preserve these constraints until the coding phase, e.g., in the form of SQL triggers.

[14] Several DBMS do not manage correctly candidate keys comprising a nullable column.

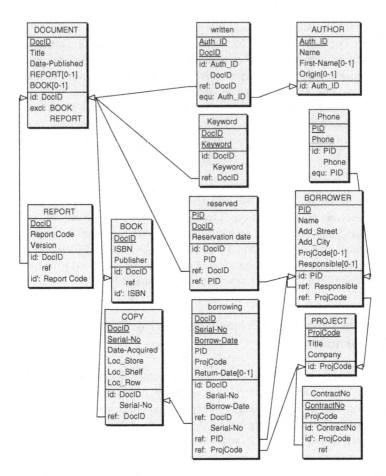

Fig. 20. The relational schema obtained by the application of the transformation plan of Fig. 18 on the conceptual schema of Fig. 19

7.1 Database Reverse Engineering

In complex projects, for instance when the database includes several hundreds or thousands of tables[15], the core of the process will be organized as described in Fig. 21. It comprises four main sub-processes, namely:

1. *Parsing*, that rebuilds the raw physical schema by merely parsing the DDL code (code$_{ddl}$). Only the constructs that have been *explicitly declared* in the code can be recovered.
2. *Refinement*, which enriches the raw physical schema with the *undeclared constructs* and constraints that have been elicited through the analysis of program code (code$_{prg}$), as well as other sources that we will ignore here. Sometimes more than 50% of the specifications can be retrieved in this way.

---

[15] An SAP database can comprise 30,000 tables and more than 200,000 columns.

3. *Cleaning*, which removes the technical constructs, such as the indexes, and which produces the logical schema.
4. *Conceptualization*, which derives a plausible conceptual schema from the logical schema.

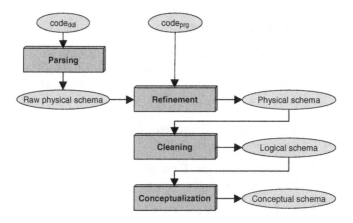

Fig. 21. The four main processes of database reverse engineeering

Calling the whole process DB-REng, and the four sub-processes Parse, Refine, Clean and Concept respectively, we can write:

Conceptual schema = DB-REng(code$_{ddl}$, code$_{prg}$)

DB-design = Concept ∘ Clean ∘ Refine ∘ Parse

An interesting, and not really surprising, aspect of database reverse engineering is that all the processes we have mentioned appear to be the **reverse** of database design processes. Indeed, we have the following relations:

Refine ∘ Parse = Coding^{-1}

Clean = PhysD^{-1}

Concept = LogD^{-1}

This observation has a deep influence on the specifications and the strategies of the reverse processes. For instance, since the Conceptualization process is the inverse of Logical design, it should be possible to derive a transformation plan for the former just by reversing the plan of Logical design. Though this approach has proved successful, the problem is a bit more complex due to the undisciplined way legacy databases were designed. When the logical schema was built, it had to meet not only functional requirements (that is, to express all the semantics of the conceptual schema), but also non-functional requirements such as time-space optimization, security or privacy. The satisfaction of the latter requirements can deeply affect the readability of the logical schema to such an extent that it has become quite difficult to understand.

In the next section, we will very shortly describe the Conceptualization process as a transformation process, and elaborate a representative transformation plan.

7.2 Logical Schema Conceptualization

Reversing a transformation plan is a new concept that would deserve some further discussion [22]. Due to space limit, we will give a simplified definition that is valid for linear plans only, that is, plans which do not include if-then-else or loop constructs:

> *Considering a transformation Σ implemented by transformation plan T, T' is an inverse of T if it implements the inverse of Σ.*

If T is a linear transformation plan, T' can be built as follows: *each operator of T is replaced with its inverse, then the resulting sequence is reversed.*

Deriving a linear plan from the plan proposed for Logical design in Fig. 18 is not too difficult, provided we target simpler schemas, that meet such realistic

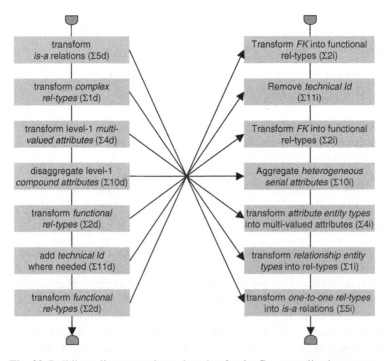

Fig. 22. Building a linear transformation plan for the Conceptualization process

restrictions as the following: *a multivalued attribute can be compound, but no compound attributes can have components that are themselves compound or multivalued.* Fig. 22 depicts the linearized plan for *Logical design* (left), and a tentative transformation plan for *Logical schema Conceptualization* obtained by inverting the former (right).

The resulting plan introduces new processes and terms that deserve some explanation. Removing a <u>technical Id</u> is valid provided it does not represent any application domain concept. A series of <u>heterogeneous serial attributes</u> is a pattern in which a sequence of attributes, generally of different types, have names that present strong similarities, and that suggest that these attributes form an implicit aggregate (Example: Address-City, Address-Street, Address-Number). An <u>attribute entity type</u> AE is an entity type the goal of which obviously is just to add an elementary information to another entity type. It comprises one or a few attributes that are all part of the identifier of AE, and is linked to another entity type only, through a mandatory role. A <u>relationship entity type</u> is an entity type the role of which obviously is just to link two or more entity types. Transforming <u>one-to-one rel-types</u> into is-a relations must be carried out with caution, since it must be semantically pertinent. A one-to-one rel-type between MANAGER and CAR does not mean that CAR is a subtype of MANAGER!

Finally, let us observe that the second step of the resulting transformation plan (right) is useless and can be discarded, though it does no harm[16].

7.3 Case Study

The application of this transformation plan to the logical relational schema of Fig. 20 is left as an exercice to the reader, preferably with the help of the Transformation assistant of the DB-MAIN CASE tool. Some observations:

1. identifying serial attributes forming attributes Location and Address is a manual process,
2. deleting the technical id of AUTHOR is a manual process,
3. the conceptual names of most one-to-many rel-types cannot be recovered (default names are suggested but they generally are not suitable), and must be assigned manually.

8 Transformations in CASE Tools

Following the discussion of this paper, it is not surprising that the transformational paradigm is particularly suited to build CASE tools. All CASE tools rely, often implicitly, on some kind of schema transformations. Due to the popularity of the MDE approaches, we can expect future CASE tools to include programmable transformation toolsets. In the past, some examples of transformation-based tools have been described, e.g., in [42]. We can also mention Silverrun, a CASE tool that explicitly makes use of transformations.

---

[16] A desirable property of these plans is their *idempotence*. It is not guaranteed in general.

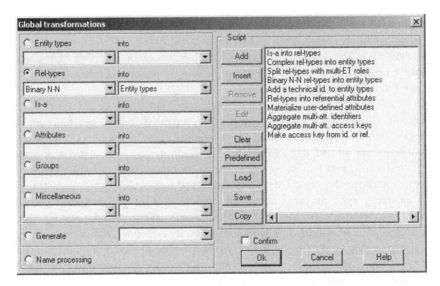

Fig. 23. The elementary transformation assistant of DB-MAIN

We will describe briefly the transformation facilities of DB-MAIN[17], a CASE tool dedicated to the support of the main database engineering processes, including non standard ones, such as database reverse engineering, interoperability, active and temporal database design, wrapper generation and XML engineering. DB-MAIN is based on the GER model and offers a toolset of about 30 elementary transformations.

DB-MAIN includes a collection of programmable assistants that are intended to help the analysts in complex and tedious tasks. Two of them are of particular interest, namely the *Transformation assistant* and the *Advanced transformation assistant*. Both allow the analyst to apply predicate-driven transformations on the current schema and to build transformation plans through a scripting facility.

Fig. 23 shows a typical screen of the first assistant. Its left part proposes a list of labelled patterns (a *user-friendly* interface to built-in structural *predicates*), accompanied by a set of possible actions that are performed on all the instances of the pattern in the current schema. The right part allows the analyst to build linear transformation plans that can be saved and reused later.

The second assistant is more powerful, and therefore more complex. It is based on predicate-driven transformations following the syntax $\Sigma(p)$ described in Section 5.4, and illustrated in Fig. 16. It allows non-linear transformation plans to be developed.

Part 2   Formal Aspects of Database Transformations

These sections which follow provide the bases for building a formal system in which GER transformations can be rigorously defined and such properties as semantics preservation can be studied.

---

[17] The free Education edition of DB-MAIN is available at the following address: http://www.info.fundp.ac.be/libd, select "DB-MAIN CASE".

9   The Extended Relational Model (ERM)

ERM is a variant of the N1NF relational model. It includes the concepts of domain, relation (schema and instance), attribute and constraints.

9.1   Domain

A domain is a named set of elements. It is declared by its name and the specification of the set of elements. A domain is *dynamic* if its set can change over time. Some *predefined basic domains* are provided, such as number, string or date. The model includes a special dynamic basic domain, called entities, whose structure is immaterial, but the goal of which could be to denote application domain entities. A *user-defined domain* is defined by an element set which is a subset of that of another domain. A relation is a valid domain. Any domain defined as a subset of the domain entities is an *entity domain*, and so forth transitively.

Example of user-defined domains

```
birth_Date:   date;
name:         string;
PERSON:       entities;
EMPLOYEE:     PERSON;
CONTACT:      address;
```

9.2   Relation and Attribute

According to the relational theory, a relation is a subset of the cartesian product of domains. An element of a relation is a tuple. A relation is described by its *schema*, that specifies the format and the constraints that its instances must satisfy. The current *instance* of a relation is the current set of tuples.

The schema of a relation comprises its name, a set of attributes and a set of constraints. An *attribute* has a name and is defined on a domain. It represents a participation of a domain in the relation. A domain can appear more than once, defining as many distinct attributes. An attribute defined on an entity domain is an *entity attribute*.

In general, the value of an attribute of a tuple is a subset of its domain. To specify the size of this subset, a cardinality property [i-j] is associated with each attribute A. It states the minimum and maximum numbers of domain values that are assigned to A in any tuple. If j = 1, A is single-valued otherwise it is multivalued. If i = 0, A is optional otherwise it is mandatory. The default cardinality property is [1-1].

Examples

```
address (    Street:         name,
             City:           name );
employee (   Pld:            number,
             Name:           name,
             1st-name[0-1]:  name,
             Phone[1-5]:     phone,
             Contact:        address);
```

Interpretation: an employee has one (default [1-1], that is, *from 1 to 1*) personal ID, one name, from 0 to 1 first name, from 1 to 5 phone numbers, and one contact, which is made up of one street and one city.

If the concept of *address* is not considered important (for instance, it is not referred to elsewhere), the domain address could be specified in line as follows:

employee (..., Contact: (Street: name, City: Name));

In some situations, the specification of the domain will be ignored for simplicity. Consequently, the following notation will be allowed.

employee (PId, Name, 1st-name[0-1], Phone[1-5], Contact: address);

In particular, specially in formal declarations, if an attribute is given the name of its domain, we will use the following shorthand, where A is both the name of a domain and an attribute defined on it:

$$R(A,B,C) \equiv R(A:A, B:B, C:C)$$

9.3 Non-set Attributes

By default, the value of an attribute is a *set* of domain values. Due to the generality of the GER, that is intended, among others, to describe logical and physical schemas, we need more poweful data structures, such as set, bag, list and array attributes:

R (A, B[0-5]set:number, C);   *also defined as*:   R (A, B[0-5]:number, C)
R (A, B[0-5]bag:number, C);
R (A, B[0-5]list:number, C);
R (A, B[0-5]array:number, C);

When the values in a list or in an array have to be *unique*, we write:

R (A, B[0-5]u-list:number, C);
R (A, B[0-5]u-array:number, C);

9.4 Constraints

ERM includes the **uniqueness** and **inclusion** constraints, as well as various dependencies, such as functional (**FD**) and multivalued (**MV**), of the standard relational model[18]. Candidate key {A,B,C} of R will be declared by the clause id(R): A,B,C. When possible, and where no ambiguity may arise, this specification can be replaced by continuously underlining the components of the key. Inclusion constraints between algebraic expressions are allowed.

---

[18] These constraints have been defined on 1NF models, and their generalization to N1NF models is far from trivial. Due to the limited scope of this paper, and without loss of generality, we will ignore the complexity of the constraint patterns of N1NF models.

Examples

1. R (A, B, C, D); id(R): A,B; *also defined as*: R (<u>A, B</u>, C, D)[19]
2. S(E, G, H); S[G,H] ⊆ R[A,B];
3. T(A, B, C); T[A] = A;

Example 1 declares a *candidate key* in both alternative syntaxes. Example 2 declares a *foreign key* through an inclusion constraint. Expression R[G,H] denotes the projection of the current instance of R on attributes (A,B). Example 3 expresses a domain constraint. Every element of domain A must appear as the value of attribute A of at least one tuple of the current instance of T.

In a N1NF structure, a local key can hold in a multivalued compound attribute. In the following example, we declare that, for each product tuple, the candidate key {Year} holds in each instance of Sales (no two sales the same year):

product (	ProNbr:	number,
	Description:	name,
	Sales[0-N]:	(Year: date, Volume: number));

The notation is extended as follows:

id(product.Sales): Year;

or by underlining the components:

product (<u>ProNbr</u>, Description, Sales[0-N]: (<u>Year</u>, Volume));

ERM includes a special form of **cardinality constraint**, through which we can state how many tuples of the current instance of a relation must/can share a common domain value.

Considering the relation schema R(A,B,C) and an instance r of R,

$$card(R.A): [I-J],$$

is interpreted as[20]

$$\forall a \in A, I \le |r(A=a)| \le J$$

Examples

1. R (A, B, C); card(R.A): [0-5];
2. R (A, B, C); card(R.(B,C)): [1-3];

Example 1 declares that any value of domain A may not appear in more than 5 tuples of (any instance of) R. Example 2 shows a generalization of the constraint. It declares that any couple of values of domains B and C must appear in 1 to 3 tuples of (any instance of) R.

Note that candidate keys as well as the domain constraint T[A] = A are special cases of cardinality constraint. Note also that cardinality properties and cardinality constraints serve different purposes, and that none can replace the other one.

---

[19] The graphical convention is as follows: the key of R(<u>A,B</u>,C) is {A,B} while R(<u>A</u>,<u>B</u>,C) has two keys {A} and {B}.

[20] Expression r(A=a) denotes the set of tuples of r where A=a.

9.5 An ERM Schema Example

We are now able to propose a more comprehensive example of ERM schema.

- **domains**

  CUSTOMER: entities;
  VEHICLE: entities;
  CAR, BOAT: VEHICLE;
  Name: string;

- **relations**

  cust (<u>CUSTOMER</u>, Cld: number, Name: name, Phone[0-3]: string),
  owns (owner: CUSTOMER, <u>CAR</u>);

- **constraints**

  VEHICLE = CAR ∪ BOAT;
  id(cust): Cld;
  card(owns.owner): [0-5];
  owns(CAR) = CAR;

10 Formal Semantics of the GER

The mapping Σger>erm (Section 3.3) is fairly straighforward for most GER constructs. The inverse mapping is easy to derive as well. The main rules are presented in Fig. 24, and need little explanation, except for the representation of an entity type, since it seems to differ from the usual way one translates a conceptual schema into relational structures, as illustrated in Fig. 1 for example. First, let us recall that the goal of this section is not to produce relational databases, as discussed in Section. 6.2, but rather to give an operational model rigorous semantics.

An entity type E is merely represented by an entity domain, with name E, independently of any other feature, such as attributes, it may be concerned with.

When entity type E participates in relationship type (rel-type for short) R, with role r, its representation also appears as the domain of ERM attribute r of the relation R that expresses this rel-type (see rel-types of and export in Fig. 24).

Now, how to express the GER attributes of E? Through a special relation that aggregates each entity with its GER attribute values. The relation is given the conventional name desc-E, for *description of E*. This relation comprises an entity attribute, with name E, and defined on entity domain E. This attribute is a key of the relation. Then, for each GER attribute, it comprises an ERM attribute, with the same name and the same domain. Later on, we will see that, in some circumstances, this relation can include other entity domains.

In this way, we can easily describe, beyond plain GER structures, an entity type without attributes, or without identifiers, or with complex constraint patterns.

GER constructs	ERM constructs

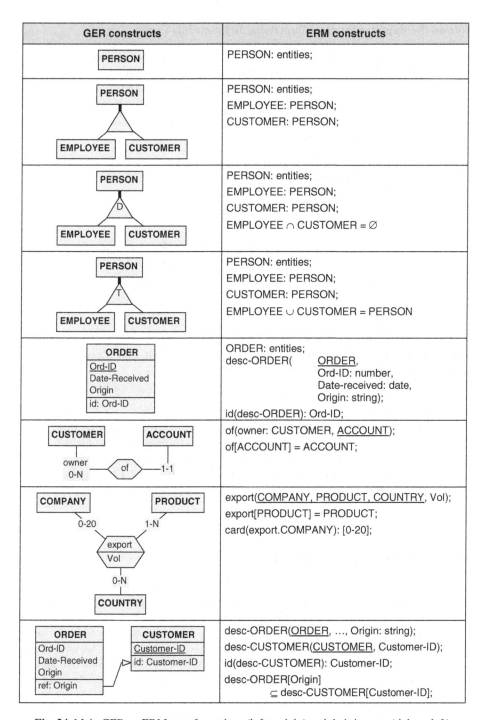

Fig. 24. Main GER-to-ERM transformations (left to right) and their inverse (right to left)

Note on the Representation of Functional Relationship Types

A rel-type is *functional* if it is binary, has no attributes and if at least one of its roles has cardinality [i-1]. Let us consider the functional rel-type of, between ACCOUNT and CUSTOMER, in Fig. 4, and recalled in Fig. 24. These three constructs translate in ERM as follows (note that the identifier of ACCOUNT has not been translated yet):

```
CUSTOMER, ACCOUNT: entities;
desc-CUSTOMER(CUSTOMER, ...);
desc-ACCOUNT(ACCOUNT, Account-Nbr, Amount);
of(CUSTOMER, ACCOUNT);
desc-CUSTOMER[CUSTOMER] = CUSTOMER;
desc-ACCOUNT[ACCOUNT] = ACCOUNT;
of[ACCOUNT] = ACCOUNT;
```

This schema happens to meet the preconditions of the semantics-preserving *project-join* transformation that will be studied in Section 11.1. Its application yields the following equivalent, but simpler, schema, in which the relations desc-ACCOUNT and of have been joined:

```
CUSTOMER, ACCOUNT: entities;
desc-CUSTOMER(CUSTOMER, ...);
desc-ACCOUNT'(ACCOUNT, Account-Nbr, Amount, Customer: CUSTOMER);
desc-CUSTOMER'[CUSTOMER] = CUSTOMER;
desc-ACCOUNT'[ACCOUNT] = ACCOUNT;
```

This form is quite interesting. Indeed, it allows us to specify, in a particularly simple and elegant way, complex constraints, such as hybrid identifiers, that is, identifiers that combine attributes and/or remote roles. Such an identifier is associated with entity type ACCOUNT in Fig. 4, the legend of which tells us that *the accounts of a customer have distinct Account numbers, which makes [ACCOUNT] a dependent or weak entity type*. Specifying this identifier is straightforward:

```
id(desc-ACCOUNT)': Customer, Account-Nbr
```

11 The ERM Transformations

In this section, we describe five important families of semantics-preserving parametric transformations that can be applied to ERM schemas. Basically, they are relational transformation and could be applied to any N1NF schema as well.

For each family, after a description of the principles, we specify the structural mapping **T**, through conditions **P** and **Q** (expressed in an intuitive way, through abstract structural patterns), if available, the description of useful variants, the signature of direct and inverse transformation, a discussion of their properties and an example. The **t** part will be ignored here. See [20] for a more detailed description of these transformations.

In the following descriptions, U is the set of attributes of relation R, while I, J and K denote subsets of U.

11.1 Project-Join Transformations

Principle

A relation R in which a multivalued dependency (e.g., a FD) holds can be decomposed into smaller fragments according to this dependency [13].

Structural mapping

P	$R(U); \{I,J,K\}$ is a partition of U; $I \twoheadrightarrow J \mid K$;
Q	$R1(I\ J); R2(I\ K); R1[I]=R2[I];$

Variants

The project-join transformation can be particularized to relations in which I, J and/or K are made up of one attribute only, in which K is optional, in which K is multivalued, in which J is empty, and in which J and K are multivalued.

Signatures

direct : $(R1,R2) \longleftarrow \textbf{PJ}(R,I,J)$

reverse : $R \longleftarrow \textbf{PJ}^{-1}(R1,R2,I)$

Discussion

This transformation is the variant of the relational decomposition theorem mentioned in Section 4.3. It is therefore symmetrically reversible.

Example

Source schema   works(who:EMP,in:PROJ,for:DEPART)
                  works:who $\longrightarrow$ for

Transformation   (works-in,works-for) $\longleftarrow$ **PJ**(works,{who},{in})

Target schema   works-in(who:EMP,in:PROJ)
                  works-for(<u>who</u>:EMP,for:DEPART)
                  works-in[who] = works-for[who]

11.2 Denotation Transformation

Principle

The result of a query E defined by, say, an algebraic expression, and the schema of which comprises attributes AE, is explicitly represented in schema S with a denotational domain X. Bijective relation D acts as a dictionary for the elements of X. This operator is mainly technical and is used as a basis for the next transformation. It is trivially symmetrically reversible.

Structural mapping

P	schema S; algebraic expression $\textbf{E}$ with schema $SE(A_1, ..., A_n)$
Q	schema S; domain X; $D(\underline{X}, \underline{A_1, ..., A_n})$; $D[A_1, ..., A_n] = \textbf{E}[A_1, ..., A_n]$; X appears in D only

Signatures

direct : $(X, D, \{A_1, \ldots, A_n\}) \longleftarrow \textbf{den}(S, E)$

reverse : $() \longleftarrow \textbf{den}^{-1}(X, D)$

11.3 Extension Transformations

Principle

The projection of a relation R on a subset $\{I_1, \ldots, I_n\}$ of its attributes is explicitly represented by surrogate domain X. Bijective relation D acts as a dictionary for the elements of X. This domain replaces I in R, leading to relation T.

Structural mapping

P	$R(U)$; $\{I, J\}$ is a partition of U
Q	domain X; $D(\underline{X}, \underline{I})$; $T(X, J)$; $D[X] = T[X]$; X appears in D and T only

Variants

When $I = U$, J is empty, so that the transformation degenerates into:

P	$R(U)$;
Q	domain X; $D(\underline{X}, \underline{U})$; X appears in D only

If I comprises at least 2 attributes, it can be partitioned into subsets $\{I_1, \ldots, I_m\}$. Considering the FD $D : X \longrightarrow I$, we can apply the project-join transformation to D according to this partition. Expressing the lost FD $D : I \longrightarrow X$ on the join of the fragments, we get the two **extension-decomposition** transformations (according to whether J is not empty or empty):

P	$R(U)$; $\{I_1, \ldots, I_m, J\}$ is a partition of U; $m > 1$
Q	$D_i(\underline{X}, I_i)$; $T(X, J)$; $D_i[X] = T[X]$; $i \in [1..m]$ $(*D_i, i \in [1..m]) : I_1, \ldots, I_m \longrightarrow X$; X appears in D_i and T only; $i \in [1..m]$

P	$R(U)$; $\{I_1, \ldots, I_m\}$ is a partition of U; $m > 1$
Q	$D_i(\underline{X}, I_i)$; $D_i[X] = D_j[X]$; $i, j \in [1..m]$ $(*D_i, i \in [1..m]) : I_1, \ldots, I_m \longrightarrow X$; X appears in D_i only; $i \in [1..m]$

Signatures

Extension

direct : $(X, D, T) \longleftarrow \textbf{ext}(R, I)$

reverse : $R \longleftarrow \textbf{ext}^{-1}(X, D, T)$

Extension decomposition

direct : $(X, \{D_1, D_2, \ldots, D_m\}, T) \longleftarrow$ **ext-dec** $(R, \{I_1, I_2, \ldots, I_m\})$

reverse : $R \longleftarrow$ **ext-dec**$^{-1}(X, \{D_1, D_2, \ldots, D_m\}, T)$

For transformations where J is empty, parameter T is void.

Discussion

This family of operators is particularly powerful, since it allows us to generate most entity-generating and entity-removing transformations [17]. Based on the **den** and **PJ**[-1] transformations, it is symmetrically reversible. The role of the parameter I can be interpreted as follows: *the subset I of attributes of R seems to represent an outstanding concept which would deserve being described by a new surrogate domain X.*

Example of the extension transformation

Source schema   program (TEACHER, SUBJECT, DATE)

Transformation   (LECTURE, defined-as, program) $\longleftarrow$
                   ext (program, {TEACHER, SUBJECT})

Target schema   domain LECTURE
                   program (LECTURE, DATE)
                   defined-as (LECTURE, TEACHER, SUBJECT)
                   defined-as [LECTURE] = program [LECTURE]

11.4 Composition Transformations

Principle

A relation S is replaced by its composition T with another relation R.

Structural mapping

P	R($\underline{I}$ K); S(K L); S[K] $\subseteq$ R[K]; I, K, L not empty;
Q	R($\underline{I}$ K); T(I L); T[I] $\subseteq$ R[I]; R*T: K $\rightarrow\!\!\!\rightarrow$ L|I

Variants

The transformation simplifies when R is bijective:

P	R($\underline{I}\,\underline{K}$); S(K L); S[K] $\subseteq$ R[K]; I, K, L not empty;
Q	R($\underline{I}\,\underline{K}$); T(I L); T[I] $\subseteq$ R[I];

The latter form generalizes to N-ary relations:

P	R($\underline{I}\,\underline{K}$ J); S(K L); S[K] $\subseteq$ R[K]; I, J, K, L not empty;
Q	R($\underline{I}\,\underline{K}$ J); T(I L); T[I] $\subseteq$ R[I]

Signatures (simple form)

direct : $T \longleftarrow$ **comp** (R, S, K)
reverse : $S \longleftarrow$ **comp**$^{-1}(R, T, I)$

Signatures (N-ary form)

direct : $T \longleftarrow$ **comp** (R, S, K, I)

reverse : $S \longleftarrow$ **comp** $^{-1}(R, T, I, K)$

Discussion

These operators derive from transformations **PJ** and **PJ⁻¹**. Therefore they are symmetrically reversible. In the bijective variants, the transformation is symmetrical and can be seen as substituting in S a key I of R for the key K.

Example

Source schema	`manages(`<u>`MANAGER`</u>`,DEPART)`
	`works-in(`<u>`EMPLOYEE`</u>`,DEPART)`
	`works-in[DEPART]` $\subseteq$ `manages[DEPART]`
Transformation	`works-for` $\longleftarrow$
	`comp(manages,works-in,{DEPART})`
Target schema	`manages(`<u>`MANAGER`</u>`,DEPART)`
	`works-for(`<u>`EMPLOYEE`</u>`,MANAGER)`
	`works-for[MANAGER]` $\subseteq$ `manages[MANAGER]`

11.5 Nest-Unnest Transformations

Principle

A N1NF relation R that comprises a multivalued attribute B is replaced by S, its equivalent 1NF version [43] [31].

Structural mapping

P	`R(`<u>`I`</u>`,B[1-N]);`
Q	`S(`<u>`I,B`</u>`);`

Variants

The cardinality of attribute B prohibits empty sets (otherwise values of I are lost), which can be too strong a precondition. Hence the following variant, in which the tuples of R with an empty B set can be rebuilt from the elements of the evaluation of E that do not appear in S:

P	`R(`<u>`I`</u>`,B[0-N]);R[I] = `**E**`;` where **E** is any algebraic expression over the database schema
Q	`S(`<u>`I,B`</u>`);S[I]` $\subseteq$ **E**`;`

If B is a compound but single-valued attribute, this operator degenerates into a disaggregation transformation as follows, where K is a set of attributes:

P	`R(I,B(K));`
Q	`S(I,K);`

Signatures

direct :   S ⟵—— **unnest** (R,B)
reverse :   R ⟵——**unnest**$^{-1}$ (S,B)

Discussion

Unnest, together with its inverse *nest,* are the main algebraic operators specific to N1NF relational models. This version of **unnest** is symmetrically reversible. Indeed, R meets the following criterion of reversibility (see [10] for instance): considering the relation R(A,B[0-N],C), the application of the *unnest* relational operator on B is (symmetrically) reversible *iff*:

- no tuple of R has an empty B value (as if the cardinality property of B actually was [1-N]),
- B is functionally (possibly non minimally) dependent on the set of all the other attributes of R.

Examples

Source schema	contacts(<u>EMPLOYEE</u>,PHONE[1-N])
Transformation	contact ⟵——**unnest**(contacts,PHONE)
Target schema	contact(<u>EMPLOYEE,PHONE</u>)
Source schema	descr(<u>EMPLOYEE</u>,CHILD[0-N]) descr[EMPLOYEE] = EMPLOYEE
Transformation	children ⟵——**unnest**(descr,CHILD)
Target schema	children(<u>EMPLOYEE,CHILD</u>)

Note in this example the instance "descr[EMPLOYEE] = EMPLOYEE" of the pattern "R[I] = **E**".

12 Analyzing and Generating GER Transformations

12.1 Analyzing GER Transformations

The issue is to prove that a known, but possibly ill-defined, practical transformation is *correct* and *complete* as far as semantics preservation is concerned. In this context, we will revisit the three transformations that we have informally used in the introductory example of Fig. 1, and that also are the most popular, notably in database logical design. Due to space limit, only the main patterns will be discussed. For any variant of the source schema, such as those that are suggested below, the reader is invited to examine the ERM expression and to infer the actual resulting schema. For example, in the transformation of attribute A2 into an entity type, no hypothesis is made on the participation of A2 in an identifier of A. If this is the case, the ERM expression clearly shows how to deal with this pattern, based on the dependency theory[21]. This is left as an exercise.

---

[21] More precisely the rules that govern the propagation of FD in the projection, the join and the selection.

12.2 Transforming an Attribute into an Entity Type

In Fig. 1, this transformation was applied to attribute Author of BOOK, leading to entity type AUTHOR. Its abstract GER pattern is as follows.

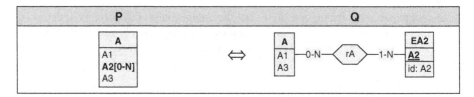

Fig. 25. Transforming an attribute into an entity type

Variants. The reader is invited to examine the following extensions: A2 is single-valued; A2 is an identifying attribute for A; A2 is a component of an identifier of A; A is a compound attribute; the cardinality property is [0-5] or [1-5]; A2 is a set of attributes of A.

Signatures

direct :   (EA2,rA) ⟵ **att-to-et**(A,A2)

reverse :   A2 ⟵ **att-to-et**$^{-1}$(EA2)

Analysis

We express the source schema (left) in ERM, then we extract and flatten the multivalued attribute:

```
A: entities;
desc-A(A,A1,A2[0-N],A3);
desc-A[A]=A;
```

⇕   (desc-A',R) ⟵ **PJ**(desc-A,{A},{A2})

```
A: entities;
desc-A'(A,A1,A3);
R(A,A2[1-N]);
desc-A'[A]=A;
```

⇕   R' ⟵ **unnest**(R,A2)

```
A: entities;
desc-A'(A,A1,A3);
R'(A,A2);
desc-A'[A]=A;
```

Now, we define a new entity domain EA2 based on attribute A2 of R':

$\updownarrow$ (EA2,{desc-EA2},rA) $\longleftarrow$ **ext**(R',{A2})

```
A,EA2: entities;
desc-A'(A,A1,A3);
desc-EA2(EA2,A2);
rA(A,EA2);
desc-A'[A]=A;
desc-EA2[EA2]=rA[EA2]=EA2;
```

Interpreting this schema in the GER gives the expected target schema (right). We conclude that **att-to-et** is an SR-transformation.

12.3   Transforming a Relationship Type into an Entity Type

In the illustration of Fig. 1, we transformed relationship type write into entity type WRITE. Here is a generalization of this operator for N-ary relationship types, that can also have attributes (Fig. 26).

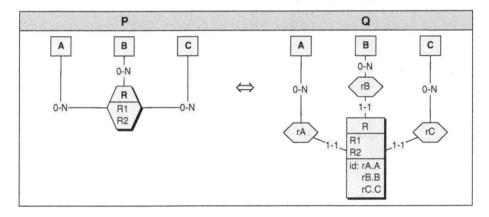

Fig. 26. Transforming a relationship type into an entity type

Variants. The roles of R have cardinality constraints other than [0-N]; R is binary; one (or more) of the roles of R has cardinality [0-1]; R has one (or more) explicit identifier[22].

Signatures

  direct :   (R,{(A,rA),(B,rB),(C,rC)}) $\longleftarrow$ **rt-to-et**(R)
  reverse :   R $\longleftarrow$ **rt-to-et^{-1}**(R)

---

[22] The default (not necessarily minimal) identifier of a relationship type is made up of the set of its roles.

Analysis

We express the source schema (left) in ERM, then we represent the set of roles by the new entity domain R:

```
A,B,C: entities;
R(A,B,C,R1,R2);
desc-A[A]=A;
```

$\quad\Updownarrow\quad$ (R,{rA,rB,rC},desc-R) $\longleftarrow$ **ext-dec**(R,{{A},{B},{C}})

```
A,B,C,R: entities;
rA(R,A); rB(R,B); rC(R,C);
desc-R(R,R1,R2);
rA*rB*rC: A,B,C ⟶ R;
rA[R]=rB[R]=rC[R]=desc-R[R]=R;
```

Interpreting this schema in the GER gives the expected target schema (right). We conclude that **rt-to-et** is an SR-transformation.

12.4 Transforming a Binary Relationship Type into an Attribute

In Fig. 1, we transformed all the one-to-many relationship types into attributes, then we declared them foreign keys.

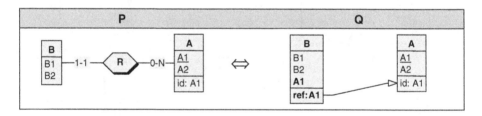

Fig. 27. Transforming a relationship type into an attribute (foreign key)

Variants. R is optional for B ([1-1] replaced by [0-1]); R is many-to-many ([1-1] replaced with [0-N]); the identifier of A is made up of more than one attribute; R is functional from A to B ([0-N] replaced by [0-1]); R is bijective; R is mandatory for A ([0-N] replaced by [1-N]); R.A appears in an identifier of B.

Signatures

direct :   {A1} $\longleftarrow$ **rt-to-att**(R.B)

reverse :   R $\longleftarrow$ **rt-to-att^{-1}**(B,{A1},A)

Analysis

We express the source schema (left) in ERM, then we apply the composition transformation:

```
A,B: entities;
desc-A(A,A1,A2); desc-B(B,B1,B2); R(A,B);
R[B]=B; desc-A[A]=A; desc-B[B]=B;
```

$\Updownarrow$ R' $\longleftarrow$ **comp**(desc-of-A,R,{A},{A1})

```
A,B: entities;
desc-A(A,A1,A2); desc-B(B,B1,B2); R'(A1,B);
desc-B[B]=R'[B]=B; desc-A[A]=A;
R'[A1] ⊆ desc-A[A1];
```

$\Updownarrow$ desc-B' $\longleftarrow$ **PJ⁻¹**(desc-B,R',B)

```
A,B: entities;
desc-A(A,A1,A2); desc-B'(B,B1,B2,A1);
desc-A[A]=A; desc-B'[B]=B;
desc-B'[A1] ⊆ desc-A[A1];
```

Interpreting the latter schema in the GER gives the expected target schema (right). We conclude that **rt-to-att** is an SR-transformation.

12.5 Generating GER Transformations

This process consists in exploiting the parametric nature of most ERM transformations to discover new practical GER transformations. This problem is open, but we can illustrate it through a more in-depth examination of the extension-decomposition transformation.

Let us consider the transformation depicted in the Fig. 26. Its analysis is based on the ERM **ext-dec** transformation of the ERM relation R(A,B,C,R1,R2) that models the relationship type R.

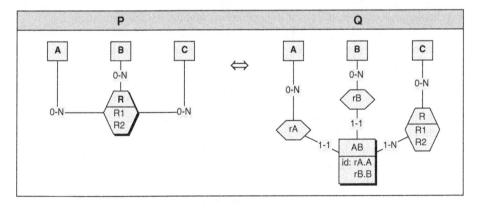

Fig. 28. An unusual transformation deriving from the **ext-dec** transformation

The GER rt-to-et transformation we have developed was obtained by choosing, in the ERM ext-dec transformation, the parameter I to be {A,B,C}. In fact, I is any non empty subset of the attributes of relation R. For instance, I can be any of the following subsets, that will generate 31 different equivalent target schemas:

{A}, {A,B}, {A,B,C}, {R1}, {R1,R2}, {A,R1}, {A,R1,R2}, {A,B,R1}, {A,B,R1,R2}, {A,B,C,R1}, {A,B,C,R1,R2}, and all the similar patterns obtained by permutation within {A,B,C} and {R1,R2}.

The reader is invited to prove the correctness of the transformation of Fig. 28 following the reasoning of Section 12.3.

13 Conclusions and Perspectives

Database engineering intrinsically has been model-driven for more than three decades. Designing, normalizing, merging, optimizing data structures can be performed at an abstraction level that is, to a large extent, platform independent.

The transformational approach enriches this framework considerably, since it opens the way to more structured and more reliable engineering processes. This paper shows that such an approach brings several essential benefits.

- Being formal, it can be used to study rigorously basic properties such as semantics preservation, that states how the operators preserve the information contents of the schemas;
- To be fruitful, and to avoid combinatorial explosion, a pivot model, with which we associate a relational semantics, has proved necessary;
- From the pedagogical view point, this approach provides a disciplined and reliable way to conduct important processes such as logical design, which many students too often tend to consider as some kind of *magic*;
- Developing CASE tools based on the transformational approach leads to more reliable products, notably as far as generation completeness is concerned;
- A transformational approach based on a pivot model is by construction scalable; introducing a new model M involves the development of components independent of the existing models.

Several problems still are to be addressed, of which we mention a sample.

- How to integrate transformational database engineering into emerging MDE framework(s)?
- How to cope with the other aspects of data structures, in particular how do integrity constraints propagate?
- How can data structure transformations be propagated to the other components of the information system, notably the data (data conversion), the human/computer interfaces and the programs?

References and Resources

1. Alves, T.L., Silva, P.F., Visser, J., Oliveira, J.N., Strategic Term Rewriting and Its Application to a Vdm-SL to SQL Conversion, in *Proc. FM 2005*, LNCS, No 3582, Springer-Verlag. (2005) 399-414

2. Baader, F., Horrocks, I., and Sattler, U. Description logics. In Staab, S. and Studer, R. (Ed.), *Handbook on Ontologies*, International Handbooks on Information Systems, pages 3-28. Springer, (2004).

3. Balzer, R. Transformational implementation : An example. *IEEE TSE*, Vol. SE-7(1). (1981)

4. Batini, C., Ceri, S., & Navathe, S., B. *Conceptual Database Design*, Benjamin/Cummings. (1992)

5. Batini, C., Di Battista, G., Santucci, G. Structuring Primitives for a Dictionary of Entity Relationship Data Schemas, *IEEE TSE*, Vol. 19, No. 4. (1993)

6. Bolois, G., & Robillard, P. Transformations in Reengineering Techniques. *Proc. of the 4th Reengineering Forum "Reengineering in Practice"*, Victoria, Canada. (1994)

7. Boyd, M., McBrien. Towards a Semi-Automated Approach to Intermodel Transformation, In *Proceedings of EMMSAD'04,Volume 1, CAiSE Workshop Proceedings*, Riga Technical University. (2004) 175-188

8. Casanova, M., A., Amaral De Sa. Mapping uninterpreted Schemes into Entity-Relationship diagrams : two applications to conceptual schema design. *IBM J. Res. & Develop.*, 28(1). (1984)

9. Clève, A., Henrard, J., Hainaut, J-L. Co-transformations in Information System Reengineering, in *Proc. of WCRE'04/ATEM-04*, (2004)

10. Darwen, H., Date, C., J. Relation-valued Attributes, in Date, C., J., Darwen, H., *Relational Database Writings* 1989-1991, Addison-Wesley (1993)

11. D'Atri, A., & Sacca, D. Equivalence and Mapping of Database Schemes, *Proc. 10th VLDB conf.*, Singapore. (1984)

12. Estiévenart, F., François, A., Henrard, J., Hainaut, J-L. Web Site Engineering. *Proc. of the 5th International Workshop on Web Site Evolution*, Amsterdam, Sept. 2003, IEEE CS Press. (2003)

13. Fagin, R. Multivalued dependencies and a new normal form for relational databases, *ACM TODS*, 2(3). (1977)

14. Fikas, S., F. Automating the transformational development of software, *IEEE TSE*, Vol. SE-11. (1985)

15. Hainaut, J-L. Theoretical and practical tools for database design, in *Proc. of the Very Large Databases Conf.*, pp. 216-224, September, IEEE Computer Society Press. (1981)

16. Hainaut, J.-L. A Generic Entity-Relationship Model. *Proc. of the IFIP WG 8.1 Conf. on Information System Concepts: an in-depth analysis*, North-Holland. (1989)

17. Hainaut, J-L. Entity-generating Schema Transformations for Entity-Relationship Models, in *Proc. of the 10th Entity-Relationship Approach*, San Mateo (CA), 1991, North-Holland. (1992)

18. Hainaut, J-L., Chandelon M., Tonneau C., & Joris M. (1993). Contribution to a Theory of Database Reverse Engineering. *Proc. of the IEEE Working Conf. on Reverse Engineering*, Baltimore, May 1993, IEEE Computer Society Press.

19. Hainaut, J-L, Chandelon M., Tonneau C., Joris M. Transformational techniques for database reverse engineering. *Proc. of the 12th Int. Conf. on ER Approach*, Arlington-Dallas, ER Institute (and LNCS Springer-Verlag in 1994). (1993)

20. Hainaut, J-L. *Transformation-based database engineering*. Tutorial notes, *VLDB'95*, Zürich, Switzerland, (1995) (available at http://www.info.fundp.ac.be/libd).
21. Hainaut, J-L. Specification preservation in schema transformations - application to semantics and statistics, *Data & Knowledge Engineering*, 11(1). (1996)
22. Hainaut, J.-L., Henrard, J., Hick, J-M., Roland, D., Englebert, V. Database Design Recovery, in *Proc. of the 8th Conf. on Advanced Information Systems Engineering* (CAiSE•96), Springer-Verlag (1996)
23. Hainaut, J.-L., Hick, J.-M., Englebert, V., Henrard, J., Roland, D. Understanding implementations of IS-A Relations, in *Proc. of the conference on the ER Approach*, Cottbus, Oct. 1996, LNCS, Springer-Verlag (1996).
24. Hainaut, J-L. Transformation-based Database Engineering. In: [47]. (2005) 1–28
25. Halpin, T., A., & Proper, H., A. Database schema transformation and optimization. *Proc. of the 14th Int. Conf. on ER/OO Modelling* (ERA). (1995)
26. Henrard, J., Hick, J-M. Thiran, Ph., Hainaut, J-L. Strategies for Data Reengineering, in *Proc. of WCRE'02*, IEEE Computer Society Press. (2002)
27. Hick, J-M., Hainaut, J-L. Strategy for Database Application Evolution: the DB-MAIN Approach, in *Proc. ER'2003 conference*, Chicago, Oct. 2003, LNCS Springer-Verlag. (2003)
28. Jajodia, S., Ng, P., A., & Springsteel, F., N. The problem of Equivalence for Entity-Relationship Diagrams, *IEEE Trans. on Soft. Eng.*, SE-9(5). (1983)
29. Kobayashi, I. Losslessness and Semantic Correctness of Database Schema Transformation : another look of Schema Equivalence, *Information Systems*, 11(1). (1986) 41-59
30. Lämmel, R. Coupled Software Transformations (Extended Abstract), In *Proc. First International Workshop on Software Evolution Transformations (SET 2004).* (2004) [http://banff.cs.queensu.ca/set2004/set2004_proceedings_acrobat4.pdf]
31. Levene, M. *The Nested Universal Relation Database Model*, LNCS 595, Springer-Verlag. (1992)
32. Lien, Y., E. On the equivalence of database models, *JACM*, 29(2). (1982)
33. Ling, T., W. External schemas of Entity-Relationship based DBMS, in *Proc. of Entity-Relationship Approach : a Bridge to the User*, North-Holland. (1989)
34. McBrien P., & Poulovassilis, A. Data integration by bi-directional schema transformation rules, *Proc 19th International Conference on Data Engineering* (ICDE'03), IEEE Computer Society Press. (2003)
35. Motro, Superviews: Virtual integration of Multiple Databases, *IEEE Trans. on Soft. Eng.* SE-13, 7, (1987)
36. Navathe, S., B. Schema Analysis for Database Restructuring, *ACM TODS*, 5(2), June 1980. (1980)
37. Partsch, H., & Steinbrüggen, R. Program Transformation Systems. *Computing Surveys*, 15(3). (1983)
38. Poole, J. Model-Driven Architecture : Vision, Standards And Emerging Technologies. in *Proc. of ECOOP 2001*, Workshop on Metamodeling and Adaptive Object Models, (2001)
39. Rauh, O., & Stickel, E. Standard Transformations for the Normalization of ER Schemata. *Proc. of the CAiSE•95 Conf.*, Jyväskylä, Finland, LNCS, Springer-Verlag. (1995)
40. Roland, D. *Database engineering process modelling*, PHD Thesis, University of Namur. *http://www.info.fundp.ac.be/~dbm/publication/2003/these-dro.pdf* (2003)
41. Rosenthal, A., & Reiner, D. Theoretically sound transformations for practical database design. *Proc. of Entity-Relationship Approach.* (1988)
42. Rosenthal, & A., Reiner, D. Tools and Transformations - Rigourous and Otherwise - for Practical Database Design, *ACM TODS*, 19(2). (1994)

43. Schek, H-J., Scholl, M., H. () The relational model with relation-valued attributes, *Information Systems*, 11. (1986) 137-147
44. Thalheim, B. *Entity-Relationship Modeling: Foundation of Database Technology*. Springer-Verlag, (2000)
45. Thiran, Ph., Hainaut, J-L. Wrapper Development for Legacy Data Reuse. *Proc. of WCRE'01*, IEEE Computer Society Press. (2001)
46. Thiran, Ph., Estiévenart, F., Hainaut, J-L., Houben, G-J, A Generic Framework for Extracting XML Data from Legacy Databases, in *Journal of Web Engineering*, Rinton Press, (2005)
47. van Bommel, P. (Ed.). *Transformation of Knowledge, Information and Data: Theory and Applications*, Information Science Publ., Hershey. (2005)
48. van Griethuysen, J.J., (Ed.). Concepts and Terminology for the Conceptual Schema and the Information Base. Publ. nr. ISO/TC97/SC5-N695. (1982)

Program Optimizations and Transformations
in Calculation Form

Zhenjiang Hu, Tetsuo Yokoyama, and Masato Takeichi

Department of Mathematical Informatics
Graduate School of Information Science and Technology
The University of Tokyo
7-3-1 Hongo, Bunkyo 113-8656, Tokyo, JAPAN
{hu, takeichi}@mist.i.u-tokyo.ac.jp
yokoyama@ipl.t.u-tokyo.ac.jp

Abstract. The world of program optimization and transformation takes on a new
fascination when viewed through the lens of program calculation. Unlike the traditional fold/unfold approach to program transformation on arbitrary programs,
the calculational approach imposes restrictions on program structures, resulting in
some suitable calculational forms such as homomorphisms and mutumorphisms
that enjoy a collection of generic algebraic laws for program manipulation. In
this tutorial, we will explain the basic idea of program calculation, demonstrate
that many program optimizations and transformations, such as the optimization
technique known as loop fusion and the parallelization transformation, can be
concisely reformalized in calculational form, and show that program transformation in calculational forms is of higher modularity and more suitable for efficient
implementation.

Keywords: Program Transformation, Program Calculation, Program Optimization, Meta Programming, Functional Programming.

1 Introduction

There is a well-known Chinese proverb: aFs (one cannot have both fishes and bear
palms at the same time), implying that one can hardly obtain two treasures simultaneously. The same thing happens in our programming: clarity is and is not next to good-
ness. Clearly written programs have the desirable properties of being easy to understand, show correct, and modify, but they can also be extremely inefficient. In software
engineering, one major design technique for achieving clarity is *modularity*: breaking a
problem into independent components. But modularity can lead to inefficiency, because
of the overhead of communication between components, and because it may preclude
potential optimizations across component boundaries.

However, it is possible to have both fishes and bear palms *at different times*: we
start by writing clean and correct (but probably inefficient) programs, and then use
program calculation techniques to transform them to more efficient equivalents. To see
this, consider the problem of summing up all bigger elements in an array. An element is
bigger if it is greater than the sum of the elements that follow it till the end of the array.
We may start with the following C program, which clearly solves the problem.

R. Lämmel, J. Saraiva, and J. Visser (Eds.): GTTSE 2005, LNCS 4143, pp. 144–168, 2006.

```
/* copy all bigger elements from A[0..n-1] into B[] */
count = 0;
for (i=0; i<n; i++) {
    sumAfter = 0;
    for (j=i+1; j<n; j++) {
        sumAfter += A[j];
    }
    if (A[i] > sumAfter)
        B[count++] = A[i];
}

/* compute the sum of all elements in B[] */
sumBiggers = 0;
for (i=0; i<count; i++) {
    sumBiggers += B[i];
}
return sumBiggers;
```

This program, though being straightforward, is inefficient due to (1) some unnecessary repeated computations of `sumAfter` and (2) the use of additional array `B[]` passing from the upper for-loop to the lower for-loop. We may expect that an automatic transformation can produce the following efficient linear-time program.

```
sumBiggers = 0;
sumAfter = 0;
for (i=n-1; i>=0; i--) {
    if (A[i] > sumAfter)
        sumBiggers += A[i];
    sumAfter += A[i];
}
return sumBiggers;
```

In this paper, rather than writing programs using C or Java, we use the functional language Haskell [1, 2]. The special characteristics and advantages of functional programming are two-fold. First, it is good for writing clear and modular programs because it supports a powerful and elegant programming style. As pointed by Hughes [3], functional programming offers important advantages for software development. Second, it is good for performing transformation because of its nice mathematical properties.

We can express the above two C programs, inefficient and efficient, in Haskell, where loops are represented by recursions.

$$sumBiggers = sum \circ biggers$$
$$\textbf{where}$$
$$biggers\ [] = []$$
$$biggers\ (a : x) = \textbf{if}\ a > sum\ x\ \textbf{then}\ a : biggers\ x\ \textbf{else}\ biggers\ x$$
$$sum\ [] = 0$$
$$sum\ (a : x) = a + sum\ x$$

$$sumBiggers\ x = \textbf{let}\ (b,c) = sumBiggers'\ x\ \textbf{in}\ b$$
$$\textbf{where}$$
$$sumBiggers'\ [] = (0,0)$$
$$sumBiggers'\ (a:x) = \textbf{let}\ (b,c) = sumBiggers'\ x$$
$$\textbf{in if}\ a > c\ \textbf{then}\ (a+b, a+c)\ \textbf{else}\ (b, a+c)$$

One methodology that offers some scope for making the construction of *efficient* programs more mathematical is *transformational programming* [4, 5, 6]. *Program calculation* is a kind of program transformation based on the theory of *Constructive Algorithmics* [7, 8, 9, 10, 11, 12]. It is a kind of *transformational programming* that derives an efficient program in a step-by-step way through a series of "transformations" that preserve the meaning and hence the correctness. A significant practical problem in traditional transformational programming is that a very large number of steps seem needed: the individual steps are too small, while in program calculation, formalisms and theories are developed with which a whole series of small steps can be combined into one single step at a higher level.

Program calculation proceeds by means of manipulation of programs based on a rich collection of identities and transformation laws. It resembles the manipulation of formulas as in high school algebra: a formula F is broken up into its semantic relevant constituents and the pieces are assembled together into a different but semantically equivalent formula F', thus yielding the equality $F \equiv F'$. The following example shows a calculation of the solution of x for the equation $x^2 - c^2 = 0$.

$$x^2 - c^2 = 0$$
$$\equiv \quad \{\ \text{by identity: } a^2 - b^2 = (a-b)(a+b)\ \}$$
$$(x-c)(x+c) = 0$$
$$\equiv \quad \{\ \text{by law: } ab = 0 \Leftrightarrow a = 0 \text{ or } b = 0\ \}$$
$$x - c = 0 \text{ or } x + c = 0$$
$$\equiv \quad \{\ \text{by law: } a = b \Leftrightarrow a \pm d = b \pm d\ \}$$
$$x = c \text{ or } x = -c$$

Here we calculate x rather than guess or *just invent*, based on some identities and laws (rules). Particularly, we make use of the transformation law that a higher order equation should be factored into several first order ones whose solution can be easily obtained.

In this tutorial, we will see that *program calculation* provides a powerful tool to formalize various kinds of program transformations [13, 14, 15, 16], besides its usefulness in guiding people to derive efficient algorithms. We will explain the basic idea of program calculation from the practical point of view, demonstrate that a lot of program optimizations and transformations, including the well-known loop fusion and parallelization, can be concisely reformalized in calculational forms, and show that program transformation in calculational forms is of higher modularity and more suitable for efficient implementation.

It is worth noting that all transformations in this tutorial have been tested with the Yicho system [17], a transformation system developed at the University of Tokyo. We encourage the reader to play with the Yicho system when reading this material. The Yicho system is available at the following site.

http://www.ipl.t.u-tokyo.ac.jp/yicho/

The rest of this tutorial is organized as follows. We start with a simple example to illustrate the basic concepts of program calculation, and clarify its difference from the traditional fold/unfold transformations in Section 2. Then, we demonstrate how to formalize two nontrivial transformations, namely loop fusion and parallelization, in calculational forms in Sections 3 and 4 respectively. And we show that program calculations can be efficiently implemented by the Yicho system in Section 5. Finally, we conclude the paper with a summary of the advantages of formalizing program transformations in calculational forms in Section 6.

2 Program Calculation vs Fold/Unfold Transformations

In this section, we illustrate with a simple example the basic concepts of program calculation, show the main idea of calculational approach to program transformation, and clarify its difference from the traditional fold/unfold approach to program transformations and program optimizations.

2.1 Notational Conventions

First of all, we briefly review the notational conventions known as Bird-Meertens Formalisms [7]. The notations are similar to those in Haskell [2].

Functions. Programs are defined as functions. Function application is denoted by juxtaposition of function and argument. Thus $f\,a$ means $f\,(a)$. Functions are curried, and application associates to the left. Thus $f\,a\,b$ means $(f\,a)\,b$. Function application is regarded as more binding than any other operator, so $f\,a \oplus b$ means $(f\,a) \oplus b$, but not $f\,(a \oplus b)$. Function composition is denoted by a centralized circle $\circ$. By definition, $(f \circ g)\,a = f\,(g\,a)$. Function composition is an associative operator, and the identity function is denoted by id.

Lambda expressions are sometimes used to define a function without giving it a name. So $\lambda x.\,e$ denotes a function, accepting an input x, computing e, and returning its value as result. For example, $\lambda x.2 * x$ simply denotes a function doubling the input.

Infix binary operators will often be denoted by $\oplus, \otimes$ and can be *sectioned*; an infix binary operator like $\oplus$ can be turned into unary functions as follows.

$$(a\oplus)\,b = a \oplus b = (\oplus b)\,a$$

Lists. Lists are finite sequences of values of the same type. The type of the *cons lists* with elements of type a is defined as follows.

$$\textbf{data}\ [a] = [] \mid a : [a]$$

A list is either empty or a list constructed by inserting a new element to a list. We write $[]$ for the empty list, $[a]$ for the singleton list with element a (and $[\cdot]$ for the function taking a to $[a]$), and $x + y$ for the concatenation of two lists x and y. Concatenation is associative, and $[]$ is its unit. For example, the term $[1] + [2] + [3]$ denotes a list with three elements, often abbreviated to $[1, 2, 3]$. As seen above, we usually use a, b, c to denote list elements, and x, y, z to denote lists.

Recursive Functions. Functions may be defined recursively. The following are two recursive functions for sorting a list.

$$
\begin{aligned}
sort\ [] &= [] \\
sort\ (a : x) &= insert\ a\ (sort\ x) \\
insert\ a\ [] &= [a] \\
insert\ a\ (b : x) &= \textbf{if}\ a \geq b\ \textbf{then}\ a : (b : x) \\
&\quad\quad \textbf{else}\ b : insert\ a\ x
\end{aligned}
$$

Here *sort* is recursively called in its definition body, and so does *insert*.

Higher Order Functions. Higher order functions are functions which can take other functions as arguments, and may also return functions as results. A simple but useful higher order function is *map*, which applies a function to each element of a list. For instance, we may write *map* $(1+)$ to increase each element of a list by 1.

$$
map\ (1+)\ [1, 2, 3, 4, 5] = [2, 3, 4, 5, 6]
$$

2.2   The Fold/Unfold Approach to Program Transformation

Before explaining the calculational approach [7, 18, 9, 12] to program transformation, the topic of this tutorial, let us take a look at the traditional unfold/fold approach [4, 5, 6, 19] and explain its problems.

To be concrete, consider the problem of finding a maximum in a list. Suppose that we already have *sort* (as defined above) in hand. Then, a direct solution is to sort the input and to return the first element:

$$
max\ x\ =\ hd\ (sort\ x)
$$

where *hd* is a function to return the first element from a list if the list is not empty, and to return $-\infty$ otherwise:

$$
\begin{aligned}
hd\ [] &= -\infty \\
hd\ (a : x) &= a.
\end{aligned}
$$

This solution is obviously inefficient; it is a quadratic algorithm.

Let us demonstrate how to apply the fold/unfold transformations to obtain a new efficient recursive definition for *max*. For the base case, we unfold the definition step by step.

$$
\begin{aligned}
&max\ [] \\
=\ &\{\ \text{unfold } max\ \} \\
&hd\ (sort\ []) \\
=\ &\{\ \text{unfold } sort\ \} \\
&hd\ [] \\
=\ &\{\ \text{unfold } hd\ \} \\
&-\infty
\end{aligned}
$$

Then for the recursive case, we do unfolding similarly.

$$max\ (a : x)$$
$$=\quad \{ \text{ unfold } max \}$$
$$hd\ (sort\ (a : x))$$
$$=\quad \{ \text{ unfold } sort \}$$
$$hd\ (insert\ a\ (sort\ x))$$

We get stuck here; we cannot perform folding to get a recursive definition unless more information is exposed. To expose more information, we unfold *insert*, by assuming $b : x' = sort\ x$, that is

$$b\ = hd\ (sort\ x)$$
$$x' = tail\ (sort\ x)$$

and continue our transformation.

$$hd\ (insert\ a\ (b : x'))$$
$$=\quad \{ \text{ unfold } insert \}$$
$$hd\ (\textbf{if}\ a \geq b\ \textbf{then}\ a : (b : x')\ \textbf{else}\ b : insert\ a\ x')$$
$$=\quad \{ \text{ law: } f\ (\textbf{if}\ b\ \textbf{then}\ e_1\ \textbf{else}\ e_2) = \textbf{if}\ b\ \textbf{then}\ f\ e_1\ \textbf{else}\ f\ e_2 \}$$
$$\textbf{if}\ a \geq b\ \textbf{then}\ hd\ (a : (b : x'))\ \textbf{else}\ hd\ (b : insert\ a\ x')$$
$$=\quad \{ \text{ unfold } hd \}$$
$$\textbf{if}\ a \geq b\ \textbf{then}\ a\ \textbf{else}\ b$$
$$=\quad \{ \text{ unfold } b \}$$
$$\textbf{if}\ a \geq hd\ (sort\ x)\ \textbf{then}\ a\ \textbf{else}\ hd\ (sort\ x)$$
$$=\quad \{ \textbf{ fold } max \}$$
$$\textbf{if}\ a \geq max\ x\ \textbf{then}\ a\ \textbf{else}\ max\ x$$

The last folding step is the key to the success of the derivation of the following efficient program.

$$max\ []\qquad = -\infty$$
$$max\ (a : x) = \textbf{if}\ a \geq max\ x\ \textbf{then}\ a\ \textbf{else}\ max\ x$$

The fold/unfold approach to program transformation is general and powerful, but it suffers from several problems which often prevent it from being used in practice.

- It is difficult to decide when unfolding steps should stop while guaranteeing exposition of enough information for later folding steps.
- It is expensive to implement, because it requires keeping records of all possible folding patterns and have them checked upon any new subexpressions produced during transformation.
- Each transformation step is very small, but an effective way is lacking to group and/or structure them into bigger steps.

2.3   Program Transformations in Calculational Form

A distinguished feature of the calculational approach to program transformation is *no use of folding during transformation*, which solves the first two problems the fold/unfold approach has, and the challenge is how to formalize necessary folding steps by means of calculation laws (rules). Transformations that are based on a set of calculation laws but exclude the use of folding steps will be called *transformation in calculation form* in this paper. The calculational approach to program transformation advocates more *structured* programming, where the inner structure of a loop (recursion) is taken into account.

Procedure to Formalize Transformations in Calculational Form

The procedure to formalize a program transformation in calculational form consists of the following three major steps.

1. Define a specific form of programs that are best suitable for the transformation and can be used to describe a class of interesting computations.
2. Develop calculational rules (laws) for implementing the transformation on programs in the specific form.
3. Show how to turn more general programs into those in the specific form and how to apply the newly developed calculational rules systematically.

The first step plays a very important role in this formalization. The specific form defined in the first step should meet two requirements. First, it should be powerful enough to describe computations of our interest. Second, it should be manipulable and suitable for later development of calculational laws. In fact, the *Constructive Algorithmics* theory [7, 18, 9, 10] provides us a nice theoretical framework to define such specific forms and to develop calculational rules.

In Constructive Algorithmics, the calculations are based on calculation rules that are built upon the algebra of programs, a collection of identities. These identities can be provided by exploiting the algebraic structure of the algebraic data concerned, such as lists or trees. In particular, there is a close correspondence between data structures (terms in an algebra) and control structures (homomorphisms mapping from that algebra to another). This correspondence is well captured by categorical functors, which are very theoretical and fall outside the scope of this tutorial.

Homomorphisms: General Structured Recursive Functions

Recall the structured programming methodology for imperative language, where the use of arbitrary goto's is abandoned in favor of structured control flow primitives such as conditionals and while-loop so that program transformation becomes easier and elegant. For high level algorithmic programming like functional programming, recursive definitions provide a powerful control mechanism for specifying programs. Consider the following recursive definition on lists:

$$f (a : x) = \cdots f\, x \cdots f\, (g\, x) \cdots f\, (f\, x) \cdots$$

There is usually no specific restriction on the right hand side; it can be any expression where recursive calls to f may be of any form and appear anywhere. This somehow resembles the arbitrary use of goto's in imperative programs, which makes recursive definitions hard to manipulate. In contrast, the calculational approach imposes suitable restrictions on the right hand side resulting in a suitable calculation form. Homomorphisms are one of the most general and important calculational forms.

Homomorphisms are functions that manipulate algebraic data structures such as lists and trees. They are derivable from the concerned structure of the algebraic data. Recall the list data structure $[\alpha]$. It can be considered as the algebra of

$$([\alpha], [] :: [\alpha], (:) :: a \to [\alpha] \to [\alpha])$$

in which the carrier $[\alpha]$ denotes all lists whose elements are of type α, and two operations, namely $[]$ with type $[\alpha]$ and $(:)$ with type $a \to [\alpha] \to [\alpha]$, are the data constructors for building up lists. An important recursive form known as list homomorphism hom_l, capturing a basic recursive form of recursive functions over lists, maps from this algebra to another similar one, say $(R, e :: R, (\oplus) :: a \to R \to R)$, and is defined by

$$
\begin{aligned}
hom_l & :: [\alpha] \to R \\
hom_l \ [] & = e \\
hom_l \ (a : x) & = a \oplus hom_l \ x.
\end{aligned}
$$

In essence, hom_l is a *relabeling*: it replaces every occurrence of $[]$ with e and every occurrence of $:$ with $\oplus$ in the cons list. Since such a list homomorphism is uniquely determined by e and $\oplus$, we usually describe it by

$$hom_l = ([e, \oplus])_l$$

and when it is clear from the context, we may omit the subscript l which is used to denote homomorphism on lists.

List homomorphisms are important in defining functions to manipulate lists. The following lists several useful functions: *sum* sums up all elements of a list, *prod* multiples all elements of a list, *maxlist* returns the maximum element of a list, *reverse* reverses a list, *inits* computes all initial prefix lists of a list, and *map f* applies function f to every element of a list.

$$
\begin{aligned}
sum &= ([0, +]) \\
prod &= ([1, \times]) \\
maxlist &= ([-\infty, \uparrow]) && \textbf{where } a \uparrow r = \textbf{if } a \geq r \textbf{ then } a \textbf{ else } r \\
reverse &= ([[], \oplus]) && \textbf{where } a \oplus r = r ++ [a] \\
inits &= ([[[]], \oplus]) && \textbf{where } a \oplus r = [] : map \ (a :) \ r \\
map \ f &= ([[], \oplus]) && \textbf{where } a \oplus r = f \ a : r
\end{aligned}
$$

For a complicated computation on lists, it may be difficult to define it by a single homomorphism, but it should be easy to define it by composition (combination) of simpler homomorphisms. For example, the following gives a clear program for computing the maximum sum of all initial segments of a list:

$$mis = maxlist \circ (map \ sum) \circ inits$$

which is defined by composition of several list homomorphisms.

Similar studies can be addressed on trees or other algebraic data structures. In this tutorial, we shall focus ourselves on lists.

Promotion Rule

Homomorphisms enjoy many calculation properties. Among them, the following promotion rule is of great importance, saying that a composition of a function with a homomorphism can be merged into a single homomorphism under a certain condition.

$$\text{promotion:} \quad \frac{f\,(a \oplus x) = a \otimes f\,x}{f \circ (\![e, \oplus]\!) = (\![f\,e, \otimes]\!)}$$

If functions are defined only by homomorphisms rather than by arbitrary recursive definitions, we can use the promotion rule to manipulate them. Recall the example of computing the maximum from a list early this section:

$$max = hd \circ sort$$

Inefficiency of this program lies in that $sort\ x$ computes a result that contains too much useless information for the later computation by hd. The standard way is to fuse the two functions hd and $sort$ into a single one which does not include unnecessary computation. Fusion based on the fold/unfold transformations has been explained before. Let us see how to calculate an efficient max with the promotion calculation rule. Notice that $sort = (\![[], insert]\!)$. The promotion rule tells us that if we can derive $\otimes$ such that

$$\forall a, x.\ hd\ (insert\ a\ x) = a \otimes hd\ x$$

then we can transform $hd \circ sort$ to $(\![-\infty, \otimes]\!)$. This $\otimes$ may be obtained via a higher order matching algorithm [20]. Here, we show another concise calculation.

$$
\begin{aligned}
a \otimes b = \quad & \{\text{ let } x \text{ be any list }\} \\
& a \otimes hd\ (b : x) \\
= \quad & \{\text{ the condition in the promotion rule }\} \\
& hd\ (insert\ a\ (b : x)) \\
= \quad & \{\text{ definition of } insert\ \} \\
& hd\ (\textbf{if } a \geq b \textbf{ then } a : (b : x) \textbf{ else } b : insert\ a\ x) \\
= \quad & \{\text{ if property }\} \\
& \textbf{if } a \geq b \textbf{ then } hd\ (a : (b : x)) \textbf{ else } hd\ (b : insert\ a\ x) \\
= \quad & \{\text{ definition of } hd\ \} \\
& \textbf{if } a \geq b \textbf{ then } a \textbf{ else } b
\end{aligned}
$$

In summary, we have derived the following definition for max.

$$max = (\![-\infty, \otimes]\!)$$
$$\textbf{where } a \otimes b = \textbf{if } a \geq b \textbf{ then } a \textbf{ else } b$$

And it is equivalent to

$$
\begin{aligned}
max\ [] \quad &= -\infty \\
max\ (a : x) &= \textbf{if } a \geq max\ x \textbf{ then } a \textbf{ else } max\ x
\end{aligned}
$$

which is the same as the result obtained by the fold/unfold program transformation before. It is worth noting that the transformation here does not need any folding step, rather we focus on deriving a new operator from the condition of the promotion rule.

3   Loop Fusion in Calculation Form

In this section, we demonstrate how to formalize *loop fusion* in calculational form. Loop fusion, a well-known optimization technique in compiler construction [21, 22], is to fuse some adjacent loops into one loop to reduce loop overhead and improve run-time performance. In the introduction, we have seen an inefficient program for *sumBiggers* which consists of three loops, and an equivalent efficient one which uses only a single loop.

In our framework, loops are specified by recursive definitions. There are basically three cases for two adjacent loops: (1) one loop is put after another and the result computed by the first is used by the second; (2) one loop is put after another and the result computed by the first is not used by the second; and (3) one loop is used inside another. The second case is much simpler. We have seen the first and the third cases in the definition of *sumBiggers* in the introduction. Recall the following definition of *sumBiggers*:

$$
\begin{aligned}
\textit{sumBiggers} \quad &= \textit{sum} \circ \textit{biggers} \\
\textit{biggers} \; [] \quad &= [] \\
\textit{biggers} \; (a : x) &= \textbf{if } a > \textit{sum } x \textbf{ then } a : \textit{biggers } x \textbf{ else } \textit{biggers } x \\
\textit{sum} \; [] \quad &= 0 \\
\textit{sum} \; (a : x) \quad &= a + \textit{sum } x
\end{aligned}
$$

The use of one loop after another is specified by a composition of two recursive functions (*sum* ∘ *biggers*), and a nested loop is specified by other function calls applying to the same input data in the definition body (*sum x* appears in the definition body of *biggers*).

We shall illustrate how to formalize the loop fusion in calculational form by the three steps in Section 2.3.

3.1   Structured Recursive Form for Loop Fusion

Now we are facing the problem of choosing a proper structured form for recursive functions. There are two basic requirements for this form. First, it should be powerful enough to describe computation that manipulates lists. Second, it should be suitable for loop fusion, where the three cases of loop combination can be coped with. We would like to show that list mutumorphism is a suitable form for this purpose.

Definition 1 ((List) Mutumorphism). A function f_1 is said to be a list mutumorphism with respect to other functions $f_2, \ldots, f_n$ if each f_i $(i = 1, 2, \ldots, n)$ is defined in the following form:

$$
\begin{aligned}
f_i \; [] \quad &= e_i \\
f_i \; (a : x) &= a \oplus_i (f_1 \, x, f_2 \, x, \ldots, f_n \, x)
\end{aligned}
$$

where e_i $(i = 1, 2, \ldots, n)$ are given constants and $\oplus_i$ $(i = 1, 2, \ldots, n)$ are given binary functions. We represent f_1 as follows.

$$
f_1 = [\![(e_1, \ldots, e_n), (\oplus_1, \ldots, \oplus_n)]\!].
$$

$\square$

List mutumorphisms have strong expressive power, covering all primitive recursive functions on lists. It should be noted that list homomorphisms are a special case of list mutumorphisms:

$$([e, \oplus]) = [\![(e), (\oplus)]\!]$$

Recall the *sumBiggers*. We may redefine *sum* and *biggers* in terms of mutumorphisms (or homomorphism) as below.

$$sumBiggers = ([0, +]) \circ [\![([], 0), (\oplus_1, \oplus_2)]\!]$$
$$\textbf{where } a \oplus_1 (r, s) = \textbf{if } a > s \textbf{ then } a : r \textbf{ else } r$$
$$a \oplus_2 (r, s) = a + s$$

3.2   Calculational Rules for Loop Fusion

After formalizing loops by mutumorphisms, we turn to develop calculation rules (laws) for fusing such loops. We will consider the three cases for loop combination.

First, we consider merging nested loops. Mutumorphism itself is actually a nested loop, as seen in the definition of *biggers*. We may flatten this kind of nested loops by the following flattening calculation rule [14].

Lemma 1 (Flattening).

$$[\![(e_1, e_2, \ldots, e_n), (\oplus_1, \oplus_2, \ldots, \oplus_n)]\!] = \textit{fst} \circ [\![(e_1, e_2, \ldots, e_n), \oplus]\!]$$
$$\textbf{where } a \oplus r = (a \oplus_1 r, a \oplus_2 r, \ldots, a \oplus_n r)$$

Here, *fst* is a projection function returning the first element of a tuple.   □

The flattening calculation rule, as its name suggests, flattens a nested loop represented by a mutumorphism to a homomorphism. Consider, as an example, to apply the flattening rule to *biggers* to flatten the nested loop.

$$biggers$$
$$= \quad \{ \text{ mutumorphism for } biggers \ \}$$
$$[\![([], 0), (\oplus_1, \oplus_2)]\!]$$
$$= \quad \{ \text{ flattening rule } \}$$
$$\textit{fst} \circ [\![([], 0), \oplus]\!]$$
$$\textbf{where } a \oplus (r, s) = (\textbf{if } a > s \textbf{ then } a : r \textbf{ else } r, a + s)$$

Inlining the homomorphism in the derived program gives the following readable recursive program, which consists of a single loop.

$$biggers \; x = \textbf{let } (r, s) = hom \; x \textbf{ in } r$$
$$\textbf{where } hom \; [] = ([], 0)$$
$$hom \; (a : x) = \textbf{let } (r, s) = hom \; x$$
$$\textbf{in } (\textbf{if } a > s \textbf{ then } a : r \textbf{ else } r, a + s)$$

Second, we try to merge two independent loops. Since mutumorphism can be transformed into homomorphism, it is suffice to consider merging of two independent homomorphisms that manipulate the same lists. This can be done by the tupling transformation [23], whose calculation form is summarized as follows [14].

Lemma 2 (Tupling).

$$(([\![e_1, \oplus_1]\!]) \ x, \ ([\![e_2, \oplus_2]\!]) \ x) = ([\![(e_1, e_2), \oplus]\!]) \ x$$
$$\textbf{where } a \oplus (r_1, r_2) = (a \oplus_1 r_1, a \oplus_2 r_2) \qquad \square$$

For example, the following program to compute the average of a list:

$$average \ x = sum \ x / length \ x$$

which has two loops can be merged into a single loop by applying the tupling rule.

$$average \ x = \textbf{let } (s, l) = tup \ x \textbf{ in } s/l$$
$$\textbf{where } tup = ([\![(0, 0), \lambda a \ (s, l). \ (a + s, 1 + l)]\!])$$

Here, to save space we choose to use lambda expression to define the new binary operator, which accepts a and (s, l), and returns $(a + s, 1 + l)$.

Finally, we consider fusion of two loops where the result of one loop is used by the other. When the loops are formalized as homomorphisms, we can use the promotion rule in Section 2.3 for this fusion, as seen in the example of fusing $hd \circ sort$. The promotion rule fuses function f to a homomorphism from left:

$$f \circ ([\![e, \oplus]\!])$$

and the following calculation rule [24, 25] shows how to fuse a function to a homomorphism from right.

Lemma 3 (Shortcut Fusion).

$$([\![e, \oplus]\!]) \circ build \ g = g \ (e, \oplus)$$

Here, the function *build* is a list production function defined by[1]

$$build \ g = g \ ([], (:)). \qquad \square$$

The shortcut fusion rule indicates that if one can express a function in *build*, then it can be cheaply fused into a homomorphism from its right. Compared with the promotion rule, the shortcut fusion rule is much simpler and cheap to implement, because it is just a simple expression substitution. On the other hand, it needs a preparation of deriving a build form from a homomorphism. The following warm-up rule is for this purpose.

Lemma 4 (Warm-up).

$$([\![e, \oplus]\!]) = build \ (\lambda(d, \otimes). \ ([\![d, \otimes]\!]) \circ ([\![e, \oplus]\!])) \qquad \square$$

Note that the warm-up rule may introduce an additional loop, but this loop is usually easier to be fused with others. Recall that we have obtained the following definition for *biggers*.

---

[1] Strictly speaking, it requires parametricity on the type of g, as studied in [24].

$$biggers = fst \circ ([([], 0), \oplus])$$
$$\textbf{where } a \oplus (r, s) = (\textbf{if } a > s \textbf{ then } a : r \textbf{ else } r, a + s)$$

We can obtain the following build form:

$$biggers = build \ (\lambda(d, \otimes). \ fst \circ ([(d, 0), \oplus']))$$
$$\textbf{where } a \oplus' (r, s) = (\textbf{if } a > s \textbf{ then } a \otimes r \textbf{ else } r, a + s)$$

Now applying the shortcut fusion rule to

$$sumBiggers = ([0, +]) \circ bigger$$

soon yields the following single-loop program for *sumBiggers*:

$$sumBiggers = fst \circ ([(0, 0), \otimes])$$
$$\textbf{where } a \otimes (r, s) = (\textbf{if } a > s \textbf{ then } a + r \textbf{ else } r, a + s)$$

which is actually the same as that in the introduction.

Before finishing our development of calculation rules for loop fusion, we give another calculation rule for fusing a function with a mutumorphism. This may not be necessary as mutumorphism can be transformed into homomorphism, but it may provide us with more flexibility in rule application.

Lemma 5 (Mutumorphism Promotion).

$$\frac{f_i(a \oplus_i (x_1, \ldots, x_n)) = a \otimes_i (f_1 \ x_1, \ldots, f_n \ x_n) \quad (i = 1, \ldots, n)}{f_1 \circ [[(e_1, \ldots, e_n), (\oplus_1, \ldots, \oplus_n)]] = [[(f_1 \ e_1, \ldots, f_n \ e_n), (\otimes_1, \ldots, \otimes_n)]]} \qquad \square$$

3.3 A Calculational Algorithm for Loop Fusion

This is the last step, where we should make it clear how to turn a program into our specific form and how to apply the newly developed calculational laws in a systematic way for loop fusion, as seen in [26, 14, 15]. Below we summarize our calculational algorithm for loop fusion.

1. Represent as many recursive functions on lists by mutumorphisms as possible.
2. Apply the flattening rule to transform all mutumorphism to homomorphisms.
3. Apply the promotion rule and shortcut fusion rule as much as possible.
4. Apply the tupling rule to merge independent homomorphisms.
5. Inline homomorphism/mutumorphism to output transformed program in a friendly manner.

We have indeed followed this algorithm in fusing the three loops in *sumBiggers*. One remark should be made on the first step above. It would be unnecessary if programs are restricted to be strictly written in terms of mutumorphisms, but there are two reasons to have it. First, it makes our system extensible; we may extend our system by showing that a wider class of functions can be transformed to mutumorphisms by some preprocessing. For example, the following recursive function

$$foo\ [] \qquad = 0$$
$$foo\ [a] \qquad = a$$
$$foo\ (a : b : x) = a + foo\ (b : x) + foo\ x$$

may not be target for loop fusion at the start. When we find a way to express functions like *foo* in terms of a mutumorphism, we can empower our system by adding it as a pre-processing. In fact, it has been shown that *foo* belongs to the class of tuplable functions which can be automatically transformed to a function defined in terms of homomorphisms [14]. Second, we may want to apply our loop fusion to legacy programs. As a matter of fact, it is possible to obtain mutumorphism automatically from many recursive functions on lists.

4   Parallelization in Calculation Form

Our second example is about Parallelization [27, 15], a transformation for automatically generating parallel code from high level sequential description. Parallelization is of key importance to the wide spread use of high performance machine architectures, but it is a big challenge to clarify what kind of sequential programs can be parallelized and how they can be systematically parallelized.

Program calculation suggests a new way to face this challenge. We know from the theory of Constructive Algorithmics that the control structure of the program should be determined by the data structure the program is to manipulate. For lists, there are two possible views. One view is known as cons lists, which is "sequential": a list is constructed by an empty list, or from an element and a list.

$$ConsList\ a\ =\ []\ |\ a : ConsList\ a$$

Another view is known as join lists, which is "parallel": a list is an empty list, or a singleton list, or a list joining two shorter lists.

$$JoinList\ a\ =\ []\ |\ [.]\ a\ |\ JoinList\ a + \!\!\!+ JoinList\ a$$

So given a list $[1, 2, 3, 4, 5, 6, 7, 8]$, we may represent it in the following two ways:

$$1 : (2 : (3 : (4 : (5 : (6 : (7 : (8 : [])))))))$$
$$(([1] +\!\!\!+ [2]) +\!\!\!+ ([3] +\!\!\!+ [4])) +\!\!\!+ ((([5] +\!\!\!+ [6]) +\!\!\!+ ([7] +\!\!\!+ [8]))$$

Programs defined on cons lists inherit sequentiality from cons lists, while programs defined on join lists gain parallelism from join lists. The following are two such versions for *sum*.

$$sumS\ (a : x)\ \ = a + sumS\ x$$
$$sumP\ (x +\!\!\!+ y) = sumP\ x + sumP\ y$$

With the above in mind, we may consider parallelization of functions on lists as mapping a function on cons lists (e.g., *sumS*) to an equivalent one on join lists (e.g., *sumP*).

4.1 J-Homomorphism: A Parallel Form for List Functions

As in loop fusion, we introduce a recursive form, J-homomorphism[2], to capture parallel computations on lists.

Definition 2 (J-Homomorphism). *J-homomorphisms* are those functions on finite lists that *promote* through list concatenation — that is, function h for which there exists an associative binary operator $\oplus$ such that, for all finite lists x and y, we have

$$h\,(x +\!\!+ y) = h\,x \,\oplus\, h\,y$$

where $+\!\!+$ denotes list concatenation.   □

In fact, it has been attracting wide attention to make use of J-homomorphisms in parallel programming [28, 30, 31]. Intuitively, the definition of J-homomorphisms means that the value of h on the larger list depends in a particular way (using binary operation $\oplus$) on the values of h applied to the two pieces of the list. The computations of $h\,x$ and $h\,y$ are independent of each other and can thus be carried out in parallel. This simple equation can be viewed as expressing the well-known divide-and-conquer paradigm of parallel programming.

As a running example, consider the *maximum segment sum problem*, which finds the maximum of the sums of contiguous segments within a list of integers. For example,

$$mss\ [3, -4, 2, -1, 6, -3] = 7$$

where the result is contributed by the segment $[2, -1, 6]$. We may write the following sequential function *mss* to solve the problem, where *mis* is to compute the maximum initial-segment sum of a list.

$$
\begin{aligned}
mss\ [] &= 0 \\
mss\ (a : x) &= a \uparrow (a + mis\ x) \uparrow mss\ x \\
mis\ [] &= 0 \\
mis\ (a : x) &= a \uparrow (a + mis\ x)
\end{aligned}
$$

How can we find an equivalent parallel program in J-homomorphism?

4.2 A Parallelizing Rule

In Section 3, we have seen that list homomorphisms play a very important role in describing computations on lists. Our parallelization rule is to show how to map a list homomorphism to a J-homomorphism. As a preparation, we define the composition-closed[3] property of a function.

Definition 3 (Composition-closed). Let $\overline{x}$ denote a sequence $x_1\ x_2\ \cdots\ x_n$, and $\overline{y}$ denote a sequence $y_1\ y_2\ \cdots\ y_n$. A function $f\ \overline{x}$ is said to be composition-closed if there exist n functions $g_i\ (i = 1, \cdots, n)$, so that

$$f\ \overline{x}\ (f\ \overline{y}) = f\ (g_1\ \overline{x}\ \overline{y})\ (g_2\ \overline{x}\ \overline{y})\ \cdots\ (g_n\ \overline{x}\ \overline{y})\ r   □$$

---

[2] It is usually called list homomorphism in many literatures [7, 28, 29]. We call it J-homomorphism here because we have used the word list homomorphism in loop fusion.

[3] This property is called context-preservation in [32].

For example, the function

$$f\ x_1\ x_2\ r = x_1 \uparrow (x_2 + r)$$

is composition-closed, as seen in the following calculation.

$$
\begin{aligned}
&f\ x_1\ x_2\ (f\ y_1\ y_2\ r)\\
=\quad &\{\text{ definition of } f \}\\
&x_1 \uparrow (x_2 + (y_1 \uparrow (y_2 + r)))\\
=\quad &\{\text{ since } a + (b \uparrow c) = (a + b) \uparrow (a + c) \}\\
&x_1 \uparrow ((x_2 + y_1) \uparrow (x_2 + (y_2 + r)))\\
=\quad &\{\text{ associativity of } + \text{ and } \uparrow \}\\
&(x_1 \uparrow (x_2 + y_1)) \uparrow ((x_2 + y_2) + r)\\
=\quad &\{\text{ define } g_1\ x_1\ x_2\ y_1\ y_2 = (x_1 \uparrow (x_2 + y_1)),\ g_2\ x_1\ x_2\ y_1\ y_2 = x_2 + y_2 \}\\
&(g_1\ x_1\ x_2\ y_1\ y_2) \uparrow (g_2\ x_1\ x_2\ y_1\ y_2 + r)
\end{aligned}
$$

The following is our main calculation rule for parallelizing homomorphisms to J-homomorphisms.

Lemma 6 (Parallelization of Homomorphism to J-Homomorphism). Given a homomorphism $([e, \oplus])$, if there exists a composition-closed function f with respect to $g_1, g_2, \ldots, g_n$, such that

$$a \oplus r = f\ e_1\ e_2\ \cdots\ e_n\ r$$

where e_i is an expression which may contain a but not r, then

$$([e, \oplus])\ x = \mathbf{let}\ (a_1, a_2, \ldots, a_n) = h\ x\ \mathbf{in}\ f\ a_1\ a_2\ \cdots\ a_n\ e$$

where h is a J-homomorphism defined by

$$
\begin{aligned}
h\ [a]\quad &= (e_1, e_2, \ldots, e_n)\\
h(x +\!\!+ y) &= h\ x \otimes h\ y\\
&\mathbf{where}\ \overline{x} \otimes \overline{y} = (g_1\ \overline{x}\ \overline{y})\ (g_2\ \overline{x}\ \overline{y})\ \cdots\ (g_n\ \overline{x}\ \overline{y}) \qquad \square
\end{aligned}
$$

To see how this parallelization rule works, consider to parallelize the function *mis*, which is actually a homomorphism:

$$mis = ([0, \oplus])\ \mathbf{where}\ a \oplus r = a \uparrow (a + r)$$

The difficulty is to find a composition-closed function from $\oplus$. In fact, such function f is

$$f\ x_1\ x_2\ r = x_1 \uparrow (x_2 + r)$$

whose composition-closed property has been shown. Now we have

$$a \oplus r = f\ a\ a\ r.$$

Applying Lemma 6 to *mis* gives the following parallel program:

$$mis\ x = \mathbf{let}\ (a_1, a_2) = h\ x\ \mathbf{in}\ a_1 \uparrow (a_2 + e)$$

where

$$h\ [a] \quad\ = (a, a)$$
$$h\ (x + y) = h\ x \otimes h\ y$$
$$\textbf{where}\ (x_1, x_2) \otimes (y_1, y_2) = (x_1 \uparrow (x_2 + y_1), x_2 + y_2).$$

4.3   A Parallelization Algorithm

After developing a general calculation rule for parallelizing general homomorphisms to J-homomorphisms, we propose the following algorithm to systematically apply it to parallelize sequential programs in practice. The input to the algorithm is a program defined in terms of mutumorphisms, and the output is a new program where parallelism is explicitly described by J-homomorphisms.

1. Apply the loop fusion calculation to the program to obtain a compact program defined in terms of homomorphisms.
2. Apply the parallelizing rule to map homomorphisms to J-homomorphisms.

The first step has been explained in details in Section 3. The second step is the core of the algorithm, where the key to applying the parallelizing rule is to find a suitable composition-closed function from the definition of the binary operator in a homomorphism. It has been shown in [33] that a powerful normalization algorithm can be applied to derive such composition-closed functions. The details of the normalization algorithm is beyond the scope of this tutorial.

Return to the program of *mss*. First, we apply the loop fusion calculation to obtain

$$mss = fst \circ mss\_mis$$

where *mss_mis* is the homomorphism defined below:

$$mss\_mis = (\![(0, 0), \oplus]\!)$$
$$\textbf{where}\ a \oplus (s, i) = (a \uparrow (a + i) \uparrow s, a \uparrow (a + i)).$$

Then, we apply the parallelizing rule to map *mss_mis* to a J-homomorphism to make parallelism explicit. To this end, we define the following composition-closed function by the algorithm in [33]:

$$f\ x_1\ x_2\ x_3\ x_4\ x_5\ (s, i) = (x_1 \uparrow (x_2 + i) \uparrow (x_3 + s), x_4 \uparrow (x_5 + i))$$

with respect to g_1, g_2, g_3, g_4, g_5 defined by

$$g_1\ x_1\ x_2\ x_3\ x_4\ x_5\ y_1\ y_2\ y_3\ y_4\ y_5 = x_1 \uparrow (x_2 + y_4) \uparrow (x_3 + y_1)$$
$$g_2\ x_1\ x_2\ x_3\ x_4\ x_5\ y_1\ y_2\ y_3\ y_4\ y_5 = (x_2 + y_5) \uparrow (x_3 + y_2)$$
$$g_3\ x_1\ x_2\ x_3\ x_4\ x_5\ y_1\ y_2\ y_3\ y_4\ y_5 = x_3 + y_3$$
$$g_4\ x_1\ x_2\ x_3\ x_4\ x_5\ y_1\ y_2\ y_3\ y_4\ y_5 = x_4 \uparrow (x_5 + y_4)$$
$$g_5\ x_1\ x_2\ x_3\ x_4\ x_5\ y_1\ y_2\ y_3\ y_4\ y_5 = x_5 + y_5$$

And we have

$$a \oplus (s, i) = f \, a \, a \, 0 \, a \, a \, (i, s).$$

By applying the parallelizing rule we soon obtain the following efficient parallel program for mss_mis:

$$mss\_mis \; x = \mathbf{let} \; (a_1, a_2, a_3, a_4, a_5) = h \, x \; \mathbf{in} \; f \, a_1 \, a_2 \, a_3 \, a_4 \, a_5 \, (0, 0)$$

where h is a J-homomorphism defined as follows.

$$
\begin{aligned}
h \, [a] &= (a, a, 0, a, a) \\
h(x +\!\!+ y) &= h \, x \otimes h \, y \\
\mathbf{where} \; (x_1, x_2.x_3.x_4.x_5) &\otimes (y_1, y_2, y_3, y_4, y_5) \\
&= (x_1 \uparrow (x_2 + y_4) \uparrow (x_3 + y_1), \\
&\quad (x_2 + y_5) \uparrow (x_3 + y_2), \\
&\quad x_3 + y_3, \\
&\quad x_4 \uparrow (x_5 + y_4), \\
&\quad x_5 + y_5)
\end{aligned}
$$

As an exercise, the readers are invited to parallelize the homomorphism for *sumBiggers* in Section 3.

5 Yicho: An Environment for Implementing Transformations in Calculational Forms

Program Calculation rules are short and concise, but their implementations are not as easy as one may expect. Many attempts [20, 17] have been made to develop systems for supporting direct and efficient implementation of calculation rules. Yicho is such a system built upon Template Haskell [34] and designed for concise specification of program calculations [35]. Its main feature lies in its *expressive deterministic higher-order patterns* [17] together with an efficient deterministic higher-order matching algorithm. This leads to a straightforward description of calculation rules.

In this section, we briefly review the Yicho system, before illustrating with some examples how calculation rules and calculation algorithms can be implemented efficiently.

5.1 Program Representation

We manipulate programs as values by meta-programming. Template Haskell [34] provides a mechanism to handle abstract syntax trees of Haskell in Haskell itself. Enclosing a program in brackets `[| |]` yields its abstract syntax tree of type `ExpQ`, and the inverse operation is unquote described by a dollar `$`. For example, given a function to calculate the sum of a given list, `sum`, which has type[4] `[Int] -> Int`. Quotation of this function `[| sum |]` has type `ExpQ`, whereas `$([| sum |])` has the same type as `sum`, i.e., `[Int] -> Int`.

---

[4] Strictly speaking, the type of function sum is $Num \; a \Rightarrow [a] \rightarrow a$ in Haskell. Here, for simplicity, we ignore type classes and polymorphism.

The following gives the representation of the initial program of *max*.

```
def =
  [d|
        max = hd . sort

        sort [] = []
        sort (a:x) = insert a (sort x)

        insert a [] = b
        insert a (b:x) = if a >= b then a : (b : x)
                                   else b : insert a x
  |]
```

Here, quasi-quote bracket [d| _ |] is syntax of Template Haskell. It quotes a list of declaration whose type is Q [Dec]. These definitions are spliced by unquote $ by $(def).

5.2   Basic Combinators for Programming Calculations

Yicho is implemented as a monadic combinator library for program transformation in Haskell. The combinator library uses *deterministic higher-order patterns* as first-class values which can be passed as parameters, constructed by smaller ones in compositional way, returned as values, etc. As a result, Yicho's patterns provide more flexible binding than first-order ones, and enables more abstract and modular descriptions of program transformation.

We define the calculation monad Y, a combination of the state monad and the error monad, to capture updating of transformation environments and to handle exceptions that occur during transformation, and we use ExpY

$$ExpY = Y\ ExpQ$$

to denote an expression in the calculation environment. We use liftY to lift ExpQ into ExpY, and use runY to go back to ExpQ from ExpY.

$$liftY :: ExpQ \rightarrow ExpY$$
$$runY\ :: ExpY \rightarrow ExpQ$$

There are five important combinators in our Yichi library, as listed below.

Match	(<==) :: ExpQ -> ExpQ -> Y ()	
Rule	(==>) :: ExpQ -> ExpQ -> RuleY	
Sequence	(>>) :: Y () -> Y () -> Y ()	
Choice	(<+) :: ExpY -> ExpY -> ExpY	
Case	casem :: ExpQ -> [RuleY] -> ExpY	

In the following, we explain them one by one with some examples.

Match

The most essential combinator is the match combinator, which is used to match a pattern with a term and produce a substitution (embedded in monadic Y).

```
(<==) :: ExpQ -> ExpQ -> Y ()
pat <== term
```

As an example, consider that we want to express the expression

```
\a x -> if a >= sum x then a : biggers x
        else biggers x
```

in the form of $a \oplus (biggers\ x, sum\ x)$ where $\oplus$ is a binary operator. We may code this intention by

```
[| \a x -> $oplus a (biggers x, sum x) |]
    <== [| \a x -> if a >= sum x then a : biggers x
                    else biggers x |]
```

which will yield the following match:

```
{ $oplus := \x (b,s) ->
              if x > s then x : b else b }.
```

Note that Function $oplus is a second-order pattern variable and can be efficiently obtained by the deterministic higher-order matching algorithm [17]. Note also that $ means unquote, so the above match is equivalent to

```
{ oplus := [| \x (b,s) ->
              if x > s then x : b else b |] }.
```

Rule

The rule combinator is used to build a transformation rule mapping from one program pattern to another. A rule is described in the form of

```
(==>) :: ExpQ -> ExpQ -> RuleY
lhs ==> rhs
```

where RuleY, which is defined by RuleY = ExpQ -> Y ExpQ, is to map a program to another under the transformation environment Y. For instance, we may define the shortcut fusion rule by

```
[| hom $e $oplus . build $g |] ==> [| g $e $oplus |]
```

where we represent a homomorphism $([e, \oplus])$ by (hom e oplus). The semantics of a rule may be clear from the following where we define a rule by the Match combinator.

```
(==>) :: ExpQ -> ExpQ -> RuleY
(pat ==> body) term = do pat <== term
                         ret body
```

Note that in the above, the function ret implicitly applies the match (i.e., substitution) kept in the transformation monad to body.

Sequence

Sequential updates of transformation environments can be realized by combining matches with the sequence combinator (>>).

```
(>>) :: Y () -> Y () -> Y ()
(pat1 <== term1) >> (pat2 <== term2)
```

which can be written as sequence of matchings using *do notation*.

```
do pat1 <== term1
   pat2 <== term2
```

Deterministic Choice and Case

The combinator (<+) is designed to express deterministic choice.

```
(<+) :: ExpY -> ExpY -> ExpY
transExp1 <+ transExp2
```

It returns the first argument if the transformation in it succeeds. Otherwise, it returns the second argument as the result. For instance, we may write

```
(rule1 e) <+ (rule2 e)
```

to first apply `rule1` to transform e, and if it succeeds, we return the result; otherwise we try to apply `rule2` to e.

Using the choice combinator, we can define a meta version of the case expression, which tries to apply a list of rules one by one until one rule succeeds.

```
casem :: ExpQ -> [RuleY] -> ExpY
casem sel (r:rs) = r sel <+ casem sel rs
```

5.3   Code Calculation Rules in Yicho

To get a flavor of Yicho, we show how to use Yicho to code the promotion rule in Section 2, and how it is used to optimize the program. Since the list homomorphism $([e, \oplus])$ is in fact the standard Haskell function *foldr* $(\oplus)$ e, we rewrite the promotion theorem as follows.

$$\text{promotion:} \quad \frac{f(a \oplus x) = a \otimes f\, x}{f \circ foldr\, (\oplus)\, e = foldr\, (\otimes)\, (f\, e)}$$

This rule is defined in Yicho as follows.

```
promotion :: ExpQ -> Y ExpQ
promotion exp = do
    [f,oplus,e,otimes] <- pvars ["f","oplus","e","otimes"]
    [| $f . foldr $oplus $e |] <== exp
    [| \a x -> $otimes a ($f x) |]
        <== [| \a x -> $f ($oplus a x) |]
    ret [| foldr $otimes ($f $z) |]
```

The promotion rule is defined as a function that takes code and returns code with its environment. In the third line, `f,oplus,e,otimes` are declared to be variables; the unquote $ is actually splicing the expression, but, intuitively we can regard expression $x as meta variable with the name of $x. In the fourth line, exp is matched with the pattern `[| $f . foldr $oplus $e |]`, with the variables $f, $oplus, $e being bound in the environment. The next two lines are a straightforward translation of the original promotion rule. $f and $oplus are instantiated and the both sides of <== are matched and the resulting match is added to the environment. The pattern instantiation contributes to the modularity of patterns. It should be noted here that the higher-order patterns such as

```
[| \a x -> $otimes a ($f x) |]
```

play an important role in this concise definition. Finally, the result expression with its environment are returned by ret.

We can enhance the promotion rule with a rule (say for unfolding the definition or simplification), and add it as an argument to the promotion function.

```
promotionWithRule :: RuleY -> ExpQ -> Y ExpQ
promotionWithRule rule exp = do
    [f,oplus,e,otimes] <- pvars ["f","oplus","e","otimes"]
    [| $f . foldr $oplus $e |] <== rule exp
    [| \a x -> $otimes a ($f x) |]
        <== rule [| \a x -> $f ($oplus a x) |]
    ret [| foldr $otimes ($f $z) |]
```

To see how to apply the promotion rule, consider the following expression

```
oldExp = [| sum . foldr (\x y -> 2 * x : y) [] |]
```

and suppose that we hope to apply to this code the promotion rule together with some other rule `rule` to obtain a new efficient expression, say newExp. We can define this newExp as follows.

```
newExp = runY (promotionWithRule rule ex1)
```

We may confirm the result of newExp under the GHCi Environment:

```
GHCi> prettyExpQ newExp
foldr (\x_1 -> (+) (2 * x_1)) 0
```

where we use function prettyExpQ :: ExpQ -> IO () to print out an expression.
Now we can compare efficiency of the two expressions.

```
GHCi> $oldExp (take 100000 [1..])
10000100000
(0.33 secs, 21243136 bytes)

GHCi> $newExp (take 100000 [1..])
10000100000
(0.27 secs, 19581216 bytes)
```

It is worth noting that the promotion theorem is applied at compile time, and the function $newExp is actually improved both in the execution time and consumed heap size.

The other calculation rules in this tutorial can be specified similarly. The readers are invited to visit the Yicho home page for more examples.

6   Concluding Remarks

In this tutorial, we explain the basic technique of formalizing and implementing program transformations and optimization in calculational form based on the Constructive Algorithmics theory. We illustrate the idea with two important transformations, loop fusion and parallelization, and we show how the transformations in calculational form can be efficiently implemented with Yicho.

We summarize the main advantages of program transformations in calculational form as follows.

- *Modularity*. A program transformation in calculational form does not require any global analysis as other transformation systems often need. Instead, it only uses a local program analysis to obtain the specialized form, and it can check locally the applicability of their calculational rules. Therefore, it can be implemented in a modular way, and is guaranteed to terminate.
- *Generality*. In this tutorial, we focus on the transformation of programs on lists. In fact, most of our calculational laws are polytypic, i.e., parameterized with data types. They can be generalized to transformation of programs on any algebraic data types.
- *Cheap Implementation*. Transformations in calculational form are more practical than the well-known *fold-unfold* transformations [4]. Fold/unfold transformation basically has to keep track of all occurring function calls and introduce function definitions to be searched in the folding step. The process of keeping track of function calls and controlling the steps cleverly to avoid infinite unfolding introduces substantial cost and complexity, which often prevents it from being practically implemented. Though they may be less general than fold/unfold transformations, transformations in calculational form can be implemented in a cheap way [24, 36, 25, 14] by means of a local program analysis and simple rule application.
- *Compatibility*. It is usually difficult to make several transformations coexist well in a single system, but transformations in calculational form can solve this problem well. For instance, fusion calculation can coexist well with tupling calculation [14]. There are two reasons. First, each transformation is based on the same theoretical framework, Constructive Algorithmics. Second, local program analysis and local application of laws make it easier to check compatibility of transformations.

It should be noted that program transformations in calculation forms can be applied only to those programs that can be turned into the form a calculation rule is applicable. To increase the power, as seen in Section 4.3, we may have to design a normalization algorithms with global analysis in order to obtain the required form. We believe that more optimizations and transformations can be formalized in calculational form to gain the advantages discussed above, and we are looking forward to see more practical applications.

References

1. Jones, S.P., et al., J.H., eds.: Haskell 98: A Non-strict, Purely Functional Language. Available online: http://www.haskell.org (1999)
2. Bird, R.: Introduction to Functional Programming using Haskell. Prentice Hall (1998)
3. Hughes, J.: Lazy memo-functions. In: Proc. Conference on Functional Programming Languages and Computer Architecture (LNCS 201), Nancy, France, Springer-Verlag, Berlin (1985) 129–149
4. Burstall, R., Darlington, J.: A transformation system for developing recursive programs. Journal of the ACM **24** (1977) 44–67
5. Feather, M.: A survey and classification of some program transformation techniques. In: TC2 IFIP Working Conference on Program Specification and Transformation, Bad Tolz, Germany, North Holland (1987) 165–195
6. Darlington, J.: An experimental program transformation system. Artificial Intelligence **16** (1981) 1–46
7. Bird, R.: An introduction to the theory of lists. In Broy, M., ed.: Logic of Programming and Calculi of Discrete Design, Springer-Verlag (1987) 5–42
8. Backhouse, R.: An exploration of the Bird-Meertens formalism. In: STOP Summer School on Constructive Algorithmics, Ameland. (1989)
9. Meijer, E., Fokkinga, M., Paterson, R.: Functional programming with bananas, lenses, envelopes and barbed wire. In: Proc. Conference on Functional Programming Languages and Computer Architecture (LNCS 523), Cambridge, Massachuetts (1991) 124–144
10. Fokkinga, M.: A gentle introduction to category theory — the calculational approach —. Technical Report Lecture Notes, Dept. INF, University of Twente, The Netherlands (1992)
11. Jeuring, J.: Theories for Algorithm Calculation. Ph.D thesis, Faculty of Science, Utrecht University (1993)
12. Bird, R., de Moor, O.: Algebras of Programming. Prentice Hall (1996)
13. Hu, Z., Iwasaki, H., Takeichi, M.: Deriving structural hylomorphisms from recursive definitions. In: ACM SIGPLAN International Conference on Functional Programming, Philadelphia, PA, ACM Press (1996) 73–82
14. Hu, Z., Iwasaki, H., Takeichi, M., Takano, A.: Tupling calculation eliminates multiple data traversals. In: ACM SIGPLAN International Conference on Functional Programming, Amsterdam, The Netherlands, ACM Press (1997) 164–175
15. Hu, Z., Takeichi, M., Chin, W.: Parallelization in calculational forms. In: 25th ACM Symposium on Principles of Programming Languages, San Diego, California, USA (1998) 316–328
16. Hu, Z., Iwasaki, H., Takeichi, M.: Calculating accumulations. New Generation Computing **17** (1999) 153–173
17. Yokoyama, T., Hu, Z., Takeichi, M.: Deterministic second-order patterns. Information Processing Letters **89** (2004) 309–314
18. Malcolm, G.: Data structures and program transformation. Science of Computer Programming (1990) 255–279
19. Pettorossi, A., Proiett, M.: Rules and strategies for transforming functional and logic programs. Computing Surveys **28** (1996) 360–414
20. de Moor, O., Sittampalam, G.: Higher-order matching for program transformation. Theor. Comput. Sci. **269** (2001) 135–162
21. Goldberg, A., Paige, R.: Stream processing. In: LISP and Functional Programming. (1984) 53–62
22. Aho, A., Sethi, R., Ullman, J.: Compilers – Principles, Techniqies and Tools. Addison-Wesley (1986)

23. Chin, W.: Towards an automated tupling strategy. In: Proc. Conference on Partial Evaluation and Program Manipulation, Copenhagen, ACM Press (1993) 119–132
24. Gill, A., Launchbury, J., Jones, S.P.: A short cut to deforestation. In: Proc. Conference on Functional Programming Languages and Computer Architecture, Copenhagen (1993) 223–232
25. Takano, A., Meijer, E.: Shortcut deforestation in calculational form. In: Proc. Conference on Functional Programming Languages and Computer Architecture, La Jolla, California (1995) 306–313
26. Onoue, Y., Hu, Z., Iwasaki, H., Takeichi, M.: A calculational fusion system HYLO. In: IFIP TC 2 Working Conference on Algorithmic Languages and Calculi, Le Bischenberg, France, Chapman&Hall (1997) 76–106
27. Banerjee, U., Eigenmann, R., Nicolau, A., Padua, D.A.: Automatic program parallelization. Proceedings of the IEEE **81** (1993) 211–243
28. Cole, M.: Parallel programming, list homomorphisms and the maximum segment sum problems. Report CSR-25-93, Department of Computing Science, The University of Edinburgh (1993)
29. Hu, Z., Iwasaki, H., Takeichi, M.: Formal derivation of efficient parallel programs by construction of list homomorphisms. ACM Transactions on Programming Languages and Systems **19** (1997) 444–461
30. Skillicorn, D.: Foundations of Parallel Programming. Cambridge University Press (1994)
31. Gorlatch, S.: Constructing list homomorphisms. Technical Report MIP-9512, Fakultät für Mathematik und Informatik, Universität Passau (1995)
32. Chin, W., Takano, A., Hu, Z.: Parallelization via context preservation. In: IEEE Computer Society International Conference on Computer Languages, Loyola University Chicago, Chicago, USA (1998)
33. Xu, D.N., Khoo, S.C., Hu, Z.: Ptype system : A featherweight parallelizability detector. In: Second ASIAN Symposium on Programming Languages and Systems(APLAS 2004), Taipei, Taiwan, Springer, LNCS 3302 (2004) 197–212
34. Sheard, T., Peyton Jones, S.L.: Template metaprogramming for Haskell. In: Haskell Workshop, Pittsburgh, Pennsylvania (2002) 1–16
35. Yokoyama, T., Hu, Z., Takeichi, M.: Deterministic second-order patterns and its application to program transformation. In: International Symposium on Logic-based Program Synthesis and Transformation (LOPSTR 2003), Springer, LNCS 3018 (2003) 165–178
36. Sheard, T., Fegaras, L.: A fold for all seasons. In: Proc. Conference on Functional Programming Languages and Computer Architecture, Copenhagen (1993) 233–242

Mappings Make Data Processing Go 'Round
An Inter-paradigmatic Mapping Tutorial

Ralf Lämmel and Erik Meijer

Microsoft Corp., Data Programmability Team, Redmond, USA

Abstract. Whatever programming paradigm for data processing we choose, data has the tendency to live on the other side or to eventually end up there. The major paradigms for data processing are Cobol, object, relational and XML; each paradigm offers many facets and many versions; each paradigm provides specific forms of data models (object models, relational schemas, XML schemas, etc.). Each data-processing application depends on a horde of interrelated data models and artifacts that are derived from data models (such as data-access layers). Such conglomerations of data models are challenging due to paradigmatic impedance mismatches, performance requirements, loose-coupling requirements, and others. This ubiquitous problem calls for a good understanding of techniques for mappings between data models, actual data, and operations on data. This tutorial lists and discusses mapping scenarios, mapping techniques, impedance mismatches and research challenges regarding mappings.

Keywords: Data processing, Mapping, XML data binding, Object-XML mapping, Object-relational mapping, Cross-paradigm impedance mismatch, Data modeling, Data access, Loose coupling, Software evolution.

1 Introduction

We steal the beginning of our tutorial from elsewhere: *"Once upon a time it was possible for every new programmer to quickly learn how to write readable programs to Create, Read, Update and Delete business information. These so-called CRUD applications, along with reporting, were pervasive throughout business and essentially defined IT or MIS as it was called in those days."* [92] (Dave Thomas: "The Impedance Imperative Tuples + Objects + Infosets = Too Much Stuff!").

Instead, today we face the following diversity:

- Cobol applications with keyed files are still developed and they make sense.
- Relational databases have fully matured and they are unarguably omnipresent.
- OO databases innovate, perhaps at a slow pace, but they must be taken seriously.
- The XML hype is over. XML types and XML documents are everywhere now.
- All these paradigms have triggered a myriad of query languages and 4GL tools.
- Much current CRUD development is done with OO languages with various APIs.

This tutorial is about the challenges implied by such diversity in data modeling and data processing. Either there are respectable, perhaps fundamental reasons for all this diversity, or it is just plain IT reality. No matter what, we need to map amongst these

R. Lämmel, J. Saraiva, and J. Visser (Eds.): GTTSE 2005, LNCS 4143, pp. 169–218, 2006.
© Springer-Verlag Berlin Heidelberg 2006

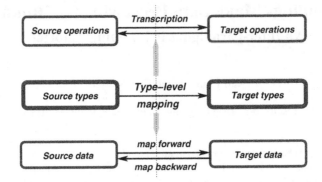

Fig. 1. Levels in mapping

paradigms, and everyone is trying to do that anyhow. According to a designated online resource[1], there are roughly 60 established products for X/O mapping, also known as XML data binding, i.e., XML schemas or DTDs are mapped to object models. We reckon that practice is ahead of foundations in this area, but this surely implies ad-hoc approaches with unnecessary limits and complexities. We need basic and applied research on inter- and intra-paradigm mappings.

What Is a Mapping Anyway?

We should make more precise what we mean by 'mapping'. We have to disappoint those readers looking for a detailed or even formal definition. Instead we offer the following explanation and the illustration in Fig. 1.

- Mapping is essentially about the transformation of values between data models.[2]
- The data models typically involve different paradigms (Cobol, OO, relational, XML).
- Fig. 1 opts for a type-based mapping (described at the type level).
- By contrast, instance-based mappings directly define value transformations.
- Other mappings may implicitly define data models for source and target.
- CRUD operations may need transcription from the source to the target or vice versa.
- There may be more levels than those in the figure, e.g., the level of protocols.

Road-Map for the Tutorial

- Sec. 2 presents diverse illustrative *mapping examples.*
- Sec. 3 is an attempt to collect (some) *mapping concepts.*

---

[1] http://www.rpbourret.com/xml/XMLDataBinding.htm
[2] The term 'data model' is ambiguous as it may refer to both the general data model of a paradigm such as the 'relational model'; it may also refer to domain-/application-specific data models such as a particular 'relational schema' or 'object model'; http://en.wikipedia.org/wiki/Data_model. In this tutorial, we favor the latter meaning.

- Sec. 4 reveals *impedance mismatches* for inter-paradigmatic mappings.
- Sec. 5 calls to arms regarding *engineering and research challenges*.
- Sec. 6 concludes the article.
- The appendix collects a good number of exercises.

2 Mapping Examples

We will walk through a few data-processing scenarios that involve mappings. We strive for diversity so that we show the ubiquitousness of the mapping notion in programming and software development. As we go, we hint at established techniques, typical requirements and recurring problems.

2.1 From Concrete to Abstract Syntax

Language processing, including compiler construction, involves mappings in abundance. Most notably, a parser needs to map concrete syntax to reasonable parse trees or proper ASTs (i.e., abstract syntax trees). In fact, a non-trivial, well-organized language processor may involve several abstract syntaxes related to different components in front- and middle-ends. Yet other mappings in language processors can be concerned with immediate representations such as PDG and SSA [28, 20]. We will discuss some forms of mapping concrete syntax to parse trees or ASTs.

Concrete Syntax as Mapping Source. Consider the following ANTLR[3] grammar for the concrete syntax of arithmetic expressions.[4] The actual encoding represents operator priorities by 'grammatical layers' — as it is common for top-down parsing. That is, expression forms are grouped per operator priority using an auxiliary nonterminal for all groups — except the top-most one:[5]

```
// ANTLR grammar
expr          :  mul_expr (addOP mul_expr)* ;
mul_expr      :  sign_expr (mulOP sign_expr)* ;
sign_expr     :  (MINUS)? primary_expr ;
primary_expr  :  IDENT
              |  constant
              |  ( LPAREN! expr RPAREN! ) ;
```

Option: Untyped, Canonical Mapping. ANTLR offers the option to construct parse trees in a canonical manner using a language-independent format (which is a sort of universal representation type). The problem with such a generic approach is that no abstraction is carried out (in the sense of ASTs), and no typing discipline for parse trees is enforced. So we are seeking different mapping options.

---

[3] ANTLR web site: http://www.antlr.org/

[4] Source: http://www.bearcave.com/software/antlr/antlr_examples.html

[5] We will start code fragments with a comment that identifies the used programming language.

Option: Mapping in 'All Detail'. The attribute grammar paradigm [55, 81] can be used for a mode of parse-tree construction that improves on the above-mentioned problems. All parser generator tools like ANTLR (and Yacc, PRECC, BTYACC, etc.) support this technique (with more or less strong typing). ANTLR presupposes type declarations for the intended parse-tree format. The actual mapping has to be described in the parser specification: semantic actions synthesize parse-tree fragments.

The following ANTLR snippet is a refinement of the last context-free production in the earlier grammar for expressions. The added semantic actions build a binary expression from two operands and an operator.

```
// ANTLR production with in−lined C++ code
expr returns [binaryNode a_expr]
  { exprNode m1 = NULL;
    exprNode m2 = NULL;
    opNode op = NULL;
  }
  : m1 = mul_expr { a_expr = m1; }
    ( op = addOP m2 = mul_expr
    { a_expr = new binaryNode( op, a_expr, m2 ); }  )∗
  ;
```

We omit the declarations for the referenced C++ classes: exprNode (the abstract base class for expressions), binaryNode, opNode. A problem with this approach is that it is 'a lot of work'. First, the abstract syntax has to be worked out in all tedious details, even though it may be 'intentionally' similar to the concrete syntax. Second, the mapping has to be 'coded' in all detail, again without leveraging any similarities between concrete and abstract syntax. Furthermore, we end up with a poor separation of concerns in so far that the original context-free productions get invaded by declarations and semantic actions for parse-tree construction.

Option: Generative Mapping. One can improve on these problems by means of generative programming [23], namely a grammar-oriented form of it; cf. [50, 57, 9, 40] for related work. (We need meta-grammarware according to [54].) We briefly summarize an approach actually offered by an existing technology: GDK (the Grammar Deployment Kit [57]). That is, GDK processes pure grammars (without any semantic actions) and generates a typed parse-tree format as well as the bloated parser specification that comprises the tedious mapping. The type declarations for parse-tree formats are also valuable for consumers of the constructed parse trees. The generated parser specification can be processed by a conventional parser generator. Various programming languages and parser generators are supported. Here is an example of a generated Yacc [49] production for parenthesized expressions.

```
// Generated Yacc production with embedded C code
expr_in_parens
  : T_QPOPEN
    expr
    T_QPCLOSE
    { $$ = build_expr_in_parens($1, $2, $3); }
  ;
```

The function symbol build_expr_in_parens is one of the term constructors that is generated from the pure grammar. Consumers of the parse trees can use accordingly generated matching functions. This approach still does not solve the problem of abstraction in the sense that the constructed parse trees mirror (too) precisely the concrete syntax.

Option: Simplify Concrete into Abstract Syntax. There exist declarative mapping approaches such that the abstract syntax and the mapping from concrete to abstract syntax can be controlled more explicitly without switching to the other extreme of defining the mapping in all detail — as it was the case for the attribute-grammar approach, unfortunately. We will discuss a particularly advanced approach that is supported by the compiler generator Eli [35]. That is, Eli provides designated tool support, Maptool [51], for concrete-to-abstract syntax mappings.

Consider the following context-free syntax using Eli's grammar notation:[6]

```
// Eli's grammar notation
Program      ::=  Statement + .
Statement    ::=  Computation ';' .
Computation  ::=  Expr/LetExpr/WhereExpr .
LetExpr      ::=  'let' Definitions 'in' Expr .
WhereExpr    ::=  Expr 'where' Definitions .
Definitions  ::=  Definition // ',' .
Definition   ::=  Identifier '=' Expr .
Expr         ::=  Expr '+' Term / Expr '−' Term / Term .
Term         ::=  Term '*' Factor / Term '/' Factor / Factor .
Factor       ::=  '−' Factor / Primary .
Primary      ::=  Integer / Identifier / '(' Computation ')' .
```

As in the earlier example, there are several layers of expressions: Computation, Expr, Term, Factor, Primary. These layers are biased towards parsing concrete syntax while only adding irrelevant complexity to subsequent phases. Hence, we would prefer to unite these layers in the abstract syntax. This is accomplished by the following fragment of a Maptool mapping specification:

```
// Eli's Maptool notation
MAPSYM
  Expr ::= Computation Term Factor Primary .
```

That is, the various nonterminals on the right-hand side of the MAPSYM declaration are placed in an *equivalence class*, which effectively implies an abstract syntax as if Expr were defined by a flat list of alternatives. This simplification enables more concise language processing code. For instance, expression evaluation does not need to handle all the concrete syntactical variations implied by the different nonterminals.

---

[6] Eli uses an EBNF-like notation. That is, '+' is for repetition (i.e., lists), and '/' is for alternatives (elsewhere denoted as '|'). There is notation for separator lists: '$e//c$', where e is the phrase to be repeated and c is the character for separation.

Option: Refine Abstract into Concrete Syntax. Rather than simplifying the concrete syntax such that a suitable abstract syntax is derived, we can also start from a simple abstract syntax and refine it into the existing concrete syntax — thereby defining a mapping. Let us design an abstract syntax that is as abstract and suggestive as it could be for the purpose of, say, *name analysis*. (In compiler construction, name analysis tends to refer to the concept of resolving (or better: establishing) the links between using (referring) occurrences and defining (declaring) occurrences.)

```
// Eli's ( abstract ) grammar notation
Program                    LISTOF Statement
BoundExpr      ::=    Definitions  Expr
Definitions               LISTOF Definition
Definition     ::=    IdDef '=' Expr
Primary        ::=    IdUse
IdDef          ::=    Identifier
IdUse          ::=    Identifier
```

It happens that several of the nonterminals in the abstract syntax correspond to nonterminals in the concrete syntax. Hence, they are automatically mapped by 'name coincidence'. However, there are major idioms for completing name coincidence into a concrete-to-abstract syntax mapping, which we will discuss in the sequel.

The abstract sort BoundExpr does not have an immediate counterpart in the concrete syntax. We use it as a general form of a binding group (say definitions). In fact, BoundExpr is meant as an abstraction for let and where expressions. This intent can be expressed by the following bits of mapping specification:

```
// Eli's Maptool notation
MAPSYM
BoundExpr   ::=   LetExpr WhereExpr .

MAPRULE
LetExpr     ::=   ' let '  Definitions  'in'  Expr  <$1$2> .
WhereExpr   ::=   Expr 'where' Definitions  <$2$1> .
```

That is, the nonterminals LetExpr and WhereExpr are placed in an equivalence class with BoundExpr. The productions for LetExpr and WhereExpr are associated with directions for AST construction. (The phrases <$1$2> and <$2$1> express the subtrees of the AST in terms of indexes of the subtrees of the concrete parse tree.)

The abstract sorts IdDef and IdUse *partition* the nonterminal Identifier from the concrete syntax. The distinct nonterminals are used for defining vs. using occurrences of Identifier. The nonterminal Definition is defined in both grammars, while the abstract syntax points out that the occurring identifier is actually a defining occurrence. This mapping leads to a useful abstract syntax design because it enables a language-independent name analysis. That is, the name analysis can identify the defining vs. using role of an identifier solely by means of the nonterminal symbols IdDef and IdUse. Without this distinction, the name analysis would need to have intimate knowledge about grammar productions and positions in which identifiers occur in this or that role.

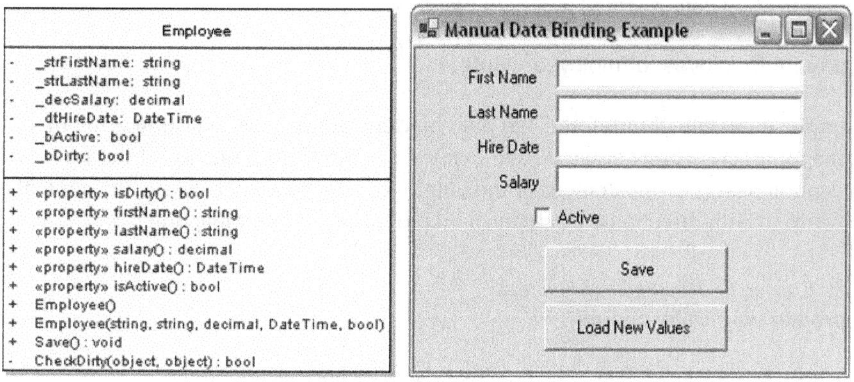

Source: http://www.15seconds.com/issue/040908.htm

Fig. 2. Data to be bound in a GUI

2.2 Data Binding in User Interfaces

Interactive applications require mappings of the kind that application data is bound to user-interface elements.[7] In the small, an archetypal example would be about associating a field, such as the first name of an employee object, to the text property of a text box in a form. The term (GUI) 'data binding' is nowadays used for this problem, but the overall issue is not tied to modern platforms such as Java and .NET. For instance, forms-based Cobol applications have dealt with the same problem for ages: application data must be mapped to user-interface elements of screens (or forms), user-input validation has to be carried out, and a protocol for change notification must be provided.

Option: Point-to-Point Programmatic Mapping. Let us consider an example of GUI data binding. In Fig. 2, on the left-hand side, we see the class structure of an employee object; on the right-hand side, we see a GUI form for operating on an employee object. Let us also assume controls for the various fields and buttons:

```
// C# 1.0 code (using System.Windows.Forms)
public class myForm : Form
{
    private TextBox txtFirstName;
    private TextBox txtLastName;
    private TextBox txtHireDate;
    private TextBox txtSalary;
    private CheckBox chkIsActive;
    private Button btnLoadNewValues;
    private Button btnSave;
    // to be cont'd
}
```

---

[7] A comment on terminology: 'data binding' is often implicitly taken to mean 'binding data to a GUI'. For an unambiguous terminology, we say 'GUI data binding'.

Our application data is stored in a field like this:

```
private Employee _oEmployee = null;
```

A simple approach ('brute force') to data binding commences as follows, the binding (or mapping) code boils down to two explicit *move* routines; one to fill the form with application data (i.e., the content of the employee field); another to save the content of the form. In both directions, we define a kind of *point-to-point* mapping:

```
//  Exception—handling code omitted
private void DataToForm()
{
  this.txtFirstName.Text      = _oEmployee.firstName;
  this.txtLastName.Text       = _oEmployee.lastName;
  this.txtSalary.Text         = _oEmployee.salary.ToString();
  this.txtHireDate.Text       = _oEmployee.hireDate.ToShortDateString();
  this.chkIsActive.Checked    = _oEmployee.isActive;
}

private void FormToData()
{
  _oEmployee.firstName = txtFirstName.Text;
  _oEmployee.lastName  = txtLastName.Text;
  _oEmployee.salary    = Convert.ToDecimal(txtSalary.Text);
  _oEmployee.hireDate  = Convert.ToDateTime(txtHireDate.Text);
  _oEmployee.isActive  = chkIsActive.Checked;
}
```

This coding style is well in line with common practice. There is one striking weakness of this approach: we end up coding the mapping *twice*. Another weakness is that we code conversions allover the place and thereby bypass static type checking; cf. the use of Convert.ToDecimal.

Option: Point-to-Point Mapping Declarations. We can improve on this brute-force approach by exploiting the designated data-binding interface of GUI controls. That is, we can actually inform each and every control about the associated application data:

```
private void MyBind()
{
  txtFirstName.DataBindings.Add("Text", _oEmployee, "firstName");
  txtLastName.DataBindings.Add("Text", _oEmployee, "lastName");
  txtSalary.DataBindings.Add("Text", _oEmployee, "salary");
  Binding bindHireDateText = new Binding("Text", _oEmployee, "hireDate");
  bindHireDateText.Format +=
      new ConvertEventHandler(DateTimeToShortDateString);
  txtHireDate.DataBindings.Add(bindHireDateText);
  chkIsActive.DataBindings.Add("Checked", _oEmployee, "isActive");
}
```

As a result, the mapping is specified only *once*, and the amount of conversion code is restricted to cases in which defaults are not sensible; cf. DateTimeToShortDateString. Unfortunately, we have to pay a considerable price for the improvement of conciseness. The mapping description is largely string-based:

- "Text"   vs.   this.txtFirstName.Text,
- "firstName"   vs.   _oEmployee.firstName.

Hence, one dimension of subsequent improvement is to provide static typing for such mappings, but we will first consider a more operational issue. The trouble is that the form is filled only *initially* when the binding is issued, but subsequent changes of the application data are not passed on to the form. Updating only works one way: changes in the form are mapped back to the bound setters, but not vice versa.

Two-Way Updates. More generally, a mapping approach might need to maintain some degree of bi-directional tracking between source and target. In this example of GUI data binding, change propagation can be arranged as follows. The data bindings of Windows.Forms can be made to listen to changes in the application data. The relevant idiom is that a setter on application data should trigger a change event:

```
public class Employee
{
    // The private field for application data
    private string _firstName;

    // An event for changes on _firstName
    public event EventHandler firstNameChanged;

    // The firstName property; note the setter
    public string firstName
    {
        get { return _firstName; }
        set {
            _firstName = value;
            firstNameChanged(this, new EventArgs());
    }}

    // ... likewise for other data ...
}
```

Change tracking is name-based: the name of a bound property + 'Changed' is the name of the event (if defined by the programmer) observed by the GUI data binding framework so as to learn about state changes; cf. the couple firstName and firstNameChanged in the code snippet. Various GUI frameworks leverage similar idioms. It is also common to leverage design patterns that help modeling some aspects of update protocols and consistency checking; e.g., the observer design pattern [33], the model-view-controller architecture [59], and friends.

Initial state   **State after user interaction**

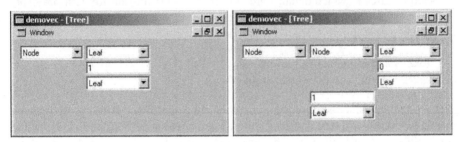

Fig. 3. GUI states with different trees (adopted from [2])

Typed *and* Canonical *and* Customizable *and* Live Mapping. Regarding the remaining typing weakness, we would like to contrast Windows.Forms with a strongly typed approach that uses the modern functional language Clean [2, 1]. At the same time, this approach also illustrates a callback-based technique for two-way change tracking. So the bound GUI is always in sync with the data layer.

The ambition of the Clean-based approach is to allow for editing data in a highly systematic manner. To this end, a generic programming approach (in the sense of induction on type structure) is employed. The generated GUI controls are called GECs — Graphical Editor Components. The overall assumption is that a reasonable GEC for a specific value v can be constructed just by observing the structure of v's type. In Fig. 3, the GECs for two values are shown. The left GEC represents a binary, node-labeled tree of the form Node Leaf 1 Leaf. When the user changes the upper Leaf to Node, through the pull-down menu, the GEC evolves as shown on the right-hand side of the figure. *Any* GEC is constructed via the following Clean function mkGEC.

```
−− A generic Clean function ( looks  like  Haskell,  almost)
generic mkGEC t ::    [GECAttribute]          −− Control appearance
                      t                       −− The initial  value
                      (CallBackFunction t ps) −− Call back for  changes
                      (PSt ps)                −− Program state
               −> (GEC t (PSt ps),PSt ps)     −− Constructed GEC + state
```

The type of the function hints at the status of the mapping to be canonical and customizable and live. The canonical mapping status is implied by the fact that mkGEC is a generic (polytypic) function with the type parameter t. The customization capability is modeled by the first argument that anticipates a list of attributes that control the appearance of the GEC. The live status of a GEC is implied by the fact that its creation must define an initial value (cf. second argument) and a CallBackFunction to be invoked when the edited value is changed (no matter whether the change is caused by editing or by programmatic access). The constructed GEC also provides read and write access to the bound value. (The rest of the function's signature deals with the fact that GEC construction and GEC usage involves state transformation. In Haskell terms, we would expect some use of the IO or state monad.)

2.3   XML Data Binding

The term 'XML data binding' [70, 15] refers to the problem of providing an object model that is meant to represent an XML schema (an XSD description) in the object world (or vice versa). This is a modern mapping scenario in which either an XML schema or an object model is given, and the counterpart (i.e., the object model or the XML schema) is to be derived. In the subsequent illustrations, we are going to use an XML schema sample for widgets (rectangle, squares, circles), as they may occur in a drawing application:[8]

```
<!-- XML schema -->
<xs:element name="Widgets">
 <xs:complexType>
  <xs:choice minOccurs="0" maxOccurs="unbounded">
   <xs:element name="Rectangle" type="Rectangle"/>
   <xs:element name="Square" type="Square"/>
   <xs:element name="Circle" type="Circle"/>
  </xs:choice>
 </xs:complexType>
</xs:element>

<xs:complexType name="Rectangle">
 <xs:sequence>
  <xs:element name="XPos" type="xs:int"/>
  <xs:element name="YPos" type="xs:int"/>
  <xs:element name="Width" type="xs:int"/>
  <xs:element name="Height" type="xs:int"/>
 </xs:sequence>
</xs:complexType>

<!-- ... Square  elided  ... -->
<!-- ... Circle  elided  ... -->
```

While this a perfectly reasonable XML schema, we may encounter challenges when mapping this schema to objects. There exist many different XML-data binding technologies; each technology defines its own canonical mapping (and one may argue at times which one is better).

Schema-Derived Classes. The following class has been generated by the .NET 2.0 technology xsd.exe. The fields of class Rectangle resemble the structure of the corresponding complex type definition. The XSD simple type xs:int is mapped to the VB.NET type Integer.

---

[8] This example explores the XSD variation on the ingenious 'shapes example' — an OO benchmark that has been designed by Jim Weirich and deeply explored by him and Chris Rathman. See the code collections http://onestepback.org/articles/poly/ and http://www.angelfire.com/tx4/cus/shapes/.

```
' VB.NET 8.0 code
' Note: all generated custom attributes omitted
Partial Public Class Rectangle
 Private xPosField As Integer
 Private yPosField As Integer
 Private widthField As Integer
 Private heightField As Integer
 Public Property XPos() As Integer
  Get
    Return Me.xPosField
  End Get
  Set
   Me.xPosField = value
  End Set
 End Property
 ' ... other properties elided ...
End Class
```

Adaptation of Mapping Results. xsd.exe's XML-to-object mapping is fully canonical; there are no means of influencing the mapping. However, one may adapt the mapping *result*, as we will discuss. Suppose we want to process collections of shapes by exploiting subtype polymorphism such that the executed functionality (e.g., for drawing) is specific to the kind of shape. So we want the classes Rectangle, Square and Circle to engage in a subtype hierarchy rooted by a new class, say Shape:

```
' A base class for all shapes
Public MustInherit Class Shape   ' Abstract class
  Public MustOverride Sub draw() ' Abstract method
End Class
```

How can we make it so that Rectangle etc. inherit from Shape and implement draw? A naive and problematic approach would be to manually adapt the generated classes. Adapting generated code is almost universally a bad idea for obvious reasons. It turns out that we can employ linguistic means to adapt the mapping result. That is, we can use VB.NET 8.0's *partial classes*, which admit compile-time extension of classes. In particular, we can resolve the aforementioned problem without touching the generated code at all. We provide another slice of the (partial) class Rectangle; the idea is that both 'slices' are merged by the compiler.

```
Partial Public Class Rectangle
  Inherits Shape
  Public Overrides Sub draw()
      WriteLine("Drawing a rectangle.")
  End Sub
End Class
```

Dead Ends in Mapping. Here is the generated code for Widgets:

```
' The class that corresponds to the Widgets element declaration
Partial Public Class Widgets
  Private itemsField() As Object
  Public Property Items() As Object()
    ' ... trivial implementation elided ...
  End Property
    ' ... rest of class elided ...
End Class
```

The use of normal arrays for collecting widgets is reasonable as long as we *observe* de-serialized XML content. However, should we want to add widgets, we may prefer a more 'dynamic' collection type such as List. Also, the widgets are exposed in a rather untyped manner (cf. Object). We may want to use a strongly typed, generic collection whose item type is Shape. The partial-class mechanism and other available programming idioms do not help in these cases.

One may argue that the canonical mapping at hand is simply suboptimal and needs to be improved, no matter what. However, any mapping technology must eventually adopt some mapping rules and options. There is always a chance that someone ends up wanting a different rule or another option later. Ideally, there would be a fundamental way of defending the quality and the completeness of a mapping.

3 Mapping Concepts

Let us raise the level of abstraction and focus on concepts. Throughout the section, we continue discussing examples so that we can illustrate the identified concepts and collect more data points. Ideally, we would like to deliver the perfect, comprehensive, formal and meaningful framework for the categorization and assessment of existing and new mapping approaches. We are unable to complete such a task at this point in time. Incidentally, the purpose of this tutorial is to motivate research that may enable the completion of the envisaged framework.

3.1 Universal Representations

Many mapping scenarios regularly call for (or take advantage of) universal representations. This concept is based on a relationship between types in a given type language (CLR classes, Haskell data types, etc.) and a universal (fixed) representation type for that type language ('the universe'). Here are applications of universal representations:

- Serialization of data (to text or XML) for persistence.
- Serialization for interoperability using XML again.
- Type erasure for foreign-language interfacing.
- Type erasure to escape to a dynamically typed or untyped coding style.

A good example for the last item is the need to escape from strong typing in cases where a given mapping problem can be more easily addressed using the simple structure of the universal representation type. We will illustrate this scenario in a Haskell context, but similar examples could be provided in an OO context (using reflective programming). We face the following mapping pipeline:

```
-- Haskell 98 code
myMapping = tree2data        -- Step 3: get back into typed world
          . trickyMapping    -- Step 2: untyped but powerful mapping
          . data2tree        -- Step 1: get out of typed world
```

In this pipeline, typed data (i.e., Haskell terms) is first exposed in an untyped tree format (cf. data2tree); then a 'tricky' mapping can be defined without running into the limitations imposed by the type system; finally the universal representation is mapped back into strongly typed data. The last step may fail of course.

A good example of a tricky mapping is a data conversion due to *type evolution* (i.e., evolution of the data model). In this case, there are two versions of the same system of data types which only differ in some details. Strongly typed programming fails to provide a concise way of mapping version A to version B; the *verbose* way would be to exhaustively cover all types and their cases in equations of functions that define a mapping. Untyped programming makes it easy to generically process the input data and to focus on the differences between the two versions.

For clarity, these are the types of the functions involved in myMapping:

```
data2tree      :: Data a => a -> Tree String
trickyMapping  :: Tree String -> Tree String
tree2data      :: Data a => Tree String -> Maybe a
```

We use n-ary, labeled trees as the universal representation type. Haskell's standard libraries readily provide the following algebraic data type; the type parameter of Tree denotes the label type, which is String in the example at hand:

```
data Tree a = Node a [Tree a]
```

3.2   Canonical Mappings

The above mappings from and to the universal representation type are canonical mappings. These are mappings that can be defined once and for all for a given class of data models (namely for all arbitrary (algebraic) data types in the example at hand). So let us define the mappings data2tree and tree2data. We employ Haskell's 'Scrap your boilerplate' style of generic programming [62, 63]. The mapping from data to trees is concisely defined as follows:

```
-- Haskell 98 + common extensions
-- Tree-alize data
data2tree :: Data a => a -> Tree String
data2tree x = Node
                (showConstr (toConstr x)) -- label
                (gmapQ data2tree x)       -- subtrees
```

As the type clarifies, the function data2tree is a generic function: it is polymorphic in the type to be mapped to the representation type. The definition of the mapping reads as follows. Using the primitive access function toConstr, we retrieve the constructor of the datum, which we turn into the string label of the tree using showConstr. Using the primitive traversal combinator gmapQ, we apply data2tree recursively to all the immediate subterms of the datum at hand, resulting in a list of untyped subtrees.

Here is also the inverse mapping — trees to data:

```
-- De-tree-alize tree
tree2data :: Data a => Tree String -> Maybe a
tree2data (Node l ts) = result
  where result = do
                  con <- readConstr resultType l
                  fromConstrL tree2data con ts
        resultType = (dataTypeOf (fromJust result))
```

The application of readConstr maps the string label into an actual constructor of the type to be populated. To this end, we use reflective information about the data type in question; cf. dataTypeOf. We construct a datum from the constructor by applying tree2data recursively on subtrees. The builder primitive fromConstrL takes a function to recursively build subterms, it also takes a constructor from which to build a term, and it takes the list of subterms in the universal representation.

3.3   Mapping Customization

The idea is that a canonical mapping is defined by a sort of generic procedure. Hence, we face an extreme form of a *non-canonical* mapping when the mapping is defined 'in all detail'. For instance, recall the point-to-point mappings in GUI data binding. However, we may also leave the grounds of canonical mappings due to customization. That is, a canonical default may exist, while the mapping setup is prepared to accommodate 'special cases'.

Let us look into object de-/serialization as a scenario that typically involves customization. A serialized default representation is available for each and every object type; the default can be overridden though by the OO programmer on a per-object-type basis. The following VB.NET fragment illustrates plain OO serialization; an object of type BinaryNode is serialized to an XML file (using a SOAP formatter):

```
' VB.NET 7.0 code
Dim myExp = New BinaryNode("")
' ... further object instantiation omitted ...
Dim s = File.Open("foo.xml", ...)
Dim f = New SoapFormatter
f.Serialize(s, myExp)
s.Close()
```

This direction corresponds to the data2tree function given above, except that we serialize (or tree-alize) to XML this time. An OO class is made fit for (de-)serialization by attaching a custom-attribute Serializable to the class:

```
<Serializable()> Public Class BinaryNode
'  ... elided  ...
End Class
```

The Serializable attribute tells the serialization library that it is 'allowed' to leverage reflective programming to carry out the mapping from objects to XML (and vice versa) in a canonical fashion. Customization of the canonical default is enabled by the following provisions. One can implement a designated ISerializable interface, and in particular, a GetObjectData method to override the generic reflection-based behavior for the serialization of the object's content:

```
Sub GetObjectData(ByVal info As SerializationInfo, _
                  ByVal context As StreamingContext)
Implements ISerializable.GetObjectData
'  Identify data for  serialization
info.AddValue("field1",  field1 );
info.AddValue("field2",  field2 );
End Sub
```

3.4   Type- vs. Instance-Based

A *type-based mapping* is defined as a relationship between the two involved data models, while it is assumed that this type correspondence (more or less) directly implies the actual value transformation for the two data models. By contrast, an *instance-based mapping* expresses value transformations directly. Type-based mappings are less expressive because they are also more abstract and canonical. In return, they make it easier to provide *updateability* (i.e., pushing back target-side value modifications to the source) and *composability* (i.e., performing target queries directly on the source).

A clear-cut example of a type-based mapping is canonical XML data binding where any given XML schema is mapped to a corresponding object model based on fixed rules that only refer to type patterns in XML schemas and object models; cf. Sec. 2.3. For instance, a specific mapping for XML-data binding could involve the following type-based mapping rule:

> *Any global element declaration without attribute declarations, with a sequence group for its content model such that the children of the sequence are local element declarations with distinct element names and nominally specified (as opposed to anonymous) content types is mapped to an object type with the global element name as class name (after name mapping), with fields for the local element declarations such that the local element names serve as field names (after name mapping) and the content types of the elements serve as field types (after type mapping).*

We leave it as an exercise to the reader to attempt a classification with regard to the 'type- vs. instance-based mapping' dichotomy for each of the examples of Sec. 2. (As we will argue shortly, such a classification may be difficult at times.) Let us consider a non-trivial but clear-cut example of an instance-based mapping. Suppose we want to extract a problem-specific XML view on some tables in a relational database. There are these tables: Orders, Employee and Customer; the XML view should look as follows:[9]

```
<Customer CustomerID="ALFKI">
  <Order OrderID="10643"/>
  <Order OrderID="10952"/>
  <Order OrderID="11011"/>
  <Employee LastName="Davolio"/>
  <Employee LastName="Leverling"/>
</Customer>
  ...
```

The XML view can be derived through a nested SELECT statement on the database. Some annotations like FOR XML AUTO, TYPE clarify that the result indeed should be 'rendered' as XML data rather than a list of queried rows:

```
// SQL with XML extensions of SQL Server 2005
SELECT CustomerID AS "CustomerID",
    (SELECT OrderID AS "OrderID"
     FROM Orders "Order"
     WHERE "Order".CustomerID = Customer.CustomerID
     FOR XML AUTO, TYPE),
    (SELECT DISTINCT LastName AS "LastName"
     FROM Employees Employee
     JOIN Orders "Order" ON "Order".EmployeeID = Employee.EmployeeID
     WHERE Customer.CustomerID = "Order".CustomerID
     FOR XML AUTO, TYPE)
FROM Customers Customer
FOR XML AUTO, TYPE
```

Let us also look at a less clear-cut example — the generic function for mapping Haskell terms of arbitrary types to trees according to a universal representation type. Do we face an example of a type-based or an instance-based mapping, or is it neither of these?

```
-- Tree-alize data
data2tree :: Data a => a -> Tree String
data2tree x = Node
                (showConstr (toConstr x)) -- label
                (gmapQ data2tree x)       -- subtrees
```

The mapping is type-based because it is fully generic. Likewise, any reflection-based mapping (such as object serialization) counts as type-based. Once customization enters the scene, the mapping may become partially instance-based. Here we assume that customization is regarded as a means of providing type-specific value transformations. The XML view example, given above, is clear-cut instance-based since it defines a query that is fully specific to certain tables, columns thereof and key-value relationships. One could impose a certain XML schema ('type') on the result of the instance-based

---

[9] Source: http://msdn.microsoft.com/library/en-us/dnsql90/html/
forxml2k5.asp

mapping, or one could even attempt to infer such a schema ('type'), but the mapping is nevertheless defined as a value transformation.

3.5   The Programmatic-to-Declarative Scale

It is common to say about mappings that they are defined *programmatically* or *declaratively*. These are not absolute concepts, but we attempt to justify these terms anyway since they are in common use and they may eventually turn out to be useful — once we better understand the scale; once we are in possession of proper definitions. (This is a future-work item.)

Programmatic Mapping. We use this term to refer to a mapping that is defined through program code such as in a general purpose programming language or a (typically Turing-complete) data processing language such as SQL, XSLT, XQuery, C#, Haskell, Java or VB. Hence, the FOR XML AUTO example from the previous section would count as programmatic. Let us review another programmatic mapping example. That is, let us map a business-object type, Order, to an XML type, Invoice. The following programmatic mapping code 'dots' into the business object, it eventually reaches sub-objects for customers and addresses, and it assembles new XML objects (using XML data binding) for invoices and items thereof; the encoding uses LINQ's SQL-like query syntax to iterate over object collections [73]:

```
// C# 3.0 / LINQ code (as of May 2006)
public static XmlTypes.Invoice Map(ObjectTypes.Order ord)
{
    return new XmlTypes.Invoice {
        name  = ord.cust.name,
        street = ord.cust.addr.street,
        city  = ord.cust.addr.city,
        zip   = ord.cust.addr.zip,
        state = ord.cust.addr.state,
        items = (from i in ord.items
                    select new XmlTypes.Item {
                        prodid   = i.prod.prodid,
                        price    = i.price,
                        quantity = i.quantity }).ToList(),
        total = ord.computeTotal()
    };
}
```

Declarative Mapping. We use this term to refer to a mapping that is not defined as an immediately executable program with an intrinsic operational semantics by itself; instead the mapping (description) is associated with an operational semantics by means of a separate interpretation, translation or code generation. For instance, the MAPSYM and MAPRULE constructs of Sec. 2.1 suggest that Maptool descriptions amount to declarative mappings. The implicit assumption is that a declarative mapping lends itself 'more easily' to different analyses and interpretations. For instance, one should expect

that declarative mappings are amenable to updateability (or reversibility, two-way updates) 'more easily'.

Let us review another declarative mapping example. That is, let us look at object-
relational mapping as it is done in HIBERNATE — an approach for relational persistence for 'idiomatic Java'.[10] The following fragment of a *class-centric mapping
specification* defines the structure of a class Cat in terms of a table CATS. Class properties are associated with table columns; a generator class is associated with the id
column:

```
<class name="Cat" table="CATS">
  <id name="id" column="uid" type="long">
    <generator class="hilo"/>
  </id>
  <property name="birthdate" type="date"/>
  <property name="color" not-null="true"/>
  <property name="sex" not-null="true" update="false"/>
  <property name="weight"/>
  <many-to-one name="mate" column="mate_id"/>
  <set name="kittens">
    <key column="mother_id"/>
      <one-to-many class="Cat"/>
  </set>
</class>
```

This declarative mapping admits the derivation of an actual Java class and a relational
schema such that the derived class facilitates the population of objects from relational
data and the persistence of objects as relational data.

3.6 Annotations vs. References

The Hibernate mapping of the previous section essentially prescribed both the ultimate
Java class and the associated relational schema. In many mapping scenarios, the actual
source and/or target types of a mapping predate the mapping effort, in which case the
purpose of a (declarative) mapping specification is really just to associate two existing
data model(s) with mapping rules or to define a new data model in terms of a given one.
In these cases, there exist two major options:

- *Annotations*: A data model is physically annotated with mapping rules.
- *References*: The mapping specification refers to components of the data model(s).

We illustrate this variation point in the context of XML data binding using the JAXB
technology for Java [91]. JAXB admits mapping customization using both inline
schema annotations and a standalone mapping specification with schema references.
Let us pick up the 'shapes example' again, which we started in Sec. 2.3, when we
discussed some drawbacks of xsd.exe's canonical mapping. The mapping of JAXB is
largely different from xsd.exe's mapping, and so we encounter different issues:

---

[10] Source: http://www.hibernate.org/hib_docs/reference/en/html/
mapping.html

- Recall the choice group of the Widgets element:

```
<xs:choice minOccurs="0" maxOccurs="unbounded">
  <xs:element name="Rectangle" type="Rectangle"/>
  <xs:element name="Square" type="Square"/>
  <xs:element name="Circle" type="Circle"/>
</xs:choice>
```

The canonical default mapping results in the following field:

```
protected List<Object> rectangleOrSquareOrCircle;
```

This mapping mostly illustrates Java's (as much as .NET's) weak story regarding 'old-style' discriminated unions. Still, there is room for improving the mapping result. In particular, we would like to use customization to replace the generated 'ugly' name rectangleOrSquareOrCircle by a more reasonable name, say Shapes.

- As we discussed for the xsd.exe technology, it is limiting that Rectangle, Square, Circle are unrelated base classes. Again, we would like to enable polymorphism by establishing a common base class using customization. As an aside, the .NET technique of using partial classes (cf. Sec. 2.3) cannot be adopted here because Java (1.5) does not offer an equivalent mechanism. (We could use aspect-oriented language extensions though [53].)

We will address both issues by using JAXB's customization mechanisms.[11]

Annotation-Based Mapping. We start the XML schema for shapes all over again. The annotation-based approach requires that we use JAXB-specific annotations in our schema. Hence, we need to bring all namespaces for JAXB into the scope:

```
<!-- XML schema -->
<xs:schema xmlns:xs="http://www.w3.org/2001/XMLSchema"
           xmlns:jaxb="http://java.sun.com/xml/ns/jaxb"
           xmlns:xjc="http://java.sun.com/xml/ns/jaxb/xjc"
           jaxb:version="2.0" jaxb:extensionBindingPrefixes="xjc">
<!-- Cont'd below -->
```

Right at the top level of the schema, we attach a new default base class, where we follow the rules of JAXB's schema for such binding declarations, and we also adhere to the rules for placing annotations in an XML schema. That is:

```
<!-- Cont'd from above -->
<xs:annotation>
  <xs:appinfo>
    <jaxb:globalBindings>
      <xjc:superClass name="drawApp.Shape"/>
    </jaxb:globalBindings>
  </xs:appinfo>
</xs:annotation>
<!-- Cont'd below -->
```

---

[11] Source: http://www.onjava.com/pub/a/onjava/2003/12/10/jaxb.html

We should note that this is a poor man's solution because Shape will now serve as the base class for *all* classes that are derived from the schema at hand. This is acceptable for the particular shapes schema. We also note that subclassing of the generated classes Rectangle etc. will be necessary once implementations of the draw method are to be added. (In the VB.NET version we were able to add the subclass-specific implementations of the draw method retroactively to the generated classes Rectangle etc. with the help of the partial-class technique. Again, we could use Java extensions, such as open-class mechanisms of aspect-oriented programming in similar ways [53].)

The other issue — provision of a reasonable name for the widgets collection — is resolved as follows. We add an annotation to the Widgets element such that the name of the generated Java property is defined as Shapes:

```
<!-- Cont'd from above -->
<xs:element name="Widgets">
  <xs:complexType>
    <xs:choice minOccurs="0" maxOccurs="unbounded">
      <xs:annotation>
        <xs:appinfo>
          <jaxb:property name="Shapes"/>
        </xs:appinfo>
      </xs:annotation>
      <xs:element name="Rectangle" type="Rectangle"/>
      <xs:element name="Square" type="Square"/>
      <xs:element name="Circle" type="Circle"/>
    </xs:choice>
  </xs:complexType>
</xs:element>
```

We elide the rest of the schema because it does not contain further annotations.

Reference-Based Mapping. JAXB offers a reference-based technique for customization that simply exploits the following facts. First, XML schemas are XML documents. Second, fragments in XML document can be addressed precisely through XPath expressions. It is indeed straightforward to transcribe the earlier annotation-based mapping description such that all binding declarations are gathered separately, and they are attached to schema parts through XPath references. So we reuse the earlier annotations, as is, but we collect them in designated JAXB bindings elements. For brevity, we only show the customization of the choice group:

```
<jxb:bindings node="//xs:element[@name='Widgets']//xs:complexType//xs:choice">
  <jxb:property name="Shapes"/>
</jxb:bindings>
```

We can see that the XPath expression under node descends into the element declaration of @name='Widgets', then into the complexType component underneath, until it hits on the subtree for the choice. One may argue whether or not the use of a low-level (schema-unaware, very syntactical) selector technique like XPath provides a sufficient level of abstraction. One alternative is offered by XML schema *component designators* [97] — an XML language for identifying XML Schema components.

3.7   Updateability

Various mapping scenarios require updateability in the sense that target-side value mod-ifications must be pushed back to the source. We have discussed this issue already in the specific context of GUI data binding. Object-relational mappings constitute another general class of mappings with an updateability requirement. That is, the database in-stance and its manifestation as an object graph are supposed to stay in sync. In the source-to-target direction, syncing is potentially just seen as a 'refresh' issue. In the target-to-source direction, syncing may require building the converse of a mapping (a 'view') that was originally thought of as being directed from source to target. For in-stance, an SQL-like view seems to be directed in that sense. Indeed, the *view-update translation problem* for databases [10, 34] is the classic form (and challenge) of an updateable mapping. The subsequent discussion is meant to provide an account on sce-narios for updateability, overall attacks, practical challenges and available foundations such as *data refinement* and *bi-directional transformations*.

Alleviated or Missing Updateability Requirement.   Updateability (or reversibility) is not a universal requirement for mappings. For instance, concrete-to-abstract syntax mappings are mostly not expected to be invertible. However, some degenerated form of updateability (such as origin tracking [22]) may still be required. Consider a language implementation with a type checker that consumes abstract syntax; when type errors are found, the type checker must be able to refer back to the original part of the input — for the programmer's convenience who needs to understand the error message.

'Near-to' Bijections.   Let us consider a basic (restricted) form of updateability:

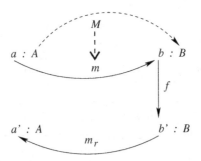

In this figure, we face types (data models) A and B and instances (elements) a and b. We also indicate the possibility of a type-level mapping M from A to B, but M is not essential. It is essential though that there an instance-level mapping m that maps a to b. Updateability of the mapping means that there is instance-level mapping m_r with which a changed target value, b', can be mapped back to an accordingly changed a'.

It is clear that m_r should be the converse of m. For a bijective m, updateability is trivially implied. However, this assumption is quite restrictive. For instance, a mapping that provides a *view* on a source (just as an SQL view) will be non-injective. In other scenarios, injectivity may be feasible but surjectivity cannot be delivered. For instance, the target types of a mapping may be intrinsically richer (say, more liberal). In the sequel, we identify deviations from bijectivity.

For a non-injective m, we have to come up with a heuristic to resolve the choice points when mapping back b' to a'. Suppose m projects *away* data (such as in a general SQL SELECT statement), we would have to expect that m_r somehow puts back the eliminated data. This is mathematically impossible for the shown diagram. We really need to have access to more information such as the original value a. We get to this different scheme in a second.

For an injective but non-surjective m, there are essentially two major cases. The first one is that B is representationally richer, but m and modifications on B do not (or are not supposed to) exploit this generality. In this case, we are still able to define a suitable m_r such that the composition of m and m_r is the identity. This case is nicely backed up by research on data refinement [42, 74, 78, 79, 6]. (The functions m and m_r are called the 'representation' and 'abstraction' mappings in standard data refinement terminology.) For instance, one can easily see that the following types are in refinement order:

$$X \subset X + 1$$
$$X \to (Y + Z) \subset (X \to Y) \times (X \to Z)$$

The first inequality is the abstract version of mapping a non-nullable type to a nullable type such as mapping a NOT NULL column of a 'value type' to an object type (which is 'nullable' because it is reference type). The second inequality demonstrates the elimination of sums through refinement. Again, the right-hand side admits more values such as a $y \in Y$ and a $z \in Z$ both being associated with the same $x \in X$. However, if the contract is such that the richer representation must not (cannot) be explored, then the mapping is still updateable.

For an injective but non-surjective m, we could also face the case that B is designed to maintain extra data along the life cycle of the mapped data on the target side. In this case, we assume that any b' can be narrowed down to the range of m in a meaning-preserving manner. Here is a simple example: change flags on the target side. These change flags may be essential for the optimized propagation of updates from the target to the source, but they are semantically irrelevant because we could (in theory) assume that all rows were changed.

Facilitation of Original Value. There are several ways to improve on the discussed notion of 'near-to' bijections. Perhaps the must general and fundamental improvement is to take the original value, a, into account when mapping b' to a':

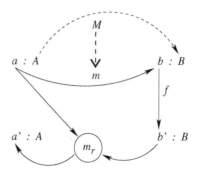

That is, when mapping back a piece of target data, b', we may also observe the associated piece of source data, a. Therefore, m_r can now compensate for a non-injective facet of m. (We may want to pass b to m_r too, or we may assume that m_r 're-evaluates' $m(a)$ in case it needs b.)

The data sets of Microsoft's ADO.NET technology for object-relational mapping instantiate this idea.[12] In-memory rows from the database carry identities (based on real or made-up primary keys). Hence, client-side changes can be pushed back to the database using 'keyed' UPDATE statements.

Bi-directional Transformations. Pierce, Hu and others have recently developed a formal notion of bi-directional transformations [36, 45, 13] that provide updateability for mappings on data. This approach facilitates the original value, but its real insight is centered around the discipline of transformation. What they call 'transformation' is (intuitively) a source-to-target instance-level mapping function which however comes with two 'interpretations' *get* and *put* for performing the mapping both ways. The bi-directional transformation literature studies the various primitive transformations and composition operators that can be fitted into this conceptual framework. Initially, this line of work applied to tree data only, but very recent developments also cover relational data. In fact, it had been observed from the very beginnings that bi-directional transformations are quite related to view-update translation for databases [10, 34].

It will be interesting to apply such theory to actual mapping problems such as object-XML mapping or object-relational mapping. We think that it is necessary to study updateability (say, bi-directional transformations) in a context that pays attention to all relevant concerns including these: remoting queries and DML operations, dealing with transient state, making scalar types vs. structured types updateable, making mapping lazy, and so on.

3.8 Usage Protocols

A very complex topic that we can only touch upon here is the provision of protocols as a complement of the mere data-modeling aspects of mapping. When talking about mappings, one may easily focus on typing issues and neglect the protocol that goes with the mapped data. An intuitive definition of the term 'usage protocol' is this: a usage protocol describes *order and conditions for the invocation of methods* in a (data access) API.

Protocols in XML Data Binding. For instance, let us consider the protocol for using a schema-derived object model in the context of XML data binding (i.e., object-XML mapping). The simple version of the protocol goes as follows:

1. De-serialize XML document into objects.
2. Operate on bound object structure using plain OO programming.
3. Serialize objects back to XML document.

---

[12] Source: http://msdn2.microsoft.com/en-us/library/y2ad8t9c(VS.80).aspx

This list is superficial. Here are some neglected protocol issues:

- Construction of structured content follows a certain protocol.
- Mixed content observation and injection requires special protocols.
- On-demand validation of global or other constraints may be provided.
- The tree semantics of XML imposes a certain contract on DML operations.
- Access to low-level XML views may require on-the fly (de-) serialization.
- There may be a protocol to handle transiently invalid content.

The Data-Sets Protocol. Let us consider the usage protocol for multiple-tier architectures using ADO.NET, in particular the ability of changing disconnected data sets that need to be committed later to the database.[13] The protocol identifies the following steps for creating and refreshing a data set, and in turn, updating the original data:

1. Build DataSet.
2. Fill DataSet with data from a data source using a DataAdapter.
3. Change DataSet by adding, updating or deleting DataRow objects.
4. For 2-tier apps:
   (a) Invoke Update on DataAdapter with the above DataSet as an argument.
   (b) Invoke AcceptChanges on DataSet.
5. For n-tier apps:
   (a) Invoke GetChanges to create a 2nd DataSet that features only the changes.
   (b) Send the second DataSet to the middle-tier via WebServices.
   (c) On the middle-tier,
       invoke Update on DataAdapter, with the 2nd DataSet instance as an argument.
   (d) From the middle-tier,
       send the updated DataSet back to the client via WebServices.
       (This DataSet may have server generated columns set to the latest value).
   (e) On the client-side,
       invoke Merge on original DataSet to merge the received DataSet, and then
       invoke AcceptChanges on the original DataSet.
6. Alternatively, invoke RejectChanges to cancel the changes.

The general observation is that the definition of a mapping is only complete when protocol issues are clearly defined, too. Unfortunately, in practice, mappings are not rigorously defined in this respect.

3.9 Further Reading

There are several fields in software engineering and programming language theory that involve notions of mapping with similarities to mappings in data processing. We do not dive into those fields here, but we document them as related work:

- As mentioned before: data refinement [42, 74, 78, 79, 6].
- As mentioned before: bi-directional transformations [36, 45, 13].

---

[13] Source: http://msdn.microsoft.com/library/default.asp?url=/library/
en-us/cpref/html/frlrfSystemDataDataSetClassTopic.asp

- Consistency maintenance in software modeling [60, 46].
- Consistency maintenance in cooperative editing [24, 90].
- Data views in functional programming (patterns for ADTs) [98, 16, 77].
- Program views in intentional programming and fluid AOP [88, 5, 52].
- Reconcilable model transformation in model-driven development [85, 26].
- Source-code modeling in re-/reverse engineering [83, 58, 69, 44, 56].
- The general notion of coupled transformations [61].

4   Cross-Paradigm Impedance Mismatches

Having discussed mapping examples and concepts, we still need to get a better handle on the following question: 'Why is it that inter-paradigmatic mappings are so difficult?'. The present section identifies and illustrates the impedance mismatches amongst the major paradigms for data modeling and processing: Cobol, object, relational and XML. We focus on the technical dimension; we attempt to circumvent the 'cultural' dimension of impedance mismatches [7]. (This separation is not always easy to mark off though.)

4.1   Characteristics of Major Paradigms

The impedance mismatches are rooted in the different characteristics of the paradigms. So we recall these characteristics here — as a means of preparation.

Object-Oriented Programming

For simplicity, we focus on mainstream, class-based, imperative, typed, object-oriented programming languages like C++, C#, Java, and VB.

- *Reference semantics*. Object structures are graphs that are basically assembled by storing references to objects in data fields of objects. An OO language may prefer not to surface the distinction between objects and object references (say pointers), but the semantics of objects is reference-based anyhow. Object construction returns a reference to the newly constructed object. Objects are passed by reference to methods. Objects can be compared for equality in the sense of object identity (i.e., object reference equality).
- *Encapsulation*. The data part of object structures does not exist in isolation. Instead, an object is a capsule of data *and* behavior (i.e., methods). The interface of an object typically provides restricted access to the data fields (i.e., to the low-level state) of an object. Consistent changes of an object's state (as well as conglomerations of objects) are to be achieved through the behavioral interface of an object. (In object-based languages and advanced frameworks, methods may be part of an object's state, too.)
- *Properties*. Data fields are often not directly exposed through an object's interface, but the object's state is instead published through *properties* adding a level of indirection. This idiom allows one to hide representation details while still providing a structural view on the object's state.

– *Abstract classes and interfaces*. An object model defines its data model potentially also through types that cannot be directly instantiated. That is, OO languages allow for abstract classes, and most typed OO languages support interfaces by now.

– *Subtype polymorphism*. Classes and interfaces are arranged in subtype hierarchies. Each variable is declared with a static type that serves as a bound for the type of objects that may be assigned to the variable. A subtype may add components to the state, and it may enrich the interface. Ideally, subtypes preserve the observable behavior of the supertype; cf. the *substitution principle* [66].

– *Generics*. Most typed OO languages support generics (parametric polymorphism) by now. That is, classes, interfaces and method types can be parameterized in types.

Relational Databases

We restrict ourselves to SQL databases in the sequel.

– *Relational algebra*. Conceptually, database tables are mathematical relations in the sense of sets of tuples over *scalar* data [19, 21]. One can process these relations in terms of set-theoretic operations (such as union, difference and intersection) as well as relational algebra operations (such as projection, selection, Cartesian product and join). In practice, we deviate from this mathematical ideal a bit, e.g., order of rows does matter in tables; SQL's SELECT statement combines several operations.

– *Keys*. Both at a fundamental level (i.e., relational algebra) and in practice, table columns may specifically serve for the global identification of table rows (cf. primary key) such that other tables may refer to the identified rows (cf. foreign key). It is a crucial ingredient of relational schema design to identify such primary and foreign keys as they will be used in queries (for joins) and in ensuring the referential integrity of the database as a whole.

– *Data integrity*. More generally, a database schema makes contributions to the effective maintenance of data integrity. To this end, integrity constraints (such as foreign key constraints), cascading operations and triggers can be used.

– *Transactions*. DML operations on a database are scoped in groups that are called transactions. Only the successful completion of such groups leads to an observable state change of the database. Transactions facilitate consistency in databases. For instance, the insertion or deletion of a row in one table may only be valid in combination with updating rows in other tables. Transactions may be expressed as stored SQL procedures that consist of SQL DML statements.

– *Schema evolution*. Within limits, a database schema can be adapted, perhaps even while the database is on-line. The schema may evolve in such a way that all or most previously valid queries continue to be valid.

– *Views*. In addition to physical tables, there can be views, which are defined by SQL queries. Views are never materialized; the defining queries are executed once the view itself is queried. Updates on views are relatively restricted.

XML Document Processing

We have in mind XML processing using XPath, XSLT, DOM, XQuery and friends. We also include uses such that XPath or other XML languages are embedded into general-purpose languages such as Java or C#.

- *Tree structure.* XML elements are normally organized as trees — as opposed to flat tuples or arbitrary graphs. One may use IDREFs to refer to remote elements, but this idiom is only occasionally used in practice. Also, XML *types* may be recursive, but the prevailing concept in XML is hierarchical, tree-like organization of data.
- *Element vs. attribute dichotomy.* "A perennial question arising in the mind [... of XML designers ...] is whether to model and encode certain information using an element, or alternatively, using an attribute. ... Experienced markup-language experts offer different opinions ..."[14]
- *Mixed content.* One may mix structured content (elements) and text. Processing instructions (PIs) and comments may occur, too. Some XML use cases require high fidelity: all details of text, PIs and comments are to be preserved. This issue is very similar to layout and comment preservation for programming language processing [93, 56] (also known as syntax retention).
- *Order matters.* Element tags are not meant to be (unambiguous) selectors or labels. Multiple element particles with the same element name may occur in a content model. XML processing functionality may care about the order of elements. Order also matters with regard to querying. That is, queries (based on XPath and friends) are normally supposed to return elements in *document order*.
- *The XML infoset.* The representation-biased view on XML is complemented by a more abstract interpretation of XML documents: the *infoset* [95]. This semantic domain regulates what sort of information is associated with each node in a well-formed (and not necessarily valid) XML document. The infoset hints at the *axis-based navigation* style for XML. That is, one can navigate to the children, to the parent, and to the siblings. In fact, the document object model (DOM [94]) almost directly implements the infoset semantics. In reality, there is not just a simple data model for XML. Most notably, each XML API implements a slightly different variation on the infoset. Also, the data model of XPath is yet again slightly different from plain infoset.

Cobol

Cobol is not just the most widely used programming language for data-processing applications; it is in fact a language that has been designed to specifically serve this role. More than that, Cobol continuously evolves to co-exist with other paradigms. (For instance, Cobol has been turned into a proper OO language over the last decade or so [48]. Admittedly, OO Cobol sees limited adoption.) Here are Cobol's characteristics:

- *Files as a language concept.* Unlike development platforms of the last 10 years or so, persistent data processing is not viewed as an 'API issue' in Cobol. Instead, statically typed language constructs for keyed and sequential file access amount to an intrinsic component of the language since the 1960s. ("No strings".) The concept of keyed files is similar to the relational model except that file access is record-based and general joins need to be rolled out as nested loops.
- *Database support.* Embedded SQL (optionally combined with transaction monitors like CICS) allows for processing relational data in Cobol code. Embedded SQL can

---

[14] Source: http://xml.coverpages.org/elementsAndAttrs.html

be pre-compiled (including compile-time data dictionary access), which implies static typing and enables optimizations. SQL queries are executed using a cursor model, and result rows are stored in accordingly structured (potentially generated) group fields, based on a simple mapping of SQL data types to Cobol types.

- *XML support.* Conceptually, records (and Cobol data in general) are described through arbitrarily nested group fields. This is already a good fit with the tree-like organization in XML except for the issue of unbounded occurrence constraints and choice types. Also, Cobol readily offers 'representation-oriented' data types, just as XML schema. Additional native XML support is being added to the standard [8]. This addition allows file processing on XML data and validation. Content models can be described more or less like normal file records. A cursor-based model resolves the issue of unbounded occurrence constraints. Choices may be treated procedurally by tag inspection.

4.2   An Open-Ended List of Mapping Issues

We attempt to pinpoint 'issues' that witness impedance mismatches for inter-paradigm mappings. The issues are phrased as questions. We reckon that each such question does not lend itself to a trivial, unambiguous and non-debated answer.

Map a Relational Schema to an Object Model

Such a mapping is needed when an OO application requires access to business data that happens to reside in a relational database. This is perhaps the most common mapping scenario in IT today up to a point that experts have labeled this problem as the 'Vietnam of Computer Science'. There are various more or less complex technologies in existence that attempt to address this problem, e.g., EJB and Hibernate, and some technologies were never completed. We phrase some issues as questions:

- How to map database schemas to class hierarchies?
  (What data is going to be private if any? What to use inheritance for, if at all?)
- How to perform queries on objects (that represent relations)?
  (Should we mimic SQL? Should we use OOQL, XPath or XQuery?)
- How do foreign key constraints show up in the behavior of objects?
  (How to map foreign key constraints to an OO design?)
- How would we possibly carry out schema evolution on the OO program?
  (Also, can we achieve independent evolution of database schema and object model?)
- How to map SQL views and stored SQL procedures to objects?
- How to enable transactions in the object-life cycle?
- Can we make any use of interface polymorphism?
- How to map object access to SQL queries?

Map an Object Model to a Relational Schema

Such a mapping is needed in the following situations: (i) the database is meant to serve for plain object persistence; (ii) the architecture of an OO application is constrained to expose its object model as a relational schema, which may be considered as a strong version of (i). In both cases, the mere mapping problem might couple up with a migration problem. That is, we may need to re-engineer the OO application that pre-dated the mapping requirement. 'Normal objects' are to be replaced or complemented by database-access objects.

- What classes, fields and properties are mapped to relations?
  (In particular, what private fields have to be persisted if any?)
- How do we map single/multiple OO inheritance to relations?
  (How does this affect querying tables that correspond to subclasses?)
- How to extract foreign key constraints from OO designs?
- How to extract NOT NULL constraints from OO designs?
- How to map Eiffel's, Java's or .NET's generics to the database?
- What to do about interface polymorphism, if anything?

Map an Object Model to an XML Schema

Such a mapping is needed in the following situations: (i) data import and export for the sake of open, interoperable software applications; (ii) XML-based persistence; (iii) remote-method invocation and web services. Object models seem to lend themselves to reasonably restricted XML schemas. However:

- What classes, fields and properties need to be mapped anyhow?
  (In particular, what private fields are part of the intrinsic object state?)
- How do we draft the hierarchical organization of the XML data?
  (What associations to represent through hierarchy? Should we use IDREFs?)
- What to do about sharing or cycles in the object graph?
  (How do we even know for sure where sharing and cycles may occur?)
- How to enable platform interoperability (cf. Java vs. .NET)?
- What to do about interface polymorphism, if anything?
- Which XSD organization style to use when?
- How to map generics to XML schema?

Map an XML Schema to an Object Model

That is, the XML schema serves the role of a 'first-contract' data model in this case. The overall scenarios for this mapping direction are more or less the same as for the other direction: objects to XML, but this time we face the full generality of XML schemas as opposed to the subset that is targeted by a given 'objects to XML' approach.

- How to group tree elements in objects?
- How to provide fidelity for mixed content?
- How to map ID literals into object references?
- Do simple XSD types constitute wrapper classes?
- How to map identity constraints to OO behavior?
- How to map facets (maxInclusive etc.) to OO methods?

- How to represent order constraints in OO code if at all?
- How to map type derivation by restriction to OO mechanisms?
- How do we cope with XML data that does not comply to the schema?
- Do we need to distinguish elements from complex types in OO types?
- How to map anonymous model groups to fields/properties in OO code?
- Can we enable independent evolution of XML schema and object model?

Map an XML Schema to a Relational Schema

Such a mapping is needed when we want to use a relational database as an XML store. (In practice, we even may want to store untyped XML data or to neglect the XML schema for the purpose of storing XML data.) Another scenario for XML-to-relational is that we actually aim at a faithful relational schema so that we can operate on the data in two worlds: XML and SQL.

- How to 'normalize' the XML schema?
- How to map XSD's built-in simple types to SQL data types?
- How to avoid clashes of XML IDs from different documents in the database?
- How to (efficiently) support XPath et al. on the relational image?

Map a Relational Schema to an XML Schema

Such a mapping is needed for the provision of an XML view on relational data. As in the case of several previous mapping couples, we may have a choice between canonical mappings (that take any relational schema and expose it as XML without any contribution from a programmer) or custom mappings, where the programmer specifically describes the shape and the content of the desired XML view relative to the relational schema. (These two options are sometimes also referred to as *prescriptive* vs. *descriptive* mappings.)

- When to use IDs/IDREFs and when to use nesting?
- How to deal with circular reference chains in tables?
- How to map SQL data types to XSD's built-in simple types?
- *Exercise to the reader: find some more variation points.*

4.3   Exemplar Frictions

We increase the level of detail by discussing exemplar frictions.

OO Lacks Foreign Key Constraints

Foreign key constraints in relational databases serve foremost for referential integrity in a database. One cannot accidentally delete a master row if there are still references to this row from elsewhere through foreign keys. Modern databases (such as SQL 92 variants) provide support for *cascading deletes and updates* such that update or delete operations are distributed automatically from the table with the primary key to tables with corresponding foreign keys. (In addition, there is also the *trigger* technique to achieve this behavior with slightly more effort.)

An example follows. Let us assume a stock table that contains a list of items that a shop stocks and sells, as well as a stock transaction table that contains a list of purchases and sales for each stock item. We can only delete a stock item if there are no transactions left that refer to the stock item. However, a cascading delete makes sense here: the deletion of the stock item should imply the deletion of the transactions for this stock item. This is expressed by the ON DELETE CASCADE phrase as part of the foreign key constraint.

```
// SQL Server 2000 code
CREATE TABLE stock_trans
(
trans_id int NOT NULL IDENTITY PRIMARY KEY,
stock_id int NOT NULL REFERENCES stock(stock_id) ON DELETE CASCADE,
// ... further columns elided ...
)
```

Cascading operations are not readily available in the OO paradigm. Let us assume that there are classes for stock items and transactions. Each transaction object holds a reference to the corresponding stock-item object. Also, let us assume that we maintain a collection of stock items. The trouble is that there is no primitive OO operation for the effective eradication of a stock item including all objects that refer to it. One may employ a range of techniques for the encoding of cascading deletes: weak references, explicit memory management with bi-directional references, the publish-subscriber design pattern, designated design patterns [76, 75], and ownership types [18, 14, 17] (which would call for language extensions).

Cobol's REDEFINES

We are asked to migrate the file-based data management layer of an existing Cobol application to database technology. Such a migration consists of three parts: (i) reverse engineering of the file-based data model with the goal to derive a reasonable relational schema; (ii) data conversion to populate the database; (iii) re-engineering of the Cobol code to perform database access in place of file access. We will focus on (i) because we want to illustrate an impedance mismatch between keyed or sequential Cobol files and the relational model. Once we understand the data-model mapping, the actual data conversion (i.e., ii) is relatively straightforward. (iii) is rather involved. Clearly, migration is not the only option. There are cases in which a Cobol system reaches the end of its conceded life, and we are requested to convert the legacy data to a database. In this case, we can ignore (iii).

Cobol offers (unsafe) variants through its REDEFINES clause: a given record can assume different types. The reverse engineering part needs to identify such records and eradicate them in some way. (The relational model does not comprise designated expressiveness for variant records.) Let us consider an example. The following record description for orders distinguishes *header* records vs. *position* records, which both start with a common structure for key data:

```
* Cobol '85 code
FILE SECTION.
 FD   ORDER-FILE.
 01   ORDER-RECORD.
* The level 05 group item holds common key data.
  05   ORDER-KEY-DATA.
   10 ORDER-NUMBER    PIC 9(8).
   10 ORDER-ACCOUNT   PIC 9(10).
   10 ORDER-PRODUCT   PIC 9(8).
   10 ORDER-POSNR     PIC 9(4).


* Note:
*   - ORDER-HEADER-DATA is redefined by ORDER-POSITION-DATA
*   - If ORDER-POSNR <= 9, then we face a HEADER.
*   - If ORDER-POSNR > 9, then we face a POSITION.
  05   ORDER-HEADER-DATA.
   10   ... details of header elided ...


  05   ORDER-POSITION-DATA
       REDEFINES ORDER-HEADER-DATA.
   10   ... details of position elided ...
```

The comment reveals that the condition ORDER-POSNR > 9 is supposed to hold for position records. Here, ORDER-POSNR is a data item that contributes to the key of any ORDER record. We may not always find such a helpful comment, neither do we necessarily trust such documentation. Ultimately, we need to engage in reverse engineering indeed. The following code pattern supports the claim in the comment; it aims to read position records while it initializes ORDER-POSNR with 10:

```
* MOVE ALL POSITION RECORDS TO FORM FOR DISPLAY
INITIALIZE ORDER-RECORD.
MOVE FORM-ORDER    TO ORDER-NUMBER.
MOVE FORM-ACCOUNT TO ORDER-ACCOUNT.
MOVE FORM-PRODUCT TO ORDER-PRODUCT.
MOVE 10            TO ORDER-POSNR.
START ORDER-FILE KEY IS >= ORDER-KEY-1.
READ ORDER-FILE NEXT RECORD.
PERFORM WITH TEST BEFORE UNTIL NOT FILE-STATUS-OK
  MOVE CORRESPONDING
     ORDER-POSITION-DATA TO FORM-FOR-ORDER
  READ ORDER-FILE NEXT RECORD
END-PERFORM.
```

Based on such evidence, we define two database tables corresponding to the variants:

```
// SQL Server 2000 code
CREATE TABLE Order_Header
(
  Order_Number int NOT NULL IDENTITY PRIMARY KEY,
  Order_Account int NOT NULL,
```

```
Order_Product int,
// ... other data items elided ...
)
CREATE TABLE Order_Position
(
  Order_Number int NOT NULL
    REFERENCES Order_Header(Order_Number),
  Order_Posnr int NOT NULL,
  // ... other data items elided ...
)
```

That is, the order number is designed to be the primary key of the table for header records, while it is a foreign key in the table for position records. The position number only shows up in the table for position records. All general key data (account, product, ...) is centralized in the table for header records. The illustrated mapping requires relatively deep insight, when done manually, or very much advanced program analyses, if the mapping should be automated.

5   Call to Arms

For *some* of the above mapping couples, substantial research work has been delivered. For instance, the couple 'map a relational schema to an XML schema' has received ample interest [86, 32, 27]. For *all* of the above mapping couples, actual technologies do exist and serve business-critical roles everywhere in IT. For *most* of the above mapping couples, the scientific understanding is largely unsatisfactory. Progress is mainly achieved through industrial drive. No integrated foundation of mapping is available. When we compare the situation in mapping with the one in compiler construction, we are clearly in need of a 'Dragon Book' [3] for mapping. However, before someone can write this book, more research is needed. Also, previous and current mapping projects should be carefully analyzed so that the observations (often failures) can be effectively used in new mapping projects and as driving forces for mapping research.

5.1   Overall Goals

Foundations — we are in need of general and scalable foundations across paradigms;
Robustness — data access in data processing must not 'go wrong';
Evolvability — data models, APIs and code must not resist change;
Productivity — we need a simpler way of developing data-access layers.

5.2   A List of Challenges

Here is a list of challenges that we see ahead of us. We reckon that progress in the area of data-processing application development boils down to progress regarding these challenges.

– *Data models as contracts.* While data-modeling languages such as OCL (UML) and Schematron provide rich *constraint mechanisms*, the transcription of such models to program types may not transport all constraints to the static type system of the programming language at hand. Extending the (static) type system of languages is one direction [72, 71, 12]. Delivering a language design with support for general pre- and post-conditions is another direction. In fact, a blend of verification, static typing, soft typing [25, 101] and dynamic typing seems to be most promising. We quote from [29]:

> *"We believe that the development of an assertion system [...] serves two purposes. On one hand, the system has strong practical potential because existing type systems simply cannot express many assertions that programmers would like to state. On the other hand, an inspection of a large base of invariants may provide inspiration for the direction of practical future type system research."*

Further work on the tension between conservative (static) type-system extensions vs. more flexible language support for typing and verification should also benefit from the body of work on OO specification languages such as VDM++; cf. [30].

- *Data-model evolution.* Research on database schema evolution has a history of about 20 years [11, 65]. In practice, simple forms of relational schema evolution are established; think of ALTER TABLE in SQL. Related foundations and techniques have been contributed by the field of data re-engineering and reverse engineering [37, 67, 39] with focus on relational schemas and ER models in information systems. The problem of XML schema evolution may just gain momentum. In OO programming and design, several refactorings address object-model evolution — in particular class refactorings [80, 31]. In reality, data-model evolution is a complex topic, and existing methods are difficult to apply (because of restrictions and engineering reasons).

- *Co-evolution of programs.* Assuming that we master the evolution problem for data models themselves, we get to the next hurdle: co-evolution of data-processing programs. This is a particularly challenging (and potentially beneficial) mode of evolution. We need *cross-paradigm transformations* to push changes of relational and XML schemas into application programs, 4GL code, and others.

- *Loose coupling of data models.* Rather than thinking in terms of the propagation of transformations from the data model to the data-model-dependent code, we may also anticipate the problem up-front, and employ an architecture with loose coupling. That is, most business logic would be coded against a more stable object model, which is intelligently mapped to a less stable 'external' data model. Loose coupling would not just help with localizing impact of evolution, it would also allow us to use the preferred internal object model, which may differ from a potentially suboptimal, external data model. Unfortunately, we lack comprehensive foundations of loose coupling.

- *Data model reverse engineering* When we talked about mapping so far, we mostly focused on the technical provision of the mapping assuming that we have a reasonable understanding of the data source and its conceptual, logical as well as physical data model. In practice, we also need to address the problems of 'data-model rot' or 'data-model legacy'. To this end, we need to engage in data-model reverse engineering and re-engineering. These activities may concern both external data models (such as relational schemas) and object models.

5.3   Challenges in Detail

We pick out two of the above items for a detailed discussion.

Re-/reverse Engineering of Data Models

Defining mappings on existing data (or object) models in a concise and robust manner is one issue, knowing the concepts *to map from and to* is another issue that easily dominates the picture whenever we face complex data models, whenever we specifically want to provide a simple-to-digest view.

Let us consider an example. The emerging *Mendocino* project (an effort in which SAP and Microsoft Corp. participate) is aimed at the integration of SAP processes (such as time management, budget monitoring, organizational management and travel and expense management) directly into Microsoft Office.[15] We may ask how difficult it is to provide such interoperability. One thing to notice is that interoperability is more than a technical term. For Mendocino to be *useful* in the context of office-ware integration, the business processes need to be exposed through *lean data models and APIs*.

In [89], the implementation of SAP R/3 is analyzed in several respects. The published data points lead us to the conclusion that a useful interoperation of SAP with Office is very challenging. We quote some details. For the record, SAP R/3 is implemented in the 4th generation language ABAP/4 (short for Advanced Business Application Programming). According to the results of the study, SAP R/3 consists of 40,000 programs, 34,000 functional modules, 11,500 tables. Regarding the internal data model, it was found that 69% of all data type declarations were not reused (i.e., they were just declared and used *once*); 6.2% were not used at all. For most of the remaining declarations, the number of reuses (in this huge system) is surprisingly small. For four fifths of the reused declarations, reuse was restricted to 2–5 times.

These figures indicate that any reasonable SAP API or any data model for SAP integration would need to make a major effort in order to hide the complexity of the 'as-implemented' data model and to furnish a concise and clear data model that can actually be used by programmers. (The Mendocino project does not start from zero because it can leverage previous interoperability efforts that have gone into the SAP software.)

In the context of software re-/reverse engineering, effective and well-founded methods for data re-/reverse engineering [37, 4, 43, 39] have been developed. We wonder whether these methods can also be adopted in a mapping context that aims at the delivery of programming APIs. In this context, we are not interested in the extraction of relational schemas or ER models for the sake of understanding, system modification or new development; instead we are interested in the provision of programming-enabled views on as-implemented data models.

Loose Coupling for Data and Object Models

In Fig. 4, we illustrate the not so obvious point that a given data model could correspond to quite different object models in an application. The first object model is 'flat' — just

---

[15] http://www.sap.com/company/press/press.epx?pressID=4520

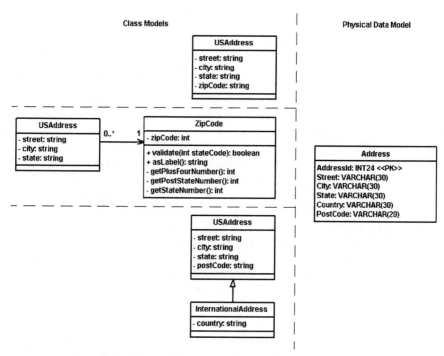

(Source: http://www.agiledata.org/essays/drivingForces.html)

Fig. 4. Different object models for the same physical model

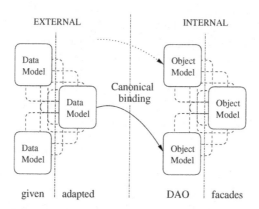

Fig. 5. A mapping web for data-processing applications

like the physical model. The second object model separates out zip-code objects and extra information about them. Both the first and the second model only deal with US addresses; they omit the country code. The third model defines a flat address structure, but it uses subclassing (in a somewhat pragmatic way) to enable the representation of international addresses.

Differences between external and internal models may arise for various reasons:

- We changed the external data model, but did not change the object model.
- We want to bind to the external data model but favor a different object model.
- We face a legacy object model to be bound to a new external data model.

Mapping techniques should help us to realize different internal (and even external) models at a high level of abstraction. Unfortunately, in practice, the various models in an application are typically hand-crafted and laborious low-level mapping code is needed to move data back and forth.

In Fig. 5, we sketch the idea of a flexible architecture for data-processing applications. One assumption is that external data models can be combined and transformed *before* entering the software application as canonically derived object models for *data-access objects* (DAO).[16] (The intent of DAOs is the provision of a data-access layer that does not expose implementation details of the underlying data management; see Fig. 6 for an example.) Another assumption is that any number of canonical object models, in turn, can be combined and transformed into 'facades' — these are the object models that are considered useful for implementing the business logic. We may want to assume that the architecture makes it unnecessary to materialize data in interim data-model layers.

For mappings on external models, one can readily use techniques that are specific to the underlying data-modeling paradigm, e.g., XQuery or XSLT for XML, or SQL views for relational databases. (Creating new data models with contributions from different paradigms is more involved.) In Fig. 7, we illustrate tool support for XML schema mapping. (The actual example encounters schema composition by instance-level join.) The tool at hand generates XSLT scripts from the visually designed mapping. Under certain preconditions, one obtains scripts that map both ways.

The situation for mappings on internal models is in flux. There are various design patterns that could be said to help (somewhat) with the design and implementation of mappings: composite, facade, bridge, factory, model-view controller, and most notably, mediator [59, 33]. The *mediator* pattern directly allows for the systematic translation of an API into another API (APIs) using connectors as the primary concept. (Notice how well this corresponds to the XML schema mapping exercise in Fig. 7.) The overall notion of mediator is of profound use in the related field of data integration [82, 84], but the design pattern is still too weak to do the heavy lifting for mappings in data-processing applications. The mediator pattern does not (nor does any other pattern we know of) provide higher-level operations on data or object models. We can describe the sought-after improvement:

> *The design and the implementation of programmatic object-model-to-object-model mappings is normally carried out at a low level of abstraction, in terms of free-wheeling, basic OO code. We need higher-level language concepts and programming techniques and APIs that enable these mappings more directly.*

Language-integrated query mechanisms (such as LINQ [73]) may serve this agenda.

---

[16] http://java.sun.com/blueprints/corej2eepatterns/Patterns/Data-AccessObject.html http://java.sun.com/blueprints/patterns/DAO.html

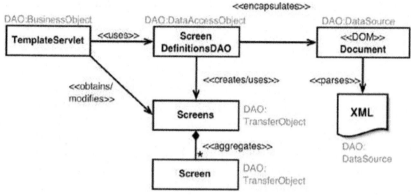

(Source: http://java.sun.com/blueprints/patterns/DAO.html)

Fig. 6. The design pattern for 'data-access objects' — instantiated for the case of a XML-based data for screen definitions. The business object accesses screen definitions through the data-access object without commitment to the general or particular XML format used underneath.

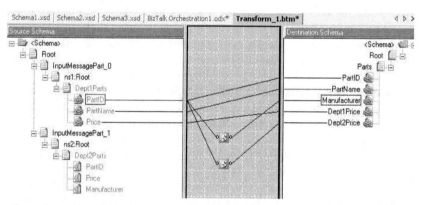

(Source: http://geekswithblogs.net/synboogaloo/archive/2005/04/22/37335.aspx)

Fig. 7. Join two XML schemas (based on the Biztalk technology)

6   Concluding Remarks

We have compiled a survey on mapping practices and mapping issues for data modeling and data-processing with Cobol, object, relational and XML. We have provided rich literature and on-line references. However, the problem is that the intricacies of intra- and inter-paradigm mappings are not fully appreciated by the archetypal research agenda on programming languages and software engineering. As a result, this important field of computer science ends up being driven by industry — not surprisingly more or less in an ad-hoc fashion.

We too adopt an ad-hoc method here to make our point — 'Google' science:

- http://www.google.com/search?q=object-relational+mapping
- http://www.google.com/search?q=XML+data+binding
- http://www.google.com/search?q=model-driven+transformation
- http://www.google.com/search?q=aspect-oriented+programming

At the time of writing this conclusion, we observe the following situation. The Google results for the first two links on *object-relational mapping* and *XML data binding* do not lead to *any* research content on the first two pages. (We didn't continue beyond that.) The Google results for the last two links on *model-driven transformation* and *aspect-oriented programming* readily list several research papers and research projects on the first page. We reckon that, in principle, mappings are worth the same scale of attention in research. Given the fact that IT industry is fighting with various impedance mismatches and data-model evolution problems for decades, it seems to be safe to start a research career that specifically addresses these problems.

One could perhaps think that the bulk of impedance mismatches will be resolved by language extensions soon. (Why not earlier?) The fix-point of this argument is that we end up with a language in which all mainstream data-modeling paradigms and programming paradigms are 'happily' united. We may need to try indeed, just to see whether the resulting paradigm soup is still digestible. However, the fix-point may be hard to reach anyway. New data modeling and data processing ideas come up all the time. Also, platform providers as much as compiler, IDE, API and tool vendors use differentiation as an intrinsic element of their business strategies. The increasing use of standards in IT (think of reference schemas etc.) is a good thing, but the increasing number of standards (and their size) challenges fix-point iteration, too. So it is essential to continuously cope with diversity. It is therefore a good idea to intensify research efforts on mapping problems that concern Create-Read-Update-Delete applications.

Acknowledgments. We are grateful for the insightful proposals by the GTTSE referees and for the mapping discussions with members of the Data Programmability Team at Microsoft. In particular we want to acknowledge contributions by Avner Aharoni, Brian Beckmann, Kawarjit Bedi, Dan Doris, Sergey Dubinets, Charlie Heinemann, Priya Lakshminarayanan, Chris Lovett, Michael Rys, Soumitra Sengupta, Dave Remy and Adam Wiener.

References

1. P. Achten, M. C. J. D. van Eekelen, and M. J. Plasmeijer. Compositional Model-Views with Generic Graphical User Interfaces. In B. Jayaraman, editor, *Practical Aspects of Declarative Languages, 6th International Symposium, PADL 2004, Dallas, TX, USA, June 18-19, 2004, Proceedings*, volume 3057 of *LNCS*, pages 39–55. Springer, 2004.
2. P. Achten, M. C. J. D. van Eekelen, and M. J. Plasmeijer. Generic Graphical User Interfaces. In P. W. Trinder, G. Michaelson, and R. Pena, editors, *Implementation of Functional Languages, 15th International Workshop, IFL 2003, Edinburgh, UK, September 8-11, 2003, Revised Papers*, volume 3145 of *LNCS*, pages 152–167. Springer, 2004.
3. A. Aho, R. Sethi, and J. Ullman. *Compilers. Principles, Techniques and Tools*. Addison-Wesley, 1986.

4. P. Aiken, A. H. Muntz, and R. Richards. Dod legacy systems: Reverse engineering data requirements. *Communications of the ACM*, 37(5):26–41, 1994.
5. W. Aitken, B. Dickens, P. Kwiatkowski, O. de Moor, D. Richter, and C. Simonyi. Transformation in intentional programming. In P. Devanbu and J. Poulin, editors, *Proceedings, Fifth International Conference on Software Reuse*, pages 114–123. IEEE Computer Society Press, 1998.
6. T. L. Alves, P. F. Silva, J. Visser, and J. N. Oliveira. Strategic Term Rewriting and Its Application to a VDMSL to SQL Conversion. In J. Fitzgerald, I. J. Hayes, and A. Tarlecki, editors, *FM 2005: Formal Methods, International Symposium of Formal Methods Europe, Newcastle, UK, July 18-22, 2005, Proceedings*, volume 3582 of *LNCS*, pages 399–414. Springer, 2005.
7. S. W. Ambler. The Object-Relational Impedance Mismatch, 2002–2005. Amysoft Inc.; online article
   http://www.agiledata.org/essays/impedanceMismatch.html.
8. ANSI. Information Technology — Programming languages, their environments and system software interfaces — Native COBOL Syntax for XML Support, Feb. 2005. J4/05-0049, WG4n0229, ISO/IEC JTC 1/SC 22/WG4, ISO/IEC TR 24716:200x(E).
9. J. Aycock. Extending Old Compiler Tools with Meta-Tools. In H. R. Arabnia and H. Reza, editors, *Proceedings of the International Conference on Software Engineering Research and Practice, SERP '04, June 21-24, 2004, Las Vegas, Nevada, USA, Volume 2*, pages 841–845. CSREA Press, 2004.
10. F. Bancilhon and N. Spyratos. Update semantics of relational views. *ACM Transactions on Database Systems*, 6(4):557–575, 1981.
11. J. Banerjee, W. Kim, H.-J. Kim, and H. F. Korth. Semantics and implementation of schema evolution in object-oriented databases. In *SIGMOD '87: Proceedings of the 1987 ACM SIGMOD International conference on management of data*, pages 311–322, New York, NY, USA, 1987. ACM Press.
12. G. M. Bierman, E. Meijer, and W. Schulte. The Essence of Data Access in Cω. In A. P. Black, editor, *ECOOP*, volume 3586 of *LNCS*, pages 287–311. Springer, 2005.
13. A. Bohannon, J. A. Vaughan, and B. C. Pierce. Relational Lenses: A Language for Updateable Views. In *Principles of Database Systems (PODS)*, 2006. Extended version available as University of Pennsylvania technical report MS-CIS-05-27.
14. C. Boyapati, B. Liskov, L. Shrira, C.-H. Moh, and S. Richman. Lazy modular upgrades in persistent object stores. In *OOPSLA '03: Proceedings of the 18th annual ACM SIGPLAN conference on object-oriented programing, systems, languages, and applications*, pages 403–417, New York, NY, USA, 2003. ACM Press.
15. A. Brookes. XML data binding. *Dr. Dobb's Journal of Software Tools*, 28(3):26, 28, 30, 32, 35–36, Mar. 2003.
16. F. Burton and R. Cameron. Pattern Matching with Abstract Data Types. *Journal of Functional Programming*, 3(2):171–190, 1993.
17. D. Clarke and S. Drossopoulou. Ownership, encapsulation and the disjointness of type and effect. In *OOPSLA '02: Proceedings of the 17th ACM SIGPLAN conference on object-oriented programming, systems, languages, and applications*, pages 292–310, New York, NY, USA, 2002. ACM Press.
18. D. G. Clarke, J. M. Potter, and J. Noble. Ownership types for flexible alias protection. In *OOPSLA '98: Proceedings of the 13th ACM SIGPLAN conference on object-oriented programming, systems, languages, and applications*, pages 48–64, New York, NY, USA, 1998. ACM Press.
19. E. F. Codd. A Relational Model of Data for Large Shared Data Banks. *Communications of the ACM*, 13(6):377–387, June 1970. Also published in/as: 'Readings in Database Systems', M. Stonebraker, Morgan-Kaufmann, 1988, pp. 5–15.

20. R. Cytron, J. Ferrante, B. Rosen, M. Wegman, and F. Zadeck. Efficiently computing static single assignment form and the control dependence graph. *ACM Transactions on Programming Languages and Systems*, 13(4):451–490, Oct. 1991.

21. C. J. Date. A formal definition of the relational model. *SIGMOD Rec.*, 13(1):18–29, 1982.

22. A. van Deursen, P. Klint, and F. Tip. Origin Tracking. *Journal of Symbolic Computation*, 15:523–545, 1993.

23. U. Eisenecker and K. Czarnecki. *Generative Programming: Methods, Tools, and Applications*. Addison-Wesley, 2000.

24. C. Ellis, S. Gibbs, and G. Rein. Groupware: some issues and experiences. *Communications of the ACM*, 34(1):39–58, 1991.

25. M. Fagan. *Soft typing: an approach to type checking for dynamically typed languages*. PhD thesis, Rice University, 1991.

26. J.-M. Favre. Meta-models and Models Co-Evolution in the 3D Software Space. In *Proceedings of International Workshop on Evolution of Large-scale Industrial Software Applications (ELISA 2003)*, 2003.

27. M. Fernandez, Y. Kadiyska, D. Suciu, A. Morishima, and W.-C. Tan. Silkroute: A framework for publishing relational data in xml. *ACM Transactions on Database Systems*, 27(4):438–493, 2002.

28. J. Ferrante, K. Ottenstein, and J. Warren. The Program Dependence Graph and Its Use in Optimization. *ACM Transactions on Programming Languages and Systems*, 9(3):319–349, July 1987.

29. R. B. Findler and M. Felleisen. Contracts for higher-order functions. In *ICFP '02: Proceedings of the seventh ACM SIGPLAN international conference on Functional programming*, pages 48–59, New York, NY, USA, 2002. ACM Press.

30. J. Fitzgerald, P. G. Larsen, P. Mukherjee, N. Plat, and M. Verhoef. *Validated Designs for Object-Oriented Systems*. Springer, 2005.

31. M. Fowler. *Refactoring: Improving the Design of Existing Code*. Addison Wesley, 1999.

32. J. E. Funderburk, S. Malaika, and B. Reinwald. XML programming with SQL/XML and XQuery. *IBM Systems Journal*, 41(4):642–665, 2002.

33. E. Gamma, R. Helm, R. Johnson, and J. Vlissides. *Design Patterns: Elements of Reusable Object-Oriented Software*. Addison-Wesley, 1994.

34. G. Gottlob, P. Paolini, and R. Zicari. Properties and update semantics of consistent views. *ACM Transactions on Database Systems*, 13(4):486–524, 1988.

35. R. Gray, V. Heuring, S. Levi, A. Sloane, and W. Waite. Eli: A complete, flexible compiler construction system. *Communications of the ACM*, 35(2):121–130, Feb. 1992.

36. M. B. Greenwald, J. T. Moore, B. C. Pierce, and A. Schmitt. A language for bi-directional tree transformations. Technical Report MS-CIS-03-08, University of Pennsylvania, 2003. Revised April 2004.

37. J.-L. Hainaut, C. Tonneau, M. Joris, and M. Chandelon. Schema Transformation Techniques for Database Reverse Engineering. In *Proceedings, 12th Int. Conf. on ER Approach*, Arlington-Dallas, 1993. E/R Institute.

38. J. Hannemann and G. Kiczales. Design pattern implementation in Java and AspectJ. In C. Norris and J. J. B. Fenwick, editors, *Proceedings of the 17th ACM conference on object-oriented programming, systems, languages, and applications, OOPSLA'02*, volume 37, 11 of *ACM SIGPLAN Notices*, pages 161–173, New York, Nov. 4–8 2002. ACM Press.

39. J. Henrad, J.-M. Hick, P. Thiran, and J.-L. Hainaut. Strategies for Data Reengineering. In *Proceedings, Working Conference on Reverse Engineering (WCRE'02)*, pages 211–220. IEEE Computer Society Press, Nov. 2002.

40. A. Herranz and P. Nogueira. More Than Parsing. In F. J. L. Fraguas, editor, *Spanish V Conference on Programming and Languages (PROLE 2005)*, pages 193–202. Thomson-Paraninfo, 14–16 September 2005.

41. R. Hirschfeld and R. Lämmel. Reflective Designs. *IEE Proceedings Software*, 152(1): 38–51, Feb. 2005. Special Issue on Reusable Software Libraries.

42. C. A. R. Hoare. Proof of Correctness of Data Representations. *Acta Informatic*, 1:271–281, 1972.

43. K. Hogshead Davis and P. Aiken. Data Reverse Engineering: A Historical Survey. In *Working Conference on Reverse Engineering, WCRE 2000*, pages 70–78. IEEE Computer Society Press, 2000.

44. R. Holt, A. Winter, and A. Schürr. GXL: Toward a Standard Exchange Format. In *Proceedings of the Seventh Working Conference on Reverse Engineering (WCRE'00)*, pages 162–171. IEEE Computer Society Press, Nov. 2000.

45. Z. Hu, S.-C. Mu, and M. Takeichi. A programmable editor for developing structured documents based on bidirectional transformations. In *Proceedings of ACM SIGPLAN symposium on Partial evaluation and semantics-based program manipulation*, pages 178–189. ACM Press, 2004.

46. Z. Huzar, L. Kuzniarz, G. Reggio, J. Sourrouille, and M. Staron. Consistency Problems in UML-based Software Development II, 2003. Workshop proceedings; Research Report 2003:06.

47. ISO. ISO/IEC 14977:1996(E), Information technology — Syntactic metalanguage — Extended BNF, 1996. International Organization for Standardization.

48. ISO/IEC. Information technology — Programming languages — COBOL, 2002. Reference number ISO/IEC 1989:2002(E).

49. S. Johnson. YACC - Yet Another Compiler-Compiler. Technical Report Computer Science No. 32, Bell Laboratories, Murray Hill, New Jersey, 1975.

50. M. de Jonge and J. Visser. Grammars as Contracts. In *Proceedings, Generative and Component-based Software Engineering (GCSE'00)*, volume 2177 of *LNCS*, pages 85–99, Erfurt, Germany, Oct. 2000. Springer.

51. B. Kadhim and W. Waite. Maptool—supporting modular syntax development. In T. Gyimothy, editor, *Proceedings, Compiler Construction (CC'96)*, volume 1060 of *LNCS*, pages 268–280. Springer, Apr. 1996.

52. G. Kiczales. The Fun has Just Begun. AOSD'03 Keynote Address, available from http://www.cs.ubc.ca/~gregor, 2003.

53. G. Kiczales, E. Hilsdale, J. Hugunin, M. Kersten, J. Palm, and W. G. Griswold. An Overview of AspectJ. In *Proceedings European Conference on Object-Oriented Programming (ECOOP'901)*, pages 327–353, 2001.

54. P. Klint, R. Lämmel, and C. Verhoef. Toward an engineering discipline for grammarware. *ACM Transactions on Software Engineering and Methodology*, 14(3):331–380, 2005.

55. D. Knuth. Semantics of context-free languages. *Mathematical Systems Theory*, 2:127–145, 1968. Corrections in 5:95-96, 1971.

56. J. Kort and R. Lämmel. Parse-Tree Annotations Meet Re-Engineering Concerns. In *Proceedings, Source Code Analysis and Manipulation (SCAM'03)*, pages 161–172, Amsterdam, Sept. 2003. IEEE Computer Society Press.

57. J. Kort, R. Lämmel, and C. Verhoef. The Grammar Deployment Kit. In M. van den Brand and R. Lämmel, editors, *Proceedings, Language Descriptions, Tools, and Applications (LDTA'02)*, volume 65 of *ENTCS*. Elsevier Science, Apr. 2002. 7 pages.

58. R. Koschke and J.-F. Girard. An intermediate representation for reverse engineering analyses. In *Proceedings, Working Conference on Reverse Engineering (WCRE'98)*, pages 241–250. IEEE Computer Society Press, Oct. 1998.

59. G. E. Krasner and S. T. Pope. A cookbook for using the model-view-controller user interface paradigm in Smalltalk-80. *Journal of Object-Oriented Programming*, 1(3):26–49, Aug. 1988.

60. L. Kuzniarz, G. Reggio, J. Sourrouille, and Z. Huzar. Consistency Problems in UML-based Software Development, 2002. Workshop proceedings; Research Report 2002:06.
61. R. Lämmel. Coupled Software Transformations (Extended Abstract). In *Proceedings of the First International Workshop on Software Evolution Transformations*, Nov. 2004. 5 pages; Online proceedings available at http://banff.cs.queensu.ca/set2004/.
62. R. Lämmel and S. Peyton Jones. Scrap your boilerplate: a practical design pattern for generic programming. *ACM SIGPLAN Notices*, 38(3):26–37, Mar. 2003. Proceedings of the ACM SIGPLAN Workshop on Types in Language Design and Implementation, TLDI'03.
63. R. Lämmel and S. Peyton Jones. Scrap more boilerplate: reflection, zips, and generalised casts. In *ACM SIGPLAN International Conference on Functional Programming (ICFP'04)*, pages 244–255, Snowbird, Utah, Sept. 2004. ACM Press.
64. R. Lämmel and G. Wachsmuth. Transformation of SDF syntax definitions in the ASF+SDF Meta-Environment. In M. van den Brand and D. Parigot, editors, *Proceedings, Language Descriptions, Tools and Applications (LDTA'01)*, volume 44 of *ENTCS*. Elsevier Science, Apr. 2001.
65. B. S. Lerner. A model for compound type changes encountered in schema evolution. *ACM Transactions on Database Systems*, 25(1):83–127, 2000.
66. B. Liskov. Keynote address - data abstraction and hierarchy. In *OOPSLA '87: Addendum to the proceedings on object-oriented programming systems, languages and applications (Addendum)*, pages 17–34, New York, NY, USA, 1987. ACM Press.
67. C.-T. Liu, P. K. Chrysanthis, and S.-K. Chang. Database Schema Evolution through the Specification and Maintenance of Changes on Entities and Relationships. In P. Loucopoulos, editor, *Entity-Relationship Approach - ER'94, Business Modelling and Re-Engineering, 13th International Conference on the Entity-Relationship Approach, Manchester, U.K., December 13-16, 1994, Proceedings*, volume 881 of *LNCS*, pages 132–151. Springer, 1994.
68. W. Lohmann, G. Riedewald, and M. Stoy. Semantics-preserving migration of semantic rules after left recursion removal in attribute grammars. In *Proceedings of 4th Workshop on Language Descriptions, Tools and Applications (LDTA 2004)*, volume 110 of *ENTCS*, pages 133–148. Elsevier Science, 2004.
69. E. Mamas and K. Kontogiannis. Towards portable source code representations using XML. In *Proceedings, Working Conference on Reverse Engineering (WCRE'00)*, pages 172–182. IEEE Computer Society Press, Nov. 2000.
70. B. McLaughlin. *Java and XML data binding*. Nutshell handbook. O'Reilly & Associates, Inc., 2002.
71. E. Meijer and W. Schulte. Unifying tables, objects and documents. In *Proceedings of Declarative Programming in the Context of OO Languages (DP-COOL)*, Sept. 2003.
72. E. Meijer, W. Schulte, and G. Bierman. Programming with circles, triangles and rectangles. In *XML Conference and Exposition*, Dec. 2003.
73. Microsoft Corp. http://msdn.microsoft.com/netframework/future/linq/.
74. C. Morgan. *Programming from Specifications*. Prentice Hall International, 1990.
75. J. Noble. Basic relationship patterns. In *Second European Conference on Pattern Languages of Programming*, 1997. Siemens Technical Report.
76. J. Noble and J. Grundy. Explicit Relationships in Object Oriented Development. In C. Mingins, R. Duke, and B. Meyer, editors, *Proceedings of TOOLS 18: Technology of Object-Oriented Languages and Systems Conference*, pages 211–225. Prentice Hall, Sept. 1995.
77. G. S. Novak Jr. Creation of views for reuse of software with different data representations. *IEEE Transactions on Software Engineering*, 21(12):993–1005, 1995.
78. J. Oliveira. Software Reification using the SETS Calculus. In *Proceedings of the BCS FACS 5th Refinement Workshop, Theory and Practice of Formal Software Development, London, UK*, pages 140–171. Springer, 8–10 January 1992.

79. J. Oliveira. Calculate databases with 'simplicity', Sept. 2004. Presentation at the IFIP WG 2.1 #59 Meeting, Nottingham, UK.

80. W. Opdyke. *Refactoring Object-Oriented Frameworks*. PhD thesis, University of Illinois at Urbana-Champaign, 1992.

81. J. Paakki. Attribute Grammar Paradigms — A High-Level Methodology in Language Implementation. *ACM Computing Surveys*, 27(2):196–255, June 1995.

82. J. Park and S. Ram. Information systems interoperability: What lies beneath? *ACM Transactions on Information Systems*, 22(4):595–632, 2004.

83. J. Purtilo and J. Callahan. Parse tree annotations. *Communications of the ACM*, 32(12):1467–1477, 1989.

84. K.-U. Sattler, I. Geist, and E. Schallehn. Concept-based querying in mediator systems. *The VLDB Journal*, 14(1):97–111, 2005.

85. B. Selic. The Pragmatics of Model-Driven Development. *IEEE Software*, pages 19–25, Sept./Oct. 2003. Special Issue on Model-Driven Development.

86. J. Shanmugasundaram, E. J. Shekita, R. Barr, M. J. Carey, B. G. Lindsay, H. Pirahesh, and B. Reinwald. Efficiently Publishing Relational Data as XML Documents. In *VLDB '00: Proceedings of the 26th International Conference on Very Large Data Bases*, pages 65–76, San Francisco, CA, USA, 2000. Morgan Kaufmann Publishers Inc.

87. T. Sheard. Generic unification via two-level types and parameterized modules. In *ICFP '01: Proceedings of the sixth ACM SIGPLAN International Conference on Functional Programming*, pages 86–97, New York, NY, USA, 2001. ACM Press.

88. C. Simonyi. The death of programming languages, the birth of intentional programming. Technical report, Microsoft, Inc., Sept. 1995. Available from `http://citeseer.nj.nec.com/simonyi95death.html`.

89. T. Spitta and F. Werner. Die Wiederverwendung von Daten in SAP R/3. *Information Management & Consulting (IM)*, 15:51–56, 2000. In German.

90. C. Sun, X. Jia, Y. Zhang, Y. Yang, and D. Chen. Achieving convergence, causality preservation, and intention preservation in real-time cooperative editing systems. *ACM Transactions on Computer-Human Interaction*, 5(1):63–108, 1998.

91. Sun Microsystems. The Java architecture for XML binding (JAXB). `http://java.sun.com/xml/jaxb`, 2001.

92. D. Thomas. The Impedance Imperative Tuples + Objects + Infosets = Too Much Stuff! *Journal of Object Technology*, 2(5):7–12, Sept.–Oct. 2003. Online available at `http://www.jot.fm/jot/issues/issue_2003_09/column1/`.

93. M. Van De Vanter. Preserving the documentary structure of source code in language-based transformation tools. In *Proceedings, Source Code Analysis and Manipulation (SCAM'01)*. IEEE Computer Society Press, 2001.

94. W3C. Document Object Model (DOM), 1997–2003. `http://www.w3.org/DOM/`.

95. W3C. XML Information Set (Second Edition), 1999–2004. `http://www.w3.org/TR/xml-infoset/`.

96. W3C. Extensible Markup Language (XML) 1.0 (Third Edition) W3C Recommendation, Feb. 2004. `http://www.w3.org/TR/2004/REC-xml-20040204/`.

97. W3C. XML Schema: Component Designators, W3C Working Draft, 29 Mar. 2005. `http://www.w3.org/TR/xmlschema-ref/`.

98. P. Wadler. Views: a way for pattern matching to cohabit with data abstraction. In *POPL '87: Proceedings of the 14th ACM SIGACT-SIGPLAN symposium on Principles of programming languages*, pages 307–313, New York, NY, USA, 1987. ACM Press.

99. P. Wadler. Deforestation: transforming programs to eliminate trees. *Theor. Comput. Sci.*, 73(2):231–248, 1990.

100. P. Walmsley. *Definitive XML Schema*. Prentice Hall, 2001. 556 pages, 1st edition.
101. A. K. Wright and R. Cartwright. A practical soft type system for Scheme. *ACM Transactions on Programming Languages and Systems*, 19(1):87–152, Jan. 1997.

A   Exercises and Riddles

We list exercises on a scale of '*' to '***'. Excellent, generalized solutions to the exercises in the three-stars category have the potential to lead to a workshop or conference paper. We also annotate exercises by 'G' to admit that googling might help, and we use 'P' for an indication that advanced programming skills are to be leveraged.

A.1   Mappings in Parsing and Un-parsing

We start with some old-fashioned mapping problems that work fine as warm-up. Parsers and un-parsers, at some level of abstraction, describe highly systematic mappings. However, occasionally, these mappings need to work hard to bypass a kind of 'impedance mismatch' between concrete and abstract syntax representations, or they need to account for implementational restrictions.

Exercise 1 (*, G). Given is a set of binary operators with associated priorities. Using your programming language of choice, give a concise description of a mapping that parses a list of operators and operands into the correctly parenthesized term. (Note that the actual operators and their priorities are a parameter of the mapping.) For instance, the list [1,+,2,*,3] should be parsed into the term '+'(1,'*'(2,3)) assuming common priorities for '+' and '*'.

Exercise 2 (*, G). Continue Ex. 1 to include explicitly parenthesized expressions.

Exercise 3 (**, G?). Continue Ex. 2 as follows. Given is a term. Describe an 'unparsing' mapping that generates the concrete representation (a list of operators and operands) with the minimum number of necessary parentheses.

Exercise 4 (**, G?). Continue Ex. 3 so that it will definitely preserve all parentheses that were explicit in the original input. That is, the composition of parsing and unparsing should be the identity function on the set of all parseable strings. (Hint: the term representation needs to be refined.)

Exercise 5 (**,G,P). Here is a definite clause grammar (DCG) for the language $(a|b)^*$

```
% Prolog/DCG code
aorbs(snoc(Xs,X)) --> aorbs(Xs), aorb(X).
aorbs(lin)        --> [].
aorb(a)           --> [a].
aorb(b)           --> [b].
```

The grammar also describes the synthesis of a *left-associative* list (cf. snoc rather than cons and lin rather than nil). Such left-associativity suggests a left-recursive grammar, as shown indeed. However, Prolog's normal left-to-right computation rule implies non-termination for left recursion. Hence, we need a right-recursive grammar. Assignment: develop the corresponding DCG.

We could build an intermediate cons list, and rephrase it eventually:

```
aorbs(SL) --> aorbsCons(CL), { rephrase(CL,SL) }.
aorbsCons(cons(X,Xs)) --> aorb(X), aorbsCons(Xs).
aorbsCons(nil)        --> [].

rephrase(CL,SL) :- rephrase(CL,lin,SL).
rephrase(nil,SL,SL).
rephrase(cons(X,Xs),SL1,SL2) :- rephrase(Xs,snoc(SL1,X),SL2).
```

This solution involves an unnecessary traversal. We ask for a solution that avoids such an inefficiency. As an aside, general descriptions of left-recursion removal are available [3, 68]. Also, one may consider techniques for deforestation [99], which could even be useful to automatically derive an efficient solution from the inefficient encoding that we have shown.

A.2 Mappings for XML Grammars

When programming language folks first looked at DTD [96], some might have said "This is just a verbose variation on EBNF [47]." — leaving implicit that there are a few issues that go beyond context-free grammars, e.g., IDREFs. This proposition does not so easily generalize to the XML schema language (XSD), which is a relatively rich XML grammar formalism. In general, the differences between grammar notations (XML schema, DTD, Relax NG, Schematron, EBNF, BNF, SDF, ASDL, ASN.1, ...) invite insightful mapping exercises. Some XSD-based riddles follow.

Exercise 6 (*,G?). The EBNF formalism is orthogonal in itself in the sense that it offers regular operators that can be applied to other grammar phrases in arbitrary ways. In what sense does XML schema deviate here? (Hint: think of occurrence constraints.) Argue regarding the pros (if any) and cons of this deviation.

Exercise 7 (**). The content model <choice/> (i.e., the empty choice) is invalid according to the XML Schema recommendation by the W3C. Why is that a sensible restriction, and how does the notion of empty choice transcribe to context-free grammars? Suppose <choice/> was not forbidden, how does it compare to <sequence/>, and again, what does this comparison mean in context-free grammar terms? Give a few more algebraic equations on content models. For instance, give equations that involve occurrence constraints.

Exercise 8 (**). Consider the following schema:

```
<!-- XML schema -->
<xs:schema ... elided for  brevity ...>
  <xs:element name="foo">
    <xs:complexType>
```

```
<xs:sequence>
  <xs:element name="bar" type="xs:string"/>
  <xs:element ref="foo"/>
</xs:sequence>
      </xs:complexType>
    </xs:element>
  </xs:schema>
```

According to the WC3 recommendation, this schema is valid. When considered as a context-free grammar, what basic property is violated by this schema? (Hint: it is the same property that is violated by <choice/>.) Argue that this property is valuable from an XML-centric point of view. Also explain the formal means to enforce such a restriction by adopting context-free grammar techniques.

Exercise 9 (***). Provide a detailed mapping for, what you might call, 'DTDification' of XML schemas. (We choose this name to hint at the similar process of YACCification, where EBNF-like expressiveness is normalized to BNF-like notation [64].) That is, how can you compile away the extra expressiveness of XSD such that the resulting schemas can be mapped to DTDs rather directly. Argue that the resulting DTD accepts a 'reasonable' superset of the XML instances that are accepted by the initial schema.

A.3   Compensation of Semantical Impedance Mismatches

Mapping operations on data models may lead us to semantical challenges (as opposed to merely typing mismatch challenges). The following exercises focus entirely on fundamental properties of language semantics in the context of data processing.

Exercise 10 (**,G,P). We will be concerned with the simulation of a lazy semantics. This is clearly necessary when we want to transcribe data-processing problems from a lazy encoding to a non-lazy encoding (i.e., perhaps to an eager language). Consider the following Haskell session that demonstrates lazy list processing:

```
haskell> take 10 [0..]
[0,1,2,3,4,5,6,7,8,9]
```

For the record, the function take is defined in the Haskell Prelude as follows:

```
-- Haskell 98 code
take n _        | n <= 0 = []
take _ []                = []
take n (x:xs)            = x : take (n−1) xs
```

Also, the notation [0..] is a shortcut for incForever 0, where:

```
incForever n = n : (incForever (n+1))
```

Detailed assignments:

- Redefine lists, take and incForever such that an eager semantics would be sufficient.
- Transcribe the eager Haskell solution to an OO language as verbatim as possible.

- Use streams (as of C# 2.0 etc.), i.e., lazy lists, instead.
- Describe a data-processing scenario that calls for lazy structures other than lists.

Exercise 11 (***,P). We want to do data processing in Haskell with an OO-like reference semantics. Consider the following algebraic data types, given in Haskell syntax; they describe a fragment of an abstract syntax for an imperative, statement-oriented language with nested scopes for declarations of variables and procedures:

```
type Block  =  ([Dec],[Stm])
data Dec    =  VarDec Id Type | ...              -- procedures etc.
data Id     =  Id String
data Type   =  IntType | StringType
data Stm    =  Assign Id Exp | BlockStm Block | ...   -- other statements
data Exp    =  Var Id | ...
```

Hence, blocks in this language are lists of statements combined with the new declarations for this block. Each block opens a nested lexical scope. Now let us assume that we are interested in a richer AST format, which faithfully models ref/dec relationships. That is, whenever a variable is referenced in an expression or a statement, we want to be able to navigate from such a 'ref' side to the corresponding 'dec' side, i.e., to the binding block that holds the visible declaration.

Detailed assignments:

1. Extend the algebraic data types, given above, to include constructor components for ref/dec relationships. Take into account that these relationships may not be represented in terms initially, as they might be computed separately. Employ lazy, pure functional programming (rather than explicit references of the IO or the ST monad) to navigate from ref to dec sides.

2. Refactor the data types to use Haskell's IORefs. Illustrate the use of 'smart' constructors so that user code is not blurred by the allocation of references and assignments to references. A useful literature reference: [87].

3. How can we avoid cycles of *generic* algorithms that walk over the Haskell graphs? For instance, an algorithm for showing a Haskell term must not run into a cycle when hitting on a ref/dec relationship? Describe a technique that does not require intimate knowledge of the problem-specific data types.

A.4 XML, Object, Relational Mapping

These exercises illustrate cross-paradigm impedance mismatches as discussed in Sec. 4.

Exercise 12 (*). Suppose we store XML documents with IDs and IDREFs in a relational database. What extra measures are necessary in case we want to (i) store multiple documents in the database, or (ii) extract new XML views from the database that potentially involve multiple documents?

Exercise 13 (**). Consider the following XSD identity constraints:

```
<!-- XML schema -->
<xs:element name="order" type="OrderType">
  <xs:keyref name="prodNumKeyRef" refer="prodNumKey">
    <xs:selector xpath="items/*"/>
    <xs:field  xpath="@number"/>
  </xs:keyref>
  <xs:key name="prodNumKey">
    <xs:selector xpath=".//product"/>
    <xs:field  xpath="number"/>
  </xs:key>
</xs:element>
```

These constraints read as follows: *"Each child of items must have a number attribute whose value is unique within the order. All product descendants of order must have a number child whose value matches one of these unique product numbers."* [100]. Let us assume that the schema with those constraints is bound to objects. How can we enforce the identity constraints within the object model?

Exercise 14 (**). We recall the discussion of cascading deletes in Sec. 4.3. A deletion of a stock item was supposed to lead to the deletion of all relevant transaction items. We seek the object-oriented counterpart for this cascading delete. Here, we assume that stock items and transactions reside in OO collections whose implementation has to be made aware of cascading.

To hint at the solution, we provide an SQL-based encoding that does not use the cascading annotations that we facilitated in Sec. 4.3. Instead, we create a trigger to kick in when a delete operation is about to affect the stock table:

```
// SQL Server 2000 code
CREATE TRIGGER stock_cascade_delete ON stock FOR DELETE AS
    DELETE FROM stock_trans
    WHERE stock_id IN
              ( SELECT stock_id FROM deleted )
```

Provide an OO encoding of the cascading behavior.

Exercise 15 (***). Continue Ex. 14 as follows. We seek a general, aspect-oriented solution that can be reused for cascading deletion. To this end, we note that the overall problem is similar to design patterns like 'observer' for which indeed modular, AOP-based solutions have been proposed [38, 41]. Such an AOP-based solution may illustrate whether AOP can be useful for mastering cross-paradigm impedance mismatches.

On the Use of Graph Transformations
for Model Refactoring

Tom Mens

Service de Génie Logiciel
Université de Mons-Hainaut, Belgium
`tom.mens@umh.ac.be`
`http://w3.umh.ac.be/genlog`

Abstract. Model-driven software engineering promotes the use of models and transformations as primary artifacts. Several formalisms can be used for the specification of model transformations. We propose to represent models as graphs, and model transformations as graph transformations. In particular, we focus on the activity of model refactoring, and show how graph transformation theory can provide formal support for this activity. We also show how such support can be implemented in state-of-the-art graph transformation tools such as *AGG* and *Fujaba*, and provide two concrete experiments. Critical pair analysis in *AGG* enables the analysis of dependencies between model refactorings. The round-trip engineering facility of *Fujaba* enables the automatic generation of code for model refactorings.

1 Introduction

Model-driven engineering is a software engineering approach that promotes the use of models and transformations as primary artifacts. Its goal is to tackle the problem of developing, maintaining and evolving complex software systems by raising the level of abstraction from source code to models. As such, model-driven engineering promises reuse at the domain level, increasing the overall software quality. *Model transformation* is the heart and soul of this approach [1].

Graph transformation seems to be a suitable technology and associated formalism to specify and apply model transformations for the following reasons:

- Graphs are a natural representation of models that are intrinsically graph-based in nature (e.g., statecharts, activity diagrams, collaboration diagrams, class diagrams, Petri nets), as opposed to source code for which a tree-based approach is likely to be more appropriate. In Bézivin's tutorial on model-driven engineering [2], this link between models and graphs is explained as follows: "... we will give a more limited definition of a model, in the context of MDE only, as a graph-based structure representing some aspects of a given system and conforming to the definition of another graph called a metamodel."
- Graph transformation theory provides a formal foundation for the analysis and automatic application of model transformations. As such, one can reason

R. Lämmel, J. Saraiva, and J. Visser (Eds.): GTTSE 2005, LNCS 4143, pp. 219–257, 2006.

about many interesting formal properties such as confluence, sequential and parallel dependence, and so on.
- Tool support for model-driven development based on graph transformation engines is starting to emerge (e.g., *GReAT* [3], *MOLA* [4] and *VIATRA* [5]).

An important activity within the domain of model transformation is *model refactoring*. The term refactoring was originally introduced by Opdyke in his seminal PhD dissertation [6] in the context of object-oriented programming. Martin Fowler [7] defines this activity as "the process of changing a software system in such a way that it does not alter the external behavior of the code, yet improves its internal structure". Recently, research interest has shifted from program refactoring to model refactoring [8, 9, 10, 11, 12, 13, 14], which aims to apply refactoring techniques at model level as opposed to source code.

The objectives of this tutorial are manifold:

- To raise the technique of refactoring from the level of programs to the level of models;
- To introduce the notion of model refactoring as a special kind of model transformation activity, and to motivate the importance of this activity in the MDE process;
- To introduce graph transformation as a promising technique (covering both theoretical foundations and tool support) for model transformation;
- To show how graph transformation can provide formal support to automate the activity of model refactoring, and to compare graph transformation to related approaches.

The remainder of this article will be structured as follows. Section 2 provides a high-level overview of model transformation and model refactoring, and introduces the necessary terminology. In Section 3 we provide a formal definition of typed graphs, and illustrate how they can be used as an underlying representation of different kinds of design models. Section 4 formally defines graph transformations and illustrates how they can be used to specify model refactorings. Both sections make use of the notation used by *AGG* and *Fujaba*, two general-purpose graph transformation tools. Sections 5 and 6 continue with two concrete experiments we have performed with *AGG* and *Fujaba* for model refactoring. Section 7 discusses the benefits and drawbacks of graph transformation for the purpose of model refactoring. Finally, section 8 concludes.

2   Model Transformation

The aim of this section is to give a general high-level overview of model transformation, and to show where model refactoring fits in. In order to do this, it is important to be aware of the fact that model refactoring represents only a very specific kind of model transformation. To illustrate this, we briefly discuss a taxonomy of model transformation in the first subsection.

2.1 Taxonomy

In earlier work [15, 16] we presented a detailed taxonomy of model transformation and showed how it could be applied to graph transformation. We will summarise some important ideas of the model transformation taxonomy here. Applying graph transformations to model transformation in general, however, is outside the scope of this paper.

In order to transform models, these models need to be expressed in some modeling language, the syntax of which is expressed by a *metamodel*. Based on the metamodels that are used for expressing the source and target models of a transformation, a distinction can be made between *endogenous* and *exogenous* transformations. Endogenous transformations are transformations between models expressed in the same metamodel. Exogenous transformations are transformations between models expressed in different metamodels. A typical example of an exogenous transformation is *migration* of a model a program written in one particular (programming or modelling) language to another one. A typical example of an endogenous transformation is *refactoring*, where the internal structure of a model is improved (with respect to a certain software quality characteristic) without changing its observable behaviour [7]. The *pull up method* transformation that will be introduced later is an example of such a refactoring.

Other examples are:

- *Optimization*, a transformation aimed to improve certain operational qualities (e.g., performance), while preserving the semantics of the software
- *Simplification* and *normalization*, used to decrease the syntactic complexity, e.g., by translating syntactic sugar into more primitive language constructs. The statechart flattening transformation that will be introduced later is an example of such a simplification.

Besides this distinction between endogenous and exogenous model transformations, we can also distinguish horizontal and vertical model transformations. A *horizontal transformation* is a transformation where the source and target models reside at the same abstraction level. A typical example is again *refactoring* (an endogenous transformation). A *vertical transformation* is a transformation where the source and target models reside at different abstraction levels. A typical example of a vertical transformation is *synthesis* of a higher-level, more abstract, specification (e.g., a UML design model) into a lower-level, more concrete, one (e.g, a Java program). A concrete application of synthesis is *code generation*, where the source code is translated into bytecode (that runs on a virtual machine) or executable code, or where the design models are translated into source code.

Table 1 illustrates that the dimensions *horizontal versus vertical* and *endogenous versus exogenous* are truly orthogonal, by giving a concrete example of all possible combinations. As a clarification for the *Formal refinement* mentioned in the table, a specification in first-order predicate logic or set theory can be gradually refined such that the end result uses exactly the same language as the original specification (e.g., by adding more axioms).

Table 1. Orthogonal dimensions of model transformations

	horizontal	vertical
endogenous	refactoring; optimization	formal refinement
exogenous	language migration	synthesis (e.g., code generation); reverse engineering

2.2 Model Refactoring

An emerging research trend is to port the idea of refactoring to the modeling level, for example by applying refactoring techniques to UML models. Boger *et al.* developed a refactoring browser integrated with a UML modeling tool [9]. It supports refactoring of class diagrams, statechart diagrams, and activity diagrams. For each of these diagrams, the user can apply refactorings that cannot easily or naturally be expressed in other diagrams or in the source code.

Statechart diagrams are particularly interesting in the context of refactoring, as these diagrams represent the dynamic behaviour of a model. Geiger and Zündorf [17] illustrated an example of statechart refactoring by flattening complex (i.e., nested) statecharts into plain statemachines, thereby illustrating how to use the *Fujaba* CASE tool for model refactoring. Van Kempen *et al.* addressed the behaviour preservation aspect of statechart refactoring, by mapping statecharts on CSP processes as a formal representation of the behaviour, and proving equivalence of these CSP processes before and after the refactoring using a model checker [14]. Sunyé *et al.* defined some statechart refactorings using OCL pre- and postconditions [8].

OCL was also used by Van Gorp *et al.* in a UML extension that allows to express the pre- and postconditions of source code refactorings in OCL [10]. The proposed extension allows an OCL empowered CASE tool to verify nontrivial pre and postconditions, to compose sequences of refactorings, and to use the OCL query engine to detect bad code smells. Such an approach is desirable as a way to refactor designs independent of the underlying programming language. Correa and Werner built further on these ideas, and implemented the refactorings in OCL-script, an extension of OCL [18]. Markovic and Baar defined a graph-grammar based formalism to preserve the syntactical correctness of OCL constraints expressed on UML class diagrams [12] .

An alternative approach is followed by Porres [19], who implements model refactorings as rule-based update transformations in SMW, a scripting language based on Python. Last but not least, Zhang *et al.* developed a model transformation engine that integrates a model refactoring browser that automates and customises various refactoring methods for either generic models or domain-specific models [13].

In the remainder of this tutorial, we will only provide examples of model refactoring for UML class diagrams and statecharts. Obviously, most of the ideas that will be explained are directly applicable to refactorings of other kinds of models as well. Even domain-specific models and non-UML-compliant models (e.g. database schemas in ER notation) can be targeted. The primary restriction is that the models have to be expressible in a diagrammatic, graph-like notation.

2.3   Model Consistency

Another crucial aspect of model transformation, and model refactoring in particular, is *model consistency*. It will not be treated in this paper, but we briefly mention some relevant related work here.

Spanoudakis and Zisman [20] provided an excellent survey on inconsistency management in software engineering. According to them, an inconsistency is "a state in which two or more overlapping elements of different software models make assertions about aspects of the system they describe which are not jointly satisfiable". They claim that the following activities are essential for inconsistency management: detection of overlaps, detection of inconsistencies, diagnosis of inconsistencies, handling of inconsistencies, tracking, specification and application of an inconsistency management policy.

Since a UML model is typically composed of many different diagrams, the consistency between all these diagrams needs to be maintained when any of them evolves. Sunyé *et al.* explored how the integrity of class diagrams and statecharts could be maintained after refactorings [8]. Van Der Straeten *et al.* explored the use of description logics as a way to specify and implement consistency rules and behaviour preservation rules [21, 11].

As a simple example of an inconsistency that can arise in a UML model, consider a design consisting of a class diagram expressing the static structure, together with a collection of statecharts expressing the dynamic behaviour of each class. For the sake of the argument, let's make the oversimplification that each class has an associated statechart, and that all transitions in each statechart are labelled by messages that correspond to operations (methods) understood by the class. Suppose now that we change the location of operations specified in the class diagram, for example by performing a *Move Method*, *Pull Up Method* or *Push Down Method* refactoring. It is possible that the statecharts of the classes that have been modified become inconsistent, because they now use messages on the transitions that may no longer correspond to operations defined in, or understood by, the class.

The problem of consistency maintenance becomes even more problematic when we acknowledge the obvious fact that models are only an intermediate step in the software development life-cycle, where the actual executable program is the most important deliverable. In this context, consistency should be maintained between the modeling level and the implementation level. Modifications to the models should be automatically reflected in the source code and vice versa. To a certain extent, automatic generation of code from the design, and reverse engineering design from the code can offer a great deal of help. But even in those cases, inconsistency problems may arise when the generated code or the reverse engineered design is being edited manually. It is outside the scope of this paper to treat this problem of co-evolution between design and implementation in detail. Some interesting work on this topic can be found in [22, 23].

3   Models Are Graphs

In order to specify model refactorings by means of graph transformations, one first needs to agree upon a way to specify the models that need to be transformed. This requires the definition of a metamodel that specifies what it means to be a valid (i.e., well-formed) model. We will use type graphs to represent metamodels, and graphs to represent models. A model will be well-formed if its graph representation conforms to the type graph. This is visualised in Figure 1.

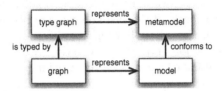

Fig. 1. Relationship between models and their graph representation

3.1   Typed Graphs

According to Bézivin and many others, a model can naturally be represented as a graph-based structure. In this subsection, we will formally define the notions of graph and type graph, as well as how they are related.

Definition 1. *Directed labelled graphs.*
A (directed, labelled) graph $G = (V_G, E_G, s_G, t_G, l_G)$ has a set of vertices V_G and a set of edges E_G such that $V_G \cap E_G = \emptyset$, functions $s_G : E_G \to V_G$ and $t_G : E_G \to V_G$ to associate to each edge a source and target vertex, and a labelling function $l_G : V_G \cup E_G \to \mathcal{L}$ to assign a label to each vertex and edge.

A direct and useful extension of the above definition would be to attach additional information to vertices and edges by attributing them. In that case, we talk about *attributed graphs*. Each vertex or edge can contain zero or more attributes. Such an attribute is typically a name-value pair, that allows to attach a specific value to each attribute name. These values can be very simple (e.g., a number or a string) or more complex (e.g., a Java expression). Examples of both will be shown later.

Definition 2. *Graph morphism.*
Let G and H be two graphs. A (partial) graph morphism $m : G \to H$ consists of a pair of partial functions $m_V : V_G \to V_H$ and $m_E : E_G \to E_H$ that preserve sources and targets of edges, i.e., $s_H \circ m_E = m_V \circ s_G$ and $t_H \circ m_E = m_V \circ t_G$. It also preserves vertex labels and edge labels, i.e., $l_H \circ m_V = l_G$ and $l_H \circ m_E = l_G$.

A (partial) graph morphism $m : G \to H$ is injective (surjective) if both m_V and m_E are injective (surjective). It is isomorphic if m is injective and surjective. In that case, we write $G \cong H$.

Note that the functions m_V and m_E are required to be *partial* in order to allow for vertex deletions and edge deletions. All vertices in $V_G \setminus dom(m_V)$ and all edges in $E_G \setminus dom(m_E)$ are considered to be deleted by m.

In order for a graph to serve as the representation of a model, we need to determine its well-formedness, by checking whether it conforms to a so-called *type graph*. The formal definition of typed graphs is taken from [24]. Basically this boils down to the same idea as the one that is taken in model-driven engineering, where each model (e.g. a UML design model) needs to conform to a metamodel (e.g., the UML metamodel) [2]. The correspondence between both ideas is depicted in Figure 1.

Definition 3. *Typed graph.*
Let TG be a graph (called the type graph*). A typed graph (over TG) is a pair (G, t) such that G is a graph and $t : G \to TG$ is a total graph morphism. A typed graph morphism $(G, t_G) \to (H, t_H)$ is a (partial) graph morphism $m : G \to H$ that also preserves typing, i.e., $t_H \circ m = t_G$.*

The above definition of typed graph requires a *total* graph morphism $t : G \to TG$ in order to ensure that each node and edge in the graph G has a corresponding type in TG. The definition can be extended in many different ways to put additional constraints on concrete typed graphs that are instances of the type graph:

- the type graph can be *attributed* to constrain the names and types of attributes of vertices and edges in concrete typed graphs;
- the type graph can contain *cardinalities* on nodes and edges to provide a lower and upper bound on the number of vertices and edges of a certain type that are allowed in concrete typed graphs;
- the type graph can contain *inheritance* relationships between vertices to express the fact that all attributes, cardinalities, and adjacent edge types of the supertype are inherited by the subtype. This is similar to the use of the generalization relationship in the UML metamodel.

In the remainder of the paper, when we use the term *graph*, we will always refer to an attributed, typed, directed labelled graph, unless indicated otherwise. Obviously, other variants of graphs exist but they will not be treated here, as they are not used by the graph refactoring tools we will employ for our experiments in the following subsections.

3.2   Graph Representation of Class Diagrams

As a first concrete example, let us see how we can provide a graph representation for class diagrams. The notation that we will use in this subsection to represent graphs and type graphs is the one that is used by the AGG^1 graph transformation tool [25, 26].

The example that we want to model is the class structure of a local area network simulation (LAN). This particular example has been used at different

---

[1] http://tfs.cs.tu-berlin.de/agg/

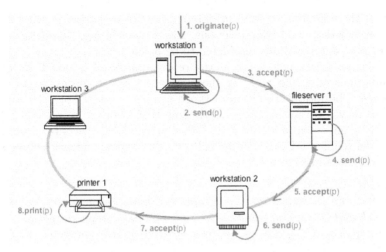

Fig. 2. Visualisation of the behaviour of a Local Area Network (LAN)

universities to teach object-oriented design and programming concepts, as well as to teach refactoring principles [27, 28].

The behaviour of this LAN is visually represented in Figure 2. The class diagram representing the static structure of the LAN is shown in Figure 3.

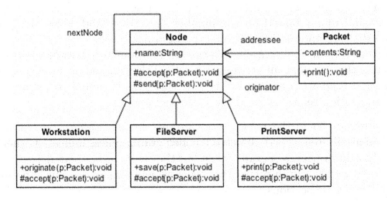

Fig. 3. UML class diagram of the LAN simulation

Now the question arises how we can model such a class diagram using a graph representation. One such representation is proposed in Figure 4. In a certain sense, this graph can be considered as an abstract syntax representation of the class diagram. We have used an *attributed* graph to attach specific information to vertices such as their `name`, `visibility` and so on. Similarly, some edges are attributed with name `order` (to reflect the order of parameters in a method signature).

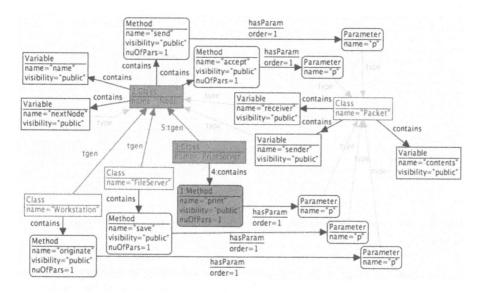

Fig. 4. Graph representing the abstract syntax of a UML class diagram for the LAN simulation modeled in Figure 3

In order to specify which concrete graphs represent well-formed class diagrams, we need to specify a *type graph*, representing a simplified object-oriented metamodel for class diagrams. All graphs that conform to this type graph will be considered as well-formed graphs.

The attributed type graph that we will use is shown in Figure 5. The graph of Figure 4 is a concrete instance graph of this type graph. The type graph expresses the following constraints on concrete graphs:

Constraints between nodes and edges: Classes can be related by generalization (*gen*-edges, or their transitive variant *tgen*). Classes contain Methods and Variables. Methods send Messages to each other and have a number of Parameters. Methods access or update Variables. Variables and Parameters are typed by Classes. The return type of a Method is also a Class.

Multiplicity constraints on edges: For example, each Variable or Method is contained in exactly one Class. A Class contains zero or more Variables and Methods. A Method contains zero (in the case of void) or one return type.

Multiplicity constraints on nodes: In the considered type graph, there are no multiplicity constraints on nodes. We could easily have decided to only allow graphs that contain at least one vertex of type Class (by attaching the cardinality 1..* to Class).

Attribute constraints: The number of Parameters of a Method, as well as the name and visibility of Methods and Variables, is represented by vertex attributes. The order of a Parameter in a Method declaration is represented by an edge attribute.

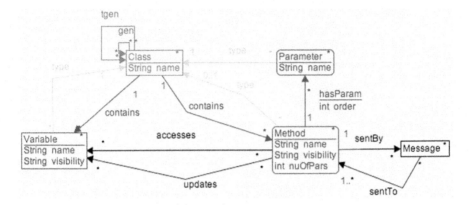

Fig. 5. Type graph representing a simplified object-oriented metamodel for class diagrams

Note that not all possible well-formedness constraints can be expressed in the above type graph. In *AGG*, this problem can be resolved by adding additional *global graph constraints*. We used this mechanism to express the following well-formedness constraints:

- no two classes should have the same name
- no two methods contained in the same class should have the same name
- no two variables contained in the same class should have the same name
- If there are multiple methods with the same name in the same class hierarchy, any message sent to one of these methods should also be sent to all other methods with the same name in the hierarchy (since it is impossible to determine the actual receiver method statically due to the mechanism of dynamic method binding)

3.3   Graph Representation of Statecharts

As a second illustrative example, we provide a graph representation for UML statechart models. A simple example of a statechart simulating part of the behaviour of a telephone is shown in Figure 6. This example is borrowed from Figure 3-71 of the UML specification version 1.5 [29]. It contains two top-level states Idle and Active with a transition between them in both directions. By lifting the receiver one can reach the Active state, and by hanging up the receiver, the state becomes Idle again. The Active state is a so-called *OrState*, i.e., a composite state that contains a large number of mutually exclusive substates.[2]

In order to model the abstract syntax of statecharts, we will use the notation used by the *Fujaba*[3] CASE tool to represent graphs and type graphs [30]. Figure 7

---

[2] So-called *AndStates* are composite states that contain concurrent substates, but they are not needed to model this example.

[3] http://www.fujaba.de/

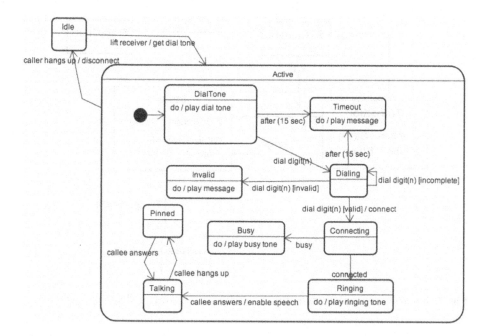

Fig. 6. Example of a statechart simulating part of the behaviour of a telephone

shows the part of the type graph for a simplified version of statecharts. As can
be seen, the notation for specifying type graphs in *Fujaba* is quite different from
the one in *AGG*. In fact, because *Fujaba* is a UML CASE tool, type graphs
are represented as class diagrams, in exactly the same way as the specification
of the UML metamodel. Classes in the diagram represent vertices of the type
graph (e.g., *State*, *Transition*, *OrState*), and associations represent edges of the
type graph (e.g., *source* and *target* edges between *Transition* and *State*, and
superState edges between a *State* and its containing *OrState*.

Class attributes are used to represent attributes of vertices. For example, a
State has a *name*, a boolean value *init* denoting whether or not it is an initial
state, and a *doAction* value representing the action to be performed. *AGG*'s
ability to specify edge attributes in the type graph is **not** allowed in *Fujaba*. The
practical reason for this is that dangling edges are treated in a different way in
AGG and *Fujaba*, but a detailed explanation of this falls outside the scope of
the current paper.

On the other hand, *Fujaba* does include a feature that is not provided by
the version of *AGG* that we used (version 1.2.6), namely the ability to use the
generalization notation of class diagrams to represent inheritance between nodes.
For example, a statechart can contain two kinds of *SCElements*: *Transitions* and
States, and an *OrState* is a special kind of *State*. This implies that all attributes,
incoming edges and outgoing edges of *State* will be inherited by *OrState*. Note
that, from a theoretical point of view, it would not pose a problem to introduce
this feature in a new version of *AGG* [31].

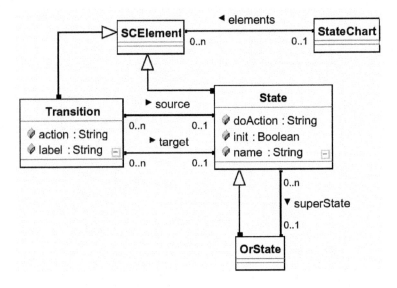

Fig. 7. Fujaba type graph representing a simplified object-oriented metamodel for statecharts

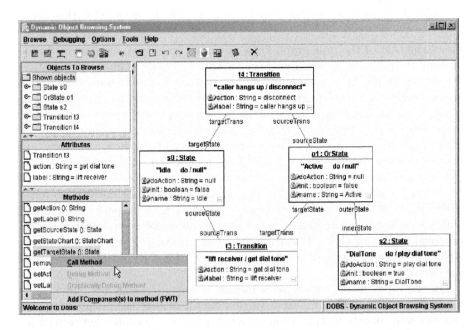

Fig. 8. Graph representing the abstract syntax of part of the statechart modeled in Figure 6. It is shown in *Fujaba*'s graph-based object browser DOBS.

An example of a well-formed statechart graph corresponding to the type graph of Figure 7 is shown in Figure 8. As can be seen, a graph is represented in *Fujaba*'s dynamic object browser DOBS as an object diagram. Objects correspond to vertices, and links between them to edges.

4   Model Refactorings Are Graph Transformations

4.1   Introduction

Graph transformation theory has been developed over the last three decades as a suite of techniques and tools for formal modeling and visual programming. Graph transformation systems can typically be found in two flavours: *graph grammars* and *graph rewriting*. *AGG* is an instance of the former category of tools, whereas *Fujaba* is an instance of the latter.

Graph grammars are the natural extension of Chomsky's generative *string grammars* into the domain of graphs. Production rules for (string-) grammars are generalized into production rules on graphs, which generatively enumerate all the sentences (i.e., the "graphs") of a graph grammar. Similarly, *string rewriting* can be generalized into graph rewriting. A string rewriting consists of a pattern and a replacement string. The pattern is matched against an input string, and the matched substring is replaced with the replacement string of the rule. In analogy, a graph rewriting consists of a pattern graph and a replacement graph. The application of a graph rewriting rule matches the pattern graph in an input graph, and replaces the matched subgraph with the replacement graph.

Many tools, even full-fledged programming environments, have been developed that illustrate the practical applicability of the graph transformation approach. These environments have demonstrated that:

1. complex transformations can be expressed in the form of rewriting rules, and
2. graph rewriting rules can be compiled into efficient code.

In recent years, a number of model transformation tools have emerged that use graph transformation as an underlying transformation engine. Concrete examples are *GReAT* [3], *MOLA* [4] and *VIATRA* [5]).

4.2   Formal Definitions

Now that we have introduced an example of how two different kinds of UML models (class diagrams and statecharts, respectively) can be represented as typed graph, let us see how we can formally specify graph transformations as an internal representation of model refactorings.

Definition 4. *Production rule and graph transformation.*
Let L and R be two graphs. A production rule *is a partial graph morphism $p : L \to R$. A graph transformation $G \Rightarrow_t H$ is a pair $t = (p, m)$ consisting of a production rule $p : L \to R$ and a total injective graph morphism (called* match*) $m : L \to G$.*

Using a category-theoretical construct called pushout, *one can automatically compute the morphisms* $m' : R \to H$ *and* $p' : G \to H$ *that make the diagram* (p, m) *commute. The graph* H *obtained through this process is the result of applying the graph transformation* t *to* G.

The above formal definition corresponds to the algebraic single-pushout approach with injective graph morphisms [32]. It is visualised in Figure 9. Because many readers may not be acquainted with category theory, we provide a more informal definition below. Essentially, the application of a production rule $p : L \to R$ in the context of a concrete graph G can be performed by carrying out the following steps:

1. finding a match m of the left-hand side L of the production rule in the graph G;
2. creating a context graph by removing the part of the graph G that is mapped to L but not to R;
3. gluing the context graph with those vertices and edges of R that do not have a counterpart in L.

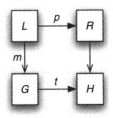

Fig. 9. Graph transformation $G \Rightarrow_t H$ consisting of a production rule $p : L \to R$ and match $m : L \to G$

In graph transformation systems with a large number of production rules it is often necessary to restrict the application of productions. We can use the notion of *negative application conditions* (NAC) for this purpose [33, 34]. It makes graph transformation considerably more expressive. Intuitively, a NAC is a graph that defines a forbidden graph structure (e.g., the absence of some vertices or edges). The mechanism of graph transformation can be extended easily to deal with application conditions, by checking all NACs associated to the production rule in the context of the concrete input graph G.

Definition 5. *Negative application condition.*
Let $p : L \to R$ *be a production rule. A* negative application condition *for* p *is a total graph morphism* $nac : L \to \hat{L}$. *A graph transformation* $G \Rightarrow_{(p,m)} H$ *satisfies a* negative application condition nac *if no graph morphism* $\hat{m} : \hat{L} \to G$ *exists such that* $\hat{m} \circ nac = m$.

In practice, several NACs can be attached to a single production rule, i.e., each production rule p has an associated set N of NACs.

Definition 6. *Applicability of a graph transformation.*
Let $\hat{p} = (p, N)$ be a production rule $p : L \rightarrow R$ together with a set N of nega-
tive application conditions. A graph transformation $G \Rightarrow_{(\hat{p},m)} H$ is applicable if
$G \Rightarrow_{(p,m)} H$ satisfies each negative application condition in N.

4.3   Specifying Model Refactorings in *AGG*

Model refactorings can be implemented in a straightforward way as *AGG* production rules. Obviously, these productions have to respect the constraints imposed by the type graph.

Coming back to our example of class diagrams, a *Pull Up Method* refactoring
can be specified as a production rule, as shown in Figure 10 (using *AGG* notation). Informally, the refactoring moves a given method one or more levels up in
the class hierarchy. (We use the edge *tgen* to denote transitive generalization of
a class, i.e., any direct or indirect superclass or the class itself.)

The left-hand side L of the production rule is shown on the left of Figure 10,
the right-hand side R is shown on the right of the figure. Vertices and edges that
are preserved have the same number in L and R. In this example, one edge of
type *contains* is removed in L, and another edge of the same type is added in
R. All other vertices and edges are preserved.

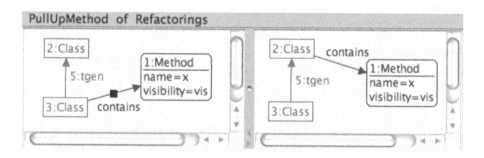

Fig. 10. A graph production rule representing part of the *Pull Up Method* refactoring

This production rule can be applied in the context of the graph G of Figure 4
by matching the nodes and edges (numbered from 1 to 5) in the left-hand side L
of Figure 10 to the nodes and edges with corresponding numbers in G. (For ease
of reference, the nodes belonging to the match m are highlighted in Figure 4.)
The result of applying this graph transformation is depicted in Figure 11.

The *Pull Up Method* production rule can be made more precise by adding
additional constraints that specify when it is allowed to apply the refactoring.
In Figure 12, two such constraints are shown. The first constraint, shown in the
upper left pane of Figure 12, is a negative application condition (NAC) called
`MethodAbsentInAncestors`. It specifies that the method cannot be pulled up if
a method with the same name (referred to by variable x) already exists in an
ancestor class belonging to the inheritance chain between the source class and

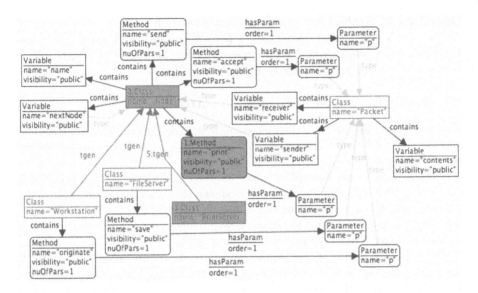

Fig. 11. Result of applying the *Pull Up Method* production rule to the graph of Figure 4

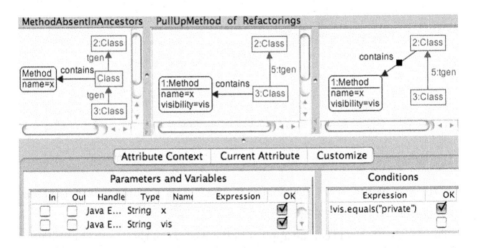

Fig. 12. The *Pull Up Method* production rule with negative application condition (NAC) in the upper left pane. The upper middle pane specifies the production's left-hand side, the upper right pane the production's right-hand side. The bottom left pane shows all parameters and variables used by the production rule. The bottom right pane shows additional constraints, that cannot be expressed graphically as NACs, but have to be implemented as Java expressions.

destination class of the method to be pulled up. In a similar way, many other NACs can be expressed for the production rule, but they are not shown here for the sake of brevity.

Figure 12 also shows a second constraint on the production rule that cannot be expressed graphically as a NAC because it has to do with the value of one of the vertex attributes, namely the visibility `vis` of the method to be pulled up. More specifically, we want to express that only methods with a non-private visibility can be pulled up. This can be achieved by adding the condition `!vis.equals("private")`, shown as a Java expression in the bottom right pane.

The *AGG* tool implements the *graph grammar* variant of graph transformations. This implies that no control structure is imposed on the production rules to be applied. Instead all applicable production rules are applied in a non-deterministic fashion until no more production rule is applicable. As such, a given initial graph G can give rise to a whole range of possible result graphs, which is referred to as $L(G)$, the language generated by the graph grammar. Each word in this language corresponds to a possible sequence of graph transformations that can be applied to G.

For the purpose of model refactoring, the mechanism of graph grammars is more a limitation than an advantage. In many practical situations, we would like to be able to control the order in which production rules have to be applied.

For instance, in the case of the *Pull Up Method* production rule introduced above, we actually need a second production rule to make the refactoring complete. The first production, P_1 (shown in Figure 12), takes a method in a class C and moves it to its parent class. A second production P_2 is needed to look for the same method signature in a sibling of C (i.e., a class with the same parent as C) and to delete this method. This production should be repeated as long as possible, i.e., for each occurrence of a sibling of C where the same method signature can be found.

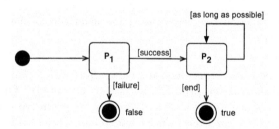

Fig. 13. An example of a programmed graph production rule composed of two productions rules P_1 and P_2. First P_1 is applied, and if it succeeds, P_2 is aplied as long as possible.

In order to be able to specify such a composition of production rules, we need an additional control structure that specifies how to combine production rules using sequencing, branching and loop constructs to control their order of application. Figure 13 shows what this could look like, using an activity diagram notation for combining the two parts P_1 and P_2 of the *Pull Up Method* refactoring. Because *AGG* does not support such control structures for specifying the composition of production rules, we will use the *Fujaba* tool to illustrate it in the next subsection.

4.4   Specifying Model Refactorings in *Fujaba*

While the *AGG* tool implements *graph grammars*, *Fujaba* implements *programmed (or controlled) graph transformation*. As such, *Fujaba* does provide a structuring mechanism to control the order in which production rules can be applied.[4]

Fujaba provides an intuitive and compact notation, called *story diagrams*, to represent both the production rules as well as their order of application. As a concrete example of how this works, we will revisit the example of a statechart flattening, and show how it can be expressed as a combination of production rules in *Fujaba* using the story diagram notation.

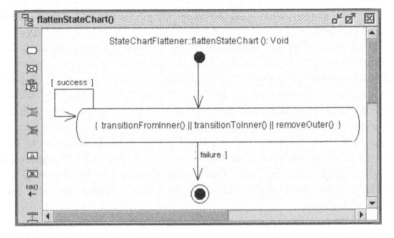

Fig. 14. Graph production rule representing the main control flow of a statechart flattening in Fujaba

Figure 14 shows a first story diagram, called *flattenStatechart* that expresses the main control flow of the production rules to be applied. One can see that the flattening of a statechart consists of three more primitive production steps (*transitionFromInner, transitionToInner* and *removeOuter*) that have to be repeated as long as possible. The order in which these three steps are applied is irrelevant, since they are parallel independent.

The *transitionFromInner* production rule, shown in Figure 15, replaces a transition originating from a composite OrState by a transition with the same attribute values from each of its substates. This can be specified by a story diagram containing three activities:

1. finding a transition originating from a composite OrState **or** to another state **a** and deleting it (while keeping the source and target states intact);

---

[4] Another well-known graph transformation tool that supports programmed graph transformation is *PROGRES* [35]. In some way, *PROGRES* can even be seen as the predecessor of *Fujaba*.

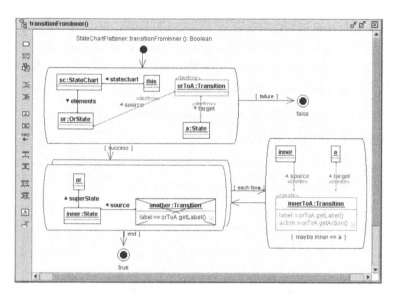

Fig. 15. Production rule *transitionFromInner*

2. looping over all substates **inner** of the composite state **or** that do not have an outgoing transition with the same label as the one that was deleted in the first step;
3. adding a transition from each of these **inner** substates to the state **a**.

Each activity box in the story diagram of Figure 15 can be considered as a separate production rule. Observe that the left-hand and right-hand sides of each production rule are compactly represented in a single graph structure. Vertices and edges to be removed by the production rule are denoted in red, with the stereotype ≪ *destroy* ≫. Vertices and edges to be added by the production rule are denoted in green, with the stereotype ≪ *create* ≫. Finally, negative application conditions specifying the absence of a vertex are denoted by crossing out this vertex.

The *transitionToInner* production rule, shown in Figure 16 is considerably more simple. There is only one activity, which consists of finding a composite OrState **or** and a substate **inner**, finding a transition whose target is the composite state, and moving the target edge of this transition to the **inner** state.

The *removeOuter* production rule, shown in Figure 17, checks whether there are no incoming or outgoing transitions of the composite OrState, and removes it if these conditions hold. As a side effect, all edges linking the substates with the composite state will be removed as well.

4.5 Comparing *AGG* and *Fujaba*

In this section we introduced the basic notions of graph transformation, and exemplified how to use them for model refactoring. Motivating examples

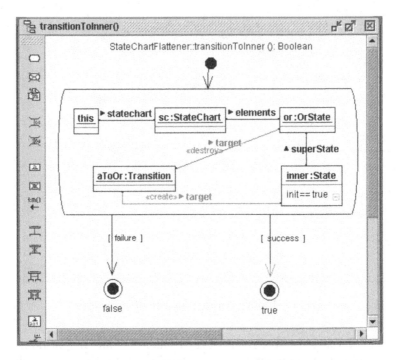

Fig. 16. Production rule *transitionToInner*

where provided for class diagrams and statecharts using two concrete tools, *AGG* and *Fujaba*.

AGG is a rule-based visual programming environment supporting graph transformation. A screenshot of *AGG* (version 1.2.6) in action is shown in Figure 18. *AGG* aims at the specification and prototypical implementation of applications with complex graph-structured data. It contains a general-purpose graph transformation engine that is implemented in Java. In *AGG*, production rules are stored as part of an attributed graph grammar. Given a start graph, the graph grammar can be applied by selecting rules that are applicable. *AGG* supports the specification of type graphs with multiplicities and attributes, such as the one shown in Figure 5. In *AGG*, vertex and edge attributes act like ordinary Java variables to which a value can be assigned. By means of Java expressions, the production rules can specify how attribute values need to be updated by the transformation. The production rules can also contain NACs and extra constraints (context conditions) that need to be satisfied when the production rule is applied in the context of an input graph. This is quite useful in practice, since the type graph and NACs are not always sufficiently expressive.

The *Fujaba* graph transformation tool is implemented in Java and uses the UML notation for design and realisation of software projects. A screenshot of *Fujaba* (version 4.3.1) in action is shown in Figure 19. It uses a combination of activity diagrams and a specific variant of collaboration diagrams (called story diagrams) for the specification of operational behaviour. The semantics of these

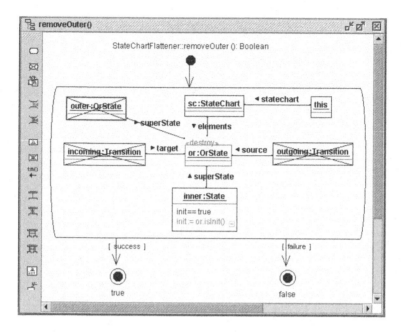

Fig. 17. Production rule *removeOuter*

story diagrams are based on programmed graph transformations. Story diagrams offer many powerful constructs of graph transformation such as multiobjects, non-injective matching, negative application conditions, and many more. This makes it a powerful language that allows to model even complex problems in an elegant way. The operational behaviour modeled with such story diagrams can then be tested using *Fujaba*'s graph-based object browser DOBS. Fujaba generates standard Java code that is easily integrated with other Java programs and that runs in a common Java runtime environment. This enables the use of graph transformation concepts in all kinds of Java applications.

If we perform a more detailed comparison of the functionality of the graph transformation tools *AGG* and *Fujaba* we observe that there are many similarities:

- They both make use of attributed type graphs with multiplicities
- They both make use of some variant of graph transformation
- They are both implemented in Java
- They both provide mechanism to specify negative application conditions and additional graph constraints

On the other hand, there are also a number of notable differences between both tools:

- *AGG* belongs to the Berlin school, which adheres to the algebraic double-pushout (DPO) approach to graph transformation, whereas *Fujaba* belongs

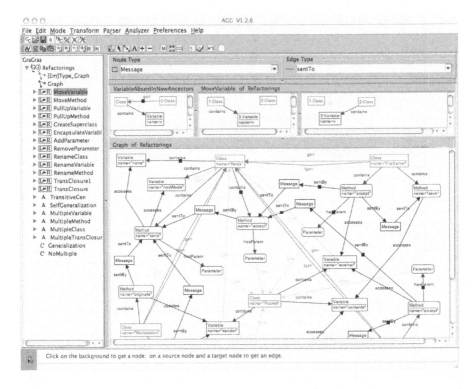

Fig. 18. Screenshot of the AGG version 1.2.6, after opening the Refactorings graph grammar

to the Aachen school, which adopts the algebraic single-pushout (SPO) approach to graph transformation. This distinction has a concrete impact at a number of places. First, the way in which dangling edges are dealt with in *Fujaba* is different from the one in *AGG*. In *Fujaba*, when a node is deleted, all dangling edges after deletion of this node will be removed as well. In *AGG*, if the deletion of a node would result in a dangling edge, then the production rule is simply not applicable. Second, the fact that edge attributes are not allowed in *Fujaba* is also a side-effect of the decision to use the SPO approach. If an edge would carry a certain attribute, then the edge has its own value and may survive in case of the deletion of an adjacent node.

- The *Fujaba* tool is actually a UML CASE tool. As a result, its notation is very close to UML notation. First of all, a type graph can be expressed as a simple UML class diagram. As a side-effect, on gets type inheritance for free. Second, Fujaba's story diagrams are actually a mixture of UML activity diagrams and object diagrams. Production rules are specified using a very compact notation (using the ≪ *destroy* ≫ and ≪ *create* ≫ stereotypes). An advantage of this adherence to the UML standard is that the tool tends to be more intuitive to users already acquainted with UML.

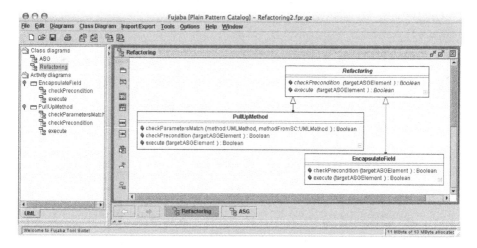

Fig. 19. Screenshot of the Fujaba Tool Suite version 4.3.1, after opening the Refactoring project

- A striking difference between both tools is the way in which the application of production rules is controlled. *AGG* relies on a graph grammar approach. This means that the control structure is implicit and non-deterministic: whenever a production rule is found that is applicable in the context of the host graph, it is applied, and this process continues with the result graph as the new host graph. The only mechanism that can control the order or production rules somewhat is the notion of layered graph grammars, but this is not sufficiently expressive in general. *Fujaba*, on the other hand, relies on programmed graph transformation. As such, the control structure is explicit and deterministic: the programmer can provide explicit sequencing, branching and loop constructs to control the order of application of production rules. More specifally, the story diagram notation is used for this purpose.
- A very useful feature of *AGG*, that is absent in other graph transformation tools, is that graph grammars may be validated using the techniques of *critical pair analysis* and *consistency checking*. These will be explained in detail in the experiment of section 5.
- A very useful feature of *Fujaba* that is absent in *AGG* is its ability to generate Java code from the story diagrams. This ability will be explored in detail in the experiment of section 6.

To shed some more light on the commonalities and differences between AGG and Fujaba, let us try to express the same model refactoring in both tools. The refactoring that we have chosen for this purpose is *Encapsulate Field*. Its goal is to change the visibility of a class attribute (called a field in Java) from `public` to `private`, and to redirect all direct accesses to this attribute by calls to a newly introduced getter and setter method for this attribute.

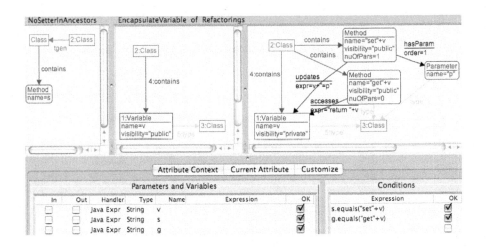

Fig. 20. *Encapsulate Variable* refactoring expressed as a production rule in *AGG*. The NAC in the left pane specifies that the name of the newly created setter method for the encapsulated variable should not exist in one of the ancestor classes. Note that this NAC also requires an extra context condition stating a relation between the value v of the name attribute of the variable and the value s of the name attribute of the method: `s.equals("set"+v)`.

The specification of this production rule in *AGG* is given in Figure 20. The production rule is parameterised by the class and its attribute that needs to be encapsulated. The name of the setter and getter methods depends on the name of the variable. This constraint can be expressed by means of the Java expressions `s.equals("set"+v)` and `g.equals("get"+v)` where v is the name of the variable, s the name of the setter method, and g the name of the getter method. The production rule also contains NACs, stating that the setter and getter methods introduced by the refactoring should not exist yet in the inheritance chain. One such NAC, called "noSetterInAncestors" is shown in the upper left pane of Figure 20.

Note that the specification of the refactoring *Encapsulate Field* shown in Figure 20 is not complete. It does not express the fact that all direct accesses to the public variable still need to be redirected by a call to its new setter method, and all direct updates to the public variable by a call to its new getter method. While it is fairly straightforward to express such a production rule in *AGG*, we cannot specify how this production should be related with the former one, since this would require some additional fine-grained control structure, which is absent in *AGG*.

The specification of the *Encapsulate Field* refactoring in Fujaba is shown in Figure 21 and Figure 22, respectively. It is implemented by means of two methods `checkPreconditions` and `execute`. This separation allows us to check the precondition of a refactoring separately from its actual execution. As usual both methods are specified in Fujaba using the story diagram notation. Note

EncapsulateField::checkPrecondition (target: ASGElement): Boolean

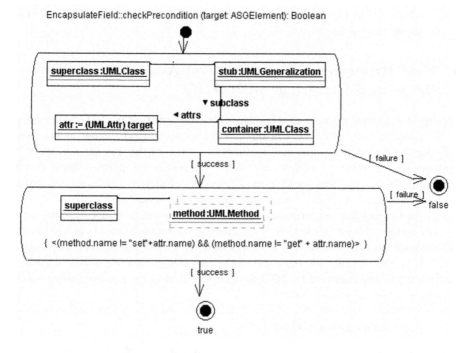

Fig. 21. Encapsulate Variable refactoring in Fujaba - Preconditions check

EncapsulateField::execute (target: ASGElement): Boolean

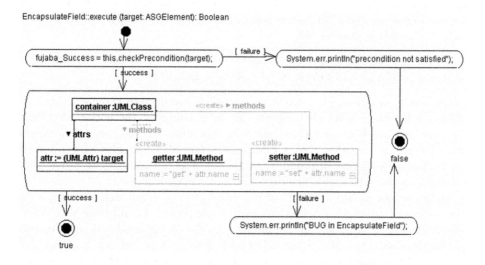

Fig. 22. Encapsulate Variable refactoring in Fujaba - Execution

that, to be consistent with the specification of the same refactoring in AGG, we did not specify that, after creating the `setter` and `getter` methods, all direct accesses or updates to the (previously public) attribute `attr` should be replaced by a method call to the `getter` and `setter` method, respectively. We leave this as an exercise to the reader.

5   First Experiment: Detecting and Analysing Conflicts Between Refactorings with *AGG*

Having introduced the basic graph transformation notation in *AGG* and *Fujaba* in the preceding sections, we will now conduct two concrete experiments that will allow us to exploit particular features of each tool. In this section, we will explore *AGG*'s ability to analyse and verify interesting properties about graph grammars. In section 6, we will explore *Fujaba*'s ability to generate code from model refactorings specified using story diagram notation.

The goal of our first experiment consists in finding out to which extent graph transformation theory can help us with identifying dependencies between model refactorings, as well as detecting conflicts between model refactorings applied in parallel. To this extent, we make use of the mechanism of *critical pair analysis*, that has been implemented in *AGG*. Before we can do this, however, we need to introduce some additional theory.

5.1   Confluence and Critical Pairs

Confluence is well-known in term rewriting, and is used to check whether a term rewriting systems (i.e., a term grammar) has a functional behaviour. Irrespective of the order in which the term rewritings are applied the end result should always remain the same. These confluence results can also be shown for the more general notion of graph grammars [36].

Definition 7 (Confluence). *A relation $R \subseteq A \times A$ is called* confluent *if $\forall a, b, c \in A$: if aRb and aRc then $\exists d \in A$: bRd and cRd*

Given a term grammar (or a graph grammar), it is crucial to know whether this grammar has the confluence property. To determine this, the notion of *critical pair analysis* has been introduced for term rewriting, and has been generalised later for graph rewriting [36]. Critical pairs formalize the idea of a minimal example of a conflicting situation. From the set of all critical pairs we can extract the vertices and edges which cause conflicts or dependencies.

To find all conflicting productions in a graph grammar, minimal critical graphs are computed to which productions can be applied in a conflicting way. Basically, one has to consider all overlapping graphs of the left-hand sides of two productions with the obvious matches and analyze these rule applications. All conflicting rule applications are called critical pairs. If one of the rules contains NACs, the overlapping graphs of one left-hand side with a part of the NAC have to be considered in addition.

Definition 8 (Conflict). *Two graph transformations $G_1 \Rightarrow_{(p_1, m_1)} H_1$ and $G_2 \Rightarrow_{(p_2, m_2)} H_2$ are in conflict if p_1 may disable p_2, or, vice versa, p_2 may disable p_1.*

There is a conflict if at least one of the following three conditions are fulfilled. The first two are related to the graph structure while the last one concerns the attributes of vertices or edges:

1. *delete/use conflict:* One graph transformation deletes a vertex or edge which is in the match of another graph transformation;
2. *produce/forbid conflict:* One graph transformation generates vertices or edges in a way that a graph structure would occur which is prohibited by a NAC of another graph transformation;
3. *change-attribute conflict:* One graph transformation changes attributes being in the match of another graph transformation.

Definition 9 (Critical pair). *A critical pair is a pair of graph transformations* $G \Rightarrow_{(p_1,m_1)} H_1$ *and* $G \Rightarrow_{(p_2,m_2)} H_2$ *which are in conflict, such that* m_1 *and* m_2 *are jointly surjective graph morphisms.*

The above definition is visualised in Figure 23. G is called the glue graph of p_1 and p_2. It is minimal by construction. In other words, it is impossible to find a subgraph of G that yields a critical pair between p_1 and p_2. For more details about critical pairs, and how to use them to achieve efficient conflict detection in graph-based model transformation, we refer to [37].

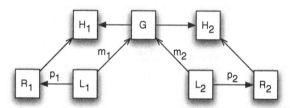

Fig. 23. Critical pair of graph transformations with glue graph G

The set of all critical pairs represents precisely all potential conflicts between a given pair of production rules (p_1, p_2). Therefore, we can apply critical pair analysis to a set of production rules, by performing a pairwise comparison of all rules. After computation of all critical pairs, the production set will be divided into conflict-free pairs and conflicting pairs.

As a concrete illustration of a critical pair, let us reconsider the *Pull Up Method* production rule of Figure 12 in combination with the *Move Method* production rule of Figure 24. *Move Method* is similar to *Pull Up Method*, except that a method is moved to a target class that does not belong to the inheritance chain of the source class. Trying to apply both production rules to the same host graph may give rise to a critical pair situation, as depicted in Figure 25. The same method m is pulled up and moved by different production rules. This clearly leads to a conflict, since both productions cannot be applied in sequence. Once the method m is pulled up, it can no longer be moved from its original location c, since it is no longer present there. The part of the glue graph that identifies this particular critical pair is shown as a gray ellipse in the figure.

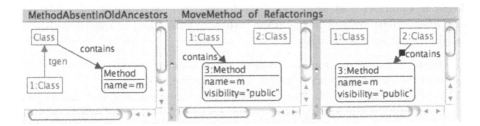

Fig. 24. A *Move Method* production rule with negative application condition. The three panes indicate, from left to right: a negative application condition, the left-hand side of the production rule, the right-hand side of the production rule.

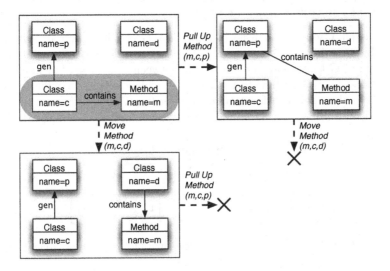

Fig. 25. Concrete example of a critical pair situation between the production rules *Move Method* and *PullUpMethod*

5.2 Detecting Refactorings Conflicts in AGG

We already saw *Pull Up Method*, *Encapsulate Field* and *Move Method* as concrete examples of production rules for class diagram refactorings in Figures 12, 20 and 24. In a similar way, other class diagram refactorings can be specified. For all these refactoring specifications, the preconditions are specified as NACs. For some refactorings, such as *Pull Up Method* and *Encapsulate Variable*, additional context conditions are needed for those constraints that cannot be expressed in terms of the type graph. These context conditions are specified as ordinary Java expressions.

In Definition 9 of Section 5.1, we explained the notion of critical pairs and how it can be used to detect conflicts between production rules. A concrete example of such a conflict was shown in Figure 25. *AGG* supports critical pair analysis

first \ second	1: Mo...	2: Mo...	3: Pul...	4: Pul...	5: Cr...	6: En...	7: Ad...	8: Re...	9: Re...	10: R...	11: R...
1: MoveVariable	3	0	4	0	0	2	0	0	0	2	0
2: MoveMethod	0	3	0	4	0	2	2	2	0	0	2
3: PullUpVariable	3	0	4	0	0	2	0	0	0	1	0
4: PullUpMethod	0	4	0	3	0	2	3	3	0	0	1
5: CreateSuperclass	0	0	0	0	0	0	0	0	3	0	0
6: EncapsulateVariable	2	2	2	2	0	0	0	0	0	0	1
7: AddParameter	0	0	0	0	0	0	0	2	0	0	0
8: RemoveParameter	0	0	0	0	0	0	2	2	0	0	0
9: RenameClass	0	0	0	0	2	0	0	0	2	0	0
10: RenameVariable	2	0	2	0	0	1	0	0	0	2	0
11: RenameMethod	0	2	0	2	0	1	1	1	0	0	2

Fig. 26. Critical pair analysis

for typed attributed graph transformations. Given a graph grammar, AGG can compute a table showing the number of conflicting situations for each critical pair of productions.

We applied AGG's critical pair analysis algorithm to a representative selection of refactorings. The results are shown in the table of Figure 26. Among others, this table shows that four critical pairs are reported between *Pull Up Method* and *Move Method*. Two of the critical graphs computed by AGG for this situation are shown in Figure 27. Both critical graphs report similar conflict situations in the glue graph that correspond to the conflict illustrated in Figure 25. The additional two conflicts not depicted are less interesting, since they report possible conflicts that cannot occur in our setting. This is due to the fact that AGG's critical pair algorithm abstracts away from concrete attribute interrelations. Since arbitrary

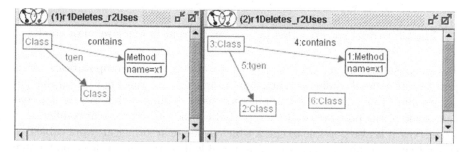

Fig. 27. Posible conflicts of *Move Method* and *Pull Up Method*

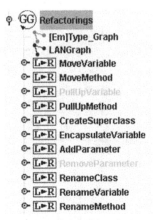

Fig. 28. Verifying applicability of refactoring productions in *AGG*. Those that are applicable in the context of the given input graph are shown in black, the others are shown in gray.

first \ second	1: Mo...	2: Mo...	3: Pul...	4: Pul...	5: Cr...	6: En...	7: Ad...	8: Re...	9: Re...	10: R...	11: R...
1: MoveVariable	3	0	4	0	0	2	0	0	0	2	0
2: MoveMethod	0	3	0	4	0	2	2	2	0	0	2
3: PullUpVariable	3	0	4	0	0	2	0	0	0	1	0
4: PullUpMethod	0	4	0	3	0	0	3	3	0	0	1
5: CreateSuperclass	0	0	0	0	0	0	0	0	3	0	0
6: EncapsulateVariable	2	2	2	0	0	0	0	0	0	0	0
7: AddParameter	0	0	0	0	0	0	0	2	0	0	0
8: RemoveParameter	0	0	0	0	0	0	2	2	0	0	0
9: RenameClass	0	0	0	0	2	0	0	0	2	0	0
10: RenameVariable	2	0	2	0	0	1	0	0	0	2	0
11: RenameMethod	0	2	0	2	0	0	1	1	0	0	2

Fig. 29. Critical pairs reported by *AGG* in the context of a given host graph

Java expressions can be used for attribute conditions and computations, *AGG* just reports general conflicts on attribute usage, i.e., one rule application changes an attribute that another rule application uses. Acting in this way, it happens that some of the possible conflicts reported can never become real conflicts.

In *AGG* it is also possible to check which of the refactorings are applicable to a concrete host graph: A refactoring is applicable if there exists at least one match of its left-hand side (taking into account the NACs). Figure 28 gives an example that shows that certain refactorings are not applicable in a particular situation.

It is obtained by using *AGG*'s menu item "Check Rule Applicability". *Pull Up Variable* and *Remove Parameter* are reported as non-applicable because, in the considered host graph, none of the subclasses had variables, and because all methods having parameters are called by others, thus prohibiting their removal.

While the critical pair table of Figure 26 shows all potential conflicting situations that can occur between any pair of refactoring productions, the number of "real" conflicts in the context of a concrete host graph is of course much lower, since not all refactorings may be applicable to this host graph. Therefore, *AGG* can also show the conflicts in the host graph by selecting only the relevant critical pairs and showing how the corresponding conflict graphs are matched to the host graph. An example is given in Figure 29. All previously computed critical pairs that are not relevant in the host graph are "grayed out".

For a more detailed discussion of the analysis we performed on the critical pairs of refactoring productions, we refer to [38].

6   Second Experiment: Generating Refactoring Code with *Fujaba*

In *Fujaba*, there is a seamless integration between UML modeling and Java programming.[5] As a result, the user of the tool can simply express his design as a UML class diagram, or directly write Java code and perform a reverse engineering step to automatically generate the class diagrams. The only place where graph transformation comes in is at the level of method implementations. In *Fujaba*, a method can be implemented as a production rule using a story diagram. An example of this was shown in Figure 21, which represents the implementation of the `checkPrecondition` method of the *EncapsulateField* class, and Figure 22, which represents the implementation of the `execute` method of the *EncapsulateField* class.

An important feature of *Fujaba* is its very flexible plug-in mechanism. One such plug-in has been developed by the University of Kassel to provide support for some simple refactorings. When a refactoring is selected via the refactoring plug-in, the corresponding refactoring will be executed. In version 4.3.2, the following list of refactorings has been implemented: *Extract Method, Override Method, Implement Method*, and *Change Method Signature*. However, the implementation of these refactorings was hard-coded in Java. Hence, this cannot be used as a proof of concept that graph transformation can effectively be used to implement model refactorings in the way suggested above.

Therefore, Pieter Van Gorp and Niels Van Eetvelde from the University of Antwerp (Belgium) conducted an experiment to specify class diagram refactorings, such as the *Pull Up Method* refactoring, in Fujaba using the story diagram notation, and to generate Java code from this graphical specification in an automatic way [39]. This has the advantage that the refactoring designer can stick to the graphical notation, and only needs to write a very limited amount of Java code.

---

[5] FUJABA is an acronym for "From Uml to Java And Back Again".

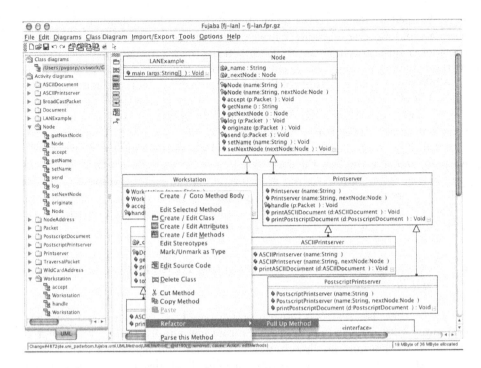

Fig. 30. Refactoring plugin for Fujaba

It is possible to go even one step further, and link the executable refactoring code into a refactoring plugin that can be used by the *Fujaba* tool. As such, after having specified and generated the refactoring code, it immediately becomes available for use. Figure 30 shows how the *Pull Up Method* refactoring, whose specification has been given as a story diagram, can be selected from a context-sensitive menu in *Fujaba*, once its corresponding Java code has been generated.

In this initial experiment, a number of important limitations were identified that were overcome in later experiments [40, 41]:

- The refactoring specifications (represented as story diagrams) could not be exchanged with other tools because story diagrams are not part of the UML standard. This problem was overcome by designing a UML profile for *Fujaba*'s graph transformation language.
- The code generated by *Fujaba* could only be executed on repositories conforming to *Fujaba*'s API conventions. This limitation was resolved by building a tool that generates MOF compliant code from transformation models conforming to *Fujaba*'s UML profile. This allowed us to repeat the class diagram refactoring experiment with general purpose UML tools such as *MagicDraw* and *Poseidon*. See Figure 31 for a screenshot illustrating the use of Poseidon (or rather, an extension of it supporting the story diagram UML profile) for specifying model refactorings and generating the associated Java code.

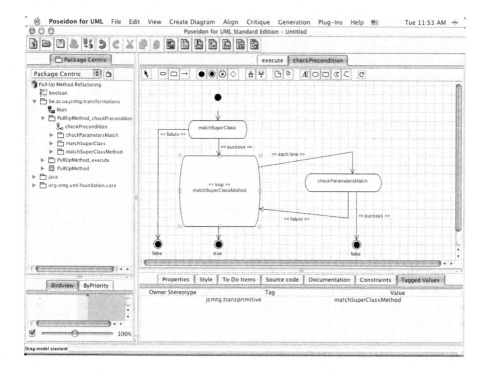

Fig. 31. Screenshot of part of the specification of the *PullUpMethod* refactoring using story diagram notation in Poseidon

7 Benefits and Drawbacks of Graph Transformation

Until now we have illustrated how and why graph transformations can be used to represent model refactorings. Table 2 provides a summary of the various notions of graph transformation, and how they represent related notions in model refactoring.

In this section we present some additional arguments why graph transformation is a good underlying foundation for refactoring technology, and point out some references to relevant literature for the interested reader.

7.1 Guaranteeing Behaviour Preservation

We can rely on graph transformation theory to determine whether a refactoring preserves the correctness or the behaviour. Mens *et al.* [42, 43] showed that graph transformation is a promising formalism to do this, but also indicated a number of limitations with respect to the expressiveness of existing graph transformation formalisms. Therefore, Van Eetvelde and Janssens [44] proposed to extend graph transformations with new mechanisms to enhance their expressive power.

Obviously, graph transformation theory is not the only formalism that may be used to check behaviour preservation. For proving the preservation of statechart

Table 2. Representing model refactoring by graph transformation

Graph transformation	Refactoring
type graph and global graph constraints	well-formedness constraints
negative application conditions	refactoring preconditions
parameterised production rules with NACs and context conditions	refactoring transformation
programmed graph transformations, story diagrams	composite refactorings
critical pair analysis	detecting refactoring conflicts
confluence analysis	detecting sequential dependencies
code generation from story diagrams	refactoring plug-in facility

refactorings, Van Kempen *et al.* use a model checking approach, by comparing the behavioural equivalence of CSP processes using refinement in the failures-divergences model [14].

Various authors have tried to deal with refactorings in presence of OCL constraints [10, 18, 12]. In particular, Markovic and Baar [12] formally describe how the OCL constraints expressed on UML class diagrams have to be refactored to preserve their syntactical correctness. To this extent, they make use of a graph-grammar based formalism.

7.2   Composition of Refactorings

Another very important question in refactoring research is how to compose primitive refactorings into more complex, composite refactorings [45, 46, 47]. An essential question in this context is how, given a sequence of refactorings, one can compute the preconditions of the composite refactoring without needing to apply each refactoring in the sequence. As a partial answer to this question, in his masters thesis, Reiko Heckel theoretically showed how a sequence of graph transformations with application pre- and postconditions could be transformed into an equivalent composite graph transformation with pre- and postconditions [48]. Kniesel and Koch [47] explored this idea in the context of refactoring, and showed how it can be used to build tools that facilitate the static composition of refactoring transformations. They implemented such a tool in Prolog using the notation of conditional transformations.

7.3   Co-evolution and Consistency Maintenance

To be able to focus on different aspects of a program, software engineers usually employ different views on the software. For example, a UML model usually consists of a class diagram to describe the static structure, a set of use case diagrams to specify the user interaction, and a set of interaction diagrams and statecharts to specify the dynamic behaviour. All these diagrams represent a different view that is represented using a different modeling notation. Hence techniques are required to maintain the consistency between all these different views when one of them evolves (e.g., by means of a refactoring).

When we also take the source code into account, we even need to maintain the consistency between the models and the corresponding program. To ensure that both views remain consistent when applying refactorings, Bottoni *et al.* [49] proposed a framework based on distributed graphs to maintain consistency between the code (represented as a flow graph) and the model (given by several UML diagrams of different kinds). Each refactoring is specified as a set of distributed graph transformations, structured and organized into transformation units.

Other formal approaches based on graph transformations that seem promising to address the consistency problem are pair grammars and triple graph grammars [50].

7.4 Graph Rewriting Versus Tree Rewriting

During our experiments in *AGG* as well as *Fujaba* we encountered an issue that has to do with the expressiveness of graphs and graph transformations. When trying to specify certain class diagram refactorings, in particular those that have to perform non-trivial manipulations of method bodies (e.g., *Extract Method*, *Move Method* and *Push Down Method*), the graph transformations quickly become very complex. This issue has already been acknowledged in [42,44].

Because a method body is essentially an abstract syntax tree, an alternative approach would be to make use of tree rewriting techniques [51,52], as they may be better suited for these kinds of manipulations. In practice, this implies that the ideal refactoring specification language may need to incorporate the best of both worlds: graph transformation for those parts of the model that are essentially graphical in nature (e.g., the class structure of a class diagram, including all inheritance, typing and association relationships), and tree transformation for those parts of the model that are essentially tree-based in nature (e.g., method parse trees).

8 Conclusion

In this article we explored the idea of model refactoring and we suggested to use the formalism of graph transformation as an underlying foundation. We provided concrete examples using a simplified version of both UML class diagrams and statecharts as our metamodel.

In addition, we conducted some concrete experiments to show how graph transformation technology can be used to support model refactoring. Using the graph transformation tool *Fujaba*, we explained how a refactoring plug-in can be developed to refactor UML class diagrams, where each refactoring is expressed as a graph production rule in *Fujaba*'s story diagram notation, and the corresponding Java code is generated automatically. Using the graph transformation tool *AGG*, we explained how to use the built-in technique of critical pair analysis to detect potential conflicts between refactorings, and to help the developer decide which refactoring should be selected when different choices are applicable.

Acknowledgements

I express my gratitude to many persons. Ralf Lämmel, João Saraiva and Joost Visser, for organising a very successful summer school, and for inviting me to give a tutorial on the topic of the current article. Pieter Van Gorp, for carrying out the experiment on generating Java code from model refactorings in *Fujaba*. Gabriele Taentzer and Olga Runge, for collaborating on the experiment with critical pair analysis in *AGG*. Albert Zuendorf and Ralf Geiger, for granting me permission to reuse their statechart flattening example.

This research has been carried out in the context of several research projects and networks. The FWO project on "A formal foundation for software refactoring", the FNRS/FRFC "Research Center on Structural Software Improvement", and the ESF scientific network RELEASE.

References

1. Sendall, S., Kozaczynski, W.: Model transformation: The heart and soul of model-driven software development. IEEE Software **20**(5) (2003) 42–45 Special Issue on Model-Driven Software Development.
2. Bézivin, J.: Model driven engineering: Principles, scope, deployment and applicability. In: Proc. Summer School on Generative and Transformation Techniques in Software Engineering (GTTSE 2005), Springer (2006)
3. Sprinkle, J., Agrawal, A., Levendovszky, T., Shi, F., Karsai, G.: Domain model translation using graph transformations. In: Proc. Int'l Conf. Engineering of Computer-Based Systems, IEEE Computer Society (2003) 159–168
4. Kalnins, A., Barzdins, J., Celms, E.: Model transformation language MOLA. In: Proc. Model-Driven Architecture: Foundations and Applications. (2004) 14–28
5. Csertán, G., Huszerl, G., Majzik, I., Pap, Z., Pataricza, A., Varró, D.: VIATRA - visual automated transformations for formal verification and validation of UML models. In: Proc. Int'l Conf. Automated Software Engineering, IEEE Computer Society (2002) 267–270
6. Opdyke, W.F.: Refactoring: A Program Restructuring Aid in Designing Object-Oriented Application Frameworks. PhD thesis, University of Illinois at Urbana-Champaign (1992)
7. Fowler, M.: Refactoring: Improving the Design of Existing Code. Addison-Wesley (1999)
8. G. Sunyé, Pollet, D., LeTraon, Y., J.-M. Jézéquel: Refactoring UML models. In: Proc. UML 2001. Volume 2185 of Lecture Notes in Computer Science., Springer-Verlag (2001) 134–138
9. Boger, M., Sturm, T., Fragemann, P.: Refactoring browser for UML. In: Proc. Int'l Conf. on eXtreme Programming and Flexible Processes in Software Engineering. (2002) 77–81
10. Van Gorp, P., Stenten, H., Mens, T., Demeyer, S.: Towards automating source-consistent UML refactorings. In Stevens, P., Whittle, J., Booch, G., eds.: UML 2003 - The Unified Modeling Language. Volume 2863 of Lecture Notes in Computer Science., Springer-Verlag (2003) 144–158

11. Van Der Straeten, R., Jonckers, V., Mens, T.: Supporting model refactorings through behaviour inheritance consistencies. In Thomas Baar, Alfred Strohmeier, A.M., ed.: UML 2004 - The Unified Modeling Language. Volume 3273 of Lecture Notes in Computer Science., Springer-Verlag (2004) 305–319

12. Markovic, S., Baar, T.: Refactoring ocl annotated uml class diagrams. In: Proc. Int'l Conf. Model Driven Engineering Languages and Systems (MoDELS 2005). Volume 3713 of Lecture Notes in Computer Science., Springer (2005) 280–294

13. Zhang, J., Lin, Y., Gray, J.: Generic and domain-specific model refactoring using a model transformation engine. In: Model-driven Software Development - Research and Practice in Software Engineering. Springer Verlag (2005)

14. Van Kempen, M., Chaudron, M., Koudrie, D., Boake, A.: Towards proving preservation of behaviour of refactoring of UML models. In: Proc. SAICSIT 2005. (2005) 111–118

15. Mens, T., Van Gorp, P.: A taxonomy of model transformation. In: Proc. Int'l Workshop on Graph and Model Transformation (GraMoT 2005). Electronic Notes in Theoretical Computer Science, Elsevier (2006)

16. Mens, T., Van Gorp, P., Varró, D., Karsai, G.: Applying a model transformation taxonomy to graph transformation technology. In: Proc. Int'l Workshop on Graph and Model Transformation (GraMoT 2005). Electronic Notes in Theoretical Computer Science, Elsevier (2006)

17. Geiger, L., Zündorf, A.: Statechart modeling with Fujaba. In: Proc. Int'l Workshop Graph-Based Tools (GraBaTs). Electronic Notes in Theoretical Computer Science, Elsevier (2004)

18. Alexandre Correa, C.W.: Applying refactoring techniques to UML/OCL models. In Thomas Baar, Alfred Strohmeier, A.M., ed.: UML 2004 - The Unified Modeling Language. Volume 3273 of Lecture Notes in Computer Science., Springer-Verlag (2004) 173–187

19. Porres, I.: Model refactorings as rule-based update transformations. In Stevens, P., Whittle, J., Booch, G., eds.: UML 2003 - The Unified Modeling Language. Volume 2863 of Lecture Notes in Computer Science., Springer-Verlag (2003) 159–174

20. Spanoudakis, G., Zisman, A.: Inconsistency management in software engineering: Survey and open research issues. In: Handbook of Software Engineering and Knowledge Engineering. World scientific (2001) 329–380

21. Van Der Straeten, R., Mens, T., Simmonds, J., Jonckers, V.: Using description logics to maintain consistency between UML models. In Stevens, P., Whittle, J., Booch, G., eds.: UML 2003 - The Unified Modeling Language. Volume 2863 of Lecture Notes in Computer Science., Springer-Verlag (2003) 326–340

22. D'Hondt, T., De Volder, K., Mens, K., Wuyts, R.: Co-evolution of object-oriented design and implementation. In: Proc. Int'l Symp. Software Architectures and Component Technology: The State of the Art in Research and Practice, Enschede, The Netherlands, Kluwer Academic Publishers (2000)

23. Wuyts, R.: A Logic Meta-Programming Approach to Support the Co-Evolution of Object-Oriented Design and Implementation. PhD thesis, Department of Computer Science, Vrije Universiteit Brussel (2001)

24. Corradini, A., Montanari, U., Rossi, F.: Graph processes. Fundamenta Informaticae **26**(3 and 4) (1996) 241–265

25. Taentzer, G.: AGG: A tool environment for algebraic graph transformation. In: Proc. AGTIVE 99. Volume 1779 of Lecture Notes in Computer Science., Springer-Verlag (1999) 481–488

26. Taentzer, G.: AGG: A graph transformation environment for modeling and validation of software. In: Proc. AGTIVE 2003. Volume 3062 of Lecture Notes in Computer Science., Springer-Verlag (2004) 446–453

27. Demeyer, S., Janssens, D., Mens, T.: Simulation of a LAN. Electronic Notes in Theoretical Computer Science **72**(4) (2002)

28. Demeyer, S., Van Rysselberghe, F., Gîrba, T., Ratzinger, J., Marinescu, R., Mens, T., Du Bois, B., Janssens, D., Ducasse, S., Lanza, M., Rieger, M., Gall, H., El-Ramly, M.: The LAN simulation: A refactoring teaching example. In: Proc. Int'l Workshop on Principles of Software Evolution (IWPSE 2005). (2005)

29. Object Management Group: Unified Modeling Language specification version 1.5. formal/2003-03-01 (2003)

30. Niere, J., Zündorf, A.: Using Fujaba for the development of production control systems. In Nagl, M., Schürr, A., Münch, M., eds.: Proc. Int. Workshop Agtive 99. Volume 1779 of Lecture Notes in Computer Science. Springer-Verlag (2000) 181–191

31. Taentzer, G., Rensink, A.: Ensuring structural constraints in graph-based models with type inheritance. In: Proc. Int'l Conf. Fundamental Approaches to Software Engineering. Volume 3442 of Lecture Notes in Computer Science., Springer-Verlag (2005) 64–79

32. Ehrig, H., Löwe, M.: Parallel and distributed derivations in the single-pushout approach. Theoretical Computer Science **109** (1993) 123–143

33. Ehrig, H., Habel, A.: Graph grammars with application conditions. In Rozenberg, G., Salomaa, A., eds.: The Book of L, Springer-Verlag (1986) 87–100

34. Habel, A., Heckel, R., Taentzer, G.: Graph grammars with negative application conditions. Fundamenta Informaticae **26**(3,4) (1996) 287–313

35. Schürr, A., Winter, A., Zündorf, A.: PROGRES: Language and Environment. In: Handbook of Graph Grammars and Graph Transformation. World scientific (1999) 487–550

36. Heckel, R., Jochen Malte Küster, Taentzer, G.: Confluence of typed attributed graph transformation systems. In: Proc. 1st Int'l Conf. Graph Transformation. Volume 2505 of Lecture Notes in Computer Science., Springer-Verlag (2002) 161–176

37. Lambers, L., Ehrig, H., Orejas, F.: Efficient detection of conflicts in graph-based model transformation. In: Proc. Int'l Workshop on Graph and Model Transformation (GraMoT 2005). Electronic Notes in Theoretical Computer Science, Elsevier (2006)

38. Mens, T., Taentzer, G., Runge, O.: Analyzing refactoring dependencies using graph transformation. Software and System Modeling (2006) To appear.

39. Van Gorp, P., Van Eetvelde, N., Janssens, D.: Implementing refactorings as graph rewrite rules on a platform independent metamodel. In: Proc. Fujaba Days. (2003)

40. Schippers, H., Van Gorp, P., Janssens, D.: Leveraging UML profiles to generate plugins from visual model transformations. In: Proc. Int'l Workshop Software Evolution through Transformations (SETra). Volume 127 of Electronic Notes in Theoretical Computer Science., Elsevier (2005) 5–16

41. Schippers, H., Van Gorp, P.: Standardizing story-driven modeling for model transformations. In: Proc. Int'l Fujaba Days. (2004)

42. Mens, T., Demeyer, S., Janssens, D.: Formalising behaviour preserving program transformations. In: Proc. 1st Int'l Conf. Graph Transformation. Volume 2505 of Lecture Notes in Computer Science., Springer-Verlag (2002) 286–301

43. Mens, T., Van Eetvelde, N., Demeyer, S., Janssens, D.: Formalizing refactorings with graph transformations. Int'l Journal on Software Maintenance and Evolution **17**(4) (2005) 247–276

44. Van Eetvelde, N., Janssens, D.: Extending graph rewriting for refactoring. In: Proc. Int'l Conf. Graph Transformation. Volume 3526 of Lecture Notes in Computer Science., Springer-Verlag (2004) 399–415

45. Roberts, D.B.: Practical Analysis for Refactoring. PhD thesis, University of Illinois at Urbana-Champaign (1999)

46. Ó Cinnéide, M., Nixon, P.: Composite refactorings for java programs. Technical report, Department of Computer Science, University College Dublin (2000)

47. Kniesel, G., Koch, H.: Static composition of refactorings. Science of Computer Programming **52**(1-3) (2004) 9–51

48. Heckel, R.: Algebraic graph transformations with application conditions. Master's thesis, Technische Universität Berlin (1995)

49. Bottoni, P., Parisi Presicce, F., Taentzer, G.: Specifying integrated refactoring with distributed graph transformations. Lecture Notes in Computer Science **3062** (2003) 220–235

50. Königs, A., Schürr, A.: Tool integration with triple graph grammars - a survey. Electronic Notes in Theoretical Computer Science (2005)

51. Visser, E.: A language for program transformation based on rewriting strategies. In Middeldorp, A., ed.: Rewriting Techniques and Applications. Volume 2051 of Lecture Notes in Computer Science., Springer-Verlag (2001) 357–

52. van den Brand, M., Klint, P., Vinju, J.: Term rewriting with traversal functions. Transactions on Software Engineering and Methodology **12** (2003) 152–190

Part II

Technology Presentations

Forms2Net - Migrating Oracle Forms to Microsoft .NET

Luis Andrade[1], João Gouveia[1], Miguel Antunes[1],
Mohammad El-Ramly[2], and Georgios Koutsoukos[1]

[1] ATX Software S.A, Rua Saraiva de Carvalho, 207C, 1350-300 Lisbon, Portugal
{luis.andrade, joao.gouveia, miguel.antunes,
georgios.koutsoukos}@atxsoftware.com
[2] Department of Computer Science, University of Leicester,
University Road, Leicester, LE1 7RH, UK
mer14@le.ac.uk
http://www.cs.le.ac.uk/~mer14

Abstract. Forms2Net is an ATX Software commercial reengineering tool that automatically converts Oracle Forms applications to the equivalent .NET (C#) ones, with approximately 75% rate of automatic conversion. From the reengineering and transformation theoretical viewpoint, Forms2Net falls in the general category of language-platform conversion tools. As theory and practice indicate, for such tools to be effective, there are two major issues that must be handled: (a) the resolution of the semantic gap between the pair of source-target languages and (b) the resolution of the dependencies (e.g., API dependencies) on functionalities provided by default by the source platform or on programming idiosyncrasies of the source platform (in this case Oracle Forms). This paper presents the important practical aspects of Forms2Net and the underlying technology. We discuss the semantic gap between Oracle Forms and .NET forms and the design principles and solution strategies used to bridge this gap.

1 Introduction

Software application transformation is an active area in research and practice [10,12]. For many reasons organizations decide to migrate from one language to another, from a platform to another, from an operating system to another or a combination of these. The reasons for such migration are diverse ranging from moving away from an obsolete technology, to creating an integrated corporate information system, to moving from client-server architecture to a multi-tier or three-tier architecture. A few examples of such migration are [6, 7, 11]:

- Converting to a newer version of a language (COBOL 68 to COBOL 85),
- Converting from a language to another (COBOL to C or Java)
- Migrating an application to a different system that supports a different dialect of the same language (Cobol on IBM Mainframe to AS/400 Cobol)
- Migrating from a file system storage or a hierarchal database to a relational database (from VSAM files to DB2)
- Converting from an application framework to another (Oracle Forms applications to .NET applications in VB or C# or to Java applications for J2EE).

R. Lämmel, J. Saraiva, and J. Visser (Eds.): GTTSE 2005, LNCS 4143, pp. 261–277, 2006.

The width of the semantic gap between the source and target languages and/or platforms decides the feasibility and complexity of the conversion. The wider the gap, the less feasible, more complex and less automated the conversion is. This paper presents the challenges faced, design decisions made and solution strategies implemented in Forms2Net [1], a commercial tool for transforming Oracle Forms applications to C# applications for .NET. It gives an overview of Oracle Forms platform and discusses the reasons for converting Oracle Forms applications to .NET ones, the challenges in this conversion and the semantic gap between both frameworks (Sections 2 to 4). Then, it explains the strategies and design principles followed in designing Forms2Net (Section 5) and the conversion approach implemented in Forms2Net (Section 6). Next, the related work is discussed (Section 7). Finally, some conclusions are drawn (Section 8). Oracle Forms might be referred to as Forms only in the rest of the paper.

2 An Overview of Oracle Forms Applications

Oracle Forms is a 4GL rapid database application development environment plus a runtime environment where these database applications run [13]. Table 1 summarizes the elements of a Forms application. [9]

Figure 1 shows the structure of an Oracle Forms application from a developer's viewpoint and the relationships between its main components. The arrows represent a general relation that can be association or aggregation.

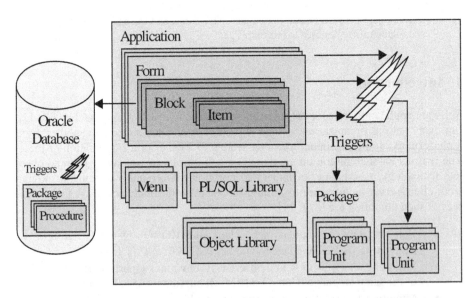

Fig. 1. The Structure of an Oracle Forms Application from a Developer's Viewpoint

Table 1. The Elements of an Oracle Forms Application

Oracle Concept	Description
Form	A Form is a collection of objects and code, including windows, items, triggers and program units. A form can include any number of separate windows.
Window	The usual window concept. A form may have several windows that are closely related.
Canvas	A canvas is a content area placed inside a window. A window may display several canvases.
Block	Represents a logical container for grouping related items into a function unit for storing, displaying, and manipulating records. Only item objects contained in a block are visible in the application interface.
Item	Items display information to users and enable them to interact with the application. Item objects include the following types: button, check box, display item, image, list item, radio group, text item and/or user area, among others.
Trigger	Represents a block of code that adds functionality to an application by one or more PL/SQL statements. A trigger object is associated with an event.
Program unit	Represents a named PL/SQL function or procedure that is written in a form, menu, or library module. It allows the reusability of code across different trigger behaviors.
Package	A package is a PL/SQL construct that groups logically related types, objects, procedures, and functions. Packages usually have two parts, a specification and a body, although sometimes the body is unnecessary.
Record Group	Represents a set of column/row values similar to a database table. However, unlike database tables, record groups are separate objects that belong to the form module in which they are defined.
LOV (list of values)	A LOV object is a scrollable popup window that provides the end user with either a single or multi-column selection list. It represents a set of column/row values similar to a database table.
Alert	An alert is a modal dialog box that displays a message notifying the operator of some application condition.
Visual Attribute	Represents a named visual attribute that should be applied to an object at runtime. A visual attribute defines a collection of font, color, and pattern attributes that determine the appearance of an object.
Menu	A collection of menus (a main menu object and any number of submenu objects) and menu item commands that together make up an application menu.
Library	A collection of user-named procedures, functions, and packages that can be called from other modules in the application.

Note in Figure 1 that the database may have some elements beside data, which are triggers and packages of procedures that are left untouched by the Oracle Forms application migration process. From the presentation or user interface viewpoint, an Oracle Forms application looks like Figure 2 [6]. Frames in Oracle Forms are visual containers similar to Group Box Controls in Windows Forms.

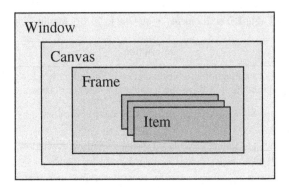

Fig. 2. The Organization of an Oracle Forms Application from a Presentation Viewpoint

3   Why Convert Oracle Forms Applications to .NET?

A .NET Windows Forms application in its essence is based on similar concepts for the presentation elements (Forms, Panels, Controls, Event handlers) and the code elements (class libraries). These are the building blocks of a .NET application and there are different ways to use them and organize them to make an application – this is the role of the application architecture. Microsoft makes available several application blocks based on the .NET Framework, but they are still low-level isolated blocks targeting a specific task/feature (logging, cache, exceptions, data access, etc.) [5].

Oracle Forms is already a legacy environment for Forms applications. J2EE and .NET are the major platforms to develop this kind of applications nowadays. They both have their own strengths. Forms2Net targets only the migration to .NET Framework. Although Oracle Forms was considered a powerful and productive environment for application development, the resulting applications lack the flexibility and the interface features available in modern applications. Several other factors may influence the decision to move from Oracle Forms to .NET:

- Easy to find and cheaper workforce
- Cost savings (database costs)
- Increased development productivity
- Platform harmonization/migration.
- Customer/partner alignment;

The conversion of legacy Forms applications is also an opportunity to integrate existing legacy applications into a service-oriented architecture if one is being constructed as the backbone of the company's information system. Applications may provide new (migrated) services to other applications or reuse already built services to replace or add functionality.

Forms2Net provides options to adapt the converted applications to multi-tier environments, enabling an easy path to an integrated service environment. Currently, Forms2Net supports Oracle Forms version 4.5 to 6i.

4 The Semantic Gap

As mentioned above there are several similarities between Oracle Forms and .NET Windows Forms, as well as some important and relevant differences that make an automated migration a complex process. For better understanding of the gap between the two approaches we present here the main differences.

4.1 Interface Elements

The most common interface elements are present in both platforms (windows, panels, labels, text boxes, combo-boxes, check-boxes, etc.). Nevertheless some differences also exist; an example is the radio group. In .NET Windows Forms, a radio group is created by a set of `System.Window.Forms.RadioButton` instances belonging to the same visual container. However, in Forms migration it is also necessary to allow the creation of radio groups that have no visual relation, i.e., they can be children of different containers and still act as a group of mutual exclusive radio buttons. In general, .NET framework provides richer pre-defined controls for better user interaction, e.g.:

- Data grids with scrolling/column sorting
- Calendar date pickers

The major semantic gap to be solved is to correctly map Oracle Forms multi-record display to a data grid preserving the associated interaction behaviour (validations, triggers, etc.). For instance, .NET data grids need to be extended with new column types (e.g., Combo Boxes) and corresponding event validation (the `validate` event) on data grid cells. Also, there is no direct mapping between Oracle Forms REQUIRED property and .NET control validation mechanisms. Hence, suitable extensions to the .NET control classes should also be provided for such Oracle Forms properties.

4.2 Data Organization

Oracle uses the data block concept to represent simple data (items) or data collections (table rows) that may be mapped to database entities. By using this concept, a lot of database read/write/commit behaviour is pre-defined in Oracle Forms without writing too many lines of code. This was one of the basics of 4GL applications, which results in minimum coding effort when following the typical patterns of Forms applications.

The major semantic gap to be solved is to ensure that access and management of data is done in a simple and uniform way, consistent with the original semantics and allowing an easy mapping of PL/SQL instructions (PL/SQL is Oracle's SQL language, with additional language constructs). For example, in Forms applications direct calls to database stored procedures are allowed (Listing 1) and, in fact, are a common practice. In .NET this is not possible and therefore a suitable mechanism must be devised (e.g., wrapping as in Listing 2) for accommodating this. The same applies to the Oracle cursors that are not present in .NET.

```
:EMP_CREATE.EMPNO := GET_NEW_EMPLOYEE_ID;
```

Listing 1. PL/SQL Call to a Stored Procedure

```
public class StoredProcedures {
      public static NullableDecimal GetNewEmployeeId() {

          IDataCommand cmd =
          DbManager.DataAccessFactory.CreateDataCommand
          ("GET_NEW_EMPLOYEE_ID", DbManager.DataBaseFactory);

          cmd.AddReturnParameter(typeof(NullableDecimal));

          cmd.Execute();

          object _retVal = cmd.GetReturnValue();
          return _retVal == DBNull.Value ? NullableDecimal.Null
          : Convert.ToDecimal(_retVal);
          }
      }

      //.NET invocation for previous stored procedure wrapper
      Model.EmpCreate.Empno = StoredProcedures.GetNewEmployeeId();
```

Listing 2. A Wrapper for the Stored Procedure and the Respective Invocation in .NET

4.3 Events

Oracle provides the Trigger concept. Triggers are events that are propagated up the object hierarchy as a chain of responsibility. In .NET the event concept is also provided but event propagation is flat, i.e., all event handlers of an event are fired and there is no event propagation from a child component to its parent component. The existing 'alphabet' of events used in Oracle is significantly different from the ones available in .NET, although some similarities may be found.

The semantic gap to bridge here is to define a correct mapping between both sets of available events, in a way that preserves most of the original semantics. By semantics here we mean 'when' the event happens, and its 'purpose'. For instance, Oracle Forms triggers can be organized in two categories: Model Triggers, fired by operations made on data or by data manipulation operations (ON-POPULATE-DETAILS, ON-COMMIT, ON-INSERT, ON-DELETE) and View Triggers, fired by user interaction at the UI level (WHEN-BUTTON-PRESSED, WHEN-NEW-BLOCK-INSTANCE, WHEN-NEW-ITEM-INSTANCE). Adequate mappings for .NET, such as the definition of such events, the event handlers and the event registration code together with the corresponding method signatures, must therefore be devised.

The mapping should be complete when semantic preservation is guaranteed, and partial when semantics are not the same. Partial here means that the mapping is provided as a possibility that should be completed during the manual 'completion' phase by a Forms2Net user. As an example consider the navigation between the several components of a Form (Next-Block, Previous-Block, Next-Item, etc.). It is common to have handlers for these operation triggers that just prevent the operation from execution or display an error message (e.g., forbid the navigation from block B1 to block B2).

.NET applications don't use this kind of navigation restrictions. If such behaviour is required, the conditions to enable/disable the relevant controls, must be performed in the code completion phase. Finally, some events are also discarded during the process. This aspect is closely related to the following one.

4.4 Behaviour

Oracle Forms runtime has a huge set of runtime features and implicit behaviour. An example of this is the behaviour associated with Execute and Commit actions that loads / saves the data being edited in the forms according to the form block types and definitions. Only some of these features are present by default in .NET framework. Some others are not relevant because .NET applications have different patterns of behaviour. For instance, validation of data in Oracle Forms is done in a complex way, with several levels of validation (item, block, form) that occur when some actions are taken. Standard validations in .NET applications are simpler, performed on single controls, when editing is finished.

Furthermore, in some cases, a Forms application may have a lot of code that overrides, controls and disables Oracle Forms implicit behaviour.

Mapping the behaviour correctly between the two approaches is the most challenging semantic gap to solve. This is typically where some rules and conversion tables may be used, but human effort is required in the migration process to check or complete the automated conversion.

4.5 Language

PL/SQL control constructs are not so different from C# constructs. The SQL part is what makes the difference, including embedded database operations (queries, cursors, etc). One of the gaps to be solved is correctly migrating all the SQL code instructions into corresponding ones using the .NET databases access infrastructure. However, the major semantic gap to be solved is the ability to work with null values on every PL/SQL data type (numbers, dates, booleans, etc.), that has no counterpart in .NET Framework 1.1. In .NET 1.1, data types (decimal, boolean, integer, etc.) do not accept null values. The only type that has this ability is string. Oracle Forms code is written with the implicit existence of null, and a straightforward transformation for C# code will not have the same behaviour, without adding lots of constraints and different rules. Therefore, the concept of Nullable type should be introduced to cope with this semantic gap. However, .NET Framework 2.0 has support for Nullable types through the `System.Nullable<T>` generic. For migration tools, such as Forms2Net, this implies a strategic decision: either change the current code generation to incorporate such a feature or just alter the current implementation of the Nullable types support library (for instance, via inheriting from the .NET Nullbale generics). In other words, a decision has to be made on whether to abandon a support library and hence the corresponding support for Visual Studio 2003 or continue with the support library and support for VS 2003.

Another gap is that Oracle Forms has support for object inheritance. Objects can inherit from other objects defined in the same module or from objects defined in a different module. However, .NET does not support multiple inheritance. One solution is to deal with inheritance at the module level and only support one base module for each module being converted. The conversion tool user can then configure the base modules for the modules being converted. Then, during the module conversion, an object is considered as inherited if it was inherited from the module's base module. This implies that any objects inherited from a different module will not be considered as inherited.

5   Forms2Net Design Principles and Strategies

Before describing how Forms2Net deals with the semantic gap between the two plat-forms in the next section, it is necessary to describe the design principles enforced throughout Forms2Net and the solution strategies adopted. Three design principles were adopted:

- **100% Pure .NET Code.** The generated code should be pure .NET code fol-lowing Microsoft's Best Practices. It should only bridge the semantic gap problems with solutions that are 100% based on .NET Framework.
- **Preserve the code structure as much as possible.** Although the converted application architecture has significant differences, the structure of the origi-nal code units should be preserved as much as possible to keep the functional model of the original application and to ease comprehending the converted code.
- **Do not impose key conversion decisions upon the user.** Keep it simple. If there are several possible alternatives to a particular semantic gap problem, the program maintainers should decide what to do. This is very important be-cause some semantic gap problems may require minor changes to be made and it is important to allow the future developers to choose how to perform them so that the final result is the desired one.

The semantic gap problems were generally addressed by the following four differ-ent but related strategies:

- Well Defined Target Architecture.
- Semantic Oriented Migration.
- Well Documented Migration Process
- Lightweight Support Libraries.

5.1 Well Defined Target Architecture

Having a well-defined target architecture simplifies the code conversion process as it allows having well-defined conversion rules for certain objects, code patterns, and semantic gap problems. Although being different from the original, the target architecture adopted by Forms2Net was defined so that most of the concepts existing in the original application could be represented. The main objective was to build a semantic map or bridge between the original application architecture and the target architecture. However, this does not mean that there are one-to-one mappings between the artefacts of the original and target architectures. On the contrary, most mappings are one-to-many which means that an artefact in the original architecture is represented in the target architecture by two or more artefacts, their relations and their behaviour. Forms2Net adopts a target architecture based on the Model-View-Controller pattern [3], with some additional concepts that are particular to Forms applications.

5.2 Semantic-Oriented Migration

Semantic-oriented migration means that Forms2Net does not focus only on the conversion of PL/SQL code into .NET. It works on a semantic level by taking into account the target architecture. Also, Forms2Net was designed so that specific plug-ins can be developed to convert specific code constructs. The following further illustrates these points:

- **Original artefacts are converted and rearranged in order to fit in the target architecture.** The conversion process works from a model of the target architecture created from the original application, i.e., the first conversion step is to map the original architecture model into the target one.
- **Certain code patterns are recognized and transformed into more adequate code patterns.** For instance, PL/SQL code routines are analysed and depending on the manipulated blocks and Oracle Forms built-ins, the converted routines are parameterized in order to reduce the dependencies between the code and the model, allowing the business logic to be easily identified and isolated.
- **Conversion of Oracle Forms runtime built-in calls can be performed on one-by-one basis.** By using the extensible architecture of .NET, it is possible to develop new plug-ins to convert a particular usage of a particular Oracle Forms built-in. Since the number of Oracle Forms built-ins is very high, the extensible architecture of Forms2Net allows built-ins conversions to be dealt with in an incremental way, starting with the most used built-ins and adding new conversions when necessary.

5.3 Well Documented Migration Process

Every time the semantic gap cannot be solved or when there are several alternatives to solve a particular problem, comments are generated in the code that point out to the user the possible directions to be taken. These comments have links to a generated migration guide specific for each form. This generated migration guide is customized for the converted forms and the specific issues encountered in the original code, and refers to the more generic documentation that is distributed with the tool.

By promoting a well-documented migration process, Forms2Net avoids imposing sensitive migration decisions on the user, and at the same time eases the code completion process by supplying code comments and a migration guide that help the user perform the necessary code changes.

5.4 Lightweight Support Libraries

Forms2Net supplies two lightweight support libraries that the converted code uses to help reduce the semantic gap and preserve the original code structure:

- **Application Data Layer Library.** ADO.NET is a set of .NET Framework classes containing the data access technologies used to manipulate databases through specific ADO.NET providers. This library is built on top of ADO.NET to allow code to be independent of the provider. It provides several other features like:
  - Simple classes to perform database operations: select/update/delete commands, cursor operations, etc.
  - Alternative interfaces to make the converted database manipulation code simpler (less verbose) while maintaining its original structure;
  - Manipulation of database null values in a transparent way
- **Application Support Library** is a set of utility classes that help reduce the semantic gap when there is not an alternative in the .NET Framework and when the solution to the problem is straightforward. It is composed mostly of user interface components that extend .NET Windows Forms Framework; and most of them are components that any user of .NET Windows Forms will eventually need. It is possible to find different flavours and implementations on the World Wide Web for these components, supplied by third party vendors or even as open-source code. The library uses .NET Windows Forms extension mechanisms (class inheritance or `IExtenderProviders` implementations) to extend .NET Windows Forms native controls.

6 Architectural Centric Conversion in Forms2Net

Forms2Net follows a 4-phases architectural centric conversion approach:

- **Target Architecture Definition.** This phase defines the architectural elements, their characteristics and relations.
- **Architectural Mapping.** In this phase, an architectural mapping of the source application elements into the target architecture is performed. Original application elements are rearranged and mapped into the target architecture according to specific rules.

- **Artefacts Generation.** In this phase, all the static architectural elements like models and views and all their components are generated into the target platform (Windows Forms).
- **PL/SQL code conversion.** In this phase all PL/SQL code existing in Forms' triggers and program units is converted into .NET taking into account their localization in the target architecture.

6.1 Target Architecture Definition

Forms2Net provides an architecture based on the well-known MVC (Model-View-Controller) pattern [3]. Forms2Net MVC architecture for migrated Oracle Forms applications decouples data access, business logic, and data presentation in a well-organized and scalable structure, mapping Oracle Forms concepts into core .NET framework concepts, using Microsoft's best practices.

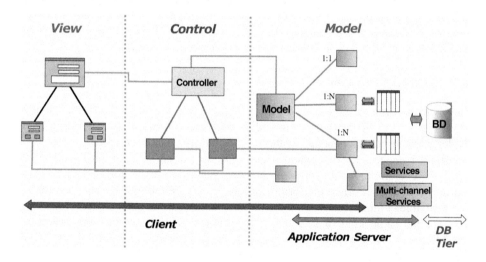

Fig. 3. MVC Architecture Targeted by Forms2Net

Using the MVC model as in Figure 3, the resulting application's design minimizes the interdependencies among the different parts. The role of each element in the MVC model architecture adopted by Forms2Net is described below.

- **The Model** component maintains and manages the information manipulated by the form. It manages the communication with the database, using Datasets[1] to store the data.
- **The View** component's role is visualizing the model state. It is responsible for handling user interaction.

---

[1] The DataSet is a component of the ADO.NET architecture, which is an in-memory cache of data retrieved from a data source. It consists of a collection of DataTable objects that you can relate to each other with DataRelation objects.

- **The Controller** is responsible for the relation and coordination between the other two components, as well as for the form's functional interface:
  - o It manages user interactions by mapping user actions and events into application responses.
  - o It translates the actions within the view to actions performed on the model.

Note that although the MVC architecture is the only target architecture currently supported by Forms2Net as an architectural centric migration tool, other architectures could be supported as well.

6.2 Architectural Mapping

In this phase, Oracle Forms objects of the source application are mapped into the target architecture. Table 2 shows some examples of how Oracle Forms objects are mapped into the target MVC architecture. Note that some of the mappings are one-to-many. For instance, each Oracle Forms Block is mapped into one *model* and one *controller*. The *model* maintains the block's state, whereas the converted code for the block's triggers and all of its items' triggers resides in the *controller*.

6.3 Artefacts Generation

In this phase architectural artefacts are generated into the target platform. Table 2 shows some of the mapping into .NET Windows Forms platform. Forms2Net is designed to be independent of the target platform. For each artefact there is a configured generator. Different platforms are supported by configuring different sets of generators. At the present moment generators exist for both Windows Forms and Web Forms platforms although only Windows Forms generators are available commercially. Also, Forms2Net design allows using different generators for the same kind of artefacts. For instance, this allows having generators for Microsoft .NET Windows Forms controls or generators for third-party .NET Controls suites.

6.4 PL/SQL Code Conversion

At this phase, all PL/SQL code is converted into .NET code. This conversion is not limited to language translation; it also applies some reengineering techniques in order to obtain better quality and higher conversion rate[2]:

- **Code routines Parameterization.** In Oracle Forms, a block item can be referenced anywhere in PL/SQL code (trigger, program unit, etc.). To reduce as

---

[2] In order to associate as much as possible the percentage of conversion with the effort needed to manually complete the application, the conversion rate measure adopted by Forms2Net is the percentage of the number of Oracle objects (e.g., interface items, Forms, triggers, properties, built-ins etc) that are supported for a given application and not the lines of code or number of Forms converted.

much as possible references to the Model objects, Forms2Net uses control flow analysis to parameterize the generated services methods and controller methods.

- **Code pattern recognition and transformation.** Certain code patterns are recognized in the original code and transformed into code patterns that are more suitable for .NET. Listings 3 and 4 illustrate a transformation of a block iteration pattern.

Table 2. The Architectural Mapping of Oracle Forms Objects into The Target MVC Architecture and The Native Target Objects of .NET Windows Forms Platform

Oracle Forms Object	.NET Code Replacement		
	Model	View	Controller
Window		System.Windows.Forms.Form subclass	Windows Controller class
Canvas		System.Windows.Form.UserControl subclass	UserControl Controller class
Block	.NET Model class	If the block has multiple records, a Data grid will be generated.	Controller class with all the block's and item's triggers
Item	Properties of the Model class (columns of DataSet table if the block is data-based)	Instances of .NET Framework System.Windows.Forms.Control class	
Form Module	A .NET Model class that aggregates all the block models. ADO .NET typed DataSet with all the DataTables, relations for all database blocks defined in the converted Form module.		Controller with all the form triggers. This is the base class for all the Window's Controllers
Relation	DataRelation in the DataSet		Master detail coordination logic
Program Units	Methods in a service class		
Triggers		Event registration and event handlers that call the correspondent Controller methods	A method for each trigger to be called by event handlers from view classes.
LOV		IExtenderProvider component that associates a ChooseValue form to each control (item) that has a LOV property	
...			

```
FUNCTION CALCULATE_REVENUES RETURN NUMBER IS
  total number;
BEGIN
  if :system.current_block != 'ord' then
    go_block('ord');
  end if;
  FIRST_RECORD;
LOOP
    EXIT WHEN (:SYSTEM.LAST_RECORD = 'TRUE' );
    total := total + GET_ORDER_COST(:ord.ordid);
    NEXT_RECORD;
END LOOP;
return total;
END;
```

Listing 3. Original PL/SQL Code for Iterating over The Records of a Block

```
FUNCTION CALCULATE_REVENUES RETURN NUMBER IS
  total number;
BEGIN
  if :system.current_block != 'ord' then
    go_block('ord');
  end if;
  FIRST_RECORD;
LOOP
    EXIT WHEN (:SYSTEM.LAST_RECORD = 'TRUE' );
    total := total + GET_ORDER_COST(:ord.ordid);
    NEXT_RECORD;
END LOOP;
return total;
END;
```

Listing 4. The Equivalent Converted C# .NET Code of a Block

7 Related Work

Software transformation is a multifaceted problem, with many applications and also many challenges, not just on the technical side but also on planning, management and risk-control side [12]. The specific version addressed here is language and architecture transformation, where not only the application will move to a different language and platform, but also its architecture has to significantly change to adapt to the architectural model of the target platform. Architecture transformation is a challenging problem, especially when the gap between the source and target architectures is wide. In this case, as Klusener et al. [4] explain is their discussion of architectural modifications to deployed software, the changes (transformations in our case) need to happen at system-wide level rather than on a per-function or per-module basis. This makes the problem harder and requires creating and possibly integrating advanced and sophisticated transformation tools. Realizing this need, The Object Management Group (OMG) created and Architecture-Driven Modernization (ADM) Task Force (ADMTF) to create a set of standards to facilitate the interoperability of modernization tools. These interoperability standards are being established in a series of meta-models that facilitate the collection, analysis, refactoring and transformation of existing systems [8].

Having decided on the need for a certain type of transformation, one faces the issue of automated versus manual transformation. Or in more the precise words, the issues of availability of transformation tools, the cost of building such tools, the cost of transformation and the quality of the produced code. Klusener et al. [4] discuss and compare automated vs. manual transformations. They conclude that for any non-trivial transformation project, automation is vital to success, but the issue is how much automation is needed and at what cost. Baxter et al. [2] discuss the requirements of building robust automated tools for "practical scalable software evolution", as they describe it. They present their effort and approach in building DMS, a generic transformation environment and tool generator.

8 Conclusions

This paper presented Forms2Net, a tool for transforming Oracle Forms applications to .NET applications that use Windows Forms. The paper gave an overview of Oracle Forms platform, the motivations for transformation, the semantic gap between both platforms, the design principles and solution strategies adopted, and finally a general overview of Forms2Net implementation. It is important to draw some useful lessons from this experience.

First, despite the similarities of the two platforms, significant semantic differences exist. This makes transformation complex in the sense that there is a considerable effort involved in building an automated conversion tool. Moreover, it is important for similar transformation problems to focus on bridging the semantic gap using semantic transformations rather than trying to just find syntactic mappings between elements of both platforms. It is expected that some manual transformation will still be needed. Our experience advocates the Klusener et al. [4] view that:

"A fully automatic solution is not always feasible, and it is sometimes not cost-effective. For instance, a modification problem that involves heuristics to determine affected parts of the system often necessitates interactive steps for approval by maintenance programmers. In an extreme case, the automation could be restricted to the generation of a report, which is then applied by maintenance staff in a manual manner. To this end, special interactive tool support can be provided such that programmers basically walk through the generated report and navigate to the affected code locations without ado. Similarly, there is a tension between handling less frequent or highly complex idioms by specific, manual changes per occurrence rather than providing a general rule for the underlying code pattern(s). The decision how much automation is necessary and whether generic modification rules are required has to be made while relating to the technical analysis of the problem at hand, and to the drivers for the project."

Second, several code generation techniques and technologies are available in the market or in the open-source community. In a complex process like Forms2Net migrations, one should not rely only on one technique. One should have a master driver for the generation, but then use the most appropriate technique in each situation. External generation configuration and a plug-in architecture for generators are also advisable solutions.

Third, one should give great attention to designing the target architectural model. On a process like this, the architecture model of a generated application is one of the most important issues, not only because it is the centre of the process, but also because it is the base or stable component of the final solution.

Fourth, invest in pattern recognition facilities. A migrated application has a much higher level of quality and satisfaction to the clients when the final result looks like it was 'written' in the target language and is able to use the language constructs in a 'natural' way. This can be highly improved using pattern detection and influencing the generation process according to those patterns.

Lastly, developers like to have control over the code that they will be in charge of. Whenever transformation rules are not clear, i.e., there is no solution or there are multiple-solutions, Forms2Net reports the case in the generated code and gives its user the choice of deciding what to do.

Acknowledgements

The authors like to thank the reviewers for their thorough reviews, detailed feedback and invaluable advice and comments. We also like to thank the editors for the great effort they put in editing and producing this volume.

References

1. ATX Software, Forms2Net. Available at http://forms2net.atxsoftware.com/
2. Baxter, I., Pidgeon, P., Mehlich, M.: DMS: Program Transformations for Practical Scalable Software Evolution. Proceedings of the International Conference on Software Engineering. IEEE Press (2004)
3. Buschmann, F., Meunier, R., Rohnert, H., Sommerlad, P.: Pattern-Oriented Software Architecture, Vol. 1: A System of Patterns. John Wiley & Sons (1996)
4. Klusener, A., Lämmel R., Verhoef, C.: Architectural Modifications to Deployed Software. Science of Computer Programming, Vol. 54, Issue 2-3 (2005) 143-211
5. Microsoft Patterns and Practices Center: Application Blocks and Libraries. Available at http://msdn.microsoft.com/practices/AppBlocks/default.aspx
6. Microsoft: Solution Guide for Migrating Oracle on UNIX to SQL Server on Windows, Chapter 17 - Developing: Applications - Migrating Oracle Forms. Microsoft TechNet (2005)
7. Mossienko, M.: Automated Cobol to Java recycling. Proceedings of the 7th European Conference on Software Maintenance and Reengineering (CSMR), IEEE Computer Society (2003) 40-50

8. Object Management Group (OMG): Architecture-Driven Modernization Scenarios (2006). Available at http://adm.omg.org/adm_info.htm.

9. Oracle: Oracle Forms Developer's Guide, Release 4.5. Oracle Corporation (1994)

10. Seacord, R., Plakosh, D., Lewis, G.: Modernizing Legacy Systems: Software Technologies, Engineering Processes, and Business Practices. Addison Wesley (2003)

11. Sneed, H.: Risks Involved in Reengineering Projects. Proceedings of the 6th Working Conference on Reverse Engineering (WCRE), IEEE Computer Society (1999) 204-211

12. Ulrich, W.: Legacy Systems: Transformation Strategies. Prentice Hall (2002)

13. Zoufaly, F., Dermody, P.: Issues & Challenges Facing Oracle Forms to J2EE Evolution. Available at SearchWebServices.com (2003)

Applications of the Asf+Sdf Meta-Environment

M.G.J. van den Brand

Technical University Eindhoven,
Department of Mathematics and Computer Science,
Den Dolech 2, NL-5612 AZ Eindhoven, The Netherlands
m.g.j.v.d.brand@tue.nl

Abstract. Generic language technology research focuses on the development of fundamental techniques for language processing. The Asf+Sdf Meta-Environment, an interactive development environment for the automatic generation of interactive systems, is an example of research in this field. The Meta-Environment has been applied in various projects in order to enable the development of high quality tools for the analysis and transformation of large software systems written in languages such as C, Java, Cobol, and PL/I. The Meta-Environment offers the interactive construction of language definitions and the generation of tools given these definitions. Over the years, this system has been used in a variety of academic and industrial projects ranging from formal program manipulation to conversion of industrial Cobol systems.

1   Introduction

The focus of research in the field of generic language technology is on the development of fundamental techniques for (programming) language processing: analysis, transformation, and compilation. The results of this research are formalisms for describing the syntax and semantics of programming languages and tools for processing languages and programs. The formalism Asf+Sdf [4, 22] and the corresponding integrated development environment, the Asf+Sdf Meta-Environment [29, 7] are excellent examples of results obtained in this field of research. The scope of research with respect to Asf+Sdf and the Meta-Environment is on exploring new fundamental concepts, such as declarative description of (programming) languages, incremental generation techniques, efficient term rewriting engines, advanced parsing technology, and new analysis techniques.

There exists a broad range of formalisms to describe the syntax and semantics of (programming) languages, for example (E)BNF, Lex+Yacc [32, 27], a wide variety of attribute grammar based formalisms [1] and Action Semantics [34]. The Asf+Sdf formalism [4, 22] is yet another formalism for the definition of syntactic and semantic features of (programming) languages. In addition it can be used for the formal specification of a wide variety of software engineering problems. The software coordination architecture, ToolBus [5] for instance has been prototyped using Asf+Sdf.

Several (industrial) applications of ASF+SDF are discussed in [8]. However, all those case studies used an older version of the Meta-Environment [29]. This

R. Lämmel, J. Saraiva, and J. Visser (Eds.): GTTSE 2005, LNCS 4143, pp. 278–296, 2006.

paper discusses applications that use the current version of ASF+SDF and the Meta-Environment [7]. We give a detailed introduction to ASF+SDF and discuss some of the engineering characteristics of the Meta-Environment. Then we briefly discuss the relation between our work and other similar systems and draw some conclusions on the applicability of ASF+SDF with respect to certain applications.

2   ASF+SDF

ASF+SDF is a general-purpose, executable, algebraic specification formalism. Its main application areas are the definition of the syntax and the static semantics of (programming) languages, program transformations and analysis, and for defining translations between languages. ASF+SDF provides the following features:

- General-purpose algebraic specification formalism based on (conditional) term rewriting.
- Modular structuring of specifications.
- Integrated definition of lexical, context-free, and abstract syntax.
- User-defined syntax, allowing you to write specifications using your own notation.
- Traversal functions (for writing very concise program transformations), memo functions (for caching repeated computations), list matching, and more.

The ASF+SDF formalism is a combination of two formalisms: ASF (the Algebraic Specification Formalism [4, 22]) and SDF (the Syntax Definition Formalism [25]). SDF is used to define the concrete syntax of a language, whereas ASF is used to define conditional rewrite rules; the combination ASF+SDF allows the syntax defined in the SDF part of a specification to be used in the ASF part, thus supporting the use of user-defined syntax when writing ASF equations. ASF+SDF also allows specifications to be split up into named modules, enabling reuse.

2.1   Syntax Definition Formalism

SDF is a declarative formalism used to define the concrete syntax of languages: programming languages, for example Java and Cobol, and specification languages, such as Chi, Elan, and Action Semantics. SDF does not impose any restrictions on the class of grammars used, it accepts arbitrary, cycle-free, context-free grammars, which may even be ambiguous. Since the class of all context-free grammars is closed under union, a modular definition of grammars is possible in SDF, unlike other (E)BNF formalisms.

Although the full power of arbitrary context-free grammars is hardly necessary when defining the syntax of a programming language (except for languages like Cobol and PL/I), modularity is essential for reuse of specific language constructs in various language definitions.

The downside of the use of arbitrary context-free grammars is the possibility to have ambiguous grammars. The underlying parsing technology must be able to cope with these ambiguities and it is necessary to have disambiguation filters in the parser [16]. Even given these filters, there is no guarantee that all ambiguities will be resolved. Tools/formalisms like Lex+Yacc guarantee the absence of ambiguities if no conflicts are detected during the construction of the table. If a conflict is detected, a shift/reduce or reduce/reduce conflict, the Yacc engine uses a fixed strategy to resolve the conflict.

See Figure 1 for an example of an SDF module. This module defines the concrete syntax of the language of Boolean expressions. The constructors `true` and `false` are defined in a separate module `basic/BoolCon` which is imported in this module. The variable `Bool` is defined in order to write the ASF equations in Figure 2.

```
module basic/Booleans

imports basic/BoolCon
exports
  sorts Boolean

  context-free syntax
    BoolCon                   -> Boolean
    Boolean "|" Boolean     -> Boolean {left}
    Boolean "&" Boolean     -> Boolean {left}
    "not" "(" Boolean ")"   -> Boolean
    "(" Boolean ")"         -> Boolean {bracket}

  context-free priorities
    Boolean "&" Boolean -> Boolean >
    Boolean "|" Boolean -> Boolean

hiddens
  context-free start-symbols Boolean

  variables
    "Bool" -> Boolean
```

Fig. 1. The SDF module of the Boolean language

2.2 Algebraic Specification Formalism

ASF is a declarative formalism used to define the semantics of (programming) languages, for instance the static semantics of Pascal [37] was specified using ASF+SDF. It provides conditional equations, also allowing negative conditions. The concrete syntax defined in the corresponding SDF module and in the transitive closure of any imported modules (only the exported sections, of course) can be used when writing the conditional equations of an ASF module. Traversal functions [12] provide a concise way of defining an ASF function which traverse the term and perform transformation and/or accumulation operations on specific nodes in the underlying term without providing all intermediate rewrite steps.

See Figure 2 for an example of an ASF module. The equations defined in this figure are unconditional and define the operational semantics of the Boolean language. The equation will be interpreted as rewrite rules and if a term is matched with one of the left hand sides, it will be reduced to the corresponding right hand side. The term `Bool` in some of equations represents a variable and matches any boolean expression.

```
equations

  [B1]    true | Bool   = true
  [B2]    false | Bool  = Bool

  [B3]    true & Bool   = Bool
  [B4]    false & Bool  = false

  [B5]    not ( false ) = true
  [B6]    not ( true )  = false
```

Fig. 2. The ASF module of the Boolean language

3 ASF+SDF Meta-Environment

The development of ASF+SDF specifications is supported by an interactive integrated programming environment, the Meta-Environment [29, 7]. This programming environment provides syntax directed editing facilities for both the SDF and ASF parts of modules as well as for terms, well-formedness checking of modules, interactive debugging of ASF equations, and visualisation facilities of the import graph and parse trees. The Meta-Environment provides the following features:

- Interactive support for writing a formal specification of a problem.
- An interactive environment for a new (application) language.
- Support for analyzing or transforming programs in existing languages.

The Meta-Environment offers the following basic functionality:

- Syntax directed editing in combination with text editors such as `gvim` and `gnu-emacs`.
- Visualization of the module graph and parse trees.
- Rewriting and debugging facilities.
- Well-formedness checkers for both SDF and ASF.
- refactoring operations at the specification level, such as renaming, copying of modules.

Furthermore, the Meta-Environment offers the specification writer integrated access to predefined modules containing the following:

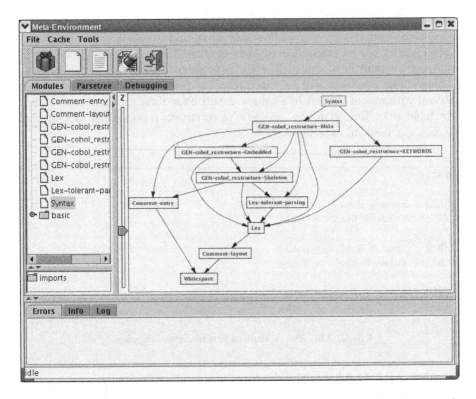

Fig. 3. The user-interface of the Meta-Environment is a browser that provides a graphical and a textual view of the modules

- A collection of grammars of programming and specification languages, such as Java, C, BOX, and SDF itself.
- Basic data types such as **Booleans**, **Naturals**, and **Strings**.
- Basic data structures, such as **Sets**, **Tables**, the basic data structures are parameterized.
- Box operators to guide the formatting of text in a declarative manner.
- A data structure to manipulate warnings and error messages.
- Functionality to access the underlying position information of subterms.

The user interface of the Meta-Environment is shown in Figure 3. The figure shows the modules of a Cobol grammar. The left pane shows a tree-structured view of the modules, and the right pane shows the graph module with import relations.

4   Applications

The obvious application areas for ASF+SDF and the Meta-Environment technology are the design and implementation of domain specific languages, software renovation, and advanced code generators. This section discusses several recent applications. In Section 4.1 we discuss a few of the most important academic applications and in Section 4.2 we will discuss a number of industrial applications. We conclude with a discussion of the use of Asf+Sdf within the Meta-Environment itself in Section 4.3.

4.1   Academic Applications

The academic applications of Asf+Sdf are mainly in the field of programming language prototyping, transformation, and compilation. In this section we consider applications which are not related to Asf+Sdf itself. There are three projects in the area of language prototyping:

- The prototyping of the syntax of the algebraic specification language Casl [15]. The project consisted of prototyping the concrete syntax of Casl and defining the mapping from the concrete syntax to the abstract Casl syntax.
- The prototyping of the next generation of the action semantic formalism [23, 26]. Besides the prototyping of this formalism an environment for this formalism is developed [10].
- The prototyping of RScript formalism and tooling. RScript provides a relational approach to software analysis [30].

Projects in the area of program transformation and compilation are as follows:

- The validation of distributed algorithms with a rewriting kernel dedicated to TLA+ specifications [31] at IRIT (University of Toulouse). This project mainly uses traversal functions in order to describe the transformations in a very concise way. Furthermore our Box pretty printing technology is used to regenerate parseable TLA+ specifications again.
- The implementation of a compiler for the formalism Chi [3] at the Mechanical Engineering Group at the Technical University of Eindhoven. The goal of Chi formalism is the specification of the dynamics and control of production plants and mechanical modeling.
- The migration of legacy databases to relational databases together with the adaptation of the corresponding program code [19].

4.2   Industrial Applications

There are three main industrial applications areas of Asf+Sdf which are very similar to the academic application areas: prototyping of domain specific languages (DSLs), software renovation, and code generation. In this section we discuss the software renovation activities in more detail. The prototyping of DSLs and code generation is discussed in [8].

Various projects in the field of software renovation, such as reverse engineering and re-engineering have been carried out in cooperation with industrial partners since 1998. The powerful generalized parsing technology allowed us to tackle both the problem of handling various dialects of Cobol as well as the problem of embedded languages in Cobol, such as SQL, assembler, and CICS.

In various software renovation projects ASF+SDF has been applied to define the restructuring of Cobol programs, see [17, 38]. We will elaborate on the restructuring of Cobol code as described in [38]. The main goal of this work was to restructure Cobol code in order to improve maintenance of the code. The restructuring consisted of quite a number of steps, for example:

- The introduction of scope terminators, such as END-IF.
- The removal of as many GOTOs as possible.
  The introduction of subroutines by means of PERFORM statements.
- The introduction of loops by means of inline PERFORM statements.
- The prettyprinting of the resulting Cobol program.

Figure 4 shows a Cobol program with a messy flow of control, this flow of control is visualized in Figure 7. The arrows without numbers in Figure 7 represent the so-called fall-through control flow. If the end of paragraph 7201 is reached the execution continues with paragraph 7203, unless paragraph 7201 was entered via a subroutine call. The numbers on the arrows correspond to the GOTOs in the corresponding paragraph, so 1 corresponds to the first GOTO, 2 corresponds to the second GOTO, and so on. The combination of fall-through semantics with gotos makes Cobol programs hard to maintain.

The goal of the restructuring operations as described in [38] is to improve maintainability. This is achieved via reducing the number of fall-throughs and gotos by introducing subroutines (procedures in modern languages) and subroutine calls, and loops via PERFORM statements. Figure 6 shows an ASF equation to remove a goto pattern which in fact implements a loop. Loops in Cobol are implemented via PERFORM statements. Perform statements are relative new in the Cobol language.

The result of applying restructuring rules such as the one presented in Figure 6 is shown in Figure 5. The paragraphs in Figure 7 are transformed into subroutines, if the execution of such a subroutine is finished the control is transferred back to the caller instead of continuing with the next paragraph. Goto based loops are replaced by PERFORM statements as well. The flow of control of the transformed program is visualized in Figure 8. An important observation with respect to these restructurings is that one of the requirements was that no code duplication was allowed. One of the consequences of this requirement is that not *all* GOTOs can be removed.

4.3   ASF+SDF Specific Applications

The core business of the Meta-Environment is language processing. ASF+SDF is suited to be used as an algebraic specification formalism for specifying language processing tools. So, it is logical to use ASF+SDF to implement the components of the Meta-Environment. ASF+SDF has been used to implement:

- The ASF2C compiler [9].
- Box toolset [18, 13]R.
- SDF normalizer as part of the parsetable generator for SDF [39].
- SDF well-formedness checker.

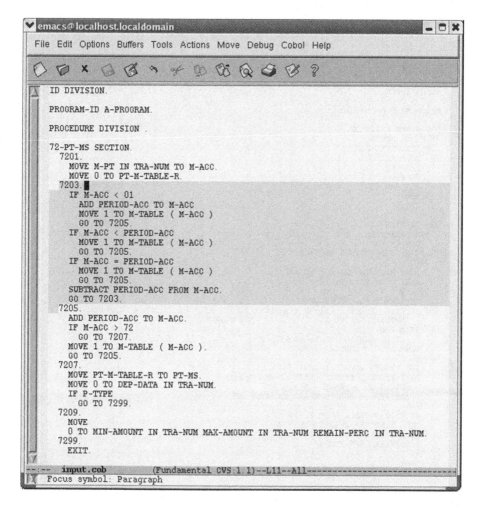

Fig. 4. A Cobol program with a messy flow of control

For other components, such as the ToolBus [5], an ASF+SDF specification was made for prototyping use only. That specification formed the basis of an optimized, handcrafted implementation in C. The underlying socket programming made it impossible to use the ASF2C compiler [9] to compile this specification.

The ASF2C compiler [9] compiles ASF+SDF specifications to efficient C code. Every SDF function (with ASF equations) is translated to a C function that contains an optimized matching automaton for the left-hand sides of the equations and conditions. The ASF+SDF functions in conditions and the right-hand side of a matched equation are translated to direct function calls.

The Box toolset [18, 13] provides a fully integrated way of defining the unparsing of terms manipulated via ASF+SDF. It consists of the Box formalism and a Box interpreter (Pandora) for translating Box expressions to either ASCII text,

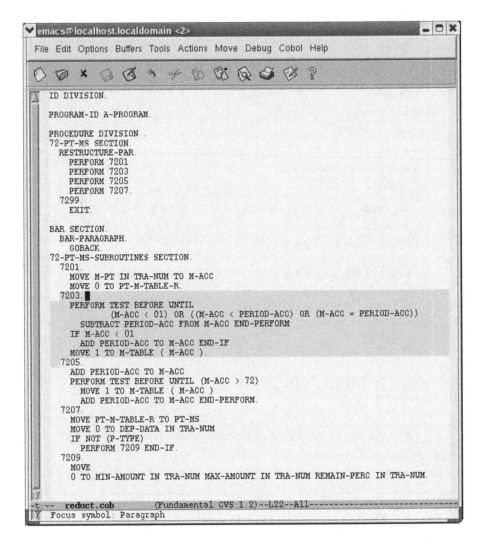

Fig. 5. The Cobol program after restructuring

HTML code, or LATEX. The unparsing of language constructs is defined using plain ASF equations.

The SDF normalizer is described in Visser's PhD thesis [39], see Chapters 6 through 10. The SDF well-formedness checker is very specific to ASF+SDF and is not yet described in an accessible publication. In the rest of this section will be devoted to a detailed discussion of the well-formedness checker, in order to understand the behaviour of the well-formedness checker it is necessary to give some internal details of SDF and the normalizer.

SDF **Normalizer.** One of the characteristics of SDF is the integrated definition of lexical and context-free syntax. This, in combination with modularity, provides

```
[] complex-stats(#Statement*1) == false
   ===>
   elim-go-trav-paragraph(
     #Label-name.
       #Statement*1
       IF #Condition
         #Statement*2
         GO #Label-name
       ELSE
         #Statement*3
       END-IF
       #Statement*4.) =
   elim-go-trav-paragraph(
     #Label-name.
       #Statement*1
       PERFORM TEST BEFORE UNTIL NOT (#Condition)
         #Statement*2
         #Statement*1
       END-PERFORM
       #Statement*3
       #Statement*4.)
```

Fig. 6. An ASF equation for eliminating GOTO's

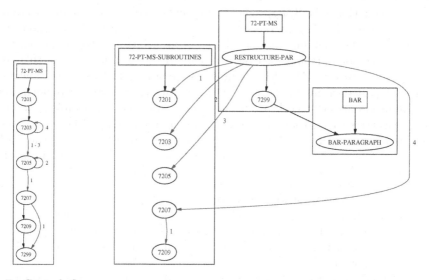

Fig. 7. Control flow
before

Fig. 8. Control flow after

a powerful way of defining the concrete syntax of a large class of (programming)
languages in a declarative way.

SDF is in fact a collection of syntax definition formalisms. The core of SDF is formed by kernel-SDF, which provides normalized syntax rules. On the kernel level there is, for instance, no distinction between lexical and context-free syntax and the modular structure has been resolved. Kernel-SDF is very similar to plain BNF, except for the direction of the syntax rules. An SDF specification is *normalized* to this kernel-SDF, by performing grammar transformations. The main operations are as follows:

- Renaming nonterminals to reflect their origin, if the ID is used in a lexical syntax section it is renamed `<ID-LEX>`. If ID is used in a context-free syntax section it is renamed to `<ID-CF>`. In order to bridge the gap a new production rule `<ID-LEX> -> <ID-CF>` is added.
- Resolution of the modular dependencies, renamings and parametrization in order to obtain one flat syntax definition.

This normalized definition in kernel SDF is input for the actual parsetable generator, a C program which was initially specified in ASF+SDF as well. The ASF+SDF specification of the normalizer strongly reflects the modular structure of SDF itself. The specification consists of about 70 small modules, where each module takes care of a specific operation (for example renaming) for a specific part of SDF (for example sorts).

SDF Well-Formedness Checker. An SDF definition used in combination with ASF may not contain kernel syntax constructions. Furthermore, in order to parse the ASF equations, the SDF specification is "extended" with a module containing the syntax rules for the equations. In order to prevent "clashes" the nonterminals used in this ASF module are not allowed in an arbitrary SDF definition. Some other restrictions are imposed on SDF constructs in order to able to rewrite the parsed terms via ASF, for example, the separator in lists should always be a literal (`{Statement ","}*` is a legal list, but `{Bool Bool}+` is not). These requirements are not checked during normalization nor parsetable generation. The reason for this is that the normalization and parsetable generation support the broadest class of SDF. Therefore, a separate SDF well-formedness checker has been developed. The most important checks performed by the well-formedness checker are as follows:

- No kernel syntax constructions are used.
- No nonterminals are used which are part of the "ASF language".
- All nonterminals (sorts in SDF terminology) used in the left-hand side of a production rule or as start symbol are defined in some right-hand side of a production rule.
- All production rules used in the priority section are defined somewhere.
- At least one visible start symbol is defined.
- The traversal functions have the correct combination of attributes.

The result of running the well-formedness checker is a list of warnings and errors. The generated messages contain position information to connect the error to the exact location in a module where the error occurred. This specification uses traversal functions in order to collect information from all parts of an SDF definition.

Figure 9 shows a rule for finding nonterminals which are in fact used within the ASF syntax. The function `check-asf-sorts` traverses the parse tree of an SDF module. The operational details of the traversal mechanism in ASF are described in [12]. If the function encounters a node of sort `Sort` the equation `cas` will be activated. This means that the corresponding conditions are checked. The first condition of `cas` checks explicitly whether the `Sort` is an ASF-specific sort. In the second condition the `get-location($Sort)` obtains the position information for the sort `$Sort`. This `get-location` function is a function defined in the module `utilities/PosInfo`. The function `symbol2str($Sort)` converts the internal representation of a symbol to a human readable string. In the right hand side of this equation a new error message, created via the function `make-error`, is added to the accumulated list of errors. The signature of the warnings and errors is defined in a predefined library module.

```
...
imports
    utilities/PosInfo[Sort]
    basic/Errors
...
exports
  context-free syntax
    check-asf-sorts(Sort, {Error ","}*) -> {Error ","}* {traversal(accu,break,top-down)}
    ...
hiddens
  variables
    "$Msgs"[0-9]*      -> {Error ","}*
    "$Sort"[0-9]*      -> Sort
    "$String"[0-9]*    -> StrCon
    "$Location"[0-9]* -> Location

equations
  ...
  [cas]  is-asf-sort($Sort) == true,
         $Location := get-location($Sort),
         $String := symbol2str($Sort)
         ====>
         check-asf-sorts($Sort, $Msgs) =
           $Msgs, make-error("Usage of asf equation sort is not allowed ",
                        $String, $Location)
  ...
```

Fig. 9. The SDF function and ASF equation for finding ASF nonterminals in SDF

5   Re-usability of Asf+Sdf Meta-Environment Components

The implementation of Meta-Environment consists of a number of components which communicate with each other via a software bus, the ToolBus [5]. The architecture of the Meta-Environment is shown in Figure 10. The components connected with the ToolBus are either homemade or third-party, for example graphviz[1] and GNU Emacs[2]. The homemade components are implemented in various languages, such as ASF+SDF, C, and Java. The Meta-Environment consists of three layers:

1. The kernel layer containing all language independent functionality, such text editor, structure editors, and a database to store information.
2. The SDF layer containing all SDF specific functionality.
3. The ASF layer containing all ASF specific functionality.

The principle design goal of the Meta-Environment was the development of a system which offers openness, reuse, and extensibility. The generation of stand-alone environments was another important goal. A first step was to develop re-usable components which can be used by others (independent of both ToolBus and Meta-Environment). This can be one single software artifact, such as the ATERM library [11], or a collection of components. The components related to parsing, such as the parser (SGLR [39]) and the parsetable generator, are distributed in one software package along with the SDF formalism.

The development of re-usable software components poses a number of challenging problems. First, it is necessary to develop both a ToolBus interface as well as a command-line interface for such a component. Second, if it is a collection of components instead of a single component, for instance the SDF package, scripts should be included to take care of the proper activation of the separate components. Third, the component or package needs to be distributed independently of the Meta-Environment. Fourth, components and packages should be well documented so that they are easily usable and/or can be easily integrated in other software.

The implementation of the Meta-Environment is based on a number of these re-usable software artifacts. We briefly discuss the most important ones:

ToolBus is a lightweight programmable software coordination architecture based on process algebra [5]. The main purpose of this software bus is to separate coordination from computation. It allows the components to be written in any programming language.

ATerms is a library to manipulate and exchange tree-like data structures in a very efficient way [11]. The ATERM library is implemented in both C and Java. Its main characteristics are maximal subterm sharing and automatic garbage collection.

ApiGen is a software generator which generates application programming interfaces (APIs), in C and Java, from both annotated datatype descriptions (ADTs) and SDF definitions [14, 28]. The generated APIs provide a type-safe interface to manipulate ATERMS.

Sdf is the combination of the formalism SDF, parsetable generator, well-formedness checker, and SGLR. It provides the minimal set of tools needed to parse strings given an SDF definition.

---

[1] http://www.graphviz.org
[2] http://www.gnu.org/software/emacs/emacs.html

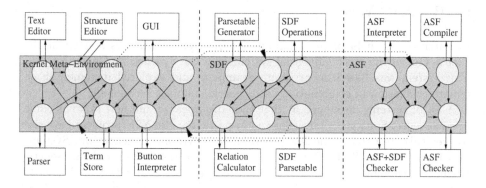

Fig. 10. The layered implementation of the Meta-Environment

Asf is the combination of the formalism ASF, well-formedness checker, interpreter, and compiler. It provides the minimal set of tools needed to reduce terms given an ASF specification.

Meta is the collection of tools which allows the user to actually develop a specification. It consists of the graphical user interface, (syntax directed) editors, term database, etc.

Box is the combination of the formalism BOX and the BOX interpreter. This is the set of tools needed to construct BOX terms and translate them into ASCII text.

Components of the Meta-Environment are used as stand-alone tools in a variety of applications. Table 1 gives an overview of which components are used in other applications. The first column contains the name of the application, tool, language, project, or company. The second column contains an indication of the type of application. We distinguish between different (language) specification, transformations, analysis, modeling, and proving. The third column contains references describing this application. The fourth upto tenth column specifies whether this Meta-Environment specific component has been used. The last column indicates whether ASF+SDF has been used as implementation language.

Table 1. ASF+SDF technology transfer

Application	Type	Refs	ATERMS	SDF	ASF	Meta	ToolBus	Box	ApiGen	ASF+SDF
Meta-Environment	Specification		x	x	x	x	x	x	x	x
STRATEGO/XT	Transformation	[41, 21]	x	x				x		
Action Notation	Specification	[23, 26]	x	x	x	x	x			x
Chi	Modeling	[3]	x					x		x
ELAN	Modeling,proving	[6]	x	x	x	x	x		x	
μCRL	Modeling	[24]	x							
Lucent	Transformation	[42]	x	x						
TLA+	Modeling	[31]								x
TOM	Transformation	[33]	x						x	

6   Related Work

Research in the field of programming environment generators started in the 1980's. One of the most influential systems was the Synthesizer Generator [36]. This system was based on attribute grammars and explored incremental attribute evaluation in combination with generic language technology.

A lot of systems developed at that time disappeared and new systems came into existence. Software renovation and in particular the Y2K problem gave rise to a revival of research in the field programming environment generators. Systems like TXL [20] and REFINE[3] were used to tackle the Y2K problem. Generic language technology proved to be a valid technique to deal with Cobol dialects and embedded languages, like CICS and SQL. Recent developments, such as Eclipse[4], has motivated people to investigate in (generic) language technology as well.

It is possible to make a selection of comparable systems on various criteria and in this paper the main selection criterium is applicability in the field of software transformation. Given this selection criterium we will discuss the following systems: STRATEGO/XT [40, 21], TXL [20], TOM [33], and DMS [2]. The list of aforementioned systems is not exhaustive, we selected these systems because they are very close with respect to concepts of the Meta-Environment. The following aspects play an important role when comparing these systems:

- The expressiveness of the *formalism*.
- The *parsing* technology used to parse the terms to be transformed.
- The *evaluation engine* to implement the transformations.
- The *environment* to support user-interaction.

Table 2 gives a concise overview of the most important characteristics between the various systems. The application area is comparable for all the systems. There are a number of observations that can be made. First, all systems, except TOM, use some kind of generalized parsing technology. Second, only TOM and the Meta-Environment have an interactive interface to develop specifications. Third, the evaluation engines are for all systems completely distinct.

Table 2. System overview

System/Formalism	Parsing	Evaluation	Environment	Availability
DMS	GLR	Attribute grammars	Command-line	Commercial
STRATEGO/XT	SGLR	Strategic rewriting	Command-line	Free
TOM	None	Java with matching	Eclipse plug-in	Free
TXL	Backtracking	Functional	Command-line	Free
Meta-Environment	SGLR	Conditional rewriting	Interactive	Free

---

[3] http://www.reasoning.com

[4] http://www.eclipse.org

Each of these five systems has its weak and strong points. DMS [2] is used in industrial projects. It is a commercial tool. The use of a generalized parsing technology indicates an easy specification of a broad range of (programming) languages.

TOM [33] adds matching primitives to Java, via these matching primitives it is possible to perform complex transformations on abstract syntax trees and XML documents. TOM is often used in combination with ApiGen [14] in order to have type-safe access to these abstract syntax trees. The TOM compiler is implemented using TOM itself. There are only a few other projects that have used TOM. The fact that TOM is available as an Eclipse plug-in makes it easier for other people to use it.

TXL [20] is a well-known system with a lot of users. The use of backtracking as parsing technology ensures a broad range of (programming) languages that can be processed via TXL. However, TXL chooses in case of an ambiguity the first parse, instead of reporting all possible derivations. There is no guarantee that the backtrack parser makes a correct choice in such a situation.

STRATEGO/XT [40, 21] is a very powerful system with a lot of users. The combination of rewriting with strategies provides a powerful engine for performing transformations. STRATEGO/XT has been extended with a number of features to deal with concrete syntax and dynamic scoping [35]. The specifications are very concise and not very easy to read.

ASF+SDF is on one hand a complex formalism, it is not easy to write a good grammar definition in SDF, on the other hand a simple formalism, the definition of operations in ASF is rather straightforward. The Meta-Environment supports writing specifications and offers a range of facilities, such as predefined modules, well-formedness checkers, and debuggers.

7   Conclusions

The application areas of ASF+SDF and Meta-Environment are very diverse. However the unifying factor is language processing. The shift from prototyping small languages, DSLs, to software renovation has had a tremendous effect on the underlying technology. It triggered the development of scalable language processing technology. The Meta-Environment was completely redesigned using component-based software development technology. The focus shifted from incremental techniques to scalability, flexibility, re-usability and efficiency of tools. This development not only opened new application areas, but also enabled us to promote and distribute the underlying technology to other research groups.

Obtaining the ASF+SDF Meta-Environment

The Meta-Environment can be downloaded from: http : //www.asfsdf.org/.

Acknowledgements

I would like to thank all current and former members of the Generic Language Technology group at CWI for making the Meta-Environment work. Furthermore I would like to thank all people who have used and still use ASF+SDF and the Meta-Environment, either to do research or to apply it to solve (complex) problems. I like to thank Niels Veerman who provided me with the Cobol restructuring examples.

References

1. H. Alblas. Introduction to attribute grammars. In H. Alblas and B. Melichar, editors, *International Summer School on Attribute Grammars, Applications and Systems*, volume 545 of *Lecture Notes in Computer Science*, pages 1–15, Berlin Heidelberg New York, 1991. Springer Verlag.
2. I.D. Baxter, C. Pidgeon, and M. Mehlich. DMS: Program transformations for practical scalable software evolution. In *ICSE '04: Proceedings of the 26th International Conference on Software Engineering*, pages 625–634, Washington, DC, USA, 2004. IEEE Computer Society.
3. D.A. van Beek, K.L. Man, M.A. Reniers, J.E. Rooda, and R.R.H. Schiffelers. Syntax and consistent equation semantics of hybrid Chi. *Journal of Logic and Algebraic Programming*, 2005. To appear.
4. J.A. Bergstra, J. Heering, and P. Klint, editors. *Algebraic Specification*. ACM Press/Addison-Wesley, 1989.
5. J.A. Bergstra and P. Klint. The discrete time ToolBus – a software coordination architecture. *Science of Computer Programming*, 31(2-3):205–229, July 1998.
6. P. Borovanský, C. Kirchner, H. Kirchner, P.-E. Moreau, and C. Ringeissen. An overview of ELAN. In C. Kirchner and H. Kirchner, editors, *WRLA*, volume 15 of *ENTCS*. Elsevier Sciences, 1998.
7. M.G.J. van den Brand, A. van Deursen, J. Heering, H.A. de Jong, M. de Jonge, T. Kuipers, P. Klint, L. Moonen, P. A. Olivier, J. Scheerder, J.J. Vinju, E. Visser, and J. Visser. The ASF+SDF Meta-Environment: a component-based language development environment. In R. Wilhelm, editor, *CC'01*, volume 2027 of *LNCS*, pages 365–370. Springer-Verlag, 2001.
8. M.G.J. van den Brand, A. van Deursen, P. Klint, S. Klusener, and E.A, van den Meulen. Industrial applications of ASF+SDF. In M. Wirsing and M. Nivat, editors, *Algebraic Methodology and Software Technology (AMAST '96)*, volume 1101 of *LNCS*. Springer-Verlag, 1996.
9. M.G.J. van den Brand, J. Heering, P. Klint, and P.A. Olivier. Compiling language definitions: The ASF+SDF compiler. *ACM Transactions on Programming Languages and Systems*, 24(4):334–368, 2002.
10. M.G.J. van den Brand, J. Iversen, and P.D. Mosses. An action environment. *Science of Computer Programming*, 2005. to appear.
11. M.G.J. van den Brand, H.A. de Jong, P. Klint, and P. Olivier. Efficient annotated terms. *Software, Practice & Experience*, 30:259–291, 2000.
12. M.G.J. van den Brand, P. Klint, and J.J. Vinju. Term rewriting with traversal functions. *ACM Transactions on Software Engineering and Methodology*, 12(2):152–190, 2003.

13. M.G.J. van den Brand, A.T. Kooiker, N.P. Veerman, and J.J. Vinju. An industrial application of context-sensitive formatting. Technical Report SEN-R0510, Centrum voor Wiskunde en Informatica (CWI), Amsterdam, 2005.

14. M.G.J. van den Brand, P.-E. Moreau, and J.J. Vinju. A generator of efficient strongly typed abstract syntax trees in java. *IEE Proceedings — Software*, 152(2):70–79, 2005.

15. M.G.J. van den Brand and J. Scheerder. Development of parsing tools for CASL using generic language technology. In D. Bert, C. Choppy, and P. Mosses, editors, *Workshop on Algebraic Development Techniques (WADT'99)*, volume 1827 of *LNCS*. Springer-Verlag, 2000.

16. M.G.J. van den Brand, J. Scheerder, J.J. Vinju, and E. Visser. Disambiguation filters for scannerless generalized LR parsers. In R. Nigel Horspool, editor, *Compiler Construction (CC'02)*, volume 2304 of *LNCS*, pages 143–158. Springer-Verlag, 2002.

17. M.G.J. van den Brand, M.P.A. Sellink, and C. Verhoef. Generation of components for software renovation factories from context-free grammars. *Science of Computer Programming*, 36:209–266, 2000.

18. M.G.J. van den Brand and E. Visser. Generation of formatters for context-free languages. *ACM Transactions on Software Engineering and Methodology*, 5:1–41, 1996.

19. A. Cleve, J. Henrard, and J-L. Hainaut. Co-transformations in information system reengineering. In *Second International Workshop on Meta-Models, Schemas and Grammars for Reverse Engineering (ATEM'04)*, volume 137-3 of *ENTCS*, pages 5–15, 2004.

20. J.R. Cordy. TXL — a language for programming language tools and applications. In G. Hedin and E. van Wyk, editors, *4th International Workshop on Language Descriptions, Tools and Applications (LDTA'2004)*, Electronic Notes in Theoretical Computer Science, pages 1–27. Elsevier, 2004.

21. M. de Jonge, E. Visser, and J. Visser. XT: A bundle of program transformation tools. In M. G. J. van den Brand and D. Parigot, editors, *Workshop on Language Descriptions, Tools and Applications (LDTA'01)*, volume 44 of *Electronic Notes in Theoretical Computer Science*. Elsevier Science Publishers, 2001.

22. A. van Deursen, J. Heering, and P. Klint, editors. *Language Prototyping: An Algebraic Specification Approach*, volume 5 of *AMAST Series in Computing*. World Scientific, 1996.

23. K.-G. Doh and P.D. Mosses. Composing programming languages by combining action-semantics modules. *Science of Computer Programming*, 47:3–36, 2003.

24. J.F. Groote and A. Ponse. The syntax and semantics of μCRL. In A. Ponse, C. Verhoef, and S.F.M. van Vlijmen, editors, *Algebra of Communicating Processes '94*, Workshops in Computing Series, pages 26–62. Springer-Verlag, 1995.

25. J. Heering, P.R.H. Hendriks, P. Klint, and J. Rekers. The syntax definition formalism SDF: Reference manual. *SIGPLAN Notices*, 24(11):43–75, 1989.

26. J. Iversen and P.D. Mosses. Constructive action semantics for Core ML. *IEE Proceedings — Software*, 152(2):79–98, 2005.

27. S.C. Johnson. YACC—yet another compiler-compiler. Technical Report CS-32, AT&T Bell Laboratories, Murray Hill, N.J., 1975.

28. H.A. de Jong and P.A Olivier. Generation of abstract programming interfaces from syntax definitions. *Journal of Logic and Algebraic Programming*, 59, April 2004.

29. P. Klint. A meta-environment for generating programming environments. *ACM Transactions on Software Engineering and Methodology*, 2:176–201, 1993.

30. P. Klint. *A Tutorial Introduction to RScript — a Relational Approach to Software Analysis*, 2005.
    `http://homepages.cwi.nl/~paulk/publications/rscript-tutorial.pdf`.
31. L. Lamport. *Specifying Systems: The TLA+ Language and Tools for Hardware and Software Engineers*. Addison-Wesley Longman Publishing Co., Inc., Boston, MA, USA, 2002.
32. M.E. Lesk and E. Schmidt. LEX — A lexical analyzer generator. Technical Report CS-39, AT&T Bell Laboratories, Murray Hill, N.J., 1975.
33. P.-E. Moreau, C. Ringeissen, and M. Vittek. A pattern matching compiler for multiple target languages. In G. Hedin, editor, *12th Conference on Compiler Construction, Warsaw (Poland)*, volume 2622 of *LNCS*, pages 61–76. Springer-Verlag, May 2003.
34. P.D. Mosses. *Action Semantics*. Cambridge Tracts in Theoretical Computer Science 26. Cambridge University Press, 1992.
35. K. Olmos and E. Visser. Composing source-to-source data-flow transformations with rewriting strategies and dependent dynamic rewrite rules. In Rastislav Bodik, editor, *14th International Conference on Compiler Construction (CC'05)*, volume 3443 of *Lecture Notes in Computer Science*, pages 204–220. Springer-Verlag, 2005.
36. T. Reps and T. Teitelbaum. *The Synthesizer Generator: A System for Constructing Language-Based Editors*. Springer-Verlag, third edition, 1989.
37. A. van Deursen. An Algebraic Specification of the Static Semantics of Pascal. In J. van Leeuwen, editor, *Conference Proceedings Computing Science in the Netherlands (CSN'91)*, pages 150–164, 1991.
38. N. Veerman. Revitalizing modifiability of legacy assets. *Software Maintenance and Evolution: Research and Practice, Special issue on CSMR 2003*, 16(4–5):219–254, 2004.
39. E. Visser. *Syntax Definition for Language Prototyping*. PhD thesis, University of Amsterdam, 1997. http://www.cs.uu.nl/people/visser/ftp/Vis97.ps.gz.
40. E. Visser. Stratego: A language for program transformation based on rewriting strategies. System description of Stratego 0.5. In A. Middeldorp, editor, *RTA'01*, volume 2051 of *LNCS*, pages 357–361. Springer-Verlag, 2001.
41. E. Visser, Z. Benaissa, and A. Tolmach. Building program optimizers with rewriting strategies. In *International Conference on Functional Programming (ICFP'98)*, pages 13–26, 1998.
42. D.G. Waddington and B. Yao. High-fidelity C/C++ code transformation. In J. Boyland and G. Hedin, editors, *Fifth Workshop on Language Descriptions, Tools and Applications*, pages 6–26, 2005.

MetaBorg in Action: Examples of Domain-Specific Language Embedding and Assimilation Using Stratego/XT

Martin Bravenboer, René de Groot, and Eelco Visser

Department of Information and Computing Sciences,
Universiteit Utrecht, P.O. Box 80089 3508 TB, Utrecht, The Netherlands
{martin, rcgroot, visser}@cs.uu.nl

Abstract. General-purpose programming languages provide limited facilities for expressing domain-specific concepts in a natural manner. All domain concepts need to be captured using the same generic syntactic and semantic constructs. Generative programming methods and program transformation techniques can be used to overcome this lack of abstraction in general-purpose languages.

In this tutorial we describe the METABORG method for embedding domain-specific languages, tailored syntactically and semantically to the application domain at hand, in a general-purpose language. METABORG is based on Stratego/XT, a language and toolset for the implementation of program transformation systems, which is used for the definition of syntactic embeddings and assimilation of the embedded constructs into the surrounding code.

We illustrate METABORG with three examples. JavaSwul is a custom designed language for implementing graphical user-interfaces, which provides high-level abstractions for component composition and event-handling. JavaRegex is a new embedding of regular expression matching and string rewriting. JavaJava is an embedding of Java in Java for generating Java code. For these cases we show how Java programs in these domains become dramatically more readable, and we give an impression of the implementation of the language embeddings.

1 Introduction

Class libraries are reusable implementations of tasks in a certain domain. The library is used via some API, which constitutes a 'language' for using the library implementation. The syntax of this language provided by the API is based on the syntax of the general-purpose language in which the API is used. Unfortunately, general-purpose programming languages provide limited facilities for expressing domain-specific concepts in a natural manner. This syntax of the general-purpose language does not always allow the appropriate notation and composition of domain concepts.

Examples of this issue are available everywhere. For example, user-interface code is typically a tangled list of statements that constructs a hierarchical structure. XML document construction is verbose or unsafe. Java libraries often return this only for making sequential composition of calls possible, thereby confusing users, compilers, and other meta-programs. Regular expressions need to be escaped heavily since they have to be

R. Lämmel, J. Saraiva, and J. Visser (Eds.): GTTSE 2005, LNCS 4143, pp. 297–311, 2006.

encoded in strings. Not to mention the run-time errors or security risks involved in composing SQL, XPath or XQuery queries by concatenating strings [7, 9]. Clearly, this is a serious issue.

Generative programming methods and program transformation techniques can be used to overcome this lack of abstraction in general-purpose languages. To this end, we proposed the METABORG[1] [6] method, which is a general way of providing domain-specific notation for domain abstractions to application programmers. METABORG is a way of implementing an embedding of a domain-specific language in a general-purpose language. METABORG starts off with the idea that there should be no restrictions (1) on the syntactic extension, (2) on the interaction with the host language, and (3) on the translation to the general-purpose code (a process we call assimilation).

In [6] several METABORG examples have been presented, but the implementation of these examples could not be discussed in detail. In this paper, we give a more extensive account of the implementation of three METABORG examples, thus providing more insight in the METABORG method for embedding domain-specific languages. We focus on the METABORG examples and experience we gained from this. For an extensive account of alternative approaches and related work, we refer to [6].

METABORG is based on modular syntax definition in SDF, which is implemented by scannerless generalized-LR parsing [4, 11] and source to source transformation in the high-level language for program transformation Stratego [13]. Stratego is a general-purpose language for the implementation of program transformation systems. On top of a small core language for pattern matching, abstract syntax tree construction, and term traversal, Stratego provides abstractions such as rewrite rules whose application can be controlled by a rewrite strategy. Context-sensitive rewritings are handled by defining rewrite rules dynamically at the location where the context information is available. Stratego is distributed as part of Stratego/XT, which is the combination of the Stratego program transformation language and an extensive set of transformation tools for parsing, pretty-printing, and so on.

In this paper, we present three examples of METABORG applications. These examples illustrate the capabilities of the METABORG method and provide an introduction to the implementation of such embeddings. In Section 2 we given an extensive overview of the implementation of JavaSwul, the embedding of a custom designed language for implementing graphical user-interfaces. In Section 3 we give a short overview of Java-Regex, which is an embedding of regular expression matching and string rewriting, and JavaJava, which is an embedding of Java in Java, intended for Java code generation.

2   Embedding Swul in Java

Swul is a domain-specific language for writing user-interfaces based on the Swing library. In this section, we will discuss in more detail why and how we implemented an embedding of Swul in Java. The Swul implementation described in this section is a major extension of the first sketch of Swul presented in [6].

---

[1] METABORG provides generic technology for allowing a host language (collective) to incorporate and assimilate external domains (cultures) in order to strengthen itself. The ease of implementing embeddings makes resistance futile.

```
JMenuBar menubar = new JMenuBar();
JMenu filemenu = new JMenu("File");
JMenuItem newfile = new JMenuItem("New");
JMenuItem savefile = new JMenuItem("Save");
newfile.setAccelerator(KeyStroke.getKeyStroke(KeyEvent.VK_N, 2));
savefile.setAccelerator(KeyStroke.getKeyStroke(KeyEvent.VK_S, 2));
filemenu.add(newfile);
filemenu.add(savefile);
menubar.add(filemenu);


JPanel buttons = new JPanel(new GridLayout(1, 2));
JPanel south = new JPanel(new BorderLayout());
buttons.add(new JButton("Ok"));
buttons.add(new JButton("Cancel"));
south.add(BorderLayout.EAST, buttons);


JPanel panel = new JPanel(new BorderLayout());
panel.add(BorderLayout.CENTER, new JScrollPane(new JTextArea(20, 40)));
panel.add(BorderLayout.SOUTH, south);
```

Fig. 1. Simple user-interface implemented in plain Java

First of all, why did we develop a domain-specific language for implementing user-interfaces? Despite all the advances in user-interface libraries, typical user-interface code is still difficult to read. The composition of a complete user-interface from its basic components is a tangled list of statements, that makes it difficult to see how the user-interface is structured. A typical implementation of a simple graphical user-interface is shown in Figure 1. The composition of the user-interface components and panels in separate statements results in spaghetti-like code: the connections between the definitions and uses of components are unclear. In plain Java, the *implementation* of a graphical user-interface is not close enough to the *domain* of graphical user-interfaces. That is, it is very hard to understand the structure of the user-interface by studying the code. This makes user-interface code hard to maintain.

Swul sets out to solve this problem by using a syntax that is closer to the conceptual idea of the Swing library. The central idea of Swul is that the implementation of a user-interface should reflect its hierarchical structure, i.e. subcomponents are subexpressions of their containers. They are not added afterwards in separate statements, which inevitably leads to tangling. Properties of components, such as widgets, containers, and layouts, can be set immediately on the component as well, thus defining all the aspects of a user-interface component at a single location.

However, the disadvantage of a separate DSL is that the integration with the rest of the program, written in a general-purpose language is cumbersome. Usually, escaping to the general-purpose language is restricted to certain places in the DSL and the connections between the domain-specific code and the general-purpose code are not verified by the compiler. For example, event handlers are often invoked by reflection if there is a separate user-interface specification.

```
menubar = {
  menu {
    text = "File"
    items = {
      menu item { text = "New"    accelerator = ctrl-N }
      menu item { text = "Save"   accelerator = ctrl-S }
    }}}

content = panel of border layout {
  center = scrollpane of textarea { rows = 20   columns = 40 }

  south = panel of border layout {
    east = panel of grid layout {
      row = {
        button of "Accept"
        button of "Cancel"
      }}}}
```

Fig. 2. Simple user-interface implemented in Java and Swul

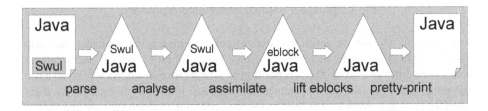

Fig. 3. Pipeline for the processing of Swul in Java

To integrate the user-interface, implemented in Swul, seamlessly with the rest of the program, we have embedded Swul in Java (JavaSwul). Swul components can be used as Java expressions (embed) and Java expressions can be used in place of Swul expressions (escape). For example, a custom border or component can be used in a Swul specification of a user-interface and event-handling code can be written in plain Java inside Swul. Figure 2 shows the implementation of the user-interface encoded in Figure 1 in Swul [2]. Here it is much easier to understand the structure of the user-interface, since this is directly reflected in the code. We will discuss the various aspects of Swul in more detail later.

Implementation Overview. A JavaSwul source file is processed by a series of components, which are of course available as a single tool to users of JavaSwul. The pipeline through which a source file is processed, is shown in Figure 3. The components will be discussed in the next few sections.

Note that the implementation, although it acts as a pre-processor to the Java compiler, is more solid than most pre-processors for several reasons. First, it operates on

---

[2] More examples are available at http://www.strategoxt.org/JavaSwulExamples

```
context-free syntax
  ComponentType Props?      -> Component  {cons("Component")}
  "{" Prop* "}"             -> Props      {cons("Props")}
  PropType "=" PropValues   -> Prop       {cons("Prop")}

  "{" Component* "}" -> PropValues {cons("PropMultiValue")}
  Component          -> PropValues {cons("PropSingleValue")}

context-free syntax
  "panel"            -> ComponentType {cons("JPanel")}
  "border" "layout" -> ComponentType {cons("BorderLayout")}
  "grid" "layout"   -> ComponentType {cons("GridLayout")}

  "content" -> PropType {cons("Content")}
  "layout"  -> PropType {cons("Layout")}
  "title"   -> PropType {cons("Title")}
```

Fig. 4. General productions of the Swul syntax definition

a complete abstract syntax tree, i.e. it is not based on lexical processing. Second, the pre-processor performs semantic analysis and type checking on the mixed AST. Hence, it is able to report semantic errors in terms of the original program. Most pre-processors only have knowledge of the lexical syntax and leave error reporting to the compiler. More advanced macro systems, such as [1, 3, 8], avoid lexical processing as well. For a discussion of the relation to macro systems see [6].

2.1 Syntax and Parsing

The syntactical part of the implementation of JavaSwul consists of a syntax definition for Swul itself and the embedding of Swul in Java. In all our embeddings we reuse an existing, modular syntax definition for Java 5.0.

Swul Syntax Definition. The syntax of Swul is defined in SDF, a modular language for syntax definition that integrates context-free and lexical syntax in a single formalism. Swul uses a combination of a general syntax and some sugar for specific circumstances. The most relevant productions from the syntax of the general syntax are shown in the first context-free syntax section of Figure 4. The general syntax is based on component types with the values of properties set between curly braces after the component type. Component types are for example panel, button etc. Examples of properties are layout, text, horizontal gap, and border. Some examples of component specific production rules of the syntax definition are shown in the second context-free syntax section of Figure 4.

In contrast to the general syntax of Swul presented here, the first edition of Swul [6] used component specific production rules and non-terminals. While extending the Swul language to cover more of the Swing library it became clear that this approach leads to a lot of duplication in the syntax definition, lots of non-terminals and, worse, poor error reports in case of syntactical errors in a JavaSwul source file. Therefore, we adopted this

```
context-free syntax
  (Modifier "-")* KeyEvent -> Prop {cons("Accelerator")}
  "ctrl"  -> Modifier {cons("CtrlModifier")}
  "alt"   -> Modifier {cons("AltModifier")}
  "shift" -> Modifier {cons("ShiftModifier")}
  "meta"  -> Modifier {cons("MetaModifier")}
```

Fig. 5. More domain-specific syntax in Swul

```
context-free syntax
  SwulComponent -> JavaExpr      {avoid, cons("ToExpr")}
  JavaExpr      -> SwulComponent {avoid, cons("FromExpr")}
```

Fig. 6. Syntactical Embedding of Swul in Java

general syntax and introduced a separate analysis phase that checks if the component types and properties are used in the right way.

Swul also supports user-friendly syntax for some domain-specific concepts that are hard to construct using the Swing API. For example, Swul introduces a concise notation for accelerator keys (key combinations to access a user-interface component with the keyboard). Figure 5 shows the SDF production rules for accelerators.

Keywords. The keywords used in the Swul production rules, such as panel and border, are not automatically *reserved* keywords. In general, reserved keywords are only necessary if ambiguities arise, for example between the keyword null and the identifier null. Moreover, if a separate scanner is used, then the scanner-parser combination cannot handle tokens that have different meanings in different contexts, i.e. if there is not interaction between the scanner and the parser. However, the META-BORG method is based on *scannerless* generalized-LR parsing, which can determine the meaning of a token based on the context in which it occurs, since there is no separate scanner. Thus, reserving these keywords (i.e. disallowing them as identifiers) is not required. However, they can still be declared as reserved keywords if this is desirable.

Embedding. The syntactic embedding of Swul in Java is defined in an SDF module that imports the Swul and Java syntax and defines where Swul components can be used in Java and vice versa. This embedding is defined by two productions, which are shown in Figure 6. The two production rules of this embedding define that a Swul component can be used as a Java expression (also known as a quotation) and that a Java expression can be used in Swul as a component (also known as escape or anti-quotation). Note that the embedding is a strictly modular combination of Java and Swul: we do not have to modify the Java or Swul syntax definition, thus we do not need to know the details of these syntax definitions either.

Renaming. To avoid unintended mixing of Swul and Java code, the non-terminals of the two languages have to be unique. Therefore, the embedding module imports SDF modules that prefixes all the Java and Swul non-terminals with the prefixes Swul and

```
module Java-15-Prefixed
imports Java-15
            [ CompilationUnit  => JavaCompilationUnit
              TypeDec           => JavaTypeDec
              PackageDec        => JavaPackageDec
              ...
              Expr              => JavaExpr ]
```

Fig. 7. Prefixing all non-terminals of Java

Java respectively. These renaming modules are generated from the syntax definitions of Java and Swul. Figure 7 illustrates such a generated renaming module for Java. This renaming module imports the Java syntax definition (`Java-15`) and renames all non-terminals in this syntax definition by prefixing them with `Java`.

Cyclic Derivations. The METABORG method does not require the use of quotation and anti-quotation symbols to separate the embedded domain-specific language from the code written in the host language. Indeed, we do not use a quotation and anti-quotation symbol in the embedding of Swul in Java. Nevertheless, a problem with the two production rules for embedding Swul in Java is that they lead to cyclic derivations: a Swul component can be an expression, an expression can be a Swul component, which can be an expression, and so on. Scannerless generalized-LR cannot handle cycle derivations, so we have to disallow a cyclic derivation in some way. In [10] a trick was presented to cut off such cyclic derivations by using an existing language construct for disambiguation: *priorities* [4]. Priorities allow a concise specification of derivations that should be removed from the parse table by the parser generator. Usually, priorities are used for declaring the priority and associativity of operators, but in fact they can be used to disallow any production as the child of another production.

The following priority declares that the production for the escape from Swul to Java can never be applied immediately below the production that allows Swul to be used as a Java expression. This effectively cuts off the cycle in the derivations, and does not reject any useful interaction of Swul and Java.

context-free priorities
```
JavaExpr -> SwulComponent > SwulComponent -> JavaExpr
```

2.2   Semantic Analysis

In the previous section we described how the Swul language is syntactically embedded in Java using the modular syntax definition formalism SDF. From this embedding we can generate a parser. Parsing a JavaSwul program results in an abstract syntax tree that is a mixture of Java and Swul language constructs. Before the Swul constructs are translated to plain Java code, we need to make sure that the source file does not contain semantic errors. If these errors will not be detected until compilation of the plain Java code, then the user of JavaSwul will have to map this error report to the original source file, which is undesirable.

```
dryad-type-of :
  Component(ct , _, Some(ComponentProps(ps )) ) -> <swul-to-swing> ct
  where <map(type-attr; check-property(|ct ))> ps

properties-of :
  BorderLayout() -> [North(), South(), East(), West(), Center() | xs]
  where <properties-of> Layout() => xs
```

Fig. 8. Type checking of embedded Swul

Therefore, we need to perform semantic analysis of the source file. To this end, we extend a type checker for Java, which is written in Stratego, with support for typing Swul code and the connections between Java and Swul. For example, we have to check that the Swul components are used correctly in the surrounding Java code and that the used Swul properties exist for the subject components. The code for this property check is sketched in Figure 8. Here, the type checker is extended with a new type rule dryad-type-of [3] that checks if a Swul component is used correctly. In this case, the properties of the component are checked, where the properties-of strategy is used by check-property to retrieve the available properties of a component. Thus, the existing type checker for Java, which invokes dryad-type-of to type expressions, is extended with a new type rule for the domain-specific Swul extension. If the Swul expression cannot be typed, then this will be reported.

2.3 Assimilation

Assimilation transforms a program with embedded domain-specific code to a program in the plain host language, in this case Java. So, the assimilation of Swul transforms the embedded Swul code to the corresponding invocations of the Swing API. A typical assimilation implemented in Stratego consists of a set of rewrite rules and a traversal strategy that controls the application of these rewrite rules. For most of the Swul language constructs, the rewrite rules are straightforward mappings of the convenient Swul syntax to more involved Swing library calls. However, some Swul constructs, such as event handling, require a more advanced treatment in the assimilation, since the generated Java code in these cases is not just locally inserted, as we will explain later.

Traversal. The traversal used in the assimilation is shown in Figure 9. The strategy is a generic top-down traversal where some Java and Swul language constructs are given a special treatment. A generic traversal is very useful for implementing assimilations of languages embedded in Java, since Java contains many different constructs. Implementing a specific traversal for Java and the domain-specific language by hand would take a lot of code and time. In all of the Stratego code fragments of this paper, the *italic* identifiers indicate meta-level (Stratego) variables. The Stratego code also uses concrete object syntax for Java and Swul (between |[and]|).

In the main traversal strategy (swul-assimilate), the special cases are preferred over the generic traversal combinator all(s), which applies the argument s to all the

---
[3] Dryad is the name of the package that contains the Java type checker.

```
swul-assimilate =
       class-declaration
   <+ class-initializer
   <+ class-method
   <+ swul-expression
   <+ all(swul-assimilate)

class-initializer :
   ⟦ static { bstm1* } ⟧ -> ⟦ static { bstm2* } ⟧
   where {| FieldModifier
          : rules(FieldModifier :+ _ -> ⟦ static ⟧)
          ; <swul-assimilate> bstm1* => bstm2*
          |}

swul-expression = ?ToExpr(<SwulAs-Component>)
```

Fig. 9. Traversal strategy for Swul assimilation

subterms of the current term. The preferred alternatives (e.g. class-declaration) implement a more specific traversal for the cases where a generic traversal is not sufficient. One of the specific cases is class-initializer, which is shown in Figure 9. This special case keeps track of the context in which the assimilation traversal currently is: non-static (instance method) or static (class method). In a static context, fields that are generated by the assimilation, for example for event-handling, have to use a static modifier and therefore we have to keep track of this context. The assimilation of Swul uses a dynamic rule FieldModifier for this purpose. In the static context of a class initializer, the set of FieldModifier rules is dynamically extended with a new rule that produces the static modifier. If the dynamic rule strategy bagof-FieldModifier, which applies all FieldModifier rules, is invoked, then all current modifiers will be produced and these can be used in a fresh field declaration.

Another special case, illustrated in Figure 9, is the strategy swul-expression, which handles the transition from Java to Swul. This strategy is applicable to a ToExpr term, which is the constructor attached to the embedding production in Figure 6. For this term, the swul-expression strategy switches the traversal to Swul mode by invoking the SwulAs-Component rewrite rule.

Assimilation Rules. Figure 10 illustrates a number of Swul assimilation rules. In the assimilation of Swul we use a small extension of Java, called an eblock, that allows the inclusion of block statements in expressions. The syntax for eblocks is {| statements | expression |}. The value of an eblock is the expression. The statements are lifted by a separate tool to the statement before the statement in which the eblock occurs. There are also alternative eblocks for lifting statement the context *after* and before *and* after the context of the current expression. This small extension of Java has proven to be very effective for introducing new variables or performing side-effects in pure rewrite rules that need to transform an expression-level construct to a Java expression.

We now return to the rewrite rules of Figure 10. The first rule shows a typical rewriting for a Swing widget. The rewrite rule is a simple translation of the Swul construct to

```
SwulAs-JButton :
  [[ button { ps* } ]]{x} -> [[ {| x = new JButton(); bstm* |x|} ]]
  where <map(SwulAs-JButtonProp(|x))> ps* => bstm*

SwulAs-JPanel :
  [[ panel of c ]]{x} -> [[ {| x = new JPanel(); x.setLayout(e); |x|} ]]
  where <SwulAs-LayoutManager(|x)> c => e

SwulAs-GridLayout(|x) :
  [[ grid layout {ps*} ]]{y} -> [[ {| y=new GridLayout(i,j); |y|bstm*|} ]]
  where <nr-of-rows> ps*    => i
      ; <nr-of-columns> ps* => j
      ; <map(SwulAs-LayoutProp(|x,y))> ps* => bstm*

SwulAs-LayoutProp(|x,y) :
  [[ horizontal gap = c ]] -> [[ y.setHgap(e); ]]
  where <SwulAs-Component> c => e
```

Fig. 10. Some rewrite rules for assimilating Swul to Java

invocations of the Swing library. Note that a pre-eblock is used to create the JButton and set the properties of it. The second and third rule illustrate the rewriting of panels with a specified layout and the handling of the grid layout. Note that Swul does not require a specification of the number of rows and columns in a grid layout, since this can be calculated by the assimilator from the number of components in the columns and rows. The fourth rule assimilates the setting of the horizontal gap between components of a layout manager. The identifier of the subject layout manager is passed a term argument to the rewrite rule.

However, not all assimilation rules are that straightforward. For example, consider the event handling support of Swul. An example menu bar defined in Swul is shown in Figure 11. The action event properties of the menu item can contain a list of arbitrary statements that have the scope of the class declaration in which the menu bar is defined. A sketch of the code after assimilation is shown in Figure 12. The event handling code has been moved to a fresh inner class and the standard EventHandler class of Java is used to invoked the method declared in this inner class. A single instance of the fresh inner class is created and declared as a field of the class MenuEvent. This non-local assimilation of embedded Swul code is beyond simple rewriting (and also beyond typical macro expansion). The non-local assimilation is implemented by collecting the non-locally generated code in dynamic rules and inserting it in the right place on the way back in the traversal.

Producing Java. After assimilation, the abstract syntax tree is a plain Java abstract syntax tree, except for the expression block extension. These can be removed by invoking a tool in the Java support package for Stratego/XT. After this, we have a pure Java abstract syntax tree that can be pretty-printed using a standard pretty-printer for Java. The resulting source file can now be compiled with an ordinary Java compiler. Ideally, this should not result in additional semantic errors, since the semantic analysis phase

```
class MenuEvent {
  static void newFileEvent() { ... }
  static void main(String[] ps) { ...
    menubar = {
      menu {
        text = "File"
        items = {
          menu item {
            text = "New"
            action event = { newFileEvent(); }
          }
          menu item {
            text = "Exit"
            action event = { System.exit(0); }
          } ...
```

Fig. 11. Swul event handling

```
class MenuEvent {
  private static ClassHandler_0 classHandler_0 = new ClassHandler_0();
  public static void newFileEvent() { ... }

  public static void main(String[] ps) { ...
    JMenuItem_0 = new JMenuItem();
    JMenuItem_0.setText("New");
    JMenuItem_0.addActionListener(
      EventHandler.create(..., ClassHandler_0, "ActionListener_0", ""));
    ... }

  public static class ClassHandler_0 {
    public void ActionListener_0(ActionEvent event) { newFileEvent(); }
    public void ActionListener_1(ActionEvent event) { System.exit(0); }
}}
```

Fig. 12. Swul event handling after assimilation

has already performed a full type check of the source file. However, the Java Language Specification defines many semantic rules, of which many are not related to type checking. Some of these are not yet implemented, so there is no absolute guarantee that errors will not occur after pre-processing until we have a fully compliant front-end for Java.

3   Other Examples

We have implemented several large embeddings to gain experience with the META-BORG method. For example, we have embedded Java, AspectJ, XML, ATerms, XPath, and regular expressions in Java. In this section we will give a brief overview of two of these embeddings: regular expressions in Java and Java in Java.

```
regex ipline = [/
   ( ( [0-1]?\d{1,2} \. ) | ( 2[0-4]\d \. ) | ( 25[0-5] \. ) ){3}
   ( ( [0-1]?\d{1,2}   ) | ( 2[0-4]\d   ) | ( 25[0-5]   ) )
 /] ;

if( input ~? ipline )
  System.out.println("Input is an ip-number.");
else
  System.out.println("Input is NOT an ip-number.");
```

Fig. 13. Regular expression syntax embedded in Java

JavaRegex. We have designed an extension of Java, called JavaRegex, for string match-ing and rewriting using regular expressions. The purpose of JavaRegex is to provide compile-time checking of the syntax of regular expressions and to introduce new, high-level operators specific to regular expressions and string processing. This extension makes regular expressions much easier to use in Java. Compared to Perl, which has such facilities built in the language, writing regular expressions in plain Java is cumber-some, since they have to be encoded in string literals. The regular expressions are first interpreted as strings and secondly as regular expressions, meaning that the programmer needs to deal with special characters in the first and in the second interpretation at the same time. This results in an escaping-hell, where even experienced regular expression users carefully have to count the number of escapes that are used. Furthermore, basic operations in string processing are often compositions of several method invocations of the standard Java regular expression library, which makes the library harder to use. Nevertheless, the basic functionality of the library is quite well designed, so we would only like to provide a different syntax to the operations provided by this library.

Figure 13 shows a basic application of JavaRegex. In this example, the basic fea-tures of JavaRegex are used: regular expression syntax ([/ /]), regular expression types (regex), and testing if a string matches a regular expression (~?). In the quotes of a regular expression there is no need to escape the special characters of Java, hence solving the escaping-hell by providing a literal regex context. Note that the regular expression syntax is easy to implement due to the use of scannerless parsing, since context-sensitive analysis of lexical syntax is supported by design. JavaRegex also sup-ports named capture groups in a regular expression, where the names immediately refer to Java variables. Furthermore, JavaRegex provides *rewrites* as a more abstract operator for string processing. Rewritings can be composed using sequential and choice opera-tors and can be used in string traversals.

The assimilation of JavaRegex translates the regular expressions to Java string literals and the operators to invocations of the standard Java library for regular expressions. The assimilation not only translates the JavaRegex extensions to straightforward API invocations, but also generates control-flow to deal with the rewriting extensions of JavaRegex. The assimilation acts as a pre-processor of the Java compiler, but, we would like to avoid that the user of JavaRegex gets compiler errors in terms of the generated Java code, which would be hard to track down in the original source file.

```
dryad-type-of :
  ToBooleanExpr(x,y) -> Boolean()
  where <type-attr> x => TypeString()
      ; <type-attr> y => Regex()

dryad-type-of :
  Assign(x, y) -> Regex()
  where <type-attr> x => Regex()
      ; <type-attr> y => Regex()
```

Fig. 14. Regular expression syntax embedded in Java

Therefore, the assimilation phase performs semantic analysis of the source file. For this, we have have extended a type checker for Java with type checking rules for the JavaRegex extensions. The type checker is based on abstract interpretation, where each expression rewrites to its type. Thus, rewrite rules are added that rewrite the JavaRegex extensions to their types and check the types of the arguments. Figure 14 shows the rules for matching ~? (ToBooleanExpr) and regex assignments (Assign). This last rule extends the existing type checking rule for assignments. This shows that the type checking of existing language constructs can be extended in a modular way using rewrite rules.

JavaJava. A common problem in the embedding of domain-specific languages are ambiguities. The ambiguities can arise between different constructs of the domain-specific language or between the host language and the domain-specific language. In particular, this is a problem in meta-programming with concrete object syntax [12], where quotations and anti-quotations usually have to be disambiguated explicitly by indicating the non-terminal of the quotation (e.g. Jak, which is part of of the JTS/AHEAD Tool Suite [2]). In a meta-language with a manifest type system this explicit disambiguation is redundant.

In [5] we present a meta and object language independent method for solving the ambiguity problem in meta-programming with concrete object syntax. The method uses scannerless generalized-LR parsing to parse meta-programs that use concrete object syntax. This produces a forest of all possible parses. An extension of a type-checker for the host language disambiguates the forest to a single tree by removing alternatives that cannot be typed. If more than one alternative can be typed, then an ambiguity is reported. This method of disambiguation extends the METABORG method by providing a *reusable* tool for disambiguating programs that use an embedded domain-specific language. Indeed, this tool is also useful for the disambiguation of the embedding of Swul in Java. This method of disambiguation generalizes the language-specific and not reusable approach of, for example, Meta-AspectJ [14], where explicit disambiguation is not necessary either.

We have used this method to embed AspectJ (similar to [14]) and Java in Java for generative programming without requiring explicit disambiguation. The implementation of the embedding of Java in Java consists of assimilation rules that translate embedded Java 5.0 abstract syntax to the Eclipse JDT Core DOM. Figure 15 shows an example of a JavaJava program. The quotation in this program (between |[and]|) is ambiguous.

```
CompilationUnit dec;
String x = "y";
dec = ⟦ public class Foo {
            public int bar() {
              return #[x] * x;
            }} ⟧;
```

Fig. 15. Java embedded in Java witout explicit disambiguation

For example, the code in the quotation can represent a full compilation unit, a single type declaration, or a list of type declarations. The scannerless generalized-LR parser will produce all these possible parses. Next, the type checker will eliminate the alternatives that cannot be typed, leaving only the compilation unit alternative, since *dec* is declared as a compilation unit in this program. JavaJava also supports anti-quotations (#[]), which are disambiguated in a similar way. The second *x* in the quotation represents a meta-variable (a variable in the meta program) and is inserted in the resulting abstract syntax tree without requiring an explicit anti-quotation.

Note that the implementation of disambiguation is independent of the embedding of Java in Java and can therefore be used for the disambiguation of other ambiguous embeddings of domain-specific languages.

4   Conclusion

We have presented examples and an overview of the METABORG method for introducing embedded domain-specific syntax to overcome the lack of abstraction in general-purpose languages. We have presented three different examples of the embedding of a domain-specific language, designed syntactically and semantically for three different application domains: user-interfaces (JavaSwul), string processing (JavaRegex), and code generation (JavaJava). These examples illustrate that modular syntax definition and scannerless generalized-LR parsing are excellent tools for syntactically embedding a domain-specific language in a general-purpose host language. Furthermore, we have shown how Stratego's rewrite rules, traversal strategies, and dynamic rules can be applied to concisely assimilate the embedded code to the host language. Also, we have sketched how a type checker for the host language can be extended to support semantic analysis of the combination of the host language and the domain-specific language.

Availability. Stratego/XT and the Java support packages are Free Software (LGPL) and available from www.stratego xt.org. More information on METABORG is available at www.metaborg.org, where you can find references to related publications and applications (including JavaBorg, JavaSwul and JavaJava).

Acknowledgments. We want to thank Rob Vermaas for his extensive contribution to the development of JavaJava. We thank the reviewers for their detailed feedback.

References

1. J. Baker and W. Hsieh. Maya: multiple-dispatch syntax extension in java. In *PLDI '02: Proceedings of the ACM SIGPLAN 2002 Conference on Programming language design and implementation*, pages 270–281. ACM Press, 2002.
2. D. Batory, B. Lofaso, and Y. Smaragdakis. JTS: tools for implementing domain-specific languages. In *Proceedings Fifth International Conference on Software Reuse (ICSR'98)*, pages 143–153. IEEE Computer Society, June 1998.
3. C. Brabrand and M. I. Schwartzbach. Growing languages with metamorphic syntax macros. In *Proceedings of the 2002 ACM SIGPLAN Workshop on Partial Evaluation and Semantics-based Program Manipulation (PEPM'02)*, pages 31–40. ACM Press, 2002.
4. M. G. J. van den Brand, J. Scheerder, J. J. Vinju, and E. Visser. Disambiguation filters for scannerless generalized LR parsers. In N. Horspool, editor, *Compiler Construction (CC'02)*, volume 2304 of *LNCS*, pages 143–158, Grenoble, France, April 2002. Springer-Verlag.
5. M. Bravenboer, R. Vermaas, J. J. Vinju, and E. Visser. Generalized type-based disambiguation of meta programs with concrete object syntax. In R. Glück and M. Lowry, editors, *Proceedings of the Fourth International Conference on Generative Programming and Component Engineering (GPCE'05)*, volume 3676 of *LNCS*, pages 157–172, Tallinn, Estonia, September 2005. Springer.
6. M. Bravenboer and E. Visser. Concrete syntax for objects. Domain-specific language embedding and assimilation without restrictions. In D. C. Schmidt, editor, *Proceedings of the 19th ACM SIGPLAN Conference on Object-Oriented Programing, Systems, Languages, and Applications (OOPSLA'04)*, pages 365–383, Vancouver, Canada, October 2004. ACM Press.
7. C. Gould, Z. Su, and P. Devanbu. JDBC checker: A static analysis tool for SQL/JDBC applications. In *ICSE '04: Proceedings of the 26th International Conference on Software Engineering*, pages 697–698, Washington, DC, USA, 2004. IEEE Computer Society.
8. B. M. Leavenworth. Syntax macros and extended translation. *Communications of the ACM*, 9(11):790–793, November 1966.
9. Z. Su and G. Wassermann. The essence of command injection attacks in web applications. In *POPL'06: Conference record of the 33rd ACM SIGPLAN-SIGACT symposium on Principles of programming languages*, pages 372–382, New York, NY, USA, 2006. ACM Press.
10. J. J. Vinju. *Analysis and Transformation of Source Code by Parsing and Rewriting*. PhD thesis, University of Amsterdam, November 2005.
11. E. Visser. *Syntax Definition for Language Prototyping*. PhD thesis, University of Amsterdam, September 1997.
12. E. Visser. Meta-programming with concrete object syntax. In D. Batory, C. Consel, and W. Taha, editors, *Generative Programming and Component Engineering (GPCE'02)*, volume 2487 of *LNCS*, pages 299–315, Pittsburgh, PA, USA, October 2002. Springer-Verlag.
13. E. Visser. Program transformation with Stratego/XT: Rules, strategies, tools, and systems in StrategoXT-0.9. In C. Lengauer et al., editors, *Domain-Specific Program Generation*, volume 3016 of *LNCS*, pages 216–238. Spinger-Verlag, June 2004.
14. D. Zook, S. S. Huang, and Y. Smaragdakis. Generating AspectJ programs with Meta-AspectJ. In G. Karsai and E. Visser, editors, *Generative Programming and Component Engineering: Third International Conference, GPCE 2004*, volume 3286 of *LNCS*, pages 1–19, Vancouver, Canada, October 2004. Springer.

Agile Parsing to Transform Web Applications

Thomas Dean[1] and Mykyta Synytskyy[2]

[1] Electrical and Computer Engineering, Queen's University
dean@cs.queensu.ca
[2] Amazon.com
nikita@mondenet.com

Abstract. Syntactic analysis lies at the heart of many transformation tools. Grammars are used to provide a structure to guide the application of transformations. Agile parsing is a technique in which grammars are adapted on a transformation by transformation basis to simplify transformation tasks. This paper gives an overview of agile parsing techniques, and how they may be applied to Web Applications. We give examples from several transformations that have been used in the Web application domain.

1 Introduction

Many program transformation tools [3,4,6,7,8,21,25] are syntactic in nature. That is, they parse the input into an abstract syntax tree (AST) or graph (ASG) as part of the transformation process. There is good reason for this: syntax is the framework on which the semantics of most modern languages is defined. One example is denotational semantics [24], which maps the syntax to a formal mathematical domain.

The syntax of the language, and thus the structure of the tree or graph used by these tools is determined by a grammar. The grammar is typically some form of context free grammar, although it might be augmented with other information [1,2]. In most cases, the transformation rules that may be applied to the input are constrained by the resulting data structure. Grammars are used by transformation languages to impose a structure on the input that can be used by the rules.

These grammars are general grammars and represent the compromise of authoring the best grammars that are suitable for a wide variety of tasks. However, for some tasks, minor changes to the grammar can make significant differences in the performance of the transformations. We call changing the grammar on a transformation by transformation basis *agile parsing* [13]. One particular area of analysis that agile parsing is useful for is web applications. Web applications are written in a variety of languages, and are the subject of a variety of analysis and transformation tasks. We have used agile parsing techniques on several web application transformation projects [11,14,16,22,23,26,27]. We do not discuss the details of the transformations as they are covered elsewhere. Instead we focus on how grammars can be crafted for the web applications and how they are customized for each of the particular transformation tasks.

R. Lämmel, J. Saraiva, and J. Visser (Eds.): GTTSE 2005, LNCS 4143, pp. 312–326, 2006.

2   Agile Parsing

Agile parsing means customizing the grammar to the task. It is a collection of techniques from a variety of sources that we have found useful for transformation tasks. In this section, we give an introduction to agile parsing, how it is accomplished in the TXL programming language and a quick overview of some of the techniques.

The parsing techniques generally serve several needs. One is to change the way the input is parsed. One example is that in the C reference grammar the keyword *typedef* is simply given in the grammar as a storage specifier, eliminating any syntactic difference between variable and type declarations. That is, there is a single non-terminal declaration, that consists of a sequence of declaration specifiers followed by the declarator list. A declaration of a global variable and a type definition using typedef are parsed as the same non-terminal. For many transformations, this is a reasonable choice. However a transformation that targets only type definitions must include conditions in the rule to match only those declarations that include the typedef keyword. Splitting the declaration productions into two non-terminals, one which requires a typedef keyword, and one that does not, lets the parser make the distinction. Those rule sets that depend on the distinction become much simpler since they no longer have to code the distinction directly as conditions in the rule. They can simply target the appropriate non-terminal. The change to the grammar is local and only applies for the given transformation task.

The second need is to modify the grammar to allow information to be stored within the tree. An example is to modify the grammar to allow us to add XML style markup to various non-terminals in the grammar. While some transformation systems permit metadata to be added to the parse tree, sometimes data more complex than can be handled in the metadata is more appropriate for the problem. Thus the markup can be used to store temporary information part way through the transformation. Markup can also be used as a vehicle for communicating the results of an analysis to the user. The third need is to robustly parse a mixture of languages such as embedded SQL in COBOL[18] or in this case, dynamic scripting languages in HTML. The last need is to unify input and output grammars so that the rules may translate from one to the other while maintaining a consistent and well typed parse tree.

2.1   Agile Parsing in TXL

TXL is a pure functional programming language particularly designed to support rule-based source-to-source transformation [7,8,10]. Each TXL program has two parts: a structure specification of the input to be transformed, which is expressed as an unrestricted context-free grammar; and a set of one or more transformation rules, which are specified as pattern/replacement pairs to define what actions will be performed on the input. Each pattern/replacement pair in a transformation rule is specified by example, and may be arbitrarily parameterized for more rule flexibility.

Figure 1 shows a simple TXL grammar for expressions. Square brackets denote the use of a non-terminal. Prefixing a non-terminal symbol with the keyword *repeat* denotes a sequence of the non-terminal and the vertical bar is used to indicate alternate productions. The terminal symbols in the grammar are either literal values, such as the operator symbols in Fig. 1, or general token classes which are also referenced using square brackets ([id] for identifier in Fig 1).

```
define expression              define term
  [term] [repeat addop_term]     [factor] [repeat mulop_factor]
end define                     end define

define addop_term              define mulop_factor
  [add_op] [term]                [mul_op] [factor]
end define                     end define

define add_op                  define factor
  + | -                          [id]
end define                     end define
```

Fig. 1. Simple Expression Grammar in TXL

Agile parsing is supported in TXL through the use of the ***redefine*** keyword. The **redefine** keyword is used to change a grammar. Figure 2 shows an example. In this example, the factor grammar production is changed to include XML markup on the identifier. The ellipses ('...') in the factor redefinition indicate the previous productions for the factor non-terminal. Thus a factor is whatever it was before, or it may be an identifier annotated by XML markup. Subsequent transformation programs may choose to insist that all such identifiers be marked up when parsing the input by removing the first line and the vertical bar from the factor redefinition.

The TXL processor first tokenizes the input using a standard set of tokens which may be extended by the grammar definition, parses the input using the grammar and then applies the rules. In TXL, the rules are constrained by the grammar to keep the tree well formed. Thus the grammar includes not only the productions for parsing the input, but also the productions for the output and intermediate results. This may lead to ambiguities which are resolved through the use of an ordered parse. That is, the order of the rules in the grammar is used to determine the form of the input.

3   Agile Parsing in Web Applications

Web applications deliver services over the HTTP protocol, usually to a browser of some sort. Early web applications provided dynamic content to standard web browsers using server side scripting such as CGI scripts, servlets, JSP and ASP. Recent innovations include Real Simple Syndication (RSS), SOAP and AJAX.

```
redefine factor                define XMLEnd
  ...                            </[id]>
  | [XmlStart][id][XMLEnd]     end define
end redefine
define XmlStart                define XMLParm
  <[id] [repeat XMLParm]>        [id] = [stringlit]
end define                     end define
```

Fig. 2. Adding XML Markup to Identifiers in Expressions

Web applications present a particular challenge for parsing and for transformation. While some of the files in the web application contain conventional languages such as Java, the core files of the web application (the web pages) are typically comprised of a mixture of several languages. The web pages typically contain HTML, augmented with JavaScript, and server side languages such as Java, Visual Basic, or PHP. Other components of the application may be in XML such as various configuration files, or the XML transfer schema such as that used in SOAP.

For some web transformation tasks, it may be possible to convert to a single language [12], but if it is desired to translate between client and server side technologies, we must be able to represent all of the languages in a single parse. A grammar for web applications must also be robust. Most browsers accept malformed HTML and our approach must also accept and deal with the malformed HTML.

3.1 Island Grammars and Robust Parsing

The first agile parsing technique is island grammars [5,16,18,19,23]. Island grammars, originally introduced by van Deursen et al. [5], are a technique where the input is divided into interesting sequences of tokens, called islands and uninteresting tokens called water. Grammar productions that recognize the islands are given precedence over the water grammar productions which typically match any token or keyword. The productions can be nested, with islands containing lakes (sequences of tokens within the island that are uninteresting), which may in turn contain nested islands. Island grammars provide a natural way to handle mixed languages and to handle unexpected input in a robust way [18]. It can also be used to identify interesting sequences of tokens without performing a detailed parse of the entire input [19]. Island grammars must be crafted with care since errors in the grammar may cause interesting token sequences to be parsed as water.

In the context of web applications, we use island grammars to find and parse application elements within the natural language on the web page and to handle erroneous input in a reasonable way. Island grammars provide us with a mechanism to identify the interesting elements. However, what constitutes an interesting element depends on the task. In some contexts we are only interested in the Java or Visual Basic code that is embedded within the web page and the links from that code to other components such as other code modules or databases. In other contexts we may be interested in some of the structural components of the web pages such as tables, forms, anchors and links. Agile parsing permits us to change what sequences of tokens are considered islands based on the task.

Island grammars provide robustness. The general access by almost anyone to web publishing means that browsers have to deal with errors in the HTML markup in the pages. Two common errors are that style markup tags in web documents be improperly nested and that closing tags for some constructs may be missing. The following, although technically illegal, is accepted: "<B><I>bold italic text </B></I>". An example of the second is the closing tags for tables, table elements and forms. In some cases, the tags are implicitly closed when a surrounding markup is closed (table rows closed by the table, nested tables closed by surrounding tables, tables closed by the end of the document.

```
define program                        define interesting_element
  [repeat html_document_element]        [html_interesting_element]
end define                            end define


define html_document_element          define uninteresting_element
   [interesting_element]                 [html_uninteresting_element]
 | [uninteresting_element]             |[token_or_key]
end define                            end define
```

Fig. 3. Core HTML Grammar in TXL

Since browsers allow these errors, any analysis or transformation must also allow these errors and more importantly, interpret them in the same way as browsers do. We have developed an HTML island grammar that is the basis of our approach to analyzing and transforming web applications. Figure 3 shows the core of our HTML grammar. The predefined non-terminal program is the goal symbol of the grammar. In this case, it is a sequence (i.e. repeat) of document elements (html_document_element). Each document element is either an interesting element or an uninteresting element. Since TXL uses an ordered parse, only input that cannot be parsed as interesting elements can be parsed as uninteresting elements.

The base grammar defines interesting elements as interesting html elements (the non-terminal html_interesting_element). In our case interesting elements include anchors (including links), tables and forms. The main purpose of the interesting_element non-terminal is to act as a extension point when adding other languages to the grammar. Uninteresting elements use the grammar production token_or_key which is defined as any token or keyword.

The html_uninteresting_element production called from uninteresting element is used to handle formatting issues. TXL uses a generalized unparser to write out the results of the transformation. Each token is written out separated from the previous by a space. This formatting is occasionally inappropriate for HTML text. The html_uninteresting_element production allows the parser to recognize those cases and provide formatting cues in the grammar to handle them.

Figure 4 shows the grammar productions used to recognize the form elements (one of the interesting elements). The production html_form_tag (which is one of the alternatives of html_interesting_element) is rather straightforward. It is a form tag with parameters (html_any_tag_param) followed by form content and an optional end element. The end element must be optional since non-terminated forms are accepted by most browsers. The SPOFF, SP, SPON, and NL symbols are formatting cues. The SPOFF cue turns off spacing between the tokens as they are written to the output until the SPON cue is encountered. The SP cue inserts a space and the NL cue inserts a newline into the output. These elements exist in the grammar only, they are not included in the parse tree, and are only used when the parse tree is written out. They have no effect on the construction of the parse tree from the input.

The content is either legitimate form content which includes form elements or other content which are html_document_elements such as arbitrary text and other islands such as tables. The TXL **not** modifier is used to guard the other content

```
define html_form_tag                    define html_form_content
  [SPOFF] <form [SP]                        [html_legitimate_form_content]
  [repeat html_any_tag_parm>              |[html_form_other_content]
  [SPON][NL]                             end define
  [repeat html_form_content]
  [opt html_form_tag_closing]           define html_form_other_content
end define                                [not html_form_tag_stop]
                                             [html_document_element]
define html_form_tag_closing            end define
  [SPOFF]</form>[SPON][NL]
end define                              define html_form_tag_stop
                                          </form | <form | </table
                                        end define
```

Fig. 4. Grammar for Form Elements

and make the grammar more robust. As menioned earlier one common error is to omit some of the closing tags of tables and forms. Before attempting to parse html_document_element as part of html_form_other_content, the parser must first attempt to parse html_form_tag_stop. If it succeeds in parsing html_form_tag_stop, then the parse of html_form_other_content fails, and no tokens are consumed. Thus other content is guarded by html_form_tag_stop which prevents any of the form or table close tags from being parsed as other content. It prevents nested forms, so another form tag causes the previous form to be closed (i.e. a missing form close tag). This shows the advantage of island grammars over a conventional grammar using an simple optional close tag. The island grammars allow us to consume the text within the form in the same manner as the browser does. Similar approaches are used to parse tables and anchor elements as interesting elements of the grammar.

Extending the grammar to handle scripting languages (server or client side) is done by extending the interesting_element non-terminal from Figure 3. Figure 5 shows how the grammar can be extended to handle Java server pages. As mentioned

```
redefine interesting_element            define jsp_interesting_element
  ...                                       [jsp_start]
  |[jsp_interesting_element]                [jsp_expression]
end redefine                                [jsp_end]
                                          |[jsp_start]
define jsp_delimiter                        [repeat jsp_scriptlet]
  [jsp_start] | [jsp_end]                   [jsp_end]
end define                                |[jsp_useBean]
                                          |[jsp_formal_declaration]
                                          |[jsp_include_directive]
                                          |[jsp_include_action]
                                          |[jsp_forward]
                                        end define
```

Fig. 5. Grammar for JSP Elements

before, the `interesting_element` production is extended to include the JSP elements. The tokens `jsp_start` and `jsp_end` represent the "<%" and "%>" tokens respectively. So interesting elements are java expressions and scriptlets that are enclosed between `jsp_start` and `jsp_end` elements, jsp bean declaratives, declarations include directives, include actions and forward directives.

The other side of the extension is the ability of java statements to include HTML. For example:

```
<table><%
for(i = 0; i < 10; i++){
  %> <TR><TD><%=i%></TD></TR><%
}
%></table>
```

In this case we have a Java `for` loop that generates the first 10 integers in a table. With the grammar additions shown in Figure 6, the end of the first scriptlet (containing the start of the for statement, will be treated as if it was a Java statement. The statement consists of HTML elements which in turn contain a nested java expression. The `jsp_html_segment`, is the reverse of a `jsp_interesting_element`. It starts with a `jsp_end` token and ends with a `jsp_start` token. The content is similar to the regular html content, but does not include scriptlets. Opening another scriplet thus results in a statement at the same scope level as the html text.

One final wrinkle is that Java code may also be invoked within the attribute values of tags. They are usually enclosed in double quotes. This causes some difficulty in TXL since string literals are primitive tokens in TXL. We handle this with a simple lexical preprocessor that translates double quotes containing java scriptlets into double square brackets. The grammar for attributes in html tags is then extended to permit double square brackets as well as identifiers and string literals.

3.2 Markup Grammars

Another agile parsing technique we use for analyzing and transforming web applications is markup grammars. Markup grammars extend the original grammar for some language to recognize a markup that has been applied to the input. Sometimes

```
define jsp_element_or_html_seg        define jsp_html_segment_content
   [jsp_declaration_or_statement]        |[jsp_useBean]
  |[jsp_expression]                      |[jsp_formal_declaration]
  |[jsp_html_segment]                    |[jsp_include_directive]
end define                               |[jsp_include_action]
                                         |[jsp_forward]
define jsp_html_segment                  |[html_only_interesting_element]
 [jsp_end]                               |[not jsp_delimiter]
 [repeat jsp_html_segment_content]          [html_element]
 [jsp_start]                           end define
end define
```

Fig. 6. Grammar for JSP Islands

```
<varset set="rs, con, userName">
<backslice distance=2>if(! rs.next())</backslice></varset>{
    <varset set="con, userName"><backslice distance=1>
        Preparedstatement stm = con.preparedstatement("INSERT INTO Employee"
        + "(Username,Password,FirstName,LastName) VALUES(?,?,?,?)");</uid>
    </backslice></varset>
    <varset set="username, stm"><slice>
      stm.setstring(1,request.getparameter("userName"));
    </slice></varset>
```

Fig. 7. Implementing Slicing in Web Applications Using Markup

the markup is used as part of a transformation. For example, the use of a variable may be marked up with unique identifier linking the declaration and all uses of the variable[14]. Markup can be used to store details about a transformation. Some transformations can be complex to identify, but rather simple to carry out once they have been completed. The complex identification problem can be broken down into multiple simple transformations, each of which analyses some part of the application and adds markup to encode the information that has been deduced. Subsequent transformations can combine markup to produce more sophisticated markup [9,12,17]. Once the information has been identified and the appropriate elements annotated, then the final transformation is straightforward.

Markup can also be used to convey information to further transformations or back to the user. For example, a slice is the minimal subset of a program that can affect the slicing criteria[16]. The slicing criteria is the value of one or more variables at a particular point in the program. Markup can be used to show both the slice and how the slice was computed in the context of the larger program. Figure 7 shows an small example of a slice in the Java portion of a JSP application using markup. The slicing criteria is identified using the slice tag which annotates the stm.setstring method call near the end of the code sequence. The set of variables active at each statement is calculated by a transformation and stored using the varset tag, and finally the elements of the slice are identified using backslice tag. This markup is intended for further transformations and is not very readable. One of the transformations[16] used to present the result for human consumption wraps the entire JSP page in <pre>...</pre> tags, translates all of the angle brackets of the HTML tags to ampersand notation (i.e. < >) and translates all of the slicing markup to font tags with color (i.e. <FONT COLOR="#FFEECB">). This allows the code to be viewed in a standard web browser.

4 Tasks

We have used the island based web application grammar as a core for several tasks. These include identical and near miss clone detection and conversion of classic Java Server Pages (JSP) to JSP with custom tags. For each task, we make small modifications to the grammar using TXL's grammar redefinition mechanism.

```
include "HTML.Grm"                rule exportEachIsland
include "ASP.Grm"                   replace $ [interestingElement]
                                        I [interesting_elemnet]
function main                     import Seq [number]
   export Seq [number]            construct FileName
      1                                 CloneCandidate_ [+ Seq]
   replace [program]              export Seq
      P [program]                      Seq [+ 1]
   by                             by
      P [exportEachIsland]              I [write FileName]
end function                      end define
```

Fig. 8. Island Extraction Transform

4.1 Clone Detection

The first task is clone detection. One may wish to limit clone detection to significant syntactic units. This is particularly important if you are looking for structural clones in web sites. Cloned text in the body of the page is not as interesting, except to the extent that participates in the cloned structure. An example is a menu bar on the top or side of a web page that was implemented directly within HTML. Such a menu bar might be implemented using tables. Since islands represent the significant structural elements, then they form an ideal basis for clone detection and resolution.

Our approach [11,22] to clone detection is to write each island out to a separate file. This is accomplished with a very simple transformation, shown in Figure 8. As explained previously, TXL grammars contain standard formatting cues, so each island is written in a standard format. The detection of identical clones is accomplished by comparing the files. This essentially turns a structural comparison into a lexical comparison. Figure 9 shows an example table clone candidate. Since we are dealing with identical clones, we only show a single instance of the clone. While this is essentially the same as using a pretty printer to print the code and use lexical analysis to find the clones, the difference is that the use of the island grammars limits the output to individual islands. Thus the clone candidates are limited to the structural elements of the page identified by the islands.

```
File CloneCandidate_3:
    <table border-1>
        <tr>
            <td colspan = 2>foo bar </td>
        </tr>
        <tr>
            <td> abc</td>
            <td>xyz</td>
        </tr>
    </table>
```

Fig. 9. Formatted Table Island

```
define div_table_tag              define html_div_content
  [SPOFF]<div [SP]                     [not div_table_tag_close]
    [repeat                                [html_document_element]
html_table_tag_param]>            end define
  [SPON][NL]
  [repeat html_div_content]       redefine interesting_element
  [opt div_table_tag_close]          [div_table_tag]
end define                        | ...
                                  end redefine
define div_table_tag_close
  [SPOFF]</div>[SPON][NL]
end define
```

Fig. 10. Adding Div Islands

To change the structural elements that are considered for the clone analysis, you need only change the grammar to identify what elements are possible clones. This is analogous to our typedef example earlier where we changed the grammar to simplify the rules. In our system, islands were tables, forms and links, thus only tables forms and links are potential clones. One of the latest trends in web sites is to use the HTML *div* tag to build the navigation menus rather than HTML tables. Adding the definitions from Figure 10 to the program in Figure 8 adds the div tag island to the grammar (by redefining `interesting_element` to include `div_table_tag`) and thus makes them clone candidates. Once identified, clones in web applications can be resolved using a variety of techniques[22]. The multilingual island grammar provides a framework for such transformations.

A similar approach can be used for locating identical clones in conventional programming languages. Rather than parse the entire language, the elements that you wish to consider as clones can be isolated using an island grammar. For example, one might construct an island grammar which selects java method headers and a water grammar that balances braces (i.e. '{' and '}') inserting newlines at all semicolons (';'). This would permit the identification of identical method clones. One could also add control statements as islands. Since islands nest, it would both make control statements candidates for clones as well as change the formatting of control statements within method islands. The change of formatting would change the way in which control statements contribute to the identification of identical method clones.

This method can also be easily extended to handle near miss clones. Near miss clones are clones that differ only by a small amount. A web application example is the same menubar, but one in which the current page is highlighted. So the menubar on the home page will have the home entry shown in a different color, while the contact page will have the contact entry on the menu shown.

We extend our approach to handle near miss clones by modifying the grammar to include different formatting cues. Figure 11 shows the redefinitions to the table grammar to handle near-miss clone detection. The only difference is the addition of the [NL] tokens in the appropriate places. In this case, we add newlines after the tag identifiers table, tr and td, after each attribute, and after the closing angle bracket. Figure 12 shows two near miss table clone islands formatted by this grammar. The arrows identify the different lines. One line is an attribute of the table, the other is the

```
redefine html_table_tag              redefine html_table_row
  <table                    [NL]       <tr                      [NL]
   [repeat html_tag_param]              [repeat html_tag_param]
  >                         [NL]       >                        [NL]
  [repeat html_table_content]          [repeat html_th_or_td]
  [opt html_table_tag_closing]         </tr>                    [NL]
end  redefine                        end  redefine

redefine html_tag param              redefine td
  [id]=[stringlit_or_id]  [NL]         <td                      [NL]
end  redefine                          [repeat html_tag_param]
                                       >                        [NL]
redefine html_table_tag_closing      [repeat html_document_lement]
  </table>                  [NL]       </td>                    [NL]
end  redfine                         end  redefine
```

Fig. 11. Near Miss Clone Islands

contents of one of the table cells. Near miss clones are then identified using a threshold on the ratio of the number of changed lines to the number of identical lines.

The formatting control allows us to control the balance between the structural and the water elements of the islands. Most islands have some water in them. Tables usually have some content in each of the cells. By formatting the tag and HTML attributes on separate lines and leaving the water on a single line, we control the balance between the weight of structural elements and the water elements. A single difference in a tag (e.g. TH instead of TD) or attribute produces an additional line difference, while multiple changes the same section of water will only produce a single line change.

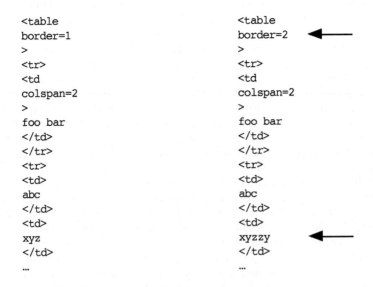

Fig. 12. Near Miss Clone Islands

define ctag_start
  <[tag_name]
   [**repeat** tag_attr]>
end define

define ctag_end
  </[tag_name]>
end define

define custom_tag
  [ctag_start]
  [repeat ctag_element]
  [ctag_end]
end define

define tag_name
  [id] : [id]
end define

define ctag_element
  [**not** ctag_end]
  [html_document_element]
end define

redefine interesting_element
  ... | [custom_tag]
end redefine

Fig. 13. CustomTag Grammar Module

4.2 JSP Custom Tag Translation

JavaServer Pages (JSP) is one of the popular technologies for building web applications that serve dynamic contents [1]. As indicated by the name, the scripting language in JSP is, by default, Java. In particular, scriptlets, which take the form of "<% Java code %>", are used to embed Java code within HTML. The explicit use of scriptlets facilitates rapid prototyping but introduces complexity into the implementation. The mixture of HTML and Java blurs this distinction between the presentation and business logic which is   needed in larger applications. Such separation can not only make a web application easier to maintain and evolve, but also allow individual developers with different skills to cooperate more efficiently.

The transformations of our approach to the migration from embedded Java to custom tags [26,11] require support from the grammar. This support takes several forms. We extend the HTML island grammar to handle custom tags (as well as Java). Figure 13 shows the grammar for the custom tags. It is very similar to the other markup grammars. The major addition, is that tag names are now two identifiers separated by a colon.

We also require unique naming markup for Java code to keep track of variables during control and data flow analysis. Each of the scriplets and each java variable is identified with a unique identifier. For example:

```
<tag id="Block2_Block1_Else">
   String[] <uid id="items ex.jsp Block2_Block1_Else">items</uid>
      = <uid id="cart ex.jsp Block0">cart</uid>.getItems ();
</tag>
```

This information is supplemented with information in the tags to which each statement will belong. The markup is used by the transformation that removes the scriplets from the JSP pages, replaces them with custom markup and generates the java classes that implements the custom tags. Since the variables may end up in

324 T. Dean and M. Synytskyy

different classes (for different custom tags), the unique naming is also used to do dependency analysis to ensure that all variables accessed between different custom tags have appropriate get and set methods.

5 Conclusions

This paper has presented some of the ways agile parsing can be used as a basis for analyzing and transforming web applications. Web applications provide a particular challenge to transformation since they often contain multiple languages, some of which are executed on the server side, while others are executed on the client side. We have examined two techniques in particular: the use of robust island grammars to uniformly represent all of the languages in a single parse and markup grammars which allow us to add annotations to web applications as part of various analysis and transformation tasks.

We have also examined how agile parsing has been used in several transformations tasks for web applications: structural clone detection and JSP migration. In both cases the general island grammar used to parse and transform the complex HTML pages was modified as part of the transformation task. In the clone identification task, the island grammar was used to identify clone candidates based on the syntactic structure provided by the islands. Changing which features are parsed as islands changes what may be considered clones. The JSP migration task needed two changes to the grammar. The first change is a markup that associated uses of java variables with the declaration of those variables. The other is the addition of the custom tag grammar productions for the result of the transformation.

References

1. Badros, G.: "JavaML: a Markup Language for Java source code", *Computer Networks* Vol 33, No. 6 (June 2000), pp. 159-177.
2. Bell Canada, Datrix *Abstract Semantic Graph: Reference Manual*, version 1.4, Bell Canada Inc., Montreal Canada, May 01, 2000.
3. van den Brand, M., van Deursen, A., Heering, J., de Jong, H., de Jonge, M., Kuipers, T., Klint, P., Moonen, L., Olivier, P., Scheerder, J., Vinju, J., Visser, C., and Visser, J., "The ASF+SDF Meta-Environment: a component-based language development environment", *Compiler Construction 2001 (CC 2001)*, Lecture Notes in Computer Science, R. Wilhelm, ed., Vol 1827, Springer Verlag,, 2001, pp. 365–370.
4. van den Brand, M., Heering, J., Klint, P., and Olivier, P., "Compiling Rewrite Systems: The ASF+SDF Compiler", *ACM Transactions on Programming Languages and Systems*, Vol 24, No 4, July 2002, pp. 334–368.
5. van Deursen, A., and Kuipers, T., "Building Documentation Generators", *Proc. International Conference on Software Maintenance (ICSM 99)*, Oxford, England, 1999, pp. 40–49.
6. Baxter, I.D., and Pidgeon, C.W., "Software Change Through Design Maintenance", *Proc. 1997 International Conference on Software Maintenance.* Bari, Italy, 1997, pp. 250–259.

7. Cordy, J.R., Halpern, and C.D., and Promislow, E., "TXL: A Rapid Prototyping System for Programming Language Dialects", *Computer Languages*, Vol 16, No 1, 1991, pp. 97-107.

8. Cordy, J.R., "TXL - A Language for Programming Language Tools and Applications", *Proc. LDTA 2004, ACM 4th International Workshop on Language Descriptions, Tools and Applications*, Edinburg, Scotland, January 2005, pp. 3-31.

9. Cordy, J.R., Schneider, K., Dean, T., and Malton, A., "HSML: Design Directed Source Code Hot Spots", *Proc. 9th International Workshop on Program Comprehension(IWPC 01)*, Toronto, Canada, 2001, pp. 145–154.

10. Cordy, J., Dean, T., Malton, A., and Schneider, K., "Source Transformation in Software Engineering using the TXL Transformation System", *Special Issue on Source Code Analysis and Manipulation, Journal of Information and Software Technology*, Vol. 44, No. 13, 2002, pp. 827-837.

11. Cordy, J.R., Dean, T., Synytskyy, N., "Practical Language-Independent Detection of Near-Miss Clones" *Proc 14th IBM Center for Advanced Studies Conference*, Toronto, Canada, Oct 2004, 29-40.

12. Dean, T., Cordy, J., Schneider, K., and Malton, A. "Experience Using Design Recovery Techniques to Transform Legacy Systems", *Proc. International Conference on Software Maintenance (ICSM 2001)*, Florence, Italy, 2001, pp. 622-631.

13. Dean, T.R., Cordy, J.R., Malton, A.J. and Schneider, K.A., "Agile Parsing in TXL", *Journal of Automated Software Engineering* Vol. 10, No. 4, October 2003, pp. 311-336.

14. Guo, X., Cordy, J., and Dean, T., "Unique Renaming in Java", *3rd International Workshop on Source Code Analysis and Manipulation*, Amsterdam, Netherlands, September 2003.

15. Hassan,   A.E.,   and   Holt,   R.C.,   "Migrating   Web   Frameworks   Using   Water Transformations", *Proceedings of COMPSAC 2003: International Computer Software and Application Conference*, Dallas, Texas, USA, November 2003, p296-303,

16. Li, X., *Defining and Visualizing Web Application Slices*, M.Sc. Thesis, School of Computing, Queen's University, 2004.

17. Malton, A.J., Schneider, K.A., Cordy, J.R., Dean, T.R., Cousineau, D., and Reynolds, J. "Processing Software Source Text in Automated Design Recovery and Transformation", *Proc. 9th International Workshop on Program Comprehension (IWPC 2001)*, Toronto, Canada, 2001, pp. 127-134.

18. Moonen, L.,"Generating Robust Parsers using Island Grammars", *Proc. 8th Working Conference on Reverse Engineering (WCRE 01)*, Stuttgart, Germany, 2001, pp 13-22.

19. Moonen, L., "Lightweight Impact using Island Grammars", *Proceedings 10th International Workshop on Program Comprehension (IWPC 02)*, Paris France, 2002, pp 343-352.

20. Neighbors, J., "The Draco Approach to Constructing Software from Reusable Components", *IEEE Transactions on Software Engineering*, Vol 10. No. 5, 1984,564-574.

21. Reasoning Systems, *Refine User's Manual*, Palo Alto, California, 1992.

22. Synytskyy, N., Cordy, J.R., Dean, T., "Resolution of Static Clones in Dynamic Web Pages", Proc IEEE 5th International Workshop on Web Site Evolution, Amsterdam, September 2003, pp. 49-58.

23. Synytskyy, Mykyta, Cordy, J., Dean., T, "Robust Multilingual Parsing Using Island Grammars", *Proc. IBM Center for Advanced Studies Conference*, Toronto, Canada, Nov 2003.

24. Tennent, A., *Semantics of Programming Langauges*, Prentice Hall, 1990.

25. Visser, E. "Stratego: A Language for Program Transformation Based on Rewriting Strategies. System description of Stratego 0.5." *Rewriting techniques and Applications (RTA '01), Lecture Notes in Computer Science*, A Middeldorp, ed. SpringerVerlag, 2001, pp. 357–361.
26. Xu, Shannon, Dean, T., "Transforming Embedded Java Code into Custom Tags", *Proc 5th International Worshop on Source Code Analysis and Manipulation*, Budapest, Hungary, Oct 2005, 173-182.
27. Xu, Shannon,*Modernizing Java ServerPages by Transformation*, M.Sc. Thesis, School of Computing, Queen's Univeristy, 2005.

Data Cleaning and Transformation Using the AJAX Framework

Helena Galhardas

INESC-ID and Instituto Superior Técnico, Avenida Prof. Cavaco Silva, Tagus Park,
2780-990 Porto Salvo, Portugal
hig@inesc-id.pt

Abstract. Data quality problems arise in different application contexts
and require appropriate handling so that information becomes reliable.
Examples of data anomalies are: missing values, the existence of duplicates, misspellings, data inconsistencies and wrong data formats. Current
technologies handle data quality problems through: *(i)* software programs
written in a programming language (e.g., C or Java) or an RDBMS programming language, *(ii)* the integrity constraints mechanisms offered by
relational database management systems; or *(iii)* using a commercial
data quality tool. None of these approaches is appropriate when handling non-conventional data applications dealing with large amounts of
information. In fact, the existing technology is not able to support the
design of a data flow graph that effectively and efficiently produce clean
data.

AJAX is a data cleaning and transformation tool that overcomes these
aspects. In this paper, we present an overview of the entire set of functionalities supported by the AJAX system. First, we explain the logical
and physical levels of the AJAX framework, and the advantages brought
in terms of specification and optimization of data cleaning programs.
Second, the set of logical data cleaning and transformation operators
is described and exemplified, using the declarative language proposed.
Third, we illustrate the purpose of the debugging facility and how it is
supported by the exception mechanism offered by logical operators. Finally, the architecture of the AJAX system is presented and experimental
validation of the prototype is briefly referred.

1   Introduction

Data cleaning aims at removing errors and inconsistencies from data sets in order
to produce high quality data. Data quality concerns arise in three different contexts: *(i)* when one wants to correct data anomalies within a single data source
(e.g., duplicate elimination in a file); *(ii)* when poorly structured or unstructured
data is migrated into structured data (e.g., when fusing data obtained from the
Web); or *(iii)* when one wants to integrate data coming from multiple sources
into a single new data source (e.g., in the context of data warehouse construction). In these contexts, the following data quality problems, also called as dirty
data, are typically encountered:

R. Lämmel, J. Saraiva, and J. Visser (Eds.): GTTSE 2005, LNCS 4143, pp. 327–343, 2006.

- Data coming from different origins may have been created at different times, by different people using different conventions to map real world entities into data. For instance, the same customer may be referred to in different tables by slightly different but correct names, say "John Smith", "Smith John" or "J. Smith". This problem is called the object or instance identification problem, duplicate elimination or record linkage problem in the case of a single source.
- The fact that fused data is produced and used by different entities also enables the existence of missing values. To be aware of a client's age, for instance, is important for a marketing department but not relevant at all for the accounting one.
- Data may be written in different formats. Since no standard notation is generally imposed, data fields may embed data of different natures (the so called free-form fields). An example is a street field that incorrectly contains the zip code and the country name. Moreover, abbreviations as well as synonyms may be used to refer to an object that is represented by their full names in another record.
- Data can contain errors, usually due to mistyping, such as "Joh Smith", even when the same naming conventions are used in different databases.
- Data can have inconsistencies: for instance, two records corresponding to the same person may carry two different birth dates.

Current technologies try to solve these data quality problems in three different ways [1]: (i) ad-hoc programs written in a programming language like C or Java, or in an RDBMS (Relational Database Management System) proprietary language; (ii) RDBMS mechanisms for guaranteeing integrity constraints; or (iii) data transformation scripts using a data quality tool. The use of a general purpose or an RDBMS proprietary language makes data quality programs difficult to maintain and optimize. The mechanisms supported by an RDBMS to enforce integrity constraints do not address the major part of data instance problems. Finally, there is an extensive market of tools to support the transformation of data to be loaded in a data warehouse, the ETL (Extraction, Transformation and Loading) tools, that enclose some data cleaning functionalities. Other data quality tools have been developed from scratch to address specific data quality problems as address standardization and name matching[1].

When an application domain is well understood (e.g., cleaning U.S. names and addresses in a file of customers), there exists enough accumulated know-how to guide the design and implementation of a data cleaning program [9]. Thus, designers can easily figure out which data transformation steps to follow, the operators to use and how to use them (e.g., adjusting parameters). However, for non-conventional applications, such as the migration of largely unstructured data into structured data, or the integration of heterogeneous scientific data sets in cross disciplinary areas (e.g., environmental science), existing data quality tools are insufficient for writing data cleaning programs. The main challenge

---

[1] The reader can find a recent classification of the existing commercial and research data quality tools in [1].

with these tools is the design of a data flow graph that effectively generates clean data, and can perform efficiently on large sets of input data. This two-fold task can be difficult to achieve, because: (i) there is no clear separation between the logical specification of data transformations and their physical implementation, and (ii) there is no support for debugging the reasoning behind cleaning results nor interactive facilities to tune a data cleaning program.

We have proposed the AJAX tool[2][10] to overcome these two aspects. The main contributions of AJAX with respect to existing data cleaning technology are the following:

- A data cleaning *framework* that attempts to separate the logical and physical levels of a data cleaning process. The logical level supports the design of a data flow graph that specifies the data transformations needed to clean the data, while the physical level supports the implementation of the data transformations and their optimization. An analogy can be drawn with database application programming where database queries can be specified at a logical level and their implementation can be optimized afterwards without changing the queries.

  We propose *five logical data transformation operators* encapsulating distinct semantics that are orthogonal and complete. These operators derive from an analysis of the types of mappings with respect to input and output tuples that are expressed by intuitive and conceptual data transformations. This approach is original when compared to commercial data cleaning tools in the sense that it prevents from having a large number of operators that are sometimes redundant. Our operators were proposed to extend SQL in order to specify those mappings.

- A *declarative language* for specifying these data cleaning logical operators. A *mechanism of exceptions* is associated to each logical operator and provides the foundation for explicit user interaction.

- A *debugger (or explainer mechanism)* that helps the user in debugging and tuning a data cleaning application program. Such a debugger facility, commonly used in programming environments, is new in the domain of data cleaning applications. An audit trail mechanism allows the user to navigate through the results of data transformations in order to discover why some records are not automatically treated. To solve those cases, the user may refine some cleaning criteria or manually correct data items.

AJAX does not provide any method to discover data problems that need to be cleaned. Before specifying a data cleaning and transformation program using AJAX, the user must be aware of the data anomalies that need to be solved. An interesting direction for future work would be to enrich the set of operators already provided by AJAX with new operators that are able to analyze data and automatically (by applying statistical techniques or data mining algorithms) detect the data quality problems that need to be solved. However, this issue is not addressed in the current version of the system.

---

[2] The first prototype of AJAX was designed and implemented at Inria Rocquencourt.

This paper presents an overview of the entire set of functionalities supported by the AJAX system. First, we explain the logical and physical levels of the AJAX framework, and the advantages brought in terms of specification and optimization of data cleaning programs. Second, the set of logical data cleaning and transformation operators is described and exemplified, using the declarative language proposed. We also illustrate the SQL equivalent of two of the AJAX operators. Third, we illustrate the purpose of the debugging facility and how it is supported by the exception mechanism offered by logical operators. Finally, the architecture of the AJAX system is presented and experimental validation of the prototype is briefly referred.

Most of these aspects have been published separately elsewhere [10], [11], but none of the previous publications concerning AJAX provided a broad description that covers all details.

The rest of this paper is organized as follows. In Section 2, we present our motivating example. Then, Section 3 details the principles of the AJAX framework. Section 4 explains the debugger mechanism. The architecture of the AJAX system and experimental validation are presented in Section 5. Related work is summarized in Section 6 and we conclude in Section 7.

2   Motivating Example

We illustrate the functionalities of AJAX using a case study. The application consists of cleaning and migrating a set of textual bibliographic references, extracted from postscript or pdf files that were obtained by a Web crawler[3], into a set of structured and duplicate-free relations.

Suppose we wish to migrate the original Citeseer dirty set of strings that correspond to textual bibliographic references, into four sets of structured and clean data, modeled as database relations: *Authors*, identified by a key and a name; *Events*, identified by a key and a name; *Publications*, identified by a key, a title, a year, an event key, a volume, etc; and the correspondence between publications and authors, *Publications-Authors*, identified by a publication key and an author key. The purpose of the underlying input-output schema mapping is to derive structured and clean textual records so that meaningful queries can be performed (e.g., how many papers a given author has published in 2005).

Figure 1 presents an example for two dirty citations that represent the same bibliographic reference. The corresponding cleaned instances are produced by the data cleaning process and stored in the four resulting relations. In the figure, the Publications table contains a single tuple that stores the correct and duplicate-free information represented by the two dirty citations. The title in this tuple, "Making Views Self-Maintainable for Data Warehousing", is the correct one among the two dirty titles, and the event key value ("PDIS") references the standardized event name ("Parallel and Distributed Information Systems") stored into the Events table. The fields concerning the location ("Miami Beach"

---

[3] This information was used to construct the Citeseer Web site [17].

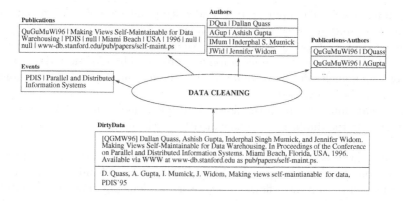

Fig. 1. Cleaning textual bibliographic references - an example

and "USA") and the url where the paper is available, have been correctly extracted by the cleaning process and associated to the cleaned publication instance. Finally, "1996" was identified as the correct year of publication. The Authors table stores one row for each real author. The data cleaning process recognizes the two distinct forms of writing the same author name and chooses the longest one. The Publications-Authors table keeps the references for cleaned authors and cleaned publications.

3   AJAX Framework

The development of a data cleaning program able to solve problems as the ones described in Section 2 actually involves two activities. One is the design of the graph of data transformations that should be applied to the input dirty data and whose main focus is the definition of "quality" heuristics that can achieve the best accuracy of the results. A second activity is the design of "performance" heuristics that can improve the execution speed of data transformations without sacrificing accuracy. AJAX separates these two activities by providing a logical level where a graph of data transformations is specified using a declarative language, and a physical level where specific optimized algorithms with distinct tradeoffs can be selected to implement the transformations.

3.1   Logical Level

A partial and high-level view of a possible data cleaning strategy for handling the set of bibliographic references introduced in Section 2 is the following:

1. Add a key to every input record.
2. Extract from each input record, and output into four different flows the information relative to: names of authors, titles of publications, names of events and the association between titles and authors.

3. Extract from each input record, and output into a publication data flow the information relative to the volume, number, country, city, pages, year and url of each publication. Use auxiliary dictionaries for extracting city and country from each bibliographic reference. These dictionaries store the correspondences between standard city/country names and their synonyms that can be recognized.
4. Eliminate duplicates from the flows of author names, titles and events.
5. Aggregate the duplicate-free flow of titles with the flow of publications.

At the logical level, the main constituent of a data cleaning program is the specification of a data flow graph where nodes are data cleaning operators, and the input and output data flows of operators are logically modeled as database relations. The design of our logical operators was based on the semantics of SQL primitives extended to support a larger range of data cleaning transformations.

Each operator can make use of externally defined functions or algorithms that implement domain-specific treatments such as the normalization of strings, the extraction of substrings from a string, etc. External functions are written in a 3GL programming language and then registered within the library of functions and algorithms of AJAX.

The semantics of each operator includes the automatic generation of a variety of exceptions that mark input tuples which cannot be automatically handled by an operator. This feature is particularly required when dealing with large amounts of dirty data which is usually the case of data cleaning applications. Exceptions may be generated by the external functions called within each operator. At any stage of execution of a data cleaning program, a debugger mechanism enables users to inspect exceptions, analyze their provenance in the data flow graph and interactively correct the data items that contributed to its generation. Corrected data can then be re-integrated into the data flow graph.

3.2   Logical Operators

We now present our logical operators based on a classification of data transformations where we consider the type of mapping that they express with respect to their input and output tuples. The proposed operators are parametric in the sense that they may enclose the invocation of generic external functions. A natural choice is to use SQL queries to express these mappings. This led us to introduce a logical operator, called *view*, that corresponds to an arbitrary SQL query. There are several obvious advantages of doing this: SQL is a widespread used language, and existing RDBMSs include many optimization techniques for SQL queries. However, the relational algebra is not expressive enough to capture the new requirements introduced by data transformation and cleaning applications as stated in [3]. Our next operator, called *map*, captures all iterator-based mappings that take a single relation as input and produces several relations as output (and therefore, several tuples for each input tuple). The map operator is proposed to enable the application of any kind of user-defined function to each input tuple. A map has the general form of an iterator-based one-to-many mapping. In the Citeseer example, formatting, standardization and extraction are implemented through a map operator.

The third operator, called *match*, captures a specific sub-class of iterator-based many-to-one mappings that consists of associating a similarity value to any two input records using an arbitrary similarity metric. The match takes two relations as input and produces one output relation. This operation is obviously expressible using a view operator but having it as a distinct first-class operator considerably facilitates its optimization. The fourth operator, called *cluster*, captures a subclass of non iterator-based many-to-many mappings that consists of transforming an input relation into a nested relation where each nested set is a cluster of records from the input relation, and the clustering of records is arbitrary. One example of the cluster operator is the application of a transitive closure method to assemble similar event records. We decided to define this operator for two reasons. The first reason is the fact that it accepts a particular signature, i.e., pairs of tuples equipped with a distance. The second reason for considering it as a first-class operator is due to the possibility of optimizing the match and cluster operators. The next operator, called *merge*, captures another subclass of non iterator-based many-to-many mappings that corresponds to grouping input elements according to a given criterion, and then applying an arbitrary aggregate data mapping to the elements of each group. This operator is an extension of the SQL group-by aggregate query where user-defined aggregate functions can be used.

To illustrate the use of these operators, we show in Figure 2 the simplified graph of data transformations, that corresponds to the cleaning strategy introduced earlier in this section, in terms of our logical operators. The numbering beside each data cleaning operation corresponds to an intuitive transformation in the strategy. For each output relation of Step 2, we have to identify and eliminate duplicate records. In the figure, duplicate eliminations corresponding to Step 5 are mapped into sequences of one match, one cluster, and one merge operator. Every other transformation is mapped into a single logical operator.

3.3 Declarative Language

AJAX provides an expressive and declarative language for specifying data cleaning programs, which consists of SQL statements enriched with a set of specific primitives to express map, match, cluster, merge and view transformations. Each one of these primitives corresponds to a transformation whose physical implementation takes advantage of existing RDBMS technology. The declarative nature of the language provides opportunities for automatic optimization and facilitates the maintenance of a data cleaning program.

Syntactically, each operator specification has a FROM clause that indicates the input data flow, a CREATE clause, which names the output data flow (for further reference), a SELECT clause specifying the format of the output data and a WHERE clause to filter out non interesting tuples from the input. An optional LET clause describes the transformation logics that has to be applied to each input item (tuple or group of tuples) in order to produce output items.

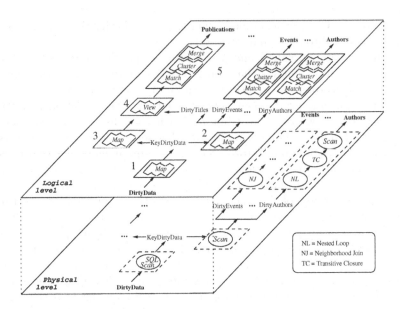

Fig. 2. Graph of logical and physical data transformations for the bibliographic references

This clause contains limited imperative primitives: the possibility to define local variables, to call external functions or to control their execution via if/then/else constructs. Finally, the cluster operator includes a BY clause which specifies the grouping algorithm to be applied, among the ones existing in the AJAX library of algorithms.

To illustrate the semantics and syntax of the AJAX operators, we exemplify the map operator that corresponds to the data transformation 1 and the match operator represented by 5 in Figure 2, in Examples 1 and 2 respectively.

Example 1. The following map operator transforms the relation DirtyData{paper} into a "target" relation KeyDirtyData{paperkey, paper} by adding a serial number to it. The LET clause contains a statement that constructs a predicate Key using an external (atomic) function generateKey that takes as argument a variable DirtyData.paper ranging over attribute paper of DirtyData. Relation Key is constructed as follows. For every fact DirtyData(a) in the instance of DirtyData[4], if generateKey(a) does not return an exception value exc, then a fact Key(a, generateKey(a)) is added to the instance of Key. Otherwise, a fact $DirtyData^{exc}(a)$ is added to the instance of $DirtyData^{exc}$ (which is the map output relation that stores exception tuples). We shall say that this statement "defines" a relation Key{paper, generateKey}[5]. The schema of the target relation is specified by the "{SELECT key.generateKey AS ...}" clause. It indicates that the schema of Key-

---

[4] Where a is a string representing a paper.

[5] For convenience, we shall assume that the name of the attribute holding the result of the function is the same as the name of the function.

DirtyData is built using the attributes of Key and DirtyData. Finally, the constraint stipulates that a paper attribute value must never be null.

```
CREATE MAP AddKeytoDirtyData
FROM DirtyData
LET Key = generateKey(DirtyData.paper)
{ SELECT Key.generateKey AS paperKey, DirtyData.paper AS paper INTO KeyDirtyData
CONSTRAINT NOT NULL paper}
```
□

A map operator that produces a single output relation and whose let-clause encloses only atomic assignment statements as the example above may be implemented by one *insert into ... select from* clause and one *create table* clause (as illustrated in Example 2). However, in a general case, a map operator may produce one or more tuples (belonging to a single or several output relations) for each input tuple. In such situation, it may not be possible to write SQL statements that represent the same semantics.

Example 2. The SQL equivalent of the map defined in Example 1 is as follows:

```
CREATE TABLE KeyDirtyData(paperKey varchar2(100),
     paper varchar2(1024) NOT NULL);
INSERT INTO KeyDirtyData
     SELECT generateKey() paperKey, dd.paper paper
     FROM DirtyData dd
```
□

Example 3 illustrates a match operation. The let-clause has the same meaning as in a map operation with the additional constraint that it *must* define a relation, named distance, within an atomic assignment statement. Here, distance is defined using an atomic function editDistanceAuthors computing an integer distance value between two author names. The let-clause produces a relation distance{authorKey1, name1, authorKey2, name2, editDistanceAuthors} whose instance has one tuple for every possible pair of tuples taken from the instance of DirtyAuthors. The where-clause filters out the tuples of distance for which editDistanceAuthors returned a value greater than a constant value given by maxDist. Finally, the **into** clause specifies the name of the output relation (here, MatchAuthors) whose schema is the same as distance.

Example 3. This (self-)match operator takes as input the relation DirtyAuthors{authorKey, name} twice. Its intention is to find possible duplicates within DirtyAuthors.

```
CREATE MATCH MatchDirtyAuthors
FROM DirtyAuthors a1, DirtyAuthors a2
LET distance = editDistanceAuthors(a1.name, a2.name)
WHERE distance < maxDist
INTO MatchAuthors
```
□

A simple match operator is mapped onto a *create table clause* and an *insert into clause* that encloses a nested query. The inner query computes the distance values and the outer query imposes a condition on the distance obtained, according to a given maximum allowed distance. Example 3 is mapped into the following SQL statements.

Example 4.
```
CREATE TABLE MatchAuthors(authorKey1 varchar2(100),
     authorKey2 varchar2(100), distance number);
INSERT INTO MatchAuthors
  SELECT authorKey1, authorKey2, distance
  FROM (SELECT a1.authorKey authorKey1, a2.authorKey authorKey2,
              editDistanceAuthors(a1.name, a2.name) distance
              FROM DirtyAuthors a1, DirtyAuthors a2)
  WHERE distance < maxDist;                                    □
```

3.4   Physical Level

At the physical level, certain decisions can be made to speed up the execution of data cleaning programs. First, the implementation of the externally defined functions can be optimized. Second, an efficient algorithm can be selected, among a set of alternative algorithms, to implement each logical operator. A very sensitive operator to the choice of execution algorithm is matching. An original contribution of our data cleaning system is the possibility to associate with each optimized matching algorithm, the mathematical properties that the similarity function used in the match operator must have in order to enable the optimization, and the parameters that are necessary to run the optimized algorithm. Then, our system enables the user to specify, within the logical specification of a given matching operator, the properties of the distance function, together with the required parameters for optimization. The system can consume this information to choose the best algorithm to implement a match. The important point here is that users control the proper usage of optimization algorithms. They first determine (in the logical specification) the matching criteria that would provide accurate results, and then provide the necessary information to enable optimized executions. Figure 2 shows the algorithms selected to implement each logical operation.

3.5   Optimization of the Match Operator

The match operator computes an approximate join between two relations. The semantics of this operation involves the computation of a Cartesian product between two input relations using an arbitrary distance function. Such semantics guarantees that all possible matches are captured under the assumption that correct record matching criteria are used. However, while doing so, a performance penalty is incurred since the Cartesian product based semantics with external function calls is usually evaluated (e.g. within an RDBMS) through a nested loop join algorithm with external function calls. The match operator is thus one of the most expensive operators in our framework once a considerable amount of data is involved.

For this reason, we dedicate particular attention to the match optimization opportunities. A match operator with an acceptance distance of ϵ computes a distance value for every pair of tuples taken from two input relations, and returns those pairs of tuples (henceforth, called *candidate matches*) that are at a maximum distance of ϵ from each other. In fact, since the distance function is an approximation of the actual closeness of two records, a subsequent step must determine which of the candidate matches are the *correct matches* (i.e., the pairs of records that really correspond to the same individual).

For very large data sets, the dominant factor in the cost of a match is the Cartesian product between the two input relations. One possible optimization is to pre-select the elements of the Cartesian product for which the distance function must be computed, using a *distance filter* that allows some *false matches* (i.e., pairs of records that are falsely declared to be within an ϵ distance), but no *false dismissals* (i.e., pairs of records falsely declared to be out of an ϵ distance). This pre-selection of elements is expected to be cheap to compute.

Distance-Filtering Optimization. This type of optimization has been successfully used for image retrieval [7] and matching of textual fields [13]. Formally, the result of a match between two input relations S_1 and S_2 in which the distance, $dist$, between two elements of S_1 and S_2 is required to be less than some ϵ, is a set:

$$\{(x, y, dist(x, y)) \mid x \in S_1 \land y \in S_2 \land dist(x, y) \le \epsilon\} \tag{1}$$

The distance filtering optimization requires finding a mapping f (e.g., get the length of a string) over sets S_1 and S_2 , with a distance function $dist'$ much cheaper than $dist$, such that:

$$\forall x, \forall y, \ dist'(f(x), f(y)) \le dist(x, y) \tag{2}$$

Having determined f and $dist'$, the optimization consists of computing the set of pairs (x, y) such that $dist'(f(x), f(y)) \le \epsilon$, which is a superset of the desired result:

$$Dist\_Filter = \{(x, y) \mid x \in S_1 \land y \in S_2 \land dist'((f(x), f(y)) \le \epsilon\}$$

Given this, the set defined by (1) is equivalent to:

$$\{(x, y, dist(x, y)) \mid (x, y) \in Dist\_Filter \land dist(x, y) \le \epsilon\} \tag{3}$$

A generic algorithm that implements this optimization is shown in Figure 3. This algorithm, called *Neighborhood Join* or NJ for short, is effective when both the number of partitions generated by the mapping f, and the number of elements in the partitions selected by the condition on $dist'$ wrt ϵ, are much smaller than the size of the original input data set. The filter used in Figure 3, map $= f$, serves to partition the input data sets and order the partitions accordingly. After applying this partitioning, only the pairs of tuples that belong to

```
Input: S₁, S₂, dist, ε, dist', f
{
    P₁ = set of partitions of S₁ according to f
    P₂ = set of partitions of S₂ according to f
    ∀s₁ ∈ p₁, p₁ ∈ P₁ : f(s₁) = cte
    ∀s₂ ∈ p₂, p₂ ∈ P₂ : f(s₂) = cte
    for each partition p₁ ∈ P₁ do {
        for each partition p₂ ∈ P₂ such that dist'(f(p₁), f(p₂)) ≤ ε do {
            for each element s₁ ∈ p₁ do {
                for each element s₂ ∈ p₂ do {
                    if dist(s₁, s₂) ≤ ε then
                        Output = Output ∪ (s₁, s₂) }}}}
}
```

Fig. 3. Neighborhood Join algorithm

partitions satisfying $dist'(f(p_1), f(p_2)) \leq \epsilon$ are compared through the distance function $dist$. This condition is imposed through the first two for cycles of the algorithm.

This optimization is illustrated below on a match operation of the Citeseer data cleaning program that takes as input the relation DirtyTitles{pubKey, title, eventKey} twice. The line between the %'s is an annotation that indicates the type of optimization and the distance filtering property of the distance function.[6] Annotations can then be used by AJAX to guide the optimizer on choosing the appropriate physical execution algorithm for the match operator. We assume that maxDist is an integer. The editDistanceTitles function is based on the Damerau-Levenshtein metric [16] that returns the number of insertions, deletions and substitutions needed to transform one string into the other.

Example 5.
    CREATE MATCH MatchDirtyTitles
    FROM DirtyTitles p1, DirtyTitles p2
    LET distance = editDistanceTitles(p1.title, p2.title)
    WHERE distance < maxDist
    %distance-filtering: map=length; dist=abs %
    INTO MatchTitles

The Damerau-Levenshtein edit-distance function has the property of always returning a distance value bounded by the difference of lengths l of the strings compared. Thus, if l exceeds the maximum allowed distance maxDist, there is no need to compute the edit distance because the two strings are undoubtedly dissimilar. This property suggests using as mapping f, the function computing the length of a string, and as $dist'$ a function abs such that $abs(x, y) = |x - y|$.

---

[6] In the Citeseer application, the distance filtering optimization was also applicable for matching author and event names.

4   Debugging Data Cleaning Programs

The goal of a data cleaning process is to produce clean data of high quality, i.e., consistent and error-free. When handling large amounts of data with a considerable level of dirtiness, automatic cleaning criteria are not able to cover the entire data set. There are two main reasons for this: cleaning criteria may need to be refined, and some cleaning decisions cannot be automatically disambiguated and thus user interaction is needed. In current technology, tuples that are rejected by the data transformations are inserted into a log file to be later analyzed by users. When the number of rejected tuples is large, which is usually the case when treating large data sets, it is fundamental to provide a user-friendly environment for discovering why some dirty records are not handled by the cleaning process. Our framework offers a facility to assist the user on this task. First, we provide a mechanism of exceptions that marks tuples that cannot be handled automatically as mentioned in Section 3. Second, a debugger mechanism is provided to allow the user to interactively inspect exceptions.

To better illustrate the problem, consider the standardization of citations and the extraction of author names, title and event names that correspond to transformation *2* in Figure 2. We may consider that the separation between the author list and the title is done by one of the two punctuation marks: {";."}. However, some citations, as the second dirty one in Figure 1 (i.e., " D. Quass, A. Gupta, I. Mumick, and J. Widom, Making views self-maintanable for data, PDIS'95"), use a comma between these two kinds of informations, so it is not easy to automatically detect where does the author list finish and the title starts. Therefore, the user may need to refine the corresponding extraction criteria so that this situation becomes automatically treated. Another example concerns the duplicate elimination applied to dirty publication records (transformation *5* in Figure 2). The two titles presented in the motivating example (starting by "Making Views...") are considered duplicates and need to be consolidated into a single title (the correctly written instance in this case). If the consolidation phase uses an automatic criterion that chooses the longest title among duplicates, then it cannot decide which is the correct one among these two titles, since they have the same length. Here again, manual intervention is required.

In order to mark input tuples that cannot be transformed automatically, a logical operator generates one *exceptional output relation* per input to store such tuples. The other output relations of an operator, called *regular output relations*, contain transformed tuples. An exceptional tuple corresponds to an input tuple that does not satisfy the cleaning criteria associated to the transformation. Given this, during the execution of a data cleaning program, a *debugger or explainer facility* offers the following functionality to the user: (i) inspection of exceptional tuples using data derivation mechanisms; (ii) navigation through the data flow graph to discover how exceptional tuples were generated, and (iii) support for refining cleaning criteria and modifying tuples to remedy exceptions. This functionality allows the user to tune a data cleaning application and, consequently to improve the accuracy of the cleaned data.

5   Architecture

The architecture of the AJAX system is represented in Figure 4. There are two types of components in the system: *repositories* that manage data or fragments of code; and *operational units* that constitute the execution core. AJAX encloses the following three repositories:

- The *data repository* stores data in a relational database management system or in a set of text files and offers a JDBC-like interface. In both cases, data include all input data of a data cleaning application (including dictionaries), the cleaned output data and the intermediate relations generated by logical operators, including exceptional output relations.
- The *library of functions* encloses the code of the external functions that are called within each logical operator. Examples of such functions are specific string matching functions (e.g., edit-distance [13]). This library contains a set of default functions and can be extended to include new user-defined functions.
- The *library of algorithms* encloses the clustering algorithms (e.g., by transitive closure) that can be invoked within a cluster operator and the physical algorithms that implement the logical operators. Analogously to the library of functions, users can add new algorithms to the set of existing ones.

The core of the AJAX system is implemented by the following operational units:

- The *analyzer,* which parses a data cleaning program and generates an equivalent internal representation;
- The *optimizer*[7], that assigns efficient physical execution algorithms to the logical operators specified and returns an optimal execution plan for a given data cleaning specification;
- The *code generator*, that generates executable code to implement each logical operator in the execution plan;
- The *execution engine*, which executes operators according to the order determined by the specification and the optimizer;
- The *debugger or explainer*, that triggers an audit trail mechanism allowing the user to discover why exceptional tuples are generated and supporting interactive data modification to correct exceptions.

5.1   Using AJAX

In [9], we present the performance results obtained when using the AJAX system to clean subsets of Citeseer bibliographic references. These results show two kinds of evidence. First, we report the execution times obtained for cleaning three subsets of the Citeseer data set with distinct sizes. We also show the percentage

---

[7] In the current version of the AJAX prototype, the optimization decisions are manually taken.

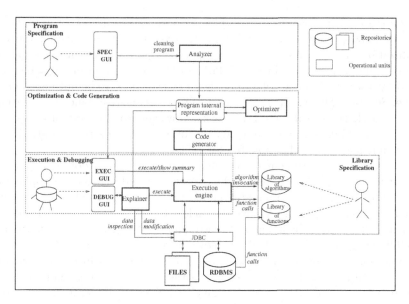

Fig. 4. Architecture of the system

of the execution time devoted to the match operations for each subset. Second, we illustrate the advantage of providing distinct physical execution algorithms for the match operator. We use different execution algorithms for the same logical semantics and we report the execution times and data quality obtained.

More recently, we applied AJAX for specifying and executing a data migration process concerning dam safety information. The main goal here was to map data that obeyed to a given schema into a distinct target data schema. In this real-world application, the exception mechanism was extensively used for detecting input data which was not automatically transformed by the specified data transformation criteria [8].

6   Related Work

The first problem with commercial tools is the existence of data transformations whose semantics is defined in terms of their implementation algorithms. To avoid this issue, a data cleaning model must be envisaged to separate logical operations from their physical implementations. There are two important results in the research literature which are concerned with the model and execution of data cleaning transformations. The main goal of the Potter's Wheel prototype [14] developed at the University of California at Berkeley, is to interleave the application of simple logical data transformations to data samples with the detection of data problems. IntelliClean [12] is another data cleaning prototype that offers a way of expressing data transformation rules through an expert system shell. None of these systems is concerned with the independence between logical and physical data cleaning operations. Recently, [15] has proposed a rigorous approach to the problem of optimizing an ETL process defined as a workflow of data transformation activities. The authors model the ETL optimization problem as a global state-space search problem. In our approach, we use local optimization, since an ETL transformation program must be represented by a set of extended relational algebra expressions to be optimized one at a time. Several RDBMSs, like Microsoft SQL Server, already include additional software packages specific for ETL tasks. However, to the best of our knowledge, the capabilities of relational engines, for example, in terms of optimization opportunities are not fully exploited for ETL tasks.

The second open problem in commercial data cleaning tools is the lack of support for user interaction during the execution of a data cleaning application. In fact, the user interaction may be required to debug the results of data transformations, refine the cleaning criteria enclosed, and manually correct data not automatically transformed. There are two important research areas that permit to fulfill this gap. First, the field of data lineage as studied in [4, 5, 2, 18] offers useful notions for browsing the results of data cleaning transformations. Second, the incremental propagation of changes in the context of view maintenance as studied in [6] supplies the basic notions for efficiently integrating data items manually corrected in the flow of data cleaning transformations.

7   Conclusions

In this paper, we provided a global overview of the AJAX system. The description intends to survey all the design and technical aspects of the system and show in which way they constitute a novelty with respect to the existing technology.

The prototype is currently being used in real-world data migration, transformation and cleaning applications so that exhaustive experimental validation can be produced. Moreover, we plan to improve AJAX functionalities according to the requirements of the application scenarios being tested. More concretely, the specification language is being extended, the mechanism of exceptions for the view operator needs to be reformulated, the debugger mechanism needs to be re-designed in order to handle a large amount of exceptions. Finally, some effort has to be put in the design and implementation of a cost-based optimizer and a graphical interface must be constructed to make it easier to specify the cleaning criteria and visualize the results.

References

1. J. Barateiro and H. Galhardas. A survey of data quality tools. *Datenbank Spektrum*, (14):15–21, August 2005. invited paper.
2. Peter Buneman, Sanjeev Khanna, and Wang-Chiew Tan. Why and Where: A Characterization of Data Provenance. In *Proc. of the International Conference on Database Theory (ICDT)*, 2001.
3. P. Carreira, H. Galhardas, J. Pereira, and A. Lopes. Data mapper: An operator for expressing one-to-many data transformations. In *Proc. of the International Conference on Data Warehousing and Knowledge Discovery (DAWAK)*, 2005.

4. Yingwei Cui and Jennifer Widom. Practical Lineage Tracing in Data Warehouses. In *Proc. of the International Conference on Data Engineering (ICDE)*, 2000.
5. Yingwei Cui and Jennifer Widom. Lineage Tracing for General Data Warehouse Transformations. In *Proc. of the International Conference on Very Large Databases (VLDB)*, 2001.
6. Françoise Fabret. *Optimisation du Calcul Incrémentiel dans les Langages de Règles pour Bases de Données*. PhD thesis, Université de Versailles Saint-Quentin, 1994.
7. Christos Faloutsos, Ron Barber, Myron Flickner, Jim Hafner, Wayne Niblack, Dragutin Petkovic, and William Equit. Efficient and effective querying by image content. *JIIS*, 3(3/4), 1994.
8. H. Galhardas and J. Barateiro. InfoLegada2gB: an application for migrating dam safety information. unpublished.
9. Helena Galhardas. *Nettoyage de Données: Modèle, Langage Déclaratif, et Algorithmes*. PhD thesis, Université de Versailles Saint-Quentin, 2001.
10. Helena Galhardas, Daniela Florescu, Dennis Shasha, and Eric Simon. AJAX: An Extensible Data Cleaning Tool. In W. Chen, J. F. Naughton, and P. A. Bernstein, editors, *Proc. of the ACM SIGMOD International Conference on Management of Data*, volume 2. ACM, 2000. (demonstration paper).
11. Helena Galhardas, Daniela Florescu, Dennis Shasha, Eric Simon, and Cristian-Augustin Saita. Declarative Data Cleaning: Language, Model, and Algorithms. In *Proc. of the International Conference on Very Large Databases (VLDB)*, Rome, Italy, September 2001.
12. Mong Li Lee, Tok Wang Ling, and Wai Lup Low. A Knowledge-Based Framework for Intelligent Data Cleaning. *Information Systems Journal - Special Issue on Data Extraction and Cleaning*, 2001.
13. Gonzalo Navarro. A Guided Tour to Approximate String Matching. *ACM Computing Surveys*, 33(1):31–88, March 2001.
14. Vijayshankar Raman and Joseph M. Hellerstein. Potter's Wheel: An Interactive Data Cleaning System. In *Proc. of the International Conference on Very Large Databases (VLDB)*, Rome, 2001.
15. A. Simitsis, P. Vassiliadis, and T. K. Sellis. Optimizing ETL processes in data warehouses. In *Proc. of the International Conference on Data Engineering (ICDE)*, 2005.
16. T. F. Smith and M. S. Waterman. Identification of common molecular subsequences. *Journal of Molecular Theory*, 147:195–197, 1981.
17. Microsoft Research (Sponsored by) NSF, NASA. CiteSeer.IST. http://citeseer.ist.psu.edu/.
18. Allison Woodruff and Michael Stonebraker. Supporting Fine-Grained Data Lineage in a Database Visualization Environment. In *Proc. of the International Conference on Data Engineering (ICDE)*, 1997.

Developing Tools with Fujaba XProM

Leif Geiger and Albert Zündorf

University of Kassel, Germany
{leif.geiger, albert.zuendorf}@uni-kassel.de
http://www.se.eecs.uni-kassel.de/se/

Abstract. Fujaba is an UML [21] based CASE tool with an emphasis on code generation from graphical behavior specifications. The Fujaba tool is accompanied by the Fujaba process, a systematic approach to use Fujaba for system development [5]. To improve the tool support for the Fujaba process, we have developed the XProM plug-in. This paper exemplifies how the XProM plug-in supports the tool developer in following the Fujaba Process. Main parts of this paper are a tutorial to XProM users. However, the paper is also useful for other CASE tool developers as a guide how developers could be supported. Therefore, we also give some hints, how such a support may be realized. As a running example we use the development of model transformations for a simple statechart editor.

1 Introduction

This paper is an extension of the position paper [8] which first introduced the concepts of the XProM plug-in. This paper elaborates those ideas and applies them to the area of Model Driven Architecture [17]. Especially, we reuse the example of developing a simple statechart editor [9].

This paper has two main targets: First, it is some kind of tutorial showing how the XProM support may be used by potential tool developers. Second, it may serve as some guideline for other CASE tools, which sophisticated process support they could offer. For the latter purpose, we also give some hints on the realization of such a tool support.

The Fujaba Process (FUP) [10] is a modern, iterative, use case driven process employing the test first principle:

- At the start of an iteration, we collect (new) functional requirements within use case diagrams.
- Then each use case is elaborated with the help of text scenarios.
- In the object oriented analysis phase, the steps of the text scenarios are modelled using (extended) object diagrams diagrams. This results in so-called story boards that model the execution of example scenarios.
- During the development of (extended object diagrams, we automatically collect declarations of classes, attributes, methods and associations within a first conceptual class diagram. Usually, this class diagram needs to be revisited in order to adjust e.g. association cardinalities.
- From the conceptual class diagram, Java code frames for the implementation are generated.

R. Lämmel, J. Saraiva, and J. Visser (Eds.): GTTSE 2005, LNCS 4143, pp. 344–356, 2006.

– Next, the story boards are automatically turned into JUnit tests.
– Now, the behavior of our application has to be specified. This may be done by coding Java directly. Alternatively, [4] shows how the behavior specification may be derived from the story boards, systematically.
– Once the implementation is done, all generated tests should be passed. Story board tests that are not yet passed give hints on missing functionality. Code coverage analysis may be used to identify implemented functionality that is not yet used within the example scenarios, cf. [10].

The next section outlines how the XProM plug-in extends the Fujaba tool with dedicated support for the Fujaba Process.

2   The XProM Project Handbook

The XProM plug-in extends Fujaba by a so-called project handbook view. The project handbook view is an HTML based text document with a predefined

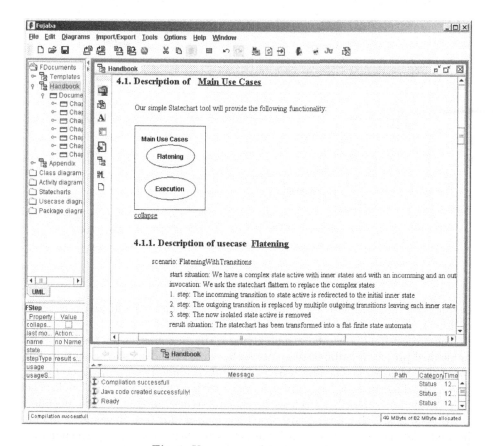

Fig. 1. Use cases and text scenarios

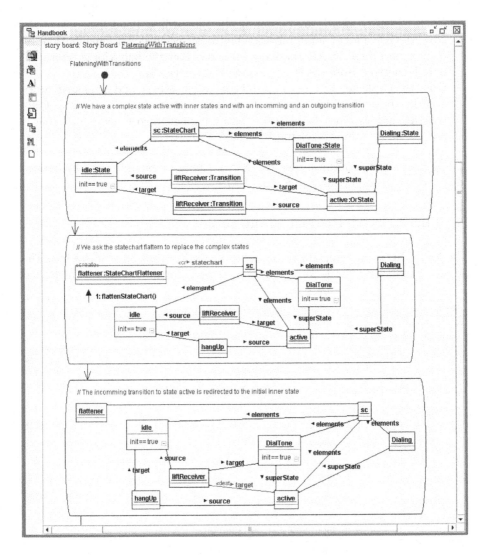

Fig. 2. Story Board First Part

overall structure and with templates for e.g. team members and text scenarios, cf. Fig. 1.

The project handbook allows embedding UML diagrams within the text. The predefined project handbook template embeds use case diagrams in section 4 of the overall handbook. The first use case diagram is found in section 4.1, cf. Fig. 1. The UML diagrams may be edited in-place within the project handbook. The XProM plug-in subscribes itself as listener to structural changes of embedded UML diagrams. Using a template based mechanism, for certain elements of embedded UML Diagrams the XProM plug-in automatically creates corresponding sections within the project handbook. Such sections are filled with documenta-

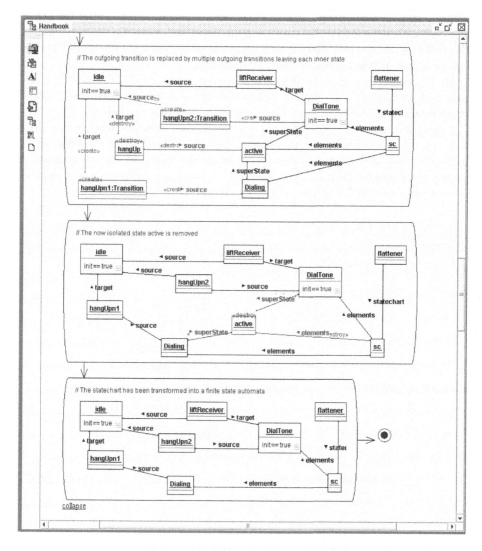

Fig. 3. Story Board Second Part

tion for the corresponding diagram elements or with additional UML diagrams refining the referred element. In Fig. 1, for the use case Flattening the XProM plug-in has automatically created section 4.1.1 containing a template for textual scenario descriptions. In Fig. 1 we have already filled the scenario template with a meaningful scenario description.

For the next step of the Fujaba process, the XProM plug-in provides a command to turn a textual scenario into an initial story board. Figures 2 and 3 show the already completed story board.

Initially, the storyboard consists of an activity diagram with one activity for each scenario step. These activities contain the textual description of the textual scenario step as a comment. Now the developer looks at one step after the other and decides how to model this step using an object structure. To show dynamics, this object structure may include collaboration messages, attribute modifications and creation and destroying of objects and links.

We frequently use story boards to discuss requirements and functionality details with customers and domain experts. For these people scenarios are usually much easier to understand than the implementation of a method.

During editing of the story board, the Fujaba tool asks the developer to provide types for the objects, attributes and links he or she deploys. The developer may either use an existing declaration or he or she may add a new declaration on the fly. These declarations are collected in a conceptual class diagram which is located in section 5.1 of the project handbook, cf. Figure 4.

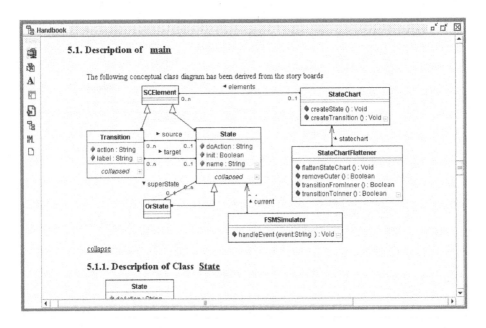

Fig. 4. Derived conceptual class diagram

For each class within a class diagram, the XProM plug-in automatically provides a subsection in the project handbook, e.g. subsection 5.1.1 in Figure 4. This subsection in turn contains subsubsections for each method of that class. If the method behavior is also modeled with Fujaba, this method subsubsection contains the Fujaba rule diagram specifying the method, cf. Figure 5. From class diagrams and method specifications, the Fujaba code generator generates a fully functional implementation of the desired application.

In order to test the implementation, the XProM plug-in provides a command that turns story boards into automatic JUnit tests, cf. [10]. These tests create the object structure modeled as the start situation of the story board. Then they

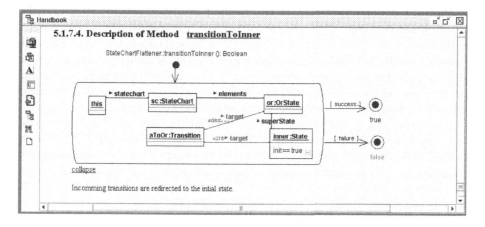

Fig. 5. Behavior Specification for method TransitionToInner

execute the operations of the invocation step and afterwards they compare the resulting runtime object structure with the result situation of the story board. Figure 6 shows a successful run of the test derived from the story board for statechart flattening.

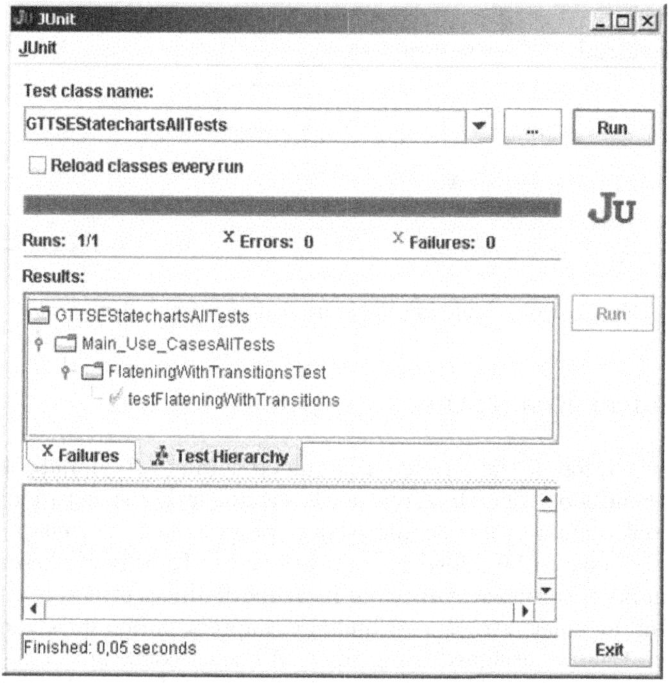

Fig. 6. JUnit test for statechart flattening

During the implementation of the method behavior, developers frequently handle additional cases that are not part of the provided scenarios. Due to our experience, it is a good idea to discuss such additional cases with customers and domain experts, too. Thus the developers should provide additional scenarios and story boards that exemplify these cases. In order to find behavior implementation or specification that is not yet triggered by an scenario, we employ a coverage tool which analyzes the execution of the generated JUnit tests.

As a prototyping environment and as a debugging aid, the Fujaba environment provides the Dynamic Object Browser DOBS. In case of a JUnit test failure, we automatically open DOBS and let it depict the actual runtime object structure as a UML object diagram. This runtime object diagram is then easily compared with the result situation of the corresponding story board which usually facilitates to identify the problem, very easily.

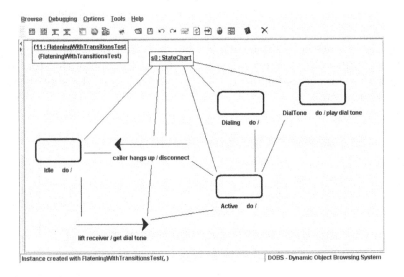

Fig. 7. Dobs depicting the start situation for a JUnit test

3 Technical Realization

As stated in section 2, the developer is guided through the Fujaba Process by the project handbook. Therefore, one needs a configurable, structured handbook. The handbook should evolve during project progress, e.g. new chapters for use case scenarios have to be added for new use cases. To achieve these goals, our project handbook is represented by an in-memory object structure as shown in Figure 8. Our document structure is build by chapters, paragraphs, and diagrams etc. This structure is designed using the well known composite design pattern. This allows arbitrary nesting of chapters and paragraphs. For the embedding of UML diagrams we use adapter objects of type FDiagram.

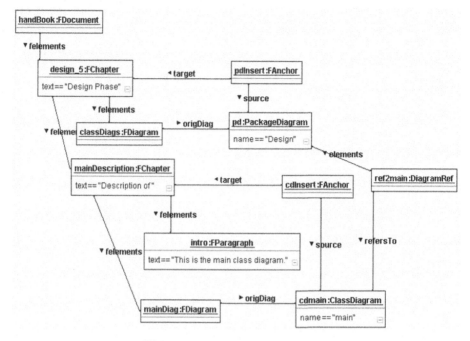

Fig. 8. XProM document structure

For the graphical user interface we use a standard HTML editor coming with the build-in java swing libraries, cf. Figure 9. This editor allows to compose an HTML document out of editable and frozen blocks. Usual HTML links may be used for cross referencing. In case of changes to the object structure, individual blocks of the HTML documents may be modified, added, or removed. In addition, block ids and a listener concept allow to propagate textual changes back to our object structure.

The XProM project handbook exploits the relationships between different parts and diagrams of the overall project handbook in two ways. First, we generate HTML links that allow to use these relationships for navigation. Second, the creation of a new item in one diagram may cause the creation of a new document chapter for the description of that diagram element.

In the example of Figure 9 the design chapter 5 contains a package diagram giving an overview of contained class diagrams. In the example, only one entry for the class diagram `main` is contained.

Now we want that the addition of an element to e.g. the package diagram causes the insertion of a describing chapter with a certain structure in the handbook. Therefore, we employ objects of type `FAnchor`, cf. Figure 8. `FAnchor` objects subscribe as listeners to UML diagrams. As soon as a new element is added to that diagram, the `FAnchor` retrieves an appropriate template for that type of element. The `FAnchor` has a `target` chapter where the template is appended to the content.

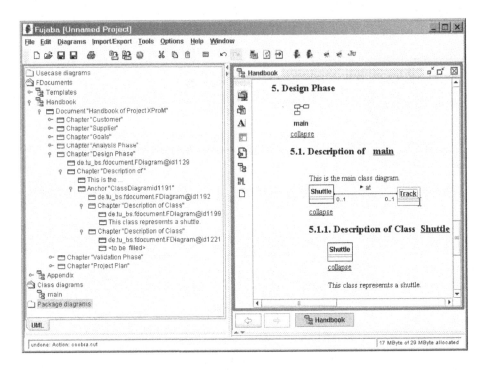

Fig. 9. XProM GUI with HTML based editor

The templates are of course modeled using the same object structures as the final document. This allows the editing of templates using the same HTML editor as used for the actual document. The composite structure provides a clone mechanism to facilitate template copying. In the example of Figure 8 the objects `mainDescription`, `intro`, `cdInsert` and `mainDiag` are clones from a template for `DiagramRef` elements. The `cdmain` object belongs to the logical structure of the UML model. The template contains a dummy diagram as a placeholder. During template instantiation, this dummy diagram has been replaced by the already existing `cdmain` diagram. The `cdmain` diagram has been identified via the predefined `refersTo` edge of the `ref2main` object. `refersTo` edges are generally used for cross referencing in our approach. Although this template mechanism is quite limited, it worked quite well for our purpose so far.

Concerning scaling one has to discuss two aspects: scaling of the project and scaling of the project team. For larger projects, the XProM project is easily split into multiple documents for different (sub)chapters. The template mechanism is working with multiple documents, too. However, currently all these documents need to be in main memory. Therefore, we are developing support for on-demand loading of subdocuments. This would allow to have one common document containing e.g. the class diagram and many separated documents e.g. for different use cases. Ideally, only one use case document and the common document would be needed simultaneously. This will allow to deal with very large projects.

In addition, Fujaba and XProM already provide multi user support based on versioning with optimistic locking and automatic merging, cf. [18]. This enables concurrent work of multiple team members on the same (sub)documents. This has been tested with large success in numerous student projects and in our own research projects.

4   Related Work

To some extend, the Rational Unified Process RUP [12] summarizes the state-of-the-art in modern software development processes. However, the RUP focuses on project organization aspects. It gives only little technical guidance how a certain use case is related to certain scenario descriptions and how such scenario descriptions are turned into interaction diagrams. The RUP does not explain how interaction diagrams are turned into automatic JUnit tests. It gives only little guidance how a class diagram and actual behavior specifications are derived and how these elements are related to each other.

Our process defines fine-grained relationships e.g. between the steps of a textual scenario description and the corresponding parts of a UML interaction diagram, i.e story boards. This idea stems from the IPSEN project, cf. [16]. Similarly, we provide fine grained relationships between story boards and JUnit tests and the methods that implement the outlined functionalities. In order to make these relationships visible for the developers, the XProM plug-in embeds the various diagrams in the pre-defined structure of a project handbook and it provides the corresponding cross referencing functionality. This embedding and cross linking of system description parts in a textual document is related to the ideas of literate programming, cf. [13, 14]. Accordingly, the template based process support that is provided by the XProM plug-in may be considered as an extension of the idea of literate programming. It would be interesting to try to establish similar project support for purely textual project specifications.

The support provided by XProM is based on the fine grained relationships between the different UML diagrams and diagram elements. In our approach, we define quite rigorous relationships between the different parts of the different UML diagrams. This goes far beyond the usual UML definitions [2] and beyond the relationships provided by the rational unified process. Since the usual UML standards do not contain such fine grained cross diagram relationships, most current UML tools do not provide such a support, either, cf. e.g. Poseidon, Rational Rose, Rhapsody, MagicDraw. Notable exceptions are the areas of requirements traceability as provided e.g. by the DOORS tool, cf. [6]. Tool chains that employ the requirements tool DOORS, frequently use the requirements ids provided by DOORS as tags in subsequent project documents. This provides fine-grained links between subsequent project artifacts and the requirements documents. In addition, most UML tools do provide fine-grained connections between the class diagrams and the various kinds of interaction diagrams. These relationships are used for consistency checking. Another frequently provided, fine-grained inter diagram relation connects statecharts to their place of use. For example, statecharts may be connected to active classes that will contain the generated code for that statechart. Or in ROOM diagrams, component ports may be connected to a statechart defining the protocol for the usage of that port, cf. [19].

Our exploitation of story boards for the generation of automatic JUnit tests has been inspired by different ideas from the area of statechart synthesis from scenarios. There exists some body of work trying to analyse e.g. sequence diagrams and to derive statecharts for the participating objects that realize at least the example behavior, cf. [20, 7, 11, 3]. These approaches employ fine-grained relationships between diagram elements of scenarios and of generated statecharts, too. Actually, we have also done some work in this area [15]. However, based on our experiences, very elaborated scenarios are required in order to generate meaningful behavior specifications, automatically. Frequently, these scenarios become somewhat artificial in order to serve the synthesis algorithms. Thus, in this work, we decided to exploit the scenarios only for the generation of JUnit tests.

5   Summary

This paper outlines the tool support provided by the Fujaba XProM plug-in for the Fujaba Process. XProM provides an editable view for a template based project handbook. The UML diagrams of the corresponding project are embedded in dedicated sections of the project handbook. Adding elements to the diagrams automatically adds corresponding description sections to the project handbook. Initially such sections may contain ToDo items. Thereby, the project handbook drives the development process and depicts the overall project state throughout the whole project life cycle. In addition, the interconnection between the different project handbook sections from earlier and later phases handles the consistency of all project artifacts.

For 3 years, we have used Fujaba and XProM in our UML courses with roughly 100 students per course. The courses are mandatory in the students second year. In these courses, we have observed that the XProM plug-in does an excellent job in guiding the students through the development process. We use an initial training round to give the students an idea of the overall process and of the role of the different project handbook sections. After that, the students quickly adapt the process and develop extended textual scenarios and story boards. They actually invest a lot of work in this phase since the story boards are simultaneously analysis aids and test specifications. These tests then drive the implementation work.

Since one and a half year, we employ the Fujaba process also with great success in an industrial project. In that project, object diagrams and story boards have proven to be extremely valuable for discussions with domain experts in this case electrical engineers. After a very short learning curve, the electrical engineers came up with their own object scenarios in order to point us to special cases and problems that we had not yet considered. With the help of the DOBS tool, these electrical engineers where even able to analyze test failures and to point us to failure causes. Overall, in that project the usage of object diagrams and story boards for analysis and test specification and the Fujaba tool support was the key to success.

With the help of the CoObRA plug-in, Fujaba XProM allows versioning of projects and provides support for concurrent development in developer teams, cf. [18]. CoObRA also protocols time and amount of contributions of different team members. Since the different sections of the project handbook contain work belonging to different phases of the Fujaba process, it should be possible to identify which developer worked how long on which use case in which process phase and how large his contribution was. Such statistical data may provide a basis for size and cost estimations for new functionalities based on the size and complexity of the corresponding scenarios and story boards. This would allow to estimate the time required to complete remaining development tasks and to compare estimated and actual efforts. Thereby the XProM plug-in may provide sophisticated support for Xtreme Project Management.

References

1. K. Beck. Extreme Programming Explained: Embrace Change. Addison-Wesley Publishing Company, 1999.
2. Grady Booch, James E. Rumbaugh, Ivar Jacobson: The Unified Modeling Language User Guide. Addison-Wesley, ISBN 0-201-57168-4, 1999
3. Yves Bontemps and Alexander Egyed (eds): proc. 4th International Workshop on Scenarios and State Machines: models, algorithms and tools; ICSE 2005
4. I. Diethelm, L. Geiger, A. Zündorf: Systematic Story Driven Modeling, a case study; Workshop on Scenarios and state machines: models, algorithms, and tools; ICSE 2004, Edinburgh, Scottland, May 24 28 (2004).
5. I. Diethelm, L. Geiger, and A. Zündorf: Applying Story Driven Modeling to the Paderborn Shuttle System Case Study; book chapter in S. Leue and T.J. Syst (Eds.): Scenarios, LNCS 3466, pp. 109133, Springer-Verlag Berlin Heidelberg (2005).
6. http://www.telelogic.com/corp/products/doors/doors/
7. Alexander Egyed, Martin Glinz, Ingolf Krger, Tarja Syst, Sebastin Uchitel, Albert Zndorf (eds.): proc. Second Workshop on Scenarios and State Machines: Models, Algorithms, and Tools; ICSE 2003
8. Leif Geiger and Christian Schneider and Albert Zündorf: Integrated, Document Centered Modelling in Fujaba; in 1st International Fujaba Days, Kassel, Germany, October 13-14 (2003)
9. L. Geiger, A. Zündorf: Statechart Modeling with Fujaba; 2nd International Workshop on Graph-Based Tools (GraBaTs); ICGT 2004, Rom, Italy, September 28 October 2 (2004).
10. Leif Geiger, Albert Zündorf: Story Driven Testing; in proc. 4th International Workshop on Scenarios and State Machines: Models, Algorithms and Tools (SCESM'05) ICSE 2005 Workshop
11. Holger Giese and Ingolf Krger (eds): proc. Third Workshop on Scenarios and State Machines: Models, Algorithms, and Tools; ICSE 2004
12. I. Jacobson, G. Booch, and J. Rumbaugh: The Unified Software Development Process; Addison-Wesley Publishing Company, 1999.
13. Donald E. Knuth: Literate Programming; Comput. J. 27(2): 97-111 (1984)

14. http://www.literateprogramming.com/
15. T.Maier, A. Zndorf: The Fujaba Statechart Synthesis Approach. in proc. Workshop on Scenarios and State Machines; ICSE 2003, Portland, Oregon, USA, May 2003
16. M. Nagl (ed.): Building Thightly-Integrated (Software) Development Environments: The IPSEN Approach, LNCS 1170, Berlin: Springer Verlag (1996)
17. The Object Management Group; http://www.omg.org/
18. C. Schneider, A. Zündorf, J. Niere: CoObRA - a small step for development tools to collaborative environments; Workshop on Directions in Software Engineering Environments; 26th international conference on software engineering, Scotland, UK 2004
19. Bran Selic, Garth Gullekson, Paul T. Ward: Real-Time Object-Oriented Modeling; Wiley, ISBN: 0471599174, 1994
20. Sebastin Uchitel, Tarja Syst, Albert Zndorf (eds.): proc. Workshop Scenarios and state machines: models, algorithms, and tools; ICSE, (2002)
21. The Unified Modeling Language; http://www.uml.org/

The COMPOST, COMPASS, Inject/J and RECODER Tool Suite for Invasive Software Composition: Invasive Composition with COMPASS Aspect-Oriented Connectors

Dirk Heuzeroth[1], Uwe Aßmann[2], Mircea Trifu[3], and Volker Kuttruff[3]

[1] www.dirk-heuzeroth.de
[2] TU Dresden, Germany
[3] FZI Karlsruhe, Germany

Abstract. Program analyses and transformations are means to support program evolution and bridge architectural mismatches in component composition. The Program Structures Group at the University of Karlsruhe und the FZI Karlsruhe, that we are or have been members of, have developed a suite of program analysis and transformation tools to attack these problems.

The basic tool Recoder offers sophisticated source code analyses and a library of common transformations in the form of Java meta programs to perform necessary component and interaction adapations. This library can be extended by the Recoder framework that offers means for implementing custom transformations. A transformation can also be a generator to produce glue code, for example.

Inject/J uses Recoder and offers a comfortable scripting language for implementing transformations. The scripting language combines declarative specifications of the program points, where the transformation should be applied, with imperative specifications of the transformation itself.

COMPASS is focused on bridging interaction mismatches among software components. It introduces architectural elements like components, ports and aspect-oriented connectors as source code transformations based on the Recoder framework.

COMPOST defines the general model of invasive software composition, where the ports of the COMPASS model are just one kind of hooks. Hooks are join points, i.e. part of a component that may be extended or replaced.

1 Introduction

Software systems evolve due to changing requirements. This evolution mostly comprises changing the programs' source code, because the new requirements have not been anticipated. Examples are performance tuning and deployment of the system in a new infrastructure requiring other interaction mechanisms. Source code adaptations are also often necessary when composing independently

R. Lämmel, J. Saraiva, and J. Visser (Eds.): GTTSE 2005, LNCS 4143, pp. 357–377, 2006.

developed components that do not completely fit each other, because of *architectural mismatches* [7], i. e., the components make different assumptions on how to interact with each other.

Indeed, program evolution very often concerns adapting component interactions. In this paper we therefore focus on source code transformations to perform the necessary interaction adaptations automatically. The underlying concept of our program adaptation approach is called *invasive software composition* [2]. It is implemented as the COMPOST (COMPOsition SysTem) framework [3]. Section 4 describes the details. As a basic infrastructure to perform automated program transformations serves our Recoder framework [24, 23]. It offers sophisticated source code analyses, a library of program transformations and means to implement custom program transformations. Section 3 introduces the concepts, design and features of Recoder. Recoder does not provide comfortable means to realize interactive transformations as well as to declaratively specify the program points where to apply transformations. These tasks are facilitated by the scripting language Inject/J [9], introduced in Section 5. All three tools Recoder, Inject/J and COMPOST are quite general program transformation tools none of which is tailored to perform interaction adaptations. This is why we have developed the COMPASS tool [12, 14, 13]. COMPASS offers means to bridge interaction mismatches among software components. It defines architectural elements like components, ports and aspect-oriented connectors as source code transformations based on the Recoder framework and as specialization of the COMPOST framework. Section 6 presents the concepts and features of COMPASS.

To enable reuse of transformations all our tools offer extensible libraries to collect the transformations implemented in the respective tool frameworks.

Figure 1 illustrates the relations among the four tools Recoder, Inject/J, COMPOST and COMPASS. COMPASS directly builds on Recoder to perform transformations, instead of using Inject/J, since COMPASS needs the comprehensive program model and Inject/J only offers an abstracted program model.

Before we start explaining the tools, we first introduce a running example (cf. Section 2 that we will use to demonstrate the concepts and features of the program transformation tools.

2   Running Example: Interaction Adaptation

In the remainder of the paper we use the adaptation of the communication in a very simple producer-consumer-system as example. We will transform the producer-consumer-system such that the direct communication of the product from the producer component to the consumer component by a method call is replaced by transferring the product via a buffer component. Such a change may arise from the requirement of increasing the concurrency in the system. Since turning the producer and consumer components into active ones is very easy to achieve in Java just letting both of them inherit from the Thread class and

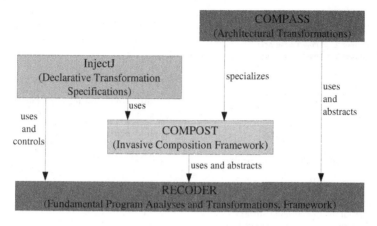

Fig. 1. The relations among the Recoder, Inject/J, COMPOST and COMPASS tools

adding a run method to both of them, we dispense with discussing this step and focus on exchanging the interaction mechanism replacing the direct call by interaction via a buffer.

Given is the following Java source code of a very simple producer-consumer-system:

```java
class Trader {
    public static void main(String[] args) {
        Consumer c = new Consumer();
        Producer p = new Producer(c);
        p.produce();
    }
}

class Producer {
    private Consumer consumer;

    public Producer(Consumer c) {
        consumer = c;
    }
    public void produce() {
        Product p = new Product();
        System.out.println(p+"_produced.");
        consumer.consume(p);
    }
}

class Consumer {
    public void consume(Product prod) {
        System.out.println(prod + "_consumed.");
    }
}
```

The Trader component represents the main program that makes the Consumer component instance known to the Producer component instance such that the latter can invoke the consume service of the Consumer component instance. The Trader drives the system by calling the produce method of the Producer object. The communication of the product from the producer to the consumer is initiated by the producer. The producer thus drives the interaction with the consumer.

The target system we aim to achieve as a result is represented by the following source code:

```java
class Trader {
  public static void main(String[] args) {
    Buffer b = new Buffer();
    Consumer c = new Consumer();
    Producer p = new Producer();

    p.setProductBuffer(b);
    c.setProductBuffer(b);

    p.produce();
  }
}

class Producer {
  private ProductBuffer productBuffer;

  public Producer() { }

  public void setProductBuffer(
      ProductBuffer productBuffer) {
    this.productBuffer = productBuffer;
  }

  public void produce() {
    Product p = new Product();
    System.out.println(p+"produced.");
    productBuffer.put(p);
  }
}
```

```java
class Consumer {
  private ProductBuffer productBuffer;

  public Consumer() { }

  public void setProductBuffer(
      ProductBuffer productBuffer) {
    this.productBuffer = productBuffer;
  }

  public void consume() {
    Product prod = productBuffer.get();
    System.out.println(prod + "consumed.");
  }
}

class ProductBuffer {
  Vector contents = new Vector();

  public BufferProduct() {}

  public Product get() {
    Object p = contents.firstElement();
    contents.removeElementAt(0);
    return (Product)p;
  }

  public void put(Product p) {
    contents.add(p);
  }
}
```

Obviously, we have to perform many invasive modifications to replace the interaction mechanism. The remaining sections discuss these modifications in detail and show how we support them by a tool. In this special case, the tool can perform the changes fully automatically.

3   The **Recoder** Tool and Framework

Recoder is a Java framework for source code meta-programming aimed to deliver a sophisticated infrastructure for many kinds of Java analysis and transformation tools, especially our tools Inject/J, COMPOST and COMPASS. The Recoder system allows to parse and analyze Java programs, transform the sources and write the results back into source code form. Figure 2 a) illustrates this cycle.

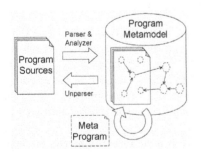

Fig. 2 a). The Recoder meta programming cycle

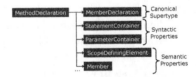

Fig. 2 b). The Recoder model for properties of a syntactic element.

3.1   The **Recoder** Program Model

To enable meta programming, Recoder derives a meta model from the entities encountered in Java source code and class files. This model contains a detailed syntactic program model (including comments) that can be unparsed with only minimal losses. The syntactic model is an attributed syntax tree (in fact a graph), where each element has links to its children as well as to its parent, in order to support efficient upward navigation. All properties of a syntactic element are modeled by corresponding types, i.e., the element has to implement the corresponding interfaces. Figure 2 b) shows this for a method declaration as an example.

The core part of the Recoder meta model is located in `recoder.abstraction` and primarily consists of entities that occur in an API documentation: Types, Variables, Methods, Packages, with some additional abstractions such as Member or ClassTypeContainer. These entities inherit from **ProgramModelElement**.

While many ProgramModelElements have a syntactic representation, the `recoder.abstraction` package also contains entities that have no syntactic representation at all, but are implicitly defined. Examples are ArrayType, DefaultConstructor, or the aforementioned Package. Figure 3 shows the elements of this abstract model and their associations.

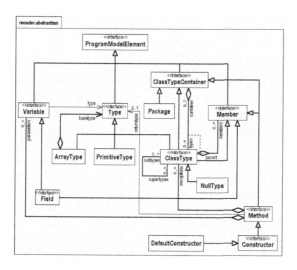

Fig. 3. The elements of the Recoder abstract model

While the syntactic model provides only the containment relation between elements, the complete model adds further relations, such as type-of, or refers-to, as well as some implicitly defined elements, such as packages or primitive types.

In order to derive this semantic information, Recoder runs a type and name analysis which resolves references to logical entities. The refers-to relation can be made bidirectional for full cross referencing which is necessary for efficient global transformations.

To construct the refers-to relation completely, Recoder was designed to be able to parse both source code as well as bytecode — when parsing bytecode, only declarations are read. Recoder does not perform a complete decompilation. In order to differentiate between model elements from source code and model elements from bytecode, Recoder maintains two class sub-hierarchies implementing interfaces from `recoder.abstraction`, one for source elements and one for bytecode elements. The topmost type for syntactic Java source elements is `recoder.java.SourceElement`, while the root of the bytecode elements sub-hierarchy is `recoder.bytecode.ByteCodeElement`.

Recoder was originally developed for Java 1.2 and constantly updated to the latest versions of the language. The currently available Recoder release is fully compatible with Java 1.4, but a sustained effort to include the Java 5 features autoboxing, methods with variable arity, static imports, enhanced for loops, enumeration types, annotations and generics is already underway.

A common trait of the new Java language features is that they define shorthands (implicit code) translated by the compiler into Java 1.4 style code. The challenge here is to find a balance between modeling this implicit code explicitly, thus adhering to the Recoder philosophy, or to preserve its original syntactical representation.

3.2   Recoder Program Transformations

Recoder program transformations operate on syntax trees. Basic transformations are attach that attaches a node or subtree to an existing node or tree, and detach that detaches a node or subtree from an existing tree. The central `ChangeHistory` service collects all change objects (performed attach and detach operations) and notifies the registered services that are responsible for keeping the program model consistent. The model is not rebuilt for every change operation, instead the services only update the model when a new model query arrives. This minimizes the number of costly model updates. Unless committed a transformation can also be rolled back. Figure 4 illustrates the interconnection of change reporting services (`SourceFileRepository` service and `Transformation` class) and model maintaining services (`SourceFileRepository`, `NameInfo`, `SourceInfo`, `CrossReferencer`) with the change history service.

Before a transformation is performed, its applicability has to be checked. This is done during an analysis phase that also collects the information necessary to perform the transformation. If the analysis phase indicates that the transformation can be performed without problems, the consecutive transformation phase performs the changes. This two pass transformation protocol ensures that a transformation is always based on valid information. This is especially required for composed transformations. Otherwise, results obtained by a model query may have been invalidated by a transformation step as a side effect, so that another transformation step of the composed transformation uses invalid information and will therefore corrupt the program.

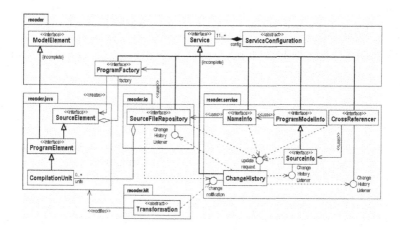

Fig. 4. Connection of Recoder services to ensure model consistency

3.3   Using Recoder

Recoder meta programs are written as follows, using our running example.

```
// Create a service configuration, first:
ServiceConfiguration serviceConfig = new CrossReferenceServiceConfiguration();

// Get the file management service:
SourceFileRepository sfr = serviceConfig.getSourceFileRepository();

// Get the program factory service:
ProgramFactory pf = serviceConfig.getProgramFactory();

try { // parse file
    CompilationUnit cu = sfr.getCompilationUnitFromFile("ProducerConsumer.java");
} catch (ParserException pe) {
    // do something
}

// Create a new syntax tree for the ProductBuffer class:
TypeDeclaration td = pf.parseTypeDeclaration("class ProductBuffer { ... }");

// Create a custom transformation object:
Transformation t = new Transformation(serviceConfig) { };

// Add the declaration of the ProductBuffer class to the compilation unit:
t.attach(td, cu);

// Similar actions for the remaining adaptation steps...

// Write the changes back to file:
PrettyPrinter pp =
    pf.getPrettyPrinter(new PrintWriter(
    new FileWriter("ProducerConsumerTransformed.java")));
cu.accept(pp);
```

3.4   Conclusion

A pure Recoder meta program to perform the transformation task of our running example is quite too complex to demonstrate here. Instead, we use the

Recoder infrastructure to construct special complex transformations to solve this task. These transformations are part of the COMPASS tool and framework (cf. Section 6). The conceptual framework is defined by invasive composition implemented as the COMPOST framework introduced in Section 4. COMPASS specializes this framework.

4   Invasive Composition and COMPOST

The idea of *invasive composition* is to compose software components by invasively modifying them using automated program transformations. The underlying model consists of the following three general elements:

box components: Represent program units to be composed. A box is a collection of program elements like a package, some compilation units, a single compilation unit, several classes or a single class. A box component maintains a set of hooks as composition interface.

hooks: Technically, a hook is a set of program elements, too. In contrast to a box, a hook always refers to a containing box. The hook's program elements are a subset of the program elements of this box. Conceptually, a hook is a join point, that identifies a part of a component that may be extended or replaced.

composers: A composer is a program transformer which transforms composables, either boxes or hooks.

Thus, invasive composition adapts or extends components at their hooks by program transformations.

4.1   Boxes

Boxes are organized in form of the composite pattern, i.e. they constitute a hierarchy of components. Each composition system (i.e. each project) has one root box. There are

– composite boxes which contain composition programs and other subboxes
– atomic boxes which consist of hand-written Java code.

Each composite box in the box hierarchy carries a composition program by which all subboxes are composed and configured. Atomic boxes do not carry composition programs.

4.2   Hooks

Box components can be configured in complex ways by program transformations. Box writers can indicate where such transformations can be applied, using the concept of *hooks*. A hook is a set of program elements that constitute a join point, identifying a part of a component that may be extended or replaced.

Hooks can be described by

- context-free or context-sensitive patterns which can be matched in the abstract syntax of a box and be replaced. The patterns may be term patterns or graph patterns. Then the hook is a reducible expression (redex) of the pattern in the program's representation.
- selection queries on the program's representations. The query language may be any language that can query graphs, such as Datalog, Prolog, OQL, or a graph database query language. Then the hook is a query result, typically a set of program elements.
- names. A rather simple kind of hooks are named program elements. The appropriate query would just look for a name and result in one program element.

Hooks are further classified into declared and implicit hooks.

Declared (Explicit) hooks denote a certain code position with a name.

Implicit hooks are hooks that are given by the programming language implicitly (here Java). Implicit hooks refer to a syntax element which can be qualified (a compilation unit, a class, a method). Each hook carries its name, and also a qualifier which determines its position in the component. Since implicit hooks need not be declared, the hook name is not a naming scheme, but the name of the hook itself; the hook qualifier plays the role of the naming scheme.

4.3 Composers

A composer is a program transformer which transforms composables, either boxes or hooks. Figure 5 illustrates the effect of a composer.

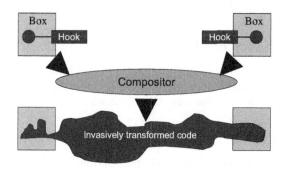

Fig. 5. The effect of a COMPOST composer

General classification criteria for composers are

- taking composables, i.e. hooks or boxes, as arguments (hook-based or box-based)
- unary, binary, n-ary
- elementary or composed

Composers for Hooks. The most important unary composer on hooks is the *bind composer*: It overwrites the hook. If it was a declared hook the hook is eliminated, i.e. cannot be rewritten anymore. Implicit hooks cannot be eliminated from the boxes since they are defined by the programming language semantics.

Composers for list hooks are:

extend: Extends a box or a hook with a mixin box or a value.
append: Appends a value to the hook and retains the hook. (Also for point hooks in list hooks)
prepend: Prepends a value to the hook and retains the hook. (Also for point hooks in list hooks)
wrap: List hooks can be wrapped with two values. The first is prepended, the second appended.
extract: Delete an element of a list hook or a point hook completely.

Composers on Boxes (Box-Based Composers). Boxes can be composed themselves without referring to their hooks. Such composers refer to the boxes' hooks implicitly; not all hook operations are applicable.

Composition Programs and Composition Terms. COMPOST is a Java library. When composers of this library are applied on boxes and hooks, composition programs in Java result. These composition programs create composition terms from composers and their arguments, as well as forests of composition terms, i.e. composition forests.

Composition terms are one of the central data structures of COMPOST since they describe compositions abstractly. Each object in a composition forest represents a composition operation, i.e. an application of a composer, and represents a Command object in terms of the design pattern Command [6].

4.4   Implementation of COMPOST

Boxes, hooks and composers are implemented as Java objects. The program elements that boxes and hooks represent are the program element objects offered by Recoder. Composers are Recoder transformations.

4.5   Using COMPOST

Composition programs which use the library should be written as in the following. Composition operations have the calling schema

Unary hooks: `<box>.findHook(HookName).<composer>(Code)`
Binary composers: `<composer>(HookName1, HookName2)`

Currently, only named hooks can be replaced by COMPOST composers. To find a hook, the hook name has to be handed over to the hook finder (`box.findHook(String)`). The hook's name is qualified with the scopes of the program in which it is contained. Qualification is by dot (.).

For our running example the composition program looks like the following.

```
// Prepare the composition by allocating a composition system with
// im- and exporter and all necessary services.
CompositionSystem project = new CompositionSystem(basepath);

// Load the box ProducerConsumer from file ProducerConsumer.coc
CompilationUnitBox pc = new CompilationUnitBox(project ,"ProducerConsumer");


// This sets lazy mode with composers as command objects and
// deferred transformations
project.setLazyMode();

// Re-compose the Producer and Consumer classes.
try {
  // Add "set" method for reference to ProductBuffer to Consumer
  pc.findHook("Consumer.members").prepend("public void setProductBuffer(
      ProductBuffer productBuffer) {
          this.productBuffer = productBuffer;
      }");

  // Add default constructor to Consumer class
  pc.findHook("Consumer.members").prepend("public Consumer() { }");

  // Add private attribute to refer to ProductBuffer to Consumer class
  pc.findHook("Consumer.members").prepend("private ProductBuffer productBuffer;");

  // Remove parameter from Consumer's consume method
  pc.findHook("Consumer.consume.parameters").extract("prod");

  // Add call to get method of buffer component
  pc.findHook("Consumer.consume.statements").prepend("Product prod = productBuffer.get();");

  // similar actions to adapt the Trader and Producer classes as well as to
  // insert the ProductBuffer class.

  // In lazy mode, this executes the transformations
  pc.execute();

  // Export the Producer-Consumer Box again
  // (Default is to ProducerConsumer.java)
  project.getBoxInfo().default.Export();

} catch (Exception e) {
  System.out.println("error: composition failed. ");
}
```

In our example, `project.setLazyMode()` sets lazy mode. By default, all compositions are directly executed on the abstract syntax tree of the box components (eager mode). In lazy mode, only composer command objects are built. When the method `pc.execute()` is called, the composer command objects are executed, and the transformations are committed in the abstract syntax tree.

4.6   Conclusion

Although we have omitted some composition operations, our composition program has still become quite complex. Before we elaborate on the complex transformations to simplify the task of replacing the direct method call by communication via a buffer (Section 6), we first introduce the scripting language Inject/J that offers means to control Recoder analyses and transformations (Section 5). Inject/J is introduced at this place, because it is also built on top of the Recoder infrastructure but only uses the conceptual framework of invasive composition, opposed to COMPASS that specializes the boxes, hooks and composers of COM-POST.

5 The Inject/J Tool

Inject/J is an operational, dynamically typed scripting language and a tool for invasive composition. It is indented to support arbitrary adaptations of Java programs. It offers means to control the analyses and transformations of Recoder and therefore provides the following operations:

Navigation with *detection patterns* and *name patterns* over the Inject/J adaptation model, which is a simplified structure graph (simplified with respect to the program model of Recoder). Detection patterns are arbitrary graph patterns selecting different program model elements based on structural and quantitative (e.g. metrics) constraints. Name patterns are used to select named program elements using regular expressions.

Example: `classes('mypackage.*')` selects all classes within package mypackage, while `method('**.*(int)')` selects all methods with a parameter of type `int`.

Transformations are used to manipulate the Inject/J model. Inject/J offers complex transformations, i.e. transformations which group semantically connected syntactic operations and hides them behind an interface. If necessary, additional transformations like expression flattening are performed automatically. These complex transformations are generally guarded by pre- and postconditions. Inject/J comes with an extensive library of these transformations which range from refactorings (e.g. `rename`) to operations known from AOP (e.g. `beforeAccess`, `afterFailure`).

Control structures like loops and if-statements are used to control the transformation. Conditions in control structures can access model queries (analyses), which are side effect free predicates and functions over the Inject/J adaptation model.

User interaction can be used to interactively parameterize transformations, e.g. to ask for the name of a new class or a temporary variable:

`ask("Please␣choose␣a␣name␣for␣a␣temporary␣variable", name);`

Inject/J provides an extension mechanism which can be used to seamlessly integrate new transformations and model queries in addition to the predefined ones. These new transformations and model queries can either be implemented using the Inject/J script language or by a Java implementation which has direct access to the Recoder framework.

For a more detailed description of Inject/J, please consult [10].

5.1 Using Inject/J

Inject/J scripts are written as follows, using our running example.

```
script IntroduceBuffer {

  // search Producer/Consumer classes
  producerClass = class('Producer').get(0);
  consumerClass = class('Consumer').get(0);
  // search produce/consume methods
  produceMethod = producerClass.getMethod("produce()");
  consumeMethod = consumerClass.getMethod("consume(java.lang.Object)");

  // Introduce new members to Producer class, e.g. reference to the
  // new buffer
  producerClass.addToMembers (${
    ProductBuffer productBuffer;

    public void setProductBuffer(ProductBuffer productBuffer) {
      this.productBuffer = productBuffer;
    }
  }$);

  // remove references to Consumer class
  foreach att in producerClass.attributes do {
    if (att.staticType==consumerClass){
      // remove the assignment in the constructor and
      // the call to the consume method
      foreach ref in att.references do { ref.delete; }
      att.delete;
    }
  }
  foreach par in produceMethod.parameters do {
    if (par.staticType==consumerClass) { par.delete; }
  }

  // add call to buffer to body of produce method:
  produceMethod.beforeExit (${productBuffer.put(p);}$);

  // introduce new members to Consumer Class
  consumerClass.addToMembers( ${
    ProductBuffer productBuffer;

    public void setProductBuffer(ProductBuffer productBuffer) {
      this.productBuffer = productBuffer;
    }
  }$);

  // remove parameter from consume method:
  productClass = class('Product').get(0);
  foreach par in consumeMethod.parameters do {
    if (par.staticType==productClass) { par.delete; }
  }

  // add call to buffer to body of consume method:
  consumeMethod.beforeEntry (${"Product␣p␣=␣productBuffer.get(p);"}$);
} // end of script
```

5.2   Conclusion

Using the Inject/J script language, the transformation to replace the direct method call by communication via a buffer is much simpler (only 53 lines of code including comments and blank lines) than implementing the transformation directly using the underlying Recoder infrastructure. Like the Recoder transformation, the Inject/J transformation can also be reused and applied to other Java classed than the ones of the running example. To do this, one has just to change the search for classes and methods at the beginning of the script or provide this information via parameters. This way the script can be used to perform the transformation multiple times on arbitrary Java source code, even very large source code.

Since Inject/J has been designed as a general purpose transformation language, it does not model complex component interactions as first class entities as needed to consistently adapt interactions. In the next section we therefore present the COMPASS tool tailored to perform such types of program transformations.

6   The **COMPASS** Tool and Framework

COMPASS (COMPosition with AspectS) [12, 14, 13] is designed to consistently exchange and adapt interactions among software units. It is based on an architectural model consisting of the three levels depicted in Figure 6 a).

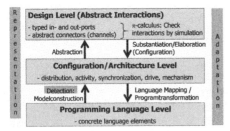

Fig. 6 a). Interaction Configuration Levels

Fig. 6 b). Configuration Level Elements, their Structure and their Links to Source Code

- The *programming language level* contains the concrete program to adapt. So the first step of COMPASS transformations is the *detection phase (model construction)* that analyzes the source code to identify components, their interactions and interaction patterns. Interaction patterns (especially design patterns [6]) are identified combining static and dynamic analyses as described in our earlier papers [17, 16, 18, 19].
- The *configuration level* results from the detection phase. It is a program representation suited to manually specify interaction configurations. This level abstracts from the concrete programming language and represents all interactions explicitly as first-class entities combining the ideas of architecture systems [8] and aspect-oriented programming [21] as well as hyperdimensional separation of concerns [26]. Figure 6 b) illustrates the elements of the configuration level and their links to corresponding source code elements. The elements of the configuration level are:
  - *components* that are the basic building blocks of every system. A COMPASS component is a box in the sense of COMPOST. Table 1 shows the mapping of Java syntax elements to COMPASS component model elements. Whenever the iterator of the detection and model construction phase encounters such a syntax node, it creates an instance of the

Table 1. Mapping of Java Syntax Elements to COMPASS Component Model Elements

Java element	COMPASS element
compilation unit	ModuleComponent
class declaration	ModuleComponent
method declaration	ProcedureComponent
field	FieldComponent
variable	VariableComponent

corresponding COMPASS component model element. Of course, components may be hierarchically composed of further components including subsystems.

- *aspect-oriented ports* that encapsulate the interaction points of components in an aspect- or hyperslice-like fashion and represent the interaction properties at these points. Interaction properties are for example the direction of the interaction (in or out), the type of the interaction (control or data), synchronization, drive (initiation of control flow), and interaction mechanism. A COMPASS port is a hook in the sense of COMPOST.

  The model construction phase constructs a COMPASS port model element instance for every syntax node denoting data or control flow, like a method call for example.

  Some ports of components are implicitly defined by the language semantics without an explicit syntactical representation in the programming language. Since our model aims at making all interactions explicit, we also create explicit port model element instances for those and associate them with their owning components. An example is the implicit first parameter (this) of a Java method, identifying the object to which the method belongs, i. e., the object which state has to be considered when referring to fields.

- *aspect-oriented connectors* that represent interactions by connecting ports. A connector also is a representation of a program transformation. Via the ports it connects, a connector has access to the interaction points buried in the components' code. It can thus substantiate or replace this code by the configured interaction code. Even connections established by private fields are considered, but the corresponding ports are marked as internal component ports. A COMPASS connector is a composer in the sense of COMPOST.

These component, port and connector entities constitute an architectural model.

In the *(re-)configuration phase*, the developer reconfigures and adapts interactions by exchanging the port and connector entities on the configuration level. This triggers corresponding source code transformations (*transformation phase*) implemented as meta programs using the Recoder framework. Since connectors are architecture and design level instances by nature, our source code transformations eliminate them in the final code by mapping them to potentially several constructs of the target language. Nevertheless, we retain the configuration level representation of the system as an architectural representation.

A program transformation consists of the two passes *analysis* and *transformation*. The *analysis pass* first collects the information necessary to perform the transformation by transitively identifying the ports and connectors affected by the transformation. These provide the relevant information already collected during the model construction phase. This especially comprises the source code elements to modify. Second, the analysis pass checks if the transformation can be executed, i. e., if the required information are available and the transformation is applicable in the given context. It might happen for example that a Java class is only available as byte code, so that we cannot transform its source code. Moreover, the configuration may define to connect incompatible ports using the wrong type of connector. The *transformation pass* carries out the transformation without performing any further analyses. This is important, since a sub-transformation may have changed the underlying system already, so that the analysis now produces different or misleading results, although the whole complex transformation should be regarded as atomic. The whole transformation is encoded as a Java program, that modifies the abstract syntax forest of the sample program. The final target code is then produced using Recoder to pretty print the modified syntax forest.

Base transformations of COMPASS are to append or remove ports and/or components, as well as to insert or remove connectors.

– The *abstract level* abstracts from the concrete interaction properties represented on the configuration level. On the abstract level interaction consists of input and output actions on typed channels. This allows to bridge architectural mismatches or mismatches caused by certain implementation techniques.

An *abstraction phase* maps configuration level elements to abstract model elements, a *substantiation phase* conversely maps abstract model elements to configuration level elements by adding implementation specific interaction properties like synchronization, drive and mechanism.

The semantics of these levels is defined formally using the π-calculus, i. e., every interaction is resolved to one or more input ($c(v)$) or output actions ($\bar{c}v$) on channels (c). We have presented the details of this model in [15].

6.1   Using COMPASS

The transformation task of our running example amounts to exchanging the procedure call connector by a buffered data transfer connector as depicted in Figure 7.

The developer performs this reconfiguration on the configuration level which results in invoking the fundamental `ReplaceProcedureCallConnectorByBuffer` transformation as follows:

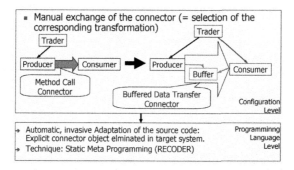

Fig. 7. Reconfiguration of Producer-Consumer-System Method Call

ProblemReport pr = **new** ReplaceProcedureCallConnectorByBuffer (config , pc) . execute ();

where

- config is a concrete COMPASS configuration that consistently bundles the source code parser, the mapping to model elements and the source code transformations including the pretty printer for a concrete programming language (Java in the current implementation of COMPASS), and
- pc is the instance of the procedure call connector to replace by a buffered communication connector.

This reconfiguration is implemented as the following single COMPASS transformation.

```
public class ReplaceProcedureCallConnectorByBuffer
    extends CompassTransformation {

  public ReplaceProcedureCallConnectorByBuffer (CompassConfiguration config ,
                                        ProcedureCallConnector procCallConnector) {
    ...
  }
  ...
}
```

To be generally applicable to exchanging a procedure call connector by buffered communication this transformation comprises several steps. As already mentioned, complex COMPASS transformations are two pass transformations like in Recoder consisting of an analysis and a transformation pass.

Figure 8 shows the producer-consumer-system as well as the procedure call connector COMPASS model element and its relation to the source code. The figure also shows the data and control flow that is relevant to replace the procedure call connector and thus illustrates the aspect-orientedness of interaction, especially the COMPASS port and connector model elements. There is no first-level encapsulation of the interaction in Java, the code dealing with this interaction is scattered over all the three classes involved.

Analysis Pass. The analysis pass starts from the method call connector to exchange and follows the links depicted in Figure 8 to identify the elements to

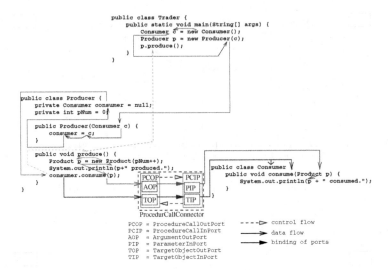

Fig. 8. Dependences in Example System

transform. These elements are stored to be accessed by the subsequent transformation pass. In particular these elements are:

1. The `ProcedureCallOutPort` to redirect to the `ProcedureCallInPort` of the put procedure component of the `ProductBuffer` module component to introduce into the system:

   srcProcOutPort = procCallConnector.getProcedureCallSource();

2. The field component of the `Producer` module component that holds a reference to the `Consumer` module component instance, because we want to exchange this field component by a field component referring to an instance of the `ProductBuffer` component to introduce.

3. The `ParameterInPort` of the `Consumer` module component to be turned into a `CallResultInPort` of a newly created `ProcedureCallOutPort` to connect to the `ProcedureCallInPort` of the get procedure component of the `ProductBuffer` module component.

4. The places where a reference to the `Consumer` component instance is provided to the `Producer` component instance — this is necessary, because in the transformed system these are the places where we need to provide the instance of the `ProductBuffer` component to the `Producer` component instance as well as to the `Consumer` component instance.

5. The places from where the **produce** method is called, i. e., from where the interaction between the producer and the consumer is (originally) initiated — this is necessary, because we need to add a call to the **consume** method of the consumer here as well, since the producer does not call the consumer directly in the transformed system:

Transformation Pass. In the description of the analysis pass, we have already explained for which transformation step the retrieved information are needed. The transformation pass simply performs these transformations, i.e.: introduces the buffer, replaces the parameter connector by communication via the intro-duces buffer and moves the call to `consume` from `Producer` to `Trader`.

6.2   Conclusion

COMPASS offers transformations tailored to reconfigure component interactions. To perform the transformation task in our running example we therefore just need to reconfigure the system by calling the corresponding transformation just writing one line of COMPASS code. So this is the easiest way to solve the given transformation task compared to 53 lines of Inject/J code or many more lines of Recoder code. So the advantages of COMPASS are, that it offers sophisti-cated analyses to detect interaction patterns, an aspect-oriented architectural model and a library of reusable transformations tailored to perform interaction adaptations.

7   Related Work

Most of the work in this area is concerned with general approaches to software de-sign, decomposition, composition and evolution [21, 26, 2], program understand-ing and refactoring. Only few works specifically deal with adapting interactions.

Architecture systems [8] like Darwin [5], UniCon [29], Rapide [22] and Wright [1] also introduce *port* entities to represent interaction interfaces of components and *connector* entities to represent interactions among components. But these architecture systems are unable to adapt the interactions of already existing code, because they do not implement architecture reconstruction algorithms.

Carriere et al. [4] generate program transformations to exchange communica-tion primitives in C source code. First, they identify communication primitives using regular expressions and naming conventions. Then, they use the mapping defined in [20] to specify pre- and post-conditions to generate corresponding program transformations to be performed by the tool Refine/C [28, 11]. These transformations then transform the abstract syntax tree of the program under consideration, automatically. This approach has the following shortcomings: the mapping of communication mechanisms is neither unique nor 1:1, thus leading to dead or superfluous code in the target system. Moreover, this includes the problem of deciding which target mechanism to use. In COMPASS this is done interactively or by providing a transformation strategy. Carriere et al. do not solve this problem. Furthermore, their approach does not detect complex inter-action patterns. This is due to the fact that their analysis is based on naming conventions and regular expressions that are not powerful enough.

Pulvermüller et al. [27] encapsulate CORBA-specific communication code in aspects implemented using AspectJ and present a few highly specialized trans-formations. But they do not define an interaction model, do neither provide gen-eral support to adapt interactions nor to adapt interaction patterns. An analysis phase to detect interactions and provide a representation suitable to adapt them is completely missing.

Altogether, we do not know any approach that deals with the complete procedure of adapting interactions, as we did. The stepwise refinement of architectures defined by the COMPASS model has now become popular using the term *model driven architecture (MDA)* [25].

8   Conclusion

We have presented a suite of program transformation tools for invasive software composition and applied them to a representative interaction adaptation task. The COMPASS tool is tailored to tackle this kind of tasks. It combines the ideas of architecture systems, aspect-oriented programming and hyperdimensional-separation of concerns to define *ports* that provide invasive access to interaction points of *components*, and *aspect-oriented connectors* as program transformations to consistently adapt interactions according to specified configurations.

All the transformations are type-safe respecting the syntactic and semantic obligations of the Java language in which the programs to be transformed are implemented. Our tools are therefore preferable to text patching approaches which inherently suffer from damaging the code to be transformed.

Our future work comprises to implement further transformations thus expanding our transformation library. Moreover, we need to deal with the problem of how to find the interactions to adapt when a problem specification or a catalog of known problems is given. The detection of anti-patterns and the application of metrics to apply refactorings are promising in this domain, but need to be extended to non-meaning-preserving transformations, in the sense that desired new observable properties can be added to the target system.

References

1. Robert Allen and David Garlan. Beyond definition/use: Architectural interconnection. In *ACM IDL Workshop*, volume 29(8). SIGPLAN Notices, 1994.
2. Uwe Aßmann. *Invasive Software Composition*. Springer, 2002.
3. Uwe Aßmann, Andreas Ludwig, Rainer Neumann, and Dirk Heuzeroth. The COMPOST project main page. http://www.the-compost-system.org, 1999 – 2005.
4. S. J. Carriere, S. G. Woods, and R. Kazman. Software Architectural Transformation. In *WCRE 99*, October 1999.
5. Darwin. http://www.doc.ac.ic.uk, 2000.
6. Erich Gamma, Richard Helm, Ralph Johnson, and John Vlissides. *Design Patterns*. Addison-Wesley, 1994.
7. David Garlan, Robert Allen, and John Ockerbloom. Architectural Mismatch: Why Reuse Is So Hard. *IEEE Software*, 1995.
8. David Garlan and Mary Shaw. An Introduction to Software Architecture. In *Advances in Software Engineering and Knowledge Engineering*. World Scientific Publishing, 1993.
9. Thomas Genßler and Volker Kuttruff. The inject/J project main page. http://injectj.sj.net, 1999 – 2005.

10. Thomas Genssler and Volker Kuttruff. Source-to-Source Transformation In The Large. In *Proceedings of the Joint Modular Language Conference*, pages 254–265. Springer LNCS, August 2003.
11. David R. Harris, Alexander S. Yeh, and Howard B. Reubenstein. Extracting Architectural Features From Source Code. *ASE*, 3:109–138, 1996.
12. Dirk Heuzeroth. The COMPASS project main page. http://www.info.uni-karlsruhe.de/~heuzer/projects/compass, 2003.
13. Dirk Heuzeroth. *Aspektorientierte Konfiguration und Adaption von Komponenteninteraktionen*. PhD thesis, University of Karlsruhe, 2004.
14. Dirk Heuzeroth. COMPASS: Tool-supported Adaptation of Interactions. In *Automated Software Engineering 2004*. IEEE, 2004.
15. Dirk Heuzeroth. A Model for an Executable Software Architecture to deal with Evolution and Architectural Mismatches. Technical report, Universität Karlsruhe, 2004.
16. Dirk Heuzeroth, Gustav Högström, Thomas Holl, and Welf Löwe. Automatic Design Pattern Detection. In *IWPC*, May 2003.
17. Dirk Heuzeroth, Thomas Holl, and Welf Löwe. Combining Static and Dynamic Analyses to Detect Interaction Patterns. In *IDPT*, June 2002.
18. Dirk Heuzeroth and Welf Löwe. *Software-Visualization - From Theory to Practice, Edited by Kang Zhang*, chapter Understanding Architecture Through Structure and Behavior Visualization. Kluwer, 2003.
19. Dirk Heuzeroth, Welf Löwe, and Stefan Mandel. Generating Design Pattern Detectors from Pattern Specifications. In *18th ASE*. IEEE, 2003.
20. Rick Kazman, Paul Clements, and Len Bass. Classifying Architectural Elements as a Foundation for Mechanism Matching. In *COMPSAC 97*, August 1997.
21. Gregor Kiczales, John Irwin, John Lamping, Jean-Marc Loingtier, Cristina Videira Lopes, Chris Maeda, and Anurag Mendhekar. Aspect-oriented Programming. In *ECOOP'97*, pages 220–242. Springer, 1997.
22. David C. Luckham, John J. Kenney, Larry M. Augustin, James Vera, Doug Bryan, and Walter Mann. Specification and Analysis of System Architecture Using Rapide. *IEEE ToSE*, 21(4), 1995.
23. Andreas Ludwig and Dirk Heuzeroth. Metaprogramming in the Large. In *GCSE, LNCS 2177*, pages 443–452, October 2000.
24. Andreas Ludwig, Rainer Neumann, Dirk Heuzeroth, and Mircea Trifu. The RECODER project main page. http://recoder.sourceforge.net, 1999 – 2005.
25. OMG. MDA Guide Version 1.0.1. Technical report, OMG, 2003.
26. Harold Ossher and Peri Tarr. Multi-Dimensional Separation of Concerns in Hyperspace. Technical report, IBM T. J. Watson Research Center, April 1999.
27. E. Pulvermüller, H. Klaeren, and A. Speck. Aspects in distributed environments. In *GCSE'99*, September 1999.
28. http://www.reasoning.com, 2003.
29. Mary Shaw, Robert DeLine, Daniel V. Klein, Theodore L. Ross, David M. Young, and Gregory Zelesnik. Abstractions for Software Architecture and Tools to Support Them. *IEEE ToSE*, 21(4), 1995.

Program Transformation Using HATS 1.84

Victor Winter and Jason Beranek

Department of Computer Science, University of Nebraska at Omaha

Abstract. This article gives an overview of a transformation system called HATS – a freely available platform independent IDE facilitating experimentation in transformation-oriented software development. Examples are discussed highlighting how the transformational abstractions provided by HATS can be used to solve various problems.

1 Introduction

Interest in program transformation is driven by the idea that, through their repeated application, a set of simple rewrite rules can affect a major change in a software artifact. From the perspective of dependability, the explicit nature of transformation exposes the software development process to various forms of analysis that would otherwise not be possible.

Within the scope of this article we will use the term *program transformation* (or *transformation*) in a general sense to refer to software manipulation processes that are restricted to the fully automatic application of rewrite rules. We will also predominantly refer to the objects that are the subject of transformation as *terms* or *trees* rather than specifications, programs, code fragments, or the variety of other artifacts over which transformation is possible.

This article gives an overview of a transformation system called HATS. HATS is freely available and provides a platform independent IDE facilitating experimentation in transformation-oriented software development [24, 23]. HATS, an acronym for High Assurance Transformation System, is a program transformation system whose continuing development is inspired by the potential benefits that *transformation-oriented programming* can offer software assurance efforts. As a result, the primitives and abstractions in HATS have been designed with thought given to verification. From a more technical perspective, HATS can be viewed as a higher-order transformation system for manipulating parse trees. Tree structures are defined using an extended-BNF notation supporting precedence and associativity. Transformations are written in TL, a language that supports first-order as well as higher-order transformation. TL also supports standard one-layer traversal constructs together with recursive definition of traversals allowing a variety of generic traversals, both first-order as well as higher-order, to be defined by the user. HATS supports several feedback mechanisms including pretty-printed text, graphical display of parse trees, and a rudimentary trace facility[1] for debugging.

---

[1] The trace facility is presently under development and is in a somewhat experimental stage.

R. Lämmel, J. Saraiva, and J. Visser (Eds.): GTTSE 2005, LNCS 4143, pp. 378–396, 2006.

The rest of this article is structured as follows: Section 2 gives an overview of HATS. Section 3 gives an overview of the HATS parser generator. Section 4 gives an overview of the transformation language TL. Section 5 presents an example showing how three algebraic laws forming part of a Verilog synthesis system can be effectively implemented in TL. Section 6 presents an example showing how the *hide* combinator has been effectively used to realize a transformational step in a class loader for an instance of the JVM. Section 7 discusses related work, and section 8 concludes.

2   An Overview of HATS (Version 1.84)

HATS is a transformation system whose development has been underway for a number of years. During this time, the design of HATS has gone through a number of changes. The earliest version of HATS [25] was influenced primarily by the TAMPR transformation system [5, 4]. In this early version of HATS, transformation was accomplished by applying collections of first-order rewrite rules to terms using a small library of traversals provided by the HATS system. Later versions of HATS drew inspiration from systems like ELAN [3], Stratego [21], ASF+SDF [2], and Strafunski [13].

In its present form, HATS (version 1.84) is a system in which transformation is realized through the execution of special purpose programs written in a language called TL [24]. The language TL provides a computational framework where transformational ideas are expressed in terms of conditional rewrite rules whose application is controlled by a variety of standard strategic combinators and traversals [12] (e.g., sequential composition, biased choice, top-down and bottom-up traversals, etc.). Distinguishing features of TL include: (1) the ability to express transformational ideas in terms of higher-order conditional rewrite rules, (2) the ability to control rule application through a variety of unique combinators including the *transient* combinator and the *hide* combinator, and (3) a semantic foundation where the failure of rule application behaves like the identity transformation (in contrast to strategic systems in which rule failure yields the strategic constant FAIL).

2.1   The Taxonomy of a Domain

In HATS, the term *domain* is used to refer to the collection of files that support the transformation of parse trees belonging to a given language. Example domains can be downloaded from the HATS homepage [9]. Figure 1 shows an example of what a user would see in a typical HATS session. The pane on the upper-left partitions the files in the domain into a variety of file types: (1) grammar files, (2) lexer files, (3) target files, (4) transformation files, (5) user-defined function files, (6) style files, (7) pretty-printed text files, and (8) parse tree files. The pane on the upper-right serves a variety of purposes including (1) a special purpose text editor, (2) a graphical tree display, and (3) an execution trace display. The pane on the bottom provides error feedback as well as a variety of execution metrics.

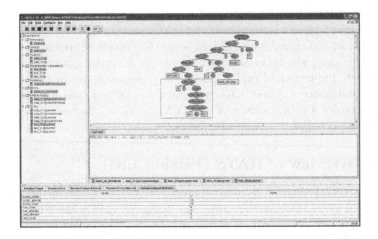

Fig. 1. Using the HATS GUI to View a Domain

2.2   Running HATS

Perhaps the most natural way to think of HATS is in terms of a collection of functions whose execution can be orchestrated from the HATS GUI. Functions that are of central importance to transformation include: (1) a parser generator, (2) a transformation engine, (3) a pretty printer, (4) a tree viewer, and (5) a trace viewer. Figure 2 gives an overview of HATS from the perspective of dataflow. In the figure, icons[2] are used to denote various functions that are available to the user, source nodes represent user input files, and sink nodes represent system feedback.

In the discussion that follows, we assume a domain whose grammar, lexer, source, transformation program, and style files are respectively named `grammar.bnf`, `lexer.spec`, `source.tgt`, `transform.tlp`, `UserDefinedFunctions.sml`, and `style.sty`.

In HATS, the transformation process is decomposed into the following phases:

1. **Parsing Phase** – The goal of this phase is to produce suitable input files for the transformation phase.

   (a) The *parser generator* ![icon] is invoked to produce a *source parser* for the language defined by `grammar.bnf` and `lexer.spec`. The *source parser* is also used by the *TL parser*, the parser for transformation programs, when parsing the portions of rewrite rules containing code fragments belonging to the source language. Thus, invoking the parser generator will in fact produce two parsers – a parser for the source language and a parser for the transformation language.

---

[2] The icons used in the figure are taken directly from the icons that are used by the HATS GUI.

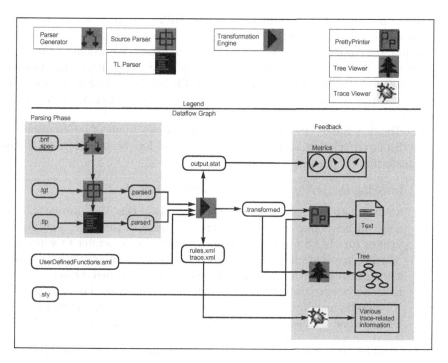

Fig. 2. The Architecture of HATS from a Dataflow Perspective

(b) Creation of .parsed files

    i. The *source parser*   can be invoked to parse the file `source.tgt`. Any errors that arise during parsing will be displayed in the bottom pane of the HATS GUI under the `Standard Error` tab. A successful parse of `source.tgt` will result in the creation of the file `source.tgt.parsed`.

    ii. The *TL parser*   can be invoked to parse the file `transform.tlp`. Any errors that arise during parsing will be displayed in the bottom pane of the HATS GUI under the `Standard Error` tab. A successful parse of `transform.tlp` will result in the creation of the file `transform.tlp.parsed`.

2. **Transformation Phase** – After completion of the parsing phase transformation is accomplished by invoking the transformation engine   . The transformation engine accepts as input the files `source.tgt.parsed`, `transform.tlp.parsed`, and `UserDefinedFunctions.sml`. Invocation will cause `transform.tlp.parsed` to be applied to `source.tgt.parsed` using the additional functionality defined in `UserDefinedFunctions.sml`. Runtime errors resulting from semantically ill-formed transformation programs

are displayed in the bottom pane of the HATS GUI. A successful transformation of `source.tgt` will produce the files: `output.stat`, `rules.xml`, `trace.xml`, and `source.tgt.parsed.transformed`. We would like to point out that transformation in HATS is accomplished in an interpretive fashion. Specifically, a denotational semantics for TL has been implemented in ML, and it is this semantics that is used to interpret the `transform.tlp.parsed` tree.

3. **Feedback Phase** – In the feedback phase, various kinds of information can be displayed relating to the computation that has been performed in the transformation phase.

(a) Invoking the *pretty-printer* will produce the file

source.tgt.transformed.pp. The contents of this file is formatted text and can be displayed in the upper-right pane of the GUI. The pretty-printer for HATS is essentially an abstract pretty-printer in which formatting is essentially inserted into BNF-style grammar productions and some control over formatting rule selection is provided. Other transformation systems also provide this kind of functionality. For example, the XT bundle includes a generic pretty-printing tool (GPP) in which a language called Box is used to describe the intended layout of text [8].

(b) Invoking the tree viewer will display the parse tree of the selected file (e.g., `source.tgt.parsed.transformed`) in graphical form in the upper-right pane of the GUI. Portions of the parse tree can be collapsed, expanded, and selected. Simultaneously, the leaves of the expanded portion of the tree are displayed in textual form with highlighted text denoting selected portions of the tree.

(c) Invoking the *trace viewer* enables the user to step through the execution of transformations that have been designated to be traced. The designation of which rules to trace can be specified within a TL program.

3   The HATS Parser Generator

HATS provides users with a GLR-style parser generator. From a technical standpoint, the HATS parser generator is not a true GLR parser because it cannot detect (and handle) nonterminating derivation sequences. Section 7.1 gives a more detailed discussion of parsing technology and its role in support of transformation.

The HATS parser generator allows users to describe context-free grammars using an extended-BNF notation. The extended-BNF notation supported can be thought of as a merging of BNF notation with regular expression notation. Figure 3 gives an overview of the meta-symbols supported by the HATS parser generator.

Symbol	Description
::=	The nonterminal definition operator.
.	The production terminator.
\<id\>	Nonterminal symbols should be enclosed in pointy-brackets.
"token"	Tokens should be decorated with (i.e., enclosed in) double quotes.
domain_vars	Terminals denoting domain variables (e.g., id) are not decorated.
|	The alternate choice operator.
[ ]	Portions of a production enclosed in square brackets are optional.
()	The constant epsilon.
( )	Used only for grouping just like in regular expression notation.
( )*	The Kleene-closure of the portion enclosed in parens. Note that this will create trees of varying degree and is not particularly useful when using first-order matching.
{ }	Equivalent to (...)*.
(* *)	Comments are similar to ML and may span multiple lines. However, comments may not be nested.

Fig. 3. Meta-symbols of the extended-BNF syntax supported by the HATS parser

3.1 Precedence and Associativity

The HATS parser generator also supports precedence and associativity rules as a mechanism for disambiguating two or more productions. The *dangling else*[3] problem is a classic example of a situation that is typically resolved using precedence rules.

There are two types of associativity: LEFT_ASSOC and RIGHT_ASSOC. LEFT_ASSOC indicates that the operator is left-associative. RIGHT_ASSOC indicates that the operator is right-associative. A BNF grammar can begin with zero or more associativity rules. An associativity rule is of the form:

$$\% assoc\_type \, quoted\_token\_list. \tag{1}$$

where *assoc_type* is one of the associativity types mentioned in the previous paragraph, and *quoted_token_list* is a list of one or more tokens separated by blanks. In this context, a token is a string enclosed in quotes. Within an associativity rule all tokens have the same precedence.

Given two associative rule declarations r1 and r2, if r1 lexically occurs before r2, then the tokens in r1 will have a lower precedence than the tokens in r2. All tokens within a given rule have the same precedence.

%LEFT_ASSOC "+" "-" "L1" . Lower precedence
%LEFT_ASSOC "*" "/" "L2" . Higher precedence

Each grammar production can have an optional precedence attribute as a suffix. The general form is as follows:

---

[3] The *dangling else* problem concerns itself with determining with which *if* construct an *else* fragment should associated.

$$nonterm ::= alpha[\%PREC\,token]. \tag{2}$$

where *token* belongs to the *quoted_token_list* of some associative rule declaration. For a detailed example of how to construct grammars having associativity and precedence rules download the type checking demo domain from the HATS homepage [9].

4   TL: The Basics

This section gives a brief overview of TL, a labelled conditional (higher-order) rewriting language supporting a variety of strategic operators and generic traversals. For a more detailed discussion of TL see [24]. In TL, parse trees are the "objects" that TL programs transform. Rewrite rules have the following form:

$$r : lhs \rightarrow s^n \; [if \; condition] \tag{3}$$

In this example, r denotes the label of the rule, *lhs* denotes a *pattern* describing a tree structure, s^n denotes a *strategic expression* whose evaluation yields a strategy of order n, and *if condition* denotes an optional Boolean-valued condition consisting of one or more *match expressions* constructed using Boolean connectives.

A *pattern* is a notation for describing the parse tree structures that are being manipulated. This notation includes typed *variables* that are quantified over specific tree structure domains, e.g., $stmt[\![\; id_1 = 5 \;]\!]$ is a tree with root $stmt$ and leaves id_1, =, and 5. In this context, the subscripted variable id_1 denotes a typed variable quantified over the domain of all trees having id as their root node. In general, a pattern of the form $A[\![\alpha']\!]$ is structurally valid if and only if the derivation $A \overset{+}{\Rightarrow} \alpha$ is possible according to the grammar and α' is obtained from α by subscripting all nonterminals occurring in α.

A *strategic expression* is an expression whose evaluation yields a *strategy* having a particular order. In the framework of TL, a *pattern* is considered to be a strategy of order 0. A rewrite rule that transforms its input tree into another tree is considered to be a strategy of order 1 (i.e., a first-order rule). Let s^1 denote a first-order strategy. Then the rule $lhs \rightarrow s^1$ denotes a second-order strategy (e.g., s^2), and so on.

A *match expression* is a first-order match between two patterns. Let t_1 denote a pattern, possibly non-ground, and let t_2 denote a ground pattern. The expression $t_1 \ll t_2$ denotes a match expression and evaluates to *true* if and only if a substitution σ can be constructed so that $\sigma(t_1) = t_2$. One or more match expressions can be combined using the Boolean connectives { *and, or, not* } to form the *condition* of a rewrite rule.

4.1   Combinators

In TL, a variety of *combinators* can be used to compose conditional rewrite rules into strategies. First-order strategies define controlled sequences of rewrites and can be applied to tree structures to produce other tree structures. Thus, a first-order strategy can be viewed as a function that rewrites or *transforms* one tree into another. Because of the important role played by strategies, transformation languages of this kind are also referred to as *strategic programming languages*. In this article we will use the terms *strategy* and *transformation* interchangeably. Figure 4 gives an overview of some of the combinator primitives provided by TL.

There are a number of combinators that have been identified as being generally useful in strategic programming [12]. Two widely used combinators are: (1) left-to-right sequential composition ($<;$), and (2) left-biased conditional composition ($<+$). Let s_1 and s_2 denote two strategies. The expression $s_1 <; s_2$ denotes the left-to-right sequential composition of s_1 and s_2. When applied to a tree t, this strategy will first apply s_1 to t and then apply s_2 to the result. In contrast, the expression $s_1 <+ s_2$ denotes the left-biased conditional composition of s_1 and s_2. When applied to a tree t, the application of s_1 to t is attempted, and if that succeeds, the result is returned; otherwise, the result of the application of s_2 to t is returned. In TL, if neither s_1 or s_2 apply then t is returned unchanged.

			Precedence	Associativity
$s_1^n <; s_2^n$	Left-to-right sequential composition.			
$s_1^n ;> s_2^n$	Right-to-left sequential composition.		(lowest) $+>$	right
$s_1^n <+ s_2^n$	Left-biased conditional composition.		$<+$	left
$s_1^n +> s_2$	Right-biased conditional composition.		$;>$	right
$transient(s^n)$	A unary combinator restricting the application of s^n.		(highest) $<;$	left
$hide(s^n)$	A unary combinator that hides the application of s^n from an enclosing conditional composition combinator.			

Fig. 4. The basic combinators of TL

The *transient* Combinator. The transient combinator is a very special combinator in TL. This combinator restricts a strategy so that it may be applied *at most once*. The "at most once" property is the hallmark of the *transient* combinator.

Transients open the door to *self-modifying* strategies. When using a traversal to apply a self-modifying strategy to a term, a different strategy may be applied to every term encountered during a traversal. For example, let $int_1 \rightarrow int[\![2]\!]$ denote a rule that rewrites an arbitrary integer to the value 2. If such a rule is applied to a term in a top-down fashion all of the integers in the term will be rewritten to 2. Now consider the following self-modifying transient strategy:

$$transient(int_1 \rightarrow int[\![1]\!]) <+$$
$$transient(int_1 \rightarrow int[\![2]\!]) <+$$
$$transient(int_1 \rightarrow int[\![3]\!])$$

When applied to a term in a top-down fashion, this strategy will rewrite the first integer encountered to 1, the second integer encountered to 2, and the third integer encountered to 3. All other integers will remain unchanged.

The *hide* Combinator. The notion of choosing the application of one rule over another is central to strategic programming. An essential component of both the left-biased and right-biased conditional composition combinators is the ability to "observe" the behavior of strategy application (i.e., whether the application of a strategy to a term has succeeded or failed). Let us consider the introduction of a unary combinator called *hide* into a strategic framework supporting left-biased and right-biased conditional composition combinators. In this context, the purpose of *hide* is to prevent the application of a strategy from being observed. As a consequence a strategy of the form $hide(s_1)$ <+ s_2 will always attempt to apply s_1 followed by s_2, in effect undoing the discriminatory nature of the conditional composition combinator.

The strategic combinator *hide* provides an interesting extension to the framework of TL. This unary combinator restricts the observability of strategy application from the perspective of the conditional composition combinators. In particular, the *hide* combinator satisfies the following properties:

$$hide(s_1) <\!\!+ s_2 \equiv s_1 <\!\!; s_2$$
$$s_1 +\!\!> hide(s_2) \equiv s_1 \;;\!\!> s_2$$

At first glance, it appears as if the *hide* combinator does not add anything new to the standard combinator set. However, section 6 gives an example showing how *hide* can be effectively utilized. We would like to point out that, although it is not shown in the example given in Section 6, the *hide* combinator is also very useful in conjunction with the *transient* combinator and higher-order strategies.

4.2   Traversals

Combinators are a control mechanism that define *how* a collection of rules should be applied to a given tree. They do not define *where* (i.e., to which trees) a collection of rules should be applied. This dimension of transformation can be defined by *traversal* mechanisms.

A *generic traversal* can be thought of as a curried function parameterized on a strategy s and a tree t. As the name suggests, a generic traversal will *traverse* its input tree structure t and apply its input strategy s at one or more points along the traversal. Two common traversals are a top-down left-to-right traversal which TL denotes by the symbol TDL, and a bottom-up left-to-right traversal which TL denotes by the symbol BUL. From a computational perspective, a TDL traversal can be understood as corresponding roughly to non-strict (outside-in) evaluation while the traversal BUL corresponds roughly to strict (inside-out) evaluation.

The *generic tree traversal* is an abstraction that is virtually essential in order for transformational ideas to scale to real-world problems (i.e., the transformation of trees whose structures are derived from large grammars). TL provides a rich mechanism (not discussed in this paper) for defining generic and pseudo-generic tree traversals. TL also supports the definition and use of higher-order generic traversals. Informally, one can think of a higher-order traversal as mechanism for dynamically collecting a number of strategies and combining them to form a new strategy. A common higher-order traversal is one that traverses a tree in a BUL fashion, applies a higher-order strategy s^{n+1}, and composes the resulting order-n strategies using the $\mathbin{<\!;}$ combinator. In TL, this traversal is denoted by the identifer *lseq_bul*. In contrast, *rcond_tdl* denotes a higher-order generic traversal that traverses a tree in a TDL fashion, applies a higher-order strategy s^{n+1} and composes the resulting order-n strategies using the $+\!>$ combinator.

5   Example I: A Verilog Synthesis Fragment

In this example, we look at how transformation can be used to realize a fragment of a logic synthesis system for a hardware description language called Verilog, whose syntax has a C-like flavor. We will look at how the three algebraic laws shown in Figure 5 can be effectively implemented in TL. These algebraic laws were initially presented in [10] and have been used by Iyoda et al [11] in the abstract design of a synthesis system for a small subset of Verilog.

Law 1 (completion). $(x, y, ... := e, f, ...) = (x, y, ..., z := e, f, ..., z)$

Law 2 (reordering). $(...y, z... := ...f, g...) = (...z, y... := ...g, f...)$

Law 3 (propagation). $(\vec{v} := g; \vec{v} := h(\vec{v})) = (\vec{v} := h(g))$

Fig. 5. Three Laws of Synthesis

An important thing to note about Laws 2 and 3 is that they cannot be directly implemented as transformations. Law 2 requires that ellipsis be matched so that the **number of variables** matched by ellipsis on the left-hand side of an assignment is equal to the **number of expressions** matched by the corresponding ellipsis on the right-hand side of the assignment. Such matching constraints lie beyond traditional associative matching. Law 3 describes constant propagation over sequentially composed assignment statements. Though its intention is clear, in the form stated, Law 3 does not directly map onto the syntax of parallel assignment statements since the right-hand side of a parallel assignment is a comma-separated list of expressions and not a function (e.g., h) as is suggested in Law 3. In spite of these issues, we will show that in the higher-order framework of TL it is possible to express the intent of Laws 2 and 3 using just two rewrite rules!

The approach to logic synthesis described here consists of passing Verilog *modules*, which are roughly the equivalent of C functions, through two canonical forms. The first canonical form is achieved when all assignments in a module are *total*. Let m denote a Verilog module and let $\vec{v}$ denote a vector consisting of all variables that occur on the left-hand side of an assignment in m. An assignment is *total* if it well-formed and has the form: $\vec{v} = \vec{e}$. A Verilog module is said to be in *Total Form* if all its assignment statements are total.

The second canonical form consists of propagating the bindings resulting from assignments over assignment sequences. This transformation is justified by Law 2 and Law 3. The following example shows how a simple sequence of Verilog assignments can be transformed into parallel normal form.

Canonical Forms

Input		Total Form		Parallel Normal Form
x = e_1;	$\overset{\Longrightarrow}{Law\ 1}$	x,y,z = e_1,y,z;	$\overset{\Longrightarrow}{Laws\ 2\&3}$	x,y,z = e_1, e_2, e_3
y = e_2;		y,x,z = e_2,x,z;		
z = e_3;		z,x,y = e_3,x,y;		

5.1   Implementation

The rules and strategies needed to place the modules in a Verilog program into parallel normal form (PNF) are shown in Figure 7 and the relevant portion of the Verilog syntax is shown in Figure 6. The strategy that achieves the transformation to parallel normal form is labelled PNF and is defined as follows:

$$\text{PNF: BUL\{Prep\}} \overset{<}{;} \text{BUL\{Law1\}} \overset{<}{;} \text{BUL\{Law3\}} \tag{4}$$

When applied to a Verilog program p_{in} the strategy PNF will first traverse p_{in} using a BUL traversal and apply the strategy *Prep*. *Prep* rewrites blocking assignments to fork/join blocks, which is what we use to model parallel assignments. For the remainder of this discussion, we will refer to such fork/join blocks as *multi-assignments* to emphasize how they are being used in this context.

*Law*1 makes all multi-assignments in a module total. Thus, the result of the traversal BUL{*Law*1} is a program p_{total} that is in Total Form. Next p_{total} is traversed, again using a BUL traversal, and the strategy *Law*3 is applied. The result is a program p_{pnf} that is in parallel normal form.

In Law1, the strategic expression $lseq\_bul\{make\_total\}[module e_0]$ will traverse the object tree module$_0$, apply the higher-order rule *make_total* to all subtrees and compose the results using the $\overset{<}{;}$ combinator. The rule *make_total* is a higher-order rule that produces an instance of the strategy $transient(check[id_1] \overset{<}{+} add[id_1])$ for each (blocking) assignment encountered in a given module. What distinguishes one instance from another is the value bound to id_1. For example, if id_1 is instantiated with the variable x then the following strategy is created:

transient (
  stmtS⟦ x = E_2; stmtS$_3$ ⟧ → stmtS⟦ x = E_2; stmtS$_3$ ⟧
  $\overset{<}{+}$
  stmtS⟦ ⟧ → stmtS⟦ x = x; ⟧
)

The semantics of an instance of the strategy $transient(check[id_1] \overset{<}{+} add[id_1])$ can be best understood in the context of its application (via a traversal) to the sequence of statements contained within a multi-assignment. When applied to

modulee	::= module module_id ";" module_item_0orMore endmodule
module_item_0orMore	::= module_item module_item_0orMore | ()
module_item	::= continuous_assign | always_stmt | ...
continuous_assign	::= "assign" lvalue "=" E ";"
always_stmt	::= "always" stmt
stmtS	::= stmt stmtS | ()
stmt_or_null	::= stmt | ";"
stmt	::= blocking_assignment ";" | seq_block | par_block | ...
seq_block	::= "begin" stmtS "end"
par_block	::= "fork" stmtS "join"
blocking_assignment	::= lvalue "=" E
...	

Fig. 6. A wide-spectrum language fragment containing a small subset of Verilog

PNF: BUL{Prep} $\lessdot$ BUL{Law1} $\lessdot$ BUL{Law3 }

Prep: stmt$[\![$ blocking_assignment$_1$; $]\!]$ $\rightarrow$ stmt$[\![$ fork blocking_assignment$_1$; join $]\!]$

Law1:   modulee$_0$ $\rightarrow$ Special_TD{ lseq_bul{ make_total }[modulee$_0$] }(modulee$_0$)

   make_total: blocking_assignment$[\![$ id$_1$ = E$_1$ $]\!]$ $\rightarrow$ transient(check[id$_1$] $\lessdot\!+$ add[id$_1$])
   check: id$_1$ $\rightarrow$ stmtS$[\![$ id$_1$ = E$_2$; stmtS$_3$ $]\!]$ $\rightarrow$ stmtS$[\![$ id$_1$ = E$_2$; stmtS$_3$ $]\!]$
   add: id$_1$ $\rightarrow$ stmtS$[\![$ $]\!]$ $\rightarrow$ stmtS$[\![$ id$_1$ = id$_1$; $]\!]$

Law3:   stmtS$[\![$ par_block$_1$ par_block$_2$ $]\!]$
      $\rightarrow$
      BUL{lseq_tdl{propagate}[par_block$_1$]}(stmtS$[\![$ par_block$_2$ $]\!]$)

   propagate: blocking_assignment$[\![$ id$_1$ = expr$_1$ $]\!]$ $\rightarrow$ expr$[\![$ id$_1$ $]\!]$ $\rightarrow$ expr$_1$

Fig. 7. Transformations implementing Parallel Normal Form(PNF)

the assignments in a multi-assignment, the rewrite rule derived from $check[id_1]$ will apply if id_1 occurs on the left-hand side of an assignment within the multi-assignment block. If this happens, the rule will fire and the *transient* combinator will remove the instance of $check[id_1]$ $\lessdot\!+$ $add[id_1]$. However, if $check[id_1]$ never applies, the traversal will proceed to the end of the multi-assignment at which point $add[id_1]$ will cause the identity assignment $id_1 = id_1$ to be added. This application will again cause the *transient* combinator to remove the instance of $check[id_1]$ $\lessdot\!+$ $add[id_1]$. Summarizing then, an instance of $transient(check[id_1]$ $\lessdot\!+$ $add[id_1])$ will leave a multi-assignment unchanged if the multi-assignment contains an assignment to id_1; otherwise $transient(check[id_1]$ $\lessdot\!+$ $add[id_1])$ will add the assignment $id_1 = id_1$ to the multi-assignment.

   In this first transformational phase, what remains is to process each multi-assignment statement within a module in the manner just described. This can be accomplished with the help of a special purpose traversal called Special_TD that has been written especially for this problem domain. What makes the traversal special is that it enables each multi-assignment in a module to receive its own individual copy of the strategy resulting from the evaluation of $lseq\_bul\{\ make\_total\}[module_0]$. This is important because, $transient(check[id_1] <+ add[id_1])$ can only be applied once. However, we want it to be applied once to **every** multi-assignment occurring in a module. The Special_TD traversal accomplishes this and, though not shown, can be defined in one line of code using standard TL primitives.

Law3 takes two multi-assignment statements, par_block_1 and par_block_2, and propagates the assignments from the first multi-assignment to the second. This is accomplished with the help of the higher-order rewrite rule *propagate*. When applied to a blocking assignment of the form $id_1 = expr_1$, *propagate* will produce the first-order rule $expr[\![id_1]\!] \rightarrow expr_1$ that rewrites occurrences of id_1 in expressions to $expr_1$. The strategic expression $lseq\_bul\{propagate\}[par\_block_1]$ creates and collects propagating rules for all assignments in par_block_1 which are then applied to par_block_2 using the traversal BUL. We would like to conclude this example with the following remarks: (1) the fact that *Law3* is applied in a bottom-up fashion in *PNF* assures that all sequences of multi-assignments will be collapsed into a single multi-assignment statement, and (2) Law 2 is never needed to transform a Verilog program into parallel normal form.

6   Example II: A Java Class Loader Fragment

In this section, we take a look at how the *hide* combinator can be effectively used to solve a problem encountered in Java class loading. In particular, we will take a closer look at class loading as it relates to the Sandia Secure Processor (SSP) [22]. The SSP is a hardware implementation of a significant subset of the Java Virtual Machine whose application domain extends to embedded high consequence systems. Class loading for the SSP is performed statically (prior to runtime) and preserves the conceptual structure of class files. These properties make the SSP class loading problem well-suited to a transformation-based solution.

To date, several full class loader designs have been implemented for the Sandia Secure Processor (SSP) [26] using the HATS system. In the discussion that follows, we join the transformation process of one such design at a time when a significant portion of the class loading transformation has already been completed. In particular, we assume that symbolic resolution has taken place, and the list of Java class files comprising the application has been partially ordered by subtype as follows: Let $c_1\ c_2\ ...\ c_n$ denote the partially ordered list of class files. Let $\prec$ denote the subtype relation on classes, and let $\Rightarrow$ denote logical implication[4]. The partial order of class files satisfies the following property:

$$c_j \prec c_i \Rightarrow i < j \tag{5}$$

---

[4] We do not wish to overload the $\rightarrow$ symbol, whose use we reserve for rewriting.

This implies that, when inspecting the class list from left-to-right (e.g., via a top-down left-to-right traversal), a parent class will always be encountered before any of its children.

The transformational goal at this stage is to further resolve symbolic references to fields so that all symbolic field references satisfy the following property.

Static Binding Property: *The class component in a symbolic field reference corresponds to the class in which the field has been declared.*

The reason why the static binding property is not universally true already is that Java makes one exception to its essentially static binding of fields. This exception arises when a reference is made to an *inherited* field. For example, suppose we have situation where (1) an integer field x is declared in class A, (2) the class B *extends* A, i.e., $B \prec A$, (3) myB is an instance of B, and (4) C is the class containing a reference to $myB.x$. In this case, the Java compiler will produce a class file for C whose constant pool will have a *constant_fieldref_info* entry corresponding to the reference $myB.x$. Standard symbolic resolution of this entry will yield:

$$constant\_fieldref\_info[\![B\ x\ I]\!] \tag{6}$$

This term represents a symbolic reference to the integer variable x belonging to the class B (even though x is not declared in B) which violates the static binding property. In this example, we would like the symbolic resolution of the constant pool entry corresponding to $myB.x$ to yield:

$$constant\_fieldref\_info[\![A\ x\ I]\!] \tag{7}$$

For a typical JVM, this extended-resolution step is performed at runtime by a dynamic search up the inheritance chain. However, the operating assumptions of the SSP enables this runtime search to be avoided by an extension to the symbolic resolution algorithm. The strategy shown in Figure 8 implements this extended-resolution step and produces a class file list in which all symbolic references to fields satisfy the static binding property.

When applied to a Java application hierarchy (app_0) the strategy x_res first evaluates the strategic expression $rcond\_tdl\{sbind\}[app_0]$. This evaluation results in a first-order strategy that is then applied to app_0, using the traversal TDL, to achieve the static binding property. The workhorse of the extended-resolution transformation is the second-order strategy $sbind$ that, for every class it is applied to, will output a strategy that abstractly has the form:

$$hide(lift\text{-}class\text{-}associated\text{-}with\text{-}field) +\!\!> check\text{-}for\text{-}declaration \tag{8}$$

Note that the control idea in the above strategy is somewhat similar to the *transient-check-add* strategy used in the Verilog synthesis example.

Within x_res, the evaluation of the strategic expression $rcond\_tdl\{sbind\}[app_0]$ will visit classes in the partially ordered class list in a top-down left-to-right (tdl) fashion, apply the $sbind$ strategy to each class encountered, and compose x_res : $app_0 \rightarrow$ TDL{ rcond_tdl{sbind}[app_0] }(app_0)

sbind: classfile⟦ cp_1 class$_{this}$ class$_{super}$ fields$_1$ mt_1 methods$_1$⟧

$\rightarrow$

(hide(lift[class$_{this}$][class$_{super}$]) +> rcond_tdl{collect_decs[class$_{this}$]}[fields$_1$])

lift: class$_{this}$ $\rightarrow$

class$_{super}$ $\rightarrow$

constant_fieldref_info⟦ class$_{this}$ name$_1$ descriptor$_1$⟧

$\rightarrow$

constant_fieldref_info⟦ class$_{super}$ name$_1$ descriptor$_1$⟧)

collect_decs: class$_{this}$ $\rightarrow$

field_info⟦ access_flags$_1$ name$_1$ descriptor$_1$ ⟧ $\rightarrow$

constant_fieldref_info⟦ class$_{this}$ name$_1$ descriptor$_1$⟧

$\rightarrow$

constant_fieldref_info⟦ class$_{this}$ name$_1$ descriptor$_1$⟧

Fig. 8. An extended-resolution step ensuring the static binding property

the resulting strategy instances using the +> combinator. The top-down left-to-right nature of the *rcond_tdl* traversal assures that in the resulting strategy, superclass strategies will be placed to the left of subclass strategies. The +> combinator used by *rcond_tdl* will compose (sub)strategies in such a fashion that an overall strategy will be created whose application will proceed from right-to-left, meaning that strategies associated with subclasses will be applied before the strategies of their corresponding superclasses.

In the strategy produced by *sbind*, the portion of the strategy abstractly denoted in (8) by *check-for-declaration* results from the evaluation of the strategic expression:

$$rcond\_tdl\{ collect\_decs[class_{this}]\}[fields_1] \tag{9}$$

In this expression, the strategy *collect_decs* is applied to the term $class_{this}$, which is the symbolic reference of the class that is currently being processed. The strategy resulting from this application is then applied to the fields section ($fields_1$) of the current class file using the traversal *rcond_tdl*. At this stage, terms in the fields section have the form $field\_info⟦ access\_flags_1\ name_1\ descriptor_1 ⟧$. The result is a strategy that applies an *identity transformation* to constant pool entries that satisfy the static binding property. Notice that, once such an identity transformation is applied, the application of the strategy to this entry is completed (since the strategy is constructed entirely using the conditional composition combinator +>). For entries that do not satisfy the static binding property none of the identity transformations associated with the current class apply an so application continues until an appropriate instance of the strategy

$hide(lift[class_{this}][class_{super}])$ is encountered. This strategy rewrites the class of the symbolic field reference to its superclass. Since the strategy is enclosed in a *hide* combinator its application does not trigger completion of the overall strategy and application continues. At this time, the symbolic reference may satisfy the static binding property. If this is the case, then an identity transformation (derived from one of the field declarations of the superclass) will apply after which the application terminates. Otherwise another lift is applied and the process repeats.

7   Related Work

This section gives a brief overview of parsing technology and briefly discusses some other approaches to transformation.

7.1   Parsing: From Strings to Terms

Parsing technology is a key enabler of transformation. In this context, a *parser* is seen as a function that is given a flat (i.e., one dimensional) string as its input and returns a (two dimensional) structure called a *term* or *tree* as its output. The structural elements in a *term* provide crucial information against which transformations are written. Without this structure, transformation degenerates to little more than an automated version of the "cut and paste" capability found in text editors.

A *parser generator* is able to automatically generate a parser for given grammar. This capability enables the development of language independent transformation systems. The ability to deal with ambiguity represents a limiting aspect of parsers and parser generators. Typical LALR(1) parser technology is effective for parsing languages provided all derivations can be disambiguated by looking ahead one token in the input. LALR(1) parsers are widely used because of their efficiency and are produced by the YACC and GNU Bison compiler-compilers.

A drawback of LALR(1) parsers [17] is that they can only effectively handle a subset of the set of unambiguous context-free grammars (i.e., not every context-free language has an LALR(1) grammar). It turns out that this restriction is significant in the realm of language independent transformation. As a result, more powerful parsing algorithms are typically employed by transformation systems. At the present time, the generalized LR (GLR) parsing algorithm is almost universally agreed upon as being necessary in order to seriously consider language independent transformation. A number of GLR parser generators are freely available. Elkhound [16] and Harmonia [1] are two systems that provide GLR parsing capabilities. In both of these systems, a grammar is defined using an EBNF syntax. In the realm of transformation, perhaps the most widely known and freely available GLR-based parser generator is that provided by the Syntax Definition Formalism (SDF) [20] [19]. SDF is a realization of a scannerless generalized LR parser (SGLR) supporting declarative disambiguation rules. Examples of disambiguation rules include rules the resolve ambiguities resulting from associativity and precedence of mathematical operators. SDF also supports modularization of grammars that enable grammars to be factored. Grammar modules can also be composed and thus reused.

7.2 Other Approaches to Transformation

In a classical setting, a strategic programming system can be viewed as a rewriting system in which constructs controlling rule application have first-class status. From a practical perspective, explicit control over rule application is essential when dealing with rule sets that are neither confluent nor terminating. Typically, it is the presence of explicit control constructs (e.g., sequential composition of rules, generic term traversals, etc.) that distinguishes a transformation system from a pure rewriting system.

ELAN [3] is a first-order strategic programming system in which rules can be grouped into labelled rule bases. An efficient AC-matching algorithm is used to control the application of such rule bases to terms. The consequence of AC matching and labelled rule bases is that the application of a rule to a specific term may yield multiple results. This form of non-determinism surrounding rule base application is central to ELAN and gives the system a deductive/declarative flavor. The ρ-calculus [7] provides the semantic foundation for ELAN [6].

Stratego [21] is a first-order strategic programming system whose control constructs include a wide range of combinators and one-layer traversals. Stratego further extends this control framework with scoped dynamic rewrite rules [15]. Though their semantics are slightly different, scoped dynamic rewrite rules can be seen as a first-order cousin of the higher-order rules of TL discussed in this article. Stratego also provides access to a number of low-level abstractions (e.g., *match* and *build*) which can be composed to define a variety of transformational ideas. As such, it provides a foundation upon which other kinds of transformation systems can be built.

ASF+SDF [2] is a first-order rewriting framework in which an extended form of matching provides the ability to perform associative matching on list structures. Recently, the ASF+SDF has been extended so that one can combine parameterized rewrite rules with a fixed set of generic traversals [18].

Strafunski is a Haskell-based system in which transformation is approached from a functional perspective. Monads are used to propagate information and traversals are described in terms of catamorphisms such as *fold b $\oplus$*. This connection between catamorphisms and strategic driven term traversal was first made in [14].

8 Conclusion

The ever increasing complexity of software systems has presented transformation-based approaches to software manipulation with unique challenges. Significant progress remains to be made with respect to problems relating to scale and reuse. Orthogonal to these issues, a ubiquitous theme in transformation concerns itself with bringing together data from unrelated portions of a term. Higher-order transformations provide an abstraction capable of distributing data throughout a term structure. However, we believe the story is far from over. HATS represents a environment in which transformational ideas can be explored. HATS gives plenty of feedback to users and the interpreted nature of the HATS transformation engine lends itself to modification allowing new transformational constructs and abstractions to be added to HATS with relatively reasonable effort. The hope is that this will encourage continued exploration and experimentation in the area of transformation-based design and development.

References

1. A. Begel, M. Boshernitsan, and S. L. Graham. Transformational generation of language plug-ins in the harmonia framework. Technical Report CSD-05-1370, University of California, Berkeley, California, January 2005.
2. J. A. Bergstra. *Algebraic specification.* ACM Press, New York, NY, USA, 1989.
3. P. Borovanský, C. Kirchner, H. Kirchner, P.-E. Moreau, and C. Ringeissen. An overview of elan. *Electr. Notes Theor. Comput. Sci.*, 15, 1998.
4. J. M. Boyle, T. J. Harmer, and V. L. Winter. The TAMPR Program Transformation System: Simplifying the Development of Numerical Software. In E. Arge, A. M. Bruaset, and H. P. Langtangen, editors, *Modern Software Tools for Scientific Computing*, pages 353–372. Birkhäuser Boston, Inc., 1997.
5. J. M. Boyle and M. N. Muralidharan. Program Reusability through Program Transformation. In *IEEE Transactions on Software Engineering*, volume 10:5, pages 574–588, September 1984.
6. Cirstea, Horatiu and Kirchner, Claude. The rewriting calculus as a semantics of ELAN. In J. Hsiang and A. Ohori, editors, *4th Asian Computing Science Conference*, volume 1538 of *Lecture Notes in Computer Science*, pages 8–10, Manila, The Philippines, Dec. 1998. Springer-Verlag.
7. Cirstea, Horatiu and Kirchner, Claude. An introduction to the rewriting calculus. Research Report RR-3818, INRIA, Dec. 1999.
8. M. de Jonge. A pretty-printer for every occasion, 2000.
9. HATS. http://faculty.ist.unomaha.edu/winter/hats-uno/hatsweb/index.html.
10. J. He and C. A. R. Hoare. *Unifying theories of programming.* Prentice Hall International Series in Comptuer Science, 1998.
11. J. Kyoda and H. Jifeng. Towards an Algebraic Synthesis of Verilog. Technical Report UNU/IIST Report No. 218, The United Nations University, July 2001.
12. R. Lämmel, E. Visser, and J. Visser. The Essence of Strategic Programming. 18 p.; Draft; Available at http://www.cwi.nl/~ralf, Oct.15 2002.
13. R. Lämmel and J. Visser. A Strafunski Application Letter. In V. Dahl and P. Wadler, editors, *Proc. of Practical Aspects of Declarative Programming (PADL'03)*, volume 2562 of *LNCS*, pages 357–375. Springer-Verlag, Jan. 2003.
14. R. Lämmel, J. Visser, and J. Kort. Dealing with Large Bananas. In J. Jeuring, editor, *Proceedings of WGP'2000, Technical Report, Universiteit Utrecht*, pages 46–59, July 2000.
15. K. O. M. Bravenboer, A. van Dam and E. Visser. Program transformation with scoped dynamic rewrite rules. Technical Report UU-CS-2005-005, Institute of Information and Computing Sciences, Utrecht University, 2005.
16. S. McPeak. Elkhound: A fast, practial glr parser generator. Technical Report UCB/CSD-2-1214, University of California, Berkeley, California, December 2002.

17. M. van den Brand, M. Sellink, and C. Verhoef. Current parsing techniques in software renovation considered harmful. In *In Proceedings of the 6th International Workshop on Program Comprehension, IWPC'98*, pages 108–117, Ischia, Italy, 1998.

18. M. G. J. van den Brand, P. Klint, and J. J. Vinju. Term rewriting with traversal functions. *ACM Trans. Softw. Eng. Methodol.*, 12(2):152–190, 2003.

19. M. G. J. van den Brand, J. Scheerder, J. Vinju, and E. Visser. Disambiguation filters for scannerless generalized LR parsers. In N. Horspool, editor, *Compiler Construction (CC'02)*, volume 2304 of *Lecture Notes in Computer Science*, pages 143–158, Grenoble, France, April 2002. Springer-Verlag.

20. E. Visser. *Syntax Definition for Language Prototyping*. PhD thesis, University of Amsterdam, 1997.

21. E. Visser, Z. el Abidine Benaissa, and A. Tolmach. Building program optimizers with rewriting strategies. In *ICFP '98: Proc. of the third ACM SIGPLAN international conference on Functional programming*, pages 13–26. ACM Press, 1998.

22. G. L. Wickstrom, J. Davis, S. E. Morrison, S. Roach, and V. L. Winter. The SSP: An example of high-assurance system engineering. In *HASE 2004: The 8th IEEE International Symposium on High Assurance Systems Engineering*, 2004.

23. V. Winter. Strategy Construction in the Higher-Order Framework of TL. *Electronic Notes in Theoretical Computer Science (ENTCS)*, 124, 2004.

24. V. Winter and M. Subramaniam. Dynamic Strategies, Transient Strategies, and the Distributed Data Problem. *Science of Computer Programming (Special Issue on Program Transformation)*, 52:165–212, 2004.

25. V. L. Winter. An overview of hats: a language independent high assurance transformation system. In *In Proc. of IEEE Symposium on Application-Specific Systems and Software Engineering and Technology (ASSET).*, pages 222 – 229, March 1999.

26. V. L. Winter, J. Beranek, A. Mametjanov, F. Fraij, S. Roach, and G. Wickstrom. A Transformational Overview of the Core Functionality of an Abstract Class Loader for the SSP. In *Tenth IEEE International Workshop on Object-oriented Real-time Dependable Systems (WORDS 2005)*, 2005.

Part III

Participants' Contributions

Using Java CSP Solvers in the Automated Analyses of Feature Models*

David Benavides, Sergio Segura, Pablo Trinidad, and Antonio Ruiz-Cortés

Dpto. de Lenguajes y Sistemas Informáticos
University of Seville
Av. de la Reina Mercedes S/N, 41012 Seville, Spain
{benavides, sergio, trinidad, aruiz}@tdg.lsi.us.es

Abstract. Feature Models are used in different stages of software development and are recognized to be an important asset in model transformation techniques and software product line development. The automated analysis of feature models is being recognized as one of the key challenges for automated software development in the context of Software Product Lines. In our previous work we explained how a feature model can be transformed into a constraint satisfaction problem. However cardinalities were not considered. In this paper we present how a cardinality-based feature model can be also translated into a constraint satisfaction problem. In that connection, it is possible to use off-the-shelf tools to automatically accomplish several tasks such as calculating the number of possible feature configurations and detecting possible conflicts. In addition, we present a performance test between two off-the-shelf Java constraint solvers. To the best of our knowledge, this is the first time a performance test is presented using solvers for feature modelling proposes

1 Introduction

Throughout the years, software reuse and quality have been two constants aims in software development. Although significant progress has been made in programming languages, methodologies and so forth, the problem seems to remain. Software Product Line (SPL) development [8] is an approach to develop software systems in a systematic way that intends to solve these problems. Roughly speaking, an SPL can be defined as a set of software products that share a common set of features. Therefore, an SPL approach could be useful for organizations that are product–oriented rather than project–oriented [7]. That is, organizations that operate in a particular market segment.

SPL engineering consists of two main activities: domain engineering (also called core asset development) and application engineering (also called product development). These two activities are complementary and provide feedback to each other. Domain engineering deals with core assets production, that is, the pieces of the products to be shared by all SPL products. On the other hand, application engineering deals with individual system production.

---

* This work was partially supported by the Spanish Science and Education Ministry (MEC) under contracts TIC2003-02737-C02-01 (AgilWeb).

R. Lämmel, J. Saraiva, and J. Visser (Eds.): GTTSE 2005, LNCS 4143, pp. 399–408, 2006.
© Springer-Verlag Berlin Heidelberg 2006

Feature Analysis [17] is an important task of domain engineering and is expected to produce a Feature Model (FM) as its main output. A FM can be defined as a compact representation of all possible products of an SPL. Furthermore, it is commonly accepted that FMs can be used in different stages of an SPL effort in order to produce other assets such as requirements documents [15, 16], portlets–based applications [11, 12] or even pieces of code [3, 9, 20]. Hence, FM becomes an important focus of research in the field of model transformation.

Automated analyses of FMs are an important challenge in SPL [1, 2]. In a previous work [4, 5] we presented how to transform a FM (without considering cardinalities) into a Constraint Satisfaction Problem (CSP). In that way, it is possible to use off–the–shelf constraint satisfaction solvers to automatically accomplish several tasks such as calculating the number of possible configurations and detecting possible conflicts. The contribution of this paper is twofold: i) to explain how a FM with cardinalities can be translated into a CSP and ii) to show the result of a performance test between two off the shelf Java constraint solvers: JaCoP and Choco. To the best of our knowledge, this is the first test that measures the performance of constraint solvers in the context of feature analyses.

The remainder of the paper is structured as follows: in Section 2 we introduce feature models. In Section 3 constraint programming is outlined and details on how to translate a FM into a CSP are presented. Section 4 focuses on the results of the experiment. Finally we summarize our conclusions and describe our future work in Section 5.

2   Feature Models

A Feature Model (FM) is a compact representation of all possible products of an SPL. FMs are used to model a set of software systems in terms of features and relations among them. Designing a software system in terms of features is more natural than doing it in terms of objects or classes. Consequently, a software system will be composed of a set of features.

Since FMs were first presented in 1990 [17] there have been many publications and proposals to extend, improve and modify the original FM diagram. However, despite years of research, there is no consensus on a FM notation. Although it would be desirable to have a common notation, it is out of the scope of this paper to give yet another FM notation. Therefore, we use the one proposed by Czarnecki [10] that was formalized as a context free grammar and integrates some previous extensions.

A FM is basically a tree structure with dependencies between features. Figure 1 represents the general metamodel of a FM (this metamodel was presented in [6]). Likewise, Figure 2 represents a FM of the James Project [13]. James is a collaborative web based system that we modeled in terms of features and can be a clear example of an SPL. Some products can be derived from the FM on Figure 2. Having a web service interface (WSInterface) is optional while it is mandatory to have user management (UserManagement), at least one module (Modules) and the core of the system (Core).

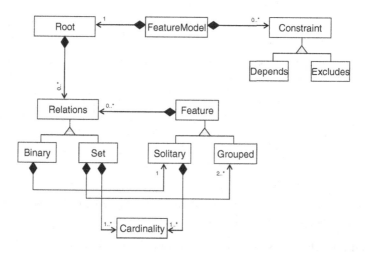

Fig. 1. CFM meta model

A FM is composed of a **root** ($JAMES$ in Figure 2) and an optional set of **constraints** (they refer to global constraints: depends and excludes; $R9$ and $R10$ in Figure 2).

A root is composed of an optional set of **relations**. Relations can be of two different types: **binary relations** which include mandatory (e.g. $R1$), optional (e.g. $R2$) and cardinality–based relations (e.g. $R4$) or **set** relations (e.g.$R7$).

A **feature** can be of two different types and is composed of zero or more relations. A binary relation is composed of one and only one **solitary feature** which is the child feature since the parent feature is the one that has this relation ($Core$ or $UserManagement$ are examples of solitary features); A set relation is composed of at least two **grouped** features ($Calendar, DB$ or PDA are examples of grouped features). In addition, a solitary feature and set relations comprise one or more cardinalities. Note that in the graphical representation it is possible not to represent a cardinality in set relations although in fact that means that the cardinality is $\langle 1\text{-}1 \rangle$. Likewise, there are graphical representations for commonly used cardinalities of solitary features like $[1..1]$ and $[0..1]$ (see Figure 2 notes).

3   Constraint Programming

Constraint programming is a well established field of research and has been successfully applied in many engineering areas such as electronics or operational engineering. In the words of Prof. Freuder "*Constraint programming represents one of the closest approaches computer science has yet made to the Holy Grail of programming: the user states the problem, the computer solves it.*" [14].

Constraint Programming can be defined as the set of techniques such as algorithms or heuristics that deal with Constraint Satisfaction Problems (CSP) to such an extent that to solve a given problem by means of constraint programming, first the problem has to be formulated as a CSP.

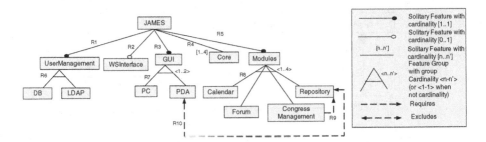

Fig. 2. James System

A CSP consist of a set of variables, domains for those variables and a set of constraints restricting the values of the variables.

Definition 1 (CSP). *A CSP is a three–tuple of the form (V, D, C) where $V \neq \emptyset$ is a finite set of variables, $D \neq \emptyset$ is a finite set of domains (one for each variable) and C is a constraint defined on V.*

Once the problem is stated as a CSP, it is possible to use off–the-shelf CSP solvers that are able to provide the solutions to the problem. Internally the solvers will be implemented by using algorithms and heuristics that have been and are being investigated during several decades.

3.1 Mapping a FM into a CSP

We presented in [4, 5] how a FM with dependencies was translated into a CSP. However we did not provide a way to do the same with cardinality–based FMs [10]. In this Section we give details on how to transform a FM with cardinalities into a CSP which is a novel contribution.

Rules for translating FMs to constraints are listed in Figure 3. First, there is a variable for each feature in the CSP. The domain of each variable depends on the cardinality associated to each variable. By default the domain is $\{0,1\}$ and if a feature is part of a cardinality relation, then the domain of the variable is added (e.g. $Core \in \{0,4\}$ in Figure 2). Then, a constraint selecting the root feature is added because all products have the root feature (e.g. root = 1). The final CSP for a FM is the conjunction of the constraints following the rules of Figure 3.

4   Experimental Results

Using CSP solvers, it is possible to automatically perform some operations on a FM such as calculating the number of possible combinations of features, retrieving configurations following a criteria, calculating the number of features in a given configuration, validating a given FM to detect possible inconsistences, finding an optimum product on the basis of a given criteria (the cheapest, the one with fewest features and so forth) or calculating the commonality factor for a given feature and the variability factor of a given FM.

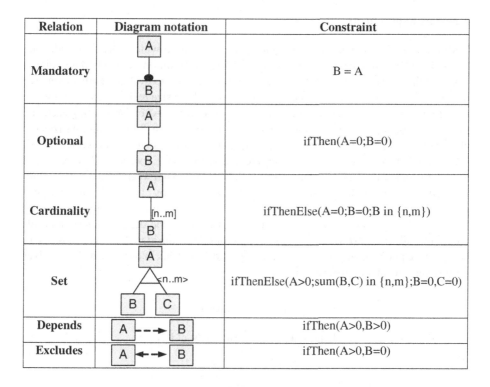

Relation	Diagram notation	Constraint
Mandatory	A / B	B = A
Optional	A / B	ifThen(A=0;B=0)
Cardinality	A / [n..m] / B	ifThenElse(A=0;B=0;B in {n,m})
Set	A / <n..m> / B C	ifThenElse(A>0;sum(B,C) in {n,m};B=0,C=0)
Depends	A - - ▸ B	ifThen(A>0,B>0)
Excludes	A ◂ - ▸ B	ifThen(A>0,B=0)

Fig. 3. Feature Models and Related Constraints

The main ideas concerning the use of constraint programming on FM analyses were stated in [4, 5] but some experimental results were left for our future work. In this Section we present an experimental comparison of two Java CSP solvers that were used to automatically analyse FMs.

4.1 The JaCoP and Choco Solvers

There are several commercial tools to work with CSPs. One of the major commercial vendors is ILOG that has two versions of CSP Solvers in C++ and Java. Because it is a commercial solution, we declined to use ILOG solvers' licenses in our empirical comparison.

To the best of our knowledge there is only one reliable and stable open source Java CSP Solver : Choco Constraint System [19]. We selected this solver because it seems to be one of the most popular within the research community and because it is the only one we know of that is available for free directly from the Internet. We selected JaCoP solver [18] because it offers a free license for academic purposes. Both solvers have similar characteristic in terms of the variables and constraints allowed, therefore the implementation of our mapping was done in a straightforward manner. For JaCoP we used FDV variables (FDV stands for Finite Domain Variables) to represent the features while IntVar variables were used in the Choco implementation.

4.2   The Experiments

With the following experiments we intend to demonstrate which solver provides the best performance in the automated analyses of FMs. In addition, we studied the robustness and the areas of vulnerability of each solver. In order to evaluate both solvers we used five FMs. Three of them represent small and medium size real systems, meanwhile the larger two were generated randomly for this experiment. After formulating each one as a CSP in both platforms, we proceeded with the execution. Table 1 summarizes the characteristics of the experiments. Experiment 1 is the FM that was presented in [4]. It is a simple FM representing a Home Integration System. Experiment 2 is the FM of Figure 2 which represents a collaborative web based system. Experiment 3 is a medium size FM of a flight booking system based on the work done by [11, 12]. Finally, we generated two larger FMs randomly (Experiments 4 and 5) with a double aim: representing more complex systems with a greater number of features and dependencies, and evaluating the solvers' performance in limit situations. We considered it was necessary to compare the performance with small, medium and large FMs in order to evaluate solver performance results in different situations.

Table 1. Experiments

Experiment	N. of Features	N. of Dep
1	15	0
2	14	2
3	26	0
4	40	14
5	52	28

The process to generate a FM randomly is based on a recursive method that has five input parameters: height levels, maximum number of children relations for a node, maximum cardinality number, maximum number of elements in a set relation and number of dependencies. Firstly, features and their relations are generated using random values. Secondly, the dependencies are created by taking pairs of features randomly and establishing a random dependency (includes or excludes) between them. We took care not to generate misconceptions (e.g. a child depends on a parent).

As exposed in [5], there are some operations that can be performed. For our experiments we performed two operations: i) finding one configuration that would satisfy all the constraints, that is, a product and ii) finding the total number of configurations of a given FM. The first is the simplest operation while the second is the most difficult one in terms of performance because it is necessary to retrieve all possible combinations.

The comparison focused on the data obtained from several executions in order to avoid as much exogenous interferences as possible. The total number of executions to calculate the average time was ten. The data extracted from the tests was:

- Number of features in the first solution obtained by solver.
- Average execution time to obtain one solution (measured in milliseconds).

- Total number of solutions, that is, the potential number of products represented in the FM.
- Average execution time to obtain the number of solutions (measured in milliseconds).

In order to evaluate the implementation, we measured its performance and effectiveness. We implemented the solution using Java 1.5.0_04. We ran our tests on a WINDOWS XP PROFESSIONAL machine equipped with a 3.2Ghz Intel Pentium IV microprocessor and 1024 MB of DDR 166Mhz RAM memory.

4.3   The Results

The experimental comparison revealed some interesting results (see Figures 4, 5 and 6). The first evidence we should mention is that JaCoP is on average 54% faster than Choco in finding a solution. It is important to observe that our approach is feasible because the necessary time to obtain a response is really low (35 milliseconds in the worst case).

However, while JaCoP is much faster than Choco in finding the total number of solutions in small CSPs, JaCoP seems to be noticeably slower than Choco in the big ones (see Figure 6). This curious result probably depends on how each solver is used to obtain the number of solutions. Choco has a simple method to know the number of solutions of a concrete problem (Solver.getNbSolutions()), while JaCoP implementation needs to find all the solutions first and count them afterwards. This simple variation implies a very important difference in performance. For instance, in test 5 JaCoP needs to create 61440 ArrayLists and fill all of them with all the solutions which produces a great time loss. On the other hand, Choco does not have this weakness as its method to find the number of solutions only returns five solutions to avoid memory deficit problems. If the user wants to obtain the other solutions he only has to make a simple iteration and take them one by one. In the three smaller experiments, JaCoP is faster than Choco so we presume that this trend would continue if JaCoP optimized this aspect. In test 5, we performed an experiment to find and return all the solutions in both solvers, that is, not only to find the number of solutions but the solutions themselves. The result was decisive: Choco required over a minute to perform this task, proving to be slower than JaCoP in this situation.

Experiment	Features in Sol.	JACOP / CHOCO				
		Time one Sol.		N° Solutions	Time all Sol.	
		JACOP	CHOCO		JACOP	CHOCO
1	7	9,9	18,8	32	37,5	45,5
2	8	9,4	22,7	68	64,4	81,3
3	13	12	24	512	225,6	265,3
4	19	20,2	34,9	34560	5619	2203,3
5	19	24,4	35,8	61440	15390,8	4817,6

Fig. 4. Experimental Results of JaCoP and Choco Solvers

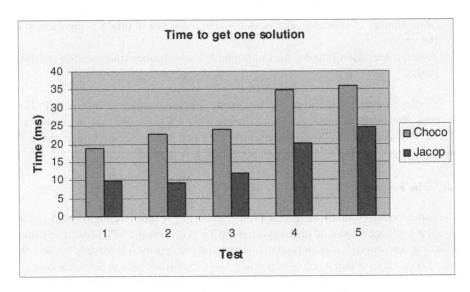

Fig. 5. Comparing JaCoP and Choco getting one solution

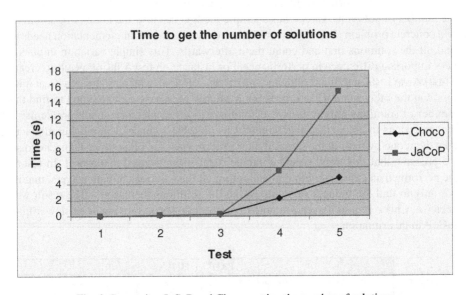

Fig. 6. Comparing JaCoP and Choco getting the number of solutions

Although memory usage was not a relevant data in our experiments we noticed that in general Choco uses more memory than JaCoP; however there is not a remarkable difference between both solvers.

Finally, we identified some interesting characteristic in both solvers. Firstly, JaCoP allows the user to obtain easily from executions more interesting information than Choco such as the number of backtracks of a search or the number of decisions taken to find a solution. In second place, we found a worrying bug when working with big problems in Choco. In most cases, executions of CSPs representing big FMs generated an exception (choco.bool.BinConjunction) which imposes an important limitation to Choco.

5   Conclusion and Future Work

In this paper we presented how to translate a cardinality-based feature model into a constraint satisfaction problem. We performed a comparative test between two off–the–shelf CSP Java solvers and offered some interesting performance conclusions. The test showed that JaCoP is faster than Choco except in finding the number of solutions. JaCoP gives more details about executions than Choco such as the number of backtracks or the number of decisions. Choco has an important bug when working with big FMs while it is a good open source alternative especially for small and medium size problems. Both solvers have a similar memory usage. Nevertheless, both JaCoP and Choco are useful for the experiments presented in the paper as executions times are really low (milliseconds).

Several challenges remain for our future work. We plan to extend the experiments in order to scale our proposal and compare the results. Bigger experiments with more features and more dependencies are needed and we plan to perform those experiments in the future. Furthermore, we think that we should compare our proposal with others using different representations like SAT or BDDs to complement our results.

References

1. D. Batory. Feature models, grammars, and propositional formulas. In *Software Product Lines Conference, LNCS 3714*, pages 7–20, 2005.
2. D. Batory. A tutorial on feature oriented programming and the ahead tool suite. In *Summer school on Generative and Transformation Techniques in Software Engineering*, 2005.
3. D. Batory, J. Sarvela, and A. Rauschmayer. Scaling step-wise refinement. *IEEE Trans. Software Eng.*, 30(6):355–371, 2004.
4. D. Benavides, A. Ruiz-Cortés, and P. Trinidad. Automated reasoning on feature models. *LNCS, Advanced Information Systems Engineering: 17th International Conference, CAiSE 2005*, 3520:491–503, 2005.
5. D. Benavides, A. Ruiz-Cortés, and P. Trinidad. Using constraint programming to reason on feature models. In *The Seventeenth International Conference on Software Engineering and Knowledge Engineering (SEKE'05)*, July 2005.
6. D. Benavides, S. Trujillo, and P. Trinidad. On the modularization of feature models. In *First European Workshop on Model Transformation*, September 2005.
7. J. Bosch. *Design and Use of Software Architectures*. Addison-Wesley, 1th edition, 2000.
8. P. Clements and L. Northrop. *Software Product Lines: Practices and Patterns*. SEI Series in Software Engineering. Addison–Wesley, August 2001.
9. K. Czarnecki and U.W. Eisenecker. *Generative Programming: Methods, Techniques, and Applications*. Addison–Wesley, may 2000. ISBN 0–201–30977–7.
10. K. Czarnecki, S. Helsen, and U.W. Eisenecker. Formalizing cardinality-based feature models and their specialization. *Software Process: Improvement and Practice*, 10(1):7–29, 2005.
11. O. Díaz, S. Trujillo, and F.I. Anfurrutia. Supporting production strategies as refinements of the production process. In *to be published at Sofware Product Line Conference (SPLC 2005)*, 2005.

12. O. Díaz, S. Trujillo, and I. Azpeitia. User-Facing Web Service Development: A Case for a Product-Line Approach. In Boualem Benatallah and Ming-Chien Shan, editors, *Technologies for E-Services, 4th VLDB International Workshop (VLDB-TES 2003)*, volume 2819 of *LNCS*, pages 66–77. Springer-Verlag, 2003.

13. P. Fernandez and M. Resinas. James project. *Available at http://jamesproject.sourceforge.net/*, 2002-2005.

14. E. C. Freuder. In pursuit of the holy grail. *Constraints*, 2(1):57–61, April 1997.

15. G. Halmans and K. Pohl. Communicating the variability of a software–product family to customers. *Journal on Software and Systems Modeling*, 2(1):15–36, 2003.

16. S. Jarzabek, Wai Chun Ong, and Hongyu Zhang. Handling variant requirements in domain modeling. *The Journal of Systems and Software*, 68(3):171–182, 2003.

17. K. Kang, S. Cohen, J. Hess, W. Novak, and S. Peterson. Feature–Oriented Domain Analysis (FODA) Feasibility Study. Technical Report CMU/SEI-90-TR-21, Software Engineering Institute, Carnegie Mellon University, November 1990.

18. K. Kuchcinski. Constraints-driven scheduling and resource assignment. *ACM Transactions on Design Automation of Electronic Systems (TODAES)*, 8(3):355–383, July 2003.

19. F. Laburthe and N. Jussien. Choco constraint programming system. *Available at http://choco.sourceforge.net/*, 2003-2005.

20. C. Prehofer. Feature-oriented programming: A new way of object composition. *Concurrency and Computation: Practice and Experience*, 13(6):465–501, 2001.

Co-transformations in Database Applications Evolution

Anthony Cleve and Jean-Luc Hainaut

Laboratory of Database Applications Engineering
University of Namur, Belgium
21 rue Grandgagnage 5000 Namur
{acl, jlh}@info.fundp.ac.be

Abstract. The paper adresses the problem of consistency preservation in data intensive applications evolution. When the database structure evolves, the application programs must be changed to interface with the new schema. The latter modification can prove very complex, error prone and time consuming. We describe a comprehensive transformation/generative approach according to which automated program transformation can be derived from schema transformation. The proposal is illustrated in the particular context of database reengineering, for which a specific methodology and a prototype tool are presented. Some results of two case studies are described.

1 Introduction

Software evolution consists in keeping a software system up-to-date and responsive to ever changing business and technological requirements. This paper focuses on the evolution of complex database applications, that is, data intensive software systems comprising a database. Database migration, database merging and database restructuring are popular evolution scenarios that involve not only changing the data components of applications, but also rewriting some parts of the programs themselves, even when no functional change occurs. In general, such evolution patterns induce the modification of three mutually dependent system components, namely the data structures (i.e., the *schema*), the data instances and the application programs [11]. When the system evolves, the consistency that exists between these three artifacts must be preserved.

In this paper, we focus on the consistency relationship that holds between the application programs and their database schema. We assume that the evolution process starts with a schema modification, potentially challenging this consistency. Our main question is the following: how can a change in a database schema be propagated to the application programs manipulating its data instances? Considering that any schema change can be modelled by a *transformation* (a rewriting rule that replaces a data structure with another one), we can formulate our question more precisely. The question can now be expressed

R. Lämmel, J. Saraiva, and J. Visser (Eds.): GTTSE 2005, LNCS 4143, pp. 409–421, 2006.
© Springer-Verlag Berlin Heidelberg 2006

as follows: how can a schema transformation be propagated to the application programs that manipulate the data stored in the database? Through this transformational approach, database applications evolution will be modelled by the derivation of program transformations from schema transformations, that is, *co-transformations*.

The paper is structured as follows. Section 2 defines the concept of schema transformation. The way program transformations are derived from schema transformations is discussed in Section 3. In Section 4, we illustrate this general approach in a particular evolution context, i.e., data reengineering. Section 5 gives an overview of a tool architecture that support the whole process. In Section 6 first experiments are presented. We discuss related work in Section 7, while Section 8 concludes the paper.

2   Schema Tranformations

2.1   Definition

A schema transformation consists in deriving a target schema S' from a source schema S by replacing construct C (possibly empty) in S with a new construct C' (possibly empty) [7]. C (resp. C') is empty when the transformation consists in adding (resp. removing) a construct. More formally, a transformation Σ is defined as a couple of mappings $<T, t>$ such that : $C' = T(C)$ and $c' = t(c)$, where c is any instance of C and c' the corresponding instance of C'. *Structural mapping* T explains how to modify the schema while *instance mapping* t states how to compute the instance set of C' from instances of C.

2.2   Semantics Preservation

The notion of semantics of a schema has no generally agreed upon definition. We assume that the semantics of a schema S_1 includes the semantics of another schema S_2 iff the application domain described by S_2 is a part of the domain represented by S_1. We can distinguish three schema transformation categories:

- T^+ collects the transformations that augment the semantics of the schema (e.g., adding an entity type).
- T^- includes the transformations that decrease the semantics of the schema (e.g., removing an attribute).
- $T^=$ is the category of transformations that leave the semantics of the schema unchanged (e.g., transforming a relationship type into a foreign key).

The transformations of category $T^=$ are called *reversible* or *semantics-preserving*. If a transformation is reversible, then the source schema can be replaced with the target one without loss of information. We refer to [6] for a more detailed analysis of semantics preservation in schema transformations.

2.3   Examples

Fig. 1[1] graphically illustrates the structural mapping T_1 of the transformation of a multivalued, compound attribute into an entity type and a relationship type R. Fig. 2 depicts the structural mapping T_2 of the transformation of a one-to-many relationship type R into a foreign key. Both transformations can be proved to be semantics-preserving.

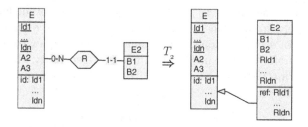

Fig. 1. Structural mapping T_1 of a semantics-preserving schema transformation that transforms a complex attribute A into entity type EA and relationship type R

Fig. 2. Structural mapping T_2 of a semantics-preserving schema transformation that transforms a one-to-many relationship type R into a foreign key $RId_1 \cdots RId_n$

3   Deriving Program Transformations

The feasibility of automatically deriving program transformations from a schema transformation depends on the nature of the latter. In the general case, the transformations of T^+ and T^- categories do not allow automatic program modifications. The task remains under the responsibility of the programmer. However, it is generally possible to help him modify the code by automatically locating the program sections where occurrences of modified object types are processed. Program understanding techniques such as pattern searching, dependency graphs and program slicing allow to locate with a good precision the code to be modified [8].

---

[1] In Fig. 1 and 2, a box represents an entity type (record type or table). The first compartment specifies its names, the second one specifies its attributes (fields or columns) and the third one specifies the keys and other constraints: **id** stands for primary identifier/key; **acc** stands for access key or index; **ref** stands for foreign key. Relationship types between entity types are represented by diamonds.

Semantics-preserving schema transformations $(T^=)$ can be propagated to the program level. Indeed, they allow the programming logic to be left unchanged, since the application programs still manipulate the same informational content. Program conversion mainly consists in adapting the related DMS[2] statements to the modified data structure. In order to define DMS-independent transformation rules, we will reason about the following abstract data modification primitives:

- `create` *var* := *rec-name condition*: creates a record of type *rec-name* satisfying *condition*. The variable *var* contains or references the created record for further manipulation.
- `delete` *var condition*: deletes the record *var* if it satisfies *condition*, according to the chosen delete mode.
- `update` *var condition*: updates the record *var* in such a way that it satisfies *condition*.

Fig. 3 presents the correspondences between the above abstract primitives and concrete statements (COBOL, CODASYL and SQL). Access (reading) primitives are both more simple and more complex than modification primitives. In the one hand, the instance mapping states how instances can be extracted from the database according to the new schema. On the other hand, the way currency registers are implemented in various DMS can be quite different. Abstracting them in a DMS-independent manner is too complex to be adressed in this paper. Therefore, we assume, without loss of generality, that propagating schema transformations to reading primitives requires DMS-specific rules.

Abstract	COBOL	CODASYL	SQL
create	WRITE	STORE	INSERT
delete	DELETE	ERASE	DELETE
update	REWRITE	MODIFY	UPDATE

Fig. 3. Correspondences between data modification primitives

The problem translates as follows: given a schema transformation Σ applicable to data construct C, how can it be propagated to the abstract primitives that create, delete and update instances of construct C. Our approach consists in associating with structural mapping T of Σ, in addition to instance mapping t, three modification primitive mappings: t_c (create), t_d (delete) and t_u (update). These three mappings specify how to modify the corresponding primitives when T is applied to the database schema.

Fig. 4 shows mapping t_{1c} we associate with structural mapping T_1 of Fig. 1. Since attribute A of entity type E has become entity type EA, the way an instance of E is created must be changed. It now involves the creation of EA instances corresponding to the old A instances (in a new loop). The created EA instances must be linked with the instance (e) of E through the relationship

---

[2] Data Management System.

type R. Fig. 5 illustrates the mapping t_{2_c} associated with structural mapping T_2 of Fig. 2. The condition $R : e$ is replaced with a condition on the foreign key value.

$$
\begin{aligned}
create\ e := E((&: A_1 = a_1)\\
and\ (&: A_2 = a_2)\\
and\ (&: A[1].B_1 = b_{11})\\
&\cdots\\
and\ (&: A[1].B_n = b_{1n})\\
&\cdots\\
and\ (&: A[N].B_1 = b_{N1})\\
&\cdots\\
and\ (&: A[N].B_n = b_{Nn}))
\end{aligned}
\qquad
\overset{t_{1_c}}{\Rightarrow}
\qquad
\begin{aligned}
create\ e := E((&: A_1 = a_1)\\
and\ (&: A_2 = a_2));\\[1em]
for\ i\ in\ 1..N\ &do\\
create\ ea := EA((&: B_1 = b_{i1})\\
&\cdots\\
and\ (&: B_n = b_{in})\\
and\ (&R : e))\\
endfor
\end{aligned}
$$

Fig. 4. Mapping t_{1_c} associated with structural mapping T_1 of Fig. 1

$$
\begin{aligned}
create\ e2 := E2((&: B_1 = b_1)\\
and\ (&: B_2 = b_2)\\
and\ (&R : e))
\end{aligned}
\qquad
\overset{t_{2_c}}{\Rightarrow}
\qquad
\begin{aligned}
create\ e2 := E2((&: B_1 = b_1)\\
and\ (&: B_2 = b2)\\
and\ (&: RId_1 = e.Id_1)\\
&\cdots\\
and\ (&: RId_n = e.Id_n)
\end{aligned}
$$

Fig. 5. Mapping t_{2_c} associated with structural mapping T_2 of Fig. 2

4 A Particular Evolution Context: Data Reengineering

4.1 Definition

Data reengineering consists in deriving a new database from a legacy database and adapting the software components accordingly. Substituting a modern data management system (relational DBMS for instance) for an outdated data manager (typically standard file manager), or improving the database schema to gain better performance are popular scenarios. Typically, this migration process comprises the following three main steps [10]:

1. *Schema conversion*: the legacy database schema is translated into an equivalent schema expressed in the target technology.
2. *Data conversion*: the database contents are migrated from the legacy database to the new one. This step consists of a schema-driven *extract-transform-load* process.
3. *Program conversion*: the legacy programs are modified so that they access the new database instead of the legacy data. In the scenario studied, the functionalities, the programming language and the user interface are kept unchanged. This conversion step is generally a complex process that relies on the schema conversion step.

Data reengineering can be seen as a particular case of database applications evolution, in the sense that it typically involves compound, *semantics-preserving* schema transformations and related program transformations [4]. However, these program transformations do not only propagate schema transformations. In addition, they must *translate* the legacy DML[3] primitives into equivalent code fragments using the target DML.

4.2   Semantics-Based Schema Conversion

There are different approaches to convert the source schema into the target schema. Our approach consists of two steps:

1. Recovering the conceptual schema (i.e., the *semantics*) of the source database through a database reverse engineering phase [8].
2. Designing the target database from the CS obtained so far, through classical database engineering techniques.

This schema conversion approach has the merit of producing a well-designed, fully-documented database rid of the flaws of the legacy data, that forms a sound basis for both existing and future applications.

4.3   Wrapper-Based Program Conversion

In migration and interoperability architectures, wrappers are popular components that convert legacy interfaces into modern ones. In this context, a wrapper is a data model conversion component that is called by the client application programs to carry out operation on the database. For instance, a set of standard files is given an object-oriented API suited to modern distributed architectures.

In the data reengineering context we suggest the opposite approach, i.e., the use of *inverse wrappers* [9]. An inverse wrapper encapsulates the new database and provide access to the migrated data through a legacy API. It converts all legacy DMS requests issued by the legacy programs into requests compliant with the new DMS. Conversely, it captures the results from the new DMS, converts them according to the legacy format, and delivers them to the calling programs.

Our program conversion approach is a three-step method:

1. From all the schema transformations that are successively applied during the schema conversion phase (described in Section 4.2), we derive the mapping between the legacy DB schema (LDS) and the target DB schema (TDS).
2. From the LDS-to-TDS mapping, inverse wrappers are automatically generated. In practice, we generate one wrapper for each migrated record type.
3. The wrappers obtained so far are interfaced with the legacy application programs. This step mainly consists in replacing the legacy DML statements with corresponding wrapper invocations.

This program conversion approach allows the legacy applications to work on the new database with minimal alteration, and therefore at low cost.

---

[3] Data Manipulation Language.

4.4 Illustration

Let us consider COBOL record type ORD (Fig. 6—left) that is converted into two
equivalent relational tables ORDERS and DETAILS (Fig. 6—right). This conversion
is the result of the combination of several schema transformations:

1. $T_1 \equiv$ transforming the compound, multivalued attribute ORD-DETAIL into an
   entity type and a relationship type R;
2. $T_2 \equiv$ transforming the relationship type R into foreign key ORD_CODE;
3. $T_n \circ \cdots \circ T_3 \equiv$ renaming some data constructs to improve expressivity and
   comply with SQL syntax.

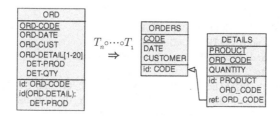

Fig. 6. Conversion of a COBOL record type into two relational tables

Each COBOL primitive that manipulate ORD records must be replaced with an
equivalent procedural fragment on the relational data structures. Then let us
examine the translation of the following COBOL statement:

```
WRITE ORD
```

This statement is first expressed as an abstract primitive:

```
create o := ORD((:ORD-CODE = ORD-CODE OF ORD)
    and (:ORD-DATE = ORD-DATE OF ORD)
    and (:ORD-CUST = ORD-CUST OF ORD)
    and (:ORD-DETAIL[1].DET-PROD = DET-PROD OF ORD-DETAIL ORD ORD(1))
    and (:ORD-DETAIL[1].DET-QTY = DET-QTY OF ORD-DETAIL OF ORD(1))
        . . .
    and (:ORD-DETAIL[20].DET-PROD = DET-PROD OF ORD-DETAIL OF ORD(20))
    and (:ORD-DETAIL[20].DET-QTY = DET-QTY OF ORD-DETAIL OF ORD(20)))
```

By applying mapping t_{1c} associated with T_1 we obtain:

```
create o := ORD((:ORD-CODE = ORD-CODE OF ORD)
            and (:ORD-DATE = ORD-DATE OF ORD)
            and (:ORD-CUST = ORD-CUST OF ORD));
for i in 1..20 do
    create det := DETAILS((:DET-PROD = DET-PROD OF ORD-DETAIL OF ORD(i))
                    and (:DET-QTY = DET-QTY OF ORD-DETAIL OF ORD(i))
                    and (R : o))
endfor
```

By applying mapping t_{2_c} associated with T_2 we refine this code fragment:

```
create o := ORD(  (:ORD-CODE = ORD-CODE OF ORD)
              and (:ORD-DATE = ORD-DATE OF ORD)
              and (:ORD-CUST = ORD-CUST OF ORD));
for i in 1..20 do
    create det := DETAILS((:DET-PROD = DET-PROD OF ORD-DETAIL OF ORD(i))
                      and (:DET-QTY = DET-QTY OF ORD-DETAIL OF ORD(i))
                      and (:DET-CODE = o.ORD-CODE))
endfor
```

Finally, the propagation of the renaming transformation $T_3 \cdots T_n$ provides us with an abstract code which is fully compliant with the structure of the SQL statements:

```
create o := ORDERS((:CODE = ORD-CODE OF ORD)
              and (:DATE = ORD-DATE OF ORD)
              and (:CUSTOMER = ORD-CUST OF ORD));
for i in 1..20 do
    create det := DETAILS((:PRODUCT = DET-PROD OF ORD-DETAIL OF ORD(i))
                      and (:QUANTITY = DET-QTY OF ORD-DETAIL OF ORD(i))
                      and (:ORD_CODE = o.CODE))
endfor
```

Generating the COBOL/SQL code is then straighforward:

```
WRITE-ORD.
  MOVE ORD-CODE OF ORD TO WR-CODE.
  MOVE ORD-DATE OF ORD TO WR-DATE.
  MOVE ORD-CUST OF ORD TO WR-CUSTOMER.
  EXEC SQL
      INSERT INTO ORDERS (CODE, DATE, CUSTOMER)
      VALUES (:WR-CODE, :WR-DATE, :WR-CUSTOMER)
  END-EXEC.
  MOVE 1 TO IND.
  PERFORM INSERT-DETAILS UNTIL IND >= 20 OR SQLCODE NOT= ZERO.

INSERT-DETAILS.
  MOVE DET-PROD OF ORD-DETAIL OF ORD(IND) TO WR-PRODUCT.
  MOVE DET-QTY OF ORD-DETAIL OF ORD(IND) TO WR-QUANTITY.
  MOVE ORD-CODE OF ORD TO WR-ORD-CODE
  EXEC SQL
      INSERT INTO DETAILS (PRODUCT, QUANTITY, ORD_CODE)
      VALUES (:WR-PRODUCT, :WR-QUANTITY, :WR-ORD-CODE)
  END-EXEC.
  ADD 1 TO IND.
```

Note that the resulting COBOL code can be equivalently generated in-line or encapsulated into an inverse wrapper. In our research, we favor the latter architecture. Therefore the initial COBOL WRITE statement is simply replaced with a corresponding wrapper invocation.

5   Tool Support

We have developped a prototype tool to support our data reengineering methodology, and particularly the program conversion phase. The architecture of this tool combines two complementary transformational technologies, namely the DB-MAIN [19] CASE tool and the ASF+SDF Meta-Environment [3].

5.1   Mapping Definition

We use the transformation toolkit of DB-MAIN to carry out the chain of schema transformations needed during the schema conversion phase. DB-MAIN automatically generates and maintains a history log of all the transformations that are applied to the legacy DB schema (LDS) to obtain the target DB schema (TDS). This history log is formalized in such a way that it can be analyzed and transformed. Particularly, it can be used to derive both the mappings between the LDS and the TDS.

5.2   Wrapper Generation

So far, wrapper generators for COBOL-to-SQL and IDS/II[4]-to-SQL have been developed. These generators are implemented through a plug-in of DB-MAIN. They take the LDS-to-TDS mapping as an input and generate the code that provides the application programs with a legacy interface to the new database. Each generated wrapper is a COBOL program with embedded SQL primitives.

The inverse wrapper generation involves two kinds of conversion rules. The first one involves API translation and is independent of the schema transformation. The legacy DMS primitives are simulated using target DMS primitives. For instance, a COBOL READ statement may require a complex procedure based on SQL cursors. This mapping layer is specific to each couple source/target models couple. The second conversion rules derives from schema transformations and are independent of API translation. The primitives initially expressed on the source schema are expanded into procedural fragments comprising primitives expressed on the target schema through rewriting rules such as those shown in Fig. 4 and 5.

5.3   Legacy Code Adaptation

The legacy application programs transformation relies on the ASF+SDF Meta-Environment. We use an SDF version of the IBM VS COBOL II grammar, which was obtained by Lämmel and Verhoef [12]. We specify a set of rewrite rules (ASF equations) on top of this grammar to obtain two similar program transformation tools. The first tool is used in the context of COBOL-to-SQL migration, while the second one supports IDS/II-to-SQL conversion.

Both program transformation tools are suitable in the context of partial migration, i.e., when only some legacy record types are actually migrated to the

---

[4] IDS/II is the BULL implementation of CODASYL.

new database platform. In this case, only the DML instructions manipulating migrated data are replaced with corresponding wrapper invocations. The other DML instructions, which still access the legacy data, are left unchanged.

We emphasize that the transformed legacy programs still manipulate the data through the legacy schema. In practice, this requires reorganizing the data declaration parts of the programs. For instance, in the case of COBOL-to-SQL reengineering, the following modifications are performed:

the migrated files declarations are removed from the INPUT-OUTPUT section of the ENVIRONMENT division;

- the migrated record types declarations are moved from the FILE section of the ENVIRONMENT division to the WORKING-STORAGE section of the DATA division. Thus, the COBOL records become COBOL variables which are used as an argument of the wrapper calls.

6   Case Studies

Two small but realistic different legacy systems have been reengineered. Fig. 7 gives an overview of both case studies. As a first experiment, we converted an academic COBOL application managing data about students, registrations, results of exams, etc. The legacy database, consisting of 8 large COBOL files, was migrated to a relational database. The 15 legacy programs were successfully interfaced with 8 generated wrappers. A second case study was performed in collaboration with the company REVER, Belgium, devoted to system reengineering. The goal of this project was to reengineer a COBOL system from a city administration. This legacy system uses the IDS/II database manager and is made of 60 programs, totaling 35 KLOC. The resulting application consists of 57 KLOC, including 24 generated wrappers.

For both case studies the program conversion phase (i.e., wrapper generation and legacy code transformation) was fully automated. Our tools have proved to be quite efficient: generating the 24 IDS-to-SQL wrappers took 4 seconds while transforming the legacy programs required a bit less than 8 minutes.

	Case Study 1		Case Study 2	
	Source	Target	Source	Target
Host Language	COBOL	COBOL	COBOL	COBOL
DML	COBOL	SQL	IDS/II	SQL
# Entity types	8 records	18 tables	24 records	24 tables
# Attributes	291 fields	276 columns	257 fields	151 columns
# Rel. types	0	15 foreign keys	13 sets	21 foreign keys
# Legacy Programs	15	15	60	60
# Wrappers	0	8	0	24
# Wrappers calls	0	365	0	936
Legacy Code Size	7 KLOC	8.2 KLOC	35 KLOC	39 KLOC
Wrapper Code Size	0	6 KLOC	0	18 KLOC

Fig. 7. Case studies overview

7   Related Work

The concept of co-transformation (or coupled transformation) has been defined by Lämmel [14] as follows: *"A co-transformation transforms mutually dependent software artifacts of different kinds simultaneously, while the transformation is centred around a grammar (or schema, API, or a similar structure) that is shared among the artifacts."*. In [13] the same author identifies the category of coupled software transformations, describes their essence and lists typical application domains for co-transformations problems. For another example, we refer to the work by Lohmann and Riedewald [15] who present an elegant approach to automatically adapting transformation rules after a change in a grammar.

The concept of transformational engineering applied to data structures has been studied for more than two decades [16], first for schema engineering, then, later on, for data conversion. A fairly comprehensive approach has been described in [2]. However, as far as the authors know, propagating data structure transformations to procedural code has not been studied yet.

The use of wrapping techniques for reusing legacy software components is discussed in [18]. Papakonstantinou *et al.* [17] present a query translation scheme that facilitates rapid development of wrappers.

An iterative process model for legacy systems reengineering is proposed in [1]. One important phase of this method aims at making the legacy programs compatible with the migrated data, by replacing the data access instructions with calls to a *data banker*.

The purpose of [20] is to apply automatic restructuring transformations to large industrial Cobol systems in order to improve their modifiability. This work shows the suitability of ASF+SDF and the IBM VS COBOL II grammar for large-scale legacy code renovation.

Defining data mappings is an important issue in our work. The MDE-based approach proposed by Didonet *et al.* [5] considers data mappings as *models*. From this starting point, the authors suggest the use of model weaving as the base to solve various data mapping problems.

8   Conclusions

We have presented a general co-transformational approach for database applications evolution. This approach consists in formally defining an evolution as the application of coupled transformations, that modify the database schema, the data instances and the application programs. A methodology and a prototype tool have been proposed for a particular scenario of evolution, namely data reengineering.

Coupling generative and transformational techniques provides us with a promising tool support for data reengineering. First experiments have shown the validity of the approach, at least for small to medium size programs. However, our methodology and tools still have to be consolidated and validated for large information systems migration. In particular, the performance impact of our wrapper-based architecture should be evaluated through industrial case studies.

Acknowledgements. Many thanks to Ralf Lämmel, João Saraiva and Joost Visser for the organization of the GTTSE 2005 Summer School and for their patient editing work. Thanks too to the anonymous reviewers for their precise and pertinent advices. This research has been carried out within the context of the RISTART project, supported by the Belgian *Région Wallonne* and the European Social Fund. We thank the SEN1 group (CWI, Amsterdam) and REVER s.a. for their fruitful collaboration in this project.

References

1. Alessandro Bianchi, Danilo Caivano, Vittorio Marengo, and Giuseppe Visaggio. Iterative reengineering of legacy systems. *IEEE Trans. Softw. Eng.*, 29(3):225–241, 2003.
2. M. Boyd and P. McBrien. Towards a semi-automated approach to intermodel transformation. In *CAiSE Workshops Proceedings*, volume 1, pages 175–188. Riga Technical University, 2004.
3. M.G.J. van den Brand, A. van Deursen, J. Heering, H.A. de Jong, M. de Jonge, T. Kuipers, P. Klint, L. Moonen, P.A. Olivier, J. Scheerder, J.J. Vinju, E. Visser, and J. Visser. The ASF+SDF Meta-Environment: A component-based language development environment. In R. Wilhelm, editor, *Compiler Construction (CC '01)*, volume 2027 of *Lecture Notes in Computer Science*, pages 365–370. Springer-Verlag, 2001.
4. Anthony Cleve, Jean Henrard, and Jean-Luc Hainaut. Co-transformations in information system reengineering. In *Proc. of the 2nd International Workshop on Meta-Models, Schemas and Grammars for Reverse Engineering*, volume 137(3) of *ENTCS*, pages 5–15. Springer Verlag, 2005.
5. M Didonet Del Fabro, J Bézivin, F Jouault, and P Valduriez. Applying generic model management to data mapping. In *Proc. of the Journées Bases de Donnes Avancées (BDA05)*, 2005.
6. J.-L. Hainaut. Specification preservation in schema transformations - application to semantics and statistics. *Data & Knowledge Engineering*, 16(1), 1996.
7. Jean-Luc Hainaut. Transformation-based database engineering. In P. van Bommel, editor, *Transformation of Knowledge, Information and Data: Theory and Applications*, chapter 1. IDEA Group, 2005.
8. Jean Henrard. *Program Understanding in Database Reverse Engineering*. PhD thesis, University of Namur, 2003.
9. Jean Henrard, Anthony Cleve, and Jean-Luc Hainaut. Inverse wrappers for legacy information systems migration. In *WRAP 2004 Workshop Proceedings*, volume 04–34 of *CS Reports*, pages 30–43. Technische Universiteit Eindhoven, 2004.
10. Jean Henrard, Jean-Marc Hick, Philippe Thiran, and Jean-Luc Hainaut. Strategies for data reengineering. In *Proc. of the 9th Working Conference on Reverse Engineering (WCRE'02)*, pages 211–220. IEEE Computer Society Press, 2002.
11. Jean-Marc Hick and Jean-Luc Hainaut. Database application evolution: a transformational approach. *Data and Knowledge Engineering*, 2006. to appear.
12. R. Lämmel and C. Verhoef. Semi-automatic Grammar Recovery. *Software—Practice & Experience*, 31(15):1395–1438, December 2001.
13. Ralf Lämmel. Coupled Software Transformations (Ext. Abstract). In *Proc. of the First International Workshop on Software Evolution Transformations*, Nov. 2004.

14. Ralf Lämmel. Transformations everywhere. *Science of Computer Programming*, 2004. The guest editor's introduction to the SCP special issue on program transformation.

15. Wolfgang Lohmann and Günter Riedewald. Towards automatical migration of transformation rules after grammar extension. In *Proc. of 7th European Conference on Software Maintenance and Reengineering (CSMR'03)*, pages 30–39. IEEE Computer Society Press, 2003.

16. S. B. Navathe. Schema analysis for database restructuring. *ACM Transactions on Database Systems*, 5(2):157–184, June 1980.

17. Y. Papakonstantinou, A. Gupta, H. Garcia-Molina, and J. Ullman. A query translation scheme for rapid implementation of wrappers. In *Proc. of the International Conference on Declarative and Object-oriented Databases*, 1995.

18. Harry M. Sneed. Encapsulation of legacy software: A technique for reusing legacy software components. *Annals of Software Engineering*, 9:293–313, 2000.

19. The DB-MAIN official website. `http://www.db-main.be`.

20. N. Veerman. Revitalizing modifiability of legacy assets. *Software Maintenance and Evolution: Research and Practice, Special issue on CSMR 2003*, 16(4–5): 219–254, 2004.

Modular Name Analysis for Java Using JastAdd

Torbjörn Ekman and Görel Hedin

Department of Computer Science, Lund University, Sweden
(torbjorn, gorel)@cs.lth.se

Abstract. Name analysis for Java is challenging with its complex visibility rules involving nested scopes, inheritance, qualified access, and syntactic ambiguities. We show how Java name analysis including ambiguities related to names of variables, fields, and packages, can be implemented in a declarative and modular manner using the JastAdd compiler construction system.

Declarative attributes and context-dependent rewrites enable the implementation to be modularized in the same way as the informal Java language specification. The individual rules in the specification transfer directly to equations in the implementation. Rewrites are used to define new concepts in terms of existing concepts in an iterative manner in the same way as the informal language specification. This enables equations to use both context-free and context-dependent concepts and leads to improved separation of concerns. A full Java 1.4 compiler has been implemented to validate the technique.

1   Introduction

The computations done on abstract syntax trees in compilers and related tools are often highly context sensitive. E.g., there are often symbolic names that have different meanings depending on their context. The purpose of name analysis is to bind each name to a declaration and hence resolve the meaning of that name. Name analysis for the Java programming language is challenging with its complex visibility rules involving nested scopes, inheritance, qualified access, and syntactic ambiguities. The purpose of this paper is to show how ambiguities related to names of variables, types, and packages, can be solved in a declarative and modular manner, using the JastAdd compiler construction system.

Consider the qualified name A.B.C and the task of binding each individual simple name to its declaration. The meaning depends on the *syntactic context*, e.g., C is expected to be a TypeName in the **extends** clause of a class declaration, and an ExpressionName when being the right hand side of an assignment. There are also *contextually ambiguous* names where the set of visible declarations are required to resolve the name. For example, A.B can be the PackageName of the top level class C, or A, B, and C can all be nested TypeNames. Such ambiguities should be resolved by reclassification to TypeNames if there are visible type declarations and otherwise to PackageNames. The Java Language Specification [3] defines the specific rules for visible declarations at each point in a program and how to first classify context-free names according to their syntactic context and then refine them by reclassifying contextually ambiguous names.

R. Lämmel, J. Saraiva, and J. Visser (Eds.): GTTSE 2005, LNCS 4143, pp. 422–436, 2006.

JastAdd supports declarative attributes and context-dependent rewrites that enable the implementation to be modularized in the same way as the informal language specification. The individual rules in the specification transfer directly to equations in the implementation. The language specification contains a set of basic language concepts captured by a context-free grammar. There are, however, additional concepts that are context-dependent, e.g., TypeNames. Rewrites are used to refine the tree to use not only the basic concepts but also the context-dependent ones. We present a transformational technique to gradually define new concepts in terms of existing concepts, in the same way that they are defined in the informal language specification. This allows for decomposition of complex problems into simpler ones, and it also better supports separation of concerns.

We define a tiny subset of Java named *DemoJavaNames* which captures all the characteristic problems in resolving contextually ambiguous names that occur in full Java. A complete name analysis implementation for DemoJavaNames is presented and included in this paper. We have implemented a full Java 1.4 compiler based on the same technique to verify that the techniques scale to full languages. The system has been validated against the Jacks test-suite and passes more tests than the production quality compilers javac and jikes [1]. While not claiming superiority over either compiler we claim that our implementation is complete while being less then half the size of the handwritten javac compiler.

The rest of this paper is structured as follows. Section 2 introduces the features of JastAdd that are used in the implementation of DemoJavaNames. Section 3 describes the implementation of name lookup, syntactic classification, and reclassification of contextually ambiguous names. Section 4 compares our work to related work and Section 5 concludes the paper.

2   JastAdd Background

The JastAdd compiler construction system combines object-orientation and static aspect-oriented programming with declarative attributes and context-dependent rewrites to allow highly modular specifications. This section gives an introduction to the JastAdd system, needed to understand the source code listings in Section 3. The evaluation algorithm is described in [7, 2] and the system is publically available [1].

2.1   Abstract Grammar

The abstract grammar models an object-oriented class hierarchy from which classes are generated that are used as node types in the abstract syntax tree (AST). Consider the grammar in Listing 1.1. A class is generated for each production in the grammar, e.g., Prog, CompUnit, ClassDecl, and may inherit another production by adding a colon followed by the super production, e.g., LocalVariableDecl : Stmt.

The right hand side of a production is a list of elements. The default name of an element is the same as its type unless it is explicitly named by prefixing the element with a name and a colon, e.g., the FieldDecl has an element named Type which is of type Name. Elements enclosed in angle brackets are values, e.g., <name:String> in

FieldDecl, while other elements are tree nodes, e.g., Type:Name and Expr in Field-Decl. The tree node element may be suffixed by a star to specify a list of zero or more elements, e.g., ClassDecl* in CompUnit.

The system generates a constructor and accessor methods for value and tree elements. The accessor method for a value element has the same name as the element, e.g., String name(), while the tree element is prefixed by get, e.g., Name getType(). List elements have an index to select the appropriate node, e.g., getClassDecl(int index), and there is an accessor for the number of elements in the list, e.g., int getNumClassDecl().

2.2 Declarative Attributes

Attribute Grammars [10] have proven useful when describing context-sensitive information for programming languages. Their declarativeness makes it easy to modularize grammars freely, and they integrate well with the object-oriented programming paradigm, in particular when augmented with *reference attributes*, allowing an attribute to be a reference to another tree node object [6]. This section gives a very brief introduction to *synthesized* and *inherited* declarative attributes.

A *synthesized* attribute is similar to a virtual method without side-effects which allows for efficient evaluation using caching. Consider the grammar in Listing 1.1 and the task to determine whether a Stmt node declares a local variable named *name* or not. This can be implemented through a synthesized attribute using the following JastAdd syntax:

```
syn boolean Stmt.isLocalVariableDecl(String name);
eq Stmt.isLocalVariableDecl(String name) { return false; }
eq LocalVariableDecl.isLocalVariableDecl(String name) =
        name().equals(name);
```

Notice that the equation for LocalVariableDecl overrides the default equation for its superclass Stmt. Notice also the functional styled short-hand for its right-hand side: it uses an expression rather than a block with a return statement. An additional shorthand is possible (but not shown): combining the attribute declaration and the first equation into a single clause by inserting the equation right-hand side before the semicolon in the declaration.

JastAdd supports inter-type declarations [9] where attributes can be added to an existing class in a modular fashion. The target class for each attribute and equation is specified by qualifying its name with the target class name, e.g Stmt and Local-VariableDecl above. The attribute is then woven into the class hierarchy generated from the abstract grammar.

An *inherited* attribute propagates the context downwards the AST. Consider the task to determine the enclosing Block for a Stmt node. A block can tell all its enclosed Stmts that it is the enclosing Block declaration. This can be implemented through an inherited attribute using the following syntax:

```
inh Block Stmt.enclosingBlock();
eq Block.getStmt().enclosingBlock() = this;
```

Equations for inherited attributes are broadcast to an entire subtree in a similar way as for the *including* construct in the Eli attribute grammar system [13]. This subtree is explicitly selected using a child accessor (getStmt() in this case). The equation should thus be read as: *define the value for the enclosingBlock attribute in the entire subtree whose root is the node returned by getStmt() in a block node. The value should be* this, *i.e., a reference to the block node defining the equation.*

2.3   Context-Dependent Rewriting

JastAdd supports declarative context-dependent rewrites to dynamically change the AST. A node of type *S* is automatically rewritten to a node of type *T* when a certain condition is true using the syntax below:

```
rewrite S {
  when(condition())
  to T new T(...);
}
```

The rewrites are context-dependent in that the conditions may depend on synthesized and/or inherited attributes. The rewrites are declarative in that they are performed automatically by a rewrite evaluation engine. In the final tree, no rewrite conditions are true. There may be multiple when-to clauses in which case they are evaluated in lexical order. The evaluation engine is demand-driven and rewrites nodes when they are being visited, interleaved with attribute evaluation. The examples discuss the resulting transformation order for each rewrite as well as interaction with other rewrites and attribute evaluation. The evaluation algorithm is presented in [2].

3   Name Analysis for DemoJavaNames

This section presents the implementation of name analysis for a tiny subset of Java that only includes compilation units, packages, nested classes with inheritance, fields, initializers, blocks, local variables, and names. We call this subset *DemoJavaNames* and, while being far from useful as a practical language, it captures all the characteristic problems in resolving contextually ambiguous names that occur in full Java.

The input of the name analysis is a context-free tree constructed by the parser. The result is an attributed tree where all names have been resolved to appropriate name kinds, and have reference attributes denoting the appropriate declaration node. The purpose of the paper is to show how ambiguities related to names of variables, types, and packages, can be solved in a declarative and modular manner, using JastAdd. We will show how each of the rules in the language maps to a specific equation in the attribute grammar.

DemoJavaNames keeps just enough language constructs to illustrate the following name related concepts: multiple kinds of nested scopes, object-oriented inheritance, qualified names, shadowing and hiding, and multiple kinds of variables. To simplify the example we removed all language concepts unrelated to names and we also removed language concepts that duplicate name analysis problems, e.g., we only use classes and not interfaces. For brevity, we also removed some language constructs that do affect name binding, i.e., imports of types and access control. While they are not included

```
ast Prog ::= CompUnit*;
ast CompUnit ::= <packageName:String> ClassDecl*;
ast ClassDecl ::= <name:String> Super:Name BodyDecl*;

ast abstract BodyDecl;
ast FieldDecl : BodyDecl ::= FieldType:Name <name:String> Expr;
ast MemberClassDecl : BodyDecl ::= ClassDecl;
ast Initializer : BodyDecl ::= Block;

ast abstract Stmt;
ast Block : Stmt ::= Stmt*;
ast LocalVariableDecl: Stmt ::= VarType:Name <name:String> Expr;

ast abstract Expr;
ast abstract Name : Expr ::= <name:String>;
ast Dot : Name ::= Left:Name Right:Name;
ast ExpressionName : Name;
ast PackageName : Name;
ast TypeName : Name;
```

Listing 1.1. DemoJavaNames abstract grammar. A minimal subset of Java used to illustrate the problems in resolving contextually ambiguous names.

in the program listings we discuss how the implementation can be extended to handle these features as well.

Listing 1.1 presents the abstract grammar for DemoJavaNames. The Dot production that represents a qualified name requires further explanation. The parser is expected to build right recursive trees where the Left child is always a simple name while the Right child may be a Dot or a simple name. It is also worth noticing that the names in the grammar are context-sensitive, e.g., ExpressionName, TypeName, Package. We introduce context-free names and transformations into context-sensitive names in Section 3.3.

The type of names and variable declarations is needed to define qualified lookups and inherited members in later modules. We therefore define the type as an attribute of expressions and declarations. Listing 1.2 implements the type attribute as a reference to the appropriate declaration. To simplify equations in name binding modules we use a null object to represent unknown types. That way it is always possible to query an expression for members instead of handling the special case where the type is unknown.

The following sections present modules for name lookup and reclassification of ambiguous names followed by a discussion on how to extend the implementation to handle full Java.

3.1   Visible Declarations

The most important contextual information used in name analysis is the set of visible declarations at each point in a program. Those declarations are then used to bind names in an actual context to their appropriate declarations. The name binding module

```
syn ClassDecl Expr.type() = unknownType();
eq Dot.type() = getRight().type();
eq ExpressionName.type() = lookupVariable(name()) != null ?
    lookupVariable(name()).type() : unknownType();
eq TypeName.type() = lookupType(name()) != null ?
    lookupType(name()) : unknownType();
syn ClassDecl LocalVariableDecl.type() = getVarType().type();
syn ClassDecl FieldDecl.type() = getFieldType().type();
```

Listing 1.2. Type binding for DemoJavaNames where each expression and variable declaration is bound to a class declaration. A null object is used for unknown types to allow for a unified member lookup.

in Listing 1.3 defines an attribute **inh** `Variable Name.lookupVariable(String name)` that provides a binding through a reference to a named visible variable-declaration.

Language constructs that change the set of visible declarations, e.g., introduce new declarations or limit scope for an existing declaration, need to provide an equation for the lookup attribute. DemoJavaNames has two kinds of variables, `LocalVariable-Declarations` declared in `Blocks`, and `FieldDeclarations` declared in `ClassDecls`. The equations for lookup need thus be placed in the `Block` and `ClassDecl` types.

Nested Scopes with Shadowing. The scope of a declaration is the region of the program in which the declaration can be referred to using a simple name. The scope of a declaration often involves nested language elements where declarations in one element are in scope in enclosed elements as well. A declaration may be shadowed in part of its scope by another declaration of the same name.

Both classes and blocks are allowed to be nested in DemoJavaNames and both implement shadowing as well. In Listing 1.3 the delegation to enclosing context, marked with ②, implements nested scopes. The eager return at first match, marked with ①, implements shadowing.

Declarations in a block have a *declare before use* policy. This is implemented by limiting the range of the block that is searched for declarations at ③. The equation is parameterized by the index of the `Stmt` in the element list and the search stops at the `Stmt` that encloses the name.

Inheritance. The member fields of a class are not only the locally declared fields but also fields inherited from the superclass. A field is inherited if there is not a local field declaration that hides the field in the superclass. The eager return at ④ implements hiding and the delegation to the superclass at ⑤ implements inheritance.

Canonical Type Lookup. The lookup of visible class declarations is implemented in a similar fashion to variable lookup. The main difference is how the lookup is handled at the compilation unit level. If the type is not found in the current compilation unit then the top level types in compilation units belonging to the same package are considered. This is implemented in Listing 1.4 by delegation ① to a canonical lookup that takes both the package name and type name into account ②. Inheritance of member classes is implemented in the same way as for variables.

```
   // visible variable or null
   inh Variable Name.lookupVariable(String name);

   // local variables in blocks
   eq Block.getStmt(int index).lookupVariable(String name) {
③    for(int i = 0; i < index; i++)
       if(getStmt(i).isLocalVariableDecl(name))
①        return (LocalVariableDecl)getStmt(i);
②    return lookupVariable(name);
   }
   syn boolean Stmt.isLocalVariableDecl(String name) = false;
   eq LocalVariableDecl.isLocalVariableDecl(String name) =
     name().equals(name);
   inh Variable Block.lookupVariable(String name);
   // member fields in classes
   eq ClassDecl.getBodyDecl().lookupVariable(String name) {
     if(memberField(name) != null)
①      return memberField(name);
②    return lookupVariable(name);
   }
   // members including inheritance
   syn FieldDecl ClassDecl.memberField(String name) {
     for(int i = 0; i < getNumBodyDecl(); i++)
       if(getBodyDecl(i).isField(name))
④        return (FieldDecl)getBodyDecl(i);
⑤    if(getSuper().type().memberField(name) != null)
       return getSuper().type().memberField(name);
     return null;
   }
   syn boolean BodyDecl.isField(String name) = false;
   eq FieldDecl.isField(String name) = name().equals(name);
   inh Variable ClassDecl.lookupVariable(String name);
   // no more nested declarations
   eq Prog.getCompUnit().lookupVariable(String name) = null;

   // abstraction for FieldDecl and LocalVariableDecl
   interface Variable {
     String name();
     ClassDecl type();
   }
   FieldDecl implements Variable;
   LocalVariableDecl implements Variable;
```

Listing 1.3. Variable binding for DemoJavaNames. Shadowing is implemented by eager return statements marked ①. Nesting is implemented using delegation marked ②. Declare before use is implemented by limiting variable search to the current node index in ③.

```
    // visible type or null object
    inh ClassDecl Name.lookupType(String name);

    // top level types in compilation unit
    eq CompUnit.getClassDecl().lookupType(String name) {
      if(topLevelType(name) != null)
        return topLevelType(name);
      // declarations in same package
①    return lookupCanonical(packageName(), name);
    }
    syn ClassDecl CompUnit.topLevelType(String name) {
      for(int i = 0; i < getNumClassDecl(); i++)
        if(getClassDecl(i).name().equals(name))
          return getClassDecl(i);
      return null;
    }
    // lookup a type using its canonical name
    inh ClassDecl Name.lookupCanonical(String pack, String type);
    eq Prog.getCompUnit().lookupCanonical(String p, String t) {
      for(int i = 0; i < getNumCompUnit(); i++)
②      if(getCompUnit(i).packageName().equals(p) &&
           getCompUnit(i).topLevelType(t) != null)
          return getCompUnit(i).topLevelType(t);
      return null;
    }
    // member classes in class declaration
    // analoguous to the member fields implementation
    eq ClassDecl.getBodyDecl().lookupType(String name) { ... }
    // no more nested declarations
    eq Prog.getCompUnit().lookupType(String name) = null;
```

Listing 1.4. Type lookup for DemoJavaNames

3.2 Qualified Lookup

The set of visible declarations for a qualified name depends on the target of the re-solved name to the left of the dot. A valid ExpressionName can be preceded by ei-ther a TypeName or an ExpressionName. Either way, the ExpressionName refers to a member field in the ClassDecl that represents the type of the preceding expression. Listing 1.5 extends the name binding module with qualified lookup. The equation at ① defines the variable lookup to search the ClassDecl (that the qualifier's type is bound to) for members.

The lookup attribute is an inherited attribute and thus defined by an equation in an ancestor node. The qualifier to the left of the dot in a qualified name should provide the equation for the name on the right hand side of the dot. This is done by the common ancestor Dot which propagates the value of the equation from left to right for variables at ① and types at ②, overriding the lookup defined by an ancestor further up in the AST.

A valid TypeName can be preceded by either a PackageName or a TypeName. If the qualifier is a PackageName then the qualified name is the canonical name of the type. But if the qualifier is a TypeName then the name refers to a member type. There are thus different rules for the lookup depending on the kind of expression that precedes the name. The Dot therefore delegates the lookup to the expression at ② and searches for member types at ③ as the default strategy for expressions while the PackageName overrides the lookup at ④ to use canonical type names.

```
    eq Dot.getRight().lookupVariable(String name) =
①      getLeft().type().memberField(name);

    eq Dot.getRight().lookupType(String name) =
②      getLeft().qualifiedLookupType(name);

    syn ClassDecl Expr.qualifiedLookupType(String name) =
③      type().memberClass(name);
    eq PackageName.qualifiedLookupType(String typeName) =
④      lookupCanonical(name(), typeName);
```

Listing 1.5. Qualified lookup of types and fields

3.3 Determine the Meaning of Names

The abstract syntax defined so far contains name nodes that are highly context sensitive and can thus not be built by a context-free parser. We now extend the abstract syntax with additional context-free name nodes that are used for gradually refining the names to reflect their semantic meaning.

The parser constructs unqualified name nodes only using the node type ParseName. These nodes are then refined by the name analysis to the resulting nodes listed in Listing 1.1. To simplify this computation, some of the refinements are done in intermediate steps, making use of two additional node types: PackageOrTypeName and AmbiguousName, see Listing 1.6.

Syntactic Classification of Names. The first step in resolving names is to reclassify the ParseName nodes based on their immediate syntactic context. This way some nodes can be directly refined to their final class: PackageName, TypeName, or ExpressionName. However, for some names, the immediate syntactic context is not sufficient, in which case the ParseName is refined to PackageOrTypeName (for names that must refer packages or types), or AmbiguousName (for names where the kind cannot yet be determined at all).

The Java language specification defines the classification process by describing a context and the expected name kind. For instance, a name is syntactically classified as a TypeName in the **extends** clause of a class declaration. We therefore introduce an inherited attribute kind() that describes the syntactic classification in a certain context by referring to an element in an enumeration of the above name kinds. Listing 1.6

shows the kind() attribute declaration at ②, the enumeration at ⑥, and the sample classification description at ③.

A qualifier in a qualified name may depend on the classification of the name it qualifies. For instance, a name is syntactically classified as a PackageOrTypeName to the left of the dot in a qualified TypeName. However, we still have the same requirement for equations in the ancestor as for qualified names. We therefore introduce another attribute predKind() which is delegated from right to left at ④ and the equation corresponding to the above example at ⑤.

The equations for kind() and predKind() complete the description of classification context and the transformation is almost trivial. The conditional rewrite at ① transforms a ParseName node into its syntactically classified counterpart. It is worth noticing that the dependences introduced by the kind() attribute equations in combination with demand driven rewriting causes qualified names to be classified from right to left.

Reclassification of Contextually Ambiguous Names. The next step is to reclassify contextually ambiguous names, i.e., AmbiguousName and PackageOrTypeName, in the context of visible declarations. An AmbiguousName is reclassified as an ExpressionName if there is a visible variable declaration with the same name. Otherwise, as a TypeName if there is a visible type declaration with the same name. Otherwise, as a PackageName if there is a visible package with the same name. The corresponding implementation is shown in Listing 1.7.

A contextually ambiguous name is resolved by binding it in the context of its qualifier. There is thus a dependence that the qualifier must be resolved before its right hand side can be resolved. We implement this dependence by making sure that all rewrite conditions in Listing 1.7 are false when the qualifier of a name is ambiguous. These conditions are false when there are no visible names. The type of an ambiguous name is unknownType() which has no visible member fields or types. To make the property hold we add an attribute hasPackage(String name) that is true when there is a visible package with that name and no ambiguous qualifiers. A qualified name a.b.c is thus first syntactically classified from right to left because of the dependences in the kind() attribute, and then reclassified from left to right.

3.4   Extensions to Handle Full Java

The DemoJavaNames language lacks some important name-related language constructs available in Java. This section describes the needed changes to the implementation to support full Java.

The implementation can be extended with more nested scopes by providing a new equation for the lookup attribute in each new scope. The various nested scopes are totally decoupled from each other using inherited attributes with parameters. The only constraint is that a scope is nested in another scope if they are on the same path to the root node. A ForStmt may for instance provide an equation (very similar to the equation for Block in Listing 1.3) that searches for LocalVariableDeclarations in its init-clause. Type imports extend the scope of type declarations and can be implemented by inserting a search for matching imports at ① in Listing 1.4. Java 5 [4] constructs such as *static imports* and the *enhanced for statement* can be supported using the same

```
  ast ParseName : Name;
  ast PackageOrTypeName : Name;
  ast AmbiguousName : Name;

① rewrite ParseName {
    when(kind() == Kind.PACKAGE_NAME)
    to Name new PackageName(name());
    when(kind() == Kind.TYPE_NAME)
    to Name new TypeName(name());
    when(kind() == Kind.EXPRESSION_NAME)
    to Name new ExpressionName(name());
    when(kind() == Kind.PACKAGE_OR_TYPE_NAME)
    to Name new PackageOrTypeName(name());
    when(kind() == Kind.AMBIGUOUS_NAME)
    to Name new AmbiguousName(name());
  }

② inh Kind ParseName.kind();
  eq Prog.getCompUnit().kind() = Kind.AMBIGUOUS_NAME;
③ eq ClassDecl.getSuper().kind() = Kind.PACKAGE_NAME;
  eq FieldDecl.getFieldType().kind() = Kind.TYPE_NAME;
  eq FieldDecl.getExpr().kind() = Kind.EXPRESSION_NAME;
  eq LocalVariableDecl.getVarType().kind() = Kind.TYPE_NAME;
  eq LocalVariableDecl.getExpr().kind() = Kind.EXPRESSION_NAME;

  // propagate information from right to left
④ eq Dot.getLeft().kind() = getRight().predKind();
  syn Kind Name.predKind() = Kind.AMBIGUOUS_NAME;
  eq Dot.predKind() = getLeft().predKind();

  eq PackageName.predKind() = Kind.PACKAGE_NAME;
⑤ eq TypeName.predKind() = Kind.PACKAGE_OR_TYPE_NAME;
  eq ExpressionName.predKind() = Kind.AMBIGUOUS_NAME;
  eq PackageOrTypeName.predKind() = Kind.PACKAGE_OR_TYPE_NAME;
  eq AmbiguousName.predKind() = Kind.AMBIGUOUS_NAME;

⑥ class Kind {
    static Kind PACKAGE_NAME = new Kind();
    static Kind TYPE_NAME = new Kind();
    static Kind EXPRESSION_NAME = new Kind();
    static Kind PACKAGE_OR_TYPE_NAME = new Kind();
    static Kind AMBIGUOUS_NAME = new Kind();
  }
```

Listing 1.6. Syntactic classification of names depending on their context. The context-free Parse-Name names are classified and rewritten to any of the five name kinds defined in Kind.

```
rewrite AmbiguousName {
  when(lookupVariable(name()) != null)
  to Name new ExpressionName(name());
  when(lookupType(name()) != null)
  to Name new TypeName(name());
  when(hasPackage(name()))
  to Name new PackageName(name());
}
rewrite PackageOrTypeName {
  when(lookupType(name()) != null)
  to Name new TypeName(name());
  when(hasPackage(name()))
  to Name new PackageName(name());
}
inh boolean Name.hasPackage(String name);
eq Program.getCompUnit().hasPackage(String name) {
  for(int i = 0; i < getNumCompUnit(); i++)
    if(getCompUnit(i).packageName().equals(name))
      return true;
  return false;
}
eq Dot.getRight().hasPackage(String name) =
    getLeft().qualifiedHasPackage(name);
syn boolean Expr.qualifiedHasPackage(String name) = false;
eq PackageName.qualifiedHasPackage(String name) =
    hasPackage(name() + '.' + name);
```

Listing 1.7. Reclassification of Contextually Ambiguous Names

technique by adding a search for imported fields in the CompUnit node type and a lookup equation for local variable declarations in the enhanced for statement AST node.

Java supports access control where modifiers impose visibility constraints on names. Access control limits inheritance in that only non private accessible members are inherited from the superclass. This is easily implemented by adding a filter at ⑤ in Listing 1.3 that removes private non accessible fields. Access control also affects qualified lookups. The type of a qualifier must for instance be accessible and there are also additional constraints when the qualifier is an ExpressionName. Such behavior can be implemented by filters at ① and ② in Listing 1.5. The specialized rules for ExpressionName may require the qualified lookup for fields to be extended to the variant used for types. The filter can then be placed on the ExpressionName qualifier.

DemoJavaNames supports inheritance from classes only while Java also supports interfaces. Interfaces complicate name analysis somewhat in that multiple inheritance may cause several fields with the same name to be inherited. This is only an error if a name refers to the ambiguous fields and the error detection can thus not occur in the ClassDecl directly but needs to be deferred to a Name node. This can be implemented by turning the lookup attribute into a set of references instead of a single reference. This does not affect the described modularization, but a few equations need to be changed to handle sets. Lookup equations defined to reference a single declaration are changed to a set of declarations, e.g., `eq` `Block.getStmt(`**int** `index).lookupVariable(String name)` in Listing 1.3 should return a set with a single reference to a variable declaration. Equations that expect a single reference need to ensure that the queried set contains a single reference and then extract that reference, e.g., `eq` `ExpressionName.type()` in Listing 1.2 should extract a single type declaration reference or return `unknownType()`. If a name binds to more than one element the name is ambiguous and a compile-time error is reported.

4   Related Work

Transformation technology is commonly used in compiler construction to refine the AST to include context-sensitive information for later passes. Our approach differs from similar techniques in the use of context-dependent rewrites interleaved with attribute computations. Rewrites allow us to gradually define new concepts in terms of existing concepts, in the same way commonly used in informal language definitions. The fine-grained interaction between attribute computation and rewriting enables the immediate use of these concepts in equations without the need of defining separate passes. This is a key mechanism that allows complex analysis problems like Java name resolution to be broken down into small simple steps. To our knowledge, there are no other systems supporting similar mechanisms. Higher-order attribute grammars [17, 12] allow the AST to be used as the only data structure, and combined with forwarding [15] it may be possible to use in a similar fashion, but as far as we know, forwarding has only been implemented in prototypes built on top of Haskell, and it is unclear how the practical performance would scale to full languages like Java.

The basic idea of name analysis for object-oriented languages based on explicit name bindings was used by ourselves earlier for simpler object-oriented languages [5], [6], and by Vorthmann in his visibility graph technique [18]. Vorthmann also uses a filtering technique to take care of constructs that limit declaration visibility. However, these approaches did not use context-dependent node types, which contribute substantially to making the approach modular. There is some other work aiming at separating the name analysis from other phases of a compiler, most notably the work on Kastens and Waite on an abstract data type for symbol tables [8]. The current version of Eli [13] contains an extensible library of modules for a large variety of scope rules, e.g., single inheritance, multiple inheritance, declare before use.

JastAdd lets context-dependent computations drive the transformations but it is interesting to compare to the opposite approach: letting transformations drive contextual computations commonly used in transformation systems such as ASF+SDF [14] and Stratego [16]. An important difference is that transformation systems typically handle contextual information by using an external database that is updated during the transformations. This requires the user to explicitly associate database updates with particular transformation rules or phases. The traversal order must thus take contextual dependences, which can be highly nonlocal, into account. In contrast, JastAdd uses the contextual dependences to derive a suitable traversal strategy. The Stratego system has a mechanism for dependent dynamic transformation rules [11], supporting certain context-dependent transformations, but it is not clear how this could be used for implementing name binding and similar problems in object-oriented languages.

5   Conclusions

We have presented a technique to implement name analysis for the Java programming language. The main contribution of the paper is to show how complex problems in name analysis including ambiguities related to names of variables, types, and packages can be solved in a declarative and modular way. The use of declarative attributes and contextual rewrites allow the implementation to be modularized in the same way as the language specification. Context-free as well as context dependent concepts in the language can be used directly in attributes and equations. It is worth noticing that the implementation can be freely modularized according to different criteria. A language extender may for instance choose to define a module with all attributes and equations related to a new language construct. The granularity of what can be modularized is a single attribute or equation, thereby providing excellent support for separation of concerns.

We have defined a small subset of Java that captures all the characteristic problems in resolving contextually ambiguous names. The implementation using JastAdd is less than 200 lines of code, most of it included in the paper. The source code and the JastAdd tool are available for download at [1]. The technique has been used to implement a full Java 1.4 compiler to verify that the technique scales to the full language. The system has been validated against the Jacks test-suite and passes more tests than the production quality compilers javac and jikes [1] while being roughly half the size of the handwritten javac compiler.

Acknowledgements

We are grateful to Calle Lejdfors and the anonymous reviewers for valuable feedback and helpful comments.

References

1. T. Ekman and G. Hedin. The JastAdd compiler compiler system. http://jastadd.cs.lth.se.
2. T. Ekman and G. Hedin. Rewritable Reference Attributed Grammars. In *Proceedings of ECOOP 2004*, volume 3086 of *LNCS*. Springer-Verlag, 2004.
3. J. Gosling, B. Joy, G. Steele, and G. Bracha. *The Java Language Specification Second Edition*. Addison-Wesley, Boston, Mass., 2000.
4. J. Gosling, B. Joy, G. Steele, and G. Bracha. *The Java Language Specification Third Edition*. Addison-Wesley, Boston, Mass., 2005.
5. G. Hedin. An overview of door attribute grammars. In *Proceedings of Compiler Construction 1994*, volume 786 of *LNCS*, pages 31–51. Springer-Verlag, 1994.
6. G. Hedin. Reference attribute grammars. In *Informatica (Slovenia)*, 24(3), 2000.
7. G. Hedin and E. Magnusson. JastAdd: an aspect-oriented compiler construction system. *Science of Computer Programming*, 47(1):37–58, 2003.
8. U. Kastens and W. M. Waite. An abstract data type for name analysis. *Acta Informatica*, 28(6):539–558, 1991.

9. G. Kiczales, E. Hilsdale, J. Hugunin, M. Kersten, J. Palm, and W. G. Griswold. An overview of AspectJ. In *ECOOP 2001*, volume 2072 of *LNCS*, pages 327–355. Springer-Verlag, 2001.
10. D. E. Knuth. Semantics of context-free languages. *Mathematical Systems Theory*, 2(2):127–145, June 1968. Correction: *Mathematical Systems Theory* 5, 1, pp. 95-96 (March 1971).
11. K. Olmos and E. Visser. Composing source-to-source data-flow transformations with rewriting strategies and dependent dynamic rewrite rules. In *Proceedings of Compiler Construction 2005*, volume 3443 of *LNCS*. Springer-Verlag, 2005.
12. J. Saraiva. *Purely functional implementation of attribute grammars*. PhD thesis, Utrecht University, The Netherlands, 1999.
13. A. Sloane, W. M. Waite, and U. Kastens. Eli - translator construction made easy. http://eli-project.sourceforge.net/.
14. M. van den Brand and P. Klint. The ASF+SDF MetaEnvironment. http://www.cwi.nl/htbin/sen1/twiki/bin/view/SEN1/MetaEnvironment.
15. E. Van Wyk, O. d. Moor, K. Backhouse, and P. Kwiatkowski. Forwarding in attribute grammars for modular language design. In *Proceedings of Compiler Construction 2002*, volume 2304 of *LNCS*, pages 128–142. Springer-Verlag, 2002.
16. E. Visser, M. Bravenboer, and R. Vermaas. Stratego: Strategies for Program Transformation. http://www.program-transformation.org/Stratego/WebHome.
17. H. H. Vogt, S. D. Swierstra, and M. F. Kuiper. Higher order attribute grammars. In *Proceedings of the SIGPLAN '89 Conference on Programming language design and implementation*, pages 131–145. ACM Press, 1989.
18. S. A. Vorthmann. Modelling and specifying name visibility and binding semantics. Technical Report CMU//CS-93-158, 1993.

Techniques for Lightweight Generator Refactoring

Holger Krahn and Bernhard Rumpe

Institute for Software Systems Engineering
Technische Universität Braunschweig, Braunschweig, Germany
http://www.sse.cs.tu-bs.de

Abstract. This paper presents an exercise to facilitate refactoring techniques not only on generated code, but also on generator templates by reusing existing refactoring techniques from the target language. Refactoring is particularly useful if not only the generated classes but also the template defining the result of the code generator can be adapted in a uniform treatment. We describe a simple demonstration prototype that illustrates our approach. The demonstration is based on the idea to define the templates for code generation themselves as compilable and therefore refactorable source code. However, this limits the directives embedded in the template used for code generation, as we have to embed those as comments. We explore how far this approach carries and where its limits are.

1 Introduction and Problem Statement

Code generation avoids repetitive and tedious programming tasks and helps to improve code quality as it "reuses" code from templates [13]. When code generators are used in agile projects, a subtle problem occurs: hand-coded source code is frequently changed using existing refactoring [7, 11] tools. To keep all existing code consistent, usually tools like Eclipse [6] also refactor the generated code. However, template and generated code are then not consistent anymore. So far two ways to handle this exist: either the generation is regarded a non-repeatable one-shot and the template is never reused, or the changes are manually applied to the template. In the latter case, it is important to ensure that generated code is in sync again, which forces re-generation and manual checks if the result is consistent. However, this approach is time consuming and therefore hinders an agile refactoring of software. This problem is illustrated further in Figure 1, where the following steps are applied within a software system that makes use of code generation.

1. A generator takes a model, in the following text also called *data*, and a given template file to generate the code. The results of this process are generated source files that typically interact with handwritten source code e.g. comprising technical interfaces, specific algorithms or reusable framework components.

R. Lämmel, J. Saraiva, and J. Visser (Eds.): GTTSE 2005, LNCS 4143, pp. 437–446, 2006.
© Springer-Verlag Berlin Heidelberg 2006

2. The source code is refactored. If the generated source code contains references like method calls or variable instantiations that are defined in the hand-written code, changes are adopted automatically by the refactoring engine. This process is usually called *updating references* [11] in the source code that is not directly refactored.
3. The model or data is changed manually, which results in the necessity to generate the classes again. One efficiency problem is that now the changes done by the refactoring engine in step 2 are discarded and the resulting source code is not necessarily interacting correctly with the generated code anymore.

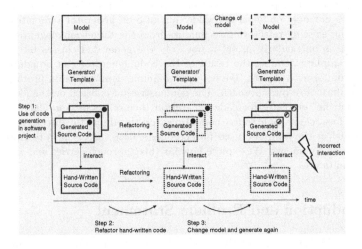

Fig. 1. Risk of incompatibility when refactoring generated source code

The problem described hadn't occurred if the template would have been refactored in the same fashion as the refactoring engine updates the generated classes in step 1. Our approach allows to write templates in a form that allows for automatic refactoring by any code refactoring engine that updates references and preserves comments. Our experiments show that e.g. the built-in Eclipse refactoring engine is sufficient for this purpose.

Various ways of code generation are already published. For a survey of the most common approaches see for example [10]. Most similar to our approach are template-based code generators like Velocity [1] which is e.g. also used in Poseidon [2]. The mainstream of these approaches uses a template that is a combination of pieces of the target language that includes "holes" where pieces of the code generator language are included. For example, if one wants to generate Java classes with Velocity, the template contains a number of Velocity tags embedded in a Java frame. Such a file is in usually not compilable, because the Velocity tags are not valid parts of the Java language. From a practical point of view, a refactoring engine thus simply ignores the template files and is therefore incapable of updating references in them. A heavyweight solution would be to enhance the refactoring engine to actually understand and transform a template as well. This is sophisticated work to do and even though the number of used templates will probably increasing a lot in future software projects, it may not be worth the effort. So the key idea of our lightweight approach is to use templates that are already compilable source files and hence allow a refactoring engine to recognize templates and update references by that.

Therefore we call our approach "language preserving" as from a point of view of the target language, the template is already syntactically valid, even though a semantically useless file. To our knowledge, there was so far no other experiment that facilitates this idea and actually built a working code generator on that idea. However, *model templates* which are written in the target modeling language and decorated with stereotypes are a similar idea [4].

The rest of this paper is organized as follows. Section 2 describes the template engine and its technical properties. In Section 3 a longer example demonstrates the applicability of the approach. Some refactorings are listed that can be applied to hand-written source code and change the template file automatically. Section 4 gives an overview of the whole process of code generation which supports the usage of the proposed template engine. Section 5 concludes this paper.

2   A "Language Preserving" Template Engine

The main idea of this template engine is not to generate code through completing the template by inserting data in the template holes, but to replace marked exemplary data with real data. The template consists of two types of elements. The main part is code of the target language which is basically copied to the output. Embedded are then special comments of the target language, so-called tags, that are interpreted as commands by the template engine to guide the code generation process. The template engine accesses the model class[1] to retrieve data and writes it to the output. In total, comments plus the exemplary data, which is usually a single word, are transformed into the real piece of code. An example of this behavior can be found in Figure 2.

A tag in this template language looks like a special Java multiline comment (/*C ... */). As described above, the word following the tag is replaced by real data. Which data is chosen depends on the tokens which are the words within the special comment. Our engine allows two possible types of tokens which are all concatenated directly without spaces to replace the word after the comment. The first type of token is surrounded by %-characters and serves as substitutable parameters. They are substituted by the value of the model attribute with the same name as shown in Figure 2. The second type of token is regarded as plain text and is copied directly to the output. This feature can be used for example to form valid strings.

---

[1] Please note that a "model class" belongs to the abstract syntax describing the model and thus to the meta-model.

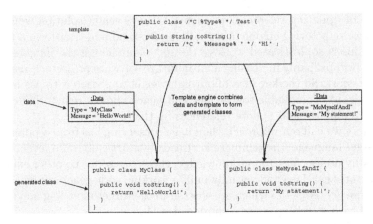

Fig. 2. Example for code generation with proposed template engine

In our template engine at each generation step one model object (that is an instance of a model class) has the "focus". This concept stems from traditional object-orientation, where exactly the *this*-object is active. This means that all tokens surrounded by % access attributes of the model object. In this point it differs from Velocity which extends to the definition of variables to access different model objects at the same time. In order to change the active model object, our template engine supports the following additional tags introducing the usual control structures:

/*for %X% */ ... /*end*/ The prerequisite for this tag is that the active model object resp. its class provides a method getX() which will be accessed by the template engine. The return value of this method becomes the active model object until the end comment (/*end*/) is reached. Then the original model object becomes the active model object again.

/*foreach %X% */ ... /*end*/ The prerequisite for this tag is that the active model object has got a method getX() which will be accessed by the template engine. The return value must be of the type java.util.List. The first entry in this list becomes the active model object and is used for code generation until the end comment (/*end*/) is reached. The resulting behavior is repeated for every entry in the list.

/*if %X% */ ... /*else*/ ... /*end*/ The prerequisite for this tag is that the active model object has a method isX() which will be accessed by the template engine and returns a boolean value. If the return value is true, the template engine uses the code written in the first clause for code generation, otherwise the else clause is used. However, this control tag does not change the focus of the used model object.

The above mentioned control structures can be nested arbitrarily to access the model tree (See Section 4 for an explanation why we make use of trees and not graphs here). Within a for or foreach environment the nodes upwards in the tree can be accessed via %number%name% where number is a natural number counting the steps upwards in the model tree (1 for direct parent) and `name` is the name of the attribute to be accessed.

In certain situations it is easier to directly output data without having example data after the comment that will be replaced. This resembles the usual behavior of a template engine and is supported via the tag `/*O ... */`.

With these mechanisms, a reasonable code generator engine is given to sufficiently demonstrate and explore our concept.

3 Example

To explore the properties of our approach, we use a comparative template engine for generating code. Martin Fowler shows in [8] different ways to realize code generation. In the following we concentrate on his solution using the template engine Velocity. The example is taken from the article, but translated from C# to Java and slightly adopted to make the concepts clearer and shorter without losing the crucial points. Especially note that while both the template and the resulting Java code are full class files, in the figures only the class body is shown.

The main idea of the example is to customize a so called reader by objects of the type `ReaderStrategy`. These are used to parse files in a line-oriented file format, where keywords at the beginning of each line determine the structure of the following data. Depending on the keyword, characters between a start and an end position have a meaning and should be extracted. For further details on the example see [8]. The example in Figure 3 shows that it is possible to invent APIs to split the code into two parts, one containing basic functions and one containing code using these basic functions in a way that is specific for a given problem.

The code from Figure 3 can be used as it is, but for complex files, one would rather like to use a form of description that just contains the information needed

```
public void Configure(Reader target) {
  target.AddStrategy(ConfigureServiceCall());
  target.AddStrategy(ConfigureUsage());
}
private ReaderStrategy ConfigureServiceCall() {
  ReaderStrategy result = new ReaderStrategy("SVCL", ServiceCall.class);
  result.AddFieldExtractor(4, 18, "CustomerName");
  result.AddFieldExtractor(19, 23, "CustomerID");
  return result;
}
private ReaderStrategy ConfigureUsage() {
  ReaderStrategy result = new ReaderStrategy("USGE", Usage.class);
  result.AddFieldExtractor(4, 8, "CustomerID");
  result.AddFieldExtractor(9, 22, "CustomerName");
  return result;
}
```

Fig. 3. Generated code (adapted from [8])

and not that much extra technical code. This form of description is usually called a domain-specific language (DSL). Figure 4 shows the condensed information garbled (or even hidden) in the Java code in Figure 3.

```
mapping SVCL ServiceCall
    4-18: CustomerName
   19-23: CustomerID
mapping USGE Usage
    4- 8: CustomerID
    9-22: CustomerName
```

Fig. 4. Domain specific description for code from Figure 3

The template for the code generation can of course be described using Velocity (cf. Figure 5) or our approach (cf. Figure 6).

```
public void Configure(Reader target) {
  #foreach( $map in ${config.Mappings})
  target.AddStrategy(Configure${map.TargetClassNameOnly}());
  #end
}
#foreach( $map in ${config.Mappings})
  private ReaderStrategy Configure${map.TargetClassNameOnly}() {
  ReaderStrategy result =
    new ReaderStrategy("$map.Code", typeof ($map.TargetClassName));
    #foreach( $f in $map.Fields)
    result.AddFieldExtractor($f.Start, $f.End, "$f.FieldName");
    #end
    return result;
} #end
```

Fig. 5. Template using Velocity (adapted from [8])

To our experience, the templates for our engine tend to be a bit easier to understand than the ones for Velocity because each replaceable tag is usually followed by an example of what could be generated from it. It turned out to be the best strategy, to either use meaningful names (as we did in the example) or to take names that obviously are meant for replacement, e.g. by beginning with double underscores.

Also typos like a forgotten semicolon at the end of a statement are usually discovered quicker, as modern IDEs compile source in the background and mistakes are highlighted immediately. This is possible because the templates for our engine are compilable. Using template engines like Velocity a generation process is required first to detect this kind of errors. As the template file is valid Java source code, various helper functions of modern IDEs can be used to create or modify the template. This includes the generation of get/set-methods, the renaming of variables, code assistants like listing all available methods by typing

```
public void Configure(Reader target) {
  /*foreach %Mappings% */
  target.AddStrategy( /*C Configure %ClassName% () */ ConfigureSCall() );
  /*end*/
}
/*foreach %Mappings% */
private ReaderStrategy /*C Configure %ClassName% () */ ConfigureSCall() {
  ReaderStrategy result = new ReaderStrategy
    ( /*C " %name% " */ "SVCL" , /*C %ClassName% */ ServiceCall .class);

  /*foreach %Entries% */
  result.AddFieldExtractor( /*C %LowerBound% */ 4 ,
    /*C %UpperBound% */ 18 , /*C " %Name% " */ "CustomerName" );
  /*end*/
  return result;
} /*end*/
```

Fig. 6. Template using proposed template engine

a dot after a class name, and the generation of method bodies for all methods of a superclass. But these features are just by-products of the main advantage, the improved possibility of refactoring the template file together with the generated files.

In our experiment, we applied a number of refactorings, including the following ones using the Eclipse built-in refactoring engine to hand-written source code that interacts with the generated source code from the example. All refactorings lead to an automatic and correct change of our template without any additional effort:

- Renaming
  e.g. Reader to Parser or ReaderStrategy to ParserStrategy.
- Change method signature
  e.g. adding an additional parameter to ReaderStrategy.addFieldExtractor with a default value or deleting one parameter of the same method.
- Extract Interface
  e.g. extracting an interface from ReaderStrategy called Strategy and use that instead of ReaderStrategy in the generated code.
- Move
  e.g. move the class ReaderStrategy to another package. The necessary imports are also updated in the template file.

This list is certainly not complete, but could give an overview on how to apply refactorings that change both the generated and the hand-written source.

In addition to the given experiment, we e.g. developed a code generation for statecharts. A result of further experiments and discussions during the summer-school was that only hand-written code and the template are refactored automatically but the model stays unchanged. Depending on the concrete template this might be a drawback because the model can contain elements like class, method or variable names which refer to elements in the implementation but are not changed by a refactoring. It is still an open question if there is a lightweight way to overcome this limitation or if only a heavyweight solution exists.

4   Easy Method for Developing a Code Generator

For a complete understanding, we describe a method to develop such a code generator that makes use of our template engine in the following three steps:

1. A prototype for the generated code is programmed manually by developing an example as it can be found in Figure 3. To our experience this first step simplifies the following steps tremendously because programming an example first is usually a lot easier than starting off directly with the template.
2. The variation points (template holes) of the class are identified and special comments are added directly before the words to be replaced. The form of these comments are described in Section 2 and the resulting template looks e.g. like the source shown in Figure 6.
3. In order to generate the resulting Java code shown in Figure 3 from the DSL description given in Figure 4, we need model classes whose instances will represent the information of the DSL description (abstract syntax) internally.

Extracting the information from a textual description is a typical task for a parser, which can be generated by parser-generator or compiler-compiler [5]. A parser generator takes a grammar as input and generates a running parser. A number of tools also generate a default set of classes representing the abstract syntax tree (AST) (e.g. [3, 9, 14]). Available tools differ in the underlying parser technology and the form of these AST classes quite heavily. Some syntax representations for example use untyped trees, others build rather deeply nested trees.

MontiCore is a project at the Institute for Software Systems Engineering at the Technical University of Braunschweig that develops techniques to simplify the definition of domain-specific languages. As MontiCore focuses on analysis algorithms, formal verification techniques and generation mechanisms, it is restricted to textual input. One of its key techniques is to enrich a grammar, such that it contains enough information to generate both parser and AST classes. Technically speaking, the description for creating an AST is identical to the parser rules. This both restricts the choices of a developer in a sense that the AST structure strongly corresponds to the grammar (similar to [9]), but it improves the effectiveness of the developer, as it allows very compact definitions of languages. As a side effect it simplifies the development of new languages for less experienced users.

MontiCore is not a parser-generator on its own, but is built on Antlr, a rather widely used tool [12], as a backend to generate the parser component. The AST class construction and the grammar description form is similar to the one used by SableCC [9]. The underlying parsing technology is a recursive-descent predicate

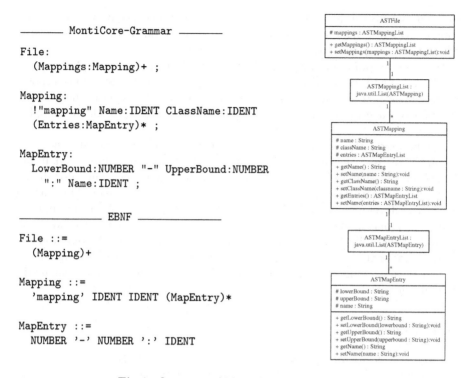

```
————— MontiCore-Grammar —————

File:
   (Mappings:Mapping)+ ;

Mapping:
   !"mapping" Name:IDENT ClassName:IDENT
   (Entries:MapEntry)* ;

MapEntry:
   LowerBound:NUMBER "-" UpperBound:NUMBER
      ":" Name:IDENT ;


————————— EBNF —————————

File ::=
   (Mapping)+

Mapping ::=
   'mapping' IDENT IDENT (MapEntry)*

MapEntry ::=
   NUMBER '-' NUMBER ':' IDENT
```

Fig. 7. Overview of MontiCore descriptions

LL-parser which simplifies the compositional embedding of languages into each other in comparison to using a LR-parser.

The following example in Figure 7 contains the MontiCore grammar, the respective EBNF grammar that describes the same language and a UML class diagram of the derived AST classes. The generated parser instantiates objects of these classes to build the internal representation of the model (abstract syntax). MontiCore is e.g. used in the example in Section 3 to parse the input data from the DSL description and to generate the AST classes which are used by the template engine. The parser and AST classes of the template engine itself are also constructed using MontiCore.

Based on our experience so far, it is worth extending the current capabilities of defining domain-specific languages and code generators for them, because it indeed speeds up the development and in particular the agile development of software systems.

5   Conclusions and Outlook

In this experiment we have shown how templates for code generation can look like, so that they allow for an automatic refactoring within an agile development process. We also have demonstrated the usability of this approach by a longer example, where we used MontiCore, a newly developed prototype, to simplify supporting work like the generation of a parser for input data and the creation of classes storing this data.

However, for our approach it was necessary to develop a new template replacement engine and we could not reuse e.g. Velocity. For demonstration purposes, it was sufficient to use the described features. However, for practical use it would be good to have more capabilities of Velocity accessible through the template engine.

Furthermore, the concrete syntax of the template engine is still not very elegant. We used it mainly for experiments first and also integrated it into MontiCore to generate the AST classes itself. But the experiments also showed that for practical usage additional tags simplify the development. This has e.g. led to the development of additional tags like /*0 ... */. Also the approach where only one model object has the focus at a certain point was weakened by adding the ability to access model objects upwards in the AST-hierarchy by %number%attribute%. These experiments encourage us to combine the idea to embed tags as comments with the comfort of a grown-up template engine like Velocity in near future.

References

1. Apache Velocity Website. http://jakarta.apache.org/velocity/.
2. Poseidon for UML Website. http://www.gentleware.com.
3. M. van den Brand, P.-E. Moreau, and J. Vinju. Generator of efficient strongly typed abstract syntax trees in Java. *IEE Proceedings - Software*, 152(2):70–78, 2005.
4. K. Czarnecki and M. Antkiewicz. Mapping Features to Models: A Template Approach Based on Superimposed Variants. In *Proceedings of GPCE '05*, pages 422–437, 2005.
5. C. Donnelly and R. Stallman. *Bison: The Yacc-Compatible Parser Generator*. iUniverse Inc., 2000.
6. Eclipse Website. http://eclipse.org.
7. M. Fowler. *Refactoring: Improving the Design of Existing Code*. Addison-Wesley Professional, 1999.
8. M. Fowler. *Generating Code for DSLs*, 2005.
   http://www.martinfowler.com/articles/codeGenDsl.html.
9. E. Gagnon and L. Hendren. SableCC – an object-oriented compiler framework. In *Proceedings of TOOLS 1998*, August 1998.
10. J. Herrington. *Code Generation in Action*. Manning Publications Co., 2003.
11. W. F. Opdyke. *Refactoring Object-Oriented Frameworks*. PhD thesis, University of Illinois at Urbana-Champaign, 1992.
12. T. J. Parr and R. W. Quong. ANTLR: A predicated-LL(k) parser generator. *Software – Practice and Experience*, 25(7):789–810, 1995.
13. B. Rumpe. *Agile Modellierung mit UML : Codegenerierung, Testfälle, Refactoring*. Xpert.press. Springer-Verlag, 2005.
14. J. Visser. Visitor combination and traversal control. In *Proc. of OOPSLA '01*, pages 270–282, New York, NY, USA, 2001. ACM Press.

E-CARES Project: Reengineering of Telecommunication Systems

Christof Mosler

Department of Computer Science 3, RWTH Aachen University,
Ahornstr. 55, 52074 Aachen, Germany
christof.mosler@rwth-aachen.de

Abstract. One important field of application for embedded real-time systems is in the telecommunications industry. In the first phase of the E-CARES reengineering project, we regarded the architecture modeling and the reverse engineering of telecommunication systems. Current work concerns the restructuring of such systems including their re-design and re-implementation. The aim is to provide concepts, languages, methods, and tools to improve the architecture and the real-time performance of the software system. Our reengineering prototype is based on a graph rewriting system by which the underlying application logic is generated.

1 Introduction

There exist many approaches concerning reengineering of legacy systems, but the majority of these approaches deals with systems in the field of business applications. Our project concerns understanding and restructuring of complex legacy systems from the telecommunications domain. Such systems are embedded real-time systems using the signaling paradigm, thus they pose additional requirements regarding fault tolerance, reliability, availability, and response time. Corresponding reengineering tools should take into account these performance aspects and provide adapted visualisation and modeling methods for their analyses.

The E-CARES research project is a cooperation between Ericsson Eurolab Deutschland GmbH (EED) and Department of Computer Science 3, RWTH Aachen University. The acronym E-CARES stands for **E**ricsson **C**ommunication **AR**chitecture for **E**mbedded **S**ystems. The current system under study is Ericsson's AXE10, a mobile-service switching center (MSC) comprising more than ten million lines of code written in PLEX (**P**rogramming **L**anguage for **EX**changes) [1].

The aim of the project is to provide a flexible and interactive reengineering environment, not only for the PLEX programming language but also for other languages used in the domain of embedded real-time systems. Figure 1 presents the different parts of the software reengineering process according to a model introduced by Byrne in [2]. The reverse engineering of telecommunication software was studied in the first phase of the E-CARES project [1]. Current work concerns the extension of the E-CARES prototype by providing restructuring support. For that reason, we study not only re-design techniques but also forward engineering methods which can propagate the changes from the design level to the implementation level.

R. Lämmel, J. Saraiva, and J. Visser (Eds.): GTTSE 2005, LNCS 4143, pp. 447–458, 2006.

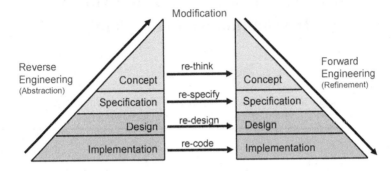

Fig. 1. General model of software reengineering [2]

The E-CARES prototype is based on the graph rewriting system PROGRES [3]. The PROGRES language is a strongly typed specification language for complex data structures. It is based on a graph model and allows the definition of graph schemes and corresponding graph transformations. The PROGRES programming environment consists basically of a syntax-directed editor and a code generator for C-code, by which the underlying application logic of the E-CARES prototype is generated. Graph grammars offer a convenient and efficient way to define the required transformations [4].

This paper describes how we use simple restructuring transformations to improve the AXE10 system. The extensions of the PROGRES specification and the new functionalities of the E-CARES prototype are presented. The implemented transformations improve the architecture of the software system and consider also aspects specific to embedded real-time systems.

The paper is structured as follows: Section 2 introduces the terminology relevant in the telecommunications context. In section 3, the current status of the E-CARES prototype is described. Section 4 explains how we use the graph rewriting system PRO-GRES to perform re-design transformations. Section 5 describes how we perform the code modifications to adapt the source code to the changes performed on the graph. In section 6, the related work is classified and the current state-of-the-art is shown. In the last section, the results are summarized and an outlook for future work is given.

2 System Under Study

The GSM network (Global System for Mobile Communication) is the current standard in mobile telecommunications. A very important part of the GSM network are the mobile-service switching centers (MSCs). They provide services like phone call, data call, and short message service (SMS). They are also responsible for the authentication and for the communication with other MSCs and networks. The AXE10 is Ericsson's implementation of an MSC. It consists of hardware and software units. Each switch has a central processor and a range of regional processors controlling various hardware devices like sensors and actors. Each processor executes the corresponding program code on its own runtime system. Incoming events are handled by the regional processors or forwarded to other processors.

The software units of the AXE10 system are implemented in PLEX (**P**rogramming Language for **EX**changes). This language was developed in about 1970 at Ericsson and is still in wide use within the company. It has a signaling paradigm, which means that only incoming signals can trigger code execution. The main unit of a PLEX program is a block and each block is stored in its own file. PLEX provides only very simple means for program structuring, therefore, engineers at Ericsson often use special implementation patterns to obtain a clear program structure. For example, it is not possible to define subsystems in the PLEX language. To group a set of blocks with similar functionality to a subsystem, they use predefined name conventions and comments. However, the concept of subsystems is still very important for the organisation and finds a wide application in the AXE10 context. For such complex legacy systems a clear and understandable architecture is essential. For that reason, we study reengineering techniques improving the software architecture, like the decomposition of subsystems and blocks. However, specific challenges of PLEX comprise primarily performance aspects. Some examples will be presented in section 4.

3 E-CARES Tool Suite

The aim of the project is to provide a flexible and interactive reengineering environment. To achieve the desired flexibility the implementation of the E-CARES prototype is extremely modular and extensible (see figure 2). The different parts of the environment are entirely exchangeable. We use formal specifications from which major parts of the prototype are generated. Hence, the scanners and parsers are generated automatically. Here, we use the lexical analyser generator *jlex* [5] and the parser generator *jay* [6]. The code modifier is based on the rule-based programming language TXL [7]. Furthermore, the PROGRES specification language offers a convenient way to specify the required graph operations. In this manner, new functionalities (e.g. new analyses, transformations, and views) can be added easily. And also extensions for other programming languages are possible, as showed in [1] for the C language by providing a corresponding graph model. However, the code generated from a PROGRES specification forms only the application logic responsible for the graph operations. We use UPGRADE [8], a framework for building graph-based applications, to provide the control over these graph operations. That is, the PROGRES generated source code is the engine of the prototype while the Java-based UPGRADE framework and its extensions provide the user interface.

In our reverse engineering approach we use different sources of information. The most important and most reliable one is the source code of the PLEX system. We parse the source code and create a textual document describing the system structure, comprising its communication, control, and data flow. Furthermore, we use some other sources of information which are also parsed; the extracted information is added to the *structure document*. For example, we use a textual file called *signal list* which provides the names of the blocks to which outgoing signals are sent during runtime. In PLEX, signal receivers are often initialized dynamically. By considering this list, we are able to exclude from the graph any signal edges which are potentially possible, but never actually used. Another example of an additional source of information is the textual *system hierarchy description* which itemizes blocks belonging to each subsystem.

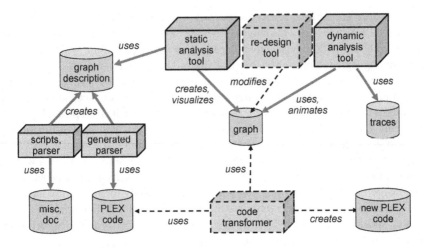

Fig. 2. Current status of the E-CARES prototype [1]

The graph described in the structure document consists of a main system node, subsystem nodes, block nodes, and the nodes for different program parts of each block. All nodes comprise different types of attributes describing where the corresponding software parts can be found and what their characteristics are. The nodes are connected to each other by various kinds of edges (e.g. contains, goto, calls, from_source, to_target). An example of a structure graph is shown in figure 3.

The main part of the reengineering environment consists of three tools whose application logic is generated from the PROGRES specification. The *static analysis tool*

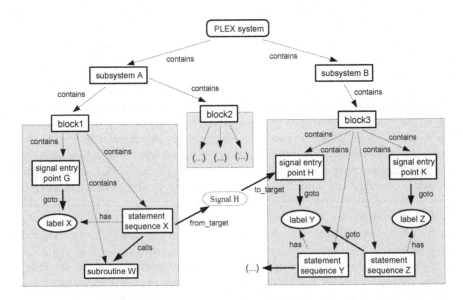

Fig. 3. Cutout of a structure graph

reads the graph description in the structure document and instantiates the graph in the underlying database. Then the user can perform various types of analyses by using different visualisation and query techniques. Also, different metrics can be used to obtain more quantitative characterizations of the analysed system. This tool provides not only the system structure but also behavioural information which can be identified by the static analysis. For instance, behavioural information allow the analysis of link chains [9] which describe how different block instances are combined at runtime to realise a certain service.

With the *dynamic analysis tool* the user is able to analyse the system behaviour during runtime. Usually, we are interested in the system behaviour for a certain scenario, e.g. an incoming phone call. The trace files containing all the information can be obtained either from an emulator or from a running AXE10 machine. For the interconnected blocks involved in the processing of the incoming event an instance graph is created which is also connected to the structure graph. Further graph transformations and queries can be used to analyse and visualise the dynamic behaviour of the system.

The basic functionalities of both tools have been already successfully implemented [9], but the graph model still must be adapted to new emerging requirements concerning implementation patterns used at Ericsson. For this purpose the missing information must be added to the graph model and new transformations defined. Furthermore, the two tools indicated by dashed lines in figure 2 are still in development. The *re-design tool* should provide an interface allowing the user to interactively improve the software system by applying different kinds of modifications. This tool uses several graph transformations which are also specified in PROGRES. The second tool, the *code transformer*, propagates the changes performed on the graph to the actual source code.

4   Graph Transformations for Architecture Re-design

Successful software restructuring requires a solid understanding of the existing system. By representing the system structure by a graph the engineer is able to work on a more abstract representation of the system. The analysis is easier and there are many aspects which can be visualised in a very effective way. To perform a restructuring on this level of abstraction means to manipulate such a graph.

To present a concrete example of a re-design rule we introduce a simplified restructuring scenario. Each subsystem consists of blocks, which all should be related to one particular functionality of the system. But, subsystems often contain blocks which are assigned to them simply because of historical reasons. Such situations make the software very difficult to understand and especially the maintenance of such a system is very painful. For this reason, engineers at Ericsson would like to have tool support for identifying such blocks and eventually for moving them to other subsystems. In a simplified scenario, we could look for blocks which are not used by any other block from the same subsystem and move them to a subsystem where they are used.

Figure 4 shows a corresponding rule in a PROGRES-like notation. From this rule, the PROGRES environment generates a corresponding C-function which can automatically be accessed by the UPGRADE-based user interface of the prototype. The left-hand side of the rule defines the subgraph we are trying to find in the instantiated structure graph.

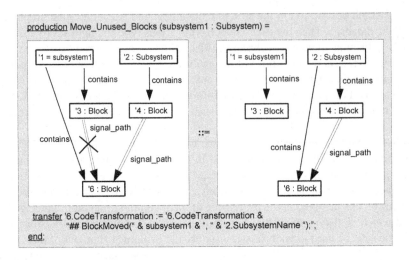

Fig. 4. Graph transformation rule for moving blocks

Given a certain subsystem as parameter, we try to find a block in it, which does not receive signals from any other block in this subsystem (expressed by the negative path expression between node '3 and node '6). As shown on the right-hand side of the rule, this block should then be moved to another subsystem where at least one other block is sending signals to it. To simplify the transformation rule we use *signal_path* to indicate inter-block communication. The definition of this complex path can be found in figure 5. Like already shown in figure 3, in the actual structure graph, blocks contain statement sequences which can send signals to entry points of other blocks. To model signals we use an edge-node-edge construction which allows storing complex attributes for the signals.

After applying this graph transformation, we obtain a clearer software architecture with more self-contained subsystems. But we also have to store information about the corresponding changes in the PLEX source code which result in the performed graph

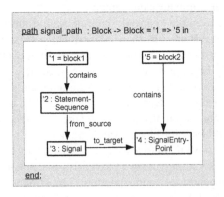

Fig. 5. PROGRES definition of signal_path

transformation. For that reason, every graph node has an attribute *CodeTransform* collecting all source code changes to be performed later. Each new transformation is indicated by the character sequence "##". In our example, only in the node of block '6 the information about moving it from subsystem1 (node '1) to the found subsystem (node '2) is assigned.

Of course, there are other restructurings possible for improving the software. When reengineering embedded real-time systems, the objective is not only to obtain a clear and understandable architecture, but also a good system performance. Algorithms concerning performance aspects in PLEX are the subject of ongoing work. The goal is to provide Ericsson engineers with proposals where to improve the software. Currently, there are two areas we are working on:

- Moving blocks from one subsystem to another does not cause any changes on the source code level. However, in a very similar way we can search through a block for subroutines and labeled statement sequences which could be moved to other blocks. For example, if we find code parts of a block which are mainly used by another block we can reduce the number of exchanged signals and temporal variable allocations by moving these parts. Alternatively, we can merge blocks with related functionalities to form a new, more complex block.
- Another promising approach to improve system performance is the analysis of *communication buffers*. Instead of transferring a large amount of data between a number of blocks, we can utilize a global memory buffer and send signals containing a pointer to such a communication buffer. We are developing algorithms supporting decisions on where usual signal communication and where communication buffers should be used. For this analysis, Ericsson provides tables with capacity breakpoints depending on the data size and the number of blocks involved in the communication.

All of these transformations require algorithms analysing complex graph patterns. Though the task of processing such patterns seemed to be very difficult in the beginning, usually some simple rule expressions are all we need to provide the operations for the graph. The PROGRES environment generates the C-code for the given graph operation and the UPGRADE framework automatically offers an adapted interface to access it. Thus, not much additional functionality needs to be coded outside the PROGRES specification.

5   Code Modifications

After the re-design phase, the tool must propagate the corresponding improvements to the implementation level. This section describes briefly how we transform the source code according to the changes performed on the structure graph.

The information about the improved software architecture is stored in the structure graph. However, this graph only forms an instantiated representation of the system; it does not contain all the information needed for the generation of the new source code. Each graph node representing a data or a control structure stores its original file name and its line numbers but not the actual source code. Therefore, to obtain the changed

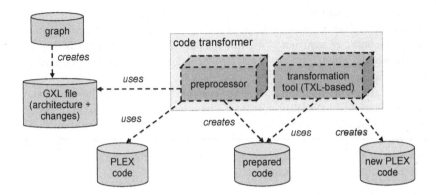

Fig. 6. Generation of the new PLEX source code

program we resort to the original source code files and enhance them by adding information extracted from the graph, describing how the particular parts should be transformed. Figure 6 shows what our *code transformer* tool looks like.

The UPGRADE framework, built around the generated application logic of our reengineering prototype, stores the instantiated structure graph in a database. It provides facilities to export the graph to a GXL[10] file. *GXL* (Graph eXchange Language) is a standard format for exchanging graph-based data. The code transformer consists of two parts: the *preprocessor* and the actual source code *transformation tool*.

The preprocessor uses the GXL file and the original source code files to generate an intermediate version of the code. According to the new system architecture, the preprocessor copies all PLEX files to a new directory and at the same time performs operations moving re-designed block parts between the files. Information about the original

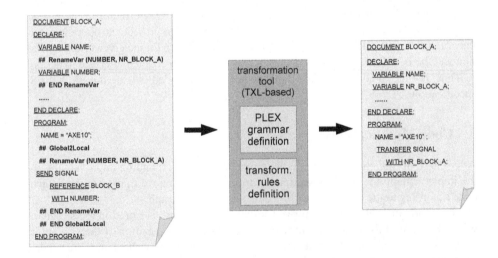

Fig. 7. Prepared PLEX source code and the TXL transformation tool

file names and line numbers have been stored in the graph, thus the program can find the corresponding source code parts easily. In the next step, the preprocessor enhances the new PLEX code by adding annotations describing source code transformations to be performed by the transformation tool. These annotations correspond to the data stored for each node in the attribute CodeTransform (see section 4) and they encapsulate the involved source code lines. If the attribute of a control or a data structure stores more than one transformation, all of them will be added to the source code, clasping the transformations to be performed beforehand. On the left side of figure 7 we see an example of the prepared source code. By using the "RenameVar" annotation we want to rename the variable "NUMBER" to "NR_BLOCK_A". The "Global2Local" annotation intends to transform a "SEND" statement, sending a signal to another block, to a "TRANS-FER", statement sending a local signal to a signal entry point within the same block. As we can see in the document on the right-hand side no "REFERENCE" variable is needed in the new code anymore. Such a transformation is used, for example, when a labeled statement sequence was moved from another block to the current one.

To avoid conflicts when applying different source code modifications we store in the graph only source code transformations for atomic PLEX parts, such as subroutines, labeled statement sequences, and data structure declarations. Such atomic parts have no child nodes in the graph and cannot be split or merged during the re-design process. By preserving the order of the code modifications for every node, we can guarantee the uniqueness of the resulting new PLEX code. This is the reason why we have used "RenameVar" for every occurrence of 'NUMBER' instead of applying it directly to the entire PLEX block. It is up to the engineer specifying the re-design transformations to take into account all graph nodes involved in the re-code process.

The syntax of this prepared code and the corresponding transformations are defined in the rule-based programming language TXL [7]. The TXL transformation system parses each of these prepared files individually and performs the transformations on the created abstract syntax trees. We do not think that we can provide TXL transformations for all possible graph re-design rules. The current set implements rules for renaming of identifiers, transforming of different signal types (e.g. local signals, goto- and call-statements to global signals and vice verse), and moving of subroutines, labeled statement sequences, and data structure declarations. This set is sufficient for all re-design operations provided by the current PROGRES specification. The introduction of new re-design rules can require the definition of new TXL transformations. However, we argue that the great advantage of declarative specifications is the possibility to add new transformations easily. This is valid for the re-design as well as for the re-code level. Although the code transformer tool is still in development we have already achieved first positive results after applying some simple re-designs on a limited number of PLEX blocks.

6   Related Work

There exist other graph-based reengineering tools. The main differences between these projects are described in the following paragraphs.

Rigi [11] is an interactive tool for reverse engineering. It can extract, navigate, analyse and document the structure of large systems. Program understanding is supported through visualisation of the software structure. Rigi is also used in the Bauhaus project [12], which offers a wide range of techniques for (semi-)automatic extraction and description of software architectures. In contrast to E-CARES, these two projects are not based on a high-level specification language. They also do not analyse dynamic data and do not support software restructuring.

GUPRO [13] (Generic Understanding of PROgrams) is a system allowing the generation of program understanding tools. The toolkit supports several programming languages. After the parsing the user can browse through the parsed software in a hypertext-like manner. A graph query language is used to define different kinds of analyses, but graph transformations can not be specified in a declarative way. GUPRO does not support restructuring.

Fujaba (From UML to Java And Back Again) [14] is a free open-source CASE tool with round-trip engineering support for Java. It provides a rule-based visual programming language for manipulating object structures using graph productions based on UML. The Fujaba Tool Suite RE [15] is a collection of Fujaba reengineering tools and plug-ins. It allows the parsing of Java source code and supports different kinds of static and dynamic analyses, such as recognition of design patterns and antipatterns [16].

The approach in [17] shows how refactorings for object-oriented software can be defined by using graph rewrite rules. Instead of PROGRES the researchers use Fujaba and AGG [18] for tool validation. AGG provides a convenient way to define source code refactorings formally. *AGG* is a general tool environment for algebraic graph transformation which follows the interpretative approach. The AGG environment consists of a graphical user interface and an interpreter which can be used for the specification and prototypical implementation of Java applications with complex graph-structured data. The paper at hand presents a very similar approach for defining software transformations. However, the E-CARES project is based on another specification language and aims at the reengineering of programs written in a different kind of programming language.

In comparison to the other graph-based reengineering projects, E-CARES follows a more complex approach to the problem. For the analyses we use not only the source code files but also *other sources of information*. We perform a structural analysis but at the same time we are able to add static behavioural information to the graph, and even *dynamic data* from trace files. Our approach comprises aspects important for the reengineering of *embedded real-time systems*, like performance restrictions and special visualisation techniques.

7   Conclusion

This paper presents the current state of the E-CARES project. It comprises research in the area of reengineering for systems in the telecommunications industry. This paper shows how graph rewriting can be used to process graphs containing information about the structure and behaviour of the systems. Graph rewriting systems like PROGRES offer a convenient way to specify the corresponding graph operations. New kinds of analyses, transformations, and views can be added easily, and also extensions for other languages are possible.

The comparison with the other projects following a graph-based approach shows that some of the other tools lack the support provided by a high-level specification language or do not support restructuring at all. Comparatively, the E-CARES tool also uses a wider range of information and concentrates on specific aspects of embedded real-time systems. As described in the introduction, the characteristics of such systems strongly impact the structuring and implementation of this kind of tool.

The first part of the project concerned the reverse engineering of telecommunication systems. The graph rewriting system was used to specify the operations needed for the analysis of the AXE10 software system. Current results show how graph rewriting systems can be used to perform transformations in order to improve the system. We have been able to successfully analyse parts of the AXE10 software system with respect to problem descriptions stated by Ericsson experts and provide suggestions how to improve the software architecture. Our current goal is to provide algorithms improving system performance by moving source code parts from one block to another, and by optimizing the use of communication buffers.

References

1. Marburger, A.: Reverse Engineering of Complex Legacy Telecommunication Systems. Shaker Verlag, Aachen, Germany (2004) ISBN 3-8322-4154-X.
2. Byrne, E.J.: A Conceptual Foundation of Software Re-engineering. In IEEE Computer Society Press: Los Alamitos CA, U., ed.: Proceedings of the 1992 International Conference on Software Maintenance (ICSM '92), Chicago, USA (1992) 226–235
3. Schürr, A., Winter, A.J., Zündorf, A.: The PROGRES Approach: Language and Environment. In Ehrig, H., Engels, G., Kreowski, H.J., Rozenberg, G., eds.: Handbook on Graph Grammars and Computing by Graph Transformation: Applications, Languages, and Tools. Volume 2. World Scientific: Singapore (1999) 487–550
4. Cremer, K., Marburger, A., Westfechtel, B.: Graph-based tools for re-engineering. Journal of Software Maintenance and Evolution: Research and Practice **14** (2002) 257–292
5. Berk, E.: JLex: A lexical analyzer generator for Java(TM). Department of Computer Science, Princeton University. (2000) http://www.cs.princeton.edu/~appel/modern/java/JLex/current/manual.html.
6. Schreiner, A.T., Kühl, B.: jay – a yacc for java. homepage (2003) URL: http://www.informatik.uni-osnabrueck.de/alumni/bernd/jay/.
7. Cordy, J.R., Halpern-Hamu, C.D., Promislow, E.: TXL: A Rapid Prototyping System for Programming Language Dialects. Computer Languages **16** (1991) 97–107
8. Böhlen, B., Jäger, D., Schleicher, A., Westfechtel, B.: UPGRADE: A Framework for Building Graph-Based Interactive Tools. In Mens, T., Schürr, A., Taentzer, G., eds.: Proceedings of the International Workshop on Graph-Based Tools (GraBaTs 2002). Volume 72 of Electronic Notes in Theoretical Computer Science., Barcelona, Spain, Elsevier: Amsterdam, The Netherlands (2002)
9. Marburger, A., Westfechtel, B.: Behavioral Analysis of Telecommunication Systems by Graph Transformations. In Pfaltz, J.L., Nagl, M., Böhlen, B., eds.: Proceedings of the 2nd Workshop on Applications of Graph Transformations with Industrial Relevance AGTIVE 2003. LNCS 3062, Charlottesville, Virginia, USA, Springer: Heidelberg, Germany (2003) 202–219
10. Holt, R.C., Schürr, A., Sim, S.E., Winter, A.: GXL - Graph eXchange Language. homepage (2006) http://www.gupro.de/GXL/.

11. Müller, H.A., Wong, K., Tilley, S.R.: Understanding Software Systems Using Reverse Engineering Technology. In: The 62nd Congress of L'Association Canadienne Francaise pour l'Avancement des Sciences ACFAS 1994, Montreal, Canada (1994) 41–48
12. Koschke, R.: Atomic Architectural Component Recovery for Program Understanding and Evolution. Doctoral thesis, Institute of Computer Science, University of Stuttgart: Stuttgart, Germany, Stuttgart, Germany (2000) 414 pp.
13. Ebert, J., Kullbach, B., Riediger, V., Winter, A.: GUPRO – Generic Understanding of Programs: An Overview. Electronic Notes in Theoretical Computer Science **72** (2002) URL: http://www.elsevier.nl/locate/entcs/volume72.html.
14. Nickel, U., Niere, J., Zündorf, A.: Tool Demonstration: The Fujaba Environment. In: Proceedings of the 22nd International Conference on Software Engineering ICSE 2000, Limerick, Ireland, IEEE Computer Society Press: Los Alamitos, CA, USA (2000) 742–745
15. Fujaba: Fujaba Tool Suite RE. homepage (2005) http://wwwcs.uni-paderborn.de/cs/fujaba/projects/reengineering/.
16. Niere, J., Schäfer, W., Wadsack, J.P., Wendehals, L., Welsh, J.: Towards pattern-based design recovery. In: Proc. of the 24th International Conference on Software Engineering (ICSE), Orlando, Florida, USA, ACM Press (2002) 338–348
17. Mens, T., Van Eetvelde, N., Demeyer, S., Janssens, D.: Formalizing refactorings with graph transformations. Journal on Software Maintenance and Evolution: Research and Practice (2005)
18. Taentzer, G.: AGG: A tool environment for algebraic graph transformation. In: Proceedings AGTIVE 99. LNCS 1779, Kerkrade, Netherlands, Springer: Heidelberg, Germany (1999) 481–488

A Feature Composition Problem and a Solution Based on C++ Template Metaprogramming

Zoltán Porkoláb and István Zólyomi

Department of Programming Languages and Compilers,
Eötvös Loránd University
Pázmány Péter sétány 1/C H-1117 Budapest, Hungary
{gsd, scamel}@elte.hu

Abstract. Separation of concerns and collaboration based design is usually a suitable concept for library implementation: it results in easily scalable and maintainable code. After specifying and implementing orthogonal features, we aim to easily assemble library components. In real life, components can be used only after appropriate refinement steps, progressively adding features in each step. Therefore the specific solution for a particular task can be produced by composing a set of refined components. Unfortunately, a subtype anomaly occurs in object-oriented languages between such composite components that have different numbers of features from different refinement stages. In this article we analyse this anomaly that we named chevron-shape inheritance and present a framework based on standard C++ template metaprogramming.

1 Introduction

The creation of large scale software systems is still a critical challenge of software engineering. Several design principles exist to keep the complexity of large systems manageable. Different methodologies are used to divide the problem into smaller orthogonal parts that can be planned, implemented and tested separately with moderate complexity. In a fortunate case such parts already exist as some foundation library module, otherwise they can be produced by reasonable efforts. This *separation of concerns* is widely discussed in [25] and [12]. In object-oriented libraries these concerns are mostly implemented as separate classes.

Possessing our premanufactured components we have several methodologies to assemble a full system from the required components. This so-called *collaboration based design* is supported by aspect oriented programming [21], subject oriented programming [27] [28], feature oriented programming [10] and composition filters [19]. Besides, the assembly can be naturally expressed by deriving from all required components using multiple inheritance in languages that support this feature, such as C++. This *mixin-based*[1] technique is highly attractive for implementing collaboration-based design [13]. Whichever approach we choose, the

---

[1] There is a number of different meanings of "mixins". We use the term *mixin* according to Batory and Smaragdakis [13].

R. Lämmel, J. Saraiva, and J. Visser (Eds.): GTTSE 2005, LNCS 4143, pp. 459–470, 2006.

basic idea is to easily create the solution as a union of components implemented in separate modules.

However, in real life it is hard to find a component that implements the required feature *exactly*. In most cases we have to customize the components to meet the requirements of the current task by adding *features* [12]. Specializations for every separate component are made orthogonally which leads to separated refinement chains, each representing refinement steps of individual features. The specific solution for a particular task can be finally produced by assembling specialized components from appropriate layers of different chains.

In object-oriented languages we represent our components as classes. Refinement is regularly expressed by inheritance, hence we gain a subtype relationship between the refined and the original component. In [11], Batory et al. claim that "the only classes that are instantiated in a synthesized application are the terminal classes of the refinement chains [...] Non-terminal classes [...] are *never* instantiated." Nevertheless, it is a frequent scenario that some client code handles the objects of terminal classes through an interface of an earlier refinement layer. For example, the client code has been implemented prior to the final refinement steps or the refinements serving implementational purposes only should be hidden. In such cases, subtyping should be provided between refinement layers.

In this article we present examples where conventional subtyping yields undesired effects, give a detailed discussion of an inheritance anomaly, dispute existing or proposed alternative solutions and introduce a solution based on code transformation using standard C++ template metaprogramming.

2   Problem Description

To define the problem, we rely on the notation and formalism of AHEAD [11]. In this model, we consider features as refinement transformations. Every feature f_i is a function that transforms a (possibly empty) component. As a result, the represented feature will be added to the component. Assuming an existing component c_i, we mark such extensions by $f_i \bullet c_i$.

For an easier creation of programs, we allow the composition[2] of features. A composition is represented by a set, e.g. a union of features is $\{f_i, f_j\}$. An extension of a compound component by a set of features is formalized as

$$f \bullet c = \{f_1, ..., f_n\} \bullet \{c_1, ..., c_n\} = \{f_1 \bullet c_1, ..., f_n \bullet c_n\} \tag{1}$$

Note that feature addition is distributive over the composition above [11]. In widely used object-oriented languages, such as Java, C++, C# or Eiffel, feature addition (component refinement) is implemented by inheritance. Additionally, composition may also be implemented by multiple inheritance[3] or aggregation.

---

[2] Such compositions are referred as *collectives* in [11].

[3] Note that some languages (e.g. Java) do not support multiple inheritance directly, but are able to simulate it (e.g. using interfaces). The problem exists in these cases, too.

What is the problem with inheritance? In object-oriented languages, reusing code and defining subtype relations is not clearly separated, they are both expressed through inheritance. Thus, composition implemented by multiple inheritance or aggregation fails to fulfil the distributive property. Hence the forementioned languages does not conform to equation (1).

The service for a specific user requirement can be constructed as a composition of refined features. In the same time, we should be able to use any subset of features from different refinement stages as an interface to this service. Therefore a subtype relation should be provided between any of these collectives irrespectively of the number and refinement level of participant concern classes. Thus we have to decide: if we derive the refined collaboration from the original collaboration class, we lose the subtype relationship with classes implementing the refined features; otherwise (deriving from the refined features) we lose the subtype relationship with the original collective. In figure 1 the general structure of the anomaly can be seen, according to the two mentioned cases respectively. We have named this anomaly *chevron-shape inheritance*.

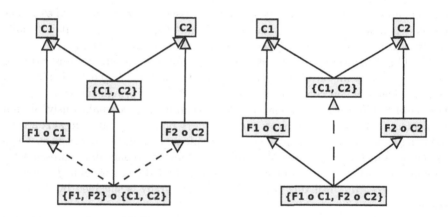

Fig. 1. Chevron-shape inheritance. (Missing subtypes are marked by dashed lines)

3   Examples

To clarify the formalism above, let us introduce an example from the C++ Standard Library. In Fig. 2 you can see the class hierarchy of the stream implementation in GNU C++ as specified by the C++ standard. (We omit the fact that all the following classes are *templates* by the standard, because this does not affect the problem).

Classes `istream` and `ostream` are representing input and output streams as orthogonal concerns. (There is a common base class `ios` for both classes that holds some general stream functionality.) Class `iostream` unifies input and output functionalities representing streams that can be both read and written. Using the formalism introduced above, $iostream = \{istream, ostream\}$. `iostream` is

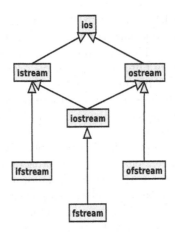

Fig. 2. I/O library according to the C++ standard

implemented by multiple inheritance from classes `istream` and `ostream`. The result is a well known anomaly called *diamond-shape inheritance*. It is usually resolved using *virtual inheritance* in classes `istream` and `ostream`.

The library contains refinements for both input and output streams. Streams opened over certain physical devices belong to classes `ifstream` or `ofstream` as refinements of `istream` and `ostream` respectively. Formalising this, we gain $ifstream = fileio \bullet istream$, class `ofstream` can be defined analogously. Similar refinements exist for streams stored in a memory buffer (e.g. `istringstream` and `ostringstream`). These refinements are implemented using inheritance. Class `fstream` (and `stringstream` also) inherits from `iostream` and represents file streams for both input and output operations. For `fstream`, we gain $fstream = fileio \bullet iostream$. Until this point, the class hierarchy is specified by the C++ standard.

Surprisingly, this construction causes some unexpected results. Intuitively, `fstream` is clearly a subtype of both `ifstream` and `ofstream`, so $fstream = \{ifstream, ofstream\}$. The inheritance hieararchy described above does not express this, hence there is no conversion from `fstream` to either `istream` or `ostream`. Thus,

$$
\begin{aligned}
fstream = fileio \bullet iostream = fileio \bullet \{istream, ostream\} \\
\neq \{fileio \bullet istream, fileio \bullet ostream\} = \{ifstream, ofstream\}
\end{aligned}
\tag{2}
$$

Clients handling input files are not able to use objects from `fstream` as an instance of `ifstream`, they are enforced to use `istream` as a more general interface losing file-specific information. After examining classes `iostream` and `istream` this may be an astonishing fact.

There is another possible construction scheme for the I/O library that is described in [29] and also referred in Stroustrup's fundamental book *The Design and Evolution of C++* [17]. Classes `ifstream` and `ofstream` are derived from `ifstream` and `ostream` respectively, and also from class `fstreambase`, which represents an orthogonal, third concern (file operations). Here, `fstream` is derived from `ifstream` and `ofstream`, therefore our previous problem is substituted with another one: `iostream` is not an ancestor of `fstream` anymore, therefore cannot be used as an interface for input and output file operations.

The implementation technique of file streams is not covered by the standard. Examining certain implementations like the one in the old GNU C++ version 2.95 we get an even more confusing picture (see figure 3). The problem arises at the implementation of file streams. Since all file streams handle files, it is highly attractive to detach file-specific functionality into `fstreambase`. The consequence of this structure is a kind of mixture of the two previous approaches: `ifstream` and `ofstream` are descendents of `istream` and `ostream` respectively, and `fstreambase` like in [29]. However, `fstream` is inherited from `iostream` and `fstreambase` as in the current standard.

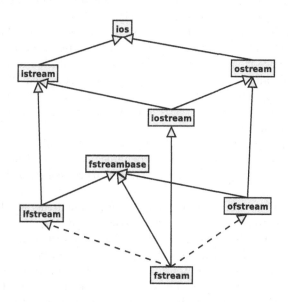

Fig. 3. The GNU implementation of the I/O library

The current C++ standard votes for the first solution. No matter, which one we choose, disturbing gaps remain in subtype relations between refinement stages. It seems we can not express the whole subtype graph that the user would find natural.

Another example is from the Eiffel programming language [18]. The kernel library of Eiffel contains several abstract classes like NUMERIC for arithmetics, COMPARABLE for sorting, HASHABLE for associative containers, etc. These classes are practical to have because in Eiffel we can require a template parameter to be a subclass of such an "interface". These classes can be combined as needed using multiple inheritance, hence we can derive a NUMERIC_COMPARABLE_HASHABLE or a NUMERIC_COMPARABLE interface directly from the bases. Again, the problem appears when we try to use an object of the first class with a generic algorithm requiring the latter type. No subtype relation is provided by the compiler, we have to resolve it by hand creating conversion functions.

4   Classical Approaches

In this section we discuss several widely used methods that may promise a possible solution for the anomaly and analyze the results.

Virtual Inheritance (opposed to conventional inheritance) guarantees that when a class occurs as a superclass several times, its members will be not duplicated in the descendants. Virtual inheritance can usually solve issues related to multiple inheritance and with a combination of abstract classes it supports a programming style where the abstract bases define interfaces and several derived classes contribute to the implementation [17] [16].

Virtual inheritance has several drawbacks in our case. Besides having memory and runtime penalties, we must explicitly mark our intention to use a class as a *virtual base*, hence it is intrusive and can not be a solution using precompiled libraries. Additionally, in the case of several feature refinement chains, the number of possible collectives grows exponentially, only an automatic mechanism provides an acceptable solution, thus it provides a suitable solution only for a small number of features.

Signatures play an important role in certain functional languages, like Standard ML. A signature prescribes the typenames, values and nested structures that must appear in a structure. That way signatures constrain the contents of structures [7].

Signatures for C++ were proposed by Gerald Baumgartner [4]. They provide a facility similar to interfaces, but in a non-intrusive way. Signatures have features similar to classes, e.g. they can inherit from other signatures, and a compiler can check whether a class has all members to meet the requirements of a signature. However, using signatures, unintentional conversions may occur: though it is conceptionally wrong, a Gun can be cast to a Camera because they both have function shoot() and signatures ignore any semantic information. Additionally, signatures are non-standard language extensions for C++.

Structural subtyping binds the subtype relation to data structures instead of inheritance. Languages like C++, Java or Eiffel declare subtyping at the point of class definition. Contrary, subtype relations are based on structural subtyping in many functional languages where existence of subtype relations can be decided based on structural conformance. The reader can find a well known implementation in the Ocaml language [8]. We suggest reading [20] on the theoretical background of structural subtyping.

Structural subtyping provides an excellent solution to our anomaly: in languages supporting this feature our anomaly does not exist. Unfortunately, structural subtyping suffers from the problem of accidental conformance the same way as signatures do. Furthermore, no widely used object-oriented language provides structural subtyping. Recently, several attempts were made to unify the object oriented and structural approaches, see [9].

Aspects address the subtyping problem a different way than structural subtyping. Instead of providing an algorithmic model to implicitly deduce subtype relations, another approach is to provide a language mechanishm external to the class definition that establishes a subtyping relation [23]. Aspect-oriented programming systems, such as AspectJ [22] allow modification of types independently of their original definitions. For example, an existing class can be modified to implement a newly created interface using static cross-cutting [21]. Though aspects are usable to weave a single feature into a hierarchy, we find the same subtyping anomaly when aspects have their own refinement chains.

5   Implementation

Beside object-orientation, the C++ language also has a rich feature set for supporting generative programming. C++ templates provide parametric polymorphism as an extension to inclusion polymorphism provided by inheritance. We can create template specializations to have a completely different implementation from the general one for some special template arguments. Thus we can create a matrix class that stores elements in a plain array except for booleans, where it stores an array of chars each representing (mostly) eight booleans. Because booleans can be passed as template arguments, we can specialize upon compile time conditions. Specializations also allow us to write algorithms running in compilation time inside the compiler instead of runtime in the program. This approach is called template metaprogramming [5].

Theoretically, template metaprogramming in C++ is a Turing complete language in itself, therefore any algorithm can be expressed as a metaprogram (see [15]). Practically, compilers have limitations in resources (e.g. a maximal depth of recursion during template instantiation) so this possibility must be used with care. Additionally, programming compile time algorithms is still an uncomfortable effort lacking standard libraries and debug tools. However, it is very useful for simple cases, especially to give a performance boost. (See expression templates [6]).

5.1   CSet

The template metaprogramming features discussed above enable us to solve the chevron-shape anomaly described in section 2. To achieve this goal we perform an automatic transformation to simulate a subtype relationship between collectives: based on the possibilities of template metaprogramming we implement automatic conversions between them. In the remaining part of the article we call these sets `CSet`s (where `C` can be pronounced as any of class, concern, collaboration, collective, chevron, etc, as conceptually needed). Presenting the technical implementation details is out of the scope of this paper, it can be found in [1].

In this article we concentrate on usage and applicability of the `CSet` framework in feature-oriented programming.

Creating `CSet`, our first task is to assemble the collaborating classes into a single entity which we implement as a C++ class using multiple inheritance. Class `CSet` is written to directly inherit from all classes in a recursive way, according to the recursive structure of typelists.

```
// --- Inherit from all types in list
typedef TYPELIST_3(Container, Rectangle, GuiComponent) WindowList;
typedef CSet<WindowList> Window;
Window win;
win.add( Button("OK") );  // --- Container method
win.move(13, 42);         // --- Rectangle method
win.draw();               // --- GuiComponent method
```

Above we assemble three features into a `CSet` called `Window`: `Container`, `Rectangle` and `GuiComponent`. The structure of the created `CSet` can be seen in Fig. 4. After having a window object we can call the methods of all three classes.

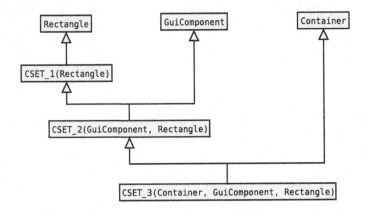

Fig. 4. Example for a CSet hierarchy

The main issue in `CSet` is the support of conversions between all appropriate collectives. The implementation is based on the fact that constructors are ordinary functions in C++, therefore they can be defined to be templates as well. This way we can make the conversion in elementary recursive steps using built-in conversions provided by the compiler. Because the conversion is built into constructors, it can be used in a completely transparent form without any function calls for conversion:

```
// --- Conversion using the constructor
CSET_2(GuiComponent, Shape) widget(win);

widget = win; // --- or the assignment operator
```

Note that CSet has CSET_N macros similar to TYPELIST_N providing an easier form of definition. Our object win can be converted to the collective of features GuiComponent and Shape because win itself is an instance of GuiComponent, furthermore it also can be converted to a shape since win has feature Rectangle which is refined from Shape. Thus the conversion is legal and the object widget can be initialized using win.

Similarly to the constructor, the assignment operator can be defined as a template, too. Template functions provide another advantage: not only CSets, but other user objects can be converted with these functions.

```
// --- Create a user class and an instance
struct MyWindow : public GuiComponent,
    public Circle, public Vector { ... };
MyWindow myObj;


// --- Conversion from user object
CSET_2(Shape, GuiComponent) widget(myObj);
```

5.2 Dynamic Binding

So far we are able to perform appropriate conversions between matching CSets. Unfortunately these conversions are done by value. This may imply the loss of dynamic data of the converted object which is often called *slicing* in C++. To avoid slicing, we have to convert our objects by pointer or reference. We follow the conventional way in our implementation and create our own smart pointers and references. Because the implementation and usage of these classes are very similar, we introduce only our smart pointer class called CSetPtr.

Conversions using class CSetPtr can be written the same way as with CSet, but using pointers we bind dynamically.

```
// --- Conversion using the constructor
CSETPTR_2(GuiComponent, Shape) widgetPtr(win);

widgetPtr = win; // --- or assignment operator
```

In CSetPtr we aggregate pointer data members instead of inheriting from ancestors to implement elementary conversion steps. As a result, the structure of CSetPtr created by the previous definition is completely different from the structure of an appropriate CSet. The created hierarchy and the essence of dynamic binding can be seen in figure 5.

CSetPtr holds a pointer member for each type in the set, so every pointer can be set to the appropriate part of an adequate CSet object. This way we can utilize dynamic binding provided by conventional pointers in C++. CSetPtr can be transparently converted to any of its pointer members, so virtual functions can be called easily.

```
Shape *shape = widgetPtr;
shape->draw(); // --- Use dynamic binding
```

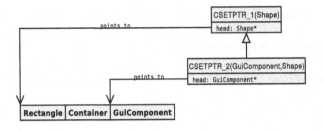

Fig. 5. Example for a CSetPtr hierarchy

The difference between `CSetPtr` and `CSetRef` comes from the type of their data members: `CSetRef` holds references instead of pointers. Thus it must be initialized and conversions are done by reference or value after initialization.

5.3   Limitations and Further Work

Though our solution relies on standard C++ features only, we encountered problems with some compilers regarding conformance to the standard. Aged compilers tend to fail providing language requirements like partial template specialization or has unacceptable compile time, exponentially growing by the number of composed features. Hopefully these problems will disappear in new compiler versions.

Another kind of problems is related to our implementation of feature composition. While we exploit the advantages of multiple inheritance, we also suffer from its usual drawbacks like possible name resolution disambiguities.

Our current version does not provide `const` correctness which is an essential language feature to improve semantical correctness of complex C++ programs, e.g. `const` member functions, pointers to `const` data or `const_iterator`.

In our future work we plan to further improve our solution by eliminating the problems enlisted above.

6   Summary

The subtyping mechanism of current object oriented languages is not flexible enough to express required subtype relationships that arise at the implementation of collaboration based designs. We described an anomaly called chevron-shape inheritance which arises assembling collectives created during the stepwise refinement of features. We have introduced a framework called `CSet` based on C++ template metaprogramming to transform the subtyping mechanism of the C++ language. `CSet`s make subtype relationships created during refinement distributive with feature composition. It supports coercion polymorphism between appropriate collectives and inclusion polymorphism allowing dynamic binding of methods with smart pointers. The framework is strictly based on standard C++ features, therefore neither language extensions nor additional tools are required.

References

1. István Zólyomi, Zoltán Porkoláb, Tamás Kozsik: An extension to the subtype relationship in C++. GPCE 2003, LNCS 2830 (2003), pp. 209 - 227.
2. Andrei Alexandrescu: Modern C++ Design: Generic Programming and Design Patterns Applied. Addison-Wesley (2001)
3. David Vandevoorde, Nicolai M. Josuttis: C++ Templates: The Complete Guide. Addison-Wesley (2003)
4. Gerald Baumgartner, Vincent F. Russo: Implementing Signatures for C++. ACM Transactions on Programming Languages and Systems (TOPLAS) Vol. 19 Issue 1. 1997. pp. 153-187.
5. Todd Veldhuizen: Using C++ Template Metaprograms. C++ Report vol. 7, no. 4, 1995, pp. 36-43.
6. Todd Veldhuizen: Expression Templates. C++ Report vol. 7, no. 5, 1995, pp. 26-31.
7. Ronald Garcia, Jaakko Järvi, Andrew Lumsdaine, Jeremy Siek, Jeremiah Willcock: A Comparative Study of Language Support for Generic Programming. Proceedings of the 18th ACM SIGPLAN OOPSLA 2003, pp. 115-134.
8. Leroy, Xavier et al.: The Objective Caml system, release 3.0.8 (July 2004), documentation and user's manual. http://caml.inria.fr/ocaml/htmlman/index.html
9. Jeremy Siek: A Language for Generic Programming. PhD thesis, Indiana University, August 2005.
10. Don Batory: A Tutorial on Feature Oriented Programming and the AHEAD Tool Suite. Technical Report, TR-CCTC/DI-35, GTTSE 2005, pp. 153-186.
11. Don Batory, Jacob Neal Sarvela, Axel Rauschmayer: Scaling Step-Wise Refinement. IEEE Transactions on Software Engineering, vol. 30, no. 6, pp. 355-371.
12. Don Batory, Jia Liu, Jacob Neal Sarvela: Refinements and multi-dimensional separation of concerns. Proceedings of the 9th European Software Engineering Conference, 2003.
13. Yannis Smaragdakis, Don Batory: Mixin-Based Programming in C++. In proceedings of Net.Object Days 2000 pp. 464-478.
14. Yannis Smaragdakis, Don Batory: Mixin Layers: An Object-Oriented Implementation Technique for Refinements and Collaboration-Based Designs. ACM Transactions of Software Engineering and Methodology Vol. 11, No. 2, April 2002, pp. 215-255.
15. Krzysztof Czarnecki, Ulrich W. Eisenecker: Generative Programming: Methods, Tools and Applications. Addison-Wesley (2000)
16. Bjarne Stroustrup: The C++ Programming Language Special Edition. Addison-Wesley (2000)
17. Bjarne Stroustrup: The Design and Evolution of C++. Addison-Wesley (1994)
18. Bertrand Meyer: Eiffel: The Language. Prentice Hall (1991)
19. Lodewijk Bergmans, Mehmet Aksit: Composing Crosscutting Concerns Using Composition Filters. Communications of the ACM, Vol. 44, No. 10, pp. 51-57, October 2001.
20. Luca Cardelli: Structural Subtyping and the Notion of Power Type. Conference Record of the Fifteenth Annual ACM Symposium on Principles of Programming Languages, San Diego, California, January 1988. pp. 70-79.
21. Gregor Kiczales, John Lamping, Anurag Mendhekar, Chris Maeda, Cristina Videira Lopes, Jean-Marc Loingtier, John Irwin: Aspect-Oriented Programming. Proceedings of the European Conference on Object-Oriented Programming (ECOOP), Finland. Springer-Verlag LNCS 1241, June 1997.

22. Gregor Kiczales et al.: An overview of AspectJ. LNCS 2072 (2001), pp. 327-355.
23. G. Baumgartner, M. Jansche, K. Läufer: Half & Half: Multiply Dispatch and Retroactive Abstraction for Java. Technical Report OSU-CISRC-5/01-TR08. Ohio State University, 2002.
24. Ulrich W. Eisenecker, Frank Blinn and Krzysztof Czarnecki: A Solution to the Constructor-Problem of Mixin-Based Programming in C++. Presented at the GCSE2000 Workshop on C++ Template Programming.
25. Harold Ossher, Peri Tarr: Multi-Dimensional Separation of Concerns and The Hyperspace Approach. IBM Research Report 21452, April, 1999. IBM T.J. Watson Research Center. http://www.research.ibm.com/hyperspace/Papers/tr21452.ps
26. Harold Ossher, Peri Tarr: Hiper/J. Multidemensional Separation of Concerns for Java. International Conference on Software Engineering 2001. ACM pp. 734-737.
27. William Harrison, Harold Ossher: Subject-oriented programming: a critique of pure objects. Proceedings of 8th OOPSLA 1993, Washington D.C., USA. pp. 411-428.
28. Subject Oriented Programming. http://www.research.ibm.com/sop
29. Jonathan E. Shopiro: An Example of Multiple Inheritance in C++: a Model of the Iostream Library. ACM SIGPLAN Notices, December, 1989.

Author Index

Lecture Notes in Computer Science

For information about Vols. 1–4121

please contact your bookseller or Springer

Vol. 4176: S.K. Katsikas, J. Lopez, M. Backes, S. Gritzalis, B. Preneel (Eds.), Information Security. XIV, 548 pages. 2006.

Vol. 4175: P. Bücher, B.M.E. Moret (Eds.), Algorithms in Bioinformatics. XII, 402 pages. 2006. (Sublibrary LNBI).

Vol. 4174: K. Franke, K.-R. Müller, B. Nickolay, R. Schäfer (Eds.), Pattern Recognition. XX, 773 pages. 2006.

Vol. 4173: S. El Yacoubi, B. Chopard, S. Bandini (Eds.), Cellular Automata. XV, 734 pages. 2006.

Vol. 4172: J. Gonzalo, C. Thanos, M. F. Verdejo, R.C. Carrasco (Eds.), Research and Advanced Technology for Digital Libraries. XVII, 569 pages. 2006.

Vol. 4169: H.L. Bodlaender, M.A. Langston (Eds.), Parameterized and Exact Computation. XI, 279 pages. 2006.

Vol. 4168: Y. Azar, T. Erlebach (Eds.), Algorithms – ESA 2006. XVIII, 843 pages. 2006.

Vol. 4167: S. Dolev (Ed.), Distributed Computing. XV, 576 pages. 2006.

Vol. 4166: J. Górski (Ed.), Computer Safety, Reliability, and Security. XIV, 440 pages. 2006.

Vol. 4165: W. Jonker, M. Petković (Eds.), Secure, Data Management. X, 185 pages. 2006.

Vol. 4163: H. Bersini, J. Carneiro (Eds.), Artificial Immune Systems. XII, 460 pages. 2006.

Vol. 4162: R. Královič, P. Urzyczyn (Eds.), Mathematical Foundations of Computer Science 2006. XV, 814 pages. 2006.

Vol. 4161: R. Harper, M. Rauterberg, M. Combetto (Eds.), Entertainment Computing - ICEC 2006. XXVII, 417 pages. 2006.

Vol. 4160: M. Fisher, W.v.d. Hoek, B. Konev, A. Lisitsa (Eds.), Logics in Artificial Intelligence. XII, 516 pages. 2006. (Sublibrary LNAI).

Vol. 4159: J. Ma, H. Jin, L.T. Yang, J.J.-P. Tsai (Eds.), Ubiquitous Intelligence and Computing. XXII, 1190 pages. 2006.

Vol. 4158: L.T. Yang, H. Jin, J. Ma, T. Ungerer (Eds.), Autonomic and Trusted Computing. XIV, 613 pages. 2006.

Vol. 4156: S. Amer-Yahia, Z. Bellahsène, E. Hunt, R. Unland, J.X. Yu (Eds.), Database and XML Technologies. IX, 123 pages. 2006.

Vol. 4155: O. Stock, M. Schaerf (Eds.), Reasoning, Action and Interaction in AI Theories and Systems. XVIII, 343 pages. 2006. (Sublibrary LNAI).

Vol. 4154: Y.A. Dimitriadis, I. Zigurs, E. Gómez-Sánchez (Eds.), Groupware: Design, Implementation, and Use. XIV, 438 pages. 2006.

Vol. 4153: N. Zheng, X. Jiang, X. Lan (Eds.), Advances in Machine Vision, Image Processing, and Pattern Analysis. XIII, 506 pages. 2006.

Vol. 4152: Y. Manolopoulos, J. Pokorný, T. Sellis (Eds.), Advances in Databases and Information Systems. XV, 448 pages. 2006.

Vol. 4151: A. Iglesias, N. Takayama (Eds.), Mathematical Software - ICMS 2006. XVII, 452 pages. 2006.

Vol. 4150: M. Dorigo, L.M. Gambardella, M. Birattari, A. Martinoli, R. Poli, T. Stützle (Eds.), Ant Colony Optimization and Swarm Intelligence. XVI, 526 pages. 2006.

Vol. 4149: M. Klusch, M. Rovatsos, T.R. Payne (Eds.), Cooperative Information Agents X. XII, 477 pages. 2006. (Sublibrary LNAI).

Vol. 4148: J. Vounckx, N. Azemard, P. Maurine (Eds.), Integrated Circuit and System Design. XVI, 677 pages. 2006.

Vol. 4146: J.C. Rajapakse, L. Wong, R. Acharya (Eds.), Pattern Recognition in Bioinformatics. XIV, 186 pages. 2006. (Sublibrary LNBI).

Vol. 4144: T. Ball, R.B. Jones (Eds.), Computer Aided Verification. XV, 564 pages. 2006.

Vol. 4143: R. Lämmel, J. Saraiva, J. Visser (Eds.), Generative and Transformational Techniques in Software Engineering. X, 471 pages. 2006.

Vol. 4142: A. Campilho, M. Kamel (Eds.), Image Analysis and Recognition, Part II. XXVII, 923 pages. 2006.

Vol. 4141: A. Campilho, M. Kamel (Eds.), Image Analysis and Recognition, Part I. XXVIII, 939 pages. 2006.

Vol. 4139: T. Salakoski, F. Ginter, S. Pyysalo, T. Pahikkala, Advances in Natural Language Processing. XVI, 771 pages. 2006. (Sublibrary LNAI).

Vol. 4138: X. Cheng, W. Li, T. Znati (Eds.), Wireless Algorithms, Systems, and Applications. XVI, 709 pages. 2006.

Vol. 4137: C. Baier, H. Hermanns (Eds.), CONCUR 2006 – Concurrency Theory. XIII, 525 pages. 2006.

Vol. 4136: R.A. Schmidt (Ed.), Relations and Kleene Algebra in Computer Science. XI, 433 pages. 2006.

Vol. 4135: C.S. Calude, M.J. Dinneen, G. Păun, G. Rozenberg, S. Stepney (Eds.), Unconventional Computation. X, 267 pages. 2006.

Vol. 4134: K. Yi (Ed.), Static Analysis. XIII, 443 pages. 2006.

Vol. 4133: J. Gratch, M. Young, R. Aylett, D. Ballin, P. Olivier (Eds.), Intelligent Virtual Agents. XIV, 472 pages. 2006. (Sublibrary LNAI).

Vol. 4132: S. Kollias, A. Stafylopatis, W. Duch, E. Oja (Eds.), Artificial Neural Networks – ICANN 2006, Part II. XXXIV, 1028 pages. 2006.

Vol. 4131: S. Kollias, A. Stafylopatis, W. Duch, E. Oja (Eds.), Artificial Neural Networks – ICANN 2006, Part I. XXXIV, 1008 pages. 2006.

Vol. 4130: U. Furbach, N. Shankar (Eds.), Automated Reasoning. XV, 680 pages. 2006. (Sublibrary LNAI).

Vol. 4129: D. McGookin, S. Brewster (Eds.), Haptic and Audio Interaction Design. XII, 167 pages. 2006.

Vol. 4128: W.E. Nagel, W.V. Walter, W. Lehner (Eds.), Euro-Par 2006 Parallel Processing. XXXIII, 1221 pages. 2006.

Vol. 4127: E. Damiani, P. Liu (Eds.), Data and Applications Security XX. X, 319 pages. 2006.

Vol. 4126: P. Barahona, F. Bry, E. Franconi, N. Henze, U. Sattler, Reasoning Web. XII, 269 pages. 2006.

Vol. 4124: H. de Meer, J.P. G. Sterbenz (Eds.), Self-Organizing Systems. XIV, 261 pages. 2006.